DISCIPLESHIP
ACCORDING TO

THE SERMON
ON THE MOUNT

DISCIPLESHIP ACCORDING TO THE SERMON ON THE MOUNT

FOUR LEGITIMATE READINGS, FOUR PLAUSIBLE VIEWS OF DISCIPLESHIP, AND THEIR RELATIVE VALUES

Daniel Patte

TRINITY PRESS INTERNATIONAL
Valley Forge, Pennsylvania

Trinity Press International, P.O. Box 851, Valley Forge, PA 19482–0851
Trinity Press International is a division of the Morehouse Publishing Group

Cover art: Elizabeth McNaron Patte
Cover design: Jim Gerhard

Library of Congress Cataloging-in-Publication Data

Patte, Daniel.
    Discipleship according to the Sermon on the mount : four
legitimate readings, four plausible views of discipleship, and their
relative values / Daniel Patte.
      p. cm.
    Includes bibliographical references.
    ISBN 1-56338-177-X (pbk.)
    1. Sermon on the mount – Criticism, interpretation, etc.
2. Christian life – Biblical teaching. I. Title.
BT380.2.P27 1996
241.5′3 – dc21   96-46647
                                           CIP

Printed in the United States of America

96   97   98   99   00   01   10   9   8   7   6   5   4   3   2   1

To   Mariano Apilado
      his colleagues and the students
      at Union Theological Seminary,
      Dasmariñas campus of Philippine Christian University.

As a sign of *utang na loob,*
      this book that does not offer any reading *for* them
            but is an invitation to *read with* other people
                  by developing and affirming their own readings.

Contents

Preface

This study of discipleship according to the Sermon on the Mount asserts that a truly critical interpretation makes explicit the specificity of all its interpretive processes. From this perspective, the bringing to critical understanding of an interpretation is a work constantly in progress that is necessarily performed *with* others. Assuming responsibility for our interpretation by understanding it critically is an ongoing task because it is threefold. It involves accounting for the *legitimacy judgments* through which we ascertain, with one or another critical method, that our interpretation is properly grounded in textual evidence. In addition, it involves accounting for the *epistemology judgments* through which we make sense of our conclusions about what the text says and for the *value judgments* through which we assess the relative value of this teaching for us *(pro nobis* or even *pro me)*. Yet we cannot assess by ourselves the specificity of these interpretive processes in our interpretation. We need to compare our interpretation to ones held by other people who also seek to assume responsibility for their own interpretations. For this, as chapter 7 emphasizes, we need to *read* the biblical text *with* these other interpreters — respecting their interpretations as legitimate and plausible until proven otherwise, even though they reflect choices different from the ones we have made in our own interpretation.

From this perspective, truly critical biblical study requires us to take the risk of personally assuming responsibility for our interpretation, of exposing ourselves to others as we reveal the reasons for our interpretive choices, and of looking at our interpretation — indeed at ourselves — through their eyes. Yet we cannot proceed with this critical task without the self-confidence that comes from *reading with* at least a few people, whom we can fully trust and respect because they themselves have shown their trust in us and their respect for us by taking the risk of being our reading partners and of revealing to us the different interpretive choices they make and their reasons for doing so.

I would not have been able to present this critical study of discipleship according to the Sermon on the Mount if I had not been empowered to do so by reading partners who generously shared with me their different perspectives, revealing to me the specificity of various aspects of the interpretive processes that characterize my own interpretation. Because the

preparation of the present book overlapped with the writing of my earlier book, *Ethics of Biblical Interpretation,* I could acknowledge here again
the help and support of the many people I thanked in the opening pages
of that book — especially the male European-American scholars who gave
me the self-confidence to acknowledge and *to affirm* my male European-
American perspective. I especially want to acknowledge the empowerment
I have received from those who *read with* me while continuing to affirm
their different perspectives and interpretations. These include many undergraduate, divinity, and graduate students at Vanderbilt University, as well as
participants in Bible study groups in Nashville churches who have offered
their very diverse interpretations in critical papers and class discussions. I
cannot name all of them here.

But I must name the students who participated in the class on "Ethics of
the New Testament" at Vanderbilt University (spring 1996) because they
directly entered into a critical dialogue with a draft of a large part of
this book and contributed to its final form through their own interpretations of the Sermon on the Mount, through their questions, through their
papers and oral presentations in which they sought to envision how to elucidate the value judgments involved in their interpretations (Part III of this
book), as well as through specific and important suggestions (as acknowledged in footnotes). This class, which met in two separate groups, included
Kelly Brandon, Cindi Brown, Carlye Clark, Caroline Davis, Michael El-
liott, Jonathan Anderson, Virginia Bain, Laura Horne, Nicole Kirk, Eric
Lee, Ellen Roberds, Stephanie Crowder, Daren Geremia, Tripp Hunt,
Grace Imathiu, Jean Kim, Philip Meckley, Tarris Rosell, and Professor Jo-
hannes A. Loubser (University of Zululand), who also participated in this
class. My thanks to each. Their passionate involvement helped me get
hold of many fleeting insights I have experienced when *reading with* other
people.

I have gained insights from James Grimshaw, Nicole Wilkinson, and
Vicki Phillips, who not only contributed to improving the style of my prose
but also, each in his or her own way, became real dialogue and reading partners concerning everything related to this study. Monya Stubbs
made me read Alice Walker and led me to *read* the Sermon *with* African-
American and womanist scholars (a revealing experience).

I am particularly indebted to three colleagues among the many around
the world who also have directly or indirectly contributed to this book.
By *reading with* me at a crucial moment in the development of this study,
each in her or his own way affirmed my stance regarding an important
point while holding on to her or his own stance. My colleague at Vanderbilt University, Amy-Jill Levine, Carpenter Professor of New Testament
Studies, *read with* me as I presented a multidimensional study of Matthew
4:18–22 far removed from her own scholarly perspective on Matthew; the
reading-with-recognition that our respective agendas are legitimate despite

their differences empowered me to develop Part I of this study — the exposition of the equal *legitimacy* of several interpretations of the Sermon on the Mount. In the context of a meeting of the Studiorum Novi Testamenti Societas and from her feminist hermeneutical perspective and her longstanding interest in "personal voices" in critical biblical studies, Dr. Ingrid Rosa Kitzberger, Katholisch-Theologische Fakultät, Münster, *read with* me as I emphasized the equal plausibility of different conceptualizations of the teaching of biblical texts by different male European-American exegetes and empowered me to develop Part II of this study. Professor Mariano Apilado, president of Union Theological Seminary, Dasmariñas and Manila, Philippines, *read with* me from the theological perspective he has gained from his study of colonialism in the Philippines and the role of the Protestant churches in it, as I struggled to recognize the relative value of my interpretation. He helped me to acknowledge the role of the European-American churches as appropriate interpretive communities of the Bible as Scripture, as long as I also affirmed the value of the interpretation affirmed by the Philippine churches. Dr. Mariano Apilado gathered diverse groups around me — his colleagues, the students at Union Theological Seminary and Philippine Christian University, teachers, and ministers — so that I might *read with* them the Sermon on the Mount. I have such a sense of indebtedness — *utang na loob* — toward them that I gratefully dedicate this book to them. Yet it must be clear that I do so because they contributed so much to this book (especially the introduction, chapter 1, and Part III) and not because this book presents an interpretation of discipleship according to the Sermon on the Mount that they should appropriate. This book does not present a reading *for* them. It is an invitation to them to continue *reading with* me and others by affirming their own interpretations and by assuming responsibility for them.

I also want to express my gratitude to Madeleine Goodman, dean of the College of Arts and Science at Vanderbilt University, for granting me a sabbatical leave and research support for completing this book, to Russell Hamilton, dean of the Graduate School, and to the University Research Council, for the financial support that allowed me to travel to Budapest, Prague, Rome, as well as the Philippines and Japan, where I attempted to *read with* people who had very different interpretations of the Sermon on the Mount. The finished form of this book owes much to the diligent work of Betsy Cagle, who helped prepare the manuscript under great time pressure, and of Chrisona Schmidt, copyeditor for Trinity Press, who has made this book so much more readable. My deep gratitude goes to Elizabeth McNaron Patte, cherished and talented daughter-in-law, for the powerful polysemic design that graces the cover and many pages of this book and expresses so well one of its central features. Finally, I could not have written this book without the constant and profuse sustenance provided by Aline, my wife, and at Westminster Presbyterian Church by K. C. Ptomey Jr., our pastor.

Introduction

Why a critical study of "discipleship according to the Sermon on the Mount"?

I chose *discipleship* as a topic in hopes of facilitating the practice of Christian discipleship in the present global context. For this purpose, this study critically examines some of the ways in which we European and North American Christians conceive of Christian discipleship.

I chose to underscore *discipleship as ethical practice* because I was surprised at the diverse ways in which persons with whom I conversed about this topic explicitly or implicitly construed the relationship of discipleship to ethical issues, be they laypersons of various churches, undergraduate students, seminarians, or biblical scholars (including preachers and teachers).

I chose the *Sermon on the Mount* (and the verses that precede it, Mt 4:18–22) because for me and for many other European-American[1] Christians this is one of the main biblical texts on which we ground our view of discipleship.

I chose both this topic and this text because, when considered against the background of our present multicultural context, they readily illustrate why we male European-American readers of the Bible need to practice critical studies of the Bible in an *androcritical, multidimensional* way — a practice that seeks to be more responsible and accountable by being as self-conscious as possible regarding the interpretive processes involved in our interpretations.

Goals of This Study of Discipleship
according to the Sermon on the Mount

A Broadened Practice of Critical Study

This study of "discipleship according to the Sermon on the Mount" strives to be rigorously critical. My acknowledging the series of personal choices

---

1. The phrase "European-American" is purposely ambiguous. It simultaneously designates European readers and North American readers of "North Atlantic" origins and cultures, as Enrique Dussel says in *Philosophy of Liberation* (Maryknoll, N.Y.: Orbis, 1985).

that shape my study does not diminish its critical quality, but rather enhances it. I want to argue and to illustrate in this book that a critical study,
i.e., a study that makes explicit its interpretive procedures, should strive to
make explicit *all* (rather than a few of) the different interpretive choices
that it involves.

Traditional critical biblical studies display how they ground their interpretations of given texts into textual, literary, historical, or other kinds of
evidence with the help of appropriate methods. In this way they make explicit the way in which the legitimacy of their conclusions is established.
As I will argue, this amounts to making explicit the *"legitimacy judgments"* through which we choose among various kinds of evidence in an
interpretive process.

Yet, as I argue here, a critical study also needs to be self-conscious about
two other types of choices that shape its interpretation: (1) choices based
on *value judgments* in terms of religious, social, and/or political commitments of the interpreter; and (2) on *epistemology judgments* in terms of the
culturally marked conceptualizations of the topic(s) at hand.

For male European-American biblical scholars, the recognition of this
broader scope of critical study as a practice has significant implications.
By acknowledging the role of a series of choices in our interpretations
and the diverse judgments on which they are based, we are led to recognize that our interpretations are contextually marked. We can no longer
imply or claim that they are "the" only legitimate and plausible ones.
They are decentered. We (male European-American biblical scholars) become *androcritical* in the sense that we acknowledge the androcentrism/
Eurocentrism — the male European-American perspective — of our interpretations. Having this perspective is not in and of itself a problem, but
pretending that our interpretations are performed from a universal or objective perspective is. Adopting an androcritical practice simply involves
making explicit our androcentrism. It does not mean that we have to
abandon our interpretations, but that we have to view them as neither
more nor less legitimate and plausible than other interpretations that reflect other contextually marked choices. The critical study thus becomes
multidimensional.

My affirmation that in order to be truly critical a study should affirm the
legitimacy and plausibility of several different interpretations might seem
to contradict traditional practices in critical biblical studies. Actually, as I
will show below, the guild of (male) European-American scholars has for
a long time sanctioned multidimensional critical practices by endorsing the
scholarly quality of very different interpretations and methods. By making explicit that each interpretation (whatever it might be) is one among
several legitimate and plausible interpretations, we put ourselves in a situation of *assessing the relative value* of this interpretation as compared
with other contextually marked interpretations. Value-laden goals of each

biblical interpretation should then be brought to light by a critical study. Similarly, a critical study itself has value-laden goals. I signal that my critical study has such goals by calling it an androcritical multidimensional study.

General Goals for This Broadened Critical Practice

My androcritical multidimensional study of discipleship according to the Sermon on the Mount is written, as stated above, with the hope of facilitating the practice of Christian discipleship in the present global context. I believe that a great impediment to this practice of discipleship has been and continues to be the traditional claims made by us, male European-American biblical scholars, who affirm that the Sermon on the Mount offers a single true teaching about discipleship. In addition to (or because of) their dubious critical character, these claims have the effect of unduly denying any plausibility, legitimacy, and/or value to any other interpretation of the teaching about discipleship found in the Sermon on the Mount. Thus the effect of our scholarship is the exact opposite of what, in my view, it should achieve.

Critical studies of the Bible have, or should have, an ultimate goal of encouraging people to read the biblical text (here the Sermon on the Mount) so as to discover its teaching about discipleship and of encouraging readers to live by the conclusions they draw from this teaching. But scholarly studies with implicit or explicit claims to offering "the" only true interpretation actually discourage readers, conveying the idea, "Do not read the Sermon on the Mount! You cannot but misread it. The specialist will provide for you 'the' only true interpretation." To those who have nevertheless read (or heard) the Sermon on the Mount for themselves and have reached some conclusions regarding its teaching about discipleship, these scholarly studies say, "Do not act according to your conclusions about this teaching![2] You are bound to be misled by them because your interpretation is certainly erroneous. Before practicing discipleship in any way, wait for our guidance and our approval." Such messages do not facilitate the practice of discipleship, to say the least. Yet they are conveyed by most European-American scholarly biblical studies and also by many sermons and Bible study classes that mimic them.

---

2. Note that my formulation leaves open all options. "Acting according to one's *conclusions about the teaching*" of the Sermon on the Mount might involve implementing this teaching in one's life or avoiding implementing it, or anything in between, according to the conclusions one has reached regarding the relative value of this teaching. A rejection of the teaching one has found in the Sermon on the Mount might be an important component of a faithful practice of discipleship. This statement makes sense in an androcritical multidimensional perspective that seeks to avoid confusing an interpreter's "conclusions about the teaching of a text" with the "teaching of the text."

Of course, biblical scholars do not intend to alienate readers of the Bible from their own readings or from the Bible. In order to avoid such alienation, it is essential to identify what causes it. In a previous study,[3] I argued that this alienation of readers from their own readings of the Bible and from the Bible itself results from the way in which critical biblical interpretation is practiced according to patterns set by male European-American scholars. As I pointed out in *Ethics of Biblical Interpretation*, overcoming this serious problem cannot include requiring male European-American scholars to abandon their traditional approaches of critical biblical studies (in order to adopt the approaches of feminist, African-American, and so-called Two-Thirds World scholars), but rather to transform their practice of traditional critical biblical studies. It amounts, on the one hand, to affirming and underscoring the legitimacy of the different kinds of critical exegesis developed on the basis of one or another of the diverse critical methods presently acknowledged by the guild; and on the other hand, to envision a *different way of practicing* critical biblical studies, which would open the possibility of acknowledging the legitimacy of other interpretations. In *Ethics of Biblical Interpretation,* I sought to underscore the moral obligation we as biblical scholars have to address this issue, and I suggested that a multidimensional androcritical conception of the practice of critical biblical studies was a plausible alternative to our current alienating practices. These ethical reflections made it clear that a radical transformation of the *practice* of critical biblical studies is already occurring in many different contexts and needs to be further developed, even though it is felt as very threatening by many biblical scholars. This book aims at promoting this transformation by deliberately challenging the resolutely *one-dimensional* practices of the most authoritative (male) European-American scholars on the Sermon on the Mount.

For this purpose, I simply propose to show that by acknowledging the legitimacy of diverse critical methods this scholarship already is *multidimensional;* it remains one-dimensional only because it represses the evidence found in the results of the different scholarly studies of the Sermon on the Mount. We male European-American biblical scholars, afraid as we are to betray our most basic commitments, remain blind to this evidence as long as we do not acknowledge the interpretive processes involved in our work. Consequently, the present study seeks to elucidate these processes and to show and affirm their respective legitimacy, plausibility, and relative value. For this purpose, I proceed to a multidimensional analysis of a few existing interpretations of discipleship according to the Sermon on the Mount proposed by male European-American scholars.

---

3. See Daniel Patte, *Ethics of Biblical Interpretation: A Reevaluation* (Louisville: Westminster/John Knox, 1995).

This androcritical analysis is not an end in itself. It calls male European-American scholars to adopt as their common way of performing their task an androcritical multidimensional practice of biblical studies which acknowledges and makes explicit that our biblical scholarship is, has been, and will continue to be an "advocacy scholarship." As such, this androcritical analysis seeks to decenter male European-American biblical scholarship,[4] so as to open the possibility of true dialogue between male European-American interpretations that at last acknowledge their advocacy and interested character and the interpretations that have done so for a long time — among them interpretations by feminist, African-American, and Two-Thirds World advocacy scholars. Ultimately, this decentered study of discipleship according to the Sermon on the Mount, as well as the dialogues it hopes to facilitate, seeks to promote biblical studies that convey the message, "Read the Sermon on the Mount! You can understand it on your own and you can reach appropriate conclusions regarding its teaching about discipleship. Do not hesitate to act according to your conclusions about this teaching, even though *you yourself* should constantly reassess and reevaluate your understanding of this teaching and your practice of it by bringing your interpretation to critical understanding."

Pro Me/Nobis Interpretations and Scholarly Interpretations

A basic presupposition I have is that each reader of this study has some kind of understanding of what the Sermon on the Mount teaches about discipleship (however vague this understanding might be)[5] and that he or she has allowed this understanding of discipleship to shape his or her life — either by striving to follow this teaching or by deciding to ignore it (e.g., because it is unrealistic or dangerous). Thus I presuppose that each of us has some kind of *pro me* or *pro nobis* interpretation, however vague, that expresses how I am or how we are affected by this text — and thus what this text means *for me* or *for us,* whether or not we are Christian believers.

If you, my reader, do not have an understanding of the teaching of the Sermon on the Mount about discipleship, please take time to read the Sermon on the Mount (Mt 5–7), asking yourself as you read, How does the teaching of this text about discipleship *affect me* (or *us*), either directly (by shaping my life in one way or another) or indirectly (by shaping the life of other people whose behavior affects me)? If you read the Sermon on the

---

4. As a response to Elisabeth Schüssler Fiorenza's call in her Society of Biblical Literature presidential address, "The Ethics of Interpretation: De-Centering Biblical Scholarship," *Journal of Biblical Literature* 107 (1988): 3–17.

5. I avoid using the term "preunderstanding" because of the negative connotations it commonly carries — "preunderstandings" being something one needs to set aside to gain a "true understanding" of the text through a "critical" interpretation (which alone is legitimate).

Mount with this question in mind, your reading will be "authentic." As is the case with any *pro me* or *pro nobis* interpretations (including "faith-interpretations" resulting from devotional readings and most "ordinary" interpretations), your *conclusions about the teaching* of the Sermon on the Mount regarding discipleship are trustworthy. Indeed, as I will argue below, such conclusions can be viewed as implicitly legitimate — that is, as appropriately based on textual features, even though in this first reading you might not be in a position to justify their legitimacy.

In sum, I presuppose that *pro me/nobis* interpretations (i.e., interpretations that are deliberately "interested") include legitimate *conclusions about the teaching* of the text, even though these conclusions may need to be complemented and/or refined, and even though the warrants (and arguments) that these interpretations propose as a demonstration of the legitimacy of these conclusions might be quite fanciful. For instance, misconceptions regarding the nature of the text and its historical, social, religious, literary contexts, which are frequently found in such nonscholarly interpretations, do not prevent these interpretations from including appropriate conclusions regarding the *teaching of the text* because they nevertheless reflect how a reader was actually affected by this text and how this reader responded to the text out of a particular religious, social, and cultural situation.

Since I presuppose that my reader has already reached his or her own conclusions regarding the teaching of the Sermon on the Mount about discipleship, I also presuppose that my reader is not a tabula rasa and is not about to forget or suppress this understanding of the Sermon on the Mount because for her or him it is already a life investment (even if it is an indirect and negative reaction to the text).

The suggestion that I do not expect my reader to be a tabula rasa might sound quite strange. We teachers often conceive of teaching as writing on a clean (or cleaned) slate or as pouring a knowledge-content into an empty container because we conceive of ourselves as being closer to the truth than our students are — an assumption that is plausible only as long as one construes scholarly studies as a quest for "the" single true interpretation of a text. But as soon as this assumption breaks down, the irony of our practice becomes quite apparent. Why should we conceive of our own interpretation as the closest to this ideal interpretation, as we affirm (or at least intimate) by our manner of teaching and of pursuing biblical scholarship? Why should we feel authorized to denounce all other interpretations as wrong (or at least insinuate such)?

My use of an androcritical multidimensional approach is a heuristic strategy intended to avoid the temptation of conducting a quest for "the" only true teaching of the Sermon on the Mount about discipleship and of presenting my interpretation as if it were the only true one.

Critical Studies as Bringing Pro Me/Nobis Interpretations to Critical Understanding

I deliberately present my interpretation of the teaching of the Sermon on the Mount about discipleship as one of four interpretations that are recognized as equally legitimate and plausible (as is verified by publications sanctioned by the guild). Thus I make it impossible for myself to claim a better legitimacy and plausibility for my own interpretation. Positively, I put myself in a position of recognizing the specific aspects of the text on which I ground my own interpretation, and thus both the particularity of my own interpretation and its legitimacy. I also put myself in a position of appreciating the specific way in which I conceptualized my *conclusions about the teaching* of the Sermon on the Mount regarding discipleship, and thus both the particularity of my conclusions and their plausibility. As it becomes clear that my interpretation represents a choice among several equally legitimate and plausible options, I am in a position of acknowledging that this choice was, implicitly or explicitly, consciously or subconsciously, made because of certain interests and concerns. In sum, through the heuristic strategy of this androcritical multidimensional study, I will have brought to critical understanding my own interpretation, by becoming aware of several of the interpretive processes that it involves.

As an extension of this heuristic strategy, I deliberately chose for this androcritical multidimensional study four interpretations by *male European-American* biblical scholars. Two of these interpretations are the most widely accepted ones in European-American academic circles, and the other two provide appropriate alternatives. My hope is to put my colleagues, male European-American biblical scholars in the pulpit as well as in the classroom, in the same position as the one in which I find myself: a position in which it will become impossible for them to claim a better legitimacy and plausibility for their own interpretation. As will become clear, this strategy does not demand them to deny the legitimacy, the plausibility, or the value of their own interpretations (and thus of their own vocation as critical biblical scholars). Yet it does require them to respect the interpretations of other biblical scholars, as they wish others to respect their own interpretation (a paraphrase of Mt 7:12 is appropriate here). As a result, each of our own scholarly interpretations is decentered; we are no longer considering it as the quest for "the" only true interpretation, there being other male European-American interpretations that are equally legitimate and plausible. The very fact that we are limiting this study to four types of interpretations of the Sermon on the Mount is a clear signal that there are other interpretations which are as legitimate and plausible as these. In this way, I hope to help my colleagues bring to critical understanding their own interpretations.

The heuristic strategy of this androcritical multidimensional study also aims to convey that many other interpretations have equal status with these four, including interpretations that have never made any universal claims about themselves, despite their scholarly character. Here I allude to feminist, African-American, and other advocacy interpretations, which make explicit their interested character. An androcritical multidimensional approach involves acknowledging and affirming the legitimacy, plausibility, and relative value of each of these interpretations.

Finally, this heuristic strategy is aimed at empowering those readers of the Bible who come to this book primarily with their *pro me/nobis* interpretations (including faith-interpretations) to bring to critical understanding their own interpretations. For this reason I want to emphasize from the outset that their interpretations have as much claim as the most sophisticated of the scholarly interpretations to have reached legitimate, plausible, and valuable *conclusions regarding the teaching* of the Sermon on the Mount about discipleship.

Of course, this strategy must be explained and justified (as it will be in the following pages). But my primary goal is *to bring to critical understanding my own interpretation and to invite you, my reader, to bring to critical understanding your own interpretation, whatever it might be.* Some explanations of what "bringing to critical understanding one's interpretation" are in order.

How Does One Bring to Critical Understanding One's Own Interpretation? An Invitation to Be Scribe for the Kingdom

Any truly critical study should have the goal of bringing to critical understanding the interpreter's own interpretation. How does one do this? By elucidating what warrants the legitimacy of one's conclusions (as is usually done through the explicit use of a critical method) and also by acknowledging the specificity of one's interpretation. Thus in my case I underscore the many interpretive choices among plausible alternatives that my interpretation reflects; I also reveal at least some of the reasons for the legitimacy judgments, epistemology judgments, and value judgments that these choices represent. As a practical way of bringing to light the distinctiveness of the interpretive choices involved in my interpretation, I compare it systematically to interpretations that reach different *conclusions about the teaching* of the Sermon on the Mount regarding discipleship because I can presuppose that such interpretations have made different choices among plausible alternatives as a result of their distinctive legitimacy, epistemology, and value judgments.

Bringing to critical understanding the specificity of my own interpretation of "discipleship according to the Sermon on the Mount" through this androcritical multidimensional study does not demand that I abandon that interpretation. On the contrary, it elucidates the basic legitimacy, plausibility, and value of my interpretation, even as I must refine my thinking whenever I recognize that I was confused about one point or another (usually because the distinctions among different interpretive judgments were not respected). Yet as I simultaneously become aware of the specificity of my interpretation and of the plausibility, legitimacy, and value of alternative interpretations, I find myself in a position of reassessing and reevaluating my choice of this specific interpretation.

Then the intended contribution of this study to my readers' understanding of "discipleship according to the Sermon on the Mount" becomes apparent: it should be similar to the contribution it makes to my own understanding. Since you, my reader, come to this book with your own interpretation of "discipleship according to the Sermon on the Mount," and since I cannot but affirm that it has at least the potential to be as legitimate, plausible, and valuable as the four interpretations I present, this study is not an invitation to abandon or forget your interpretation. On the contrary, it invites you (yourself!) to bring your own interpretation to critical understanding.

This involves recognizing that your view of "discipleship according to the Sermon on the Mount" is not simply "what the text says," but is in fact an interpretation of the text (among other interpretations) with its own characteristics and peculiarities. My study provides you with four types of interpretations with which you can compare and contrast your own, so as to elucidate its specificity. You may find that your interpretation is closely related to one of the four kinds of interpretations that are highlighted in this study. Consequently, the comparisons I make among the four selected interpretations should help you become aware of the specificity of your own interpretation. But my expectation is that in many instances this will not be the case. As my deliberate focus on interpretations by male European-Americans shows, I expect that gender, social, and cultural factors play a role in our choices of interpretations. Thus, especially if you are not a male European-American (but possibly even if you are), I anticipate that none of the four types corresponds to your own interpretation. Then the androcritical multidimensional study will play its full role for you. It illustrates, through four examples, a heuristic model that you can use for examining your own interpretation. By analyzing your interpretation and comparing it with these examples in terms of the different categories of interpretive choices that they respectively involve, you will be in a position to elucidate the characteristics of your interpretation of "discipleship according to the Sermon on the Mount."

Of course, going through this process will lead you to reassess and reevaluate your interpretive choices, and ultimately your choice of this particular interpretation, as I do for my own (and for the others). Yet I do not expect you to change your interpretation. I do not advocate a specific understanding of "discipleship according to the Sermon on the Mount" that I would like you to adopt. Rather, my hope is that this study will en-tice you to assume responsibility for your own interpretation and to strive to be accountable for it. But do not expect me to be impartial! I am ready to grant that the choice of an interpretation depends on our sense of account-ability, including our vocational, community, and political commitments. But I have quite definite views regarding which interpretations are irrespon-sible in the present sociocultural context in Europe and North America, as the concluding chapter (chap. 7) makes explicit.

At any rate, this androcritical multidimensional study in which you are invited to participate will change your view of the Sermon on the Mount and its teaching about discipleship (as my view of it would be further changed if you would share with me your own interpretation). The Ser-mon on the Mount offers a broader diversity of legitimate, plausible, and valuable teachings about discipleship than either you or I thought. This diversity of interpretations gives us a first but limited glimpse of the rich-ness of the teaching of the Sermon on the Mount about discipleship. We can then anticipate that in any given sociocultural context "scribes trained for the kingdom" will "bring out" of the "treasure" of the Sermon on the Mount either one of these "old" teachings about discipleship or a "new" one that, though surprising, would be more appropriate for this particular situation (Mt 13:52). This study invites you to be such a scribe.

The hermeneutical payoff involved in the identification of the most valu-able interpretation in a given situation should not be construed as distinct from — or in tension with — a critical study of the Sermon on the Mount and its teaching about discipleship. As has been much discussed since Bultmann and the New Hermeneutic movement,[6] critical exegesis and her-meneutics can be conceived as parts of a single interpretive process. Of course, one can make a strong legitimating argument that would also show the plausibility of a conception of hermeneutics as a secondary interpretive process, considering "what the text means for us today" on the basis of the results of a critical exegesis that has established "what the text meant" (that is, "the" true teaching of the text). This is the traditional understanding of critical biblical studies that male European-American biblical scholars de-veloped during the last one hundred years, even as they carefully sought to avoid undue positivism.[7] Conversely, one can make a strong case for the legitimacy and the plausibility of a conception of an interpretive practice, weary of the abuses committed in the name of objective exegesis, that gives complete priority to the role of the reader in the ever contextual hermeneu-tical process that any interpretation is. Yet I want to insist that it is essential to conceive of the critical practice as carefully balancing the role of the text

---

6. See, for instance, James M. Robinson and John B. Cobb Jr., eds., *The New Hermeneu-tic* (New York: Harper & Row, 1964).

7. K. Stendahl, "Biblical Theology, Contemporary," in *Interpreter's Dictionary of the Bible* (New York and Nashville: Abingdon, 1962), 1:418–32.

and the role of the reader in the interpretive process. My insistence is passionate. It is not that this view is more legitimate or more plausible than either one of the other two. It is a value judgment. It is a matter of ethics of biblical interpretation.

When the two parts of the interpretive process are conceived as separate, people become alienated from their readings of the Bible and from the Bible itself. Hermeneutics becomes a sterile application that fails to empower the readers of the Bible, and critical exegesis loses its critical edge because it ignores its kinship with all other readings of the Bible. The study proposed here seeks to avoid these twin pitfalls by insisting that in order to be truly critical, a reading must acknowledge that it is contextual and interested (and thus hermeneutical), and that in order to be truly hermeneutical (meaningful for us), a reading must also be perceived as legitimate (based on critically acceptable evidence).

In the following pages of this introduction, I briefly sketch the main features of the proposed androcritical multidimensional study of discipleship according to the Sermon on the Mount and the broader conception of critical interpretation that it involves. Chapter 1 presents in greater detail these procedures and the multidimensional conception of discipleship that they include. This chapter is formulated in such a way as to provide a first broad application of these androcritical multidimensional procedures. Chapter 2, an androcritical multidimensional study of discipleship according to Matthew 4:18–22, rehearses these procedures and identifies some characteristics of discipleship according to the Gospel of Matthew by studying this short text. With this wealth of general and concrete reflections about discipleship, we will be ready to appreciate the richness of the teaching of the Sermon on the Mount that we shall study in the subsequent chapters.

Rethinking the Practice of Critical Interpretation

The Broad Characteristics of an Androcritical Approach

Let us clarify the shift in the practice of critical interpretation of biblical texts that this book advocates and illustrates. First, I want to emphasize that different practices of critical interpretation are necessary in different cultural and social contexts because of the specificity of the epistemology and value judgments found in each context. This is what I express by designating my practice of critical interpretation as "androcritical," a term that refers to the male European-American context in which I practice critical interpretation.

Adopting an *androcritical* approach starts with the judgment (a metacritical judgment, since it is about critical interpretations) that most male European-American scholarly biblical studies have lost their critical edge because they are still conceived in terms of a dichotomy between exegesis and hermeneutics, between what the text meant and what it means, between object and subject. This critique of traditional views of *critical interpretation* obviously involves a different yet plausible conceptualization of *critical* based on a different yet legitimate theory of *interpretation* that takes into account cross-cultural and even global communication,[8] even if its choice is guided by specific ethical concerns, as mentioned above and as discussed in chapter 1.

From this perspective, holding on to the dichotomy between exegesis and hermeneutics (or between object and subject) is failing to acknowledge the very character of the interpretive processes that occur when we read and interpret texts. It is failing to be fully critical, that is, as the root of the word "criticism" in the Greek *krinein*[9] suggests, failing to offer an interpretation that acknowledges the kinds of *judgments* that led it to its conclusions. While male European-American scholarly studies carefully specify their "legitimacy judgments" (through the use of critical methods), they rarely acknowledge the "epistemology" and "value" judgments they also involve.

In sum, the proposed study of discipleship according to the Sermon on the Mount is *androcritical* for several reasons:

1. Its starting point is a judgment that most of the interpretations proposed by male European-American scholars are not fully critical because they fail to acknowledge significant features of the interpretive processes that shape and authorize their conclusions.

2. Constructively, it seeks to elucidate these undisclosed features of *selected male European-American scholarly interpretations of the Sermon on the Mount*. More specifically, through a critical analysis it seeks to make explicit the legitimacy, epistemology, and value judgments that frame and support their *conclusions about the teaching* of the Sermon on the Mount regarding discipleship.

---

8. For me this conceptualization of "interpretation" owes much to semiotic theory, as is clear from my book *The Religious Dimensions of Biblical Texts: Greimas's Structural Semiotics and Biblical Exegesis*, SBL Semeia Studies (Atlanta: Scholars Press, 1990). It also owes much to postmodern studies, most directly to The Bible and Culture Collective, *The Postmodern Bible* (New Haven and London: Yale University Press, 1995), and to feminist epistemological reflections, including Allison M. Jaggar, "Love and Knowledge: Emotion and Feminist Epistemology," in *Gender/Body/Knowledge/Feminist Reconstructions of Being and Knowing*, ed. Allison M. Jaggar and Susan R. Bordo (New Brunswick, N.J.: Rutgers University Press, 1989), 145–71. In this latter essay, Jaggar proposes an epistemological model that makes room for the roles of emotions, ideology, and interest in the construction of knowledge, in addition to the role of reason.

9. The entry of Liddell-Scott on *krino* is quite revealing in that it suggests how much "criticism" is related to choosing, picking out, deciding, and thus "making discriminating judgments." This latter phrase is used by J. C. O'Neill in his article "Biblical Criticism" in *The Anchor Bible Dictionary*, ed. David Noel Freedman (New York: Doubleday, 1992), 1:725–30.

3. *It affirms the legitimacy and plausibility of these diverse male European-American interpretations* of discipleship according to the Sermon on the Mount, and it acknowledges their relative values, which make each of them more or less appropriate for specific contexts.

By explaining these characteristics of the proposed androcritical approach, I also present how this androcritical multidimensional study of discipleship according to the Sermon on the Mount will proceed.

An Interpretation of the Sermon on the Mount in Terms of Existing Interpretations

These first comments about what constitutes an "androcritical" study have already indicated that I am proposing a critical interpretation of existing interpretations, rather than a direct interpretation of the Sermon on the Mount. Nevertheless, it will truly be a study of discipleship *according to the Sermon on the Mount.* By emphasizing that my interpretation of this text is performed in terms of other interpretations, I simply make explicit a part of the interpretive process that leads me to my *conclusions about the teaching* of the Sermon on the Mount regarding discipleship. Concurrently, my perception of these conclusions is changed: I cannot see them any longer as the presentation of the only plausible and legitimate teaching of the Sermon on the Mount about discipleship, but as the presentation of one among several equally legitimate and plausible teachings of the Sermon on the Mount about discipleship.

This polysemic conception of the teaching of the Sermon on the Mount about discipleship is, in my view, the main contribution of my study. It is much needed in order to allow male European-American biblical scholars to regain a critical sense and to abandon our phantasmagoric propensity to intimate (and even to say), each in turn, that our interpretation presents "the" only true teaching of the Sermon on the Mount about discipleship, and thus that everybody else is wrong. We could simply laugh at this parody of a critical stance, if people (including us) were not deeply affected and hurt by it, as I have discussed elsewhere.[10]

In order to expose this critical shortcoming of male European-American scholarly studies (including my own), I have chosen to focus my androcritical study on four kinds of interpretations of Matthew by male European-American exegetes. Of course, I include my own interpretation of "discipleship according to the Sermon on the Mount." This interpretation is *legitimate* (I can point to the textual evidence that warrants it), *plausible* (it involves a conceptualization of discipleship that makes sense

---

10. See Patte, *Ethics of Biblical Interpretation,* 17–30.

in the present cultural context in which I am), and most *valuable* for me
and people in similar sociocultural situations (I am ready to advocate — to
preach — that it be urgently adopted by male European-American Christians because it would help us to be responsible and accountable toward
ourselves and toward others). Yet by explaining why I hold my interpretation to be legitimate, plausible, and valuable through an androcritical
multidimensional presentation, I make it impossible for me or for anybody
else to consider this interpretation as "the" universally true interpretation. Thus I show that my interpretation of the Sermon on the Mount as
presented in my commentary[11] is, despite what might be implied by its
methodological claims, nothing more than one among several equally legitimate and plausible interpretations, which I chose because of the value I
perceived in it for my present context.

For this purpose, I compare my interpretation with other ones, which I
selected for reasons related to issues of legitimacy, plausibility, and value.
I first chose to include the two contemporary interpretations that in my
view are the most influential in the European-American cultural context in
which I am — a context that is notably androcentric. Even though these
two interpretations are quite different from each other, they nevertheless
are readily perceived as legitimate, plausible, and valuable. The works of
Strecker[12] and Kingsbury[13] represent a first kind of interpretation, while
the works of Luz,[14] Davies, and Allison[15] represent another. Despite the

---

11. Daniel Patte, *The Gospel according to Matthew: A Structural Commentary on Matthew's Faith* (Minneapolis: Fortress, 1987; 3d printing, Valley Forge, Pa.: Trinity Press
International, 1996).

12. Georg Strecker, *Der Weg der Gerechtigkeit: Untersuchung zur Theologie des Matthäus*
(Göttingen: Vandenhoeck & Ruprecht, 1962; 3d ed. 1971; all references are to the 3d edition)
and *The Sermon on the Mount: An Exegetical Commentary*, trans. O. C. Dean Jr. (Nashville:
Abingdon, 1988).

13. Particularly his interpretation of discipleship in Matthew: Jack D. Kingsbury, "The
Verb *Akolouthein* ('to Follow') as an Index of Matthew's View of His Community," *Journal of
Biblical Literature* 97 (1978): 56–73 and *Matthew as Story* (Minneapolis: Fortress, 1986). As
we shall see, although using a different method in this latter work, Kingsbury's interpretation
remains very closely related to that of his earlier redaction critical studies, and is, on many
points, not unlike Strecker's.

14. Ulrich Luz, *Matthew 1–7: A Commentary* (Minneapolis: Augsburg, 1989), "The Dis-
ciples in the Gospel according to Matthew," in *The Interpretation of Matthew*, ed. Graham
Stanton (Minneapolis: Fortress; London: SPCK, 1983), 98–128, and *The Theology of the
Gospel according to Matthew* (Cambridge: Cambridge University Press, 1995).

15. W. D. Davies, *The Setting of the Sermon on the Mount* (Cambridge: Cambridge
University Press, 1964), and primarily, W. D. Davies and D. C. Allison Jr., *A Critical and
Exegetical Commentary on the Gospel according to Saint Matthew*, ICC, vols. 1–2 (Edinburgh: T. & T. Clark, 1988, 1991). Since this latter commentary wants to be a comprehensive
discussion of the critical literature, it ends up presenting critical arguments using a diversity of
critical methods and partial conclusions related to the perspective represented by these methods. Thus at times (e.g., on Mt 4:18–22) they present critical comments that support the
interpretation of Strecker and Kingsbury (rather than Luz). Yet, as a whole, their conclusions
are akin to those of Luz. Naturally they are not in full agreement on all points, but they
reinforce each other.

polemical debates between the proponents of these two kinds of interpretations, all their works are well-respected scholarly interpretations, which are therefore broadly acknowledged as legitimate and plausible by the scholarly guild. A fourth kind of interpretation, suggested by Edwards,[16] was added for the balance of the study (and for other reasons to be discussed below). The interpretation of Strecker and Kingsbury will be most directly compared with the interpretation developed out of Edwards's suggestions because it involves easily recognizable alternative choices; for similar reasons, the interpretation of Luz and Davies and Allison will be compared with mine.

I must emphasize that I do nothing extraordinary when I conceive of my study of discipleship according to the Sermon on the Mount as a second-level interpretation. I simply make explicit one of the processes that govern any interpretation, namely, that we always read a text in terms of other readings (of this text or of other texts). Thus my title remains accurate: I propose a study of "discipleship according to the Sermon on the Mount," although I make explicit that my interpretation, as any other one, is an interpretation of this text and topic in terms of other interpretations.

I deal in this study with interpretations by Strecker, Kingsbury, Luz, Davies and Allison, and Edwards because they are particularly helpful in clarifying important characteristics of my own interpretation. They represent very common interpretations of discipleship according to the Sermon on the Mount in similar androcentric European-American cultural contexts. This andro*critical* study is by definition focused on critical analyses of male European-American interpretations. This is a necessary step in the decentering process that I hope will result in allowing them to become accountable participants in biblical interpretation in a multicultural global context, alongside interpretations framed by the perspectives of different sociocultural contexts (as is discussed in chap. 7).

Many biblical scholars might be surprised by the suggestion that any interpretation of a text is done in terms of other interpretations. But they themselves signal that they use this procedure, even though they might not acknowledge it, when they include in their work footnotes referring to other interpretations. Of course, we often use such footnotes to express our disagreement with others and to underscore the originality of our interpretations as an independent (and thus objective) reading of the text. In this way, we often successfully convey to our readers that our interpretation is atemporal, acontextual, and thus universal, presenting "the" only true teaching of the text. Yet our footnotes also perform their primary function, which is to reveal what our interpretation owes to other

---

16. Richard A. Edwards, *Matthew's Story of Jesus* (Minneapolis: Fortress, 1985), and "Uncertain Faith: Matthew's Portrait of the Disciples," in *Discipleship in the New Testament*, ed., F. F. Segovia (Minneapolis: Fortress, 1985). Since he does not present a detailed study of the Sermon, I have to develop it myself on the basis of some of his suggestions.

people. They show that the questions we address to the text and the categories with which we frame our conclusions have been formulated in terms of other interpretations. This happens even when we totally disagree with these interpretations; we read the text looking for features that will allow us to refute these "incorrect" and "misleading" interpretations, and thus we perceive these textual features in the mirror of these other interpretations.

Making explicit that our interpretation is done in terms of other interpretations is necessary if we want to claim that our study is critical because this interpretive process decisively shapes, and authorizes, our interpretation. Our interpretation claims very different kinds of authority depending on whether it hides or acknowledges that it is a second-level interpretation. In the former case, it presents itself as objective and universal, that is, as an elucidation of "the" true teaching of the text, which should be accepted by everyone in any sociocultural situation. In the latter case, it presents itself as a contextual interpretation, limited by the kinds of interpretations in terms of which it read the text.

Androcriticism as Criticism of Interpretations by Male European-American Scholars

The preceding comments express in very general terms that androcriticism is simply a form of criticism. What O'Neill says about "biblical criticism"[17] applies to androcriticism. Of course, criticism does not take at face value either a text (i.e., an interpretation by a male European-American) or its implicit or explicit claims. Criticism is "the practice of analyzing and making discriminating judgments" about this text by bringing to understanding certain features of the text, such as its origin.

Thus criticism should not be taken to mean condemnation. My critical observation that male European-American scholarly interpretations (including mine) are, despite their implicit or explicit claims, contextual interpretations in terms of other interpretations is not in itself a condemnation. After all, any (adult) reader comes to a text having read other texts. Yet it is a condemnation of the implicit or explicit claim by male European-American scholars that their interpretations are direct interpretations of the text. This claim denies (instead of making explicit, as should be the case in a critical study) one of the significant processes that shaped these interpretations.

What is at stake in a critical study is not so much to make explicit all the concrete factors, circumstances, and persons who have directly or indirectly helped to focus our interpretations in one way or another. Listing all these, besides being quite long (and boring), would soon become a very artificial exercise based on a selective autobiographical reconstruction. In order to

---

17. O'Neill, "Biblical Criticism," 725.

make explicit the contextual character of an interpretation, it is enough for a critical study to show that a limited number of interpretations with quite different conclusions are as plausible and legitimate as the one advocated in the study. Thus I present beside my interpretation those of Strecker and Kingsbury, and those of Luz, Davies and Allison, as well as one suggested by Edwards. Yet in order to be in a position to affirm the legitimacy and plausibility of all these interpretations, including mine, even as I show their contextual (rather than universal) character, I must proceed to a critical analysis of each.

Three Kinds of Interpretive Judgments That a Critical Study Must Make Explicit

The problem with traditional male European-American scholarly interpretations is that, while claiming to be transparent, they do not disclose some of the prominent interpretive processes shaping and authorizing them. More specifically, the problem with these interpretations is that they are performed without a clear perception of the different roles that these interpretive processes have. As these processes are confused with each other, misinterpretations occur. The (andro)critical analysis of these scholarly interpretations involves both acknowledging what they already disclose — their legitimacy judgments — and elucidating what remains unsaid or hidden — in most instances, their epistemology and value judgments.

The use of critical methods in scholarly interpretations discloses *one* of their important interpretive processes — their *legitimacy judgments*. As is clear to everyone in the guild, a scholarly study of a biblical text must make explicit the critical argument (including evidence, warrants, criteria, method) that establishes the legitimacy of its *conclusions about what the text is and says* (CAWs). Thus through the self-conscious use of a specific critical method, each scholarly interpretation makes explicit how it establishes that its specific conclusions (CAWs) are *legitimate*. This disclosure is appropriate, and it must remain a central part of all critical studies, including androcritical studies. Yet the effort at self-consciousness should not stop at this point.

As a casual glance through the studies on the shelves of any contemporary library shows, different scholarly interpretations of the same text use different critical methods and demonstrate in this way the legitimacy of different *conclusions about what* (CAW) the text is and says. Beyond this, our (andro)critical study must also explain *why* one critical method was chosen instead of another one and *why* a scholar perceived the necessity of establishing the legitimacy of certain features of the interpretation, and not of others. This kind of inquiry soon leads to the recognition that interpretations which use different critical methods usually propose different *conclusions about what the text is and says* (CAWs). More specifically, each method leads the interpreters to underscore specific aspects of *what the text is* (in terms of literary genre, literary conventions, relations to historical situations, relations to other texts and traditions, etc.) and/or *what the text says* (it presents, for instance, a Christological or eschatological view, exhortations and other commands, motivations to act, a symbolic world, patterns of interpretations). The critical methods ground the legitimacy of specific CAWs on different kinds of features of the text — different meaning-producing dimensions of the text. Thus, making explicit the *distinctiveness* of the legitimacy judgments of a given interpretation must take place in a multidimensional practice in which it can be compared with the different legitimacy judgments of other interpretations.

In order to elucidate other aspects of the distinctiveness of each interpretation, we must also acknowledge and make explicit (1) the cultural, intellectual, and theoretical stance and the *epistemology judgments* through which we conceptualize how certain aspects (e.g., a theme) of what the text says have the potential to affect readers and thus to be a *teaching* for these readers (be they readers in the original or in later rhetorical contexts), and thus through which we formulate a different kind of conclusion, *conclusions about the teaching* (CATs) of the text regarding this theme;[18] as well as (2) the interests, concerns, and commitments that led us to focus our interpretation on a specific theme or subtheme — following certain *value judgments*.

Self-consciousness about the main interpretive processes we use demands that we acknowledge and make explicit in our (andro)critical study the three kinds of judgments that most directly shape and authorize our interpretation of a text — legitimacy, epistemology, and value judgments — instead of pretending there is only one kind, legitimacy judgments. Similarly, we need to acknowledge the three kinds of conclusions regarding a given text.

- Legitimacy judgments lead to *conclusions about what the text is and says* (CAWs); these include conclusions about which features of the text are particularly significant (according to a certain group of interpreters).

- Epistemology judgments lead to *conclusions about the teaching* (CATs) of the text *to a specific audience* regarding a given theme or topic; CATs concern the teaching that has the potential to affect readers of the text (be they in the original or in later rhetorical sit-

---

18. The distinction between, on the one hand, legitimacy judgments and CAWs and, on the other hand, epistemology judgments and CATs corresponds approximately to the distinction between two kinds of interpretive practices, "hermeneutical practice" and "rhetorical practice," made by Elisabeth Schüssler Fiorenza in *Revelation: Vision of a Just World* (Minneapolis: Fortress, 1991). This correspondence is only approximate because I believe it is important to mark the distinctive role of *value judgments*.

uations) because it is about a theme, such as discipleship, that is *plausible* for these readers.

- Value judgments lead to *conclusions about the relative value* (CARVs) of diverse interpretations, that is, about the different ways in which their respective CATs affect the interpreter and other actual readers due to the positive or negative relationship of these interpretations to the readers' convictions and commitments in specific concrete situations.[19]

The Respective Roles of Legitimacy, Epistemology, and Value Judgments

To further clarify why an androcritical study must disclose each of these three kinds of judgments and how procedures for this disclosure can be envisioned, the respective roles of these judgments in the process of interpretation need to be clarified.[20] These roles are particularly apparent in the case of interpretations of texts, such as the Bible, which, in one sense or another, have scriptural authority for a significant segment of the society in which they are interpreted.

The Value Judgments

First, and most generally, for Christian believers (as well as for those around them), interpretations of biblical texts always matter. They are never inconsequential. They are always interested and thus reflect *specific value judgments*, even when they claim to be disinterested. This interpretive process is at work in any interpretation of the Bible[21] because directly or in-

---

19. The threefold distinction I propose here is similar to the distinction between the three functions of language that Brian K. Blount (*Cultural Interpretation: Reorienting New Testament Criticism* [Minneapolis: Fortress, 1995]) underscores, with the difference that I try more systematically to take into account the metadiscursive character of any interpretation. Thus the threefold distinction between legitimacy, epistemology, and value judgments and the corresponding three sets of conclusions — CAWs, CATs, and CARVs — describes "interpretive discourses" (metadiscourses) instead of "discourses," as proposed by Greimas and by Halliday in their respective communication/semiotic theory. In each case, this model is threefold. For Greimas (see A. J. Greimas and J. Courtés, *Semiotics and Language: An Analytical Dictionary*, trans. L. Crist, D. Patte, et al. [Bloomington: Indiana University Press, 1982]), it includes "syntactical," "semantic," and "discursive" processes and structures. For M. A. K. Halliday (*Explorations in the Functions of Language* [London: Edward Arnold, 1973]), on whose work Blount bases his proposal, it includes "textual," "ideational," and "interpersonal" dimensions. As noted above, this threefold model is closely related to the model posited by Schüssler Fiorenza in *Revelation: Vision of a Just World,* even though she is content to emphasize two components — the hermeneutic and rhetoric components.

20. Other issues concerning the plausibility of these three types of judgments will be addressed in chapter 1 as we deal with a concrete topic: "discipleship" and diverse ways in which it is understood.

21. These comments also apply to the interpretation of any text, although the role of value judgments might be more subtle in the case of nonauthoritative texts. There is no need to argue this point here.

directly people are significantly affected by any interpretation of a text that has scriptural authority for them (or for people around them). In one way or another, this interpretation expresses what is in this text for its readers and how the readers should be affected by it.

For believers (and indirectly for nonbelievers), the interpretations of a text with scriptural authority are *pro me/nobis* interpretations, i.e., interpretations by which believers live. This is explicit in the case of interpretations that emphasize the *conclusions about the teaching* of the Bible that readily support the convictions of one religious group or another. But this is also true of interpretations that relish emphasizing *conclusions about the teaching* of the text that contradict believers' convictions; these interpretations are presented with the hope that people will assume these conclusions and in so doing abandon their futile convictions. Whether interpreters believe or not in the scriptural authority of the text, in a sociocultural situation where a significant segment of the population believes in it, the interpretation of a biblical text is always interested. Interpreters and their readers alike have vested interests in (or concerns with) the *conclusions about the teaching* of the text that the interpretations present. When these CATs either support or contradict their convictions or commitments, readers cannot remain indifferent; conversely, when they express indifference, they signal that an interpretation is *value* neutral — an affirmation that obviously involves a value judgment. In sum, the emotionally charged debates over interpretations and their *conclusions about the teaching* of a biblical text, and, conversely, the strong claims to being disinterested, are clear evidence that value judgments are involved and that the interpretation implicitly or explicitly includes certain *conclusions about the relative value* (CARVs) of the teaching of the text.

The Epistemology Judgments

Since *conclusions about the teaching* (CATs) of a text require at least some conceptualization of this teaching, *epistemology judgments* have to be included among the interpretive processes through which the interpretation was generated. These conclusions have to make sense in a certain cultural context. The role of epistemology judgments is particularly clear in the case of thematic studies, which deliberately seek to elucidate the teaching of the text to its readers regarding a specific theme, such as discipleship.

A reading of the Sermon on the Mount for its teaching about discipleship reflects, as discussed above, some kind of interest in this theme and thus a general value judgment. Yet it also reflects some kind of conceptualization of discipleship, which becomes the focus of the reading and/or focalizes it on those features of the text that concern this theme. Acknowledging the role of epistemology judgments amounts to recognizing that a thematic interpretation (and actually, any interpretation) is shaped and focused by a conceptualization of the theme emphasized in its *conclusions about the teaching* of the text and that this theme, here discipleship, is conceptualized out of the reader's peculiar cultural, intellectual, and theoretical resources.

A few remarks will suffice here, starting with the observation that any given reading of the Sermon on the Mount for its teaching about discipleship asks a certain set of questions derived from a specific conceptualization of discipleship, which is in turn born out of the reader's cultural perspective. This conceptualization might be quite broad or might be sharply focused on an aspect of discipleship. It has each time a specificity that comes from emphasizing one aspect of the phenomenon of discipleship, an aspect that is viewed as its center. This choice of a specific conceptualization of the theme, and thus of the kind of questions that are addressed to the text, does not affect in any way the legitimacy of the interpretation. If someone raises a question for which the text does not have any answer, the interpretation remains legitimate (true to the evidence) when one simply states this fact. Actually, the role of epistemology judgments includes verifying that some features of the text actually express a teaching about the theme chosen for an interpretation. Thus the conceptualization of the theme, discipleship, already focuses the interpretation on specific features of the text.

Extended discussion of these issues will be necessary in the following chapters because most traditional scholarly interpretations totally fail to make explicit the epistemology judgments that they involve by presupposing (against all historical evidence) that there is only one universally recognizable understanding of discipleship according to the Sermon on the Mount, which is nothing other than Matthew's own conceptualization of discipleship. Therefore, they cannot even imagine that the understanding of discipleship and the questions they address to the text are the outcome of epistemology judgments that they have performed out of their cultural context. Of course, each (legitimate) interpretation elucidates something about Matthew's conceptualization of discipleship. But because of the focalization provided by the epistemology judgments, it is in each case a very partial understanding of Matthew's conceptualization.

In sum, each interpretation is focused on certain features of the text — a given meaning-producing dimension of the text — by the *epistemology judgments* that conceptualize its theme and thus establish its plausibility. This theme was chosen among other plausible themes through *value judgments* as the focus of the interpretation and of its *conclusions about the teaching* of the text. A third kind of judgments, the *legitimacy judgments*, establishes that these conclusions and the rest of the interpretation are grounded in appropriate evidence.

The Legitimacy Judgments

Having said that any interpretation involves some kind of *conclusions about the teaching* of the text, I hasten to add that a given interpretation might not emphasize these conclusions, but might only allude to them because it is so totally devoted to establishing warrants for them. Scholarly interpretations often do this by proposing detailed descriptions of features of the text, including *what the text says* about various themes (whether it is or is not a theme that affects readers) and warranting arguments about *what the text is* that call on evidence beyond the text, for instance, its historical setting or the literary conventions of the time. In such cases, the conclusions of these scholarly interpretations might be *conclusions about what the text is and says* (CAWs), i.e, penultimate conclusions that warrant certain *conclusions about the teaching* (CATs). Even when a scholarly interpretation exclusively emphasizes its CAWs, at least implicitly, it still includes *conclusions about the teaching* of the text.

Conversely, we need to recognize that *any* interpretation grounds its *conclusions about the teaching* in some kind of textual evidence. At minimum, it reflects how the interpreter was affected by and/or reacted to certain features of the text. Thus any interpretation presupposes that its *conclusions about the teaching* are warranted, whether or not it makes explicit its warrants, which are *conclusions about what the text is and says*. Another interpretive process and its role become apparent: the performance of *legitimacy judgments*. Since any interpretation includes at least some warrants for its *conclusions about the teaching* of the text, it implicitly or explicitly reflects the performance of legitimacy judgments that establish what counts as warranting evidence for specific *conclusions about the teaching* of the text.

Relationships between Pro Me/Nobis Interpretations and Scholarly Interpretations

How are scholarly interpretations related to *pro me/nobis* interpretations, i.e., when we read the text to understand how it affects us? I suggested above that *pro me/nobis* interpretations should not be understood as prolongations of scholarly interpretations that would first need to establish "the" true teaching of the text. Rather, the relationship between these two kinds of interpretations is best conceived of as a complex interaction. Each of them is the product of the three kinds of interpretive judgments — legitimacy, epistemology, and value judgments — and includes or presupposes corresponding conclusions (CAWs, CATs, and CARVs). The differences between them come from the fact that they make explicit and thus emphasize different kinds of interpretive judgments and conclusions.

Pro me/nobis interpretation is a category in which I include all the readings that *make explicit their interested character*, such as devotional readings by believers and advocacy readings of all kinds. They emphasize how the text directly or indirectly affects the interpreters through a specific teaching. As such, *pro me/nobis* interpretations cannot but foreground their *conclusions about the teaching* of the text and allude to the epistemology and value judgments that they reflect, even if they do not make them fully explicit. Because of this focus on their interests and on their *conclusions about the teaching* of the text, in most instances *pro me/nobis* interpretations barely mention their CAWs, that is, the warrants that point to the evidence that supports them. This is not a criticism. On the contrary, I want to affirm that *pro me/nobis* interpretations that do not pretend to be something else are "implicitly legitimate," i.e., they are appropriately grounded in textual evidence, even though they may not make it explicit. Precisely because they carefully account for the ways in which given interpreters are affected by the text, they have to make sure that the text does affect its readers in this way and thus focus themselves on features that have the potential to produce such effects. Thus I want to insist that, until proven otherwise, any authentic *pro me/nobis* interpretation — which "authentically" reflects how the text affects a given interpreter in a concrete situation — should be viewed as basically legitimate in the sense that it includes *legitimate conclusions about the teaching* (CATs) of the text, even though their legitimacy remains to be demonstrated, and that in the process of this demonstration the interpretation and these CATs will certainly be refined and complemented.

Presupposing that all authentic *pro me/nobis* interpretations are implicitly legitimate is not saying that they are free from inaccuracies — as we teachers know well from reading our students' interpretations. These inaccuracies usually concern warranting statements, not *conclusions about the teaching* of the text.[22] For instance, believers often seek to warrant their *conclusions about the teaching* of the text of their devotional readings by calling on other *conclusions about the teaching* as evidence (thus creating a circular argument), or even by calling on their interests or convictions. In this latter case, the readers/believers obtain their warranting conclusions by projecting their interests and convictions onto the text instead of pointing to those aspects of the text on which the *pro me/nobis* interpretations are grounded. In sum, *pro me/nobis* interpretations that pretend to be scholarly readings often have fanciful warrants. But this does not mean that their *conclusions about the teaching* of the text are illegitimate. It simply means that their legitimacy remains to be elucidated — one part of the task of a critical study.

---

22. The more a *pro me/nobis* interpretation pretends to be authoritative, implicitly denying its interested and contextual character, the more it includes inaccuracies, since it seeks to establish the legitimacy of its *conclusions about the teaching* without truly disclosing and becoming self-conscious about the legitimacy judgments it involves. Only a critical study, which deliberately aims at making explicit the legitimacy judgments reflected in this interpretation by distinguishing them clearly from its epistemology and value judgments, can hope to have reliable warranting conclusions.

Conversely, scholarly interpretations emphasize and make explicit their legitimacy judgments (through the use of critical methods) and may be focused entirely on descriptions of what the text is and says (CAWs) and on warranting arguments. Yet, as we noted, they always involve some kind of *conclusions about the teaching* of the text, even when conclusions remain completely implicit. As such, each scholarly interpretation can be viewed as a second-level interpretation that makes explicit the warrants and the legitimacy judgments that a *pro me/nobis* reading left implicit, since at first the reader's attention was entirely focused on the teaching of the text *for him or her* or for a group *(for us).*

Table 1

The Relationship between *Pro me/nobis* Interpretations
and Traditional Scholarly Interpretations

	Pro me/nobis Interpretations	Traditional[23] Scholarly Interpretations	Exemplary Critical Interpretations
CARVs	Explicit	Implicit	Explicit
Value Judgment	+/-Explicit	Implicit	Explicit
CATs	+/- Explicit	+/- Explicit	Explicit
Epistemology Judgment	Implicit	+/- Explicit	Explicit
CAWs	Implicit	Explicit	Explicit
Legitimacy Judgment	Implicit	Explicit (methods)	Explicit

CARVs = *Conclusions about the relative value* of the teaching of a text
CATs = *Conclusions about the teaching* of a text
CAWs = *Conclusions about what the text is and says*

Among other things, table 1 shows the features of both *pro me* and scholarly interpretations that need to be brought to critical understanding. It also shows the features of each kind of interpretations that are *reliable* (those that are *explicit*), *more or less reliable* (those that are *+/- explicit*), and those that are *not reliable* (those that remain *implicit)*. The table also shows that *pro me* interpretations cannot be directly compared with scholarly interpretations because before being brought to critical understanding in an "exemplary critical interpretation," they do not foreground the same type of conclusions. A *pro me* interpretation should not be declared illegitimate because its explicit conclusions (about the relative value of a teaching of the text) are different from a scholarly interpretation's conclusions (about what the text is and says). Vice versa, believer-interpreters should not, in the name of their *pro me* interpretations, reject as valueless

---

23. I use "traditional" as a shorthand designation of "androcentric and Eurocentric" interpretations.

(or blasphemous) the interpretations of scholars. These two kinds of interpretations are not directly comparable because the conclusions that they respectively foreground are not directly comparable. The common component that can be most easily compared is their respective CATs, which in most instances can be readily inferred from the interpretations, even if they are not explicitly stated.

Thus a complex relationship materializes between *pro me* interpretations and traditional scholarly interpretations. A scholarly critical interpretation, by means of its legitimacy judgments made explicit through the use of a critical method, "brings to critical understanding" in its descriptions of what the text is and says (CAWs) the evidence for the conclusions about the teaching (CATs) of the text — which often discretely remain in the background (+/- Explicit) because they are the basis of the scholar's own conclusions about the relative value (CARVs), which the scholar might have first formulated as a *pro me* interpretation. No wonder then that different scholars produce different kinds of scholarly interpretations. They bring to critical understanding different CARVs. They can do so and remain critical because there is a variety of legitimacy judgments, each of which is acknowledged as at least potentially appropriate by the scholarly guild. Indeed, the use of different critical methods by various contemporary scholarly studies shows that a variety of legitimacy judgments reach different *conclusions about what* (CAWs) the text is and says, which show the legitimacy of diverse *pro me* interpretations with their specific conclusions about the teaching of the text.

Finally, table 1 makes explicit that an exemplary critical interpretation should strive to make explicit all the components of the interpretive process. This ideal is never fully realized because it is by nature an ongoing process. As critical scholars, we are constantly confronted by new interpretations (including our own) which, along with all other interpretations, need to be brought to critical understandings. Table 1 makes clear that one should not proceed in the same way with *pro me* and traditional scholarly interpretations. Regarding *pro me* interpretations, CAWs and legitimacy judgments must be made explicit; regarding scholarly interpretations, CARVs and value judgments. In both cases, one needs to make more explicit CATs and epistemology judgments. This critical process enables one to compare and contrast different interpretations in terms of truly analogous components. This is what I hope to accomplish, regarding a limited number of interpretations by male European-American scholars, in this androcritical study: to make it possible for me (in chap. 7) and for you (beyond this book) to compare and contrast their relative values to those of other interpretations.

The Necessary Multidimensionality of Critical Biblical Interpretations

Finally, I want to emphasize that our androcritical study, like any critical biblical interpretation, must be *multidimensional* in order to be truly critical. In a sense, the necessity of multidimensionality was discussed throughout this introduction, as I tried to underscore that a multidimensional practice of critical biblical study is not only heuristically valuable but also legitimate and plausible.

Throughout this introduction, I have emphasized the *plausibility* of the claim that one-dimensional scholarly biblical studies fail to elucidate all the major interpretive processes they involve, and thus they can appropriately be viewed as uncritical. Being critical involves acknowledging the legitimacy, plausibility, and relative value of several interpretations, rather than claiming or implying in one's practice that a given interpretation presents "the" only true and universal teaching of a text. Thus I have said that my goal is to bring to critical understanding my own interpretation and to invite each of my readers to do the same with his or her own interpretation. By stating in addition that this can only be done through acknowledging the legitimacy, plausibility, and relative value of other interpretations, I made it quite explicit that a critical interpretation has to be multidimensional. Thus I have begun to show the plausibility of a conceptualization of critical biblical studies as multidimensional, by seeking to explain why it made sense according to a carefully thought through epistemology judgment.

The *relative value* of a multidimensional practice of biblical studies has been supported through references to my preceding book, *Ethics of Biblical Interpretation: A Reevaluation*, which proposes a detailed argument underscoring the ethical necessity of multidimensional critical biblical studies.[24] I do not need to rehearse here this *value judgment,* even though it naturally is intimately linked to my deepest convictions, interests, and concerns.

The question that remains is therefore a question of *legitimacy*. Is it legitimate to claim that quite different conclusions about the teaching of a text are equally appropriate representations of the teaching of this text? Is it legitimate to claim that these different sets of conclusions result from interpretations focused on different meaning-producing dimensions of the texts? Where is the evidence that supports these claims?

Showing this evidence is a matter of

- discussing the multidimensional character of our collective work as biblical scholars who use different critical methods that establish the legitimacy of different interpretations by calling on diverse features of the text and by pointing out how each method is appropriately

---

24. See especially chapter 2 of Patte, *Ethics of Biblical Interpretation,* 37–71.

grounded in one or another theory about history, language, literature, gender, sociology, or anthropology, for instance;[25]

- presenting in a systematic way, in terms of one or another of these theories, the plurality of textual dimensions out of which various readers produce different meanings;[26]

- showing the polysemy of specific texts — a most concrete and thus most convincing kind of evidence; the present study will show the polysemy of Matthew 4:18–22 and of the Sermon on the Mount in the following chapters.

The problem is that many biblical scholars — especially male European-American scholars — reject any discussion of multidimensional critical study as an illegitimate endeavor even before considering this evidence. This is a part of the problem that I have underscored here. Many male European-American scholars confuse issues pertaining to value judgments and to epistemology judgments with issues pertaining to legitimacy judgments.

For some, a multidimensional critical study is itself a contradiction in terms. Instead of acknowledging that they do not understand what is involved or instead of seeking to identify the epistemological issues that prevent them from making sense of it, they declare that this procedure is illegitimate because "as is well known" there is no real ground for it, and therefore, there is no point in considering this grounding. Similarly, and even more commonly, male European-American scholars reject out of hand even the possibility that a multidimensional conception of critical biblical studies might be legitimate because of ideological reasons, including theological ones. Multidimensional interpretation cannot be legitimate because "as is well known" any given text has a single true meaning. Different interpretations of the same text cannot be equally legitimate because then no interpretation is really true and then every teaching in the Bible is relative — something that cannot be, otherwise how could the Bible be word of God? In sum, under the cover of claims of illegitimacy, the rejection of

---

25. Contemporary introductions to biblical critical methods strive to respect the distinctiveness of each method. I refer to two of these that are, in my view, particularly successful in this endeavor, and are complementary due to their different origins and the ten years that separate them: Raymond F. Collins, *Introduction to the New Testament* (Garden City, N.Y.: Doubleday, 1983); Steven L. McKenzie and Stephen R. Haynes, eds., *To Each Its Own Meaning: An Introduction to Biblical Criticisms and Their Application* (Louisville: Westminster/ John Knox, 1993). See also the remarkable presentation of the relations among diverse critical interpretations using different methods in Mieke Bal, *Murder and Difference: Gender, Genre, and Scholarship on Sisera's Death* (Bloomington: Indiana University Press, 1988).

26. From the perspective of historiography, see Van Harvey, *The Historian and the Believer: A Confrontation of the Modern Historian's Principles of Judgment and the Christian's Will-to-Believe* (New York: Macmillan, 1966). From the perspective of semiotic theory, see Daniel Patte, *Religious Dimensions of Biblical Texts*.

multidimensional biblical studies is actually based on an *epistemology*, or *value*, judgment.

In the following chapters, I will try to dispel such confusions among epistemology, value, and legitimacy judgments, simultaneously presenting the evidence that explains why I am convinced of the legitimacy of multidimensional critical biblical studies. In keeping with this approach, I have to underscore that this is not the only possible way of interpreting the phenomenon "interpretation of the Bible"; the one-dimensional perspective is also plausible and legitimate (based on appropriate evidence). Thus my choice of this view of critical biblical studies is itself based on an epistemology and a value judgment. As I briefly suggested above (and as explained at length in *Ethics of Biblical Interpretation),* for me the practice of critical biblical studies must be multidimensional in order to be ethically responsible and accountable toward those it affects. This value judgment can also be formulated theologically, as I will discuss in the following pages.

Procedures Followed in This Androcritical Multidimensional Study of Discipleship according to the Sermon on the Mount

Since a critical study must make explicit its interpretive processes, in order to prevent or overcome disastrous confusions among legitimacy, epistemology, and value judgments, I will use this threefold distinction in all aspects of this work.

My study of "discipleship according to the Sermon on the Mount" is "androcritical" in the sense of being deliberately focused on interpretations of Matthew 4:18–22 and of the Sermon on the Mount by male European-Americans — interpreters who belong to sociocultural contexts similar to mine, gender being a relevant category in an androcentric culture.

In chapter 1, this study of "discipleship according to the Sermon on the Mount" begins to gain a critical edge by acknowledging the interpretive process involved in the very conception of its primary task as "the bringing to critical understanding of interpretations." For this purpose, I strive to make explicit (1) some of the *epistemology judgments* involved in the process of conceptualizing "discipleship" by taking note of the plurality of conceptualizations in present European-American sociocultural contexts; and (2) some of the *value judgments* involved in choosing to pursue this study in an androcritical and multidimensional way.

This is merely the beginning of the critical process. In subsequent chapters, as I proceed to interpret interpretations of Matthew 4:18–22 and of the Sermon on the Mount and these texts in terms of their interpretations, I deliberately seek to elucidate the legitimacy, epistemology, and value judgments involved in each interpretation.

CHAPTER 1

A Multidimensional Critical Study of Discipleship

Its Plausibility, Legitimacy, and Relative Value

Throughout this book I underscore, illustrate, and thus seek to demonstrate that a plurality of interpretations regarding the teaching of a specific text (the Sermon on the Mount) about a specific theme (discipleship) are equally plausible and legitimate. I also emphasize that they have quite different relative values; it is on the basis of a value judgment that readers ultimately assess which interpretation is the most significant for them. From this multidimensional critical perspective, the conclusions about the teaching of the text that a reader draws from a text make sense in a specific (sub)cultural context and reflect the way in which the reader was affected by an actual dimension of the text — thus, these *conclusions about the teaching* of the text result from appropriate (conscious or subconscious) epistemology and legitimacy judgments. Yet they also reflect (conscious or subconscious) value judgments through which the reader has *chosen* one among several equally plausible and legitimate interpretations.

My decision to adopt this critical perspective, rather than another one, reflects the same kind of choice. Thus in this first chapter I want to clarify that I *chose* this multidimensional critical perspective for the present study because it was one of the perspectives I perceived as both plausible and legitimate, and because I saw a greater value in it. By saying so, I acknowledge the hermeneutical circle in which my study is caught, as are all critical studies, whether they acknowledge it or not; I choose a critical perspective from the standpoint of this very perspective.

One of the main goals of this chapter is to demonstrate that the proposed multidimensional critical study is plausible and legitimate. This demonstration is necessary because for many biblical scholars the very suggestion that a "critical" study might be "multidimensional" is a contradiction in terms. I can hear my colleagues muttering now. "Of course, one can readily conceive of different interpretations of a text aimed at serving the interests of various groups! But this is hermeneutics rather than exegesis, isn't it? Or eisegesis instead of exegesis? How can you even imagine that diverging interpretations of discipleship according to the Sermon on the Mount could be equally plausible and equally legitimate?"

I offer no counterargument in response to these ironical rhetorical questions by means of which certain scholars believe they can bypass the issues I raised in *Ethics of Biblical Interpretation.* Seeking to demonstrate that their one-dimensional view of critical study is neither plausible nor legitimate is a futile endeavor.[1] I am convinced that such a one-dimensional view is both plausible and legitimate. My point is simply that a multidimensional view of biblical critical study has *equal claim* to plausibility and legitimacy. For biblical scholars in the pulpit and the classroom, who are convinced of the plausibility and legitimacy of a one-dimensional perspective, I need to justify my claim that it is *equally* plausible and legitimate to conceive of a critical study as multidimensional.

As I develop this argument, I also affirm the legitimacy and plausibility of advocacy hermeneutics, which are almost exclusively concerned with the reception of the text by readers in various cultural and social contexts — another alternative perspective. Yet the multidimensional critical perspective I adopt departs from such advocacy hermeneutical perspectives in that I emphasize the question of "legitimacy" of the several interpretations, i.e., I emphasize the importance of elucidating how each interpretation is legitimately grounded in the text, or, more specifically, in one of the meaning-producing dimensions of the text.

By the very fact that I affirm the equal plausibility and legitimacy of three critical perspectives — the ones that govern one-dimensional practices of traditional European-American exegesis, hermeneutical practices of advocacy interpretations, and the multidimensional practices proposed here — it becomes clear that I adopt a multidimensional approach because of its greater relative value. Since I acknowledge that I perceive a better relative value in this perspective from my point of view as an interpreter who happens to be a Protestant male European-American, I also signal that my multidimensional practice is "androcritical": it is because of certain concerns and interests that I have as a male European-American that I pursue it. This practice is also andro*critical* because it criticizes andro*centric* practices that do not acknowledge their interested and contextual character.

Let me be more explicit. The one-dimensional view that a critical study should aim at elucidating and formulating conclusions regarding a *single* true teaching (the single *logos*) of a text about a given theme makes sense when it is envisioned from the point of view of *modern* theories

---

1. See Daniel Patte, *Ethics of Biblical Interpretation: A Reevaluation* (Louisville: Westminster/John Knox, 1995).

of interpretation; this is a plausible epistemology judgment.[2] Similarly, the corollary one-dimensional view that a diversity of methods contributes to establishing the legitimacy of this *single* true teaching can be justified by emphasizing that it is appropriate for a *modern* critical study of biblical texts to privilege one method (or one set of methods) that is particularly well suited for the study of religious texts belonging to a distant historical past. Then it can be shown that reducing all other methods to the role of maidservants of the primary one is appropriately grounded on evidence concerning the process of interpretation of biblical texts; this is an appropriate legitimacy judgment.

But I am also convinced that a multidimensional view of critical study of the Bible is equally plausible and equally legitimate. Is it not plausible to acknowledge, without undue humility, that other people's views of "discipleship according to the Sermon on the Mount" as an ethical practice are as appropriately conceptualized as our own, even as they call on different ethical theories (that is, different "preunderstandings of the moral life," as Ogletree aptly calls them)?[3] Thus it is plausible to affirm that epistemology judgments remain appropriate, even as they vary from one cultural context to another. Similarly, is it not legitimate to recognize that the plurality of critical methods presently recognized by the guild demonstrates that a plurality of interpretations of the Sermon on the Mount are appropriately grounded in textual evidence? Thus a legitimate critical stance involves acknowledging that different critical methods elucidate different codes of a text, or different voices of a text, or as I prefer to say, different meaning-producing dimensions of a text. This is simply saying that, for instance, historical, rhetorical, literary, sociological, and anthropological critical methods study different sets of significant features of a given text.

Similarly, I readily envision the plausibility and legitimacy of hermeneutical practices, which underscore the role of the reader to the point that, implicitly or explicitly, they assume that the text which is interpreted is in fact constructed by the reader, as Fish suggested.[4] The multiplicity of

---

2. I allude to the hermeneutical theories and preunderstandings that deconstructionist and postmodern scholars call "logocentric," following Jacques Derrida, *Of Grammatology*, trans. Gayatri Chakravorty Spivak (Baltimore: Johns Hopkins University Press, 1976). Logocentrism, which involves the preunderstanding that a meaning is present in the text and is thus "the" (single) meaning of the text, is imbricated with the metaphysics of presence in *modern* Western thought. Thus Derrida notes that "Logocentrism is an ethnocentric metaphysics" (op. cit., 76), a point that is underscored by The Bible and Culture Collective, *The Postmodern Bible* (New Haven and London: Yale University Press, 1995), 122–23. It follows that a nonlogocentric perspective would also in and of itself be imbricated in an ethnocentric metaphysics: this time, the metaphysics (or antimetaphysics) of a *postmodern* culture.

3. Thomas W. Ogletree, *The Use of the Bible in Christian Ethics: A Constructive Essay* (Philadelphia: Fortress, 1983).

4. See Stanley E. Fish, *Is There a Text in This Class? The Authority of Interpretive Communities* (Cambridge: Harvard University Press, 1980). See the remarkable essay on "reader-response criticism" in The Bible and Culture Collective, *The Postmodern Bible,* 20–

interpretations — including the multiplicity of scholarly interpretations — provides ample evidence for such a claim; postmodern theories provide adequate epistemological framework for apprehending its plausibility.

Yet from the multidimensional perspective that I adopt and its balanced view of the respective roles of text and reader in the reading process, I can readily argue for the legitimacy and plausibility of envisioning a text as multidimensional (or multivoiced, or multicoded). From this perspective it is legitimate and plausible to envision that any given reading includes two processes. In each case, a text affects certain readers through *one* (but not all) of its specific meaning-producing dimensions (the role of the text); conversely, readers focus their attention on, define, and select one of the meaning-producing dimensions of the text because in one way or another it addresses specific interests and concerns that they have (the role of the reader).

In sum, without denying the plausibility and legitimacy of one-dimensional and hermeneutical views of critical biblical studies, I want to emphasize the equal plausibility and legitimacy of a multidimensional view. The adoption of one or the other of these practices of critical biblical studies results *from a choice* among (at least) three broad sets of equally plausible and legitimate options. In each instance, this choice is made in terms of a value judgment, i.e., in terms of the scholar's interests and concerns. Personally, I opt for a multidimensional critical (and androcritical) study because of ethical reasons underscored in *Ethics of Biblical Interpretation:*[5] because of my concerns for the very problematic consequences of one-dimensional critical practices, and because of my interests in the positive effects that we can expect from a multidimensional practice, but not from a reader-response hermeneutical practice.

Consequently, in this chapter I propose to show that the androcritical multidimensional study of discipleship according to the Sermon on the Mount presented in this book is conceptually plausible (i.e., that it is one of several plausible ways of conceptualizing a critical study of such a topic; an epistemology judgment); that appropriate evidence can be adduced in order to support it (this kind of critical study is one of the several kinds of study of this topic that can be grounded on appropriate evidence; a legitimacy judgment); and also that the proposed study with its specific multidimensional and androcritical character has been shaped by choices among several equally plausible and legitimate options (choices I ultimately made on the basis of certain interests and concerns; a value judgment).[6] In the concluding part of this chapter I will therefore clarify the

---

69. This reader-response perspective is partially or completely adopted by some feminist and other advocacy interpreters.

5. Patte, *Ethics of Biblical Interpretation.*

6. Despite the overlap in topic, I will not repeat here the ethical reasons that led me to adopt this androcritical multidimensional practice of biblical studies. I proposed such an ethical argument in Patte, *Ethics of Biblical Interpretation.*

interested character of my study — its theological and androcritical character — which is ultimately aimed at facilitating the practice of responsible Christian discipleship in the present global context.

The Epistemological Plausibility of Multiple Conceptualizations of Discipleship as Ethical Practice

My study of the theme of discipleship was first prompted by a puzzlement, i.e., by an epistemological issue. Discipleship, as a designation for the practice of Christian faith, seems to be a wide-open question for many of our contemporaries in Europe and North America. Yet the question they have about it is not necessarily the one that we teachers and preachers expect. For us as for them the practice of discipleship is an ethical practice. But for many of our contemporaries it raises basic ethical issues that we often ignore. Thus at the outset we are in the presence of two different types of conceptualizations of discipleship as ethical practice: ours and that of our contemporaries. Taking seriously, and therefore puzzling over, the different interpretations of our contemporaries is a most appropriate starting point for a responsible critical study.[7]

I want therefore to argue that it is as plausible to affirm as it is to deny that the various epistemologies through which discipleship is conceptualized should be respected as at least potentially appropriate in specific cultural situations. But in order to understand it, we biblical scholars, and especially male European-American ones, need to accept to change our perspective by learning to raise different questions about discipleship.

Learning to Raise Different Questions about Discipleship

As perpetual students aware of the limits of our knowledge, we teachers often assume that when people have questions about discipleship (or any other topic) it is because they lack information about it. Thus we believe that the question is, *What* does discipleship entail? *What* is Christian discipleship?

That our teaching should address this question seems to be confirmed for us by the vague, eclectic, and disparate answers we get when raising it with members of adult Sunday school classes, undergraduate students, and even seminarians. Clearly they have much to learn about "what" constitutes Christian discipleship. Our contemporaries' hesitations about discipleship are, for us, unmistakable signs that they do not properly understand the nature of discipleship, and consequently the nature of the Christian faith and identity that is implemented in discipleship. Our task as teachers is to

---

7. See Patte, *Ethics of Biblical Interpretation,* 17–36.

overcome their uncertainties by helping them to acquire a well-grounded knowledge of discipleship and its theological basis.

Our conviction that the problem to be addressed is a confusion about *what* constitutes discipleship seems to be further confirmed by the great diversity of views about discipleship, ranging from the most conservative views to those of mainline liberal churches to those championed by feminists, African-Americans, and other advocacy groups and movements. Such diversity is, of course, nothing new; in one form or another, it has existed throughout the history of the church. Yet in the present situation these diverse views more directly compete with each other because the walls separating churches have crumbled. The often incompatible views of discipleship proposed by the various churches as well as those proposed by the different groups marginalized by these churches (which as advocacy groups call for justice wherever oppression is found) are now perceived as alternatives among which we can choose, whatever might be our church affiliation.

This situation can still be interpreted to mean that our contemporaries are confused about which view of discipleship they should choose. Thus we can still conceive of our task as that of providing a teaching regarding the characteristics (the *what*) of true Christian discipleship that believers should implement in their lives. Elucidating beyond any uncertainty the actual teaching about discipleship of the Sermon on the Mount would begin to overcome this conceptual confusion about what constitutes Christian discipleship.

This suggested agenda seems quite sensible. There is no doubt that many of our contemporaries are quite ignorant about *what* discipleship entails according to the Sermon on the Mount. Since a teaching aimed at overcoming this ignorance seems most appropriate, I followed this agenda in my teaching for many years. But I will not follow it in this study because I had to recognize that through such a pedagogical practice I could not hope to reach my ultimate pedagogical goal — facilitating the practice of responsible Christian discipleship. To begin with, this kind of teaching involves a hierarchical pedagogical model, the procedures of which posit a one-directional relationship between a teacher (as a possessor of a knowledge content, the *what* of discipleship) and learners/students (as people who need to receive this knowledge that they lack, as an empty container needs to be filled up). This plausible and legitimate understanding of the pedagogical relationship is problematic for me because of its ethical implications. Recognizing that people (including students) do not have a certain knowledge that I have does not give me the right to decree that they must have it. On the one hand, they might have quite different needs, which as reasonable and intelligent persons they might already strive to meet after identifying them. On the other hand, they might have a different kind of knowledge regarding discipleship that I need to learn from them — such as a different conception of discipleship as ethical practice. Then envisioning my teaching as filling up a need that *I perceive in students/learners* might be completely beside the point and might deny their intellectual abilities and their respective identity.

My dubious ethical position in this pedagogical practice became even clearer to me when I recognized that in such a practice I present myself as someone I am not. As a teacher/scholar, I am of course aware of the fact that I am in no position to give the definitive answer to the perennial questions concerning the true nature of Christian discipleship. I cannot pretend to resolve conflicts of interpretation that have divided the church for twenty centuries. Despite the privileged situation I have as a biblical scholar who can devote much of my time to such matters, I do not have exceptional qualities or tools that would put me in a position of achieving what no other generation of interpreters was able to achieve. At any rate, I am fully aware that I do not have a privileged access to the truth. And yet, such claims are implied by the project of teaching our contemporaries what is the true nature of discipleship according to the Sermon on the Mount.

Therefore, I must distance myself from a pedagogical practice according to which *we*, the teachers, formulate the questions that in *our* view are the significant ones for our contemporaries, and according to which *we* provide the answers for these questions. We are so thoroughly convinced that our questions are identical with those of our contemporaries (including our students), that it does not occur to us that we might not truly hear them. This pedagogical practice amounts to denying any individuality and identity to our contemporaries, and to reducing them to a caricature of themselves, since their views have legitimacy and make sense only insofar as they conform with ours.

But when we are ready to affirm the otherness of our contemporaries, for instance, by allowing them to formulate their own questions, we are surprised. In many instances, their concerns are with features of discipleship that we often take for granted without having explicitly examined. This candid acknowledgment that their questions might be different from ours is a simple step, yet it is far from insignificant. In the process, we also acknowledge that our way of conceiving of discipleship is not the only plausible one; we have stepped beyond the boundaries of the hierarchical pedagogical model.

This does not mean that we should discount our own concern about the importance of knowing the characteristics of discipleship — if this is indeed our concern. In view of our contemporaries' lack of knowledge about the Bible and church traditions (which is so obvious from our perspective as scholars), at one point or another we might need to help them gain a better knowledge of "what constitutes Christian discipleship." Yet it also begins to appear that, for each of us, this is not simply a matter of teaching our own view about "what constitutes Christian discipleship," but rather of teaching the different views on this issue found in the scholarship and in the history of interpretation. Furthermore, our role as teachers and scholars also includes, as I suggested, sharing our contemporaries' concerns for other features of discipleship.

Conceiving of Discipleship as an Intuitive Ethical Practice

What are these other features of discipleship? When I let students or laypersons formulate their own questions (rather than silencing them by imposing on them my own), many of them seem to have no hesitation concerning *what* faithful Christian discipleship entails. Whether they are committed to a life of discipleship (as members of a church or one of the marginalized groups), or whether they are indifferent or even determined to have nothing to do with Christian discipleship, many of them are quite confident that their general understanding of Christian discipleship is adequate for making this decision. In "Christianized" North America, as well as in "de-Christianized" Europe, with or without Sunday school education, many are satisfied with the knowledge they have regarding "what Christian discipleship is." They are quite aware that in most instances their knowledge is quite vague and poorly informed and that they have much to learn about discipleship. But for them the question *"what* is discipleship?" is not the primary issue because discipleship is an intuitive, spontaneous ethical practice, i.e., an ethical practice that is *not* conceived of as the implementation of a previously known ideal or set of values that would define "what discipleship is."

A recent study of mainstream Protestantism and American religious and cultural life in this century notes that "polls suggest that there has been virtually no change in religious belief during the last half-century. What has changed is religious affiliation and behavior."[8] This reference to change in "religious affiliation and behavior" is a gentle way of referring to the many people (including a large proportion of baby boomers) who have dropped out of church. Yet this vocabulary also shows that they have opted out of a life of Christian discipleship (behavior), and not out of a set of beliefs (which they retain). The issue with which baby boomers struggle is *not* a lack of knowledge about *what* Christian discipleship entails. Their questions concern motivation and the conditions of a practice of discipleship. *Why* should one adopt a life of discipleship? *How* should one practice discipleship (e.g., in a given situation)? Their primary questions are *not* about the nature or the theological basis of discipleship (their beliefs are stable),

---

8. Milton J. Coalter, John M. Mulder, and Louis B. Weeks, *The Re-Forming Tradition: Presbyterians and Mainstream Protestantism* (Louisville: Westminster/John Knox, 1992), 279. See the entire book and the other volumes in the series, The Presbyterian Presence: The Twentieth Century Experience.

but about the *practice* of discipleship. These are *ethical* questions. Consequently, my strong suspicion is that their decision to practice or not to practice discipleship depends on the kind of answers they find for these ethical questions of Why? and How?

What these polls suggest goes against the grain of our intellectual habits. By considering discipleship as an actual ethical practice, our contemporaries bring to the fore features of discipleship that we do not usually consider. Of course, we would not deny that discipleship is an actual ethical practice. But because traditionally we have been so concerned to define *what* characterizes the behavior known as Christian discipleship, we have failed to ask, *How* and *why* is it to be *practiced?* How is the will to act as a disciple established? Does one need to assess the consequences of projected actions? Does one need to identify duties? To cultivate virtues? How are "projects" of a life of discipleship developed? How does one pass from such projects to their actualizations? Is the major obstacle that needs to be overcome a lack of knowledge (not knowing what to do or how to do it)? A lack of will (not being willing to do it, e.g., because it is too "costly")? A lack of competence (e.g., not having the training or ability to address problems arising out of a concrete situation)?

Two Conceptualizations of Discipleship as Ethical Practice: "Implementation of Christian Beliefs" or "Imitation as Intuitive Ethical Practice"

The fact that we did not directly focus our attention on such questions regarding discipleship as ethical *practice* — the questions raised by many of our contemporaries — does not mean that we did not conceive of discipleship as an ethical practice. We did by default, so to speak. Thus my own preoccupation with "what characterizes true Christian discipleship" initially led me to posit a certain conceptualization of this practice that I unduly considered to be the only plausible one, as long as I did not self-consciously examine how I had constructed it. Here it is enough to note that I posited that knowing the characteristics of Christian discipleship is a precondition for a correct practice of it. I understood the *practice of discipleship as the implementation of a previously known set of characteristics* or even as the implementation of a previously known ideal Christian identity. From this perspective, the how's and the why's of discipleship as ethical practice can only be raised *after* the cognitive issues about the characteristics and nature of discipleship have been settled.

This conceptualization of ethical practice as the implementation of something previously known (e.g., a set of values or an ideal) is quite plausible. It is an appropriate description of the way in which many people practice discipleship. But it does not account for the way in which at least some other people practice it; for instance, those who practice it without knowing anything about it; the "Gentiles, who do not possess the law, [but] do instinctively what the law requires" (Rom 2:14); or those who have fed, given a drink to, clothed, healed, visited in prison, and otherwise taken care of the Lord, without being aware that they were doing so as they took care of the needy (Mt 25:34–37). Interestingly, baby boomers, as well as more and more of us in the European-American culture, seem to presuppose this alternative way of envisioning discipleship as ethical practice.

According to this latter conceptualization, the actual practice of discipleship[9] is primary and takes place before reaching certainties regarding the cognitive issues about discipleship. Cognitive issues are appropriately addressed in the pragmatic context of an actual practice in progress because this practice is *not* understood as the implementation of previously known characteristics of discipleship or of Christian faith. Rather, it is in the very practice of discipleship that characteristics of discipleship, of Christian faith, and of Christian identity take shape and become known.

This latter conceptualization of the practice of discipleship might sound strange to those of us who hold the previous and more traditional one. For us, this latter conceptualization might be totally unacceptable. Yet in this case, we have to sort out why we respond to this suggestion in a negative way. Are we rejecting it because we cannot conceptualize it (an epistemology judgment)? Because it is not properly grounded in the Christian traditions and/or the Bible, and is thus an illegitimate conception of the practice of discipleship (a legitimacy judgment)? Because it is at odds with the conceptualization in which we have invested our commitments, concerns, and interests (a value judgment)? It is quite appropriate to reject this other conceptualization of discipleship on any one of these grounds. Yet if we reject this conceptualization, in a critical study we must make explicit the kind of judgment that leads us to do so.

Clearly, I want to affirm that discipleship as ethical practice can be plausibly conceptualized both as the implementation of a previously known ideal or set of values and as an intuitive ethical practice. This second type includes all the conceptualizations of discipleship as *"imitation"* — understood either as "conforming" or as "following" — when these terms entail a sense of adventure; for instance, sharing the vision of the kingdom proclaimed by Jesus and accepting re-formation as we envision ourselves in light of the kingdom and as we are formed in the image of Christ; or committing to following the living Christ without knowing exactly where he is going and what this will require. In both cases, it is not a matter of implementing an already known ideal or set of values (it is not imitating Christ in the sense of implementing the already known ideal represented by his ministry). It is in the very practice of discipleship (being conformed

---

9. This actual practice might take the form of deciding not to practice discipleship.

to the kingdom and to Jesus, following the resurrected Christ) that what discipleship entails takes shape and becomes known.

The plausibility of this plurality of conceptualizations of discipleship as ethical practice is confirmed by the fact that the moral life is conceptualized in quite different ethical theories. Consequently, in subsequent chapters (chaps. 5–6), one of my goals will be to show how different critical studies of discipleship according to the Sermon on the Mount conceptualize the practice of discipleship in terms of any number of ethical theories (such as the different kinds of consequentialist, deontological, and perfectionist ethical theories described by Ogletree),[10] which envision the moral life either as the implementation of previously known ideals and values, or as an intuitive ethical practice. In sum, my epistemology judgment (as suggested by the above comments and as presented in the rest of this study) is that several conceptualizations of discipleship as ethical practice are equally plausible. Conceptualizations of "discipleship as imitation/intuitive ethical practice" will appear as plausible as the various views of "discipleship as implementation." After all, the various views of "discipleship as intuitive ethical practice" include the several understandings of discipleship as following Jesus toward the kingdom and thus entering a life of discipleship without knowing exactly what it entails. This remark (which anticipates the discussion of subsequent chapters) suggests that several conceptualizations of discipleship have equal epistemological plausibility. It is not simply a theoretical claim; it is based on the study of actual interpretations of the Sermon on the Mount.

The Legitimacy of a Multidimensional Critical Study of Discipleship

Further justifications of the kind of critical study proposed in this book are necessary because for many the multidimensional option adopted by this study is far from being self-evident. Affirming, as we did in the preceding pages, that several conceptualizations of discipleship as ethical practice are equally plausible is one thing. But affirming that several conclusions about the teaching of the Sermon on the Mount about discipleship are *equally legitimate* representations of the teaching of this text is quite another matter.

Many objections to this affirmation are commonly raised, for example, Is it not the task of a critical study to establish what is distinctive about the teaching of the Sermon on the Mount about discipleship? Indeed it is. Thus I expect that a critical study of the Sermon on the Mount (read as part of the Gospel according to Matthew) and a critical study of the

---

10. Ogletree, *Use of the Bible*, 15–45.

Gospel according to Mark (for instance) would reach significantly different conclusions regarding their respective teachings about discipleship.

Another objection goes, Is it not the case that these critical studies establish (or should strive to establish) how discipleship is conceptualized by each of these two texts? My answer has to be ambivalent. Yes, a critical study elucidates something about the specific conceptualization of discipleship by the Sermon on the Mount. But whether or not it elucidates "the" entirety of this conceptualization is a matter of perspective. From a one-dimensional perspective, a critical study can account for the actual specificity of the conceptualization of discipleship by the text — often viewed as "what the author intended to say." I do not deny that strong arguments for the legitimacy of this understanding of the task of critical biblical studies can and have been developed. Since these arguments already exist and are widely accepted, I do not need to repeat them.[11] But I want also to affirm that it is legitimate to claim that any given critical interpretation is "partial" and that because of the nature of the reading process, it is unrealistic to expect that any single interpretation, including any single critical interpretation, can represent the entirety of the teaching of the text about discipleship.[12]

The elucidation of a specific teaching of a text (e.g., its teaching about discipleship) is always limited to certain features of it because it is necessarily focused on those aspects that can be perceived within a specific conceptualization of discipleship. This focus results from an epistemology judgment. Each time we read a text for its teaching about discipleship, our reading is framed by a specific ethical theory that we use, explicitly or implicitly, to approach the text. This ethical theory frames our interpretation by focusing our attention on a specific dimension of the text (a set of textual features) and by concealing from us other such dimensions.

This conceptualization of the process of reading was long ago articulated by Bultmann, who insisted that there is no interpretation without preunderstandings.[13] This does not mean, of course, that we read into the text the ethical theory and the conceptualization of discipleship with which

---

11. The systematic presentation and discussion of the historian's principles of judgment in Harvey's work remains the best formulation of this argument. See Van Harvey, *The Historian and the Believer: A Confrontation between the Modern Historian's Principles of Judgment and the Christian's Will-to-Believe* (New York: Macmillan, 1966).

12. The following argument is necessarily one-sided. Yet it should be remembered that, even though I need to argue for the legitimacy of multidimensional critical studies by emphasizing features of the reading process not accounted for from a one-dimensional perspective, I do not deny the legitimacy of one-dimensional critical studies (which account for features of the reading process neglected from a multidimensional perspective). I will emphasize below that from my point of view they are equally legitimate, and therefore that the choice of one approach or of another ultimately reflects a value judgment

13. See, for instance, Rudolf Bultmann, "Is Exegesis without Presuppositions Possible?" in *Existence and Faith: Shorter Writings by Rudolf Bultmann*, ed. S. Ogden (Cleveland and New York: World Publishing, 1960), 289–96.

we approach the text. But even when we conclude that the teaching of the text is unlike the ethical theory and the view of discipleship we hold, we still use the categories of this theory and of this view as a way of framing our interpretation and formulating the questions we address to the text. Thus our reading is focused on a certain aspect of the text, a certain meaning-producing dimension that displays features germane or antithetical to the presupposed conceptualization of discipleship. Or, using another metaphor, our reading is attuned to the voice of the text with which this conceptualization resonates or with which it is dissonant. In the process, other dimensions or voices of the text are left aside. Whether or not the interpretation is legitimate depends on the way it elucidates and represents this given dimension (or voice) of the text.

This is why, in my view, biblical scholarship over the years has developed a whole range of critical methods, rather than a single one.[14] While these critical methods are often viewed as contributing to the elucidation of "the" (single, true) teaching of a given text, the following chapters of our study will show that they can also be viewed as addressing different questions to the text. Their respective questions reflect different epistemological paradigms through which themes are conceptualized and through which the attention of exegetes is focused on certain meaning-producing dimensions of the text. Then we shall not be surprised to find that various critical methods focused on certain meaning-producing dimensions are correlated with specific conceptualizations of discipleship, for which they provide evidence and warrants.

For instance: an interpretation of the Sermon on the Mount as a series of parenetic instructions — best elucidated through a redaction critical study — is correlated with a *deontological* conceptualization of "discipleship as implementation." An interpretation of the Sermon on the Mount as a sermon aimed at transforming its hearers — best elucidated through either a narrative or a rhetorical critical method — is correlated with a *consequentialist* conceptualization of "discipleship as implementation," which emphasizes the ongoing process of becoming discipleship. Similarly, the various conceptualizations of "discipleship as imitation," which emphasizes conforming to the kingdom or to Christ or identifying and following Christlike religious leaders (true prophets rather than false prophets, etc.) are conceived in terms of *perfectionist* ethical theories. Thus an interpretation of the Sermon on the Mount as providing readers with a series of "figures" of discipleship primarily defined through their allusions to other texts and traditions (best critically studied in terms of the history of traditions and of the history of interpretations) is correlated with a perfectionist conceptualization of discipleship as resocialization in a new

---

14. A point that will be illustrated at length in chapters 3 and 4. I illustrated it in different ways in *Ethics of Biblical Interpretation*, 37–71.

community held together by a particular symbolic world. Similarly, an interpretation of the Sermon on the Mount as seeking to transform the readers' "convictions" (as self-evident values) through its thematic and mythical structures (best elucidated by means of either structural and anthropological critical methods) is correlated with a perfectionist conceptualization of discipleship as characterized by the particular moral discernment that allows one to identify and then follow Christlike religious leaders.

While the examination of a series of scholarly interpretations of discipleship according to the Sermon on the Mount provides the evidence for my claim that a critical study must be multidimensional, this claim makes sense only insofar as one keeps is mind the most basic definition of criticism — as a self-conscious practice of interpretation that makes explicit its interpretive judgments. To put it negatively, from this perspective and the epistemology and legitimacy choices it reflects, what makes a study of discipleship a critical study is neither its conclusions in themselves, nor its methodological argument in itself, nor again its conceptualization of discipleship in itself, but rather the explicit acknowledgment of the ways in which all of these were constructed and/or selected among several plausible alternatives. A critical study involves the recognition that various conceptualizations of the practice of discipleship presuppose equally plausible ethical theories; that the choice and use of a given critical methodology (the legitimacy judgment) is directly related to the conceptualization that frames an interpretation (the epistemology judgment); and that the conclusions about the teaching of the text about discipleship are thus shaped by these epistemological/conceptual and legitimacy/methodological frames. Furthermore, a critical study that acknowledges in this way its constructed character can and should make explicit its ideological character, including its theological, moral, and social motivations. In other words, it should also make explicit the value judgment it involves.

Conceiving of a multidimensional critical practice of critical biblical studies and implementing such a practice do not present any difficulty. Its three components can now be listed more concretely, with reference to discipleship according to the Sermon on the Mount and to the categories discussed in the introduction:

- The presentation of these different interpretations as equally legitimate by showing that each interpretation is focused on a certain meaning-producing dimension of the text that is best elucidated by a specific critical method and is expressed in its *conclusions about what the text is and says* (CAWs) (legitimacy judgment);

- The presentation of the *conclusions about the teaching* (CATs) of the Sermon on the Mount regarding discipleship of several different interpretations, so as to clarify in each case the particular conceptualization of discipleship[15] (epistemology judgment);

- The elucidation of the specific interests and/or concerns that each of these interpretations seeks to address and thus their conclusions about the relative value (CARVs) of a given interpretation (value judgment).

Such a multidimensional practice of critical biblical interpretation is a direct and logical outcome of the hermeneutical theories that traditionally inform critical biblical studies and led to the multiplication of critical methodologies.[16] This multidimensional practice of critical biblical interpretation is nothing but a description of what we collectively do as a scholarly guild, which acknowledges and respects scholars who use differing critical methods and propose diverse *conclusions regarding the teaching* of a text.

The preceding comments should be enough to suggest the legitimacy of such a multidimensional critical study. Yet biblical critical scholars resist making their practices multidimensional, and they continue to conceive of their practice of biblical studies in a one-dimensional way.[17] Why? It is not because we cannot conceptualize a multidimensional study (not because of a negative epistemology judgment). We are used to pluralities of theories on any given topic. It is not because we cannot accept the legitimacy of a multidimensional study (not because of a negative legitimacy judgment). This is what we do at the level of the guild. Why, then, do we resist the idea of practicing critical biblical studies in a multidimensional way? It is a matter of value judgment, related to our basic conviction that there is only one "truly good" interpretation.

The Value of a Multidimensional Critical Study of Discipleship: Its Androcritical Character

The proposed multidimensional study of discipleship according to the Sermon on the Mount involves choices among equally plausible options and equally legitimate options. I have argued, and will further argue in the following chapters, that it is at least as plausible to affirm as it is to deny that the various epistemologies through which discipleship is conceptualized should be respected as potentially appropriate in specific cultural situations. Note that this argument presupposes that the alternative option — denying that the various epistemology perspectives offered in different cultural settings should be respected — is also plausible. *I have chosen* to reject

---

15. As noted in the introduction, CATs concern the teaching of the text *to a certain audience* (the rhetorical dimension of the text) and how this teaching is conceptualized.

16. See Patte, *Ethics of Biblical Interpretation*, 54–59.

17. Our critical reviews of the scholarship are everything but multidimensional. See Patte, *Ethics of Biblical Interpretation*, 117–18, passim.

this latter option because it involves the affirmation that a certain culture is superior to other cultures. Thus *I have chosen* the former option as a concrete way of affirming and implementing my convictions that different cultures and their respective epistemologies are equally appropriate ways of making sense of human experience. The value involved in this choice appears.

Similarly, I have argued and will further argue below that it is at least as legitimate to affirm as it is to deny that in any given reading process, meaning is produced when a reader is affected by and responds to one of a multiplicity of meaning-producing dimensions of the text. Yet this argument presupposes that the alternative option — denying that a reader is affected by and responds to a specific dimension of the text but that he or she is affected by and respond to the text as a whole — is also legitimate. *I have chosen* the former option because, as I discuss at length in *Ethics of Biblical Interpretation,* this option opens the way to affirm the legitimacy of interpretations of biblical texts different from those of male European-Americans, including those of feminist, African-American, and so-called Two-Thirds World scholars. The value judgment involved in this choice is also clear.

By adopting these two options, *I have also chosen*[18] to include in the critical task a strong focus on the role of the text in the reading process — a focus that is the primary concern of the part of the critical exegetical process involving "legitimacy judgments" — even as I stress the role of the readers by taking into account the epistemology and value judgments that emphasize it. I opted for this *balanced view of the respective roles of readers and texts*, rather than for either an exclusive focus on the role of the text (as traditional male European-American scholars tend to do in their exegetical task) or an exclusive focus on the role of the readers (as feminists and other advocacy scholars, as well as postmodern scholars, at times prefer to do). This choice is also based on a specific value judgment. Personally, I value the power of the biblical text to affect me and many other readers and hearers.[19] I also acknowledge *its authority* — institutionalized by the church that canonized it as Scripture and affirmed by the academic world that sees it as one of the sources of Western culture. In sum, my choice to underscore the role of the text beside the role of the reader is also a political choice. This choice involves the value judgment (and confession) that through our practice of one-dimensional scholarly interpretations, we male European-American exegetes have deprived all other readers of the text.

---

18. As Grace Imathiu reminded me, in a recent seminar.

19. This value judgment is rooted in my convictions about the power/authority of the biblical text that I have as a Protestant with roots in his Huguenot ancestry. See my detailed discussion of this point in Patte, *Ethics of Biblical Interpretation,* 73–112. For further discussion of this point, see below, chapter 7.

Affirming in a multidimensional study that all (authentic) interpretations[20] can be shown to be basically legitimate because each is based on one or another of the several dimensions of the text is thus a deliberate (political) strategy to affirm that the biblical text (as well as its power and authority) belongs to all readers, not just a few of them who have usurped it.

By elucidating the varying role of the text in a series of interpretations by male European-Americans, I seek to prevent us from usurping the text and its authority. If we are claiming the authority of the text for such a diversity of interpretations, everyone should feel free to claim the authority of the text for his or her interpretation, however different it might be from ours. Indeed, anyone who wants to can claim the authority and power of the text against the text itself, for instance, by underscoring the devastating effect on its readers of patriarchal, anti-Jewish, and antisocial dimensions of the biblical text. By choosing to keep a balance between the role of the readers and the role of the text, I seek to leave open as many options as possible for contemporary readers vis-à-vis the biblical text. I leave open the possibility of acknowledging and affirming the positive authority and power of certain dimensions of the biblical text, while rejecting others. But I also leave open the option of rejecting the institutional and cultural authority/power of the biblical text because it is focused on a very oppressive dimension of the biblical text. I even leave open the possibility of defining and redefining the authority of the biblical text in many different ways. Through all this, my hope is to free the biblical text from its captivity in one-dimensional critical exegesis, so that it might once again belong to whoever wants to open it and to read it. The value judgment involved in this deliberate strategy is also clear.

By affirming that I have chosen to adopt a multidimensional andro-critical practice of biblical scholarship because of a series of value judgments, do I deny the value of one-dimensional interpretive practices? Paradoxically, I do not. Even as I underscore the equal legitimacy and equal plausibility of several interpretations in my multidimensional practice because of my value judgments I will want to affirm that, "for me" *(pro me)*, one of these interpretations is particularly significant. Thus my interpretive practice becomes once again one-dimensional, but now it is deliberately and self-consciously one-dimensional. Aware that the chosen interpretation was selected among several plausible and legitimate ones, I can ponder the

---

20. I call "authentic interpretation" any interpretation of the text that reflects how a reader (or group of readers) is affected by the text and responds to the text. An "unauthentic" interpretation is, therefore, exclusively limited to the expression of "what the text says" by people who have not actually allowed the text to affect them. This is, of course, the case of people who express "what the text says" without having actually read the text or listened to it. (This is what some of my students do, when they write a report on their reading of the Sermon on the Mount, without reading the Sermon on the Mount.)

relative value of my choice before allowing it to affect and shape my life in a "seconde naïveté."[21]

Fundamental Values Reflected by One-dimensional and Multidimensional Critical Biblical Studies

I share the conviction that, for each of us at a given moment, only one interpretation is "truly good." But the conclusion that a given interpretation is the only one that is "truly good" reflects a value judgment, which should not be confused either with an epistemology judgment (about what is "truly plausible") or with a legitimacy judgment (about what is "true," real, based on some kind of evidence).

This common confusion has its roots in the way in which one makes sense of texts and discourses. At any given moment, each reader perceives by himself or herself only one plausible and legitimate teaching of the text. In order to perceive other plausible and legitimate teachings, one needs to look at the text from the perspective of someone else, i.e., from the perspective of an other.[22] Practicing critical biblical exegesis in a multidimensional way demands a different perception of our relationship to other readers. It involves acknowledging the legitimacy of others' interpretations because ultimately it is only through this acknowledgment of the others that I can recognize and affirm the specificity of my own interpretation (and my own identity) in a given time and place.

Consequently, the basic value question regarding our practice of critical biblical studies is, Where do we find ultimate meaning (i.e., truly trustworthy teachings)? In the reading experience of the individual, and thus in the single plausible and legitimate teaching of the text perceived by an individual reader?[23] This is where people who practice one-dimensional biblical studies often find ultimate meaning. Or in the reading experience of multiple readers, and thus in the relationships among different plausible and legitimate teachings perceived by different readers, e.g., diverse members of a church? This is where people who practice multidimensional biblical studies find ultimate meaning.

Whether one adopts one or the other of these critical perspectives, one accounts for the same evidence regarding the reading process; thus, both approaches can be shown to be legitimate. As I repeatedly stated, my argument aimed at showing the legitimacy of a multidimensional approach

---

21. See Paul Ricoeur, *The Symbolism of Evil*, trans. E. Buchanan (Boston: Beacon, 1967), 351–52. Also "The Hermeneutics of Symbols and Philosophical Reflection," in *The Philosophy of Paul Ricoeur*, ed. C. E. Reagan and D. Stewart (Boston: Beacon, 1980), 36–58.

22. "An other" who might be a different person or myself in a different time and circumstance.

23. This individual reader might be "I" as a reader/believer or an authoritative reader, e.g., a bishop, the pope, a scholar.

does not deny the legitimacy of a one-dimensional approach. The choice of one or the other approach does not depend on a legitimacy judgment about the realities of the reading process. Adopting a one-dimensional perspective does not prevent one from perceiving the existence of a diversity of interpretations; yet one sees them as competing with each other for the position of "the" only true interpretation, which has elucidated "the" single teaching of the text — a teaching usually perceived as inscribed in the text as the author's intentional teaching.[24] Conversely, the multidimensional perspective does not prevent people from recognizing that each reader gives priority to a single interpretation and its teaching. What separates these two perspectives is primarily their respective ideology (or theology, as I suggest by speaking of "ultimate meaning"). To put it in theological terms, Is revelation primarily found in a vertical relationship between an individual and God? Or is it primarily found in horizontal relationships with others, who in their otherness manifest the Other for us? Obviously, I hold the latter view, which for me is consistent with a covenantal theology of a God who chose a people, Israel, as those through whom God is present among the nations, and the prolongation of this covenantal theology in an incarnational and ecclesiological theology.

Before discussing this theological/ideological grounding of my study, I need to emphasize that these issues first confront us in much more concrete ways in the present cultural situation in Europe and North America. In other words, I need to explain briefly what led me to advocate a multidimensional practice of biblical studies that is also "androcritical."

Multidimensional Practice by a One-dimensional Interpreter

I readily acknowledge that it is because of my androcritical interests and concerns that I affirm the superior value of multidimensional studies. As I have argued elsewhere, not practicing multidimensional critical biblical studies amounts to forsaking my sense of vocation as a male Protestant European-American exegete.[25] But by definition, a multidimensional practice should not exclude other kinds of interpretations, including one-dimensional interpretations. Actually, this inclusion of the one-dimensional perspective takes place quite readily because a multidimensional study is always practiced by a one-dimensional interpreter.

Even as I practice critical exegesis in a multidimensional perspective, I do so as a reader who gives priority to a single interpretation and its teaching.

---

24. One can also use reader-response criticism in this one-dimensional perspective in order to establish the single true teaching of the text as perceived by the original readers. Since the author is also the first reader of the text, one might even end up with the same conclusions. On the use of reader-response criticism in biblical studies, see the brilliant analysis in The Bible and Culture Collective, *The Postmodern Bible*, 20–69.

25. Patte, *Ethics of Biblical Interpretation*, 73–112.

For me *(pro me)*, at any given moment, there is only one interpretation of a text that is both truly valuable (in that it corresponds to my concerns and interests) and truly makes sense (in that I am quick to perceive its legitimacy and to conceptualize it). Thus my own interpretation, from its most spontaneous and intuitive origins to its most elaborated critical formulation, remains one-dimensional because in one way or another, positively or negatively, it is a *pro me* interpretation that reflects how I am affected by this text in a given circumstance. Because abandoning my one-dimensional *pro me* interpretation would amount to forsaking a part of my identity,[26] I am appropriately reluctant to adopt any critical approach that would demand that I do so.

But a multidimensional critical practice does not demand anything like this from us. On the contrary, it demands from each of us to hold on to our own interpretations, and indeed to affirm their specificity and their legitimacy. Yet in a pluralistic context, this twofold affirmation cannot but involve the acknowledgment that other people's interpretations are similarly legitimate. Such a point can only be made through a critical study that shows the different ways in which these interpretations were constructed. In sum, it is precisely when we proceed with a multidimensional critical study that we are in a position to affirm our own (one-dimensional) interpretations, as the following chapters illustrate. Nevertheless, our one-dimensional interpretation is transformed by being set in the context of several other interpretations that are shown to be equally legitimate. Thus a multidimensional practice carries within itself a dialectical tension between multidimensional and one-dimensional that can and must be maintained.

This tension between recognizing the legitimacy of a plurality of interpretations and affirming a single one is commonly found among European-American biblical critics. In most instances we are fully aware of the limitations of our critical interpretations, as contemporary hermeneutical theories underscore. We readily concede that no interpretation is absolute and that there is a plurality of legitimate interpretations (since there are several critical methodologies).[27] We are theoretically open to the possibility of multidimensional critical practices. Yet we practice our critical studies *as if* they were each time the only plausible ones and *as if* their conclusions were the only legitimate ones. Our critical practice is one-dimensional, and as such it is in tension with our hermeneutic theory.

---

26. Unless this change in *pro me* interpretation is called for by a change of context and circumstances.

27. See the discussion of "traditional pluralists" by The Bible and Culture Collective, in *The Postmodern Bible*, 48–50. My analysis is quite different from the authors' (at this point in their book), in that my concern is not with the fact that (historical) biblical critics have an inconsistent attitude (simultaneously affirming pluralism and denying it by limiting it to a "range" of legitimate interpretations), but with the fact that they fail to acknowledge that they are inconsistent.

The tension between our acknowledgment that in each case our interpretation is relative and our conviction that our interpretation is far superior to other interpretations should not be dismissed as some kind of hypocrisy or of self-deception. This tension is inherent to any interpretation understood as part of the communication process, which is necessarily both *centrifugal* or pluralist (multidimensional, in the case of interpretations), and *centripetal* or centered on itself (one-dimensional, in the case of interpretations). In order to foster communication beyond our narrow circle, we need to adopt a centrifugal or pluralist attitude by acknowledging that our interpretation is one among several legitimate ones. Conversely, in order to posit a meaningful world and/or an institution as context for meaningful life, one needs to adopt a centripetal attitude, affirming our own interpretation as superior (in one way or another) to any other.[28] True communication and interpretation require the dialectical tension between these two poles.

Thus regarding discipleship, the difference between these two conceptualizations is not found in what they account for; both account for the cognitive dimension of discipleship (the knowledge of the "what" of discipleship) and for its praxis dimension (the "how" and "why" of discipleship). The difference is that *discipleship as implementation* gives priority to the cognitive dimension — the "what" implemented in the "how" and "why" of the praxis; while *discipleship as imitation* gives priority to the praxis — the "how" and the "why" — which through its actualization in concrete situations shapes and defines "what" discipleship is about.

Prior to a multidimensional critical study, we simply assume that our conceptualization of discipleship and of the relationship between the cognitive and praxis dimensions embedded in it are the only possible ones; our interpretation is one-dimensional. A multidimensional critical study reveals to us that at least one other conceptualization of discipleship is also plausible. This multidimensional perspective puts us in the position of recognizing that our conceptualization of discipleship involves a choice between two legitimate and plausible options. It does not prevent us from holding on to and affirming our one-dimensional conceptualization of discipleship as the practice of the Christian faith; the multidimensional critical study shows that this view is legitimate. But this study also helps us to recognize the specificity of our conceptualization, marked by a particular choice among several legitimate options, and thus the specificity of our one-dimensional

---

28. Here I follow semiotic theories that underscore that any interpretation (and communication) process involves the use of "codes" that are both plural (and thus submitted to a centrifugal force) — otherwise communication among different groups would be impossible — and interested (and thus submitted to a centripetal force). For a very effective presentation of the characteristics of codes, see Mieke Bal, *Murder and Difference: Gender, Genre, and Scholarship on Sisera's Death* (Bloomington: Indiana University Press, 1988), 3–11 (whose vocabulary I use). For the complete theory, see Umberto Eco, *A Theory of Semiotics* (Bloomington: Indiana University Press, 1976), 48–150.

interpretation, which results from choosing to give priority to a specific dimension.[29]

The recognition of the specificity of our interpretation forces us to assume responsibility for it. Since we had a choice, *why* did we choose this option rather than another one? By raising this question, the multidimensional critical study asks us to own up to our own interpretation, to acknowledge the values, ideology, and other commitments that our (singular, one-dimensional) interpretation embodies. In the case of male European-American interpreters, such a study demands that we acknowledge what I call our "andro" values — ideology, and commitments — and clarify the interests and concerns reflected by our interpretations. Then the multidimensional study becomes "androcritical" and is well on its way to its ultimate goal — facilitating the practice of *responsible* discipleship.[30]

My Multidimensional Androcritical Practice as a Theological Commitment

One of the main benefits of a multidimensional practice is that it facilitates the practice of *responsible* interpretation (as well as responsible discipleship). By pointing this out, I reveal some of the values and commitments embedded in my proposal. My multidimensional androcritical practice is itself interested. It promotes values that I have as I keep in balance the two environments in which I teach New Testament: a department of religious studies in a secular university in North America, where I maintain dialogue with colleagues in other fields (especially literary theory and anthropology); and various church and seminary contexts. I have actively participated in the life of the church through many years of teaching adult Sunday school classes (in particular, in the Presbyterian church where I worship) as well as classes and sessions for preachers, ministers, and teachers from various churches in North America, Europe, Africa, and Asia. I also participate in formal and more often in informal ecumenical dialogues, and I have had opportunities to appreciate the diversity of the European-American culture in which I live and to consider it from without, thus gaining some appreciation of the global context in which it exists, whether it likes it or not.

---

29. And of course, the multidimensional critical process does not stop here. As we proceed, we discover that our interpretation of discipleship involves many other choices among plausible alternatives.

30. As stated above, this is the ultimate goal of my critical study of "discipleship according to the Sermon on the Mount." Whether or not other critical studies make it explicit, I believe they have similar ultimate goals, even though their ideological orientation might be quite different. Instead of seeking to facilitate the practice of responsible discipleship, they might seek to prevent the practice of oppressive forms of discipleship, or even of all forms of discipleship. In such cases, the critical interpretation functions in slightly different ways. Yet *mutatis mutandis* the following discussion still applies.

As an interpreter of the Bible in this twofold horizon, I strive to be accountable toward others and their interpretations. For this, my interpretive practice must make room for their different interpretations — it must be multidimensional — and must also allow me to assume full responsibility for, and ownership of, my own interpretation — it must be androcritical. Multidimensionality and androcriticism are corollary. I can affirm the specificity of my own interpretation as a male European-American only insofar as I recognize the specificity and legitimacy of interpretations by others, and thus only insofar as I have encountered, or better, I have been encountered by, others who are truly other than I.[31] Conversely, I can affirm the specificity and legitimacy of others' interpretations (multidimensionality) only insofar as I acknowledge and affirm the specificity, legitimacy, and value of my own interpretation (androcriticism).

This conception of multidimensional androcritical practice in biblical studies obviously reflects what ecumenical dialogues taught me. It is broadly recognized that true ecumenical dialogues require the participants to respect each other's points of view and thus be willing and able to affirm the legitimacy of, for example, several conclusions regarding "discipleship according to the Sermon on the Mount," and also to express and affirm his or her specific point of view as a member of a given tradition.

Yet our response to this ecumenical attitude is ambivalent. While we readily applaud its affirmation of the others in their otherness, as well as the concurrent affirmation of the specificity of our own views and beliefs, we are less convinced or even openly hostile to its corollary: the denial that any of the views is absolute. In matters of discipleship and of faith, can one be content with pluralism?

This ecumenical, pluralistic attitude could readily be set aside if it were found in ecumenical dialogues alone. But it is part of a much broader and more pervasive cultural phenomenon of which ecumenical dialogues were early manifestations. Whether we like it or not, we now find ourselves in multicultural and global contexts that result from the technological and communications revolution. Through radio and television (not to mention the Internet and the World Wide Web), what happens in countries on the other side of the world is as much a part of our lives as what happens on the other side of town. Consequently, we cannot live in our own culture, whatever it might be, without being constantly reminded that it is merely one among a multiplicity of viable cultural options.

This multicultural context in which we live is echoed by the multiplication of critical methodologies due to a great theoretical diversification over the last thirty years or so. There is no need to underscore that, as a result,

---

31. Because this encounter with the others is also an encounter with the Other, as I write this sentence I have in mind Paul's hesitation between the active and passive voices in Galatians 4:9: νῦν δὲ γνόντες θεόν, μᾶλλον δὲ γνωσθέντες ὑπὸ θεοῦ ("Now, however, that you have come to know God, or rather to be known by God," NRSV).

critical biblical studies became multimethodological. It is enough to consult the contents pages of recent textbooks introducing students to critical
exegesis.[32] What needs to be emphasized is the implication of this methodological pluralism, namely, that different critical methods yield different
conclusions regarding the teaching of each given text. One should not be
surprised. Because they are focused by their specific theoretical and methodological perspectives on different dimensions of a text, these studies reach
quite distinct (and at times contradictory) conclusions about the teaching
of the text, even though they remain rigorously critical. Thus far from
providing a way of escaping the ambivalence we have inherited from ecumenical dialogues, contemporary critical biblical scholarship reflects and
reinforces this pluralism in that it shows the critical legitimacy of several
different *conclusions about the teaching* about discipleship of the Sermon
on the Mount.

The same ambivalence is maintained and reinforced (rather than as-
suaged) as we are exposed, through the media, to the diverse ways in which
discipleship and Christian identity are conceived of and lived in different
cultures. On the one hand, we recognize a diversity of views on discipleship, which now appear to be culturally conditioned. On the other hand,
since discipleship is a weighty matter of (Christian) identity, we feel compelled to affirm that one view of discipleship is the only true one for us and
therefore worthy to be adopted as our own.

This ambivalence toward the culturally diverse understandings of discipleship that we might experience as Christian believers is not limited to
the religious domain. It is typical of the culture in which we live, a culture
that theoreticians have called "postmodern."[33] We are torn apart. We are
modern. Nostalgically, we aspire to the clarity, the unambiguity, and the
security of a modern, monocultural world, even if it is ever in the process
of being established through a long quest (according to the modern confidence in progress). But all the while we are *postmodern*. With realism and
with concerns for justice, we have a vague yet unmistakable feeling that
this nostalgia for a monocultural world is both an unrealistic dream and an
unjust quest for cultural hegemony that necessarily entails exclusion and
oppression.

This postmodern tension is unsettling. Yet it has the great advantage of
raising ethical questions (concerns for justice) regarding matters of identity
(cultural or religious).

The postmodern tension, a part of our daily life, is also unsettling

---

32. See, for instance, Raymond F. Collins, *Introduction to the New Testament* (Garden
City, N.Y.: Doubleday, 1983); Steven L. McKenzie and Stephen R. Haynes, eds., *To Each
Its Own Meaning: An Introduction to Biblical Criticisms and Their Application* (Louisville:
Westminster/John Knox, 1993).

33. For a more complete, but still congruent, definition of postmodernism, see The Bible
and Culture Collective, *The Postmodern Bible*, 8–12, and the entire book.

for Christian believers. When the implications of this globalization and multiculturalism are articulated by advocacy critics, such as feminist, post-Holocaust, African-American, and Two-Thirds World critics, we are deeply challenged in our sense of identity. Although we are confident about our identity (we know "what" Christian identity and discipleship entail, don't we?), we are confronted by the questions: How? and Why? The post-modern culture, globalization, multiculturalism, and advocacy critics — even the multiplicity of critical study of biblical texts — challenge us to reconsider how and why we conceive of Christian identity and discipleship as we do.

We are unsettled. We are disturbed. We resist. Often it is because we misunderstand this challenge. We believe that feminists and other advocacy critics are asking us to rethink "what discipleship is all about" (the question of truth, of reality, which is typical of the modern way of thinking), without realizing that it actually raises an ethical question about our choice of one rather than another view of discipleship. Why did we choose this view of discipleship? How? On what grounds? Because of this misunderstanding, even when we male European-American Christians welcome the challenge of feminists and other advocacy critics, we miss its point, believing that we should abandon our conception of discipleship for another one (such as the one that feminists or African-Americans have), when what we are called on to do is to acknowledge why and how we adopted our conception of discipleship and to consider whether or not our practice of discipleship is consistent with our reasons for choosing it.

In many instances, we fail to hear that we are called to affirm our own interpretation and its reasons. Individually and collectively, we feel threat-ened in our identity. The cries of those who are hurt and oppressed easily sound like threats, whether they are or not. Whatever might be the case, we tragically fail to hear legitimate voices in these cries. We respond by im-plicitly or explicitly reaffirming our own traditional sense of discipleship, whatever it may be, as the only legitimate one. This reaffirmation of the "fundamentals" of our Christian identity is a latent fundamentalism that readily becomes actual fundamentalism when we take our sense of disciple-ship to be nothing else than "the" only true teaching of a biblical text, such as the Sermon on the Mount.

This reactionary attitude against feminist, African-American, and other advocacy critics, including those of the so-called Two-Thirds World, is the biblical studies version as well as the Christian version of the nostalgia for modernism — its certainties and its security. If we do not hold on to old-time discipleship as the norm, how can we conceive of "faithful Christians"? Thus our knee-jerk reaction is to reject any suggestion that discipleship could be conceived of in ways different from our traditional way. Without any apparent hesitation, we affirm, sometimes through our words but mainly and most effectively through our deeds, that we have the only true conception of Christian discipleship because (accordingly!) we are the only ones who take seriously the teaching about discipleship of biblical texts, such as the Sermon on the Mount. Thus we implicitly or even explicitly claim that our conception of discipleship should be adopted by all those who want to speak about Christian discipleship.

Yet once again, our postmodern ambivalence comes to the surface. Many of us (if not all of us male European-American readers of the Bible) have then another knee-jerk reaction: we greet with cynicism any claim (by somebody else, of course) to have the only true view of discipleship. This is our attitude toward evangelical fundamentalists and their claims that they know what "the" single, true teaching of the Bible about discipleship is. But evangelical fundamentalists return the favor and quite appropriately apply the same cynicism to our critical biblical studies which, as I confessed regarding my own work,[34] implicitly claim to present "the" single, true teaching of the text in resolutely one-dimensional interpretations.

We who readily condemn fundamentalism would like to affirm that we have established — or more modestly, that we are engaged in a collective research project aimed at establishing — the fundamentals about the teaching of the Sermon on the Mount about discipleship. Is this hypocrisy? Maybe. Certainly not in any deliberate or self-conscious way. But saying this is no excuse. Being critical is being self-conscious about the interpretive process one uses; that is, in our case, being aware of the ambivalence that pervades our interpretations, whether we want it or not.

This ambivalence becomes apparent as soon as we consider the way in which we, biblical critics, commonly deal with a diversity of interpretations. We see this diversity of interpretations of discipleship according to the Sermon on the Mount as a problem to be solved. Then we end up arguing that one of the views (which just happens to be the one we practice) is true, and rejecting the others as false. Of course, those who do not practice this "true" form of discipleship do not belong to the "true" Christian community; they are heretics. From this perspective, the role of critical biblical study is to help resolve this problem of diversity of interpretations by establishing "the" true meaning of a text. Is it not clear that a text can have only one meaning (which just happens to be the one we perceive) and that the Sermon on the Mount offers only one teaching about discipleship (which just happens to be the one we hold)?

The parenthetical comments suggest appropriate cynical responses, which we readily utter with a sneer when someone else makes such claims. We readily recognize that seeing diversity as a problem generates an arrogant, if not self-serving, attitude that is necessarily exclusive; other people's views, practices, motivations, beliefs, etc., are wrong to the extent that they do not conform to ours. In our candid moments, we even adopt such

---

34. See Patte, *Ethics of Biblical Interpretation*, 75–107.

a cynicism — or what we prefer to call an ironic distance — toward our own one-dimensional interpretations when we acknowledge the plurality of critical methods and their conclusions. Yet biblical critics (and especially male European-American ones) are longing for absolute truths to such an extent that we cannot conceive of our critical interpretations as anything other than quests for certainty. Thus despite our own cynicism, despite our awareness of a multiplicity of critical methods leading to different conclusions, far from being inclined to affirm the legitimacy of several views, we proceed with a one-dimensional critical study of "discipleship according to the Sermon on the Mount" aimed at dispelling any doubts arising from the diversity of interpretations. For this purpose, through our critical studies we strive to establish "the" universally true interpretation — an immutable truth that we might want to call ultimate truth, or divine revelation, or the word of God.[35] But then we cannot but have some cynicism or irony toward our own conclusions and our own projects — and so on and so forth. The more we repress the ambivalence of our quest, the more it haunts all our interpretations, whether they are critical or not.

I intentionally described our efforts to overcome or to deny our ambivalence in terms reminiscent of the struggle Paul describes in Romans 7:18–19, "For I know that nothing good dwells within me, i.e., in my flesh. I can will what is right, but I cannot do it. For I do not do the good I want, but the evil I do not want is what I do." For me, Paul's text speaks to our situation and the ambivalence that turns our quest for certitudes about discipleship — the equivalent for us of "the law . . . and the commandment [which are] holy and just and good" (Rom 7:12) — into something which, in our cynical but ethically sensitive moments, we can eventually recognize as destructive, oppressive, exclusive, and/or sinful.

Then should we not conclude, with many of our contemporaries who have adopted a purely secular life, that the teaching about discipleship that we found through our reading of the Sermon on the Mount is wrong, misleading, sinful, either because our absolute claims about one teaching are spurious if not fraudulent, or because the diversity of irreconcilable interpretations makes it absolutely impossible to find in any of them the absolute certainty on which to commit oneself to a life of discipleship? Or should we not reject as absolute nonsense all these fanciful postmodern discussions, along with all politically correct multicultural concerns and atheistic ecumenical dialogues, so as better to hide ourselves behind the for-

---

35. Of course, biblical critics do not need to believe that the Sermon on the Mount is word of God to carry on this kind of critical study; they might simply seek to describe the teaching of the Sermon on the Mount that people who are believers (but not them) should follow. Biblical critics who reject the Christian faith and seek to establish that "the" teaching of the Sermon on the Mount about discipleship is dangerous and should not be followed end up at a similar place: a one-dimensional universal certitude; a universal and immutable truth. Thus *mutatis mutandis,* the following comments also apply to those biblical critics; they still seek to ground their behavior in an absolute truth.

tifications of absolute certitudes, be it in a fundamentalist movement or in positivistic scientific studies of the Bible? Either positively or negatively, we exclusively deal with absolutes. Are absolutes not appropriate when considering religious commitments? The difficulty is that, soon after adopting one of these attitudes, we once again find ourselves oscillating to the opposite pole, either in a quest for absolute certitudes or in cynical denial of any absolute certitudes.

Are we condemned to oscillate forever between these two poles, absolutizing one and denying the other for a while, then, confronted by the reality of the latter, absolutizing it and as a consequence denying the other? As I have already suggested, in the last analysis, this is a theological issue. Absolutizing what, in moments of sanity, we recognize to be not absolute is idolatry. Relativism (absolutizing the diversity and concluding that anything goes, or that nothing goes) as denial that there is any basis for discipleship is also a denial of Christian faith and thus of God — another form of idolatry.

Whether our critical exegetical practice is, consciously or not, a quest for an absolute ("the" true teaching of the biblical text) or whether it is, consciously or not, the cynical denial of any possibility of establishing a teaching of the biblical text that could inform a life of discipleship, our critical exegetical practice is idolatrous.

For me, an androcritical multidimensional practice of biblical studies avoids these two idolatries — these two absolutizations of what should not be absolutized — and their dire moral consequences[36] (1) by acknowledging, through the multidimensional component of this practice, the plausibility, the legitimacy, and the contingent value of a plurality of interpretations — none of which can be viewed as absolute, and (2) by affirming, through the androcritical component of this practice, and thus owning up to the value in a certain context and in a certain time of a certain interpretation — a value such that, forsaking all others, we commit ourselves to live by this interpretation at least for a certain time. To put it in theological language, this androcritical study demands that I, a male European-American, affirm a specific interpretation of discipleship according to the Sermon on the Mount as the "word of God for me." Thus this interpretation is far from being relative; indeed, it is authoritative for me. Yet I can affirm it as the word of God for me without denying that another interpretation might be the word of God for someone else, as I keep in mind my fundamental theological conviction that it is in concrete, contingent historical contexts that God reveals Godself. Consequently, I must constantly reexamine the interpretation that I value and affirm, so as to be sure it still is the word of God for me in the present context, in which I am in relation with others.

---

36. See Patte, *Ethics of Biblical Interpretation*, 17–27.

As we shall see (cf. chap. 7), the word of God needs to be affirmed by a community, even as it is also a private matter.

This theological confession shows why, in the present situation, I find greater value in androcritical multidimensional exegetical practices, as contrasted with one-dimensional critical exegetical practices. It also explains what specific kind of androcritical multidimensional study is most urgent in my view. While feminist, African-American, and other advocacy interpreters do not hesitate to affirm the contextual value of their interpretations, we male European-American interpreters fail to do so when we implicitly claim that ours have an absolute, universal value, or when we deny that they have any value at all. Thus it is essential that my multidimensional study of discipleship according to the Sermon on the Mount be focused on male European-American interpretations in order to clarify that we ourselves deny the absolute character of any of our interpretations, since in practice we as a group propose not one but several equally plausible and legitimate interpretations of discipleship according to the Sermon on the Mount. This affirmation of a diversity of interpretations that we value as a group of male European-Americans is essential because we are in great need of reexamining each of these interpretations in order to reassess their respective value for us in the present circumstances. That is, we simply need to seek to discern which of our own interpretations we should view as the word of God for us in the present situation. Regarding the diverse interpretations of the teaching of the Sermon on the Mount about discipleship as an ethical practice, this involves raising ethical questions about each interpretation. Is a given interpretation beneficial? Or harmful? For whom? Does it helpful or hinder the performance of our duties and other commitments? Is it in harmony with our convictions or in tension with them?

With the hope that the preceding pages have at least suggested the plausibility, legitimacy, and relative value of an androcritical multidimensional approach, I now begin our specific study of a series of interpretations by male European-American interpreters of "discipleship according to the Sermon on the Mount." The concrete procedures for this study are best clarified through the use of the same approach for the study of a shorter text, Matthew 4:18–22. Since these verses also are about discipleship and set the stage for the Sermon on the Mount, their study will be a good introduction to our main topic.

CHAPTER 2

Discipleship according to Four Scholarly Interpretations of Matthew 4:18-22

An Androcritical Multidimensional Study

This chapter discusses four types of scholarly interpretations of Matthew 4:18–22, including mine. I selected three of the many available studies of this passage from the Gospel of Matthew because they can be contrasted easily with each other and with mine in terms of both their scholarly approaches and their *conclusions about the teaching* of this text regarding discipleship. These four types of studies provide us with an ideal sample for illustrating the multidimensional and androcritical approach we shall use for our study of discipleship according to the much richer and complex text that the Sermon on the Mount is.

Our study of these four types of scholarly interpretations of Matthew 4:18–22 is *multidimensional*. The reasons (including the value judgments) involved in this choice of approach have been discussed above (chap. 1). Here because the emphasis is on the practice of such an approach, it becomes clear that a study becomes multidimensional by deliberately seeking to respect the scholarly character of each of the interpretations to which it refers and the critical approaches they use. In a sense, this is nothing else than reaffirming the judgment of the guild that acknowledges the legitimacy of these different approaches in congresses, publications, and academic positions. Yet this study also takes stock of the implications of recognizing the legitimacy of these different scholarly approaches, by anticipating that such a diversity of scholarly interpretations might result in different yet legitimate *conclusions about the teaching* of Matthew 4:18–22 regarding discipleship.

This study is also deliberately *androcritical*. For this reason, I purposefully selected a series of interpretations by "andros" — male European-American scholars — for the central part of this study (other kinds of interpretations will be discussed in chap. 7). Studying such interpretations from a multidimensional perspective readily leads to *androcriticism*. Because this study emphasizes the multiplicity of possible legitimate interpretations, it calls our attention to the complexity of the interpretive process that *critical* interpretations are committed to make explicit. This study is also androcritical in the sense that it contests the claim to being fully critical made by these four kinds of scholarly interpretations by male European-American exegetes, either explicitly or implicitly. *All* of these interpretations (including mine) are challenged to be more systematically critical. Constructively, this study complements and refines these scholarly interpretations by striving to make explicit what they presupposed and/or suppressed. Since the critical problem that plagues these interpretations originates in the one-dimensional practice of denying legitimacy, epistemological consistency, and validity to all other interpretations, one can readily envision how to proceed.

Each of the scholarly interpretations presents *conclusions about what the text is and says* (CAWs) as warrants for its *conclusions about the teaching* (CATs) of the text regarding discipleship, which may or may not be made explicit.[1]

Furthermore, each provides a justification for its CAWs by showing that they provide a coherent account of the textual and contextual evidence. Yet because of its one-dimensional practice, each fails to acknowledge that these *conclusions about what the text is and says* merely represent the coherence of one of the several meaning-producing dimensions of the text. The problem is *not* that these scholarly interpretations conclude that one specific dimension of the text is truly significant and thus provides coherence for the text. Any interpretation does this. The problem lies with the practice of interpreting the text as having one, and only one, true coherence, and thus one true meaning-producing dimension. Because it denies other dimensions, each of these scholarly interpretations proposes *conclusions about what the text is and says* (as well as supporting arguments) that are warped by efforts to account for textual features that belong to other dimensions and by misuses of critical methods — using a given method

---

1. Here, for quick reference is table 1 from the introduction.

	Pro me/nobis Interpretations	Traditional Scholarly Interpretations	Exemplary Critical Interpretations
CARVs	Explicit	Implicit	Explicit
Value Judgment	+/-Explicit	Implicit	Explicit
CATs	+/- Explicit	+/- Explicit	Explicit
Epistemology Judgment	Implicit	+/- Explicit	Explicit
CAWs	Implicit	Explicit	Explicit
Legitimacy Judgment	Implicit	Explicit (methods)	Explicit

CARVs = *Conclusions about the relative value* of the teaching of a text
CATs = *Conclusions about the teaching* of a text
CAWs = *Conclusions about what the text is and says*

(e.g., a historical method) to study textual features that it is not equipped to address (e.g., literary features). As we proceed to a multidimensional study that affirms the basic legitimacy of very different interpretations, we are freed from the compulsion to seek to account for all the features of the text in a single interpretation. Rather, we can recognize that each critical method is crafted so as to account for the coherence of a specific dimension of the text.

Using this comparative practice, an androcritical multidimensional study can make explicit which of the meaning-producing dimensions was chosen as the focus of a given scholarly interpretation. The warranting argument of this interpretation and its *conclusions about what the text is and says* can then be streamlined to underscore their specificity as compared with the warranting arguments and CAWs of other interpretations. Thus, the first part of this chapter shows that each scholarly interpretation has made a choice among several equally legitimate sets of *conclusions about what the text is and says*, on the basis of specific *legitimacy judgments* that find expression in the use of a given critical method.

The second part of this chapter seeks to address a second and similar problem that plagues each of these scholarly interpretations. Each fails to be truly critical because it fails to acknowledge the *epistemology judgments* through which it conceptualized the theme or subtheme that is the center of its plausible *conclusions about the teaching* of the text and that its *conclusions about what the text is and says* implicitly or explicitly support. This failure to acknowledge the epistemology judgments is not surprising, since in traditional male European-American practices, scholarly interpretations are almost always exclusively devoted to arguing for *conclusions about what the text is and says*, as if these did not have any implications for understanding the teaching of the text to one audience or another (including us).

My androcritical multidimensional study seeks to remedy this deficiency of the scholarly interpretations through a deliberate formulation of the implications of their *conclusions about what the text is and says* for an understanding of the teaching of the text (to someone). Once again, the comparative approach involved in a multidimensional practice is helpful for identifying the specificity of the (reconstructed) *conclusions about the teaching* of Matthew 4:18–22 proposed by each of the scholarly interpretations. This identification is further facilitated by focusing this comparative investigation on a specific theme — discipleship.[2] Recognizing the spe-

---

2. As I underscored in the introduction and in chapter 1, it is because of my own interests that I chose this theme. Another theme (e.g., Christology) could have been chosen. By comparing these interpretations in terms of one kind of teaching, discipleship, which the text apparently includes, I seek to make explicit what, according to our custom, these scholarly interpretations have left implicit: their respective implications for an understanding of the teaching of Matthew 4:18–22 and the Sermon on the Mount (to someone).

cific way in which the few features of this theme manifested in Matthew 4:18–22 are conceptualized in each scholarly interpretation will allow us to recognize the specific kind of epistemological categories used in envisioning its *conclusions about the teaching* of the text. This comparative multidimensional study will, therefore, help us to recognize a range of epistemology judgments through which male European-Americans make sense of this text and of discipleship. This study will bring to light some of the epistemological choices involved in each interpretation. Yet the interpretations of such a short text, Matthew 4:18–22, do not supply us with enough data for recognizing how "European-American" cultures have contributed to these epistemology judgments by providing semantic categories. We will have to wait for the data provided by the respective interpretations of the Sermon on the Mount in order to understand fully how each conceptualizes discipleship. But what we will have learned from the interpretations of Matthew 4:18–22 will provide us with essential guidelines for our study of discipleship according to the interpretations of the Sermon on the Mount.

A third problematic aspect of these scholarly interpretations of Matthew 4:18–22 will remain to be addressed, namely, their failure to acknowledge the *value judgment* through which each chose certain *conclusions about the teaching* of the text among various plausible options. Denying that a value judgment is used results from not acknowledging that there are several legitimate coherent interpretations of a text and several meaningful conceptualizations of each theme and subtheme. The discussion of the issues regarding the value judgment involved in these interpretations will not be presented in this chapter, since it needs to be preceded by a more complete assessment of the conceptualizations of discipleship in the Sermon on the Mount. We shall present this discussion in chapter 7, that is, after our study of the four kinds of interpretations of discipleship according to the Sermon on the Mount.

Basic Options Selected for This Androcritical Multidimensional Study of Matthew 4:18–22

The Text to Be Studied

By saying that our study of discipleship according to Matthew 4:18–22 lays the groundwork for our study of this theme in the Sermon on the Mount, I signal that I have chosen to study a specific kind of text: the Sermon on the Mount and other passages *as parts of the Gospel according to Matthew.* I am interested in the text studied in redaction criticism and semio-literary criticism, by contrast with Matthew 4:18–22 and the Sermon on the Mount as parts of the New Testament as a whole (as they are treated, for instance, in studies about discipleship according to the New Testament)[3] or by contrast with the Sermon on the Mount as an independent text (e.g., prior to its insertion in the Gospel according to Matthew, as Betz suggests).[4]

The Scholarly Interpretations Considered in This Androcritical Multidimensional Study

This androcritical multidimensional study involves a critical analysis of interpretations offered by male European-American scholars (including my own), which must be decentered and be ready to play, alongside feminist and other advocacy interpretations, a constructive role in helping readers of Matthew bring their own interpretations to critical understanding. The present study plays this role for me. By analyzing other interpretations by male European-Americans, I can recognize, acknowledge, and affirm the specificity of my own interpretation. You, my reader, are invited to do the same.

I already mentioned (see introduction, pp. 13–15) the specific critical interpretations I selected to examine: those by Strecker[5] and Kingsbury,[6] those by Luz,[7] Davies and Allison,[8] as well as two kinds of interpretation that function as direct alternatives to the preceding ones: an interpretation that I develop out of Edwards's suggestions[9] and the interpretation proposed in my own commentary.[10] There are several reasons for this selection.

---

3. Such as Eduard Schweizer, *Lordship and Discipleship* (London: SCM, 1960); Anselm Schulz, *Nachfolgen und Nachahmen: Studien über das Verhältnis der neutestamentlichen Jüngerschaft zur urchristlichen Vorbildethik* (Munich: Kösel-Verlag, 1962); Martin Hengel, *The Charismatic Leader and His Followers*, trans. J. Greig (New York: Crossroad; Edinburgh: T. & T. Clark, 1981).

4. See Hans Dieter Betz, *Essays on the Sermon on the Mount*, trans. L. L. Welborn (Minneapolis: Fortress, 1985), and *Synoptische Studien* (Tübingen: J. C. B. Mohr, 1992).

5. Georg Strecker, *Der Weg der Gerechtigkeit: Untersuchung zur Theologie des Matthäus* (Göttingen: Vandenhoeck & Ruprecht, 1962; 3d ed., 1971 [all references are to the 3d edition]) and *The Sermon on the Mount: An Exegetical Commentary*, trans. O. C. Dean Jr. (Nashville: Abingdon, 1988).

6. Jack D. Kingsbury, "The Verb *Akolouthein* ('to Follow') as an Index of Matthew's View of His Community," *Journal of Biblical Literature* 97 (1978): 56–73, and *Matthew as Story* (Minneapolis: Fortress, 1986).

7. Ulrich Luz, *Matthew 1–7: A Commentary* (Minneapolis: Augsburg, 1989); "The Disciples in the Gospel according to Matthew," in *The Interpretation of Matthew*, ed. Graham Stanton (Minneapolis: Fortress; London: SPCK, 1983), 98–128; and *The Theology of the Gospel according to Matthew* (Cambridge: Cambridge University Press, 1995).

8. W. D. Davies, *The Setting of the Sermon on the Mount* (Cambridge: Cambridge University Press, 1964), and primarily, W. D. Davies and D. C. Allison Jr., *A Critical and Exegetical Commentary on the Gospel according to Saint Matthew*, ICC, vol. 1 (Edinburgh: T. & T. Clark, 1988).

9. Richard A. Edwards, *Matthew's Story of Jesus* (Minneapolis: Fortress, 1985), and "Uncertain Faith: Matthew's Portrait of the Disciples," in *Discipleship in the New Testament*, ed. F. F. Segovia (Minneapolis: Fortress, 1985).

10. Daniel Patte, *The Gospel according to Matthew: A Structural Commentary on Matthew's Faith* (Minneapolis: Fortress, 1987; 3d printing, Valley Forge, Pa.: Trinity Press International, 1996).

First, I had to limit my androcritical multidimensional study to *four kinds* of interpretations for practical reasons. It is simply very difficult to compare and contrast more than four interpretations in a given study, especially in a systematic fashion. I will at times refer to other interpretations by male European-American exegetes who reach conclusions regarding discipleship according to Matthew that can be readily compared on specific points with the conclusions proposed by Strecker and by Luz, among which those by Barth,[11] Lambrecht,[12] Zumstein,[13] and Betz,[14] to name only a few. The fact that the latter studies are only occasionally mentioned and that other studies are not mentioned at all does not mean that I consider them less significant. It simply means that I had to limit my presentation for practical reasons, which will become readily apparent below.

Second, my choice was governed by my personal assessment that the two kinds of interpretations represented by the works, on the one hand, of Strecker and Kingsbury, and on the other hand, of Luz and Davies and Allison are the most influential in contemporary European-American cultures. I chose to proceed to an andro*critical* study of these two kinds of interpretations because I am *concerned* by the detrimental effects that they have in their present form and because I am *interested* by the teachings of Matthew that they underscore. Even though these interpretations do not necessarily emphasize their respective *conclusions about the teaching* of Matthew regarding discipleship, for better or for worse these conclusions are particularly significant in contemporary (androcentric) European-American cultural situations.

Because of their very preeminence, these two kinds of male European-American critical interpretations are particularly problematic. I do not mean that these interpretations lack plausibility, or legitimacy, or even value, although I will question their relative value in the present sociocultural situation (see chap. 7). The problem is that as long as each is *presented* as the one and only legitimate interpretation, and thus, as long as they are *parts of a praxis conceived as a quest for "the" single universal meaning* of the Gospel according to Matthew, each signals that all other interpretations are illegitimate. With the powerful voice given to them by

---

11. Gerhard Barth, "Matthew's Understanding of the Law," in *Tradition and Interpretation in Matthew,* by G. Bornkamm, G. Barth, and H. J. Held, trans. P. Scott (Philadelphia: Westminster, 1963), 58–164.

12. Jan Lambrecht, *"Eh bien! Moi je vous dis": Le discours-programme de Jésus (Mt 5–7; Lc 6,20–49),* Lectio Divina 125 (Paris: Cerf, 1986).

13. Jean Zumstein, *La condition du croyant dans l'Evangile selon Matthieu* (Göttingen: Vandenhoeck & Ruprecht, 1977).

14. Most of his studies are relevant even for interpretations focused on the Sermon on the Mount as a part of Matthew. See again Betz, *Essays on the Sermon* and *Synoptische Studien.* Unfortunately, when writing this book, I did not have access to his commentary, Hans Dieter Betz, *The Sermon on the Mount, Including the Sermon on the Plain (Mt 5:3–7:27 and Lk 6:20–49): A Commentary on Two Early Christian Manuals of Discipleship,* Hermeneia, ed. Adela Yarbro Collins (Minneapolis: Fortress, 1995).

their academic credentials, these studies call ordinary readers, whatever their cultural, social and/or religious contexts, to dismiss their own interpretations (and ultimately their identities) as meaningless, whenever their interpretations do not conform to the given exegetical interpretation. This is ethically problematic.

It remains that each of them includes a teaching about discipleship of the Gospel of Matthew that is particularly important in contemporary European-American cultural situations. Once decentered through an androcritical multidimensional study that presents each of them as one among several legitimate and plausible interpretations, they are each without any doubt very significant.

This affirmation of the legitimacy, plausibility, and significance (or value) of these two very different kinds of interpretations is the exact opposite of the practice they themselves implement: each dismisses the other as illegitimate in order to affirm its unique and exclusive claim to truth. The debate between Strecker and Luz over Matthew's teaching about discipleship,[15] which is summarized below, is a classical instance of the inevitable conflicts resulting from one-dimensional and exclusive practices in biblical studies. By contrast, our multidimensional practice will allow us to affirm the legitimacy, plausibility, and significance of both.

For this purpose, we first need to overcome the perception (which one-dimensional studies readily reinforce) that these two dominant types of interpretations are in competition with each other for the "title" of most complete and most accurate representation of "the" meaning of the text. This competitive perspective leads each of them to view its differences with the other as an error or deficiency on the part of the other, rather than as a signal that it represents a legitimate alternative interpretation. It follows that these differences must be accounted for and overcome, since both kinds of interpretations seek to elucidate the same thing: "the" (single, universal) meaning of the text.

The Specific Goals of This Chapter

In order to dispel this inappropriate perception of the relationships between these two dominant kinds of interpretations, I begin by comparing the first kind of interpretation (Strecker's redaction critical and Kingsbury's redaction critical and narrative interpretations) to a distinctive narrative interpretation developed following suggestions by Edwards, since through its specific critical method this latter interpretation offers an alternative way

---

15. This debate is well represented by Graham Stanton, ed., *The Interpretation of Matthew* (Philadelphia: Fortress, 1983), which sets the classical essays by Strecker on "The Concept of History in Matthew" (pp. 67–84) and by Luz on "The Disciples in the Gospel according to Matthew" (pp. 98–128) side by side.

of accounting for the coherence of the "historical" or "narrative" dimensions of the text — the primary critical concern of Strecker and Kingsbury. While they find the coherence of the text in the situation(s) to which the text refers, Edwards finds it in the unfolding of the plot of the story (and of history, or in brief "the unfolding of hi/story"). After establishing in part 1 that these two kinds of interpretations are equally legitimate — their *conclusions about what the text is and says* are based on evidence established by appropriate critical methods — we will compare in part 2 their *conclusions about the teaching* of Matthew 4:18–22 regarding discipleship. This second comparison will clarify that these two kinds of interpretations conceptualize *discipleship as implementation* of certain beliefs or principles about what Christian believers should do in order to be faithful. Yet these are clearly *alternative* interpretations because their respective *conclusions about the teaching* that needs to be implemented and how this implementation should take place are quite different. For Strecker and Kingsbury, the implementation of discipleship involves acting according to the idealized norm represented by the response of the four first disciples to Jesus' call. By contrast, for the interpretation developed out of Edwards's suggestions, the implementation of discipleship involves agreeing to enter a long process through which one is to be transformed by Jesus (and his representatives).

Similarly, I compare the second kind of critical interpretations (those by Luz and Davies and Allison) with the structural interpretation presented in my commentary because they are focused on related meaning-producing dimensions. Through the use of critical methods dealing with the history of traditions and with the history of interpretations, Luz as well as Davies and Allison seek the coherence of the text among its figures, symbolic expressions, and metaphors, that is, in a "figurative" meaning-producing dimension. Alternatively, through the use of structural critical methods, my interpretation seeks the coherence of the text among its themes, convictional expressions, and semantic trajectories, that is, in a "thematic" meaning-producing dimension. After the legitimacy of both sets of interpretations is shown through a first comparison in part 1, a second comparison will show in part 2 that both sets conceptualize *discipleship as an intuitive ethical practice,* and thus *discipleship as imitation,* understood either as "conforming to" or as "following." According to the conceptualization presupposed by Luz and Davies and Allison, the primary teaching of Matthew is viewed as conveying a vision of an ideal world (the kingdom) that Jesus during his ministry and others after him have manifested "among us." Disciples allow themselves to be "formed" by this vision and thus to conceptualize themselves in terms of this vision and thus in the image of Jesus and others who manifest this vision among us. In this way, disciples imitate Jesus as they embark on a life of discipleship without knowing exactly what this entails and/or where it will lead. According to the conceptualization presupposed by my commentary, the Gospel according to Matthew conveys to its readers a vision of discipleship, that is, the moral discernment that should allow them to identify those who should be followed as models of discipleship. As they participate in Jesus' ministry, disciples share in the vision of the kingdom toward which Jesus' ministry points. In sum, while these two kinds of interpretations are closely related, it is clear that they are *alternatives;* both are plausible and present views of discipleship which make sense and are thus epistemologically sound, even as the vision of the kingdom and the vision of discipleship (discernment of models of discipleship) have inverted roles.

After identifying for each of the dominant interpretations a first legitimate alternative, it is readily recognizable that the interpretations of Strecker and Kingsbury can also be viewed as legitimate alternative interpretations to those of Luz and Davies and Allison, and vice versa. Differences among interpretations can be viewed as signals that disparate rigorous critical interpretations account for distinct aspects of the teaching of the Gospel of Matthew about discipleship, rather than as conflicts that must be resolved by rejecting one or the other of the interpretations.

PART 1: THE LEGITIMACY OF FOUR DIVERGENT INTERPRETATIONS OF MATTHEW 4:18–22

The Legitimacy of Four Kinds of Conclusions about What the Text Is and Says: An Overview

In this first part I propose a multidimensional comparison of the four kinds of interpretations of Matthew 4:18–22 in terms of their respective critical methods and of their *conclusions about what the text is and says.* This comparison is *multidimensional* in that its goal is to show that their respective conclusions are equally legitimate because each set reflects a textual meaning-producing dimension that has as much potential to be significant for readers as any of the other dimensions.

Of course, for many contemporary historians and historically minded European-Americans, the significance (for us) of a text from the past is legitimate only insofar as it accounts for "the situation to which the text refers" — and thus the *conclusions about what the text is and says* of a critical interpretation must provide a sketch of this situation, which is essentially a "still picture" where people and institutions are stable entities with fixed characteristics. This one-dimensional view is, in brief, what Strecker and Kingsbury presuppose.

This view is most directly challenged when it is confronted with an interpretation that also proposes conclusions about what is the history (or story) represented by the text, but that finds its significance in the unfolding process that characterizes history itself. While it has become habitual in European-American scholarly circles since World War I to dismiss the significance of the unfolding of history (identified with the "progress myth"), this unfolding of hi/story remains the meaning-producing dimension that is most significant for many readers from various cultures.

After envisioning the potential legitimacy of both kinds of interpretations (Strecker, Kingsbury, Edwards), we will be in a position to acknowledge equal legitimacy for interpretations that find the significance of the text in "nonhistorical" dimensions (Luz, Davies and Allison, Patte). From their one-dimensional perspectives, Luz, Davies and Allison, and Patte (he also!) might be surprised to hear that their interpretations are "nonhistorical." In different ways, each carefully takes into account the results of historical research, and at times contributes to it (as is expressed in notes). Yet their respective *conclusions about what the text is and says* point to meaning-producing dimensions that transcend the historical period of the text — and are thus nonhistorical — as the true significance for legitimate interpretations. These conclusions are neither about what is "the situation to which the text refers" nor about what is "the unfolding of the hi/story that the text presents," but about the "figurative" or the "thematic" dimension of the text, that is, using Luz's term, about dimensions concerning the textual "transparency" through which the Gospel of Matthew transcends the historical reality to which it refers. This transparency of the figurative dimension (and, to a lesser extent, of the thematic dimension) calls for a study of the text in terms of *other periods* of history — in the context of a "history of traditions" or of a "history of interpretations" — or in terms of atemporal structures.

While the *conclusions about what* the text refers to of the two "historical" interpretations can easily be viewed as complementary, such conclusions of a "historical" interpretation and those of a "nonhistorical" interpretation are farther away from each other and are appropriately perceived as contradictory. Yet in a multidimensional approach, they are to be viewed as equally legitimate. This claim is best illustrated by the clash between Strecker and Luz regarding the interpretation of discipleship according to Matthew.

A Concrete Instance of the Problem Addressed by This Study: Luz vs. Strecker

From the perspective of traditional, one-dimensional exegetical practices, divergent interpretations of Matthew 4:18–22 and of its teaching about discipleship are problematic. One needs to resolve this conflict of interpretations so as to elucidate what is "the" (single, true, universal) legitimate interpretation. After all, Matthew as the author or redactor of this Gospel meant to convey one specific message to his audience, and thus one specific teaching about discipleship, did he not?

Luz's essay on "The Disciples in the Gospel according to Matthew" is typical of this practice. He begins by noting that there are two kinds of interpretations of the disciples in Matthew:

> There are two tendencies evident in the interpretation of this. One can be characterized by the catchword "transparency." This is stressed by Hummel: the title "disciple" remains the exhaustive ecclesiological term. G. Barth speaks of "an equating of the time of the Church with the time of the life of Jesus." The other tendency is best described by the catchword "historicizing." That Matthew's understanding of the disciples has a historicizing thrust is stressed above all by G. Strecker: "The disciples, like Jesus himself, are set in an unrepeatable, holy past."[16]

From Luz's perspective, this plurality of interpretations is a problem that must be resolved either by showing that one of these is legitimate and the other is not or by proposing a third kind of interpretation that could account for features of both. "This complex situation justifies a fresh treatment of discipleship in Matthew"; that is, Luz's essay. In it, Luz ends up rejecting Strecker's interpretation as illegitimate because "we have not found a thorough-going historicizing in the understanding of the disciples in Matthew's gospel"[17] — that would make out of the presentation of the disciples in Matthew an idealized norm to be implemented. Thus, contrary to Strecker, Luz underscores that in Matthew "disciple" is "the exhaustive ecclesiological term."[18] Through its "transparency" Matthew offers a vision of discipleship (as intuitive ethical practice). Yet in his argument Luz cannot deny that there are signs of historicizing in Matthew, and thus that Strecker's argument is based on actual textual evidence. He simply denies that these signs can be interpreted as evidence for concluding that Matthew has a "*thorough-going* historicizing in the understanding of the disciples."

Because of his thoroughness and probity as a scholar, Luz shows that his objection is not that Strecker's interpretation fails to be based on textual evidence, but that his own interpretation is based on another kind of textual evidence, as, conversely, Strecker acknowledges regarding Luz's interpretation, for instance, when noting that Peter is presented as a "type" of discipleship (as intuitive ethical practice).[19] In effect, Luz acknowledges that the text is ambivalent. Of course, it would be difficult to say against Strecker that Matthew, from his perspective in the latter part of the first century, did not consider Jesus' ministry as belonging to "an unrepeatable and holy past," and thus that he did not have a historicizing tendency. But

---

16. Luz, "The Disciples," 98. Luz refers to R. Hummel, *Die Auseinandersetzung zwischen Kirche und Judentum im Matthäusevangelium* (Munich: Kaiser, 1963); Barth, "Matthew's Understanding of the Law," in *Tradition and Interpretation;* and Strecker, *Der Weg.*
17. Luz, "The Disciples," 105.
18. See also Luz, *Matthew,* 200–201.
19. See Strecker, *Der Weg,* 198–206.

conversely, it would be difficult to say that Matthew neither conceived of Jesus' ministry in terms of the church of his time nor used the term "disciple" in an ecclesiological sense by "reading" Jesus' ministry in terms of concerns and interests of his church.

For Luz, as well as for Strecker and all other one-dimensional interpreters, the question is, Which one of these two tendencies is the one that is "thoroughgoing" and is thus to be viewed as dominant and as the key for understanding the teaching that Matthew intended to convey about discipleship? Matthew cannot have meant both of these radically different teachings about discipleship — a difference that one can sense behind the few general remarks made so far (see the detailed discussion in part 2) about the options represented in interpretations advanced by Luz and Strecker. Clearly, this polyvalence of the text must be resolved.

I agree that one cannot hold to both of these interpretations (by Strecker and by Luz) as "the Matthean teaching about discipleship *for us.*" We would need to have contradictory behaviors! We need to choose one of them (or another one still).

The question is, On which ground are we to make this choice? Not by claiming and seeking to demonstrate that one interpretation is legitimate *and that all the others are illegitimate.* Why? Because this one-dimensional demonstration is ethically dubious; denying that all the other scholarly interpretations are illegitimate is implicitly (if not explicitly) making an arrogant claim of superiority for our interpretation and for ourselves — as if other scholars had not used critical methods to scrutinize the evidence and as if they were unable to exercise sound legitimacy judgments.

Intellectual probity calls us to acknowledge that according to the kind of critical questions we raise — that is, according to the critical perspective we adopt — we end up giving priority to one set of textual evidence or to another. Thus we perceive "Matthew's intention" in one way rather than in another.[20] The fact that one kind of critical perspective (e.g., Luz's) becomes the dominant one during a given period of the history of scholarship after displacing another critical perspective (e.g., Strecker's) does not guarantee that the view of Matthew's intention it elucidates is the true historical one!

Traditional one-dimensional biblical studies view this undecidability regarding an author's intention as a problem of historical distance. This is a plausible view, and I want to underscore that it is indeed important to recognize how historical distance generates interpretive difficulties. Yet it is also plausible to consider that this distance amplifies, rather than creates, the ambiguities of the text. This involves recognizing that there is no text without a plurality of messages besides the intentional message of the author.

---

20. For other examples of this phenomenon, see Patte, *Ethics of Biblical Interpretation,* 37–71.

From this perspective, the interpretive difficulties spawned by historical distance begin as soon as an author is no longer present to answer questions regarding his or her intention. This is so because any discourse involves a semantic investment that is at least twofold.[21] For our present purpose, it is enough to note that when one speaks or writes, one always does it for a specific audience and with the intention of transforming this audience in some way. For instance, many would agree that a part of Matthew's goal was to transform his audience's (his church's) view of discipleship because for him the view that they held was inappropriate. In order to convince these people to adopt his view about discipleship, Matthew had to express it for them in terms of what they already knew, and thus *in terms of concepts and images that they already associated with discipleship*. Even when he used these concepts and images in order to transform them or to reject them, they remain associated with the audience's view of discipleship, and Matthew's text also conveys this view of discipleship. As a result, the Gospel according to Matthew gives expression to at least two views of discipleship: that of the intended audience and that of Matthew. Because we are not the original audience, we are in no position to assess which aspects of the text reflect Matthew's intentional teaching about discipleship and which the different view of his intended audience.

Traditional one-dimensional biblical scholars conceive of their critical task as an attempt at resolving such tensions in the text by identifying its intentional teaching, which would then be the true meaning of the text. A glance at the history of scholarship — or simply at the contemporary interpretations of Matthew 4:18–22 that we discuss — is enough to convince me that we are not successful in this endeavor.[22] Did Matthew intend to present the disciples as an ideal norm by setting them in an unrepeatable, holy past (Strecker)? Or was this the view of his intended audience, which Matthew seeks to overcome? Did Matthew intend to present the disciples as "types"

---

21. Here I allude to semiotic theories (such as Greimas's and Eco's) which, by seeking to account for the interrelations among linguistic, semantic, communication, and the various literary and social science theories, had to acknowledge the polyvalence of any meaning-producing cultural artifact, including and especially discourses. This is what I have tried to show in D. Patte, *The Religious Dimensions of Biblical Texts: Greimas's Structural Semiotics and Biblical Exegesis* (Atlanta: Scholars Press, 1990). See this book for bibliography on semiotics and a discussion of the different trends (especially chap. 1). The ambivalence of my own text (a discourse like any other) is shown by the fact that despite my intention to underscore a plurality of religious dimensions (plural form in the title; three separate chapters focused on three distinct religious dimensions) it was read by two reviewers as seeking to establish a single religious dimension. As I acknowledged in a response to these reviewers, their interpretation of my text is legitimate — it is based on appropriate textual evidence (my rhetorical use of terminologies and categories coming from the views I sought to challenge), even though my intentional message (which is also the interpretation of my text by myself as its first reader) is different.

22. Since in the past the claim by a generation of scholars to have established the definite intentional teaching of Matthew was dismissed by the next generation, why would it not be the same for the dominant interpretations today?

of church members by presenting them anachronistically as struggling with issues that church members needed to address in Matthew's time (Luz)? Or, was this his intended audience's view, which Matthew seeks to overcome?

As critical scholars who strive to acknowledge the interpretive processes involved in reading, we should acknowledge that we cannot resolve this ambivalence of the text. Indeed, we should agree that our task is not to resolve this ambivalence because, whether intentionally or not, both messages are potentially conveyed by the text to readers. By now it should be clear that this is not a call for a malapropos display of humility, but for intellectual probity and responsibility. It is enough to emphasize that semiotic theories as well as our ordinary experience as readers and hearers show us the *plausibility* of this conceptualization of our task.

Unintentional messages are often as significant as intentional ones, as we readily recognize in our daily life. For instance, at present in North America, if in a speech about church finance and stewardship I use sex exclusive language or even more subtle forms of sexism, even though my intended message has nothing to do with this issue, for many women in my audience the message conveyed by my speech is that a sexist or even patriarchal perspective is acceptable. Is this interpretation of my speech legitimate? Absolutely. Even though I might be quite frustrated by this unexpected interpretation, which does not pay any attention to my intended message, I have to acknowledge that my (hypothetical) speech also conveys this message, even though it is unintended. It is a consistent pattern in this speech, and thus one of its coherent meaning-producing dimensions. Many of us have learned to pay attention to what is conveyed by the many meaning-producing dimensions that are intertwined in our discourses with the dimension that conveys our intentional message. We are responsible for all these potential messages, even if we did not intend to convey them.

Recognizing the legitimacy of several interpretations of a given text is, in one sense, nothing other than the prolongation of this common experience to critical studies. Interpretations are divergent or in tension with each other because they are focused on different meaning-producing dimensions of a text. The polyvalence of a text from a distant past is even greater because as mentioned above we cannot even be sure which of its meaning-producing dimensions expresses its intentional message. Thus we should not be surprised that several critical interpretations of the same text, Matthew 4:18–22, reach quite different *conclusions about its teaching* regarding discipleship (as is discussed in part 2).

Each interpretation is focused on a specific meaning-producing dimension of the text. Even though each takes into account the entirety of the text, it remains that what is "thoroughgoing" in the text (as Luz says), and thus what holds the text together and gives unity and coherence to it, varies with the perspective that is adopted. This becomes apparent as we consider from our multidimensional perspective the critical arguments that support the legitimacy of four kinds of interpretations of Matthew 4:18–22.

The Legitimacy of Readings A and B: The History/Realistic Narrative and the Plot as Meaning-Producing Dimensions

Regarding both the dominant interpretation of Strecker and Kingsbury (reading A) and the alternative interpretation developed out of Edwards's suggestions (reading B), this subsection *first* considers their respective methodological approaches and the features of the texts on which they are focused. It *then* elucidates the *conclusions about what the text is and says* (CAWs) of these scholarly interpretations, showing in each case how a critical interpretation exclusively[23] focused on a given meaning-producing dimension of Matthew 4:18–22 verifies the coherence of these conclusions.

Reading A, CAW 1: Matthew 4:18–22 as a Window on an Event of "History" or a Scene of a "Realistic Narrative"

Strecker underscores that his study is a historical critical study, and more specifically, a redaction critical study of the Gospel according to Matthew. As is well known, this involves identifying "the genuinely redactional statements that may reflect the central thrust of a particular Gospel, as seen by the redactor himself,"[24] elucidating the specific way in which the redactor transformed sources and traditions, and thus clarifying Matthew's concept of history — that is, how Matthew understood the historical situations to which the tradition and now his text refers.[25] For this purpose, such a historical critical study pays close attention to the peculiar ways in which events, geographical locations, personages, and time periods are characterized through the redaction.[26] In sum, such an interpretation is focused on a meaning-producing dimension of the text that can be called the *"history" to which the text refers.*

---

23. As mentioned above, the interpretations "exclusively focused on a given meaning-producing dimension" are streamlined versions of the interpretations proposed by male European-American scholars. One-dimensional studies include many comments and remarks that concern other dimensions and are thus irrelevant for our specific interpretations. They are merely efforts to show that our interpretation presents "the" single, true meaning of the text. In my brief representation of these interpretations, I limit myself to highlighting the remarks about "pertinent" features.

24. Strecker, "Concept of History," 69; see *Der Weg*, 9–14.

25. For Strecker the task of the redaction critic is summarized by the question: "In what way has the redactor of the first Gospel taken into account in his modification and compilation of traditional material, the theological situation of his generation; and that means by what specific understanding of history does he respond to the problem area that exists?" ("Concept of History," 70).

26. In *Der Weg* Strecker pays special attention to time notations and geographical references (e.g., pp. 86–98), to the relationship between the church and Israel (e.g., pp. 99–118), as well as to the way in which personages (and especially Jesus and the disciples) are presented.

This textual dimension, "history," can also be studied with a literary method. As Strecker himself underscores, this "history" in the text is a construct of the redactor. It presents historical events *as conceived by the redactor* and reflects his peculiar conception of history.[27] This is what a literary critic might want to call the "realistic narrative" presented by the text. Consequently, Kingsbury has no difficulty passing from a redaction critical study of Matthew[28] to a literary narrative study, such as his *Matthew as Story*, which similarly emphasizes the elucidation of events, characters, and their settings (in time and space) as expressions of the narrator's point of view for the sake of the implied reader.[29] In sum, because of the specific literary method he uses (that of Chatman)[30] Kingsbury ends up focusing his study on the same textual dimension as a redaction critic: the "realistic narrative" or "history" presented by the text.

There is no doubt that Matthew 4:18–22 includes the presentation of a historical event — a part of the dimension of the gospel that we call "realistic narrative" or "history" — which is meaningful for certain readers. As we shall see below (part 2), redaction critical studies of Matthew 4:18–22 as a part of the "history" of Matthew and narrative studies of this text as expression of a "realistic narrative" ground the conclusion that this text presents an ideal norm of discipleship.

Readings focused on the history/realistic narrative dimension of the text necessarily hide and ignore other of its meaning-dimensions in the same way that in the well-known cognitive test reproduced in the accompanying diagram, when we perceive the vase (or candlestick), our attention is focused on features of the drawing that hide from us the two faces (persons) looking at each other, which are represented by the same image.

---

27. A "historicization" according to which, as we noted above, Jesus' ministry is "an unrepeatable and holy past."

28. See Kingsbury, "The Verb *Akolouthein*," and his other publications.

29. Kingsbury, *Matthew as Story*, 1–40.

30. Seymour Chatman, *Story and Discourse: Narrative Structure in Fiction and Film* (Ithaca, N.Y.: Cornell University Press, 1978).

This point is even clearer when we consider the less familiar drawing from the cover (reproduced below) in which people see either a cross surrounded by flower-like designs or doves.

When one is preoccupied with the way in which this text represents a specific situation in Jesus' ministry, one cannot but *freeze* this scene and thus *stop* (historical) time or *stop* the unfolding of the narrative. While it is perfectly legitimate to use the text as a window on the history/realistic narrative presented by Matthew, we should not forget that the *unfolding* of history and/or of the plot of the narrative is also meaningful.

Reading B, CAW 1: Matthew 4:18–22 as the Beginning of the Unfolding of a Plot or of a History

For reading B, an alternative interpretation, the unfolding of a story (or of a history)[31] is meaningful in and of itself for readers (i.e., it is a coherent meaning-producing dimension of the text) because of the nature of a plot.[32] In the same way that each action of a story is the transformation of a situation by an actor (an agent, which performs the action and might be human or not, individual or collective, etc.), the plot of a story represents the overall transformation of a situation.[33] The nature of this transformation and the way

---

31. For this alternative interpretation, it is best, following Edwards's *Matthew's Story*, to envision the reading of a narrative plot. Yet an interpretation that would be focused on the unfolding of a (sacred) history would reach similar conclusions.

32. According to Stephen Moore's classical definition in *Literary Criticism and the Gospels: The Theoretical Challenge* (New Haven: Yale University Press, 1989), 14, a plot is "a set of events linked by temporal succession and causality." As discussed below, according to this definition, "plot" is a feature of the "fabula." As is clear, all the components of the definition of the plot are also components of the definition of the fabula in Mieke Bal, *Narratology: Introduction to the Theory of Narrative*, trans. C. van Boheemen (Toronto: University of Toronto Press, 1985), 11–47.

33. When a story is strictly read for its plot, the characters themselves are exclusively defined by their participation in actions (performing actions or being affected by them) and

in which this transformation is brought about might be of great interest for readers, for very different reasons according to the kind of texts they read. For instance, it might offer a message of hope (or despair) by showing the possibility of a positive (or negative) transformation of a situation similar to that of the readers; it might convey a theology, if one of the necessary agents of transformation is divine; it might provide for readers an example of what they should do in order to undergo the same transformation, if those who benefit from this transformation are characters with which readers can identify themselves.

In the case of the Gospel according to Matthew, this plot is twofold: besides the story of Jesus, there is a story of the disciples.[34] This means that the story presents two intertwined narrative transformations in its plot: one concerning Jesus and the other concerning the disciples.

The story of Jesus moves from his genealogy and conception by the Holy Spirit, his birth and infancy—in the course of which we are told of the promise that Jesus "will save his people from their sins" (1:21), that "his name will be called Emmanuel" (1:23), and that this weak and threatened child will be "king of the Jews" (2:2) — to his death and resurrection through which he fulfills all that is expected of him (see, respectively, 26:28; 28:20; 27:11–37) and, at last, receives "all authority in heaven and on earth" (28:18). Despite the complexity of this plot, it is striking that Jesus has all authority in heaven and on earth only after the resurrection. In other words, this story is about the transformation of one who does not have such authority into someone who has it. It is through his ministry (and Passion) that Jesus gains or receives authority; during his ministry Jesus does not yet have it. In effect, instead of the high Christology (Jesus is already in 4:18 the exalted Kyrios with all authority, as Strecker and Kingsbury underscore; see reading A, CAW 5), the interpretations focused on the plot as a dimension of the text discover a low Christology. The Gospel is here the story of how he became the exalted Lord, through his ministry as the lowly Son of man (e.g., 8:20) who makes himself servant of all (e.g., 20:28).

Similarly, the parallel story of the disciples begins in Matthew 4:18–22, Jesus' calling of a first group of disciples, and ends in 28:16–20, Jesus' commissioning of the disciples. Since the disciples as a collective actor are acted on (called and commissioned) by Jesus, it already appears that this story is

---

by what they need to have in order to perform actions (specific qualifications; a competence). Thus, in this dimension, characters are called "actors" (or more technically, "actant") to distinguish them from full-blown characters (as in Kingsbury's interpretation). *Actant* is Greimas's technical term. See A. J. Greimas and J. Courtés, *Semiotics and Language: An Analytical Dictionary*, trans. L. Crist, D. Patte, et al. (Bloomington: Indiana University Press, 1982), 5–6. *Actor* is the more common term, although used as a technical term, which Mieke Bal substitutes for "actant" in *Narratology*, 25–37.

34. Kingsbury (*Matthew as Story*, 103–19) also notes it, but for a different purpose: in order to explain why one needs to pay special attention to the characters "Jesus" and "disciples."

about the disciples in the sense that they are those who are being trans-
formed. Thus, studying this story is elucidating how the disciples have been
progressively transformed through their interactions with Jesus, from their first
encounter with him to their commissioning. Of course, the unfolding of this
story is not straightforward; it involves many complications, as is the case in
most stories.

Comparing the beginning with the end of the story shows how much the
collective actor, the "disciples," has been transformed. It is at the end (Mt
28:16–20), and only at the end (after the Passion), that they are at last ready
to be commissioned to carry out their vocation to be "fishers of people"
(4:19, author's translation), which involves "making disciples" of all the na-
tions. Unlike the other Gospels, Matthew does not present the disciples as
going into mission before the end of the Gospel (after the missionary dis-
course, 10:5–42, the disciples do not go in mission). The opening scene,
which includes Jesus' promise, "I will make you fishers of people" (4:19,
author's translation), confirms that the story of the disciples is the story of
the transformation of would-be disciples and novice disciples into full-fledged
disciples who are ready to be commissioned and to carry out a specific
mission.[35]

It is clear that an interpretation focused on the plot of the hi/story (read-
ing B) is both distinct from reading A and readily meaningful for certain
readers. Here, discipleship is understood as a process through which people
(would-be and novice disciples) are progressively "made disciples"; they are
made ready to carry out the vocation of fishing for people (4:19). In such
a case the interpretation is focused on those qualifications of the characters
that directly contribute to the unfolding of the plot, that is, their transforma-
tion into full-fledged disciples.[36] *This amounts to following the main part of*
the method that Edwards and Kelber proposed.[37]

---

35. In our study of the plot of the disciples' story it is helpful to distinguish between several uses of the term "disciples." All those who are trained to carry out this vocation are "novice disciples"; others who are taught by Jesus, such as the crowds, can be called "would-be dis-ciples." Those who ultimately carry on this vocation by contributing in one way or another to the making of disciples are full-fledged disciples; they have been made disciples. Such is the case of the eleven in 28:16–20, but before them, of the women, who are themselves commis-sioned (28:5–7, 9–10) and contribute to bringing about the final transformation of the male disciples.

36. This is by contrast with the interpretations focused on the history/realistic narrative that most of the time emphasize features of the characters, having no bearing whatsoever on the unfolding of the plot (for instance, the names of the characters).

37. See Werner H. Kelber, *Mark's Story of Jesus* (Philadelphia: Fortress, 1979), 11, and Edwards, *Matthew's Story*, 9. We will adopt this attitude, although we shall not seek to re-construct what happens "in the reader's mind," as Edwards does; it is enough to describe what the text expresses. Against Edwards, who argues that "the absence of exposition about the disciples" demands that the readers interpret their story by "positing a set of hypotheses — that is, filling the gaps" (Edwards, "Uncertain Faith," 48–52), I will show that the text (Mt 4:18–22 and the Sermon on the Mount) does provide an exposition of the plot of the story of disciples, even though they are in most instances actors who are "acted on" (receivers)

Reading A, CAW 2: The Representation of an Event of History or a Scene of a Realistic Narrative in Matthew 4:18–22 as a Meaning-Producing Dimension of the Text

A reading of the text as a window on the history/realistic narrative presented by Matthew (or history/realistic narrative dimension) pays close attention (1) to events (or narrative scenes, which must be a complete self-contained unit to be truly realistic); (2) to geographical locations, temporal notations, and personages, or, in a literary approach, to their representations; and (3) to the role that each of these features plays in the construction of historical/realistic situations to which the text refers — a construct of the past from the perspective of the time of the intended readers. It is this construct that is the ultimate focus of this interpretation. A critical interpretation focused on this dimension should make explicit each of these foci. Since neither Strecker nor Kingsbury provides a full-fledged critical interpretation of this passage (they are content to mention their *conclusions about what the text is and says* in their monographs or thematic essays), I sketch the features of such an interpretation.

The appropriate limits of the event/scene as a textual unit need to be ascertained. When one reads the text about the beginning of Jesus' ministry (4:12ff. or 4:17ff.)[38] as a "history," one does not have any hesitation in recognizing that the first event (self-contained scene) in the history of the

---

rather than agents (subjects performing actions). By elucidating the aspects of the actors' competence that the text underscores, we show the specific features of the plot that this coherent dimension of the text proposes as an example to be emulated. See a detailed explanation of this important point in Patte, *Religious Dimensions,* 183–84, against the literary studies that aim at elucidating the gaps that the readers are expected to fill in, following W. Iser, *The Implied Reader: Patterns of Communication in Prose Fiction from Bunyan to Beckett* (Baltimore: Johns Hopkins University Press, 1974), and *The Act of Reading: A Theory of Aesthetic Response* (Baltimore: Johns Hopkins University Press, 1978). The unfolding of the plot of the hi/story is the narrative dimension that Greimas calls "surface narrative syntax," which is an "actantial" syntax: see Greimas and Courtés, *Semiotics and Language,* 5–6, 332–34. By contrast, Kingsbury's (and Chatman's) studies are focused on a part of the dimension that Greimas calls "discursive syntax" (which includes the phenomena of actorialization, temporalization, spatialization, and many of the relationships between enunciator and enunciatee, etc., all of which contribute to the production of whatever degree of verisimilitude a text has). See Greimas and Courtés, *Semiotics and Language,* 330–31.

38. For the realistic-historical interpretation, which breaks the text in units in terms of the changes in time, place, and characters (characteristics of the discursive syntax), the "history" of Jesus' ministry begins either in 4:17 (when all the criteria are taken into account) or in 4:12 (when one emphasizes change in time). Thus, by using all these criteria, Kingsbury (*Matthew: Structure, Christology, Kingdom* [Minneapolis: Fortress, 1975], 7–25) subdivides the gospel into three parts: 1:1–4:16 (the person of Jesus Messiah); 4:17–16:20 (the proclamation of Jesus Messiah); 16:21–28:20 (the suffering, death, and resurrection of Jesus Messiah). Scholars who emphasize the temporal reference ("when he heard that John had been arrested," 4:12), see the beginning of Jesus' ministry in 4:12. Among them are J. Schmid, *Das Evangelium nach Matthäus,* RNT 1 (Regensburg: F. Pustet, 1959), 69; P. Bonnard, *L'évangile selon Saint Matthieu,* CNT 1 (Neuchâtel: Delachaux & Niestlé, 1963), 47; P. Gaechter, *Das Matthäusevangelium* (Innsbruck: Tyrolia, 1963), 81; X. Léon-Dufour, "The Synoptic Gospels," in *Introduction to the New Testament,* ed. A. Robert and A. Feuillet; trans. P. W. Skehan

disciples is Matthew 4:18–22. The names Simon Peter, Andrew, James, and John are historical markers, which for Matthew's audience (or the intended readers)[39] are those of four of Jesus' companions, i.e., four disciples. From this perspective, 4:18–22 is a discrete unit that includes everything said about the disciples in Matthew 4 (contrast reading B, CAWs 2.1 and 3).

Reading A, CAW 3: Time and Space Notations as Particularly Significant

Although the scene (4:18–22) does not include any specific temporal notation, it is set at the beginning of Jesus' ministry: after John's arrest (4:12) and when Jesus began preaching ("from that time," 4:17). The location of the new scene is specified as "by the Sea of Galilee" (4:18). The context shows that this is near Capernaum "in the territory of Zebulun and Naphtali" (4:12–13, 15). Matthew displays geographical knowledge[40] that he expects his readers to share. These geographical notations make the story realistic for them, or, as Strecker prefers to say, they contribute to the "historicization" of the gospel.[41] Matthew 4:18–20 takes place in a certain time and space that belong to history—the unrepeatable and holy time of Jesus' ministry.[42]

Reading A, CAW 4: Personages or Characters as Particularly Significant

The naming of the four fishers and the mention of their family relationships (two pairs of brothers; James and John are sons of Zebedee) shows that Matthew expects his readers to recognize them readily as four of the disciples (there is no ambivalence here; contrast reading B, CAWs 3 and 4).

---

et al. (New York: Desclée, 1965), 169; W. F. Albright and C. S. Mann, *Matthew,* vol. 26 of the Anchor Bible (Garden City, N.Y.: Doubleday, 1971), 38.

39. Let us keep in mind that the historical interpretation seeks to reconstruct how the text would be read by the intended audience of the text and that the corresponding literary study seeks to elucidate a discursive dimension of the text that includes the "implied readers" as inscribed in the text, which I call the "intended reader" in order to avoid any confusion.

40. Matthew could not have derived from his sources the idea that Capernaum is in the territory of Naphtali, as noted by Davies and Allison, *Matthew,* 379. It should be kept in mind that Davies and Allison seek to be comprehensive by collecting conclusions from scholars who might use approaches that are without direct relevance for their own primary concern (here, the vision of discipleship proposed by 4:18–20 and its figures).

41. Strecker, *Der Weg,* 93–98. See also E. Schweizer, *Matthäus und seine Gemeinde* (Stuttgart: Verlag Katholisches Bibelwerk, 1974), 138–40, for whom this is a proof of the location of Matthew's community in Syria (not a primary concern for Strecker; see *Der Weg,* 37).

42. For Strecker ("The Concept of History," 67–84) this passage is one instance of the threefold phenomenon that characterizes the Gospel according to Matthew: historicization, ethicization, and institutionalization.

For the intended readers, 4:18–22 shows that the disciples were special individuals who had a unique kind of experience — an experience that cannot be repeated after the time of Jesus and that sets them apart. This means that

- they are "historicized" and "idealized" in the sense that they are personages who have a unique position due to their special call by Jesus, as Strecker underscores;[43] but also,

- they are already perceived in terms of their subsequent history, including their ministry after Jesus' death and resurrection; that is, they are already perceived as religious leaders who had a special authority in the church as its founders.

Since the intended readers read the text with a knowledge of the rest of the history of the Gospel, in studying this dimension it is quite appropriate to have in mind later parts of the Gospel, specifically the passages that refer to the church and to the disciples as apostles: 10:2 (see also 16:17–20; 18:18–19; 19:28; 28:16–20). In sum, the disciples' history is perceived by the intended readers inscribed in the text as a history of the "apostles."

Similarly, the phrase "Simon who is called Peter" (4:18) shows that Matthew expects his readers to know Simon primarily by the name Peter, and that this latter name (and this disciple) has a particular significance for them. This preeminence of Peter is also expressed by his description as one of the first two called by Jesus, as 10:2 also underscores. Peter had a special place in the group of the disciples, and thus he had, for the readers, greater authority than the other disciples.[44]

Reading A, CAW 5: The Features of the Scene Emphasized by the Redactor as Particularly Significant

Matthew's redaction of his source, Mark 1:16–20, involves adding the repetition of the realistic feature "two brothers," the repetition of "immediately" (εὐθέως) as a characteristic of the response in each case, and the repetition of the same verbal phrase, "they followed him" (ἠκολούθησαν αὐτῷ; Mark 1:20 uses another verb). This recognition of the repetitions has three major effects for the readers.

First, the recognition of the twofold pattern leads the intended readers to pay special attention to each of the repeated features, which become central for the interpretation focused on the history/realistic narrative dimension. Jesus (1) "saw two brothers" (4:18a, 21a) (2) who were at work as fishers (4:18b, 21b); (3) Jesus called them (4:19, 21c); (4) "immediately" they abandoned everything and followed Jesus (4:20, 22). The repetition

---

43. Strecker, *Der Weg,* 191–98; "The Concept of History in Matthew," 67–84.
44. See Strecker, *Der Weg,* 198–206.

of "Jesus saw [them]" underscores that Jesus took the initiative in this encounter. This is a first expression in 4:18–22 of Jesus' authority as Son of God, a high Christology that the intended readers expected, since they read the beginning of the Gospel in terms of its end. Here as well as throughout the rest of his ministry, Jesus had "all authority in heaven and on earth" (28:18).[45] The repeated descriptions of the work that the fishers abandoned[46] and of the "immediacy" of their response underscore with a realistic touch the "cost" of the disciples' obedient response to Jesus' call, as well as the authority of this call on them. The disciples acknowledged Jesus' extraordinary authority to command and to be obeyed without hesitation, despite the cost. Jesus' words were an unconditional command that the disciples could not but obey.[47] His authoritative command was sufficient basis for their decision to follow him by abandoning their vocation-identity of fishers of fish and of sons of a fisherman.

Second, by conversely focusing the readers' attention on these features of the history/realistic narrative dimension, such an interpretation pays less attention to the features that are not repeated. Thus, the fact that Jesus' words in 4:19 are not repeated, but rather summarized by the phrase "he called them" (4:21), has the effect of deemphasizing the promise included in 4:19 (contrast with reading B, CAW 5). "He called them" can then be interpreted as an unconditional command. The metaphor "fishers of people" loses much of its power (contrast with readings C and D). Actually, in this historical/realistic interpretation, it is not at all perceived as a metaphor; it is simply read as a phrase that refers to the mission of the disciples after Jesus' ministry (28:16–20).

Third, the repetition of this pattern in 4:18–22 makes a "normative" scene of the call of the disciples and of their responses, as is confirmed by the use of the same pattern in 9:9 (the call of Matthew the tax collector)[48] and an "ideal" scene, in the sense that the disciples' response to Jesus' call is perceived as an ideal response. Because this scene is read in terms of the subsequent history, the disciples are perceived as the same persons with the

---

45. From this perspective, Matthew 1–3 establishes that Jesus has all authority as Son of God. As Strecker constantly emphasizes, Jesus is perceived as the "exalted Kyrios." See, for instance, Strecker, *Der Weg*, 123–25, passim; "Concept of History," 76–77. See also Kingsbury, *Matthew as Story*, 104, passim. With such an interpretation, these scholars (and many others) read the Gospel in terms of 28:18. (Contrast this high Christology with the low Christology of the plot of the story; see above, reading B, CAW 1, and below).

46. The redaction of 4:21 — Zebedee is left alone, rather than "with hired workers" (Mk 1:20) — further underscores this cost.

47. Kingsbury, *Matthew as Story*, 104. Other interpretations will underscore the same point, but from a very different perspective: see below our comments on Davies and Allison, *Matthew*, 397, and Patte, *Matthew*, 57, when dealing with the next two readings.

48. For the intended readers, this does not in any way put into question the "historical" character of the text. On the contrary, it reflects the idealization of the past common to most historical perspectives, especially in religious history; the unity and specificity of a period of the past (here, the time of Jesus and of his disciples) is viewed as the repetition of certain patterns.

same "identities" from beginning to end; they take an atemporal character. In brief they are "idealized"; *through their ideal obedient response to Jesus' authoritative command, the four fishers became "disciples" once and for all.*[49] This does not mean that they were perfect. As the rest of their history will show, many times they failed to live up to the standard of discipleship that they exemplified by their response to Jesus' call. For the readers, these failures make more realistic the cost of discipleship, and they make even clearer the disciples' unconditional and costly obedience to Jesus' call. From this very moment and throughout their history, they were and remained disciples; in the same way that they were and remained the persons named Simon Peter, Andrew, James, and John; in the same way that they were and remained two pairs of brothers; and in the same way that James and John were and remained sons of Zebedee.[50]

Reading A, CAW 6: The Historical/Realistic Situation Constructed by the Text and Its Institutional Features

The *conclusions about what the text says* concerning the historical/realistic dimension can now be summarized. In this dimension, disciples are defined as people of the time of Jesus, whom Jesus chose to call directly, who immediately responded to his authoritative call by abandoning everything, and who became founders of the church (28:16–20). Such disciples/apostles are the Twelve (10:1–4; 19:28–29). Thus, the "history of the disciples" is exclusively limited to the passages dealing with the Twelve, as historicized and idealized personages.[51] Yet this dimension is also made realistic for the intended readers through its description of the disciples in terms of the organization of the church of their time. Of course, the church as a whole was far from meeting the high standards set by the disciples/apostles. "Matthew's community does not maintain that its reality matches such high demands," as Strecker says about the Sermon on the Mount.[52] Yet its leaders are closer to this ideal. Thus, greater and lesser implementation of this example brings about an institutional hierarchy in the community, even if offices are not clearly defined.[53] Conversely, one

---

49. We could say that by responding to Jesus' call they became disciples in the full sense of the term, i.e., "full-fledged disciples." Yet this phrase borrowed from the alternative interpretation does not make any sense here, since disciples are "full-fledged" disciples from the time of their obedient response to Jesus' call!

50. The only possibility for not remaining a disciple is to renounce totally one's relationship with Jesus by betraying him, as Judas Iscariot did (26:47–50). This is such a renunciation of one's (immutable) identity that it is renouncing oneself, one's very existence — committing suicide, as Judas did (27:5).

51. Yet it does include the passages that allude to the Twelve, even if their names are not mentioned; the word "disciples" is sufficient to evoke them.

52. Strecker, *Sermon,* 180–81.

53. Trilling emphasizes that they are not well developed. See W. Trilling, "Amt und Amtsverständnis bei Matthäus," in *Mélanges bibliques en hommage au R. P. Béda Rigaux,*

can say with Kingsbury that this passage (and others) reflects the institutional hierarchy of the church of Matthew's time, which included a special group of people who were close to embodying the ideal example of the disciples, namely, religious leaders who had responded in total obedience to a special call and had abandoned everything to be totally devoted to their missionary and teaching vocation (28:16–20).[54] These missionaries/ teachers had a special status (and authority) in the community, which is to be distinguished from the status of other members of the church — people who, even though they strove to be disciples, were far from this ideal because they could not envision abandoning everything (jobs, families) as the disciples/apostles did.[55]

Reading B, CAW 2: The Plot of Matthew 4:18–22 as a Meaning-Producing Dimension of the Text

Reading the text for its plot dimension involves paying close attention to (1) the flow of the plot, and therefore identifying narrative units in terms of their contributions to the unfolding of the story;[56] *(2) the interplay among*

---

ed. A. Descamps and R. D. A. de Halleux (Genbloux: Duculot, 1970), 29–44. Yet Strecker (e.g., "Concept of History," 77) emphasizes that "Matthew presupposes 'prophets, wise men, and scribes' as officials in the Christian community."

54. These religious leaders were not exclusively wandering prophets or missionaries, since their mission included teaching all that Jesus commanded. See Kingsbury, "*Akolouthein,*" 62–73.

55. It is quite possible that Matthew sought to resist the development of specific offices, wanting instead to affirm that all members of the church should view themselves as having equal status as disciples (a view expressed in the "story" and the "conditions of discipleship"). But if in this "*historical*" interpretation, one wants to maintain that all church members are equally and fully "disciples," that is, people abandoning jobs and families, one is led to conceive of the entire Matthean community as a group of wandering charismatic prophets. This is the tendency that one finds in Schweizer, *Matthäus und seine Gemeinde,* 27–28, 140–59; idem, "Matthew's Church," in *The Interpretation of Matthew,* ed. G. Stanton (Minneapolis: Fortress, 1983), 129–55; and idem, "Gesetz und Enthusiasmus bei Matthäus," in *Beiträge zur Theologie des Neuen Testaments,* ed. E. Schweizer (Zurich: Zwingli Verlag, 1970), 49–70. Although Schweizer acknowledges that at least an embryonic form of authority structure was found in the Matthean community and that it was established in a specific location (and not wandering), he maintains that it kept the characteristics of a community in that each member was viewed as a prophet and a teacher. Kingsbury's interpretation is more consistent as a reading of the "history" when he describes the community as involving two groups: missionaries (for whom the historical disciples were models) and the settled community (for which the teaching about discipleship only had a "paradigmatic value"). See Kingsbury, "*Akolouthein,*" 73.

56. In Kelber's words, this method requires the exegete "to read the whole story from beginning to end, to observe the characters and the interplay among them, to watch for the author's clues regarding the plot, to discern the plot development, to identify scenes of crisis and recognition, and to view the story's resolution in the light of the antecedent logic" (Kelber, *Mark's Story,* 11). It should be noted that this procedure is only a part of Kelber's agenda; he also seeks to read the Gospel of Mark against its historical background (14), that is, as referring to historical situations of the time of its writing. In so doing, he collapses the "plot" dimension with the "history/realistic narrative" dimension that has its own coherence. As is deplored by Moore (*Literary Criticism,* 18–20), Kelber ends up providing a study of Mark

characters; and (3) the characters as "actors" (i.e., as active participants to the unfolding of the plot) and to what qualifies them to act in this way (how their will is established and what kind of ability they have).[57] The ultimate focus of this interpretation rests, therefore, on the process of becoming a disciple and acting like one and on the competencies needed for this and how they are acquired. A critical interpretation elucidates each of these foci.

The delimitation of an appropriate textual unit that accounts for the unfolding of the plot is the first task at hand. When one reads the text about the beginning of Jesus' ministry (4:12ff.) as an unfolding story (that is, without assuming any knowledge of the rest of the narrative; contrast reading A, CAW 2), one finds in 4:18-22 the beginning of a substory about four fishers who are called (4:21) by Jesus and who follow him (4:20, 22). The fact that the text gives their names (which, for the plot, are simply "tags") suggests that they are significant actors whose story will be told. But it is not clear that they are disciples until 5:1, where the word "disciples" (μαθηταὶ) is used for the first time. The collective actor, "disciples," is defined in 5:1 as "coming to Jesus" after he sat down, thus, as people following Jesus. In retrospect, one recognizes that the story of the disciples began in 4:18 and thus that the four fishers who follow Jesus certainly belong to the group of disciples mentioned in 5:1. In sum, verses 18-22 cannot be read by themselves. The textual unit of the plot dimension in which they must be considered is 4:18-5:1.

Reading B, CAW 3: The Interplay among Characters as Particularly Significant

The composition of the group of "disciples" is left ambiguous, as Edwards point out.[58] It is clear that in 5:1 the story separates the disciples from the crowds. Furthermore, the fact that the four fishers are identified as individuals in 4:18-22 distinguishes them from the anonymous crowds of 4:23-25. Yet crowds and disciples are closely related because they are presented as the same kinds of actors; both the four individuals and the crowds perform the same action, they "followed him" (4:20, 22, 25). The crowds belong to the same group as the disciples: the group of the followers of Jesus.

---

that has in large part abandoned its first stated agenda. Yet we shall proceed exactly according to this agenda in our study of the story of the disciples, although we shall also pay close attention to the competence of the actors who perform the actions. As Edwards recognized, this involves adopting the position of a first-time reader of the story, "examining the narrative from the point of view of a reader who begins at the beginning" (*Matthew's Story*, 9).

57. The actors' qualifications as active participants in the unfolding of the plot, which make out of them potential examples for readers, can be understood when one keeps in mind that an actor must be properly equipped in order to be in a position to perform an action. No action can take place as long as the actor does not have the *will* and the *ability* (and knowledge) to perform the specific action. On this and what follow see Greimas and Courtés, *Semiotics and Language*, 193-95, and Patte, *Religious Dimensions*, 182-95.

58. Edwards, "Uncertain Faith," 53.

Reading B, CAW 4: The Characters as Actors/Active Participants in the Unfolding of the Plot and Their Significance

Since the crowds and the four fishers perform the same action, following Jesus, the difference between these two actors should be a matter of competence.[59] In both cases, nothing is said about the establishment of the ability to follow Jesus. The text is exclusively concerned with the establishment of the will to follow Jesus.

In 4:23–25, the motivation for the crowd's bringing to Jesus their sick (4:24) is expressed: they hope and expect that Jesus will heal their sick, as he does (4:24). Thus, the text emphasizes the establishment of the crowds' will; the "fame" of Jesus as healer motivates them to act as they do. Since the crowds' next action, following Jesus (4:25), is simply strung together with the preceding one and also involves being with Jesus, one can conclude that they follow Jesus for the same reason that they brought their sick to him. Jesus' fame as a healer motivates them (establishes their will) both to come and to stay with him; they follow him with the hope of receiving other "good things." As healer, Jesus has the power to overcome all things that might "badly," κακῶς, affect them (cf. 4:24).

In 4:18–22, Jesus' words to the four fishers, "Come with me and I will make you fishers of people" (4:19, author's translation), is a "call" (as is expressed in 4:21), a command aimed at convincing the four fishers to act in a certain way, namely, to follow Jesus. But how were they convinced to do so?

The fishers' decision to follow Jesus is much more radical than the crowds' decision. The crowds decide to follow Jesus after receiving something (the healing of their sick) from Jesus (4:23–24). The four fishers decide to follow Jesus after a few words from Jesus, a decision that entails abandoning "their nets" (4:20) and "the boat and their father" (4:22). The fishers abandon the activities that characterized their original vocation and their identity as fishers of fish and sons of a fisher. But what motivates them to do so?

The four fishers did not follow Jesus because of his fame as healer, since in the narrative development Jesus began healing after calling them. Furthermore, there is no indication that they follow Jesus because of his fame as preacher (4:17); actually, by describing a change in location in 4:18, the text clarifies that the fishers did not hear Jesus' preaching. According to the unfolding of the plot, they are totally unconnected with the previous part of the narrative, which could have given them a knowledge of Jesus' authority as Son of God. Thus, there is no indication within the plot that the fishers acknowledge an authority inherent in Jesus' person (contrast reading A). Thus, we have to conclude that the fishers are convinced by Jesus' words in and of themselves.

---

59. The "competence" of actor includes whatever gives this actor the means (including cognitive means) to act by providing him/her with will and ability. Greimas and Courtés, *Semiotics and Language*, 193–95, and Bal, *Narratology*, 33–34.

It is noteworthy then that these words include both a command and a promise: *"I will make you fishers of people" (4:19). A promise, if recognized as reliable, commonly has the role of establishing the will of people. This promise of a new vocation and identity (as "fishers of people") is what motivates the fishers to abandon their earlier vocation and identity. Because they want to become "fishers of people," and because, for some untold reason, they trust that Jesus' promise is reliable, the fishers agree to follow Jesus, and they do so with enthusiasm (as is indicated by the description of their response as "immediate," 4:20, 22).*

Reading B, CAW 5: The Process of Becoming a Disciple

The fishers' reason for following Jesus is not unlike the crowds'. As the crowds' will to follow Jesus is based on the "promise" they perceive in his healings (the promise that one can expect more "good things" from him), so the fishers' will to follow Jesus is based on their trust in his verbal promise to give them a new vocation/identity, that of "fishers of people." As the crowds recognize that Jesus has power/authority to heal, so the fishers recognize that Jesus' words (his promise) are authoritative. Here "authoritative" means trustworthy. In the story, Jesus' words are a "call" asking for a voluntary decision — being willing to follow Jesus, not simply because he commanded them to do so but also and primarily because they want to be made fishers of people.

Since in this interpretation the emphasis is on the promise to be made fishers of people, by the end of this scene the fishers are far from being full-fledged disciples. They can be called "novice disciples."

Reading B, CAW 6: The Relationship of Matthew 4:18–22 with the Rest of the Hi/Story

After such an introduction (4:18–5:1), we can expect that the rest of the story will tell us how the novice disciples are made "fishers of people" (and what being fishers of people is). Yet the story of the disciples also includes the story of the crowds, as "potential disciples." The plot does not oppose the crowds' and the fishers' motivations for "following Jesus." Both are legitimate results of Jesus' ministry. This ambiguity of the story must be respected. Our study of the story of the novice disciples must include a study of the story of the crowds, who, as "potential disciples," might be on their way to becoming novice disciples, and thus persons willing to be made fishers of people.

This brief review of the respective methodological approaches of Strecker's and Kingsbury's interpretation (reading A) and of the alternative interpretation developed out of Edwards's suggestions (reading B), the identification of the meaning-producing dimensions — the textual representation of a historical/realistic narrative event or the plot as their respective *conclusions about what the text is* — and the elucidation of their respective *conclusions about what the text says*, especially about the disciples and discipleship, demonstrate the legitimacy of these two types of readings. Both reading A and reading B are coherent legitimate interpretations in the sense that they develop their *conclusions about what the text says* on the basis of appropriate evidence, each focusing on a textual dimension that indeed has the potential of being meaning-producing for certain readers.

The Legitimacy of Readings C and D: Figurative and Thematic Meaning-Producing Dimensions

Regarding both reading C, the dominant interpretation presented in the commentaries of Luz and Davies and Allison, and reading D, the alternative interpretation presented in my commentary, this section *first* considers their respective methodological approaches and the features of the texts on which they are focused. *Then* it elucidates the *conclusions about what the text is and says* of these scholarly interpretations, and shows how, in each case, a critical interpretation exclusively[60] focused on a given meaning-producing dimension of Matthew 4:18–22 grounds coherent *conclusions about what the text says* on the basis of which the interpreters draw *conclusions about the teaching*[61] of this text regarding discipleship (elucidated in part 2).

In order to make sense of the methodological approaches of these two kinds of interpretations, one may want to note that the teaching about discipleship that both find in this text concerns discipleship as "intuitive ethical practice," which is grounded either in a vision of the kingdom preached by Jesus (cf. Mt 4:17) or in a vision of discipleship as participation in Jesus' ministry. We can recognize in a general way the potential legitimacy of these two kinds of interpretations by underscoring that from this perspective nothing (including a discourse) makes sense outside of such visions of meaningful life in society and the world as expressed, for instance, in a symbolic world (such as that of the kingdom) or a system of convictions (which gives discernment and, as in the present case, a vision of discipleship).[62]

---

60. As above the interpretations "exclusively focused on a given meaning-producing dimension" are streamlined versions of the interpretations proposed by male European-American scholars.

61. Unless these *conclusions about the teaching* (CATs) were first reached through an intuitive interpretation. In this case, the warranting arguments and the CAWs are developed in order to ground existing CATs of the text. This is actually the most frequent pattern, even though scholarly interpretations ostensibly proceed the other way around. The result is the same.

62. This vision is diversely understood according to the perspective one adopts and thus is diversely designated as a "semantic universe" in semiotics (see Greimas and Courtés, *Semiotics and Language*, 361–62), a "world view" in anthropology (see, e.g., Clifford Geertz, *The*

More specifically, we can note that discourses convey such visions to their readers through their *figurative* and *thematic* dimensions, at the very least because these discourses reaffirm and reinforce an old vision (symbolic world and/or system of convictions) that the author (as inscribed in the text) supposedly shares with the readers (as inscribed in the text). Yet many discourses have as their primary goal the communication of new visions; this is especially the case with poetic and religious discourses. In sum, at the outset one should acknowledge the potential legitimacy of interpretations of Matthew 4:18–22 read as providing a vision of the kingdom and of discipleship.

Since such visions are conveyed by the connotative dimensions of a text — including its figurative and thematic dimensions — one should not be surprised to find polysemy: several visions are expressed by a given text.[63] Luz and Davies and Allison study the *figurative dimension* of Matthew 4:18–22. I study its *thematic dimension.*

Reading C, CAW 1: Matthew 4:18–22 as a Figurative Text and the Appropriate Critical Method

Luz and Davies and Allison focus their scholarly interpretations on the figurative dimension of the text. This can be readily recognized by noting that: (a) they interpret each figure (e.g., fishers of people) of the passage in terms of other texts in which this figure is also used (e.g., Mt 13:47–50 and Jer 16:16); and (b) they seek to understand the place of each figure in the overall figurative organization of the text (and thus they read Mt

---

Interpretation of Cultures: Selected Essays [New York: Basic Books, 1973], 126–41), an "ideology" in cultural and political theories (e.g., Geertz, *Interpretation of Cultures,* 193–233), a "nomos and cosmos" in sociology of knowledge (see Peter Berger, *The Sacred Canopy: Elements of a Sociological Theory of Religion* [Garden City, N.Y.: Doubleday, 1967], 3–51), etc. For a believer, such a vision forms what can be designated as a "system of convictions" (see Patte, *Religious Dimensions,* 111–28).

63. Communicating a vision of meaningful life in society and the world is necessarily a complex and ambiguous undertaking because the addressees always already have a vision of life that establishes their identity (readers are never a tabula rasa). It is therefore a matter of modifying the implied readers' old vision(s) of life, by homologating new features (and new values) to parts of their old vision(s). This is what happens in metaphors (figures par excellence), such as "Sabbath is a palace in time," in which two semantic fields — one related to the vision of life of the implied readers (summoned by the word "palace") and one to that of the author (summoned by the word "Sabbath") — are associated. This metaphor, proposed by Abraham J. Heschel (*The Sabbath: Its Meaning for Modern Man* [New York: Farrar, Straus, and Young, 1951]), is analyzed and discussed at length in Patte, *Religious Dimensions,* 147–58. This also happens with the figure "fishers of people," which associates discipleship and fishing, and the complex semantic fields represented by these two concepts as used together or separately in different contexts. More subtly the characters, disciples, and their stories are presented by Matthew as figures of discipleship and/or as thematic features conveying a vision of discipleship. By these few words, I simply suggest the complexity of the connotative dimensions, which through their figurative and thematic features can evoke different visions of meaningful life in society and the world.

4:18–22 in terms of its context in Matthew). This is quite an appropriate critical approach. Figures make sense *as figures*[64] only insofar as readers can recognize the two different semantic fields that they bring together in a precarious relationship; saying that something is "like" something else is also implying that the two things are "unlike" each other! It is this tension between the two semantic fields and the visions of life they represent — the one represented by the traditions to which the text alludes and the other expressed by the relations among the figures in the text — which gives to a figure its fascinating and emotionally charged character as a challenge to the reader's vision and identity.

Since the discussion of the *conclusions about the teaching* of the text of reading C (see part 2) necessarily involves a presentation of the figures of the text in terms of their allusions to other texts and traditions and of their relations with other figures of the text, the presentation of the critical method (as well as of the *conclusions about what the text is and says*, and of the warranting arguments that support them) can remain relatively brief.

A history of traditions approach is obviously appropriate for elucidating in Matthew 4:18–22 all the possible allusions to other texts and traditions, including those that at first might not seem to be relevant. This is part of the method used by Davies and Allison.[65] This scholarly approach also includes taking note of the way in which the redactor transformed traditions and sources in order to construct the figures of the text. Consequently, a redaction critical approach is also appropriate. This is part of the method used by Luz, although it is not implemented in the same way as it is by Strecker and others (see reading A, CAW 1), since it now has a different focus. A significant part of Luz's approach involves elucidating how the redactor reshapes the traditional figures into new figures.

Luz and Davies and Allison also pay close attention to the *figurative organization* of the text: it is through this *structure* that the figurative dimension of the text emotionally affects readers. Studying the figurative organization of the Gospel involves identifying the way in which the redactor delimits and organizes figurative textual units and subunits, with the help of certain *literary conventions*. These poetic and thus figurative literary conventions are used by Luz and Davies and Allison as an important way of identifying the structure of the figurative dimension of the text (which in their one-dimensional study they present as "the" single structure "of the text"). For texts of the Hellenistic period, these literary conventions include inclusios, chiasms, ring compositions, use of triads, and other stylistic fea-

---

64. Of course, they will make sense in another reading, but not as a figure. Remember, for instance, how "fishers of people" is read as *referring* to missionary activities (and thus, not at all as a figure) in Strecker's interpretation as well as in the alternative interpretation.

65. See Davies and Allison, *Matthew,* 34–58. This is a long table presenting the quotations of and allusions to the LXX (and not yet including the allusions to other traditions that they discuss in their comments on each passage).

tures (discussed at length by Davies and Allison and Luz).[66] Identifying this *figurative* organization of Matthew in terms of this literary conventions is, in such scholarly interpretations, an important step toward the *conclusions about what the text is and says* because in this *figurative* dimension the *center* of each chiastic structure (including that of inclusios, ring compositions, and triads) is one of the keys for interpreting the figures of a passage. (We shall see that the key for interpreting *themes* is found in the beginnings and ends of units, rather than in their centers; see reading D, CAW 1).

Reading D, CAW 1: Matthew 4:18–22 as a Thematic Text and the Appropriate Critical Method

A scholarly interpretation focused on the thematic dimension of the Gospel according to Matthew, as the one proposed in my commentary, reaches quite different conclusions about what the text is and says (and consequently, quite different conclusions about its teaching, see below part 2) because it focuses on another dimension of the text. As in the other case, in this multidimensional androcritical study I underscore the legitimacy of these conclusions about what the text is and says by elucidating the main characteristics of the thematic dimension, which is the focus of this interpretation. This study also refines and complements the conclusions presented in my commentary through the more systematic elucidation of this dimension that becomes possible when one avoids being trapped in a one-dimensional interpretation.[67]

Here, priority is given to the internal semantic organization of the text, that is, to its internal semantic structure and to the system of convictions that this structure conveys. Elucidating the vision of discipleship as a part of the system of convictions expressed by this thematic dimension is therefore most systematically accomplished through the use of a structural method.

The structural exegetical method that I have developed for elucidating this convictional vision has been presented elsewhere.[68] It is enough to say here that themes can be formally identified by keeping in mind that each

---

66. Davies and Allison, *Matthew*, 58–96; Luz, *Matthew*, 33–46, 49–73.

67. As I wrote my "structural commentary," I imagined that the system of convictions conveyed by this structure was the author's (Matthew's) — by contrast with the implied readers' system of convictions, which I thought was expressed by the figurative dimension. See Patte, *Matthew*, 1–15, passim. Theoretical reflections and analyses of quite a few texts convinced me of the undecidability of this issue; the vision expressed by the system of convictions of a text might be that of the implied readers, rather than that of the author. In other words, my own commentary and its implicit claim to present the true meaning of the text is itself subject to criticism from an androcritical perspective.

68. See Daniel Patte, *Structural Exegesis for New Testament Critics*, Guides to Biblical Scholarship (Minneapolis: Fortress, 1990; 2d printing, Valley Forge, Pa.: Trinity Press International, 1996). In this book I strove to formalize the structural method used in different ways by various scholars in a series of six steps.

"thematic unit" (and the text as a whole) has a theme that is most directly ex-
pressed by its opening and its closing, and by their relations. The opening by
itself presents the theme, but in a way that is often veiled by its figurativiza-
tion. In didactic discourses, the opening presents the theme as a problem (or
question) that needs to be resolved. In narratives, the opening presents the
theme as an initial situation that is incomplete or less than ideal. This theme
is restated in another form in the closing. In didactic discourses, it appears as
the solution to the problem; in narratives, as a transformed situation. Thus, as
becomes clear in the concrete cases discussed below, the theme is expressed
by those features of the opening and the closing of the unit (or text) that are
in inverted parallelism with each other (as a problem is to its solution). This
procedure allows us to identify both the limits of the thematic units of the
Gospel and, in a first approximation, the convictions expressed by the themes
of these units.[69] *As is the case with the figurative dimension (but not with the*
historical dimensions), the overall structure of the text and of the thematic
dimension plays an essential role in the way in which this dimension affects
readers and thus in the way in which it is a meaning-producing dimension of
the text.

The study of the themes merely provides an approximate *identification*
of the thematic vision because the themes and their features are always
expressed figuratively, i.e., in figures that simultaneously express two sets
of convictions. Consequently, the study of the thematic convictions as ex-
pressed by the inverted parallelisms must be complemented and refined by
an identification of the convictions expressed by the semantic oppositions
associated with the oppositions of actions.[70]

Reading C, CAW 2: The Figurative Unit to Which Matthew 4:18–22 Belongs Delimited by Literary Conventions

For Luz, Matthew 4:18–22 belongs to a textual unit, 3:1–4:22, which
he calls "the beginning of the ministry of Jesus." This is a figurative unit
delimited by repetitions and *inclusios:* the identically formulated proclamation of John and Jesus ("Repent, for the kingdom of heaven is at hand,"
3:2; 4:17); the parallelism between 3:1–12 and 4:12–17, both of which
contain a Scripture quotation with a geographical statement. Matthew
4:18–22 belongs to this figurative unit because of its close connections with
4:12–17 (see reading C, CAW 5) and because the next figurative unit begins

---

69. These are, respectively, step 1 and step 5 of the above mentioned method. See Patte,
Structural Exegesis for New Testament Critics, 9–22 and 47–61. Note that by contrast with
the study of the figurative organization (which focuses on the center of chiastic structures),
here priority is given to the material found at the beginning and end of the passages (the
outside of the chiasms; the inclusios themselves). Yet as we shall see, thematic and figurative
units do not always correspond to each other; slight variations are possible.

70. These are steps 2, 3, and 4 of the above mentioned method. See Patte, *Structural*
Exegesis for New Testament Critics, 23–45.

at 4:23.[71] The figures of 4:18–22 must be understood in terms of their respective place in the figurative unit 3:1–4:22, even though they must also be studied in terms of the allusions to traditions and to other texts that shape them. Since this latter procedure allows us to identify these figures, we consider it first, as I make explicit (and thus amplify) the way in which Luz and Davies and Allison interpreted Matthew 4:18–22.

Reading C, CAW 3: A Vision of Disciples as Religious Leaders with an Ambivalent Mission: Metaphors and Figures

When one reads Matthew 4:18–22 for its figures, the metaphor "fishers of people" stands out. Ideally, this metaphor should be interpreted in terms of all the information one can recover regarding the practices of actual fishing and the similar metaphors in non-Christian and Christian texts of the period.[72] Here, it is enough to emphasize the use of this metaphor in Jeremiah 16:16,[73] where it is associated with the similar metaphor, "hunters of people." When they are read in their complex context in Jeremiah 16:14–21, the metaphors "fishers" and "hunters" refer to a twofold vocation involving both a constructive, soteriological function and a judgmental function. Disciples like prophets are sent to save people (as the prophets sent by God were to "fish" Israel out of exile, when Jer 16:16 is read with 16:15), but also to punish the wicked (when Jer 16:16 is read with 16:17–18). This ambivalence of the metaphor is preserved in Matthew 4:19,[74] through its relations in the Gospel according to Matthew with the metaphor of fishing in Matthew 13:47–50 (sorting good and bad fish has to do with judgment) and with other metaphors that express a similar ambivalence: the vocation of the disciples as compassionate "shepherds" in

---

71. The strongly marked inclusio between 4:23 and 9:35, an almost word-for-word repetition of a summary description of Jesus' threefold ministry, shows that the next figurative unit is 4:23–9:38.

72. As has been done by Wilhelm Wuellner, *The Meaning of "Fishers of Men"* (Philadelphia: Westminster Press, 1967).

73. This metaphor is also used in Ezekiel 47:10. But Jer 16:16 is more important in the pertinent traditions. See Davies and Allison, *Matthew*, 398–99. See also Samuel Tobias Lachs, *A Rabbinic Commentary on the New Testament: The Gospels of Matthew, Mark and Luke* (Hoboken, N.J.: KTAV, 1987), 58–59. Lachs argues that this reference to Jer 16:16 (and Ezek 47:10) is unlikely because the Hebrew verb *dug* is used to speak of catching people "for the purpose of punishment, and that is hardly the meaning." But it is! As Davies and Allison discuss, this metaphor expresses an ambivalent view of the disciples' vocation as being both *judgmental* and soteriological.

74. Davies and Allison (*Matthew*, 398) are more tentative. Gundry (*Matthew*, 62) opts for the positive view of the disciples' vocation (without real justification). Luz (*Matthew*, 199–201) does not deal explicitly with this issue, but implicitly supports the proposed interpretation (through his reference to Mt 13:47–50 and his remarks regarding the "painful break with the synagogue").

9:36 is juxtaposed with that of "harvesters," 9:37; cf. 13:30, 39–42, as an expression of the judgmental aspect of their missionary ministry.[75]

This suggestion is further confirmed by the fact that the ambivalence of the metaphor is retained in the Dead Sea Scrolls, where it is used in 1 QH 5:8 together with the hunter metaphor. The use of the two metaphors of Jeremiah 16:16 in 1 QH 5:8 is particularly helpful for understanding our passage:[76] in 1 QH 5:9–10 the false religious leaders (false "fishers" and "hunters" of people) are described as "venomous vipers," as the Pharisees and Sadducees are called a "brood of vipers" in Matthew 3:7.[77]

The connection established by the connotations of Matthew 4:18–22 between the figure of the disciples and the figure of the Pharisees and Sadducees in 3:7 (a part of the same figurative unit, 3:1–4:22) evokes a vision of discipleship as authentic religious leadership, by contrast with the inauthentic (and thus misleading) religious leadership represented by the Pharisees and Sadducees.

Reading C, CAW 4: A Vision of Discipleship as a Prophetic Vocation—Allusions to Other Texts and Traditions

As a redaction of Mark 1:16–20, Matthew 4:18–22 emphasizes the parallelism between the calls of the two sets of brothers (as the study of the historical/realistic dimension also notes; see reading B, CAW 5). This redaction of Mark's text has the effect of making clearer the allusion to 1 Kings 19:19–21, Elijah's call of Elisha, which includes the following steps:[78] (1) Elijah traveling finds Elisha (1 Kgs 19:19a); (2) Elisha working (19:19b); (3) Elijah throwing his mantle over Elisha, a sign of call to prophetic vocation (19:19c); (4) Elisha responding "I will follow you" yet asking to kiss his father and mother (19:20); (5) Elisha following Elijah (19:21), after sacrificing and giving away his property (oxen).[79]

The difference between 1 Kings 19:19–21 and Matthew 4:18–20 is clear: Elisha asks for permission to say farewell to his father and mother,

---

75. The missionary vocation signified by the metaphor and 13:47 is the connotation underscored by Luz, *Matthew*, 199.

76. Because of the likely connection between the Qumran community and John the Baptist. Yet I do not want to argue that John's baptism ministry should be perceived as a "fishing" ministry as is done by Wuellner, op. cit., 131–33. This is stretching the evidence, as Wuellner himself admits.

77. Davies and Allison, *Matthew*, 396–97. See Otto Betz, "Die Proselytentaufe der Qumransekte und die Taufe im Neuen Testament," *Revue de Qumran* 1 (1958): 223. Note that in Matthew, the phrase "brood of vipers" constantly refers to the Pharisees and Sadducees in 3:7, as well as in 12:34 and 23:33 (contrast with Luke 3:7, where it refers to crowds). See Sjef Van Tilborg, *The Jewish Leaders in Matthew* (Leiden: Brill, 1972), 28–29.

78. Listed by Davies and Allison, *Matthew*, 392–93. See also Lachs, *A Rabbinic Commentary*, 58.

79. It is noteworthy that Elisha transformed the tools of his trade into equipment to serve people a sacrificial meal—he uses the plough to cook the oxen that he had sacrificed (19:21; as the fishers of fish becomes fishers of people in 4:19).

while James and John abruptly abandon their father. Furthermore, Elijah's response to this request, which is ambiguous in Hebrew, was interpreted as granting Elisha the permission to do so,[80] by contrast with Jesus who responds negatively to a similar request in Matthew 8:21–22. In light of this allusion to 1 Kings 19:19–21, Jesus appears as a charismatic, prophetic figure, like Elijah, but with a greater authority than his.[81] Jesus' call is a more radical call, demanding more from his disciples than Elijah demanded from Elisha. Conversely, this confirms the above remark that the call to discipleship of the four fishers is as *a call to a prophetic vocation* (cf. 5:12 and 7:15–20, which describe disciples as "prophets"), although it is a vocation involving more than Elisha's vocation. As Jesus fulfills the type Elijah (in the same way that he fulfills the prophecies; cf. 4:14–16) and is, therefore, greater than Elijah, so the disciples fulfill the type Elisha and are greater than Elisha.

It then appears that this prophetic vocation of the disciples is unlike a rabbinic vocation.[82] Jesus (like Elijah) chooses his disciples (4:19, 21), unlike the rabbinic practice according to which the disciple chose his rabbi: "Choose a teacher and get thee a companion" (Mishnah Abot 1:6).[83] This contrast is certainly pertinent because it is related to the contrast between the Pharisees and Sadducees and the disciples established by the use of the metaphor "fishers of people" as a designation for the disciples and by the way in which 4:18–22 is contrasted with the Pharisees and Sadducees through the organization of the figurative unit to which 4:18–22 belongs: 3:1–4:22.[84]

Reading C, CAW 5: A Vision of Discipleship as Repenting from One's Sins — Organization of the Figurative Unit

We have noted that the figurative unit, Matthew 3:1–4:22, to which 4:18–22 belongs, is primarily delimited by the inclusio between 3:2 and 4:17,

---

80. According to LXX and Josephus, *Antiquities of the Jews* 8.354; see Davies and Allison, *Matthew*, 393.

81. On Jesus' charismatic authority, see M. Hengel, *The Charismatic Leader*, 17.

82. As Davies and Allison (*Matthew*, 396) underscore.

83. Cf., e.g., Gundry, *Matthew*, 62; Davies and Allison, *Matthew*, 396.

84. Luz, *Matthew*, 164, 203. This figurative unit does not correspond exactly with the thematic unit (see reading D, below), yet they are closely related. The breakdown into figurative units is based on "inclusios," that is, "parallelisms" (not "*inverted* parallelisms," see below) between features of the text that are most salient, by means of repetitions of words and figures. Thus the figurative unit does not include 4:18–25 because they are not "parallel"; rather, they express the differences between Jesus' ministry and John's (they are in "*inverted* parallelisms" with 3:1–12; see reading D). Another figurative breakdown takes into account the repetition of triadic groupings throughout the Gospel. Cf. Davies and Allison, *Matthew*, 62–72. From this perspective, 1:18–4:22 (the early history) is viewed as including three parts: 1:18–2:23 (conception and infancy of Jesus); 3:1–17 (John the Baptist and Jesus); and 4:1–22 (the beginning of Jesus' ministry). Yet even from this perspective, Davies and Allison (*Matthew*, 287) acknowledge that Matthew 3 and 4 belong together.

the repeated proclamation, "Repent, the kingdom of heaven is at hand." Consequently, 4:18–22 is certainly related to this inclusio; more specifically, it is presented as a figurative representation of 4:17.

This is confirmed by the fact that Matthew 4:18–22 is figuratively linked with the preceding verses by the mention of the "sea of Galilee" both in 4:13–15 and 4:18: what happens to the fishers by the "sea of Galilee" is fulfilling (*is like* what is expressed by) the prophecy of Isaiah 9:1–2 quoted in 4:14–16,[85] which refers to that sea. Thus, the four fishers *are like* the "people who sat in darkness," "in the region and shadow of death" and who "have seen a great light" (4:16). The coming of Jesus, the coming of that light, is for them a call to abandon this darkness, this region and shadow of death in which they live — their jobs, their boats, their families. In other words, Jesus' coming to the fishers has the very effect that is expressed by his preaching: "Repent, for the kingdom of heaven is at hand" (4:17). The fishers are called to repent; their immediate obedient response is repentance, turning away from darkness and from the shadow of death. Thus Schweizer closes his comments on 4:18–22: "All this means that the light announced in verse 16 of the quotation is Jesus' *call* to repentance. There is no way to attain salvation through adoption of a theological formula, bypassing repentance. But repentance, as the call of the first disciples shows, is a gift."[86] This interpretation maintains that "repentance" is primarily a "turning away" from one's sin, from darkness and the shadow of death (by contrast with a "turning toward"; see reading D), which is radically demanded by Jesus from his disciples, but also facilitated by him and thus a "gift." In order to "follow" Jesus and to be a disciple, one first needs to repent, i.e., to abandon one's former way of life.

As this last statement suggests, in the figurative dimension the model of the disciples offered by 4:18–22 is not an example that should necessarily be followed literally. The fishers abandoning their jobs and father are a

---

85. On the redaction of the text of Isaiah 9:1–2 (Mt 8:23–9:1), see Davies and Allison, *Matthew*, 379–86, and bibliography.

86. Schweizer, *Matthew*, 76. Note how Schweizer proceeds in this "homiletic" conclusion (by contrast with his historical work, heavily focused on the "history of the disciples"): he interprets the figure formed by 4:18–22 in terms of other figures *juxtaposed* to it. The disciples abandoning their nets, boat, and father are viewed as a figure of the "repentance" preached by Jesus (4:17). "Jesus preaching repentance" and "Jesus calling people to follow him" are viewed as equivalent figures that can be interpreted in terms of each other. Similarly, the description of Jesus as "a great light" dawning on people sitting in darkness and in the shadow of death (4:16) and Jesus coming to people and calling them to follow him (4:18–22) are equivalent figures that are interpreted in terms of each other. This is an excellent model of the way in which an interpretation focused on the figurative dimension proceeds. Schweizer moves back and forth between "historical" (critical!) interpretation and "figurative" (homiletic) interpretation — a move facilitated by the multidimensional presentation of his commentary — without acknowledging the significant differences between these interpretations.

figure of repentance; the kind of old way of life one has to abandon varies. As Luz underscores, they have a "typical" significance.[87]

Reading C, CAW 6: A Vision of Disciples Associated with Other Followers of Jesus and Contrasted with Pharisees and Sadducees

The figurative relationship between 4:18–22 as a figure of discipleship and the crowds in 4:23–25 can then be perceived. The two passages are in tension, as can be expected from passages belonging to two different figurative units (the latter belongs to 4:23–9:38). On the one hand, it seems that the crowds cannot be viewed as "disciples" because, *unlike* the fishers, it is not made explicit that they repented; they did not abandon their former way of life; nor did they sacrifice anything. On the other hand, the crowds are portrayed as being *like* the fishers by the repetition of the same phrase, "followed him" in closely related verses (4:20, 22, 25), which demands that this phrase be interpreted in a metaphorical way in 4:25. Thus we have to conclude with Luz that "following on the part of the disciples does not distinguish them from the people who are sympathetic to Jesus, but the people, by following, belong together with the disciples."[88] Furthermore, Jesus' "preaching of the gospel of the kingdom" (4:23), a call to repentance (4:17), was addressed to the crowds. In sum, the crowds are both *like and unlike* the fishers. Since they are in this traditional figurative relationship between two comparable entities, it already begins to appear that the disciples (fishers) are presented by Matthew as *models* of discipleship for the crowds (and readers).

By contrast with the four fishers as disciples (and the crowds that are on their way to becoming disciples), the Pharisees and Sadducees in 3:7–10 are a figure of "antidisciples" ("brood of vipers" instead of "fishers of people"). What makes them antidisciples (an antifigure that brings most clearly to light the characteristics of the figure of the disciples)? First, they do not repent (turn away from their present life, 3:8). In addition (and this is worse) they pretend (or suppose) that they do not need to repent because they have Abraham as their father (3:9). Unlike James and John, they do not want to abandon their father, their life in line with the heritage of this dead ancestor, and thus their life "in the shadow of death."

---

87. Luz, *Matthew,* 200. See the discussion of this issue by Schweizer, "Matthew's Church," in *Matthew,* ed. Stanton, 129–55 (against this conclusion because he ends up emphasizing the "history of the disciples"), Kingsbury, *"Akolouthein," Journal of Biblical Literature* 97 (1968): 56–73 (closer to the above conclusion), and Davies and Allison, *Matthew,* 404–6 (in favor of it, since they emphasize the figurative dimension).

88. Ibid., 201. Uncharacteristically Strecker (*Der Weg,* 230–31) proposes the same interpretation, abandoning in this case his "history" perspective.

Reading D, CAW 2: The Thematic Unit to Which Matthew 4:18–22 Belongs Delimited by Intratextual Structures

The thematic unit to which Matthew 4:18–22 belongs is 3:1– 4:25.[89] By study-ing the inverted parallelisms and other intratextual markers, one can recognize that the preceding thematic units are 1:1–25 and 2:1–23 and the follow-ing unit is 5:1–7:29. This observation is, of course, not a guarantee that the many scenes in 3:1– 4:25 form a single thematic unit.[90] Yet the inverted par-allelisms between 3:1–12 and 4:12–25 establish a thematic unity for this passage.

The theme of this unit (expressed by its inverted parallelisms) concerns the character of Jesus' ministry as clarified through a comparison of the ministry of John the Baptist (the opening) with the ministry of Jesus (the closing). John's ministry (3:1–12), explicitly presented as announcing Jesus' coming (3:11–12), foreshadows Jesus' ministry (4:12–25) that begins after John's arrest (4:12). For our present concern, this means that 4:18–22 is a part of the closing of this thematic unit. An interpretation of 4:18–22 aimed at its thematic dimension must therefore examine this passage in terms of the complex relationship be-tween its opening (3:1–12) and closing (4:12–25), and it will have to take into account the relationship between 4:18–22 and the other parts of the closing.

Reading D, CAW 3: A Vision of Discipleship as Being Associated with Jesus' Ministry — Jesus' and John's Ministries in Inverted Parallelisms

What makes John's and Jesus' respective ministries parallel is clearly marked in the text. John and Jesus preach exactly the same message, "Repent, for the kingdom of heaven is at hand" (3:2; 4:17). Both fulfill "what was spo-ken by the prophet Isaiah" (3:3; 4:14–16). In addition, we note here that both John and Jesus are associated with crowds of people from "Jerusalem" and "Judea" (3:5; 4:25; note also that "Jordan" is mentioned in both verses). Thus, in a first approximation, we can say that the theme of this unit concerns what constitutes "true ministry of servants of God" (of people fulfilling the prophecies).[91] John's ministry includes potentialities that are fulfilled in Jesus' ministry, as is expressed by the differences (amounting to inversions) between 3:1–12 and 4:12–25, which set the two scenes in "inverted parallelisms." These differences include the following:

---

89. See Patte, *Matthew*, 43–59.

90. This passage may be divided into several thematic subunits. See Patte, *Matthew*, 43–59.

91. By this phrase I seek to express what is *common* to the presentations of John's ministry and of Jesus' ministry. Therefore, I have to use the category "servant of God" as a designa-tion that can encompass both John and Jesus. *Looking for convictions expressed thematically involves looking for abstract categories,* in contrast with the study of figures (see reading C).

1. John is in Judea, while Jesus is in Galilee;

2. John preaches in the wilderness (3:1), while Jesus dwells in a town, Capernaum (4:13), and preaches in synagogues (4:23);

3. John stays in one place, and people come to him from Judea alone (3:5), while Jesus goes to various locations (4:13, 18, 23) and is followed by people from Galilee and the Decapolis as well as from Jerusalem and Judea (4:25);

4. John baptizes (3:6, 11), while Jesus heals (4:23–24); John rebukes and rejects people (Pharisees and Sadducees, 3:7–10), while Jesus calls people to follow him (disciples, 4:18–22).

These formal differences are the thematic expressions of convictions that form the thematic vision proposed by this unit. Most of these do not directly concern us here, since they are about Jesus' special kind of authority as Son of God during his ministry.[92] But the last inverted parallelism in our list (between 3:7–10 and 4:18–22) is directly related to our topic. It indicates that both John and Jesus are concerned with the issue of religious leadership (as represented by the mention of the Pharisees and the Sadducees and of fishers of people), but that John the Baptist's preoccupation with religious leadership is inappropriate, while Jesus' is appropriate. While John rebukes and sends away people whom he views as inappropriate religious leaders, Jesus calls people to become religious leaders ("fishers of people") by asking them to follow him and to associate themselves with his ministry. The significance of this difference between John and Jesus appears when we elucidate the convictions thematically expressed by this inverted parallelism. While, in the figurative dimension, John's rebuke of the Pharisees and Sadducees is viewed in a positive light (see above, reading C), the thematic dimension contrasts it with Jesus' own attitude: he associates the disciples to his ministry by calling them.

Reading D, CAW 4: Matthew 4:18–22 as Vision-Type of Discipleship: Trusting Response to the Coming of the Kingdom

In order to clarify further the convictions expressed by thematic inverted parallelisms, we need to identify the convictions most directly expressed in this thematic unit (Mt 3:1–4:25): those expressed by the semantic oppositions associated with explicit oppositions of actions. No such opposition can be found in 4:18–22,[93] but three oppositions involve John and the Pharisees and the Sadducees.[94]

The opposition between the common people coming to John (3:5, viewed positively) and "many of the Pharisees and Sadducees" coming to him (3:7,

---

92. See Patte, *Matthew*, 44–56.
93. Which is therefore purely "thematic." Patte, *Matthew*, 10–11.
94. See Patte, *Matthew*, 55–58.

viewed negatively) underscores that the latter are religious leaders (by contrast with laity). The problem is with Jewish religious leaders, their specific view of religious life and their behavior, and not with Jews in general and Judaism itself (for a quite different perspective, see reading C, CAW 5).

The opposition between "fleeing from the wrath to come" (3:7) and "bearing fruit that befits repentance" (3:8) underscores what is wrong with these leaders' attitude and what will bring about condemnation (3:10) if their attitude does not change: (1) their will to act is established by following the advice of "someone" who "warned [them] to flee from the wrath to come" (τίς ὑπέδειξεν ὑμῖν φυγεῖν ἀπὸ τῆς μελλούσης ὀργῆς; 3:7) instead of responding to John's (and Jesus') call to "repent, for the kingdom of heaven is at hand" (3:2; 4:17); consequently, (2) their actions are oriented[95] toward the wrong will: they react to the coming wrath and want to escape evil (3:7), instead of positively responding to the coming of the kingdom and thus desiring and doing deeds that befit repentance (3:8).

Finally, the opposition in 3:9 (between "do not presume to say to yourselves, 'We have Abraham as our father'" and "I tell you, God is able from these stones to raise up children to Abraham") underscores that it is wrong to put one's confidence in one's ancestry and thus to establish one's will by turning toward the past. The proper way of establishing one's will is by considering what God is able to do, and thus by trusting in God's future interventions.

In view of the relations between 3:7–12 and 4:18–22 noted above, one can readily recognize the differences between John and Jesus and those between the Pharisees and Sadducees and the disciples. Matthew 4:18–22 appears as a figurative expression — a type — of the convictions expressed by these oppositions and inverted parallelisms; it clarifies the vision of discipleship as being associated to Jesus' ministry, and thus discipleship as following Jesus, in the sense of carrying out the same ministry. Thus, Jesus' ministry is also perceived as a "type" of discipleship, in the same way that scriptural descriptions of events of sacred history (e.g., the Exodus out of Egypt or Moses on Mount Sinai) are "types" fulfilled in events of Jesus' life (see, respectively, 2:13–15 and 5:1–2).

Yet this does not mean that discipleship involves a rejection of Judaism; it is rather affirming a kind of religious leadership different from that of the Pharisees and the Sadducees (which is to be rejected). By sharing in Jesus' ministry, the disciples participate in Jesus' fulfillment of the Scriptures. Jesus' ministry in Galilee fulfills Isaiah 9:1–2, cited in 4:15–16; he is the great light that "has dawned" on "the people who sat in darkness" and "in the region and shadow of death." He is thus the light toward which people in darkness readily turn. It is significant that these people in darkness are Gentiles

---

95. Using connotations of ὑποδείκνυμι, pointing in a certain direction, translated "warned" (3:7).

(cf. "Galilee of the Gentiles," 4:15). Yet Jesus' ministry in Galilee, which fulfills the Jewish Scriptures, is in continuity with Judaism (contrast with reading C). In the "Galilee of the Gentiles," Jesus teaches "in their synagogues" (4:23). Similarly, the result of this ministry is that people from not only Galilee and Decapolis (Gentiles) but also Jerusalem and Judea follow Jesus, thus being oriented toward the kingdom. As the disciples fulfill the Scriptures by their own ministry in prolongation of Jesus' ministry, their religious leadership, which is totally oriented toward the kingdom, should also be understood in continuity with true Jewish religious leadership, even though it is now also aimed at Gentiles.

Reading D, CAW 5: The Thematic Connotations of Jesus' Calling of Disciples and the Thematic Vision of Discipleship

While John's and Jesus' ministry have the same goal — calling people to repent because of the coming of the kingdom (3:2; 4:17) — they end up being quite different because John's attitude is in tension with the convictions expressed in his own words to the Pharisees and Sadducees. John reacts to the wrong things that he sees (inappropriate religious leadership) and thus rebukes the Jewish leaders and proclaims the coming of the wrath of the judgment (3:10 – 12). By contrast, Jesus has a proactive ministry. He goes to people, to their places of worship (synagogues, 4:23, thus affirming the positive value of their world and of their religious activities), he proclaims the kingdom as "good news" (τὸ εὐαγγέλιον τῆς βασιλείας, 4:23), and he brings people healing, good things.[96] *Thus, Jesus calls disciples as a part of his positive response to the coming of the kingdom. His perception of the urgent need for additional leaders who will lead people toward the kingdom as he does — as is further expressed by the thematic dimension of 5:14 – 16 (and of other passages, such as 9:36 – 38) — is part of that positive response.*

The characteristics of the thematic vision of discipleship can be similarly elucidated by considering the contrast between the Pharisees and Sadducees as religious leaders (and not common people) and the disciples called by Jesus to be religious leaders ("fishers of people," 4:19).

Unlike the Pharisees and Sadducees, the disciples are presented as having an attitude that is a condition for being faithful religious leaders: they "bear fruit that befits repentance" (3:8). They do so by "immediately" obeying Jesus' call, "following him," and abandoning their jobs and even their family (their father). These are "fruit that befits repentance." The most basic characteristic of discipleship is that disciples do not seek to escape an evil situation (cf. 3:7), but instead respond to a positive promise, "I will make you fishers of

---

96. The question regarding the role of the frequent mentions of judgment in the thematic dimension of Jesus' subsequent speeches, including the Sermon on the Mount, will be addressed in the following chapters, as we deal with these texts.

people" (4:19); disciples act in response to the good they perceive (a promise; the kingdom as good news), not in response to the evil they perceive
(the coming wrath; the judgment).

Unlike the Pharisees and the Sadducees, the disciples are faithful. They
trust that, through Jesus, "God is able" to transform them into fishers of
people (as God is able to transform stones into children of Abraham, 3:9);
they put their trust in Jesus and his promise (see also reading B), rather than
in their "father" (Abraham, 3:9, or Zebedee, 4:21–22).

Note that repentance is a part of the thematic vision of discipleship. Yet
"repentance" is not so much a turning away (from sins, from evil) as it is a
turning toward (the kingdom, God, Jesus).[97] "Following Jesus" (which involves
turning toward Jesus) is an expression of repentance; of course, it involves
leaving nets, boats, one's father (turning away from these sources of security), but the essential movement of repentance is the turning toward Jesus
(following him), responding to the positive promise (4:19), responding to his
healings (4:23–25), turning toward the kingdom (as the good thing that God
is bringing about, 4:17, and not as the coming of the judgment, 3:10–12),
turning toward the great light that Jesus is (4:15–16).

This conception of repentance as "turning toward" expresses an essential
condition for faithful discipleship. As long as one conceives of repentance as
turning away from one's sins because one fears the judgment, one cannot be
a faithful disciple;[98] this is not "following Jesus."

In sum, in a systematic, critical interpretation of the thematic dimension the conclusions about what the text is and says are that the inverted
parallelisms between 3:7–10 and 4:18–22 provide a vision of discipleship
characterized by (1) trusting in God's ability, which is also trusting in Jesus'
promise, rather than in human sources of security (jobs, ancestors); (2) repenting, as turning toward the kingdom as coming blessing; deciding to act
(establishing one's will) on the basis of "good things" ("euphoric things" that
one expects), rather than on the basis of "bad things" (the "wrath to come,"
i.e., "dysphoric things").

Discipleship is envisioned as being associated with Jesus' ministry. Jesus'
ministry is characterized by trusting in God's ability (see the temptation story,
4:1–11), which is also trusting that the kingdom of heaven that God promised is indeed coming (as his proclamation of the good news of the kingdom
shows). By trusting in Jesus' promise that he will make them fishers of people,

---

97. Patte, *Matthew,* 49, 56. The same view of "repentance" as "turning toward" is found
in Acts by Dupont. See J. Dupont, "Repentir et conversion d'après les Actes des Apôtres," in
Etudes sur les Actes des apôtres (Paris: Cerf, 1967), 422, 449–53.

98. One can turn away from a form of evil, and go in many different directions, which are
just as evil. But more importantly, as we shall see, the problem with understanding repentance
as turning away from evil (from sins but also from dysphoric situations, such as condemnation) is that it does not establish a true will to do the will of God (doing God's will from the
heart) and that it leads to rejecting and condemning evil people (instead of forgiving them).

the disciples already display the same attitude as Jesus does during his ministry; they are already associated with his ministry. Similarly, as Jesus' ministry is characterized by its proactive and positive orientation, so the disciples are envisioned as people who decide to act on the basis of the positive "things" they perceive, who repent by turning toward the blessings of the kingdom, and who bear fruit that befits repentance. Jesus' ministry, with its "teaching in their synagogues, and proclaiming the good news of the kingdom and curing every disease and every sickness among the people" (4:23), is indeed the bearing of fruit that befits repentance; discipleship is being associated to this ministry.

Conclusions: Four Meaning-Producing Dimensions, Four Critical Methods, Four Legitimate Sets of Conclusions about What (CAWs) the Text Is and Says

The results of the preceding four-way comparative study can be summarized by listing the characteristics of the meaning-producing dimension on which each interpretation is focused, of the critical method(s) it appropriately uses for studying this dimension, and of its *conclusions about what the text is and says.*

Reading A: Strecker and Kingsbury

Meaning-Producing Dimension

The "history" represented by the text; the situation (events involving people in time and space) to which the text refers and which, as a construct, can be viewed as the "realistic narrative" dimension of the text; in Greimas's semiotics, *one* of the several meaning-producing dimensions belonging to the broad category, *discursive syntax.*[99]

Critical Methods

Historical critical method, and more specifically here, redaction critical method; or, narrative criticism focused on events and characters in space and time (Chatman).

CAWs

Matthew 4:18–22 historicizes the call of four apostles/disciples, founders of the church, so as to make clear that it represents an ideal norm for discipleship, which Matthew's church members are invited to implement in their

---

99. See Greimas and Courtés, *Semiotics and Language,* 330–31. For a discussion of the relationship of this dimension with the religious teaching of biblical texts, see Patte, *Religious Dimensions of Biblical Texts,* 173–202. In narratology, this is a dimension that includes a series of "story *aspects.*" See Bal, *Narratology,* 49–118.

lives. Yet since this ideal could only be met in the unrepeatable past when Jesus' authoritative call was directly addressed to individuals, church members are expected to implement this ideal to various degrees — wandering missionaries being the closest to it.

Reading B: Edwards (and Prolongation)

Meaning-Producing Dimension

The unfolding of the plot (or the unfolding of "history"); the process of transformation from an initial situation to a concluding one; personages defined by their participation in this unfolding of the plot, and thus as "actors" who need to be equipped with the appropriate competence (will, knowledge, and ability) before acting; in Greimas's semiotics, *one* of the several meaning-producing dimensions belonging to the broad category, *narrative syntax*.[100]

Critical Methods

Narrative critical method focused on the plot (Kelber) paying close attention to the narrative transformations and to the qualifications of actors.

CAWs

Matthew 4:18–22 presents the beginning of the story of the disciples, how they accepted the invitation to be made disciples/fishers of people, something they will finally be at the end of the gospel (Mt 28). The passage underscores the promise uttered by Jesus as a factor in establishing their will to be made disciples and, with 4:23–25, underscores the similar status of the four fishers and of the crowds.

Reading C: Luz, Davies and Allison

Meaning-Producing Dimension

The figurative dimension is characterized by (1) its organization in figurative textual units by means of literary conventions (inclusios, chiasms, etc.); and (2) its figures that allude to other texts and traditions, relate to other figures in the text, and provide a vision of meaningful human life. In Greimas's semiotics, this is *one* of the several meaning-producing dimensions belonging to the broad category, *discursive semantics*.[101]

---

100. See Greimas and Courtés, *Semiotics and Language,* 332–34. For a discussion of the relationship of this dimension with the religious teaching of biblical texts, see Patte, *Religious Dimensions of Biblical Texts,* 202–12. In narratology, this dimension is called the "fabula." See Bal, *Narratology,* 11–47.

101. See Greimas and Courtés, *Semiotics and Language,* 274–75. For a discussion of the relationship of this dimension with the religious teaching of biblical texts, see Patte, *Religious Dimensions of Biblical Texts,* 129–72. In narratology, this dimension is part of the "textual layer." See Bal, *Narratology,* 119–49.

Critical Methods

History of traditions; history of interpretations; study of the literary structure of the text established with the help of literary conventions of the time.

CAWs

Matthew 4:18–22 presents a vision of discipleship which, in its "transparency," reflects both the church's and Matthew's ecclesiology; discipleship as an ambivalent prophetic vocation (both soteriological and judgmental) that is authentic religious leadership because it is grounded in repentance as turning away from sinful lives, from "darkness," in response to Jesus' call and proclamation of the kingdom; by contrast with the false leadership of the Pharisees and Sadducees.

Reading D: Patte

Meaning-Producing Dimension

The thematic dimension is characterized by its internal semantic organization in (1) thematic textual units by the "inverted parallelisms" between their introductory and concluding sections and (2) clusters of convictions around its explicit oppositions of actions. It offers a thematic vision of meaningful human life; in Greimas's semiotics, *one* of the several meaning-producing dimensions belonging to the broad category, *narrative semantics*.[102]

Critical Methods

Structural exegesis, focused on the identification of inverted parallelisms and of narrative oppositions and on their semantic analysis through a study of intratextual semantic relationships.

CAWs

Matthew 4:18–22 presents a vision of discipleship as being associated with Jesus' proactive ministry when one repents, i.e., turns toward the kingdom, because its coming as proclaimed by Jesus is "good news" and because one trusts in God (and in God's goodness); and when one "bears fruits that befit repentance," a proactive response to the manifestations of goodness one perceives.

---

102. See Greimas and Courtés, *Semiotics and Language,* 277. For a discussion of the relationship of this dimension with the religious teaching of biblical texts, see Patte, *Religious Dimensions of Biblical Texts,* 111–28. In narratology, this dimension is another part of the "textual layer." See Bal, *Narratology,* 119–49.

Summary

This list makes clear why I could claim from the beginning that these four kinds of interpretations are basically *legitimate,* despite the fact that their respective *conclusions about what the text is and says* are so different: they are based on different meaning-producing dimensions of the text. Of course, if one reads the text for "what it refers to" (as is legitimate to do, since the text does refer to a certain situation in history), one must conclude with Strecker that this scene presents an idealized norm for discipleship, since it is set in a holy and unrepeatable past. Similarly, if one reads the text for its figurative vision of meaningful human life in the world (as is legitimate to do because the text does include figures), one must conclude with Luz that this passage offers a vision of discipleship which, because of its transparency, is also an ecclesiological vision. Furthermore, it became clear that each interpretation is focused on a *discrete* meaning-producing dimension. The limit of each focus was shown by the fact that the CAWs of any given interpretation do not take into account even closely related textual dimensions — as is illustrated by juxtaposing an interpretation derived from Edwards's work and one represented by my own commentary to those of Strecker, Luz, and Davies and Allison. Finally, it must be emphasized that beyond the four specific textual dimensions, which happen to be the focus of the interpretations that I discuss, there are many other meaning-producing dimensions.

This multidimensional presentation calls for some refinements of each of the one-dimensional scholarly interpretations — which unduly include arguments and comments concerning other dimensions in their effort to be comprehensive. For each interpretation, the needed refinements are obvious as soon one acknowledges that its *conclusions about what the text is and says* actually represent the meaning-producing features of one textual dimension. Thus, this multidimensional presentation shows that each given scholarly interpretation results from a choice among several possibilities offered by the text. The question is then, On which ground was this choice made? The answer must be twofold. A given interpretation is chosen, both because the *conclusions about the teaching* of the text one can draw from it "make sense" — an epistemology judgment — and because these *conclusions about the teaching* appear to be useful in terms of the interpreter's interests and concerns — a value judgment.

PART 2: MAKING SENSE OF FOUR SETS OF CONCLUSIONS ABOUT DISCIPLESHIP ACCORDING TO MATTHEW 4:18–22

This second part is concerned with the epistemology judgment involved in each of the four scholarly interpretations of Matthew 4:18–22. How does each of these four interpretations "make sense" as a teaching? As I raise this question, I assume that it has been established in part 1 that each proposed interpretation is legitimate.[103]

Raising this epistemological question amounts to seeking to *elucidate the semantic categories used by the interpreter* to formulate *conclusions about the teaching* of the text. Since these categories are also embedded in the warranting argument and the *conclusions about what the text is and says*, one could identify them through a detailed semantic analysis of the argument of the interpretation.[104] But one can achieve comparable results in a much more concrete and direct way through a comparative procedure similar to the one used above, yet focused on the *conclusions about the teaching of the text regarding discipleship*. This amounts to comparing the four different kinds of interpretations in terms of their respective conceptualizations of discipleship.[105] For this purpose, in many instances we need to infer from the warrants of scholarly interpretations the conclusions about discipleship toward which they point because one-dimensional scholarly interpretations usually avoid emphasizing their *conclusions about the teaching* of the text, for fear of being perceived as "interested" interpretations (be they called "hermeneutical," "advocacy," or *pro me/nobis* interpretations).

As soon as one asks the question of the conceptualizations of discipleship involved in each of the interpretations discussed above, it becomes clear that the two pairs of interpretations represent very different options in the conceptualization of discipleship. We can anticipate that according to the first pair, readings A and B, the text of Matthew seeks to teach its readers *what they should implement* in order to be faithful disciples, although what should be implemented is understood in different ways in these two kinds of interpretations. Similarly, according to the second pair, readings C and D, the text of Matthew seeks to provide its readers with *a vision of discipleship as religious leadership*, although this vision is conceptualized in different ways in readings C and D.

As we ponder the differences between the two sets of teachings about discipleship, we must first note that by contrast with the two teachings about *discipleship as implementation* (of something, such as a norm, a

---

103. The interpreters assumed all along that their respective interpretations were legitimate. Yet it should be kept in mind that an interpreter might raise the epistemological question before the legitimacy question. Male European-American biblical scholars, as long as they follow a one-dimensional practice, self-consciously raise the legitimacy question first.

104. Thus, Greimas and his collaborators analyzed the interpreter's "scientific discourse" in order to elucidate the different epistemologies of scholars in various fields of the humanities and social sciences. See A. J. Greimas, *Sémiotique et science sociales* (Paris: Seuil, 1976), and A. J. Greimas and E. Landowski, eds., *Introduction à l'analyse du discours en sciences sociales* (Paris: Hachette, 1979).

105. Of course, instead of making this comparison in terms of the conceptualization of "discipleship," one could make it in terms of many other semantic categories.

procedure, ethical principles, a law), the second pair of readings do *not* conceptualize discipleship in this way. One does not "implement" a vision. Rather — and this is a first possibility — one is shaped or "formed" by a vision, so much so that one conforms to it, receives an identity from it, and thus is resocialized by it into the community of those who share this vision. Alternatively — and this is a second possibility — one is illuminated by a vision, so much so that one receives from it a new way of perceiving all aspects of human experience, a new discernment, through which one can identify people who are worthy to be imitated and followed. When discipleship is conceptualized in terms of a vision, in either one of these two possible senses, it is an "intuitive ethical practice" (see chap. 1), rather than an implementation. From this perspective, discipleship can be envisioned in terms of a figure that is underscored by the text: as "following" Jesus by imitating him.

This brief preview of the kinds of *conclusions about the teaching* of the text regarding discipleship illustrates in a general way the approach we follow in this section: seeking to discern the implications of the *conclusions about what the text is and says* (CAWs) identified in each kind of scholarly interpretation for a conceptualization of the practice of discipleship.

Readings A and B: Discipleship as Implementing Matthew 4:18–22 either as Ideal Norm or as Procedure for Being Made Disciple

The interpretations of the first pair conclude that Matthew 4:18–22 offers an *example of behavior* that Christian believers should emulate in their lives. Most contemporary male European-American Christians might want to exclaim, What is more natural! How else could believers read the story of the call of the first disciples? Since as Christian believers we are to be disciples, we have to follow the example of the original disciples, don't we? The question is, What exactly should we emulate? It depends on our interpretation of this passage, which even in this first option includes a choice.

Reading A, The Teaching of Matthew 4:18–22 about Discipleship according to Strecker's and Kingsbury's Interpretations

Reading A, CAT[106] 1: Matthew 4:18–22 as Ideal Norm of Discipleship

On the basis of the CAWs about Matthew 4:18–22 as a window on an event of "history" or a scene of a "realistic narrative" (see above, reading A, CAW 1ff.), it is already clear that the overall teaching of Matthew

---

106. Here and below, the abbreviation "CAT" stands for *conclusion about the teaching* of the text.

4:18–22 is that it offers itself as an ideal norm for discipleship.[107] To be a disciple is to emulate what the four disciples did in this scene, i.e., obediently respond to Jesus' authoritative command. Thus, discipleship is conceptualized as a status that one acquires once and for all through one's obedient response to Jesus, as Simon Peter, Andrew, James, and John acquired the status of disciples through their own obedience.

Reading A, CAT 2: Discipleship as Unconditional and Costly Submission to Jesus' Words

The characteristics of discipleship are found, according to this kind of interpretation, in the description of the behavior of the four disciples/apostles, since they exemplify discipleship in their unconditional and costly submission to Jesus' words (4:20, 22), as well as in their perception of Jesus' words as an authoritative command that they could not but obey. As such they are unlike the crowds who also follow Jesus, but not as a response to a direct call and without abandoning anything (4:24–25).

Reading A, CAT 3: Discipleship as Acknowledging the Authority of the Exalted Kyrios

Discipleship includes acknowledging and submitting to Jesus' extraordinary authority, and thus having a high Christology — Jesus to whom one should give "total allegiance"[108] (as Kingsbury says) has "all authority in heaven and on earth" (Mt 28:18) because he is the exalted Kyrios, as Strecker repeatedly underscores.

Reading A, CAT 4: Matthew 4:18–22 as Apostolic "Ideal" in Terms of Which the Relative Status of Church Members Can Be Assessed

In sum, Matthew 4:18–22 offers a teaching about discipleship that is "normative" in the sense that all believers (church members) are called to carry it out by following this example; they are to respond to Jesus' call in an unconditional way, whatever might be the cost. On the basis of Strecker's and Kingsbury's CAWs (see reading A, CAW 6), one can add that this normative example is an apostolic "ideal," which only the apostles could truly fulfill because they belonged to the unrepeatable time of Jesus. This apostolic ideal serves as a criterion for assessing the relative status in discipleship of the various persons or groups presented in the rest of the Gospel.[109] The Twelve (10:1–4; 19:28–29) alone have the full status of disciples; no other person or group (e.g., crowds, people with faith, women) satisfies this criterion, although some might have a status that might not be far from it (e.g., those with "great faith," certain women?). Similarly, this apostolic

---

107. Strecker, *Der Weg*, 193–94, passim.
108. Kingsbury, *Matthew as Story,* 104; see also *"Akolouthein,"* 58.
109. As Kingsbury does in *"Akolouthein,"* 58–62.

ideal can serve to assess the relative status of each of the members of the church; greater and lesser implementations of this teaching signal the position of church members in the institutional hierarchy of the community. Ultimately, this norm, as reinforced and refined by other passages of the Gospel according to Matthew, is also a norm that can be used to assess whether or not people belong to the church.

Reading B, The Teaching of Matthew 4:18–22 about Discipleship according to the Alternative Interpretation Suggested by Edwards

Reading B, CAT 1: Discipleship as an Ongoing Process of Transformation

In the alternative interpretation of Matthew 4:18–22 the conclusions about what the text is (the beginning of the unfolding of a plot or of a history, see reading B, CAW 1ff.) already underscore that the text describes the process through which the four fishers have accepted the call to be made *disciples* (fishers of people), something they will finally become at the end of the Gospel (28:16–20). Thus, discipleship is conceptualized as an ongoing process of transformation by Jesus who promises, "I will make you fishers of people" (4:19). Discipleship is not static; it is not a status that one can acquire once and for all; it is a process in which one voluntarily participates.

Reading B, CAT 2: Matthew 4:18–22 as One of the Diverse Ways of Entering the Process of Discipleship

Matthew 4:18–22 presents one of the possible beginning points of the process of discipleship. Some might receive from Jesus a direct call to follow him, as the fishers did. Yet there are other ways of beginning this journey, as the text shows by using the same phrase to express that the crowds and the four fishers "followed" Jesus (ἠκολούθησαν αὐτῷ, 4:25; 4:20, 22). As Edwards notes,[110] the text maintains this ambiguity, by avoiding identification of the four fishers as "disciples" (this word is not used before 5:1). In sum, the scene presented in 4:18–22 is not normative; one can enter the process of discipleship in other ways, for instance, by following Jesus for other reasons than those of the four fishers, as the crowds did because Jesus healed their sick. Through its depiction of different characters, here as elsewhere the Gospel according to Matthew presents a diversity of ways in which one can follow Jesus and be made disciples/fishers of people.

Reading B, CAT 3: Discipleship as a Voluntary Decision to Follow Jesus

Matthew 4:18–22 says more about the way in which one enters the process of discipleship. This alternative interpretation notes that the four fishers are presented as responding to a promise, "I will make you fishers of

---

110. Edwards, "Uncertain Faith," 48–61; see especially 53.

people." By following Jesus, they signal their willingness to be made fishers of people. Thus, discipleship is far from the submission to Jesus' unconditional command; rather, it involves a voluntary decision to follow Jesus. Entering the process of discipleship is the expression of a willingness to be transformed.

The conclusions about what the text says *(see reading B, CAW 5)* note that the four fishers are presented by Matthew 4:18–22 as acknowledging Jesus' trustworthiness and authority in the sense that they view his promise as totally trustworthy. We can thus conclude that here discipleship is not conceived of as costly. Even if following Jesus involves abandoning occupation and family, discipleship is a gain: it is being made a fisher of people and thus receiving a great blessing.

Reading B, CAT 4: From "Would-be Disciples" and "Novice Disciples" to "Full-fledged Disciples"

Discipleship as a process leading to an ethical practice, which Matthew 4:18–22 presents, is here conceptualized as the ongoing training one needs in order to be ready to perform its ultimate task, "fishing for people." Discipleship involves being made fishers of people. A precondition for all this is to trust Jesus' promise included in his call — be it verbal, as for the four fishers, or in action, as for the crowds — and to be willing to be made disciples and to perform this task. It is this willingness that is represented by the decision to follow Jesus, while the act of following Jesus represents the process of transformation that discipleship involves.

In sum, in reading B, discipleship is understood as a process, going from being "would-be disciples" (like the crowds who have taken a first step toward discipleship by following Jesus with the hope of receiving from him more good things, 4:24–25), to being "novice disciples" in one or another stage of training (such as the four fishers after 4:18–22), to being "full-fledged disciples" charged with the mission of being fishers of people (28:18–20). From this perspective, Matthew 4:18–22 provides neither an "ideal" nor a "normative" example of discipleship that could function as a way of deciding who does or does not belong to the church and as a way of ranking people in the church (contrast with reading A). Rather, Matthew 4:18–22 invites its readers to be willing to enter the process of discipleship, with the understanding that there is more than one way of entering the process. One does not need to have received a personal call to be in the discipleship process; one might be part of the anonymous crowds who follow Jesus, trusting that Jesus will do the good things that he promises in words (4:18–22) or in actions (4:23–25).

Readings C and D: Matthew 4:18–22 as a Vision of Discipleship as Religious Leadership in a New Order or as Association with Jesus' Ministry

There are significant differences between the conceptualization of discipleship found in the *conclusions about the teaching* (CATs) of Matthew 4:18–22 proposed by Luz and Davies and Allison, and its conceptualization in my commentary. Before considering these differences, I must first underscore the conclusions that they have in common and that distinguish them from the first set of interpretations (readings A and B).

Reading C and D, CAT 1: Matthew 4:18–22 Conveys a Vision of Discipleship — A View Shared by Luz, Davies and Allison, and Patte

"Repent, for the kingdom of heaven has come near" (Μετανοεῖτε: ἤγγικεν γὰρ ἡ βασιλεία τῶν οὐρανῶν, 4:17; cf. 3:2). Taking seriously into account that all of Jesus' (and John's) ministry is related to the proclamation of the kingdom is what fundamentally distinguishes readings C and D (Luz, Davies and Allison, and Patte) from readings A and B. Readings C and D have quite different conceptualizations of discipleship as compared with the other set of interpretations because they read Matthew 4:18–22 as related to the vision of the good news of the kingdom (τὸ εὐαγγέλιον τῆς βασιλείας, 4:23) proclaimed by Jesus, instead of reading 4:18–22 as teaching a norm or a procedure that must be implemented by disciples.

The difference between these two kinds of conceptualization of the teaching of Matthew 4:18–22 is readily understood by comparison with the parables. As is broadly recognized, the parables communicate a new vision of human experience in light of the kingdom; yet, they can also be read as example stories.[111] Similarly, but conversely, while Matthew 4:18–22 is often read as providing an example of behavior for disciples (readings A and B), it can also be read as offering a part of Matthew's vision of the kingdom (readings C and D).

This proclamation of a vision remains an ethical teaching, as is shown by its association with repentance. The call of the disciples and the vision of discipleship that it includes is also a call to repent in view of the coming kingdom, as is expressed by Jesus' words that introduce it (4:17). The

---

111. Thus, in my androcritical multidimensional exegetical perspective, I see this major debate in parable studies as a signal that two equally legitimate interpretations of these texts focus on different dimensions. See the debate among Dan O. Via, *The Parables: Their Literary and Existential Dimension* (Philadelphia: Fortress, 1967); John Dominic Crossan, *In Parables: The Challenge of the Historical Jesus* (New York: Harper & Row, 1973); and "Parable and Example in the Teaching of Jesus," *Semeia* 1 (1974): 63–104; Bernard Brandon Scott, *Hear Then the Parable: A Commentary on the Parables of Jesus* (Minneapolis: Fortress, 1989).

vision of the kingdom and the vision of discipleship are thus related, and both visions play a central role in bringing about repentance and faithful performance of one's role as a disciple. Let me be more specific.

The *conclusions about what the text is* of Luz and Davies and Allison (above, reading C, CAW 1ff.), as well as those of my commentary (reading D, CAW 1ff.), underscore that Matthew 4:18–22 is a figurative and thematic text that offers *a vision of discipleship as a distinctive type of religious leadership* — an eschatological religious leadership, since it is associated with the coming kingdom. So, what does this mean for readers? What *conclusions about the teaching* of this text regarding discipleship should we draw? What happens when readers are invited to share a vision? Briefly, they are offered a new way of perceiving their experience. Such a vision functions for them as a pair of eyeglasses which because of their corrective lenses, allow them to see what they could not see, even though it was in front of them. Yet what is seen in this new light depends on the specific focalization of the vision that readers select.

Reading C

When the text is perceived as offering a broad vision of a new order — the kingdom — readers are invited to enter this vision, to envision themselves and their identify in this new order, and thus to conform themselves and to be conformed to the kingdom. Thus, reading C conceptualizes discipleship as seeing oneself in terms of the new order of the kingdom, rather than in terms of the old order of traditional religions and traditional societies, which then must be rejected. More specifically, the vision of discipleship concerns religious leadership conceived in terms of this new order. As readers share this vision and are conformed to it, they will want to act according to this new perception of their identity and their responsibility as religious leaders (as we shall see, all readers/believers are invited to assume religious leadership vis-à-vis the world). Thus, in this *indirect* way, readers are brought to act according to this vision. Discipleship is an "intuitive" ethical practice; disciples do what they intuitively feel is the right thing to do as they envision their vocation and their present situation in light of the vision of religious leadership in the kingdom.

Reading D

Matthew 4:18–22 can also be read as offering a more narrowly focused vision, as a spotlight or a searchlight focuses one's vision. In this case, the text provides the spotlight vision that allows identification of those people who already manifest the kingdom (at least in part); readers are invited to follow their lead. Following them, readers would then be brought to act "like them," and thus in this indirect *fashion the text governs their behavior. They in turn become religious leaders whom others might want to imitate.*

In both cases, the teaching of Matthew 4:18–22 for the readers — this vision — remains a teaching about discipleship as ethical practice. But because of the indirect way in which this text affects the readers' behavior, it is not prescriptive in the way a norm or a process to be implemented would be. The readers, whether they conform to this vision or they imitate those they have identified as true disciples among them, might end up acting as the characters in 4:18–22 did, and thus as if they had read the text as a norm or a procedure to be implemented (as in readings A and B). Yet in most instances, these readers will act in different ways because they have intuitively perceived that a concrete situation demands it.

These *conclusions about the teaching* of this text as offering a vision of discipleship are implied in Luz's *conclusion about what the text is and says* according to which the scene presented by Matthew 4:18–22 has in and of itself "typical significance"[112] (see reading C, CAW 5), and as such allows the members of Matthew's community who share in this vision to recognize themselves as disciples with leadership responsibility in the new order of the kingdom. Similarly, in my commentary, I see this scene as proposing a "type discipleship." In this phrase the word "type" is used in a technical sense. As Jesus fulfills the prophecies (e.g., 1:22–23; 2:15) and the types of Scripture (e.g., he fulfills the type "Israel called out of Egypt" in 2:15, the type "Israel tempted in the wilderness" in 4:1–11, the type "Moses on Mount Sinai" in 5:1ff.), so certain people in the past and in the present fulfill the type "discipleship" proposed by 4:18–22 and are thus to be imitated (see reading D, CAW 4).

This "typical" presentation of discipleship in either of its understandings is inscribed in the text. The crowds are depicted as fulfilling the type of discipleship by doing what the disciples also did: "following him" (ἠκολούθησαν αὐτῷ, 4:20, 22, 25) as a response to Jesus' preaching (4:17, 23). With Luz one can, therefore, speak of a discipleship of the ὄχλοι who conform to the vision of discipleship offered by the story of the four fishers (the crowds are also described as "following Jesus" in 8:1; 12:15; 19:2; 20:29).[113] The crowds are "disciples" insofar as they either conform to or imitate the disciples in this and other typical scenes.

---

112. Luz, *Matthew*, 200–201. See Rudolf Bultmann (*History of the Synoptic Tradition*, trans. J. Marsh [New York: Harper & Row, 1963], 28) and Dibelius (*Tradition*, 111–12) who call it an "ideal scene" (created by Mark out of the metaphor "fishers of people") rather than a historical scene. See also Schweizer (*Matthew*, 75) who speaks, in the same sense, of "the exemplary nature" of the scene. Regarding Luz, it is noteworthy that he does not develop his interpretation of 4:18–22 in great detail (either in his commentary or in "The Disciples," 98–128). Yet his few comments clearly indicate that he reads this scene, as well as the Sermon on the Mount, figuratively. Note also in his essay the emphasis on the "ecclesiological" presentation of the disciples. The interpretation presented in my commentary has a similar perspective.

113. Luz, *Matthew*, 201. Luz underscores that all these passages are in the Matthean redaction.

Beyond these general *conclusions about the teaching* that we can draw from the CAWs of Luz, Davies and Allison, and Patte, more specific conceptualizations further clarify their divergence. From the perspective adopted by Luz and Davies and Allison, the emphasis on the contrast between the new order of the kingdom and traditional religions leads to underscoring that discipleship involves making a clear distinction between "authentic" and "inauthentic" religious leadership.

By contrast, from the perspective I adopted in my commentary, discipleship involves a concern to identify exclusively "authentic" religious leaders. The focused vision of types of discipleship leads to underscoring that discipleship involves recognizing people who manifest the kingdom, such as Jesus and those who prolong his ministry.

Reading C, CAT 2: Distinguishing "Authentic" from "Inauthentic" Religious Leadership

Luz, Davies, and Allison interpret the "figures" of Matthew 4:18–22 in terms of texts from other biblical books or traditions and suggest that this passage provides a vision of discipleship as *authentic religious leadership* (see reading C, CAWs 3 and 4). From this perspective, they conceptualize true discipleship as a specific kind of religious leadership authenticated through its fulfillment of the Scriptures.

More specifically, let us keep in mind that here discipleship involves a missionary activity (fishing for people), which is a prophetic vocation with both positive and negative, soteriological and judgmental, aspects. This ambivalence of the vocation of disciples is consistent with the perception of a clear dichotomy between the before and after of repentance (as turning *away from evil;* see reading C, CAW 5): disciples become true religious leaders by abandoning their old way of life, their worldly occupation (fishing for fish), and their family (father), i.e., by abandoning the "darkness" in which they sat (4:16). Since discipleship demands such a rupture with one's past, it appears as a radical kind of religious leadership, whose authenticity is then defined by contrast with the false kind of leadership offered by the synagogue,[114] the leadership of the Pharisees and Sadducees, rejected as a "brood of vipers" (Mt 3:7).[115] (See reading C, CAW 6.) Thus, discipleship refers to the religious leadership of a different and new community, as Luz repeatedly points out: " 'Disciples' is an ecclesiological term in the Gospel according to Matthew."[116]

---

114. So Luz, *Matthew,* 201.
115. On the systematic rejection of religious leaders in Matthew, see A.-J. Levine, *The Social and Ethnic Dimension of Matthean Salvation History* (Lewiston, N.Y.: Edwin Mellen, 1988).
116. Luz, *Matthew,* 200, and "The Disciples," 98–128.

This brief summary of the *conclusions about what the text is and says* that we identified above in the interpretations of Luz and Davies and Allison raise a fundamental question regarding the general *conclusions about the teaching* of this text, How does this vision of discipleship help Christian readers of the Gospel according to Matthew to perceive what authentic discipleship-religious leadership entails for them? And how does it help them to conform to this vision?

Entering this vision proposed by Jesus and conforming to it involve repentance. But from the perspective of the vision, the question is, What is authentic repentance? For this purpose, it is essential to perceive clearly what and who is evil; it is a matter of discerning from what one needs to turn away, as one repents. The vision of the kingdom, the light shining in darkness (4:15–16), proposed by the text reveals the evil from which one must turn away. How? By providing the readers with "types": types of authentic repentance and discipleship, but also and most importantly, types of inauthentic repentance and religious leadership.

Reading Matthew 4:18–22 as a part of the figurative unit to which it belongs (3:1–4:22), while paying attention to the figures of this text (see above, reading C, CAW 3 and 4), shows the figures/types of inauthentic repentance and religious leadership. The Pharisees and Sadducees are posited as types of false religious leaders who have hypocritical attitudes and from whom disciples need to turn away. Their lives are still governed by evil, as John reveals (3:7–12). The figure/type of the Pharisees and Sadducees as antidisciples makes it clear that authentic repentance and faithful discipleship involve a complete break from Judaism, a radical turning away from Jewish traditions, from the means of salvation it offers (which are illusory; "do not pretend," μὴ δόξητε, 3:9a). The promise of God to Abraham does not become void; "God is able from these stones to raise up children to Abraham" (3:9b), and thus God is able to fulfill his promise in another way. Instead of fulfilling his promise with and through the Jews, God fulfills them with and through those who truly repent,[117] as the prophecies are fulfilled by Jesus' ministry (4:14–16).

Positively, the figure of authentic religious leadership provided by Matthew 4:18–22 appears: authentic disciples are people who carry out a radical prophetic vocation involving both soteriological and judgmental functions after having themselves radically turned away from their old

---

117. On all this, see the detailed discussion of 3:8–10 in Davies and Allison, *Matthew*, 305–11 (and bibliography). The authors emphasize that in many ways one is led to conclude that, at the very least, John the Baptist "places a large question mark over the covenantal nomism of his day" (308), although this may only be "the popular understanding of what the Abrahamic covenant entailed" (309). Yet Davies and Allison admit that "for Matthew" (i.e., from our perspective, for the figurative dimension of the Gospel according to Matthew) this break with Judaism is understood more radically, "given his interest in the Gentile mission" (309).

ways of life and from Judaism — indeed, from anything in which one finds illusory security in view of the impending judgment.

For the readers who adopt this vision and look around themselves through these positive and negative figures/types as through corrective lenses of a pair of eyeglasses, the world is restructured. They assign clear categories to everyone. Such and such persons are hypocrites, since their repentance fits the type of the inauthentic repentance of the Pharisees and Sadducees; those other persons are faithful disciples who show true repentance, since they fit the type of authentic repentance of the disciples. This situation is evil and needs to be abandoned or rejected, while this other situation demands their involvement because they fit respectively the types of evil situations abandoned by the disciples and the types of situations in which the disciples become involved (e.g., Jesus' ministry). In the process, these readers gain a new identity; they see themselves in a new way. The readers follow the typical transformation of the fishers/disciples. The fishers belonged to a society in which they were socialized; after encountering Jesus and abandoning their former life, they are in effect resocialized in a different community — the community of disciples. So it will be for the readers; as they enter the vision of the text, they will progressively be conformed to this vision; they will be resocialized. At least this is what we can anticipate on the basis of the CAWs of reading C, which see in Matthew 4:18–22 a type of discipleship as an ambivalent prophetic vocation with a soteriological *and* a judgmental component. The vision offered by this first and brief text provides a number of types that will allow the readers to carry out this prophetic mission by giving them the means to sort out the evil from the good (as the fisher sorts good and bad fish; 13:47–48). But one can anticipate that the Sermon on the Mount (and the rest of the Gospel according to Matthew) will provide many more such types, which offer a much more complete resocialization to the readers who enter the vision of the text.

Reading D, CAT 2: Discipleship Requires Identifying Those Who Are Associated with Jesus' Ministry

The vision of discipleship as religious leadership expressed by Matthew 4:18–22 is characterized by the disciples' association with Jesus' ministry according to the alternative interpretation that my commentary represents[118] (see reading D, CAW 3). The evidence for this CAW includes, among many things, Jesus' emphatic call to follow him: "Come after me (Δεῦτε ὀπίσω μου), and

---

118. Patte, *Matthew,* 56–57 (see also 45–58). Note that, as was the case with the other interpretations, my CAWs are "sharpened" as they are formulated for this comparison with the three other interpretations; the *conclusions about the teaching* regarding discipleship, which were implied, are now made explicit.

I will make you fishers of people" (4:19). *Since Jesus calls the disciples to become fishers of people by following him, he associates the disciples with his ministry. Discipleship as religious leadership and ministry prolongs Jesus' ministry. Thus, a first conclusion about the teaching of this text is that a clear vision of discipleship involves a clear vision of Jesus' ministry.*

The vocation of the disciples as fishers of people is, therefore, clarified by considering Jesus' ministry to the crowds, which is presented in the following verses (4:23–25). The comparison with John's ministry required by this kind of interpretation makes it clear that Jesus' ministry is entirely positive (see reading D, CAW 4): Jesus "fishes for people" by going out of his way to teach people and to preach to them in their own locations; this preaching is designated as a "good news" (4:23). He heals their sick (4:24), and the crowds follow him, as the disciples also do (4:25). That these conclusions about what the text says regarding Jesus' ministry should be taken to be a model/type for discipleship, as the conceptualization of discipleship of reading D suggests, is further confirmed by other passages in Matthew, which clearly indicate that discipleship involves duplicating Jesus' preaching and healing ministry (10:7–8) and even his teaching ministry (28:18–20). Being a disciple is being the kind of religious leader who helps other people become disciples themselves. It is an exclusively positive ministry (which does not include any negative, judgmental aspects; by contrast with reading C).

That discipleship is completely defined in positive terms is further shown by the repentance (4:17) that it demands. It is not a matter of turning away from evil, or of abandoning other ways of life (see above, reading C, CAT 2). Rather, repenting involves turning toward Jesus and adopting the orientation that Jesus' ministry has: turning toward the good things that the kingdom of heaven is.

Turning toward the kingdom and toward Jesus involves, of course, turning away from certain things (occupation, family). But this is not saying that the things one abandons are necessarily evil, as is implied by reading C. Furthermore, from the perspective of this interpretation, turning away from evil (whatever it might be) would not define discipleship in any appropriate way. When one turns away from something, one might still go in many inappropriate directions. It is only when one turns toward the truly appropriate goal – the kingdom, toward which Jesus' ministry is also directed – that one can be sure to have an appropriate ministry.

Thus, what is the conceptualization of discipleship involved in the interpretation proposed by my commentary? What are for this reading the conclusions about the teaching of Matthew 4:18–22 regarding discipleship? As above (reading C), this text offers the readers a vision of discipleship. There is no ambivalence in this vision: it is entirely positive (euphoric). The corrective lenses of this pair of eyeglasses focus the sight of the Christian readers completely on the positive manifestations of the kingdom in Jesus' ministry, which disciples are expected to imitate. Is this to say that evil is no longer recognized? That evil does not exist according to this vision? Of course not. Evil is simply not in the spotlight.

This narrowly focalized vision, incomplete as it is, does not allow the readers who adopt it to envision a new order, a new community, in which one needs to be resocialized after having repented (see reading C, CAT 2). This narrowly focalized vision has a more limited function. It offers to readers the means to discern and identify manifestations of the kingdom to be imitated, or, in other words, the characteristics of Jesus' ministry that disciples are to imitate in their daily life. Being disciples is being associated with Jesus' ministry and prolonging it.

We can anticipate that there is more. The rest of the description of Jesus' ministry in the Gospel according to Matthew will certainly refine this vision. In addition, it is clear that the disciples as described in the Gospel are also models to be imitated – since, after all, they were themselves associated with Jesus' ministry. Beyond them, we can anticipate that all the other disciples who will continue to prolong Jesus' ministry, including in our present, will also be models that readers/believers will be invited to identify with the help of the types provided by the text, and then to imitate. But this remark already points toward the Sermon on the Mount, and more specifically, toward the conclusions of reading D regarding the teaching about discipleship of the Sermon.

Such is the teaching of this passage, Matthew 4:18–22, read in its thematic context (3:1– 4:25). We can anticipate that these conclusions will hold true as we read the Sermon on the Mount, including passages where Jesus expresses condemnations. But it is clear that these conclusions are still very incomplete; as we flesh them out in the following chapters, they will also be refined.

We can now summarize the results of our review of the conclusions about the teaching of the four kinds of interpretations. For the first pair, readings A and B, the text of Matthew seeks to teach its readers *what they should implement* in order to be faithful disciples. Yet their conceptualizations of "what" must be implemented are different. For reading A (Strecker and Kingsbury), Matthew 4:18–22 is a norm — being a disciple is *implementing a norm*. For reading B, it describes a process of transformation — becoming disciples is *entering a long process and implementing its procedures*. Similarly, according to the second pair, readings C and D, the text of Matthew seeks to provide its readers with *a vision of discipleship as religious leadership*. Yet their conceptualizations of the relationship between vision and discipleship are different. For reading C (Luz and Davies and Allison), Matthew 4:18–22 sees discipleship in terms of a vision of the coming kingdom, perceived through contrast with the old religious order that is to be rejected — being disciples entails *envisioning oneself in the new order of the kingdom, where religious leadership is redefined.* For reading D (Patte), Matthew 4:18–22 proposes a vision of discipleship that includes recognizing in Jesus' ministry manifestations of the kingdom which become models of discipleship that the disciples are to imitate — being disciples entails *discerning in Jesus' ministry (and possibly beyond it) models of discipleship to be imitated.*

Many issues are left open, pending our study of the four kinds of interpretations of the Sermon on the Mount. My hope is simply that each set of conclusions might be perceived as epistemologically plausible, in the sense that one can envision that someone might want to practice discipleship in this way, even if personally one does not want to do so.

PART 3: ONE TEXT WITH FOUR LEGITIMATE AND PLAUSIBLE TEACHINGS ABOUT DISCIPLESHIP

The Question of the Relative Value of Each of These Plausible and Legitimate Interpretations

I have presented four epistemologically plausible interpretations of the teaching about discipleship of Matthew 4:18–22:

1. discipleship as implementing an ideal norm (its legitimacy being supported by a scholarly interpretation focused on the historical/realistic narrative dimension of the text);

2. discipleship as implementing procedures of a long process through which one is made a disciple (its legitimacy being supported by a scholarly interpretation focused on the plot dimension of the text);

3. discipleship as a vision of authentic religious leadership in the new order of the kingdom, which involves an ambivalent ministry (its legitimacy being supported by a scholarly interpretation focused on the figurative dimension of the text);

4. discipleship as a vision of authentic religious leadership of people who imitate Jesus and are associated with Jesus' ministry, which involves an exclusively positive ministry (its legitimacy being supported by a scholarly interpretation focused on the thematic dimension of the text).

These two pairs of contrasting conclusions about the teaching of Matthew 4:18–22 regarding discipleship do not leave any doubt: these four interpretations are quite different. If we are not yet convinced of this, we will be as soon as we envision *pro me* (or *pro nobis*) interpretations corresponding to each of these, i.e., how each of these quite distinct teachings about discipleship would affect us either as we strive to be disciples or as we interact with such people. Through my presentation I have tried to show as clearly as possible both the legitimacy and the epistemological plausibility of each set of *conclusions about what the text is and says* (CAWs) and of *conclusions about the teaching* (CATs) of Matthew 4:18–22 regarding discipleship. All these conclusions are necessarily quite partial because they are based on the limited data offered by interpretations of a short text. A similar androcritical multidimensional study of the much richer Sermon on the Mount will clarify, complement, and refine these preliminary conclusions, and it will allow us to raise another set of questions.

Let us not forget why these four kinds of interpretations were presented in such a way that the legitimacy and epistemological plausibility of each might readily be recognizable and, simultaneously, in such a way that they might easily be compared: it was in order to bring to critical understanding my own interpretation and in order to entice you to do the same with yours. In this chapter I have began elucidating the specificity of my own *conclusions about the teaching* of Matthew regarding discipleship — and thus the specificity of my conceptualization of this teaching — as well as the specificity of the textual features (meaning-producing dimension) on which my interpretation is based. Even as I refined and complemented the interpretation presented in my commentary, as I was making explicit the choices I had made on the basis of legitimacy and epistemology judgments, I could also recognize its basic legitimacy and plausibility. Yet it should be clear that my goal is not to lead you, my reader, to adopt my interpretation. Rather, my hope is that you will want to bring to critical understanding *your own interpretation,* by making explicit and affirming both *its legitimacy* (it is grounded in a meaning-producing dimension of the text) and *its epistemological plausibility* (its conceptualization of the teaching about discipleship makes sense). My hope is thus that this chapter has already begun helping you do so. But I can understand that you might have the feeling that you have not progressed much toward this goal. This process is not complete for either you or me, even if we would limit ourselves to Matthew 4:18–22.

The preceding discussion has shown that each of these four kinds of interpretations of the text has as much claim as the others to being viewed as legitimate and epistemologically plausible. If any one of these *conclusions about the teaching* on discipleship in Matthew 4:18–22 seems more plausible or more legitimate than the others, this means that there is one of two problems. A first possibility is that there might be weaknesses in the multidimensional study presented above. My presentation of the critical arguments supporting each set of *conclusions about what the text is and says* and of *conclusions about the teaching* might not be as convincing as it should be; better evidence in support of the existence of the different meaning-producing dimensions and in support of the plausibility of such interpretations might have been adduced. If so, kindly complement my presentation by a close study of the critical studies I refer to in notes; I might have failed to present clearly enough the rigor of their respective arguments.

Yet there is another possibility, namely, that you, my reader, evaluate these interpretations from a traditional one-dimensional perspective. Then you cannot but be confused by what I tried to present above. A few comments should suffice to overcome this potential confusion.

By affirming that these four interpretations of Matthew 4:18–22 are equally legitimate and equally epistemologically plausible, I do not suggest that we should try to hold on to these four kinds of interpretations as we seek to establish what is the teaching of this text *for us*. Actually because they are so different from each other, we have to make a choice among them and decide which one will provide the teaching about discipleship that we will want to implement in our lives (if we are Christian believers). Traditionally, from our one-dimensional perspective, we male European-American exegetes have convinced ourselves (1) that it is possible to make this decision by showing that one, and only one, interpretation is truly legitimate, and thus that the others are illegitimate, and (2) that it is purely accidental that our rigorous and "disinterested" critical studies always concluded that the legitimate interpretation was the one that supported our interests and concerns as male (middle class) European-Americans and that the illegitimate interpretations were those that supported the interests and concerns of other people. As I suggested in chapter 1, I do not believe that such critical studies are truly disinterested; the evidence of a consistent pattern of critical studies matching the interpreters' interests and concerns should at least make us suspicious. In addition, the multiplication of *critical* methods, which clearly produce different exegetical results, convinced me that it is *impossible* to have a critical demonstration that only one interpretation of a text is legitimate.

Thus, I want to underscore once again that what happens in one-dimensional critical exegeses is a confusion between the three kinds of interpretive judgments: (1) the *legitimacy judgment* regarding the specific textual evidence (a meaning-producing dimension of the text) chosen as meaningful, which finds expression in *conclusions about what the text is and says;* (2) the *epistemology judgment* regarding the relative plausibility of the conceptualization of each interpretation, which finds expression in *conclusions about the teaching* of the text; and (3) the *value judgment* regarding *the relative value* of each interpretation, that is, regarding the ways in which this interpretation affects people (as compared with the effects of other interpretations of this text on these people), which finds a most direct expression in *pro me* or *pro nobis* formulations. This latter judgment regarding the relative values of interpretations is a matter concerning ethical values; thus, this judgment is "interested," as is any ethical judgment.

After considering the legitimacy and the epistemological plausibility of the four sets of *conclusions about the teaching* of Matthew 4:18–22 regarding discipleship, we should now raise the question of their relative values: Why did we choose one rather another interpretation of discipleship

according to Matthew 4:18–22? This question should allow us to elucidate the *value judgment* involved in our own interpretation, whatever it
might be. Yet I propose to postpone raising this question. It will be better
to enter this discussion after our androcritical multidimensional study of
the Sermon on the Mount, which will refine and complement the preliminary observations proposed in the present chapter. Let us now turn to the
Sermon on the Mount.

A Fourfold Commentary
on the Sermon on the Mount

Four Legitimate Interpretations

W E NOW TURN to our main topic, discipleship according to the Sermon on the Mount, or, more precisely, discipleship according to four kinds of scholarly interpretations of the Sermon by male European-American scholars. The overall goals and procedures of this study should come as no surprise, following our discussion of interpretations of Matthew 4:18–22. Only a few words are necessary to introduce the more specific goals and procedures of Part I of our fourfold commentary on the Sermon on the Mount.

The study in the rest of this book undertakes a critical assessment of the two most influential kinds of interpretations of the Sermon on the Mount by male European-American scholars, represented on the one hand by those of Strecker[1] and Kingsbury,[2] and on the other hand by those of Luz[3] and Davies and Allison.[4] This critical assessment seeks to make explicit the interpretive judgments reflected by these two dominant kinds of interpretations, by comparing each with a closely related alternative interpretation: I develop (out of suggestions by Edwards) a direct alternative to the interpretation of Strecker and Kingsbury; similarly, the interpretation of my commentary[5] is a close alternative to that of Luz and Davies and Allison. In the process, we will foreground the legitimacy, epistemology, and value judgments of these four kinds of interpretations. In this way, I will have brought to critical understanding my own interpretation of the Sermon on the Mount, along with the three others. My hope is that this study will help you, my reader, to bring to critical understanding your own interpretation of discipleship according to the Sermon on the Mount.

More specifically, this critical assessment of each interpretation involves elucidating the choices that each given interpretive judgment represents. Each interpretation has chosen to focus itself on the following:

---

1. Georg Strecker, *The Sermon on the Mount: An Exegetical Commentary*, trans. O. C. Dean Jr. (Nashville: Abingdon, 1988).

2. Jack D. Kingsbury, *Matthew as Story* (Minneapolis: Fortress, 1986).

3. Ulrich Luz, *Matthew 1–7: A Commentary* (Minneapolis: Augsburg, 1989).

4. W. D. Davies and D. C. Allison Jr., *A Critical and Exegetical Commentary on the Gospel according to Saint Matthew*, vol. 1, ICC (Edinburgh: T. & T. Clark, 1988); see also W. D. Davies, *The Setting of the Sermon on the Mount* (Cambridge: Cambridge University Press, 1964).

5. Daniel Patte, *The Gospel according to Matthew: A Structural Commentary on Matthew's Faith* (Minneapolis: Fortress, 1987; 3d printing, Valley Forge, Pa.: Trinity Press International, 1996), 60–108.

- Certain textual features as a sound and coherent basis for a meaningful interpretation, and thus as the meaning-producing dimension[6] of the text on which the interpretation is focused (*legitimacy judgment*)

- Certain semantic categories, themes, and subthemes that make sense and thus frame the conceptualization of plausible *conclusions about the teaching* of the text (*epistemology judgment*)

- Relative values ascribed to legitimate and plausible interpretations on the basis of the interpreters' interests and concerns (*value judgment*)

In order to show the specificity of these judgments and choices, this study is deliberately *multidimensional* and *androcritical* in the sense that it seeks to elucidate, beyond the legitimacy judgments foregrounded by their methodologies, the kinds of epistemology judgments found in European-American cultures and the kinds of value judgments performed by male readers from these cultures.

The richness of the Sermon on the Mount, as well as its length (Mt 5:1–7:29, as compared with 4:18–22), gives us an opportunity to survey a multidimensional teaching about many facets of *a life of discipleship* (rather than an abstract concept) expressed in the discrete sections of the Sermon on the Mount. Our study needs, therefore, to deal successively with each of these sections (however they might be defined) in the form of a fourfold commentary on this text.

In order to make this fourfold commentary androcritical, we need to make explicit the judgments and choices of each interpretation. For this purpose, this fourfold commentary of the Sermon is best presented in three parts. A first part (chaps. 3–4) investigates the legitimacy and consistency of the four interpretations by exploring how each establishes the legitimacy of its particular conclusions about discipleship. This first part of the fourfold commentary retains its concreteness through its unwavering focus on specific passages of the Sermon and through its emphasis regarding each interpretation on the *conclusions about what the text is and says* (CAWs) about some specific aspect of a life of discipleship (which is the basis for certain *conclusions about the teaching* of the Sermon about discipleship). In each chapter, the contrast between the two kinds of interpretations, as one moves from one section of the Sermon to another, constantly surprises us with new insights and the unexpected specificity of each of the interpretations.

A second part (chaps. 5–6) investigates the plausibility of the different conceptualizations of discipleship found in the *conclusions about the teaching* (CATs) of the Sermon of these four kinds of interpretations. While

---

6. Although I personally prefer the metaphor of a text as "multidimensional," it is as appropriate to speak of the text as "polysemic," or as part of a communication process along a plurality of "codes," or as a "multivoiced discourse."

retaining the fourfold form, this section is organized thematically — as is appropriate for presenting these diverse conceptualizations of discipleship. This second part seeks to elucidate the epistemological preunderstandings of the four kinds of interpretations regarding discipleship *as an ethical practice*.

The third part (chap. 7) assesses the relative value of each of these four kinds of male European-American interpretations of the Sermon on the Mount. This section departs from the fourfold form in order to put the four interpretations in dialogue with interpretations that make their own value judgments explicit — advocacy interpretations by feminists and other readers from diverse cultural, social, and economic contexts. For this purpose, we male European-Americans are called to "read with" these other readers — to read with them the Sermon on the Mount itself, and also and necessarily to reread with them the four kinds of scholarly interpretations, which we should learn to consider as a few of the legitimate and plausible interpretations, even if these other interpretations are *pro me* or *pro nobis* interpretations that make their interested character explicit.

With this third part, my study will have reached its end. I will have brought to critical understanding my own interpretation. I hope it will also have facilitated the bringing to critical understanding of your own interpretation. But my work remains incomplete without your critical assessment of the four proposed interpretations in terms of your own interpretation, either after or during the process of reading this book. As you add another interpretation (yours) to those already considered, you will want to reopen my assessment of the relative value of the different interpretations. Indeed, your interpretation would call me further to reassess my own value judgment (chap. 7), as the interpretations of many people in academic and church settings have helped me to bring my interpretation to critical understanding by confronting me with the different interpretive choices they made.

Interpreting and bringing our interpretations to critical understanding is an ongoing process that must be kept open to change as we encounter other interpretations and are enlightened by other interpreters. Otherwise, the process stops. We are interpretively dead. Not knowing what we are doing, we then use interpretations as deadly weapons that we turn against others and against ourselves.

CHAPTER 3

Historical and Narrative Interpretations of Discipleship according to the Sermon on the Mount

Chapter 3 presents, in the form of a twofold commentary, the interpretations of discipleship according to the Sermon on the Mount found in Strecker's and Kingsbury's studies, as well as in an alternative narrative interpretation focused on the plot. The twofold commentary moves back and forth between the two kinds of interpretations as it presents their respective *conclusions about what the Sermon on the Mount is and says* concerning discipleship in its different sections — each CAW subtitle summarizes a specific *conclusion about what the Sermon is and/or says*. Now that we have completed our multidimensional study of Matthew 4:18–22, it is enough to make a few introductory remarks regarding the meaning-producing dimensions on which these two kinds of interpretations are focused in regard to their *conclusions about what the text is*, and thus about the textual features that are viewed as a sound and coherent basis for a meaningful interpretation. These remarks are sufficient to clarify the critical methods that help make explicit the legitimacy of both of these kinds of interpretations explicit.

Reading A: Redaction Critical and Literary Critical Interpretations Focused on the History/Realistic Dimension of the Sermon on the Mount

We have already noted, regarding Matthew 4:18–22, that Strecker's critical interpretation is a redaction critical study that bases its conclusions on the examination of a dimension of the text that can be called the "history to which the text refers" or, when viewed from the literary perspective adopted by Kingsbury, the "realistic narrative" presented by the text (see chap. 2, reading A, CAW 1). The role and place of what can be called

128

"the historical/realistic dimension" is clearly marked in a passage such as Matthew 4:18–22, which is readily recognizable as a historical (or realistic narrative) presentation of a part of Jesus' ministry. Since this historical presentation is idealized and formalized, one can conclude with Strecker that "that time" is viewed by Matthew as "an unrepeatable and holy past" offered as an ideal norm of discipleship for the reader. Thus in the preceding chapter, we could readily recognize that Matthew 4:18–22 proposes a historical/realistic dimension that has the strong potential of affecting readers and can therefore be the focus of a legitimate interpretation. In sum, we could affirm that an interpretation which takes Matthew 4:18–22 as the expression of an ideal norm for discipleship is legitimate.[1]

Although the Sermon on the Mount is quite a different kind of text, a "didactic discourse" rather than a narrative, Strecker and Kingsbury support their *conclusions about what the Sermon is and says* through an examination of the same historical/realistic dimension. There is no difficulty in conceiving of a study of the historical/realistic dimension of the Sermon on the Mount. Since the Sermon is addressed to the "disciples" (5:1–2), it can be read as a part of their historical/realistic narrative; it is presented by Matthew as the teaching of the "historical" Jesus to his "historical" disciples. The understanding of this teaching is, of course, a construct of Matthew, as the redactor of this Gospel; it is his view of the teaching of the historical Jesus, which he considers to be relevant for the first-century Christian community to whom he writes.

Thus in his redaction critical study,[2] Strecker strives to elucidate the way in which the teaching of the historical Jesus (to the historical disciples), as transmitted in traditions and sources, was redacted by Matthew for the sake of the Christian community of his time. Regarding our topic, we note that Strecker pays close attention to (1) discipleship as lived by the "historical" disciples/apostles viewed from the perspective of the intended readers, for whom they were the founders of the church; and (2) discipleship as the "reality" known to Matthew's community (the intended readers) on the basis of their own experience, namely, as the role played by the leaders of their community and as the ideal that church members strive to implement in their lives, even though they are far from this ideal goal.

From this perspective, Strecker expects to find in the Sermon on the Mount a description of discipleship that includes features that are anachronistic when viewed from the standpoint of the time of Jesus' ministry. In

---

1. An interpretation is legitimate whether it takes the form of the faith-interpretation of a believer (a *pro me* or *pro nobis* interpretation, which emphasizes the *conclusions about the teaching* of the text) or the form of a scholarly interpretation (which makes explicit the *conclusions about what the text is and says* that ground these *conclusions about the teaching* in a textual dimension).

2. Georg Strecker, *The Sermon on the Mount: An Exegetical Commentary*, trans. O. C. Dean Jr. (Nashville: Abingdon, 1988).

other words, the view of discipleship presented in this meaning-producing dimension is a composite picture of these two kinds of features, in which the "historical" is interpreted in terms of the "reality" known to the intended readers, and vice versa.

Similarly, in his *literary study*,[3] Kingsbury seeks to elucidate the coherence of the Sermon on the Mount in terms of the "story," or more precisely, in terms of the "realistic narrative" — since Kingsbury's primary concern is with "events," "characters," and "settings,"[4] i.e., with the features of the story as retold for the sake of the intended readers.[5] One should not be surprised that Kingsbury's conclusions are similar to Strecker's; their respective studies deal with the same textual dimension, although they view it from different methodological paradigms.[6]

Reading B: Narrative Critical Interpretation Focused on the Plot Dimension of the Sermon on the Mount

Our critical interpretation of the plot dimension of the Sermon on the Mount has to follow a procedure somewhat different from the one used in our study of Matthew 4:18–22 (see chap. 2, reading B), a narrative passage in which the plot dimension is quite obvious. Yet this dimension is no less important here, even if it is not as apparent.

To begin with, the plot dimension[7] is manifest in the narrative framework of the Sermon on the Mount (5:1–2 and 7:28–29). The proclamation of the Sermon by Jesus to certain actors/characters – the disciples and the crowds – is very much a part of the plot. On the basis of our interpretation of the preceding verses (4:18–25), we can already say that, by preaching or teaching this Sermon to novice disciples (the four fishers) and would-be disciples (the crowds), Jesus is beginning the process of making fishers of people out of them – he is making (full-fledged) disciples out of them. Thus a part of the plot dimension of the Sermon is elucidated by raising the question, How are

---

3. Jack D. Kingsbury, *Matthew as Story* (Minneapolis: Fortress, 1986), especially 58–70 and 103–19.

4. Kingsbury, *Matthew as Story*, 2–29.

5. Greimas would say "the features of the story as discursivized for the enunciatee." See each of these technical terms in A. J. Greimas and J. Courtés, *Semiotics and Language: An Analytical Dictionary*, trans. L. Crist, D. Patte, et al. (Bloomington: Indiana University Press, 1982). Bal would speak of the "ordering" and "narrating" of the fabula. See Mieke Bal, *Narratology: Introduction to the Theory of Narrative*, trans. C. van Boheemen (Toronto: University of Toronto Press, 1985), 11–47.

6. The realistic narrative, which is the "story discursivized for the sake of the intended readers" (the discursive syntax as defined in a semio-literary paradigm), corresponds to the "redaction of sources for the sake of Matthew's community" (the redactional dimension as defined in a historiographic paradigm). On the relations between these two paradigms, see Daniel Patte, *The Religious Dimensions of Biblical Texts: Greimas's Structural Semiotics and Biblical Exegesis*, SBL Semeia Studies (Atlanta: Scholars Press, 1990), 1–17; 173–215.

7. The "plot dimension" would be called by Greimas, "narrative syntax," and by Bal, "fabula." See Greimas and Courtés, *Semiotics and Language,* and Bal, *Narratology.*

the actors/characters to whom the Sermon is addressed affected by it? *The textual evidence for this matter is found outside the Sermon on the Mount proper — in its framework and beyond.*

We can formulate a similar question for elucidating another aspect of the plot dimension as expressed in the Sermon itself, What is the "ideal effect" of the Sermon (as a whole as well as each of its sections) on the "addressees"? When it is specified that the technical term "addressees" refers to the ideal readers implied by the text, one can recognize that this ideal effect on addressees is inscribed in the text; it is manifested by the literary form, the style, and other features that signal the rhetorical function of each passage. Since we know from the context and from the framework (4:18–5:2; 7:28–29) that this Sermon participates in the training of disciples, we can systematically examine this ideal effect of the discourse by asking of each section the more concrete question, How should this section ideally contribute to making full-fledged disciples out of these novice disciples and would-be disciples? In this light, it will appear, for instance, that because of their form and style the beatitudes function as a call to discipleship (a first explicit call for the crowds; a renewed call for the four former fishers). Additionally, it will be shown that by 7:12 the hearers should ideally have been transformed into full-fledged disciples, ready to carry out their vocation. Of course, the rest of the gospel story shows that this was not the actual effect of the Sermon on the Mount on the hearers (we will have to understand why this is the case). Yet this conclusion about what the Sermon is and says *will be quite significant for the interpretation of the effect of the concluding section, 7:13–27.*

A last and most important aspect of the plot dimension is the story of ideal disciples that the Sermon on the Mount presupposes and presents, somewhat haphazardly,[8] as a part of its rhetorical strategy to make disciples out of the addressees. In each of its sections, the Sermon on the Mount provides a preview of a part of the plot of the story of ideal disciples. We can anticipate that this ideal story includes the process of becoming full-fledged disciples, the process of carrying out one's mission as disciples, and its outcomes. The systematic study of this preview of the story of ideal disciples (performed by identifying the plot stage[s] to which each section of the Sermon refers) is all the more important in that it provides the conclusions about what the Sermon says about central aspects of discipleship (the basis for the conclusions about the teaching of the Sermon about discipleship; see chap. 5).

Since the legitimacy of the critical observations regarding the preview of the plot is further supported by showing the role of this preview in the rhetorical effect of the Sermon on its addressees, for each section we shall proceed in two steps (with additional ones as necessary): (1) a study of the preview of

---

8. The "logical (or chronological) sequence" of the plot-fabula should not be confused with the "sequential ordering" of the text aimed at realizing specific literary effects (on readers). See Bal, *Narratology*, 42–43, 51–68. What I call "story of ideal disciples," or, in short "ideal story," is what Bal would call "fabula."

the story of ideal disciples; and (2) a study of the ideal effect of the section on the addressees. The study of the framework of the Sermon on the Mount needs, of course, to be conducted in a different way.

Reading A, CAW 1: Critical Interpretations of the Historical/ Realistic Dimension — The Sermon's Framework (5:1-2; 7:28-29)

Reading A, CAW 1.1: What the Sermon Is — A Teaching Addressed to the Disciples for the Sake of the Crowds

A critical interpretation of the historical/realistic dimension spontaneously takes note of historical markers in the text. In the framework (5:1-2; 7:28-29), there is only one significant historical marker — the phrase οἱ μαθηταὶ αὐτοῦ ("his disciples," 5:1). It is read as referring to the historical disciples Peter, Andrew, James, and John who, in the unique and unrepeatable time of Jesus' ministry,[9] have abandoned everything to follow Jesus in unconditional obedience.[10] Furthermore, the mention that Jesus "sat down" is perceived as a realistic description of a teacher addressing his disciples;[11] the Sermon was a teaching addressed by Jesus to his disciples.

According to the historical/realistic dimension, the explanation that Jesus climbed on the mount "when he saw the crowds" (Ἰδὼν δὲ τοὺς ὄχλους, 5:1) indicates that this movement was made "in order to be visible and audible to the people [crowds] when he speaks."[12] In other words, as becomes clear in 7:28-29, the Sermon was not merely taught for the sake of the closed circle of the disciples/apostles, but also for the sake of the "crowds."[13]

It remains that the Sermon was most directly addressed to the disciples; the disciples formed an inner circle, and the crowds an outer circle.[14] The crowds did recognize the "authority" of Jesus and his teaching (7:29). Yet it is not enough to say "Lord, Lord" (cf. 7:21-23)! The crowds should have

---

9. Georg Strecker, "The Concept of History in Matthew," in *The Interpretation of Matthew,* ed. Graham Stanton (Philadelphia: Fortress, 1983), 70–74.

10. There are no other "historical" markers (names, temporal and geographical notations) in 5:1-2 (the "mountain" is not an identifiable location) and in the Sermon itself.

11. Strecker, *Sermon,* 25. This is noted by most commentators. See for instance, W. D. Davies, *The Setting of the Sermon on the Mount* (Cambridge: Cambridge University Press, 1964), 8; W. D. Davies and D. C. Allison Jr., *A Critical and Exegetical Commentary on the Gospel according to Saint Matthew,* vol. 1, ICC (Edinburgh: T. & T. Clark, 1988), 424; Ulrich Luz, *Matthew 1-7: A Commentary* (Minneapolis: Augsburg, 1989), 224; Robert Gundry, *Matthew: A Commentary on His Literary and Theological Art* (Grand Rapids: Eerdmans, 1982), 66; and Samuel Tobias Lachs, *A Rabbinic Commentary on the New Testament: The Gospels of Matthew, Mark and Luke* (Hoboken, N.J.: KTAV, 1987), 67. Lachs points out that this reference to sitting as a teaching position describes "a *late*-first-century practice," and is thus anachronistic realism.

12. Strecker, *Sermon,* 25.

13. Ibid., 26.

14. Ibid., *Sermon,* 25.

"done" this teaching also, but they were content to acknowledge Jesus' authority. The disciples alone were doers of Jesus' teaching, as they demonstrated by abandoning everything. In sum, this teaching is primarily for the disciples.

The crowds were in the outer circle so as to clarify that by giving this teaching to his disciples/apostles, founders of the church, Jesus was providing the instructions that they were to teach to the crowds, i.e., to the nations and to the church, in order to make out of them "disciples" (28:19–20).[15] In sum, the teaching of the Sermon on the Mount was also for the sake of the crowds, although they will receive it only indirectly through the ministry of the disciples/apostles.[16]

Reading A, CAW 1.2: Who Is Jesus? The Preacher on the Mount? The Eschatological Lord?

According to the historical/realistic dimension, the crowds' response to Jesus' teaching (Mt 7:29) confirms that Jesus' words have an unconditional authority (as in 4:18–22). This is an appropriate recognition of Jesus' exceptional authority (by contrast with reading B, CAW 1.2), which shows that the Preacher on the mount was, unlike the scribes (7:29), "the eschatological Lord and Son of God, the revealer of God's will,"[17] indeed, the one who had "all authority in heaven and on earth" (28:18)[18] — a status and eschatological authority that, in this dimension, Jesus had since his birth (1:18–25) and that he claimed during his ministry (e.g., 11:25–30).[19] This conclusion will be further supported as we examine the historical/realistic representation of Jesus in the Sermon itself.[20]

---

15. Jack D. Kingsbury, "The Verb *Akolouthein* ('to Follow') as an Index of Matthew's View of His Community," *Journal of Biblical Literature* 97 (1978): 73. In his redaction critical study, Kingsbury reaches this conclusion by taking note of the way in which Matthew redacted his sources for the sake of the Christian community of his time. See also Strecker, *Sermon*, 14, 178–81.

16. Let us not forget that the historical/realistic dimension of any passage must be read from the perspective of the time of the writing, and thus with a knowledge of the founding of the churches by the apostles, or, and this amounts to the same thing, with a knowledge of the end of the realistic narrative.

17. Strecker, *Sermon*, 26.

18. Thus Strecker (*Sermon*, 178) emphasizes that for Matthew, the one who teaches the Sermon on the Mount is "the now exalted Kyrios."

19. In contrast with the teaching expressed by the narrative plot dimension (below) and by the thematic dimension (see chap. 4), according to which Jesus receives "all authority" only after his death and resurrection. From these perspectives, during Jesus' ministry, the nature of his authority remains ambiguous; it is only after the cross and the resurrection that its actual character appears. In such readings, one interprets 1:18–21 and 11:25–30 in terms of other passages that point out the limitations of Jesus' authority (e.g., 20:23; 24:36) or that point out that the disciples and certain others have or should have an authority comparable to Jesus' (e.g., 1:1–17; 10:7–8; 21:18–22).

20. Matthew 7:29 is not sufficient to support this CAW. After all, the crowds are not necessarily trustworthy characters!

Reading A, CAW 1.3: What the Sermon as an Eschatological Teaching Is: An Absolute Expression of God's Eternal Will

Because Jesus is the eschatological Lord, his teaching is an absolute expression of God's will for disciples of all times. As Strecker says, it is "the binding Law of the *Kyrios* who is coming and has already come."[21] This teaching is normative for the historical disciples and also for the intended readers — the members of Matthew's church, who must implement it in their daily life.

Since this teaching is eschatological, we can anticipate that as we examine this dimension of the Sermon itself, we will find that those who do this teaching adopt an eschatological way of life and thus enter a domain that can be appropriately described as the "sphere of God's eschatological Rule."[22] Does this mean that the church is viewed, in this dimension of the Sermon, as the eschatological community governed by this eschatological teaching — which then would provide criteria for determining who belongs to it and who does not? This is another question we will need to keep in mind as we read Strecker's and Kingsbury's interpretations of the Sermon on the Mount itself.

Reading A, CAW 1.4: The Sermon Is an Epitome; It Teaches Basic Ethical Principles Rather Than Parenetic Sayings Demanding Literal Implementation

In an interpretation focused on the historical/realistic dimension such as Strecker's, the Sermon on the Mount is simply divided in three parts: (1) the opening, Matthew 5:3–20 (defining the nature of discipleship and the nature of the teaching of the Sermon); (2) the body of the Sermon, Matthew 5:21—7:12 (a series of commands that should govern the life of disciples); and (3) the closing, Matthew 7:13–27 (admonitions to do this teaching).[23]

This breakdown already shows that the organization of these instructions does not have a particular significance, as is the case with any parenetic text,[24] or more precisely, with any text that has a parenetic historical/realistic dimension. Cargal's summary of the characteristics of parenesis according to Dibelius can directly be applied to the Sermon on the Mount:

---

21. Strecker, *Sermon*, 179.

22. Kingsbury, *Matthew as Story*, 104–5.

23. Strecker, *Sermon*, 14–15.

24. As Martin Dibelius emphasized regarding James (*James*, Hermeneia, revised by H. Greeven [Philadelphia: Fortress, 1975], 5–11). A part of what makes a discourse realistic is its use of certain conventions, including literary genres. Hence, the importance of determining literary conventions, literary forms, and literary genres in a critical interpretation focused on the historical/realistic dimension. This point is emphasized in Timothy Cargal, *Restoring the Diaspora: Discursive Structure and Purpose in the Epistle of James* (Atlanta: Scholars Press, 1993), 9–29.

First, parenetic literature is marked by a "pervasive *eclecticism*" arising from its chief concern for "the transmission of an ethical tradition
that does not require a radical revision." Second, the "stringing together of saying after saying is the most common form of paraenesis"
that leads to the *"lack of continuity"* characteristic of all parenesis
literature. Finally, parenetic literature served as a kind of repository
of traditional ethical admonitions. As a result, these admonitions "do
not apply to a single audience and a single set of circumstances; *it is
not possible to construct a single frame into which they will all fit.*"[25]

Note the emphasis on the acontextual and thus universal character of parenesis, which is conveyed by its fragmented presentation. This literary form
is, therefore, well suited to convey the teachings of the Sermon as expressions of God's eternal will. Yet Strecker does not emphasize this literary
form of the Sermon, I suspect, because of its implications. As a universal moral teaching, each parenetic statement can easily be understood as
a teaching that must be carried out literally — a legalistic interpretation
that Strecker rejects. Although the Sermon on the Mount has a parenetic
literary form (and therefore could legitimately be interpreted in a legalistic
way), one needs to be more specific regarding its literary genre. I believe
Strecker's critical interpretation is supported by Betz's identification of a
more specific literary genre.

For Betz, the specific (parenetic) literary genre of the Sermon on the
Mount is the epitome.[26] As an Epicurean epitome does, the Sermon is
"training" (ἄσκησις) readers to theological-ethical reflection and practice
(μελετᾶν) by presenting them with the most characteristic teachings of
Jesus. In this way, the readers are put in a position of appropriating these
teachings and of creatively developing and implementing them in concrete
life situations.[27] The relative significance of these teachings depends less on
their place in the Sermon than on the concrete situations with which the
readers are confronted. Consequently, from this perspective, the Sermon is
primarily a list of ethical instructions that can be taken up independently of
each other. But these instructions do not express what one should literally

---

25. Cargal, *Restoring the Diaspora,* 17 (citing Dibelius).

26. Hans Dieter Betz, *Essays on the Sermon on the Mount,* trans. L. L. Welborn (Minneapolis: Fortress, 1985), 1–16; and *The Sermon on the Mount, Including the Sermon on
the Plain (Matthew 5:3–7:27 and Luke 6:20–49): A Commentary on Two Early Christian
Manuals of Discipleship,* Hermeneia, ed. Adela Yarbro Collins (Minneapolis: Fortress, 1995),
72–80. My only objection is that Betz claims here and implies elsewhere that any reading of
the Sermon that does not take into account its *epitome* genre is illegitimate. My point is that
while taking this genre into account is important for a reading of the Sermon focused on the
historical/realistic dimension, readings of the Sermon focused on other dimensions need not —
indeed, should not — do so.

27. See Betz, *Essays,* 7–9, 15–16. Even though Strecker did not recognize that the literary
genre of the Sermon on the Mount is the epitome, his *conclusions about what the text says*
show that he envisions the Sermon on the Mount exactly in this way.

do; they represent how certain basic principles (the actual expressions of God's will) *should be implemented in various ways in different situations* (one of Strecker's main *conclusions about the teaching* of the Sermon for us; see chap. 5, reading B, CAT 1.24).

The critical interpretation of the Sermon on the Mount (focused on the historical/realistic dimension) needs therefore to be a redaction critical study, which shows how Matthew reinterpreted his sources for the sake of the Christian community of his time. This reinterpretation process illustrates the very message that the Sermon conveys — the knowledge of how to reinterpret the law and Jesus' own teaching so as to implement them in a new situation.

Reading B, CAW 1: A Critical Interpretation of the Plot Dimension of the Sermon's Framework (5:1–2; 7:28–8:1)

Reading B, CAW 1.1: Matthew 5:3–7:27: A Sermon Addressed to Both Novice Disciples and Crowds

A critical interpretation of the plot dimension first identifies the place of the Sermon on the Mount in the unfolding of the story under study, here the story of the disciples as a subplot of the story of Jesus.

We noted (see chap. 2, reading B) that the beginning of the story of the disciples (4:18–25) is ambivalent regarding the composition of the collective actor-character, "disciples." It presents two groups of "followers" as potential disciples, either as novice disciples in the case of the former fishers who, as a result of Jesus' call, want to be made "fishers of people" or as "would-be disciples" in the case of the crowds who follow Jesus because of his fame as healer. Because of this ambivalence, one can expect that the Sermon is addressed to both groups, as is actually expressed by its narrative framework (5:1–2 and 7:28–8:1).

In Matthew 5:1–2, the Sermon on the Mount is presented as a teaching addressed to "his disciples" (οἱ μαθηταὶ αὐτοῦ), who must be identified as the former fishers because they are distinguished from the crowds, who are also present. Yet 7:28–29 explicitly describes its effect on the crowds; the Sermon is also addressed to them. After hearing it (7:28–29), the crowds, who originally followed Jesus because of his fame and his power/authority as healer, now follow him (8:1) also because they acknowledge his authority as teacher: "The crowds were astonished at his teaching, for he taught them as one having authority, and not as their scribes. When Jesus came down from the mountain, great crowds followed him" (7:28b–8:1).[28]

---

28. This conclusion is similar to that of Kennedy in his rhetorical interpretation of the Sermon on the Mount. See George A. Kennedy, *New Testament Interpretation through Rhetorical Criticism* (Chapel Hill, N.C., and London: University of North Carolina Press, 1984), 39–42. Since the interpretation of the plot demands that we consider the effect of this text as a ser-

Reading B, CAW 1.2: Jesus' Twofold Role of Preacher and Teacher of the Sermon

Are the crowds in the process of being transformed into novice disciples (as the four fishers were)? The style of the text shows that this is indeed the function of the Sermon in the plot, as we shall see below (reading B, CAW 1.3). But before discussing this point, we need to note that since Jesus addresses two groups, his narrative role is certainly twofold, as is also suggested in Matthew 4:23 (where Jesus is presented as teacher, preacher, and healer).

Jesus is a preacher. By proclaiming the Sermon on the Mount, Jesus addresses a call to the members of the crowds, inviting them to join the novice disciples — a call comparable to the one he addressed to the four fishers. Consequently, we can expect that, as in 4:18–22, Jesus' role will be to convince people to agree (establish their will) to be made disciples. For this, Jesus has to make promises to them and show them that these promises are trustworthy. There is no unconditional command and extraordinary authority here (by contrast with reading A, CAW 1.2); although Jesus' authority still needs to be acknowledged,[29] it cannot be the authority of the eschatological Lord. The unfolding of the plot of the Gospel is clear; it is only after his death and resurrection (see 28:18) that Jesus has this kind of authority, not when he preaches the Sermon on the Mount. Actually, its end (7:21–27) maintains that the confidence that one gains from acknowledging and affirming Jesus' authority as the eschatological Lord is a false confidence. Then the crowds' acknowledgment of Jesus' authority in 7:28–29 is ambivalent. At any rate, it cannot be taken as a sign that the crowds have become novice disciples.

Jesus is a teacher. He also addresses the Sermon to his (novice) disciples in order to train them; he begins to make fishers of people out of them.[30] We will have to wonder in what ways the Sermon contributes to the training of the novice disciples. We can expect that it will provide the characters (and readers) with some indications of what their transformation into disciples/fishers of people entails. The critical study of the plot dimension involves the elucidation of how this Sermon contributes to the unfolding of the plot (the transformation of ordinary people into full-fledged disciples) and the identification of the features of the Sermon that reveal the trajectory (the main stages) of this plot.

---

mon on its hearers, it necessarily overlaps with a rhetorical analysis. I will note other points at which the reading focused on the plot overlaps with Kennedy's rhetorical analysis.

29. As will be underscored in the CATs. See Kennedy, *Rhetorical Criticism*, 50.

30. Kennedy (*Rhetorical Criticism*, 47) expresses a similar point by saying that the audience does not need to be convinced to have faith. Yet he does not make a distinction between the rhetorical effect of the Sermon on two different audiences, crowds and disciples. On the other hand, Kennedy does point out how the Sermon would affect different hearers in the church (42).

Reading B, CAW 1.3: The Sermon on the Mount Is a Call to Discipleship

The style of the Sermon confirms the above suggestion that one of its narrative functions is to call the crowds to discipleship. As one seeks to elucidate how the preaching of the Sermon contributes to the unfolding of the plot, and thus how it affects actors/characters, one notes the interplay between impersonal and personal styles in this text. In most of the Sermon, we find a direct, personal style, marked by the use of "you," which is addressed to the novice disciples to whom Jesus speaks most directly (5:2). Yet both the introduction (the beatitudes, 5:3–10)[31] and the conclusion (the warnings to those who do not do these words, 7:21-27) are in the impersonal style. For instance, we do not read, "Blessed are you poor, for yours is the kingdom" (Lk 6:20), but, "Blessed are the poor in spirit, for theirs is the kingdom" (Mt 5:3). Similarly, in the conclusion, we read, "Every one who says to me, 'Lord, Lord'" (Mt 7:21).

The impersonal style of the introduction shows that the audience of the beatitudes (5:3–10) and, consequently, of the entire Sermon includes everyone who wants to listen, and thus the crowds.

The impersonal conclusion (7:21–27) confirms this observation. It is addressed to "everyone" who claims to be a (novice) disciple by calling Jesus "Lord" (7:21-23). This group clearly includes other people in addition to the former fishers. From the perspective of the story, it includes all those who follow Jesus for the wrong reasons, and more specifically those who follow him simply because they believe in him as one who has authority as the eschatological Lord (7:21-23). Is this not what the crowds do when they are astounded by his authority? By the end of the Sermon, are not at least some members of the crowds in danger of claiming that they are Jesus' (novice) disciples, although they are not really? Did they fail to respond appropriately to the call Jesus addressed to them by means of the Sermon? This is quite possible. Yet this does not prevent the Sermon from being a call to discipleship. It makes it a genuine call, which might or might not elicit a positive response.

---

31. When considering the effect of the Sermon on the actors/characters (disciples and crowds), our subdivision of the text must take into account the shift from impersonal to personal style. Thus the beatitudes must be limited to 5:3–10, with Jack M. Suggs, *Wisdom, Christology, and Law in Matthew's Gospel* (Cambridge: Harvard University Press, 1970), 121–27; Eduard Schweizer, *The Good News according to Matthew* (Atlanta: John Knox Press, 1975), 82; Gundry, *Matthew*, 73; Robert A. Guelich, *The Sermon on the Mount: A Foundation for Understanding* (Waco, Tex.: Word, 1992), 93; John P. Meier, *Matthew* (Wilmington, Del.: M. Glazier, 1980), 39; Jan Lambrecht, *"Eh bien! Moi je vous dis," Le discours-programme de Jésus (Mt 5–7; Lc 6, 20–49)* (Paris: Cerf, 1986), 61; and N. J. McEleney, "The Principles of the Sermon on the Mount," *Catholic Biblical Quarterly* 41 (1979): 552–70, among others. Yet the Sermon must be subdivided differently when considering the features that contribute to make out of the gospel a discourse addressed to the intended readers (either the historical/realistic dimension or the figurative dimension). Thus for instance, Strecker (*Sermon*, 27–47), Davies and Allison (*Matthew*, 429–67), and Luz (*Matthew*, 224–46) treat 5:3–12 as a unit.

Reading B, CAW 1.4: The Sermon Contributes to Making Fishers
of People out of the Novice Disciples

The personal part of the Sermon (the central part [5:11–7:20] addressed to
"you") is directed at novice disciples, i.e., to the four former fishers, and also
to all those from the crowds who would have been convinced by the impersonal beatitudes (5:3–10) to agree to be made fishers of people. Thus this
central part will have to be divided in terms of the function of each passage
in the training of the disciples.

   These observations show that in studying the Sermon as a part of the story
of the disciples, we must evaluate how it affects the characters. At first, we
must evaluate the ideal effect of the impersonal beatitudes (5:3–10) on two
separate groups: their effect on the former fishers (who are already novice disciples) and their effect on the crowds (who ideally are made novice disciples
by the beatitudes). Beginning with 5:11, the rest of the Sermon should ideally
have the same effect on both groups; it is presupposed that the members of
the crowds have been convinced to become novice disciples.

   In order to account for different kinds of effects on the novice disciples,
we subdivide the rest of the Sermon as follows:

1. 5:3–10: The Beatitudes: A preview of important stages of the disciples'
   story and a call to discipleship

2. 5:11–16: The Disciples' Vocation: Further preview of their story; further
   establishment of the will to be disciples

3. 5:17–19: Conditions for being great in the kingdom

4. 5:20–6:21: Conditions for entering the kingdom — adopting a radical
   behavior

5. 6:22–7:12: Conditions for adopting the radical mode of behavior
   required of disciples

6. 7:13–27: The urgency of the disciples' mission

Reading A, CAW 2: Matthew 5:3–12: The Beatitudes: An Ethical Teaching for the Eschatological Community under God's Rule

Reading A, CAW 2.0: The Beatitudes Reflect the Self-Consciousness of
the Community

In the historical/realistic dimension, the beatitudes encompass 5:3–12 (including 5:11–12, the ninth beatitudes in personal style; and not merely
5:3–10 as below, reading B, CAW 2)[32] because the "blessed ones" as well
as the "you" are unambiguously identified with the disciples.

---

32. Strecker, *Sermon*, 30. As we shall see, studies focused on the figurative dimension (Luz,
Matthew, 224–46, and Davies and Allison, *Matthew*, 430) also do not make any distinction
between impersonal and personal styles.

Since the disciples are idealized and envisioned in terms of the rest of their history as having a permanent and stable identity, the beatitudes are perceived as a threefold *description* of the actual status of the disciples: they *are* "blessed"; they *are* people with a specific way of life; they *are* people who, as a community, already belong to "the sphere of God's eschatological Rule."[33] The beatitudes reflect "the self-consciousness of the community."[34]

Reading A, CAW 2.1: Disciples Are "Blessed"

Jesus simply states, and thus reveals to the disciples, what is the reality of their status after their obedient response to his call (provided they do not forfeit their "status" as disciples). They *are* blessed.

Reading A, CAW 2.2: The "Indicative" of the Beatitudes Is Also "Imperative," Expressing an Admonition or a Command

True disciples *are* people with a specific, ethical way of life: they *are* "poor in spirit," etc. This is "the kinds of persons Jesus' disciples are"[35] from the beginning, even if they have not yet had occasion to implement these qualities. A comparison of the beatitudes in Matthew 5:3–12 with the beatitudes in Luke 6:20–23 and the reconstructed beatitudes of the historical Jesus shows that Matthew has ethicized the beatitudes.[36] True disciples are lowly in spirit, humble ("poor in spirit," 5:3);[37] grieve over the world[38] or over their sins[39] ("mourning," 5:4); have a humility demonstrated in kindness ("meek," 5:5; about Jesus, 11:29);[40] strive to behave righteously ("hunger and thirst for righteousness," 5:6);[41] are "merciful" (5:7; obvi-

---

33. Kingsbury, *Matthew as Story*, 107. I underscored the verb (*are*) so as to call attention to the atemporal way in which Kingsbury refers to the disciples, a characteristic feature of the historical/realistic dimension.

34. Betz, *Essays*, 35. Betz's studies of the Sermon on the Mount fall in two categories; at times (as here), his focus is on the historical/realistic dimension; at other times, in the history of religion essays, his focus is on the figurative dimension.

35. Kingsbury, *Matthew as Story*, 107.

36. Strecker, *Sermon*, 28–47. Of course, the ethical character of the beatitudes in 5:3–12 is also recognized by the commentators who focus their interpretation on the figurative dimension, e.g., Luz, *Matthew*, 224–46; Davies and Allison, *Matthew*, 429–67.

37. Jacques Dupont, *Les béatitudes* (Paris: Gabalda, 1969–73), 3:457–71; Strecker, *Sermon*, 30–34; Strecker, "Die Makarismen der Bergpredigt," *New Testament Studies* 17 (1970/71): 262.

38. Rudolf Bultmann, "Πένθος, Πενθέω," in *Theological Dictionary of the New Testament*, ed. G. Kittel and G. Friedrich, trans. G. W. Bromiley (Grand Rapids: Eerdmans, 1964–74), 6:40–43.

39. As in James 4:9. Strecker, *Sermon*, 34–35.

40. The translation "meek" is misleading because it suggests a nonviolent attitude that πραεῖς does not have. Strecker, *Sermon*, 35–36.

41. A behavior, and not, in this perspective, a longing for righteousness as something to be given by God (God's righteousness). Strecker, *Sermon*, 36–38. This beatitude keeps its ethical character even if one interprets it as referring to the "righteousness of God" as a gift, while underscoring that the disciples' duty is to "search" actively for this righteousness, as is expressed in 6:33; Betz, *Essays*, 114–15. It amounts to having a behavior worthy of God's righteousness.

ously an ethical behavior); "fulfill the demand of righteousness" with a good conscience[42] ("pure in heart," 5:8); are "peacemakers" (5:9; again, an obviously ethical behavior); are persecuted because of their righteous behavior ("persecuted for righteousness' sake," 5:10)[43] or because they follow the "way of righteousness" (21:32) taught by Jesus ("persecuted ... on my account," 5:11–12).[44] It is only insofar as one has such an ethical behavior that one can truly claim to be a disciple. These features of the beatitudes are comparable to "the cultic list of virtues of the Old Testament"[45] and define "the kinds of persons Jesus' disciples are,"[46] an "indicative" that is simultaneously an "imperative," expressing an admonition or a command.[47]

Reading A, CAW 2.3: God's Eschatological Rule Is Proleptically Realized in the Community of Disciples Who Carry Out God's Eternal Will

In this historical/realistic dimension, the beatitudes are at the same time what the intended readers should perceive as a realistic description of their historical situation. They are reviled and persecuted by people who "utter all kinds of evil against" them (5:11). They need admonitions to be faithful disciples (the very fact that the beatitudes are "ethicized" is a realistic feature). They nevertheless are those to whom these blessings are addressed because, despite their imperfection, they strive to obey these admonitions. Disciples *are* people who as a community already belong to "the sphere of God's eschatological Rule."[48]

In my view, this latter assertion by Kingsbury is the most adequate interpretation of the relations between present and future blessings in the historical/realistic dimension. First, it accounts for the proclamation that the disciples *are* now blessed, μακάριοι, and that this present blessing is related to the future blessing (in the future kingdom of heaven). Second, speaking of the community of disciples as "the sphere of God's eschatological Rule" indicates that it is the community formed by people who carry out God's eternal will as expressed by the eschatological Lord (as Strecker emphasizes), and who are promised eschatological blessings ("theirs is the kingdom"; "they shall be comforted"; etc.) that belong to the apocalyptic future, as the tense of the verbs in 5:4–9 shows.[49] This is the "reward"

42. Strecker, *Sermon*, 39.
43. Strecker, *Sermon*, 42.
44. When interpreted in terms of 5:10, although it can also be interpreted as persecuted for proclaiming Jesus. Strecker, *Sermon*, 43–45.
45. Strecker, *Sermon*, 33.
46. Kingsbury, *Matthew as Story*, 107.
47. Strecker, *Sermon*, 33–34. This "ethicization" of the beatitudes is seen by Strecker as a part of the general "ethicization" of Jesus' teaching by Matthew: Strecker, "Concept of History," 74–77; "Die Makarismen," 255–75.
48. Kingsbury, *Matthew as Story*, 104–10.
49. Strecker, *Sermon*, 31.

that disciples shall receive "in heaven" (5:12). Yet in this dimension, these promises about the kingdom of heaven (5:3, 10) are also proleptically real- ized, although in a quite specific sense, which is elucidated by taking note of the way in which Matthew redacted the teaching of the historical Jesus. Thus the beatitudes as ethical teachings (that will lead to these rewards) are themselves blessings for the hearers: God's demands are a gift for the believers.[50]

Since, in the historical/realistic dimension of Matthew's redaction, the beatitudes have been ethicized, the promise that "theirs is the kingdom of heaven" is no longer understood as a promise of a glorious future to the poor, the hungry, and the mourning. With its strong ethical connotations, the kingdom is understood as "the reign of heaven." "Just as the rabbis admonish people to carry already now the yoke of the reign of God, it is decisive for Matthew to live in the present in agreement with the βασιλεία τῶν οὐρανῶν so that the community will be granted at the end the entrance into the reign of heaven."[51] Thus the members of the church viewed them- selves as "disciples," because "they had taken on themselves [Jesus'] yoke and were 'learning' from him."[52] Consequently, for them God's eschatologi- cal rule (or "reign") is indeed proleptically realized in the community: both the group of historical disciples and the church of Matthew's time. Thus Strecker concludes, "The passive of the eschatological future [in 5:4, 6, 7, 9] speaks of God's action, which will be revealed at the end of the world but is already happening in the present."[53]

In this historical/realistic dimension, this statement has an ethical sense: God's action is already happening in the present *of a community of disci- ples who strive to fulfill God's eternal will* revealed by the eschatological Lord. For instance, even though such disciples are still longing for the com- plete fulfillment of these promises (these rewards "in heaven," 5:12), they are already comforted (by the very declaration that they *are* and *will be* blessed);[54] they already obtain mercy (as they pray, "forgive us our debts, as we also have forgiven our debtors" (6:12); they are already called "sons of God" (cf. 5:45);[55] they are already part of "God's eschatological rule," the kingdom as realized in the community (be it in Jesus' or Matthew's

---

50. Strecker, "Die Makarismen," 274.

51. Luz, *Matthew,* 167. This is Luz's comment on Matthew 3:2, which is in direct contrast with his interpretation of the beatitudes as "nonrealized eschatology" (*Matthew,* 235, 245– 46). In sum, as he read 3:2, Luz adopted an interpretation focused on the historical/realistic dimension, which is in tension with the rest of his interpretation, focused as it is on the figu- rative dimension. These kinds of inconsistencies (passing from one dimension to another, and thus trying to integrate interpretations in tension with each other) are common as long as one practices one-dimensional exegesis.

52. Kingsbury, *Matthew as Story,* 129.

53. Strecker, *Sermon,* 35.

54. Ibid., 29.

55. Kingsbury, *Matthew as Story,* 129. As we shall see, the sex-exclusive vocabulary is consistent with the interpretation of this meaning-producing dimension.

times). By submitting to the commands of Jesus and being "poor in spirit," etc., the disciples submitted to God's rule, and entered its sphere.

Reading A, CAW 2.4: What the Beatitudes Are: A Realistic Description of the Historical Disciples

In sum, the description of the "historical" disciples (the Twelve) in the beatitudes as "blessed" is "realistic" for the intended readers because Christians can view their own participation in the church as a blessing — the blessing of participating in the eschatological community under God's rule. Disciples *are* blessed (the indicative). Simultaneously, they are fully aware that the community and each of its members are far from perfect; consequently, the reality of their situation leads them to perceive the beatitudes as a series of admonitions (the imperative).[56] Disciples *are* those people with the way of life specified by the beatitudes. Truly belonging to the sphere of God's eschatological rule and, at the end, receiving eternal blessings demand fulfilling God's will.

In reading A, the hearers of the Sermon are *willing* to be disciples; the problem is that they do *not know* what is their status and what they should do. It is this problem the beatitudes (and the rest of the Sermon) address.

The perception of the problem that needs to be addressed is perceived in quite a different way, from the perspective of reading B.

Reading B, CAW 2: Matthew 5:3–10, The Beatitudes — A Preview of Important Stages of the Disciples' Story and a Call to Discipleship

Reading B, CAW 2.0: The Beatitudes Are Addressed to Both the Disciples and the Crowds

In the plot dimension, the beatitudes encompass 5:3 – 10 (not 5:11 – 12). Because the Sermon is considered as a discourse through which the addresser (Jesus) seeks to affect the addressees (disciples and crowds), it is necessary to take into account the change from impersonal to personal style; it signals a shift in the relationship between addresser and addressees. Thus we have to examine how 5:3 – 10 by itself affects each of the two groups of addressees. For the novice disciples, the beatitudes give a preview of the rest of their story; for the crowds, they are a call to discipleship.

---

56. Redaction critics discuss in this context the different understandings of the relationship between "indicative" and "imperative" in Paul (for whom the "indicative" is "grace" on which the "imperative" is based) and in the Sermon (in which the "imperative" is a form of "grace"). Cf., e.g., Strecker, *Sermon*, 33–34; Luz, *Matthew*, 245–46, 253; Jean Zumstein, *La condition du croyant dans l'évangile selon Matthieu* (Göttingen: Vandenhoeck & Ruprecht, 1977), 303.

Reading B, CAW 2.1: The Beatitudes Give a Preview of the Story of the Disciples

The beatitudes as proclamations of blessings invite novice disciples to identify themselves with the blessed ones, i.e., with full-fledged disciples. Consequently, the descriptions of the blessed ones (poor in spirit, mourning, meek, etc.) and the depictions of the blessings ("theirs is the kingdom," "they shall be comforted," etc.) offer a preview of various stages of the story of disciples.

The descriptions of the blessed ones express what being a disciple entails. In the first two beatitudes (5:3–4), these descriptions are related to the beginning of the story of the former fishers. Are they not "poor in spirit," οἱ πτωχοὶ τῷ πνεύματι (5:3), since they immediately obeyed Jesus' command (4:20, 22) — rather than calculating the pros and cons of this decision, as people who believe they know how to make such decisions on their own (people "rich in spirit") would do? Are not James and John mourning, πενθοῦντες (5:4) because of being separated from their father, Zebedee (4:22)? But the rest of the descriptions (the blessed ones as meek, thirsting and hungering for righteousness, merciful, pure in heart, peacemakers, and persecuted; cf. 5:5–10) do not apply to the four fishers introduced in the preceding verses (4:18–22). These are descriptions of full-fledged disciples, which specify what following Jesus to become "fishers of people" entails beyond leaving one's family and usual activities. Beyond this, discipleship involves having a specific spiritual attitude (being meek, pure in heart); acting in a specific way toward other people (being thirsty and hungry for righteousness,[57] merciful, peacemakers); and being persecuted for righteousness' sake.

These descriptions of what disciples do provide a sketch of one of the later stages of the story of the disciples: how they will behave and what will happen to them when they carry out their mission (which might itself entail other things they will have to do).

The descriptions of the disciples' blessings present still later stages of their story. As a consequence of their behavior (and thus at a later stage of their story), the disciples will receive immediate[58] blessings (they are declared "blessed," μακάριοι), the confidence that the kingdom of heaven is theirs (5:3, 10). Later on, they will receive additional blessings (in the kingdom): they will be comforted, inherit the earth, be satisfied, obtain mercy, see God, be called children of God (5:4–9). These are rewards, positive consequences for faithfully carrying out their mission, which refer to the ultimate stages of the story of the disciples.

---

57. "Righteousness" being understood, here and in the rest of the Sermon, as the right conduct required by God, especially toward other people. On this point, the understanding of righteousness differs neither from the interpretation focused on the historical/realistic dimension (see Strecker, *Sermon*, 36–38), nor from that focused on the figurative dimension (see Davies and Allison, *Matthew*, 452–53).

58. See the present tense of the verb (ἐστιν) in 5:3, 10.

In sum, these verses give the novice disciples a preview of at least three stages of the plot of their story: (1) their behavior as faithful disciples; (2) receiving rewards in the present; (3) receiving rewards in the eschatological future.

Reading B, CAW 2.2: The Ideal Effect of the Beatitudes on the Crowds as a Verbal Call to Discipleship; Many Are Called to Discipleship

The beatitudes affect the crowds like a call to discipleship because despite obvious differences the beatitudes and the call of the four fishers are similar. Jesus' call to the four fishers (4:19) has three features. It includes: (1) a command, "Come with me" (Δεῦτε ὀπίσω μου), that expresses what they should do (yet this is not an unconditional command that by itself would establish their will); (2) a promise, "I will make you fishers of people" (ποιήσω ὑμᾶς ἁλιεῖς ἀνθρώπων), that establishes their will to do what is commanded (they want to be made "fishers of people"); (3) an expression of the authority/ trustworthiness of Jesus (their positive response expresses that they trust Jesus' promise).

Each of the beatitudes also has these three components: (1) it expresses what disciples should do (being poor in spirit, mourning, etc.; cf. 5:3–10); each beatitude demands that the disciples commit themselves to a specific way of life;[59] (2) each beatitude includes a promise: "theirs is the kingdom of heaven" (ὅτι αὐτῶν ἐστιν ἡ βασιλεία τῶν οὐρανῶν), "they shall be comforted," etc. (cf. 5:3–10);[60] (3) each beatitude expresses the authority/ trustworthiness of Jesus; as blessing (macarism, cf. μακάριοι), a beatitude is a word that has the power to bring about a new reality, "blessedness." By uttering beatitudes, Jesus presents himself as one who is in a position to make such a promise in the name of God.[61]

Since the beatitudes have the same features as Jesus' call of the four fishers, they potentially have the same function — a call to discipleship aimed at establishing the will of the addressees.[62] Ideally, those to whom the blessings (including the kingdom) are promised by the beatitudes would want

---

59. The fact that the beatitudes are "ethicized," as Strecker emphasizes (see above), is thus taken into account.

60. The "promises" are particularly apparent in the central beatitudes (5:4–9), where they are in the future tense (e.g., "they *shall* be comforted"). But "theirs is the kingdom" (5:3, 10) is also a promise. Furthermore, the promises involved in the beatitudes, i.e., the effect of the beatitudes as blessings, should not be overlooked.

61. On blessings as authoritative words that transform a situation, see W. Beardslee, *Literary Criticism of the New Testament,* Guides to Biblical Scholarship (Philadelphia: Fortress, 1970), 27ff. See also Kennedy, *Rhetorical Criticism,* 50.

62. This is in general agreement with Kennedy's rhetorical interpretation of the Sermon as deliberative, i.e., as aimed at persuading the audience to take some action. This involves the establishment of the will. Thus the beatitudes display classical ploys of deliberative rhetoric, such as the reference to self-interest and thus rewards, but also the use of phrases such as συμφέρει σοι, it is expedient for you (5:29, 30), which is characteristic of classical deliberative oratory." See Kennedy, *Rhetorical Criticism,* 46.

to receive these blessings. Who would not want to receive such blessings! Thus ideally they would want to identify themselves with the blessed ones, and thus they would want to adopt the behavior demanded from disciples, and thus they would want to become disciples. To whom are the beatitudes addressed? Who are those who are called to discipleship by them? The impersonal style of the beatitudes shows that they are addressed to anyone who wants to listen. Consequently, they are addressed to the crowds as much as they are addressed to the novice disciples, as discussed below.

In sum, according to the plot dimension, many are called to become disciples. Even if it is in an impersonal style, Jesus addresses a verbal call not only to a few individuals but also to all the individuals who form the crowds. The crowds are in a position almost as good as that of the former fishers for responding positively to this call. By following Jesus (4:25), the crowds show that they trust that Jesus has the power/authority to give them blessings; he has healed their sick (4:23-24). Thus trusting in the promises that Jesus utters in the form of beatitudes should not present any difficulty for the crowds. Of course, they would want to receive the kingdom of heaven and the other blessings promised by the beatitudes, in the same way that they avail themselves of the blessings offered by Jesus by bringing him their sick (4:24).

We can conclude that, ideally, the crowds would want to identify themselves with the blessed ones; their will to become disciples would be established. Along with the former fishers, the crowds would want to accept the general and permanent commitment to adopt the attitudes requested of disciples.

Reading B, CAW 2.3: The Ideal Effect of the Beatitudes on the Novice Disciples — a Call to a More Permanent Commitment

Thus far in the story, the novice disciples (the former fishers) are exclusively qualified by their will to follow Jesus — a will established by Jesus' call (4:19; see chap. 2, reading B, CAW 4). For such hearers, the beatitudes are a renewed call, as well as a specification of their first call. Ideally, they should want to identify themselves with the blessed ones — full-fledged disciples — as they are encouraged to do by the first two beatitudes (5:3-4) in which they can recognize themselves (as being poor in spirit, and mourning).

Yet for them the beatitudes are not simply a repetition of Jesus' original call. The promise of the original call concerned the disciples' vocation: "I will make you fishers of people." The promises of the beatitudes concern rewards that the disciples will receive for carrying out their vocation. In effect, the beatitudes say to the novice disciples, "You should indeed want to be made fishers of people and disciples because of the blessings that you will receive as rewards for being disciples." Thus the beatitudes presuppose that, despite their positive response to Jesus' original call, the novice disciples' will is not yet fully and firmly established. This is not surprising. Anybody's will to do *something is quite fragile; one often changes one's mind! The fishers' "imme-diate" positive response to Jesus' laconic call was a real commitment, yet it was a blind commitment without clear awareness of what it entailed. As they discover what being made fishers of people involves, the former fishers might renege on their former commitment. Ideally, the beatitudes should further es-tablish their will to become disciples, even though it now is clear that this commitment demands more than abandoning jobs and families.*

The demands expressed by the descriptions of the blessed ones and Jesus' first command (4:19) are different in another way. Instead of a call for immedi-ate action, "come after me," which the four fishers could "immediately" obey by following Jesus, the beatitudes are a call to a more general and permanent commitment. This is clear in 5:6–10. Committing oneself to "hunger and thirst for righteousness" (5:6) is a commitment to seek[63] righteousness "earnestly and habitually."[64] In 5:7 and 5:9, the novice disciples are called to commit themselves to adopt certain attitudes that they will have to implement in ap-propriate circumstances in the future (as compared with the present in the story, when they hear the Sermon on the Mount). It is only when someone will have sinned against them that they will be in a position to be merciful (5:7). It is only when people are fighting with each other that they can be peacemakers (5:9). In 5:10, the novice disciples are called to accept certain consequences of these attitudes: "being persecuted for righteousness' sake."

In sum, becoming disciples involves committing oneself to be, in all kinds of circumstances, now and in the future, poor in spirit, meek, hungry and thirsty for righteousness, merciful, pure in heart, peacemakers, and persecuted for righteousness' sake.   ²ally, in response to the beatitudes, the four novice disciples would make tnis general and permanent commitment requested from those who are to become full-fledged disciples.

Reading B, CAW 2.4: Ideally, the Beatitudes Establish Both the Fishers' and Crowds' Will

Ideally, both the former fishers and the crowds would want to identify themselves with the "you," which, in the following verses, often refers to full-fledged disciples. Although they are not yet full-fledged disciples who im-plement this attitude in their lives, they are committed to becoming such disciples. Yet this commitment, this will, is still quite fragile, since it is primarily based on their desire to receive the blessings promised by Jesus. In order to have fully the will to be disciples, the former fishers and the crowds need to

---

63. In the plot of the story of the disciples, "hunger and thirst for righteousness" has to be interpreted as an active behavior (the early church and "Catholic" interpretation), so, "seek," instead of a passive longing for God's righteousness (the "protestant" interpretation, in terms of Paul). See Luz, *Matthew*, 237–38.

64. As Davies and Allison (*Matthew*, 451) underscore, "Righteousness is to be earnestly and habitually sought, as though it were meat and drink." Yet for them "seeking righteous-ness" is the designation of another kind of practice.

be more fundamentally transformed (made fishers of people). *This is what the rest of the Sermon on the Mount contributes to accomplishing.*

By contrast with reading B, which presupposes that the basic problem Jesus seeks to overcome is a *lack of will* to be a disciple and to act accordingly, reading A presupposes a *lack of knowledge* about what one should do as a disciple. Those to whom the Sermon is addressed are already committed to being disciples and to acting accordingly — they have the *will*, as they have demonstrated by immediately abandoning job and family to follow Jesus. But they lack the knowledge of what discipleship entails. They are ready to receive further commands and imperatives of all kinds that tell them what they should do — indeed, what they are already committed to do.

Reading A, CAW 3: Matthew 5:13–16: The Nature of Discipleship as Setting Up Duties for Disciples and Boundaries for the Church

An interplay between "indicative" and "imperative" similar to the one in the beatitudes is found in Matthew 5:13–16. These verses underscore what disciples are and what they should do; in addition, they include warnings that, in this historical/realistic dimension, are perceived as a rule for determining who belongs and who does not belong to the church.

Reading A, CAW 3.1: "Salt" and "Light of the World" Are Descriptions of the State of Discipleship — the Indicative

Disciples "are" (indicative of a present reality) "the salt of the earth" (5:13) and "the light of the world" (5:14); this is a "description of the state of discipleship."[65] In the historical/realistic dimension, these statements are perceived as a description of what disciples are by nature (contrast reading B, CAW 3.1); they "are" salt; they "are" light.

Reading A, CAW 3.2: Being "Salt" and "Light of the World" Involves Carrying Out a Universal Mission — the Imperative

Being salt and light is also a duty (an imperative).[66] This is a universal duty that must be carried out for the sake of the "earth" (τῆς γῆς) or the "world" (τοῦ κόσμου), i.e., for the sake of all humankind. While the exact duty involved in being "salt" and "light" is not specified,[67] it is clear

---

65. Strecker, *Sermon*, 49.

66. "Being salt and light expresses the duty of discipleship." Strecker, *Sermon*, 49.

67. The metaphors can receive quite diverse interpretations. Does "salt of the earth" mean being ready to "sacrifice oneself" for the earth, as Strecker tentatively suggests following Cullmann and Steinhauser (Strecker, *Sermon*, 200)? Yet note that in this case the metaphor is not really read as a metaphor (see reading C), but as a sign referring to something (here, to a specific duty).

that it involves performing "good works" before people (5:16) and that it is important, and even essential, not only for humankind, but also for God because, as a result, people give glory to God (5:16b). This universal duty is nothing but the universal mission to "all the nations" (28:16–20), a mission that, in this dimension, the historical disciples/apostles have carried out and that resulted in the church (including Matthew's church). Yet this is also a duty for the church as a community of disciples; they also must be "salt" and "light" of the world.

Reading A, CAW 3.3: "Salt without Taste" and Light "under a Bushel" Are Expressions of a Rule of Community Discipline

The references to "salt [that] has lost its taste" and to light "under a bushel" (5:15) signify the reality of the church, which includes members who tend not to live up to the duties of their discipleship and thus must be reproved. This is a polemical statement against certain members of the church or against certain communities.[68] Such people do not belong to the community of disciples;[69] they must be "thrown out" (5:13). In sum, the historical/realistic dimension of this passage provides a rule on the basis of which those who do not live up to their duties should be excluded from the community of disciples, i.e., from the church.

The same passage is read in a quite different way when attention is focused on the plot dimension. Differences in interpretation also occur because reading B includes 5:11-16 in this section (since 5:11-12 do not belong together with the other beatitudes), not merely 5:13-16 (as in reading A).

Reading B, CAW 3: Matthew 5:11–16: The Disciples' Vocation — Further Preview of Their Story; Further Establishment of the Will to Be Disciples

With the shift from impersonal to personal style in 5:11, the Sermon on the Mount as discourse anticipates a shift in the relationship between addresser and addressees. Before considering this shift, we need to note the description of the disciples' vocation in 5:11-16.

---

68. See Daniel Marguerat, *Le Jugement dans l'Evangile de Matthieu* (Geneva: Labor et Fides, 1981), 21, 124.

69. Strecker does not emphasize this point and is quite possibly reluctant to do so because of the sectarian implications for *pro me* interpretations. Yet it is very much in the logic of his exegesis. Thus he writes, "Matthew's *community* stands under the commission to evangelize all nations (28:16–20). *The matter of being disciples is decided by the carrying out of this mission assignment!*" Strecker, *Sermon*, 49 (emphases mine).

*Reading B, CAW 3.1: The Preview of the Story of the Disciples in
5:11–16 — the Performance of Their Vocation as Prophets, Salt, and
Light and Its Consequences*

*These verses provide a threefold description of disciples carrying out their
mission, as prophets, salt of the earth, and light of the world; this is a threefold
preview of another part of their story.*

*Faithful disciples are like the prophets, and like them they will be perse-
cuted (5:11–12). As was the case with the impersonal beatitudes, the positive
results for the disciples (rewards) of faithfully carrying out their mission is emphasized: "your reward is great in heaven." Thus they should rejoice and be
glad (5:12).*

*Faithful disciples are "salt of the earth" (5:13) and "light of the world"
(5:14); their mission will have positive results for other people. According to
the plot dimension,[70] the main positive result is that these people will receive
what they need (designated metaphorically as "salt" and "light"), namely,
"good works" (5:16), deeds that these people perceive as good for themselves, since they glorify God because of these deeds. The possibility of giving
glory to God is a blessing (although it is not yet clear why this is the case).*

*Ultimately, the disciples' mission will have positive results for God: God
will be "glorified," "God's name will be sanctified," as the disciples ask when
they pray "hallowed be thy name" (6:9).*

*In sum, the end of the plot of the story of the disciples can be summarized
as follows: (1) disciples faithfully carry out their vocation in the midst of persecution (5:11); (2) they nevertheless rejoice and are glad (positive result for the
disciples, 5:12); (3) other people (the "earth"; the "world") benefit from their
mission and good works; they glorify God (positive results for other people,
5:13–14); (4) God is glorified (positive result for God, 5:16); (5) disciples
receive rewards in heaven (ultimate positive result for the disciples, 5:12).*

*The text also indicates that negative actions can prevent the unfolding of
this plot. The fact that the disciples ("you") need to be exhorted to "rejoice"
and "be glad" (two imperatives) suggests that they might not do so because
people persecute them; then they would not be faithful disciples. Similarly,
the disciples, as salt and light of the world, might lose their taste (5:13) and
hide their light (5:14–15) — they might not carry out their mission (because
of persecutions?). Then they would be rejected (5:13) instead of receiving
rewards; other people would not benefit from their mission; God would not
be glorified.*

---

70. Let us keep in mind that in this perspective one focuses one's attention on the *actions*;
thus the metaphors "salt" and "light," and "giving taste" (cf. 5:13) and "giving light" (5:14–
15), are to be interpreted in terms of the actions "seeing your good works" and "giving glory
to God." Note that in the plot, the metaphorical expression "your Father in heaven" is simply read as "God." The figure "Father" is taken into account in the figurative and thematic
dimensions.

Reading B, CAW 3.2: The Ideal Effect of Matthew 5:11–16 on Novice Disciples — Benefits for Others and God as Additional Reasons to Be Disciples

For the former fishers and for the crowds who have identified themselves with the blessed ones and with the "you," and thus have committed themselves to becoming disciples, the ideal effect of 5:11–16 is to reinforce their commitment. They wanted to become disciples because of the blessings promised to them if they did so; they wanted to receive such rewards. Wanting to receive these blessings is a legitimate reason for wanting to be disciples; thus, they are warned that they should strive to avoid losing these rewards by being rejected (as tasteless salt, 5:13). Yet there are two other reasons for wanting to become disciples: their mission will benefit other people, and it will benefit God! It is not only for their own sake (for rewards) that they should want to carry out their mission, but also for other people's and for God's sake.

Reading B, CAW 3.3: The Establishment of the Hearers' Will to Be Disciples Is a Major Purpose of the Sermon on the Mount

In sum, the ideal effect of 5:11–16 should be to reinforce the novice disciples commitment (will) to become full-fledged disciples. Their commitment is still viewed as quite tentative and fragile; they might renounce their initial commitment when confronted with the demands it entails (including being persecuted). These verses seek to convince novice disciples that carrying out one's vocation faithfully despite its apparent cost and its difficulty is most desirable — something the disciples should want to do. After all, in addition to bringing blessings for oneself (5:12, cf. 5:3–10), it ultimately brings blessings to others who benefit from the good works and blessings to God who is glorified: "let your light shine before others, so that they may see your good works and give glory to your Father in heaven" (5:16).

This observation is important for our understanding of the view of discipleship expressed by the plot: the major obstacle in the process of becoming disciples seems to be that novice disciples might not truly want to become disciples. A proper and complete establishment of the will to be disciples seems to be a major step (possibly the major step) in the process of being made disciples.

This conclusion is quite far from the one we find in reading A, where the Sermon is addressed to disciples, i.e., to people who do not need to have their will established. Rather according to this reading of 5:13–16, disciples lack a clear understanding of the state of discipleship that they should implement and of the rules of community life (see above, reading A, CAW 3).

Reading A, CAW 4: Matthew 5:17–20: Sentences of "Holy Law" for Reproving or Rejecting People from the Church

Reading A, CAW 4.1: Rules for Determining the Status of People vis-à-vis the Community in 5:17–20

The polemic against members of the community of disciples continues in 5:17: "Think not..." In the historical/realistic dimension, 5:17–20 is a polemical reference to members of the church (or entire communities). Certain scholars emphasize that these verses refer to an actual polemical situation in the church of Matthew's time (against antinomians, or against the Gentile churches, or against Paul),[71] while others maintain that Matthew merely envisioned "a theoretical possibility" (rather than concrete adversaries).[72] But in the historical/realistic dimension on which Strecker's and Kingsbury's interpretations are focused these verses must be understood as expressing hermeneutical principles for the interpretation of the law[73] that are to be used as rules for determining the status of people vis-à-vis the community. Through his teaching Jesus fulfills the law (5:17) by reinterpreting it according to certain principles. Through this teaching certain people are rejected as unfit for participation in the kingdom (5:20) or judged as "least in the kingdom" (5:19) because they have a wrong understanding of Jesus' vocation. They view "the law and the prophets" as "abolished" (5:17), they "relax" the commandments (5:19), and/or they do not have the proper righteousness (5:20). As Käsemann underscores, 5:19 has the form of a statement of "holy law," on the basis of which people are reproved or rejected.[74] Thus in this perspective, this teaching is perceived as a rule to reprove people in the community of disciples (church). It follows that 5:20 can be understood as a rule to exclude people from the community. Certain people shall not enter the kingdom and thus do not belong to the sphere of God's eschatological rule because they do not have the appropriate kind

---

71. Betz, *Essays,* 40; cf. 37–53 and bibliography in notes.

72. E.g., Strecker, *Sermon,* 54. Cf. also John P. Meier, *Law and History in Matthew's Gospel: A Redactional Study of Mt. 5:17–48* (Rome: Biblical Institute Press, 1976), 66–67, and notes, who cautiously avoids identifying the people attacked as an actual antinomian group (or the Pauline churches), after conceding that "Mt's redaction does invite us to seek a definite group" as audience.

73. Although these features are more clearly emphasized and studied by Betz, *Essays,* 39–53.

74. Ernest Käsemann, "The Beginnings of Christian Theology," in *New Testament Questions of Today* (Minneapolis: Fortress, 1969), 87. Käsemann's interpretation refers to the teaching of Jewish-Christian prophets used by Matthew, who through such a teaching denied church fellowship to people who relaxed the commandments, even though the kingdom of heaven is not denied to them. In the historical/realistic dimension, since kingdom and church are closely associated, such people are not excluded from the church, but ranked as "least" in it. These remarks remain true, whether the "commandments" (5:19) are understood as referring to those of Torah (the more common view) or to those of Jesus (in 5:21ff.), as Betz (*Essays,* 46–51) argues.

of righteousness, i.e., because they do not implement the teaching of Jesus that "fulfills" the law (5:17).

Reading A, CAW 4.2: Jesus' Sovereign Authority to Fulfill the Law and the Prophets

In an interpretation focused on the historical/realistic dimension, 5:17 is not perceived as challenging the disciples' overvaluation of Jesus' authority (for contrast, see reading B, CAW 4.2); on the contrary, one cannot overvalue Jesus' authority, since he has "all authority in heaven and on earth." Thus Strecker writes, "By virtue of his authority as the Son of God (1:18ff.) Jesus stands, not under, but over the Law."[75] Jesus' authority is underscored by the emphatic "I say to you" (5:18, 20; cf. 5:21–48). The affirmation that Jesus fulfills the law and the prophets means that "the law of the Lord and the Torah of the Old Testament are not in contradiction with each other; both express the eschatological demand whose fulfillment characterizes discipleship to Jesus Christ."[76]

By fulfilling the law through his teaching[77] about the law (the antitheses, 5:21–48, but also 6:1–7:12), Jesus fully reveals the eternal will of God expressed by the law. He "brings to full measure — that is, confirms in their real meaning — the law and the prophets . . . he 'fulfills' or 'realizes' the will of God expressed in the Old Testament, . . . reveals the intended meaning of the Old Testament Torah and thus leads it to its actualization."[78] In so doing, Jesus might at times contradict the law of Scripture (cf. 5:21–48). This is so because "the Old Testament Torah in itself does not carry its own validity, but needs realizing fulfillment and authorizing confirmation through Jesus Christ."[79]

Reading A, CAW 4.3: Matthew 5:17–19 Is a Rule "Obligatory for All Followers of Jesus"

In the historical/realistic dimension, 5:17–19 is a rule that is "obligatory for all followers of Jesus"[80] and can therefore serve as an injunction to reprove members of the church (and/or communities) who either totally reject the authority of Scripture (5:17) or "relax" its authority (5:19). Yet those who relax the authority of the Law should not be excluded from the community; they are "least" in the kingdom, but nevertheless in it (5:19).[81]

---

75. Strecker, *Sermon*, 56.
76. Ibid., 53.
77. As the mention of "teaching" in 5:19 makes clear, the text emphasizes here the fulfillment of the law in Jesus' teaching, rather than in his deeds. Cf. Strecker, *Sermon*, 54.
78. Strecker, *Sermon*, 54–55.
79. Ibid., 54.
80. Ibid.
81. Ibid., 58.

Reading A, CAW 4.4: The Better Righteousness of the Sphere of God's Eschatological Rule

By contrast, those whose "righteousness" does not "exceed that of the scribes and Pharisees" (5:20) are not worthy of the kingdom and thus do not belong to the community. In the historical/realistic dimension, such a "righteousness" is not to be understood as quantitatively different from that of the scribes and Pharisees (as in reading B, CAW 4), but as *qualitatively* different, as Strecker emphasizes. It is a "better righteousness."[82] The righteousness of the scribes and Pharisees is qualitatively inferior because it is not a righteous behavior lived in the context of the sphere of God's eschatological rule; it is not the "better," eschatological righteousness. Such people do not live up to their eschatological nature as disciples. They are tasteless salt and hidden light (5:13, 15) and, therefore, are "to be thrown out" (5:13). Consequently, in this historical/realistic dimension, we find a first clearly anti-Jewish statement. "The scribes and Pharisees" are excluded from the kingdom because they are Jewish rather than members of the eschatological community of disciples. They have been excluded from the church, and those who are like them should also be excluded from it.

Reading A, CAW 4.5: In Sum: Matthew 5:3–20 Provides Rules for Inclusion and Exclusion from the Church as the Sphere of God's Eschatological Rule

In the historical/realistic dimension, the beatitudes (5:3–12) are a realistic description of the disciples (rather than a "call," see reading B, CAW 2) and 5:13–16 and 5:17–20 refer to problematic situations in the church. As a consequence, these passages (i.e., their historical/realistic dimensions) have a *legal* character. Strecker expresses it regarding the Gospel as a whole by saying that the descriptions (indicatives) have the value of ethical demands (imperatives)[83] and that Matthew "ethicizes" the traditional material about Jesus' ministry.[84] This entire passage provides realistic descriptions (indicatives) of the disciples as the blessed ones (5:3–12), of their vocation as their nature (5:13–16), and of those who do not have the proper view of the authority of Jesus and of Scripture and are thus "least" in the kingdom or are excluded from it (5:17–20). Yet these realistic descriptions also are imperatives; they set rules for identifying those who truly belong to the community

---

82. Ibid., 60–61. See also Francis W. Beare, *The Gospel according to Matthew* (San Francisco: Harper & Row; Oxford: Basil Blackwell, 1981), 142–45. The way in which Kingsbury describes the "greater righteousness" shows that he also conceives it as "qualitatively" different from that of the scribes and Pharisees (*Matthew as Story*, 107). To mark the qualitative character of this righteousness, I call it, with Strecker, a "better righteousness." Contrast this interpretation to the "quantitative" interpretations of the plot dimension (reading B).

83. Strecker, *Der Weg der Gerechtigkeit: Untersuchung zur Theologie des Matthäus* (Göttingen: Vandenhoeck & Ruprecht, 1962; 3d ed. 1971), 166–75.

84. Strecker, "Concept of History," 74–77.

of disciples, i.e., rules for inclusion and exclusion from the church. By contrast with the dynamism of the plot dimension (see reading B, CAWs 2–4), *the historical/realistic dimension is static.* It refers to the twofold reality of the historical disciples and of the church known by the readers. It defines the relative positions of people vis-à-vis the community of disciples — either in it or out of it; either "great" or "least" in it. As a consequence, what is a call to a life of discipleship in the plot is, in the historical realistic dimension, a static reality; a set of rules for inclusion and exclusion; a law with an objective reality (which "must unconditionally be done") because it is the eternal will of God revealed by the exalted Lord. It also is an expression of what disciples "are" (5:13, 14), their nature-reality in the concreteness of human experience (the "world").

Reading B, CAW 4: Matthew 5:17–19: Conditions for Being Great in the Kingdom

Reading B, CAW 4.1: A Passage Limited to Matthew 5:17–19

In the plot dimension, 5:17–19, which refers to conditions for being great in the kingdom (cf. 5:19), is to be distinguished from 5:20, which concerns conditions for entering the kingdom. This segmentation of the text has "considerable consequences for the interpretation of v. 17"[85] (contrast with reading A, CAW 4).

Reading B, CAW 4.2: The Preview of the Story of the Disciples in 5:17–19 — Conditions for Being "Great in the Kingdom of Heaven"

Matthew 5:19 refers to the end of the plot: disciples in the kingdom of heaven. Their story unfolds beyond obtaining participation in the kingdom (5:3, 10), since some of them will be "least" in it, while others will be "great" in it (5:19); some will be more blessed than others.[86] Yet in 5:17–19, the focus is primarily on earlier stages of the story: conditions for being "great in the kingdom of heaven" (5:19).

The immediate condition is to do and teach all commandments of the law (5:18–19), a stage of the plot concerning the disciples' performance of their mission. But a prior condition for doing and teaching all the commandments is to have a proper understanding of Jesus' relation to the law and the prophets (5:17); disciples need to understand that Jesus did not abolish the

---

85. As Luz says, *Matthew*, 256–57. Luz's comment regarding his own segmentation for other reasons in reading C is also appropriate here.

86. In an interpretation focused on the unfolding of the story of the disciples, one has to acknowledge that those who are "least" are *in the kingdom* and *not* excluded from it (as the scribes and Pharisees are according to 5:20), as is also recognized, for instance, by Käsemann, *New Testament Questions*, 85–87; Meier, *Law and History*, 92–95; Betz, *Essays*, 50.

law.[87] *Matthew 5:17 refers to a stage of the plot when novice disciples are still in the process of being made disciples.*

Thus 5:17–19 refers to three stages of the plot of the story of the disciples, which are in the following order (other stages can be expected in between them): (1) thinking that Jesus came to fulfill the law and the prophets, rather than to abolish them (5:17) — a condition that novice disciples must meet to become completely faithful disciples; (2) doing and teaching all the commandments (5:19) — fully carrying out one's mission as a disciple, a condition for being great in the kingdom; (3) being great in the kingdom (5:19).

Reading B, CAW 4.3: Matthew 5:17 Is a Warning against Overvaluing Jesus' Authority

The formulation of the condition for becoming a fully faithful disciple is strongly negative: "Think not," Μὴ νομίσητε *(5:17). In the plot dimension, according to this admonition novice disciples should not misunderstand Jesus' relation to the "law and the prophets." Far from being "above" the law and the prophets (which he would then abolish), Jesus is subordinated to them: "I have come not to abolish them but to fulfill them" (5:17). Novice disciples are warned against overvaluing Jesus' authority (contrast reading A, CAW 4.2).*

Not overvaluing Jesus' authority is thus posited as a condition for becoming a completely faithful (a great) disciple. This is once again a matter concerning the establishment of the will of the novice disciples. Our study of both 4:18–22 and 5:3–10 has shown that acknowledging the authority/ trustworthiness of Jesus is an essential condition for trusting his promises; without this trust in Jesus, the fishers (and the crowds) would not want to receive these blessings and thus would not want to become novice disciples and consequently would not want to be made full-fledged disciples. Thus acknowledging Jesus' authority/trustworthiness is a necessary condition for becoming disciples and ultimately for participating in the kingdom. Yet an overvaluation of Jesus' authority has negative consequences, even though it would still have the positive effect of allowing people to become disciples. It is true that such an overvaluation of Jesus does not prevent one from entering the kingdom (even if one does not do and teach all the commandments, one ends up in the kingdom, 5:19); and that it can play a positive role in the establishment of the will to become a disciple. But this is following Jesus for

---

87. Paying attention to the unfolding of the story presupposed by the discourse (as we do in this interpretation) shows that the relationship of 5:17 and 5:19 demands that the "commandments" mentioned in 5:19 be understood as commandments of the law (with most commentators), and not as commandments of Jesus (such as those found in 5:21ff.), as proposed in various ways by E. Lohmeyer, *Das Evangelium des Matthäus*, 4th ed., rev. W. Schmauch (Göttingen: Vandenhoeck & Ruprecht, 1967), 110–12; R. Banks, "Matthew's Understanding of the Law: Authenticity and Interpretation in Matthew 5:17–20," *Journal of Biblical Literature* 93 (1974): 223; Schweizer, *Matthew,* 108; Betz, *Essays,* 48. Yet this latter interpretation should not be totally rejected; it belongs to other interpretations (see reading A on a historical/realistic dimension and reading C on a figurative dimension).

the wrong reason; this will to follow Jesus is inappropriate. It prevents one from receiving all the blessings of the kingdom (one is "least in the kingdom") because it prevents one from fully carrying out what is expected of disciples.

The text specifies the source of this overvaluation of Jesus' authority: confusing the "present" with the "future" eschatological time, when the law and the prophets will indeed be abolished (cf. 5:18). At present (i.e., at the present stage of the story), Jesus does not have "all authority in heaven and on earth" (cf. 28:18)![88] Now is the time, for both Jesus (5:17) and the disciples (5:19), to fulfill the law.

In sum, in order to become a completely faithful disciple, one must recognize that Jesus' authority is not absolute; it is relative. It is an authority subordinated to the law and the prophets that he has come to fulfill (5:17b); it is an authority subordinated to another authority. It is only when one acknowledges this that one will want to submit oneself to the law and to do and teach all of its commandments. As Jesus "fulfills" the law, so completely faithful disciples should "fulfill" all the law, although it is not yet exactly clear what this entails (from the perspective of the story, 5:20–6:21 expresses it).

Reading B, CAW 4.4: The Ideal Effect of Matthew 5:17–19 on Novice Disciples — Establishing Their Will to Become Fully Faithful Disciples

The admonition not to overvalue Jesus' authority readily fits the story of the former fishers and of the crowds. The fishers' immediate positive response to Jesus' call (4:20, 22), the crowds' enthusiastic[89] response to Jesus' ministry (4:23–25), as well as the hearers' presumed positive response to the beatitudes (5:3–10) are quite ambiguous. These responses were quite possibly based on an overvaluation of Jesus' authority; the fishers and the crowds might want to become disciples for an inappropriate reason.

Thus the ideal effect of 5:17–18 on the novice disciples is to undermine one of the reasons novice disciples might have had for deciding to follow Jesus and for wanting to be made disciples. In the process, their will to become disciples might itself be undermined. Yet 5:19 reinforces another of the reasons they had for wanting to become disciples, namely, desire to receive the blessings associated with being in the kingdom. The validity of the promises about the kingdom is reaffirmed; the reward for being disciples is still receiving blessings in the kingdom. Wanting to receive such blessings is a perfectly appropriate basis for one's will to become disciple. Indeed, as a disciple, one should want to be "great in the kingdom," i.e., to receive as many blessings (rewards) as possible. For this, one should want to "do and teach" all the commandments, i.e., to fulfill them, as Jesus also does

---

88. See Meier (*Law and History*, 35–40), who emphasizes that Jesus has "all authority" only after his death-resurrection, an eschatological event that opens a new era; in this new era, when "all is accomplished" (5:18), Jesus' authority is above the law (Meier, *Law and History*, 159–61, and all the preceding demonstration).

89. Cf. Jesus' "fame" (ἡ ἀκοὴ αὐτοῦ; 4:24).

(5:17b), rather than relaxing them. In sum, 5:17–19 should ideally establish the will of novice disciples to become not only disciples but also fully faithful disciples.

Reading A, CAW 5: Matthew 5:21–7:12: The Revelation of God's Eternal Will to Be Implemented by the Eschatological Community

Reading A, CAW 5.0: What Is the Historical/Realistic Dimension of Matthew 5:21–7:12?

In this realistic-historical interpretation, Matthew 5:21–7:12 is the revelation of the eternal will of God by the exalted Lord in the form of a series of commands. Subsections can be readily identified: 5:21–48, duties toward others; 6:1–18, duties toward God (almsgiving, praying, and fasting); and 6:19–7:12, various directives (wealth, anxiety, judging, prayer). As is the case for the entire Sermon on the Mount according to this reading,[90] the organization of these teachings does not have significance in itself, although a few sayings function as conclusions (5:48; 7:12) or introduction (6:1) of sections. In light of the preceding interpretation of the historical/realistic dimension of 5:1–20, we can anticipate certain conclusions about 5:21–7:12:

- Each teaching in this section is an authoritative pronouncement by the exalted *Kyrios,* who revealed to the disciples/apostles how God's eternal will is to be implemented in specific situations.

- Each of these teachings is an admonition to "fulfill the law" (as Jesus did) and to have a better righteousness (living up to one's nature as a disciple in the sphere of God's eschatological rule, as the disciples did). The repeated mentions of the judgment[91] reinforce the "legal" character of these teachings as authoritative commands that must be obeyed urgently in light of the eschatological judgment.[92]

- Each of these teachings is a law that governs the life of *the church* ("the sphere of God's eschatological Rule"). As such, each teaching is

---

90. See above (reading A, CAW 1.2) our remarks on the parenetic genre, following Dibelius (*James,* 5–11).

91. Note that in the historical/realistic dimension, the references to heavenly rewards and deprivations from these rewards are directly interpreted as references to the impending threat of condemnation at the eschatological judgment, by contrast with their interpretation in the plot dimension (where a clear distinction is made between "deprivation of rewards," in 5:3–7:12, and "judgment-condemnation" in 7:13–27).

92. "Christian existence is envisioned in light of the judgment" ("L'existence chrétienne sous l'horizon du jugement"): Marguerat, *Jugement,* 34, 142–67. See also G. Barth, "Matthew's Understanding of the Law," in *Tradition and Interpretation in Matthew,* by G. Bornkamm, G. Barth, and H. J. Held, trans. P. Scott (Philadelphia: Westminster, 1963), 58–62.

a law to be used to evaluate (1) one's own behavior (so as to determine whether one is "great" or "least" in the kingdom, or whether one is out of it), and also (2) the behavior of others (judging whether or not they belong to the community; cf. 7:13–27).

Let us briefly review the first two sets of conclusions before closely considering how the third set of conclusions is established through a redaction-critical argument that establishes its legitimacy.

Reading A, CAW 5.1: Matthew 5:21–7:12 Is the Authoritative Proclamation of God's Eternal Will by Jesus, the Exalted Kyrios and Eschatological Judge

In the historical/realistic dimension, the very form of the antitheses (5:21– 48) as formulated by Matthew[93] — "you have heard" a command of the Mosaic law, "but I say to you" — indicates that Jesus, "the *Kyrios*, stands over the Torah; his authority makes it possible to be critical of the Torah, which leads even to dissolving individual commandments and setting up new instructions."[94] Jesus authoritatively radicalizes and intensifies the commands of Torah in 5:21–26, 27–30, 43–48, and replaces them by new commandments in 5:31–32, 33–37, 38–42.[95] Nevertheless, Jesus' teaching should not be viewed as abolishing the law (5:17) or even as neglecting or relaxing any of its commandments (5:18–19); "the Preacher on the mount does not want to teach a new law but rather to bring to expression the sovereign will of God in and in contrast to the Old Testament Torah."[96] This is how the exalted Kyrios fulfills the law.

The authority of Jesus as the exalted Kyrios is further emphasized through the series of solemn pronouncements of judgment: "Truly I tell you, they have received their reward" (ἀμὴν λέγω ὑμῖν, ἀπέχουσιν τὸν μισθὸν αὐτῶν, 6:2, 5, 16), as well as by the solemn declaration in 6:25: "Therefore I tell you." Together with the antitheses, these formulas clearly establish that all the teachings in 5:21–7:12 are pronouncements of the eschatological Lord and Judge.

Although this authoritative teaching was revealed to the historical disciples/apostles ("you"), it is also a teaching addressed to the church, since it is a revelation of God's *eternal* will. These pronouncements are uttered by the eschatological Lord and Judge *of the church,* and therefore are addressed to the church as well as to the disciples/apostles (as is confirmed by the study of their redaction; see below, reading A, CAW 5.3).

---

93. As usual we focus on the final form of the text. It is quite possible that Matthew found them in a source (e.g., special Matthean material in Q; Strecker, *Sermon,* 63).
94. Strecker, *Sermon,* 62; cf. 65, 71, 76, 94–95.
95. Ibid., 94.
96. Ibid., 95.

*Reading A, CAW 5.2: Matthew 5:21–7:12: Hermeneutical Principles for
"Fulfilling the Law" and Having a Better Righteousness in View of the
Impending Eschatological Judgment*

Through his radical reinterpretations of the law in the antitheses (5:21–48)
as well as through the teachings in 6:1–7:12, Jesus "fulfills the law," as the
concluding saying, the Golden Rule, makes clear: "So whatever you wish
that people would do to you, do so to them; for this is the law and the
prophets" (7:12). These teachings do not cover all possible situations; they
provide models of the way in which disciples should themselves "fulfill the
Law" in order to have a better righteousness in all kinds of situations. As
such, the Sermon on the Mount provides hermeneutical principles for the
interpretation of Torah.[97] Therefore, in this historical/realistic dimension,
one seeks to elucidate these basic hermeneutical principles. Three main
principles are discernable.

Reading A, CAW 5.21: The Hermeneutical Principle of Love.   "The demand of righteousness is reinterpreted in terms of the commandment of
love"[98] that is radicalized to include love for one's enemies (5:44) and
generalized by the Golden Rule (7:12), which "is identical in terms of content with the commandment of agape,"[99] and which is offered as a basic
principle for fulfilling and reinterpreting "the law and the prophets."[100]
For instance, when the commandment, "You shall not murder," is reinterpreted in terms of the commandment of love, it means, according to the
circumstances, "do not be angry" with others, or "do not insult" them,
or "be reconciled" with someone who is angry with you by abandoning
your worship activities (5:21–26), or more generally "do whatever it takes"
to restore broken relationships. This "principle of love" is essential for
Strecker because it prevents making out of the Sermon on the Mount a
"new legal norm" that would lead to legalism, since the way to implement
a commandment has to change so as to be the truly loving response to a
situation.[101]

Reading A, CAW 5.22: The Hermeneutical Principle of Perfection.   The
demands of Torah are understood as applying to the whole person, i.e.,
to both outward (e.g., killing, committing adultery) and inward behavior
(e.g., anger, lust). "Love and righteousness...attitude and action...are to

---

97. Betz, *Essays*, 39.
98. See *Strecker, Sermon*, 95. Cf. Barth, "Matthew's Understanding of the Law," 75–85.
99. Strecker, *Sermon*, 155 (see also 151–53). Other interpretations of the Golden Rule will
be discussed in chapter 6.
100. Barth, "Matthew's Understanding of the Law," 73.
101. Strecker, *Sermon*, 61–95.

become one."[102] This is the perfection ("wholeness") that is demanded of the disciples ("Be perfect, therefore, as your heavenly Father is perfect," 5:48),[103] and includes "the overcoming of the contradiction between outward appearance and true inner attitude."[104] This principle is exemplified by the internalization of the commandments: while these commandments concern outward actions, as is expected for laws that are parts of the legal system governing the life of a community (e.g., "you shall not murder," "you shall not commit adultery"), they should also be applied to one's inner life (anger, lust) and thus be internalized. This internalization of the commandments, as well as other inner attitudes, is important for the life of a community. Thus the text on anxiety (6:25–34) "is understood by the Evangelist as community admonition."[105] The principle of perfection requires that one forego any distinction between personal and community realms in doing God's will.

Reading A, CAW 5.23: The Hermeneutical Principle of Judgment. The demands of Torah, as well as Jesus' demands for love and perfection, are to be interpreted in light of the coming judgment. Jesus' demand for love is "not based on human presuppositions" (be they human rules of prudence, the stoic humanitarian ideal, or human rights). Rather, it "is to be understood...out of the divine realm: both friend and foe are nearing the coming kingdom of God. They will both have to answer for themselves before the supreme judge. There is no escape."[106] Similarly, the demand for perfection (behavior involving the whole person) becomes relevant. Of course, according to traditional views, one cannot enforce in a community the application of the law to the inner life of disciples — anger, lust, even love for enemies cannot truly be assessed from the outside. Yet inner attitudes affect the quality of the community life, and they can be demanded from disciples because they will have to account for their inner attitudes at the coming judgment, and in the meantime they can judge themselves (5:29–30).[107]

In sum, in this historical/realistic dimension, although Jesus' teaching is not "legalistic" (legalism being understood as the hypocritical attitude of the scribes and Pharisees who are content to do the literal teaching of the commandments), it is "legal." The central role given to the expectation of the coming judgment in the interpretation of the law reinforces the "legal" character of Jesus' teaching; it must be carried out urgently.

---

102. Ibid., 94; cf. 72. Thus this teaching should not be understood as an "ethic of attitude," i.e., as "a summons to a proper inner spirit" (p. 66).
103. Ibid., 93–94.
104. Ibid., 102 (on Mt 6:1–4).
105. Ibid., 141.
106. Ibid., 88.
107. This remark is in the logic of Strecker's interpretation, even though he does not emphasize this point in his comments on 5:29–30: see Strecker, *Sermon*, 70–72.

*Reading A, CAW 5.3: Matthew 5:21–7:12 Is a Series of Laws (Rules)
Governing the Life of the Community of Disciples, as a Redaction
Critical Study Shows*

As a part of the revelation of God's eternal will by the exalted Kyrios and as
a radical reinterpretation of Torah in light of the coming judgment, in the
historical/realistic dimension each of the teachings in 5:21–7:12 is a law
that disciples are to use to evaluate their own behavior and the behavior
of others in the community. This is what is shown by Strecker's study of
Matthew's redaction. This central part of the Sermon on the Mount is a
set of rules for community life, which helps to define the boundaries of the
communities of those who live in the sphere of God's eschatological rule. It
is enough to summarize Strecker's exegetical argument.

**Reading A, CAW 5.31: Matthew's Redaction Applies the First Antithesis
(5:21–22) to the Life of His Church.** Regarding the first antithesis, 5:21–
26, "not only (treacherous) murder is placed under Jesus' verdict, but also
anything that can harm one's neighbor."[108] Through his redaction, Matthew makes clear that this teaching applies to the community life of the
Palestinian church for which he writes. This becomes apparent in the pro-
gression from the condemnation of "being angry" (ὀργιζόμενος — as a part
of the "uncompromising call to repentance" of the historical Jesus (5:21–
22a)[109] — to calling a fellow member (ἀδελφῷ) of the community "Raca"
('Ρακά, "idiot," incapable of interpersonal relations) or "fool" (μωρέ, i.e.,
incapable of relating to God) — a reinterpretation for the sake of a Palestinian community familiar with the Jewish court system and the Semitic
conceptual world (ἔνοχος ἔσται τῷ συνεδρίῳ, "liable to the council," ἔνοχος ἔσται εἰς τὴν γέενναν τοῦ πυρός, "liable to the hell of fire," 5:22b–c).[110]
The condemnation of an attitude (anger) has been reinterpreted as a condemnation of excluding a neighbor from interpersonal relations in the
community for the wrong reason. In 5:23–24 we find a second level of
reinterpretation (borrowed by Matthew from another source)[111] that now
clearly takes the form of a *rule for community life:*[112] reconciliation with
other members must take precedence over cultic practice (5:23–24); those
who belong to the community under God's eschatological rule must reconcile themselves with other church members. A third level of reinterpretation
is then presented by Matthew in 5:25–26, where he reinterprets a "crisis
parable" that announced the judgment (see Lk 12:57–59) into an "in-

---

108. Strecker, *Sermon*, 65.
109. Ibid., 65–67.
110. Ibid., 67.
111. This reinterpretation presupposes the existence of the Temple in Jerusalem. Ibid., 68.
112. Ibid., 67.

struction for the life of the individual as well as for the ordering of the community as a whole."[113]

Strecker summarizes the significance of these successive reinterpretations of Jesus' teaching: "Thus like the community before him, Matthew is removed temporally and materially from Jesus' apodictic call to repentance. He sees the necessities of community organization. Hence, he is at pains to assure that the community of Christ does not lose its identity in the course of time. Therefore, he offers practical instruction."[114]

More generally, regarding each antithesis, Strecker ends up showing that through the redaction of traditions and sources according to the principles of love, perfection, and judgment that he found in Jesus' reinterpretation of the law, Matthew transforms Jesus' teaching (a call to repentance) into a series of community rules. Rather than repeating Strecker's detailed discussion of all the antitheses,[115] I simply present the characteristics of the community rules, which he elucidates in the antitheses.

Reading A, CAW 5.32: Matthew's Redaction Applies the Other Antitheses (5:27–48) to the Life of His Church.   The second antithesis, 5:27–30, emphasizes the importance of judging oneself (5:29–30) in terms of the demand for perfection (wholeness) concerning one's relation with women. This injunction presupposes a patriarchal structure (μοιχεύειν means "to make an adulteress"),[116] which is thus established as a part of the eternal will of God. Thus the community itself is understood in a patriarchal perspective; it is made up of "brothers." (Sex-exclusive language is often appropriate in the discussion of the historical/realistic dimension.)

The third antithesis, 5:31–32, displays the same patriarchal structure. Its formulation makes it clear that this teaching about divorce is understood as a community rule: it has a casuistic character ("παρεκτὸς λόγου πορνείας, "except on the ground of unchastity," 5:32) that makes out of the prohibition of divorce "a practical instruction, with whose help the current problems of order can be resolved."[117]

Similarly, Matthew's version of the fourth antithesis, 5:33–37, is a community rule: the formula ναὶ ναί, οὒ οὔ ("yes yes, no no"), although not technically an oath, is a solemn declaration, which is a practical way of meeting the needs of community life (where solemn declarations are needed in judicial investigations; cf. 18:17), without violating Jesus' prohibition against oaths.[118]

---

113. Ibid., 70; cf. 68–70.
114. Ibid., 70.
115. Ibid., 70–95.
116. Ibid., 71.
117. Ibid., 75.
118. Ibid., 80.

As a result of Matthew's redaction, the fifth antithesis, 5:38–42, including its admonition not to resist evil, becomes a practical teaching regarding the behavior that members of the community should have toward outsiders because of the "anticlimactic" way in which the examples are listed: "from the greater evil to the lesser one: violent encounter, court trial, coercion, request."[119] As a result, the radical injunction against resisting evil becomes an instruction that can be practiced by the community through an attitude of self-denial in the most common of situations.[120]

The sixth antithesis, 5:43–48, is once again formulated by Matthew so as to make clear that the injunction to love one's enemies is to be practiced by the community in the current situation; the enemies that are to be loved are those who persecute the church (5:44). Simultaneously, it indicates that this behavior distinguishes those who are in the community from those who are not part of it. Members of the community are "sons of [their] Father who is in heaven" (5:45);[121] they have God as their model (5:45, 48), unlike the tax collectors and the Gentiles (5:46–47). Those who belong to the community are those who have a "better righteousness" (5:46–47), being "perfect" as their Father in heaven is (5:48).

Reading A, CAW 5.33: Matthew's Redaction Reinforces the Character of Community Rules of the Teachings in 6:1–18. In studies focused on the historical/realistic dimension, the following section, 6:1–18, is commonly recognized as a series of rules for community life, Jewish-Christian "catechetical pieces"[122] (6:2–4, 5–6, 16–18), which Matthew appropriated and reinforced by introducing three literary units (an introduction, 6:1; the saying against the prayers of the Gentiles, 6:7–8; and the Lord's Prayer and its interpretation, 6:9–15).

The introduction, 6:1, sets up the pattern. By taking as its premises Jewish views so as to better criticize Jewish practices, this teaching becomes a rule for a community that distinguishes itself from the Jewish community. Jewish "hypocrites" who practice their piety before people (6:2–4, 5–6, 16–18) do not belong to the community under God's eschatological rule. Hypocritical Jews, as well as any other person who has the same kind of attitudes, are to be rejected from the community. The saying against the Gentiles' way of praying, 6:7–8, defines another boundary of the community; "the church made up of Jews and Gentiles understood itself as the

---

119. Ibid., 83.

120. And should not be understood either as advising compliance with the power of evil or as a maxim for governing the world. Strecker, *Sermon,* 81–85.

121. The literal translation "sons," rather than the inclusive "children" of the NRSV, is more appropriate for this dimension.

122. Strecker, *Sermon,* 96. Also called "community catechism" made up of "rules of piety" (Rudolf Bultmann, *History of the Synoptic Tradition,* trans. S. Marsh [New York: Harper & Row, 1963], 133, 145) or "Cultic *Didache*" (Betz, *Essays,* 55–69).

'third race,' as an independent entity."[123] Despite its emphasis on practicing one's piety "in secret" (6:4, 6, 18), interpretations focused on the historical/realistic dimension underscore that in this teaching "Matthew is not concerned about an inner ethic as opposed to an outer one, or a secret versus a public ethic." Rather, these teachings emphasize eschatological rewards for those who belong to the community of disciples under God's eschatological rule.[124] These teachings allow the members to distinguish who belongs or does not belong to the community and to evaluate their own behavior. As members of such a community, they must practice giving alms, praying, and fasting before God rather than before people.

Reading A, CAW 5.34: The Lord's Prayer, 6:9–13, Is Also a Set of Indirect Admonitions. The Lord's Prayer is understood in this historical/realistic dimension not merely as a set of petitions that should be prayed with the confidence that God will answer, but also and primarily as a set of indirect admonitions. Those who pray must "realize holiness so that human deeds may stand before the judicial verdict of the holy God" (6:9);[125] they must hold themselves "ready for the kingdom" (6:10a);[126] they "must strive for the realization of God's will" (6:10b).[127] As the interpretation (6:14–15) underscores, the petition for forgiveness obligates one to forgive others, the very condition for divine forgiveness (6:12).[128] Consequently, the two other petitions (for daily bread and for deliverance from evil, 6:11, 13) are also to be understood as implying admonitions to active participation in obtaining bread or in resisting evil (persecutions). In sum, the prayer calls the disciples to evaluate their own life and to commit themselves to the better righteousness.

Reading A, CAW 5.35: The Teachings of 6:19–24 Are Practical Injunctions Challenging the Absolutization of the Economic Order. The three sayings in 6:19–24 concern the attitude of individuals toward wealth; the saying about the eye (6:22–23) must be interpreted in this way, since it is bracketed by two sayings explicitly about wealth. The saying about treasures on earth and in heaven (6:19–21) remains a practical (and thus realistic) injunction that can readily be applied in the concrete situations of the life of the church members, since it "does not demand a radical renunciation of possessions.... Matthew expects the proper attitude regarding possessions to be made concrete in social deeds (cf. 6:2–4)."[129] In this perspective,

---

123. Strecker, *Sermon*, 98.
124. Ibid., 101–2.
125. Ibid., 113.
126. Ibid., 114.
127. Ibid., 116.
128. Ibid., 119–21.
129. Ibid., 132.

the saying about the eye (6:22–23) is similarly a practical injunction about wealth: it "clarif[ies] one's proper relationship to possessions."[130] This interpretation is made possible by the fact that ἁπλοῦς ("sound") can be interpreted as "generous" (as in Prov 22:9 and Jas 1:5) and πονηρὸς ("not sound," "evil") as "greedy" (as in Dt 15:9; Prov 23:6; 28:22). Thus this saying "means that whenever someone looks greedily at earthly possessions, the whole person goes bad; and conversely, whoever is generous with his wealth, to him belongs the light."[131] The saying about serving God or mammon (6:24) completes this teaching by "admonish[ing] the community to turn their vision away from earthly possessions and direct it toward God"[132] so as to be freed from enslavement to mammon. Yet it remains a practical injunction; although it challenges the economic order as an absolute (taking the place of God) and demands total commitment to God, "the saying does not demand freedom from any economic order or absolute separation from possessions."[133]

Reading A, CAW 5.36: The Teaching about Anxiety, 6:25–34, Is Also a Rule for Community Life.

Studies that focus on the historical/realistic dimension interpret the teaching about anxiety, 6:25–34, which Matthew appropriated from the tradition with some redaction, as a rule for community life. Members of the community are people who place themselves without reservation at the disposal of the promised "kingdom" and the demanded better "righteousness" (6:33).[134] They must overcome anxiety (6:25) because anxiety is pointless (worry never leads to the desired goal, 6:27), unreasonable (every day has its own trouble, 6:34), and above all needless (since God is the Creator and Sustainer of life, 6:26, 28–30).[135]

Reading A, CAW 5.37: Matthew's Redaction Transforms the Radical Prohibition of Judging, 7:1–5, into a Community Rule.

In 7:1–5, Matthew transforms the radical prohibition of judging/condemning (7:1) into a community rule for the proper use of judging "in keeping with the situation of a community that is prepared for the duration in history."[136] Judging others is necessary for order and discipline in the community (cf. 18:15–20); proper judging in the community must take place in terms of God's

---

130. Ibid., 134.

131. Ibid., 134. Note that this interpretation presupposes that "the eye is not the real cause of sin, but the *lumen internum* itself when it has turned into darkness" ["greed" for Strecker] as Betz (*Essays,* 86) says in conclusion of his careful analysis of the form of the argument and of its comparison with Greek theories of vision.

132. Strecker, *Sermon,* 135.

133. Ibid.

134. "[Matthew] continues the admonition to the community: one who is committed to the reign of God may not let himself be attacked by anxiety." Ibid., 137.

135. Ibid., 141.

136. Ibid., 144.

judgment (7:2) and with the acknowledgment that one judges oneself in the process. Therefore, true members of the community, unlike "hypocrites," not only acknowledge their own faults but also remove them, before helping others and judging them (7:5). In this dimension, the proverbial saying in 7:6 about not giving to dogs what is holy and not giving pearls to swine (the original meaning of which is quite obscure), is a qualifier to the injunction to exercise restraint in criticizing brothers (7:2–5). This proverbial saying expresses that there is "a limit to not judging. When the truth of the faith stands in the balance, it may be necessary to make an unambiguous profession and draw a clear line of demarcation."[137] Judging, condemning, rejecting "brothers" and/or outsiders is necessary when "the identity of the community [is] threatened."[138]

Reading A, CAW 5.38: Matthew 7:7–11 Is a Practical Admonition for a Distinctive Way of Praying by the Community.   The members of the community must be people who pray with the confidence that prayer will be answered (7:7–11), as they must be people characterized by a right attitude toward possessions (6:19–24), by control over anxiety (6:25–34), and by the right kind of judging (7:1–5). In other words, this teaching about prayer is once again a practical admonition for a kind of behavior (a way of praying) that distinguishes members of the community from nonmembers and outsiders.[139]

All these practical laws for community life regarding the distinctive behavior ("better righteousness") of the members of the community are then summarized in the Golden Rule (7:12). True disciples, true members of the community, are those who do to others whatever they wish others would do to them.

Reading A, CAW 5.39: This Entire Set of Community Rules "Fulfills" Jesus' Teaching as Jesus' Teaching "Fulfills" the Law.   As is clear from the preceding comments, in the historical/realistic dimension the teachings in 5:21–7:12 are not general or theoretical expressions of God's eternal will, but rather concrete rules/laws that should govern the life of the community "in the sphere of God's eschatological Rule." As such they reflect the concrete reality of discipleship in the church of Matthew's time (including its failures to carry out this teaching). They show that the church "does not maintain that its reality matches such high demands," since it needs to be admonished. Furthermore, as we noted in passing, these teachings reflect concrete situations of this community in the world. It is a community in which problems concerning relationships among its members (disputes

---

137. Ibid., 147.
138. Ibid., 148.
139. Ibid., 149.

among members, relations between the sexes, divorces, 5:21–32) need to be addressed. It is a community that suffers persecution from outsiders (5:44) and generally experiences tension with outsiders (5:38–42). It is a community that sees itself as separated from the Jewish community as well as from the Gentiles (6:1–18). It is a community that is settled in the world; its members have possessions that they need to use judiciously (6:19–24). It is a community that needs to have rules to maintain within itself discipline and order. Thus despite the restriction put on judging others (7:1–5), it needs clear procedures for judging its members (5:33–37; 7:1–6) and eventually for rejecting them when necessary as "tax collectors or Gentiles" (5:46–47), i.e., as people who do not practice a "better righteousness" and thus do not belong to the community "in the sphere of God's eschatological Rule."

In addition, we can say that Strecker's redaction critical study appropriately shows that this entire set of community rules "fulfills" Jesus' teaching as Jesus' teaching "fulfills" the law; it is the reinterpretation of the law and of Jesus' teaching for a new situation (the church situation) in terms of the very principles (love, perfection, judgment) which Jesus used in the special situation of his own ministry.

The interpretation of reading A is thus consistent — from beginning to end it is focused on the historical/realistic dimension — and coherent. One might wonder: Is it possible that any other interpretation be as consistent and coherent as reading A? Indeed! Reading B is a case in point: its *conclusions about what the text is and says* are quite different, yet it is legitimate, consistent, and coherent.

Reading B, CAW 5: Matthew 5:20–6:21: Conditions for Entering the Kingdom: Adopting a Radical Behavior

In an interpretation focused on the plot meaning-producing dimension, this long passage is viewed as a single section of the Sermon on the Mount because throughout it offers a preview of the same stages of the plot of the story of the disciples posited by this text: (1) entering or not entering the kingdom – a stage related to certain blessings of the beatitudes; (2) kinds of behaviors disciples need to fulfill their vocation in order to enter the kingdom – a stage related to the descriptions of the blessed ones in the beatitudes; (3) appropriating certain views that establish the will of novice disciples to adopt this behavior – a stage partly related to the proper acknowledgment of Jesus' authority (already expressed in 5:17-19).

In this interpretation, the conclusions about what the text is and says concern, first, the ways in which the text describes each of these stages of the plot and, second, the ideal effect of this passage and of its descriptions of the stages of the story on the implied readers. These readers are themselves "novice disciples," i.e., people who, like the four fishers, have agreed to be made full-fledged disciples, but are not yet ready to carry out their vocation as disciples.

Reading B, CAW 5.1: The Preview of the Story of the Disciples in 5:20–6:21

Reading B, CAW 5.11: Entering or Not Entering the Kingdom as Receiving or Being Deprived of a Reward. *Rather than describing the very last stage of the story (the greater or lesser number of blessings one might receive after entering the kingdom; cf. 5:17–19), Matthew 5:20–6:21 describes preceding stages: (1) entering the kingdom or (2) not entering it; (3) receiving this reward or (4) being deprived of it. I begin by listing each reference to the end of the story of the disciples. They fit into two positive categories and their negative counterparts:*

1. *Entering the kingdom of heaven (as in 5:3, 10): having treasures in heaven, 6:20, and thus having one's heart in heaven (confidence that one belongs to heaven), 6:21.[140]*

2. *Not entering (being deprived of) the kingdom of heaven: like the scribes and Pharisees, 5:20 (implicitly like the tax collectors and the pagans, 5:46–47);[141] having treasures on earth, 6:20, and thus having one's heart on earth, 6:21;*

3. *Receiving a reward: being children of your Father, 5:45 (with the confidence of entering the kingdom; cf. 5:9; all those who enter the kingdom are to be called children of God); being rewarded by the Father (without specification of the reward), 6:4, 6, 18 (cf. 5:6, being satisfied); being forgiven, 6:14 (cf. 5:7; entrance in the kingdom involves being forgiven);*

4. *Being deprived of this reward: being liable to Gehenna, 5:22; being put in prison, 5:25–26; being thrown into Gehenna, 5:29–30; having no reward, 6:1, or having received the earthly rewards one seeks, 6:2, 5, 16; not being forgiven, 6:15.*

The negative descriptions (not entering the kingdom; being deprived of reward) stand out, especially after the series of blessings of the beatitudes. In the plot dimension, they must be interpreted as deprivations of rewards or of the kingdom, rather than condemnations of nondisciples, for two reasons. First, most of the negative descriptions are clearly presented as deprivations; the introductory verses of the two subsections (5:20–48; 6:1–21) set the tone: "you will never enter the kingdom of heaven" (5:20); "you will have no reward from your Father who is in heaven" (6:1). The only mentions of actual

---

140. Reading "heaven" as a metonymic reference to the "kingdom of heaven."

141. The terms οἱ ἐθνικοὶ in 5:47 and in 6:7 and τὰ ἔθνη in 6:32 are best translated as "pagans" (not "Gentiles") because their religious attitude is the connotation that is emphasized. With Betz, *Essays*, 97.

punishments are in 5:22, 25–26, 29–30. Second, these latter cases themselves do not present irremediable condemnations (by contrast with what we find in 7:13–27), but rather they teach how to avoid such punishments, and thus implicitly how to avoid being deprived of the kingdom.

Reading B, CAW 5.12: The Disciples' Behavior as They Fulfill Their Vocation — Overabundant Righteousness.

Matthew 5:20–6:21 also refers to specific kinds of behavior that the disciples must demonstrate in order to avoid being deprived of the kingdom – or to receive entrance into the kingdom as a reward. The antitheses (5:21–48) amplify the beatitudes (5:3–10), describing concrete kinds of behavior that disciples should practice in their relations with other people, while 6:1–18 describes the kinds of behavior that should characterize their relationship with God. This is a description of the disciples carrying out their vocation, a stage of their story that precedes being confident of entering the kingdom and actually entering it.

The right attitude toward other people (δικαιοσύνη, righteousness, 5:20) entails being reconciled with others whatever might be the circumstances, even if one is not at fault (5:23; cf. 5:7, being merciful), and even if this demands interrupting a religious practice (5:21–26); avoiding at all cost evil/ lustful relations with others, including "in one's heart" (5:27–30; cf. 5:8, being pure in heart) and preserving good relations (marriage; 5:31–32); avoiding the separation of oneself from others by words (swearing), even if these words are religious vows (5:33–37); not resisting evil people (5:38–42; cf. 5:5, being meek; 5:10, 11, being persecuted); and loving one's enemies (5:43–44; cf. 5:9, being peacemakers). In sum, good relations with others should be maintained or reestablished at all cost. Anything that separates or risks separating disciples from other people should be overcome. What is demanded from disciples is an overabundant righteousness, i.e., a righteousness that involves doing more[142] than what the scribes and Pharisees (5:20) and the tax collectors and pagans (5:46–47) do (cf. 5:6, being hungry and thirsty for righteousness; contrast with reading A, CAW 4.4.)

The right attitude toward God (another aspect of "righteousness," δικαιοσύνη, 6:1, often translated "piety" in such a context) involves giving alms[143] "in secret," i.e., before God alone (6:2–4), praying "in secret" (6:5–6), and fasting "in secret" (6:16–18). In brief, one's relation to God should be exclusively directed toward God, and not simultaneously directed toward other people (in order to receive praises from them, 6:2, or human rewards, 6:1, 5, 16).

---

142. Περισσεύω (NRSV "to exceed") has, in this reading, a connotation of *quantity* (in agreement with Dupont, *Béatitudes* 3:248–49) that plays a major role in the plot dimension (by contrast with the historical/realistic dimension that underscores the connotation of quality, see reading A, CAW 4.4).

143. Almsgiving is here understood as a religious duty, and thus as an expression of one's relation to God, rather than as a direct attitude toward others, as in 5:21–48.

Reading B, CAW 5.13: Three Conditions for Wanting an Overabundant Righteousness: Acknowledging Jesus' Authority, Internalizing the Basic Intention of the Law, and Recognizing That God's Will Is Good to Do. *Finally, Matthew 5:20–6:21 refers to a prior stage of the story of the disciples presented by the Sermon: the appropriation of views that make it possible for novice disciples to want to adopt the radical behavior discussed above.*

First, they should acknowledge the authority of Jesus' teaching — "I tell you" (5:20), "you have heard...but I say to you" (Ἠκούσατε ὅτι...ἐγὼ δὲ λέγω ὑμῖν ὅτι, 5:21–22, 27–28, 33–34; and in abbreviated forms, 5:31–32, 38–39, 43–44); "truly I say to you" (ἀμὴν λέγω ὑμῖν, 6:2, 5, 16). Taken by themselves, theses phrases could be viewed as an expression of Jesus' absolute authority; the antitheses seem to say that Jesus displays an authority superior to that of the law, since several of these antitheses contradict the teaching of the Mosaic law[144] rather than simply complementing it. An interpretation focused on the plot of the disciples' story — an interpretation that seeks to elucidate the coherence of this story — necessarily interprets this description of Jesus' authority as consistent with its description in 5:17–19. Thus the authority of Jesus, which novice disciples should acknowledge at this point, is not "above" that of the law; by this teaching, Jesus submits to the authority of the law by the very fact that he "fulfills the law."[145] Yet Jesus has authority, and they must acknowledge it.

This authoritative teaching calls novice disciples to adopt Jesus' attitude toward the law. It assumes that they know the law ("you have heard that it was said"); now they are told that they must "fulfill" it, as Jesus does, by going beyond its letter. According to the first two antitheses (5:21–30), this is a matter of "internalizing" it, so much so that it applies not merely to actual actions (e.g., killing, committing adultery) but also to intentions (being angry, lusting in one's heart); thus, the "intention" of the law becomes one's personal intention. This internalization of the law transforms both the law itself and the disciples.

The internalization of the law involves identifying the basic intention of the law, i.e., the will of God that it expresses. In this way, the disciples makes God's will their own will. In the process, the law is radicalized; one perceives that the basic intention of the law is that the believers maintain and restore good relations with others (and thus avoid all that might disrupt these good relations). After internalizing the law, one is led to go beyond the letter of the

---

144. Thus Meier (*Law and History*, 125–61) argues that three of the antitheses revoke the law (5:31–32, on divorce; 5:33–37, on oaths; 5:38–42, on the *jus talionis*).

145. As many commentators note. See, e.g., Luz, *Matthew*, 279; Davies and Allison, *Matthew*, 508–9. This interpretation (against Meier) is possible even if one acknowledges that the antitheses oppose what Jesus says to what God said (cf. Meier, *Law and History*, 131–35), rather than opposing the way in which the law was interpreted (the interpretations "heard" by the novice disciples) with the way in which Jesus interprets it (another traditional interpretation; see Luz, *Matthew*, 277–78).

commandments (5:21–30) and dismiss provisions of the law,[146] such as those that permit divorce, oaths, protecting oneself, hating enemies (5:31–48).

Such an internalization of the law (adopting God's will as one's own will) presupposes that one wants to do so. The disciples' will to internalize the law is partially established through the recognition of the negative consequences of not doing so (5:22–26, 29–30, 32b, 46–47) and of the positive consequences of doing so (5:45). In short, the novice disciples should want to internalize God's will (the law) because they recognize that it is good for them. The same could be said regarding the establishment of the disciples' will to give alms, to pray, and to fast "in secret" (6:1–18); this is what they should do if they want to receive the true rewards given by God.

Reading B, CAW 5.14: A Condition for Wanting to Internalize God's Will — Being Convinced of God's Goodness. *The instruction regarding prayer (6:7–15) goes beyond the preceding point and concerns prior stages of the story of the disciples, which is posited by the Sermon. Before accepting God's will as one's own will and before trusting God for rewards, one needs to be convinced of God's goodness. One needs to recognize that God does not need to be convinced to give good things to human beings. One needs to know that God is a loving father ("our Father in heaven," 6:8, 9; cf. 5:45, 48) who is ready to give people what they need (6:8) and indeed does so (5:45). Only one who is convinced of God's goodness can be convinced that God's will (expressed in the law) is good for oneself, a conviction that is necessary to agreeing to make God's will one's own will.*

Reading B, CAW 5.2: The Ideal Effect of Matthew 5:20–6:21 on Novice Disciples

Reading B, CAW 5.21: Matthew 5:20–6:21 as Threatening the Novice Disciples' Resolve to Be Made Disciples. *For the former fishers and the crowds, this section of the Sermon makes explicit[147] what is concretely involved in becoming disciples, namely, an overabundant righteousness: doing more than the good deeds that the scribes and Pharisees (5:20), and the tax collectors and pagans (5:46–47) do; doing more than what the letter of the law requires. This is a radical kind of life, which they cannot but perceive as quite "costly" and demanding (especially 5:20–48). Their general resolve to follow Jesus and to be made disciples (their identification with the "you") is threatened. Is it not impossible to demonstrate radical behavior that includes, for instance, not being angry, not lusting in one's heart, giving up any attempt to protect oneself and one's belongings?*

---

146. On the distinction between actual "commandments" and "provisions of the law," see e.g., Davies and Allison, *Matthew,* 507. See also Matthew 19:7–8, where Matthew makes this distinction explicit.

147. The behavior that full-fledged disciples should exhibit was already presented by the descriptions of the blessed ones in the beatitudes, but in general terms.

In the plot dimension, this hesitation is indeed one of the anticipated effects on the Sermon's intended hearers. The emphases on Jesus' authority, on rewards, and on deprivation of rewards show that the discourse anticipates that the novice disciples (former fishers and former members of the crowds) need to be convinced to adopt this radical behavior as their own. One might be surprised. Should they not accept the trustworthiness of Jesus' promises of rewards, since they have acknowledged Jesus' authority by accepting his call (4:18–22 and/or 5:3–10)? Should they not be willing to adopt the behavior that will bring them valuable rewards, rather than being deprived of them?[148] *These emphases show that affirmative answers to these questions are dubious.*

The question then becomes obvious: How will the hearers be convinced to do all this teaching? Does the discourse expect the hearers to be convinced by these strong emphases on the authority of Jesus and on rewards? The oddness of the teaching about prayer as we seek to understand its place in the plot (see reading B, CAW 5.14) suggests that this is not the case. The best that the discourse can hope for (the ideal effect of this section) is that the novice disciples might want to make the prayer of 6:9–13 their own.

Reading B, CAW 5.22: Matthew 5:20–6:21 as Inviting Novice Disciples to Pray the Lord's Prayer and to Acknowledge That without God's Help They Lack the Will to Carry Out Their Mission. *When one considers the ideal role of praying in the unfolding of the story of the disciples posited by the Sermon, one recognizes that by uttering the Lord's Prayer (6:9–13), novice disciples would acknowledge that God does want to give them what they ask (6:8), including what they concretely need (daily bread, 6:11) and forgiveness (6:12). It is true that these two petitions presuppose that the praying novice disciples would view themselves as disciples carrying out the teaching found in the preceding verses; at least, it is presupposed that they would forgive others ("as we also have forgiven our debtors"; 6:12, 14–15; cf. 5:21–26, 38–48). Yet the rest of the prayer shows that even in this limited case the discourse does not expect that the intended hearers would be consistent in carrying out their mission. As they pray the Lord's Prayer, they indicate that without God's help they lack the will to carry out their mission. This is what they express by uttering the petitions.*

1. *"Hallowed be your name" (6:9) – a petition that people will give glory to their Father, something that will happen when, carrying out their mission, they do good works before others (cf. 5:16). This petition amounts to asking that they be given the will (and ability?) to carry out their vo-*

---

148. Note that in the plot dimension the novice disciples are ideally convinced to adopt this radical behavior because they *want to receive rewards* (and do not want to be deprived of these rewards), and not because they fear punishment and condemnation (because they want to avoid punishment), as is the case in the historical/realistic dimension (above).

cation as light of the world faithfully (5:14-16), and thus that God give them what they need to do so.

2. "Your kingdom come" (6:10a) — a petition that they receive God's reward, the kingdom, for fulfilling their vocation. This petition also amounts to asking that they be given by God the will (and ability) they need to carry out faithfully their vocation.

3. "Your will be done, on earth as it is in heaven" (6:10b — a petition that they (along with all others on earth) be given the will to do God's will. This petition specifies what they need to carry out their vocation faithfully, namely, the will to do it.

4. "And lead us not into temptation, but deliver us from the evil one" (6:13, author's translation) — a petition that they be freed from the evil one, who tempts them and thus seeks to prevent them from making God's will their own will.[149]

Each of these four petitions shows that the novice disciples uttering them perceive themselves as needing God's help (1) so that their will to adopt this radical kind of behavior might be truly established and (2) so that they might remain faithful to this commitment as they carry it out. This is the ideal effect of this prayer: novice disciples who utter it thus acknowledge that they lack the will to do this teaching completely. Only with God's help can they hope truly to have the will to do what is expected of disciples.

Does this section of the Sermon on the Mount (in the plot dimension) anticipate that ideally the novice disciples will want to utter this prayer? On the basis of 5:20-6:21, we cannot say. We can onl note that uttering this prayer demands an acknowledgement that God is "our Father in heaven," a good God who wants to give good things to people.[150] The question becomes, Is it expected in 5:20-6:21 that the novice disciples would view God as such a good Father? Would they view themselves as children of such a Father? Or would they remain "like pagans" (5:47; 6:7), who fail to recognize God as a good Father and thus pray another kind of prayer (heaping up empty phrases in seeking to convince a hostile or indifferent god)? Once again, on the basis of 5:20-6:21, we cannot say. But the next section (6:22-7:12) shows that the Sermon anticipates that even in the case of an ideal response the novice disciples would not yet acknowledge the goodness of God as Father, and thus they would not yet want to claim the prayer of 6:9-13. Indeed, the ideal effect of this next section is primarily to convince the novice disciples that God is a good Father.

---

149. Note that by definition a "temptation" is something that leads one to adopt the wrong kind of will (one succumbs to temptation when one wants to do the wrong thing rather than God's will).

150. A God who gives rewards, but also "what you need," 6:8, as well as sun and rain, 5:45, to disciples, the good, the just, but also to the evil, the unjust.

◆

This interpretation focused on the story of the disciples posited by the Sermon, reading B, reaches conclusions about what the text says that are different from those reached by reading A. This is most striking when we compare their respective conclusions about what the Lord's Prayer is and says. In reading B, after the call to discipleship expressed by the beatitudes (5:3–10) and the multiple promises contained in the vocation of discipleship (5:11–16), the Sermon emphasizes conditions for being great in the kingdom (5:17–19) and conditions for entering the kingdom and thus for faithful discipleship (5:20–6:21). For any individual listeners who responded to this call and thus agreed to become novice disciples, the description of these conditions and of the radical behavior demanded from them challenges their resolve to be made disciples. The cost of discipleship is in full view. The question is, Who will want to carry out such daunting vocation, despite all the promises of personal rewards and of positive effects for others and for God? In this perspective, the Lord's Prayer (6:9–13) is read as an invitation to call on God for help. Thus the question is sharpened, Will each individual novice disciple have the confidence in God as "our Father in heaven" that praying this prayer requires?

By contrast, reading A concludes that the Lord's Prayer, 6:9–13, presents a set of indirect admonitions to implement the better righteousness which, in this interpretation focused on the history/realistic dimension, is a set of rules for community life. The issue that the Sermon addresses is not the difficulty of convincing people to become disciples. It is almost the reverse — the issue of boundaries that an established community of disciples needs to define because people unduly claim to be disciples. As soon as ("immediately" 4:20, 22) one has truly heard the revelation of the eternal will of God by the eschatological Lord, one is confronted by an unconditional command. This is indeed "a call to decision,"[151] but one does not really have any choice. Discipleship and obeying Jesus' word is not voluntary in the sense that one has actually to make up one's mind about it. Not obeying is a sign that one has not truly heard this authoritative revelation. But when one has truly heard it, one obeys and wants to be part of the eschatological community of disciples under God's eschatological rule. The only issue is that members of the community need to have a clear understanding of what is required of them. This contrast is further clarified as we follow the interpretation of 7:13–27 by Strecker and Kingsbury.

---

151. Strecker, *Sermon*, 156.

Reading A, CAW 6: Matthew 7:13–27: Closing Admonitions

In the prolongation of the historical/realistic dimension of 5:3–7:12, the closing section of the Sermon on the Mount, 7:13–27, is a series of concluding admonitions that further express how the teaching of the Sermon should be implemented in the life of the church. The three categories that we used for the interpretation of 5:21–7:12 — as an authoritative teaching of the exalted Kyrios; as a series of admonitions to a better righteousness in view of the coming judgment; as rules governing the life of the church — directly apply to this concluding section. The image of the gate and the way, 7:13–14, and the parables of 7:24–27 that frame these admonitions express (1) a similar "call to decision"[152] demanding the acknowledgment of the authority of the Lord of the church and of his teaching; (2) a similar warning about the coming judgment; and (3) similar criteria for distinguishing those who belong or do not belong to the community as "the sphere of God's eschatological Rule." As for the rest of his interpretation of the Sermon on the Mount, Strecker supports his *conclusions about what the text is and says* by emphasizing how Matthew redacted his sources. These conclusions we now summarize.

Reading A, CAW 6.1: Matthew 7:13–14, a Call to Practice Jesus' Teaching That Reflects the Situation of Matthew's Church

In the historical/realistic dimension, the image of the gate and the way, 7:13–14, summarizes Jesus' demands as a whole (as did the Golden Rule, 7:12): (1) it is a call to practice Jesus' teaching, despite its demanding character: "enter by the narrow gate" (7:13) and follow the "hard way" (cf. 7:14); it "invites the community and the world to recognize the claim of the *Kyrios*";[153] (2) it is a warning to the "many" (πολλοί): by not obeying this teaching "they are pronouncing a judgment on themselves; they are on the way to destruction"[154]; the urgency of practicing this teaching, as the "few" (ὀλίγοι) do, comes from perceiving it in terms of the judgment; not practicing it is going to perdition; (3) finally, the references to the "few" and the "many" reflect the situation of the church: a small community as compared with the many and potentially hostile outsiders.[155]

Reading A, CAW 6.2: Matthew 7:15–20: Apocalyptic Warnings That Become Criteria for Exclusion and Inclusion in the Church as Eschatological Community

In the historical/realistic dimension, the warning against false prophets, 7:15–20, has three functions. First, it is an eschatological pronouncement

---

152. Ibid.
153. Ibid., 158.
154. Ibid.
155. Ibid., 216–17 (note 8).

by the exalted Lord for those in the sphere of God's eschatological rule. What was in the tradition a threat belonging to the apocalyptic future (when the elect might be led astray by false prophets and false christs; cf. Mk 13:21) is now, even more clearly than in Mark, a present threat for the community. In other words, the eschatological teaching of the Kyrios applies to the present of the community at any time because it is the eschatological community. Second, the context of judgment is clear from 7:19. Third, the primary focus of this passage is to provide criteria for exclusion and inclusion in the community. These criteria are necessary because it is difficult to distinguish false prophets from true ones: "false prophets...come to you in sheep's clothing" (7:15). They are distinct because they have fundamentally different "inward" (7:15) natures. Either one *is* a disciple, a good tree (and thus is "salt" or "light" of the world, 5:13–16) or one *is not* a disciple, a bad tree (7:17–18). But this distinction only becomes apparent when one considers the fruits of these trees: "you will know them by their fruits" (7:16, 20). Those who truly belong to the community are those who do what Jesus commanded: those who have a better righteousness. But those who do not bear good fruit are, by nature, false prophets; they are not disciples, and thus they should be excluded from the community. This might be a reference to specific groups in the time of Matthew's community, e.g., antinomians.[156] But this saying is better understood as a general warning concerning false prophecy (and leadership), "a danger that threatens the church in all times."[157]

Reading A, CAW 6.3: Matthew 7:21–23 Applies the Preceding Criteria to All Church Members

In the historical/realistic dimension, the following saying, 7:21–23, emphasizes the lordship of Jesus and the necessity of recognizing him as Lord (7:21) because he is the Judge of the end of time ("on that day," 7:22). Yet its primary aim is to show that the preceding criteria apply not merely to the case of false prophets but also to all the members of the community. Those who merely acknowledge the lordship of Jesus (7:21), speak and prophesy in his name, and perform miracles in his name, without *doing* God's eternal will as revealed by Jesus, the eschatological Lord,[158] do not belong to the community and should be excluded from it, as they will be excluded at the judgment (7:23). What defines a member of the community, a disciple, is doing what is right (better righteousness), not doing charismatic works. The latter are not rejected, but they are "relativized and subordi-

---

156. Barth, "Matthew's Understanding of the Law," 74–75.
157. Strecker, *Sermon*, 162.
158. This passage can also be interpreted as referring to specific "charismatic" groups in the time of Matthew's community. But this teaching has more general applications. Strecker, *Sermon*, 166–68.

nated to the ethical demand."[159] Those who truly acknowledge Jesus as Lord, Kyrios, obey his teaching.

Reading A, CAW 6.4: Matthew 7:24–27: Obeying or Not Obeying the Teaching of the Kyrios Is Pronouncing a Judgment on Oneself

In the historical/realistic dimension, the closing parables of the wise and foolish builders, 7:24–27, with their emphasis on the fate of the houses, rather than on the activity of the builders,[160] once again indicate that acknowledging or denying the authority of the Kyrios and obeying or disobeying his teaching is pronouncing a judgment on oneself. Thus these parables are an admonition to make the right decision: obeying Jesus' words. This is once again making a decision under constraint (the judgment) rather than voluntarily. Furthermore, this passage makes clear that for Matthew, these demands are realizable; "this demand is obligatory. No one can escape its radicality under the pretext of its unrealizability; it is rather a directive instituted to be fulfilled."[161] These demands and their fulfillment delimit the community of those who truly belong to "the sphere of God's eschatological Rule."

Reading A, CAW 7: The Sermon on the Mount as a Law That Determines the Boundaries of the Christian Community

An interpretation focused on the historical/realistic dimension of the Sermon on the Mount concludes that the Sermon is an expression of God's eternal will by the exalted Lord (Kyrios, i.e., Son of God) as a law that urgently needs to be performed because of the coming of the judgment. As such, this is a law (rule) that determines the boundaries of the Christian community (it determines who belongs or does not belong to it) and the life inside this community. The nature of this community is summarized by Kingsbury in the following words:

> The nature of this new community derives from the call Jesus extends: through Jesus, who is God's unique Son in whom God's Kingdom is a present reality, those who make up this community live in the sphere of God's eschatological rule where God is their Father (6:9) and they are sons of God [cf. 5:9, 45; 13:38], disciples of Jesus (10:1; 26:18), and brothers of Jesus (28:10) and of one another (23:8). In a word, the new community Jesus forms is a brotherhood of the sons of God and of his disciples.[162]

---

159. Ibid., 168.
160. By contrast with Luke 6:47–49. Ibid., 169–70.
161. Ibid., 172.
162. Kingsbury, *Matthew as Story*, 104. The references in brackets were in a footnote in Kingsbury's book.

One is no longer surprised by such a statement. It is an accurate summary of the main features of the teaching of the historical/realistic dimension of the Sermon on the Mount. Its sex-exclusive language ("sons of God," "brothers," "brotherhood") expresses well the androcentric and patriarchal perspective — to which would need to be added the anti-Jewish perspective — of this coherent meaning-producing dimension of the Sermon. Even though this dimension of the Sermon provides a revelation by Jesus to the disciples of the nature of discipleship — "the quality of life that is indicative of disciples who live in the sphere of God's eschatological Rule"[163] — we will need to raise the question of the relative value of this interpretation as compared with interpretations focused on other dimensions of the text (an issue to be discussed in chap. 7). These concluding remarks also point toward the *conclusions about the teaching* of the Sermon on the Mount that readers in different settings could make their own — the issue to be discussed in chapter 5.

Reading A finds in the historical/realistic dimension of the Sermon an expression of God's eternal will as a law that needs to be performed urgently because of the coming of the judgment and that determines the boundaries of the Christian community. Reading B, in contrast, focuses on the story of the disciples posited by the Sermon: the decision to be made disciples is not reached under constraint or threat. In order to be authentic, a life of discipleship must be fully voluntary.

Reading B, CAW 6: Matthew 6:22–7:12: Basic Condition for Overabundant Righteousness — A Sound Eye

Reading B, CAW 6.1: The Preview of the Story of the Disciples in 6:22–7:12: How the Lack of Will to Adopt Such a Radical Behavior Is Overcome

The plot dimension of this new section of the Sermon on the Mount presents a preview of the story of the disciples focused on basic conditions for adopting the radical behavior — overabundant righteousness — required from full-fledged disciples (5:20–6:21) as they carry out their prophetic vocation as salt and light of the world (5:11–16). The focus is therefore on the stages of the plot concerning novice disciples: the lack of appropriate will that prevents them from being full-fledged disciples carrying out their vocation, the causes of this lack of will, and the way in which the will to become full-fledged disciples with an overabundant righteousness can be established.

Reading B, CAW 6.11: Matthew 6:22–24: The Nature of the Problem — A Divided Will Resulting from a Divided Eye. *As we begin to read 6:22–*

---

163. Ibid., 107.

23, it is not clear to which stage(s) of the plot the saying about the "eye" refers. When is it essential to have a "sound (ἁπλοῦς) eye" rather than an "evil (πονηρὸς) eye"? It is not even clear how the metaphor of a "sound eye" should be interpreted: ἁπλοῦς (literally referring to an eye "in good health," in the physical sense) can be a metaphorical reference to an eye that is "undivided," "single-minded," "sincere," or even "generous."[164]

The next saying, 6:24, clarifies these issues by showing plot relations and the nature of the problem with the unfolding of the plot. The description of someone who seeks (wants) to serve two masters (God and mammon) shows that the matter at hand is the divided will of a person. Thus the "evil eye" (6:23) is a "divided" eye; people with a "divided eye" are bound to have a divided will and try to serve two masters (6:24). By contrast, people with a "sound," "undivided" eye (6:22) can be totally devoted to a single and true master, God. The latter would be full-fledged disciples; that is, people who have made God's will their own will by internalizing it, and thus are in a position to do God's will by adopting the radical behavior described in 5:20–6:21. A condition for being such a disciple is to have a sound, "undivided" eye.

But the focus is on those who have an "evil eye" and consequently seek to serve two masters; these are people who have not yet taken the decisive step of internalizing God's will. Their "divided" eye leads them to have a divided will that prevents them from being full-fledged disciples.

Reading B, CAW 6.12: Matthew 6:25–34: Anxiety Is the Source of Divided Eye and Divided Will — Overcoming Anxiety by a Sound Eye Seeing Manifestations of God's Goodness (i.e., Faith).   *The next passage, 6:25–34, describes the same stage of the plot (establishing the will of novice disciples) in terms of "anxiety." Those who are anxious about their life (or soul; ψυχή) and body (or person; σῶμα)*[165] *are concerned about food, drink, clothing (6:25, 31), and thus "strive for*[166] *all these things" as the pagans do (6:32) instead of seeking the kingdom and God's righteousness, the principal (πρῶτον) task of disciples (6:33; cf. 5:6). In sum, novice disciples, who seek the kingdom (want to receive it) and who simultaneously are anxious about their life, do not have the right priority; their anxiety makes them want to serve two masters (6:24) and makes their eye "evil," "divided." They are not entirely devoted to the search for God's kingdom and for God's righteousness.*

Matthew 6:25–34 also provides a preview of the way in which novice disciples can overcome this anxiety — this evil eye and this divided will that end up preventing them from seeking the kingdom and from seeking God's

---

164. For this latter sense, which leads to an economic interpretation, see reading A, CAW 5.35. See also Davies and Allison, *Matthew*, 637–39, who list all the possible options.

165. On the ambiguity of the terms ψυχή and σῶμα in 6:25, see Betz, *Essays*, 104–7.

166. A good way of rendering the wrong kind of searching (ἐπιζητέω, by contrast with ζητέω) proposed by Betz, *Essays*, 97.

righteousness, i.e., seeking to make God's will their will (6:33). The first step involves using their "eye," which is sound enough to be used for looking at something else than themselves: "Look (ἐμβλέψατε) at the birds of the air" (6:26). What do novice disciples learn from considering birds and lilies? They discover that God feeds and clothes birds and lilies. Thus God is all the more willing to take care of the needs of human beings (6:30). They discover that God is their "heavenly Father" who knows that they need the necessities of life (6:32) and will give all these things to disciples who are entirely devoted to seeking the kingdom and God's righteousness (6:33). This confidence in God as the provider of the necessities of life, i.e., this "faith" (cf. "you of little faith," ὀλιγόπιστοι, 6:30), frees novice disciples from anxiety. They are then free to devote themselves entirely to the search of the kingdom, which, as we know (cf. 5:20–6:21), they will receive as a reward for seeking God's right-eousness (having an overabundant righteousness, 5:20, 46–47; being hungry and thirsty for righteousness, 5:6).

Reading B, CAW 6.13: Matthew 7:1–6: A Sound Eye to Be Used for Help-ing Others, Not for Condemning. The next pericope, 7:1-5, when read for its preview of the plot of the disciples' story, needs to be understood in terms of its concluding verse (7:5). Before taking "the speck out of [their] neighbor's eye" (7:5) – an appropriate task, a part of the vocation of disciples – novice disciples should "first take the log out of [their] own eye." In terms of the pre-ceding verses, they first need to transform their own "evil eye" into a "sound," "undivided eye." In addition, the role of a "sound eye" (that disciples should have) is specified; it should not be used to condemn others ("condemn not, that you be not condemned," 7:1),[167] as an evil eye (an eye with a log) does (7:2-3), but rather to help others (7:4-5). Yet one cannot truly help others as long as one does not have a sound eye; one must see the problems that others have clearly to help them. Righteousness (helping other people; cf. 5:21-48) is possible only when one has a sound eye.

In this perspective, 7:6 refers to the same limitation of novice disciples, although the emphasis is now on the failure to recognize good things for what they are (rather than on the failure to recognize problems). This saying describes people who are unable to distinguish between what is holy and what is impure (dogs); between what is of great value (pearls) and of little value (food for swine). This is again a description of novice disciples with an "unsound eye."

Reading B, CAW 6.14: Matthew 7:7–12: Consequences of Having a Sound Eye — Faith/Confidence in God and Being Willing to Do God's Will. The concluding pericope (7:7-12) of this section describes the consequences of

---

167. "Condemn" rather than "judge," because the warning about the Last Judgment concerns avoiding condemnation.

having a sound eye (6:22–23), i.e., of making use of one's ability to distinguish between good and evil, between more serious problems and less serious ones (7:1–5), between what is holy and what is impure, between what has great value and what has little value (7:6), between bread and stone (7:9), between fish and serpent (7:9–10), between good things for one's children and what is not good for them (7:11), between good things for oneself (what one wishes to have others do to oneself) and what is not good for oneself (7:12).

First because one can recognize what is good, including the fact that God takes care of birds and lilies (6:26–30) and that human parents want to give good things to their children (7:9–11), one recognizes that this must be even more true in the case of God's relation to human beings. Thus one acknowledges that God wants to give good things to human beings (7:11); one has confidence in God as the provider of good things (6:30), as "our Father who is in heaven" (6:9, 32; 7:11). This confidence in God is faith (cf. 6:30); "faith/confidence."[168]

Second, and consequently, with this faith/confidence in God's good will toward human beings, one is in a position to "ask," "seek," "knock" (7:7–8), "pray" (6:9), with the full confidence that God will "give good things to those who ask" (7:11).

Third, because of one's faith/confidence, one is in a position to recognize that what God requires the disciples to do to others is identical with the good things that one wishes others do to oneself: "this is the law and the prophets" (7:12). In other words, one recognizes that one's own will (one's wish for good things from others) and God's will (what God wishes that people would receive from others) are identical.

Fourth, and consequently, by considering what one wishes that other people would do to oneself, one knows God's will. Because one has faith/confidence that God will provide "the good things" one needs and asks, one no longer needs to seek these good things from others (or from another "master," 6:24); one no longer needs to hope that others will do them. Thus one is in a position of turning this "wish for oneself" into a "wish for others" to internalize God's will, to internalize the law and the prophets, to make God's will one's will. Such internalization constitutes an overabundant righteousness, i.e., to internalize God's will is to become a full-fledged disciple, to do good works toward others (5:16), to be light, salt, and prophet for them (5:11–16).

Reading B, CAW 6.2: The Ideal Effect of Matthew 6:22–7:12 on Novice Disciples — Fully Establishing Their Will to Carry Out Their Mission as Disciples

For the former fishers and the crowds, the ideal effect of this section of the Sermon on the Mount is fully to establish their will to have an overabundant

---

168. I use the phrase "faith/confidence" to signal the distinctiveness of the understanding of faith in this reading.

righteousness and thus to transform them into full-fledged disciples *ready to undertake their mission. This can readily be understood after our descrip- tion of the preview of the story of the disciples presented in 6:22–7:12. It is worth summarizing what is involved in this essential stage of the story of the disciples.*

First, the plot dimension of this section of the Sermon shows the novice disciples that their lack of will to carry out this teaching (it is too costly!) is due to their anxiety about their life — about food, drink, clothing, and other necessities (6:25–34), an anxiety that leads them to have a "divided will" (di- vided allegiance, 6:24). The novice disciples are also told what is the cause of this anxiety: a "divided eye" (6:22–23), the lack of an ability to distinguish a serious problem from a small one (7:3–5), holy from impure, great value from little value (7:6).

Yet the novice disciples are also shown that this problem (having a divided eye) is not irremediable. In fact, they merely failed to use their eye! Indeed, if they would use their eye, they would see that God takes care of the birds and of the lilies, and they would recognize that God takes all the more care of human beings and especially of disciples (6:26, 30, 32). Thus they would have faith/confidence in the goodness of God as provider of the good things that they need (6:30; cf. 7:11). They would also recognize that they cannot pretend to do good things for others (taking the speck out of other people's eyes) with their eyes closed (encumbered by a log, 7:5). But most importantly, they would recognize that their "eye" is naturally "sound"; they know how to discern what is good for their children from what is bad for them, as well as what is good from what is bad for themselves (7:9–12).

Second, by identifying themselves with those who use their eyes in this way, the novice disciples should ideally be convinced that God does want to give the good things they need (6:32); they should ideally be convinced to have faith/confidence in God. Thus they should be free from anxiety; in- stead of anxiously striving to obtain the necessities of life as the pagans do (6:32), they would know that they can simply ask God to give them these good things (7:11), and thus they would be free to devote all their energy to seeking the kingdom and God's righteousness (6:33).

Finally, they would truly want to seek God's righteousness relentlessly (6:33), to hunger and thirst for righteousness (5:6) as they hungered and thirsted for food and drink, and to have overabundant righteousness, not only because they would want to receive the kingdom, but also because they would internalize God's will, making God's will their own, since after all God's will as expressed in the law and the prophets is already what they want to do for their children (7:11) and what they want others to do to them (7:12).

◆

In sum, by 7:12, the novice disciples would ideally be transformed into full-fledged disciples, ready to carry out their mission. Our systematic study of the plot dimension of the story of the disciples expressed in 5:3–7:12 provides us with an almost complete plot of this story, encompassing both the process of becoming disciples and the process of making disciples. This is the process that readers are invited to emulate (as we shall discuss in chap. 5, reading B, CAT). A brief review of this overall plot might be useful at this point.

Reading B, CAW 6.3: Overall Plot of the Story of the Disciples

(The overall plot of the story of the disciples expressed in Matthew 5:3–7:12 can be summarized in the following table as a series of stages, moving from the situation prior to becoming novice disciples (when one already knows God's will) to the present and future consequences of doing God's will, when at last the disciples do God's will.

Preview of the Story of the Disciples in Matthew 5:3–7:12

Stage 0. Prior to Becoming Novice Disciples: Knowing God's Will

Before Jesus' ministry, people already have a certain body of teachings (5:21, 27, 33, 38, 43); they know the law (and the prophets). In addition, they have the "natural" abilities of distinguishing good from bad (7:7–12) and recognizing what God is doing in their present (6:22, 26, 28).

Stage 1. Becoming Novice Disciples: Acknowledging the Authority/Trustworthiness of Jesus

Their first step toward discipleship involves acknowledging the authority/trustworthiness of Jesus and his promises as the four fishers did in 4:18–22, and as the crowds are invited to do in the beatitudes (5:3–10) — words and promises that are authoritative, effective, and transformative.

Stage 2. Recognizing God's Goodness

Because of the guidance they receive from Jesus they have a "sound eye" (6:22), i.e., the ability to recognize God's providence and to acknowledge their own blindness (6:26, 28; 7:3–5); the ability to recognize the good for self and others and not to confuse it with the impure and with the useless (7:6–12); and thus also the ability to recognize manifestations of God's goodness in the good works of others (5:16) and in Jesus' fulfillment of the law and the prophets (5:17) to which he subordinates himself.

Stage 3. Trusting in God's Goodness, Having Faith

Because they now recognize the manifestations of God's goodness, they can trust God as their loving Father (5:45, 48; 6:8, 9), who wants to take care of them.

They are no longer anxious (6:31, 34). They have "faith" (6:30, rather than "little faith"); they have confidence that God will give good things to them when they ask (7:11).

Stage 4. Making God's Will Their Own Will; Appropriating Jesus' Teaching, Internalizing the Law, Praying

Since they now recognize God as their loving Father, they can recognize that God's will is good for them, i.e., something that they truly want to do. Thus acknowledging the authority of Jesus' teaching as an expression of God's will, they can internalize the law; they are willing to go beyond the letter of the law and to renounce "provisions of the law" that would allow them to limit their quest for righteousness (5:20–48); they pray for God's help so that their will to have an overabundant righteousness be truly established and so that they might remain faithful to this commitment (6:9–13).

Stage 5. Doing God's Will

Having an Overabundant Righteousness

Because they are now aware that doing God's will is good for them and others, they are eager to do everything that might be implied by the law and other expressions of God's will. This "overabundant righteousness" (5:20, 46), the behavior of the blessed ones in the beatitudes (5:3–10) further presented in 5:21–6:18, is seeking first the kingdom and God's righteousness (6:33).

Carrying Out One's Mission

As they perform these good works of overabundant righteousness, they are prophet, salt, and light of the world and thus carry out their vocation: seeing their good works, people can give glory to God (5:16). Through them other people can recognize God's goodness (see stage 2) and thus be on their way toward becoming disciples themselves. Through their overabundant righteousness they have become full-fledged disciples, and they are making disciples of other people (28:19–20).

Stage 6. The Better Way to Carry Out the Disciples' Mission

The best way for full-fledged disciples to carry out their mission lies in recognizing that Jesus is himself subordinated to the law and the prophets and in following his example by doing and teaching all the commandments (5:19).

Stage 7. Immediate Consequences

Consequences for Others:

Being "salt" (5:13); being "light" (5:14). Others give thanks to God for the good works of the disciples (5:11–16) (i.e., they recognize God's goodness; see stage 2).

Consequences for God:

Being glorified by people (5:16); God's name being hallowed (6:9).

Consequences for Disciples:

Confidence that the kingdom is theirs, that they belong to it ("theirs is the kingdom of heaven," 5:3, 10); rejoicing and being glad (5:12); being children of the heavenly Father (5:45); being confident of receiving rewards from God (6:4, 6, 18); being forgiven (6:14); having treasures and one's heart in heaven (6:20–21).

Stage 8. Future Rewards for Disciples: The Kingdom

Entering the kingdom (5:20); receiving a reward from God (6:4, 6, 18); being comforted, inheriting the earth, being satis- *fied, obtaining mercy, seeing God, being called children of God (5:4–9); great rewards in heaven (5:12).*

Special rewards for disciples who fulfill all the law: being great in the kingdom (5:19).

Reading B, CAW 6.4: The Overall Ideal Effect of This Preview of the Story of the Disciples

The significance of the plot of the story previewed in 5:3–7:12 appears when we consider its ideal overall effect on the former fishers and the crowds.

Reading B, CAW 6.41: Matthew 5:3–7:12: Ideally Transforms the Former Fishers and the Crowds into Disciples Ready to Carry Out Their Mission. *A brief survey of the plot expressed by the previews of the story of the disciples in this dimension of 5:3–7:12 shows that by 7:12 the fishers and the crowds should ideally be ready to carry out their mission (as described in stage 5).*

For them, the beatitudes (5:3–10) should be a confirmation of the authority/trustworthiness of Jesus and of his promises (stage 1); thus, the fishers and the crowds should have agreed to become novice disciples. Yet their commitment is only tentative at this point. Despite their acknowledgment of Jesus' authority/trustworthiness, they are ready neither to undertake the mission described in 5:11–16, nor to fulfill all the law (5:17–19), nor to have the overabundant righteousness that Jesus teaches in 5:20–6:21. In sum, despite the knowledge of what discipleship entails revealed by Jesus in 5:3–6:21 — and possibly because of this revelation — the novice disciples would lack the will to adopt such a radical and "costly" behavior and to become full-fledged disciples. They would remain novice disciples, and thus at stage 1.

In order to progress toward full-fledged discipleship, fishers and crowds need to make God's will their own will by internalizing the law (stage 4). For this, they need to have "faith," i.e., full confidence in God's goodness and thus full confidence that God's will is truly "good for them" (stage 3). Yet there is no indication that up to this point (6:21) in their hearing of the Sermon anything would have established for them such a faith. In terms of the story of the disciples they would lack confidence in God's goodness (they would have "little faith," 6:30) because they would still have an "evil eye" (6:22–23) and consequently would fail to perceive the goodness of God (6:25–34 — stage 2).

But after hearing 6:22–7:12, and especially after their attention (their sight) is drawn to the manifestations of God's goodness (6:25–34), the fishers and crowds should be in a position to recognize God's goodness, and thus to have faith (stage 3). The only remaining obstacle would be that they might not trust their own ability to recognize what is truly good; in such a case, they would have doubt about what they perceive as manifestations of God's goodness, a condition for faith. But 7:7–11 should remove for them this last obstacle by demonstrating to them that even evil people know how to distinguish what is good from what is evil. Thus they should discover that they have a "sound eye" (stage 2) that they should have the confidence to use, trusting that their perception of the manifestations of God's goodness are true indications of God's care for human beings. Thus they should be in a position of having faith/confidence in God's goodness (7:11b; stage 3). Consequently, they should be ready to acknowledge that God's will is "good for them," i.e., that it is nothing other than what they perceive as good for themselves (what they "wish" for themselves, 7:12). With this acknowledgment, they would then be ready to internalize God's will; indeed, they would discover that they have already internalized God's will, since "the law and the prophets" are nothing other than what they wish others to do to them (7:12). It is just a matter of redirecting this "wish for oneself" to transform it in a "wish for others" (7:12). They should be ready to seek first God's kingdom and God's righteousness (6:33), i.e., to be willing to appropriate Jesus' teaching by internalizing the law and by praying with confidence to their "Father in heaven," asking what they need to fulfill all righteousness (stage 4).

In sum, the ideal effect of hearing 5:3–7:12 on the fishers and the crowds should be that they would be ready to carry out their mission as full-fledged disciples, at least in a minimal way. In the actual story, this is the situation of the disciples at the end of the gospel (28:16–20). Apparently, much more is actually needed to transform the fishers and members of the crowds into fishers of people! The question is, What are they still missing? How will they be made full-fledged disciples? We can anticipate that they still miss what Jesus will do for them during his ministry. Yet the Sermon on the Mount expresses it. Since the disciples' vocation is similar to Jesus' vocation — making disciples — the presentation of the disciples' mission in the Sermon clarifies what is involved in making disciples, and thus what the fishers and the crowds are still missing.

Reading B, CAW 6.42: The Mission of the Disciples — Performing Good Works toward Others in Order to Make Disciples out of Them. *How should we understand the disciples' mission according to the plot dimension of the Sermon on the Mount? What is its purpose? The descriptions of this mission in 4:19, "being fishers of people," and in 28:19, "making disciples," seem quite different from the description found in the Sermon on the Mount: the mission of prophets (5:11–12), of salt of the earth, and light of the world (5:13–16; stage 5b).*

What is most surprising is that, according to the Sermon, fulfilling this mission entails only having an overabundant righteousness, i.e., performing good works toward others (5:20–48) and carrying out one's religious duties "in secret" (6:1–21). How can this be a way of "making disciples"? Why is there no mention that the disciples should proclaim the gospel preached by Jesus (4:17, 23), thus proclaiming Jesus' authority as the one who brought this good news?

These questions reflect more our presuppositions about what making disciples entails than the concept of making disciples presented in the plot dimension of the Sermon on the Mount. To see the Sermon's view of making disciples, we need only consider once again the beginning of the story of the fishers and of the crowds in terms of the preview of the story of the disciples.

One might wrongly imagine that stage 1, the preliminary establishment of the novice disciples' will, is not the actual beginning of their story. Before acknowledging the authority/trustworthiness of Jesus and of his promises, the would-be disciples knew something about Jesus, did they not? Surely Jesus made himself known to them. Were they not confronted by his presence, an encounter that Jesus initiated by going to the fishers (4:18, 21)[169] and to the people who benefit from his ministry and become crowds of followers (4:23)? One could think that an important first stage of the story is that, by his very actions, Jesus makes himself known to the fishers and the crowds.

Yet it is striking that Matthew's text does not underscore this point at all. Indeed, it is those who have less knowledge about Jesus who unambiguously become novice disciples — there is no indication that the fishers knew anything about Jesus when he called them.[170] The crowds are described as bringing their sick to him because of his fame (4:24), and thus because they have knowledge about him. But this is a vague knowledge that concerns primarily his good works (healings).

Thus the description of the disciples' mission in the Sermon on the Mount (stage 5b) is not out of step with 4:18–25; in both cases "making Jesus known" is not at all emphasized, although one might presuppose that this is (or will be) an important part of the disciples' task. At best, the Sermon alludes to such a task when it mentions that the disciples will be persecuted "on my [Jesus'] account" (5:11).[171]

We have to let ourselves be puzzled by the fact that the Sermon on the Mount barely alludes to this eventual aspect of the disciples' mission. Why is their mission as prophets, salt of the earth, and light of the world (stage 5b) exclusively described as an overabundant righteousness (stage 5a)? We have

---

169. A point emphasized by commentators focusing on other dimensions of the text; see e.g., Davies and Allison, *Matthew*, 396; Schweizer, *Matthew*, 76.

170. The text notes that Jesus "saw" them (4:18, 21), but it does not even hint that the fishers might have seen him.

171. The same is true in the other discourses about the disciples' mission. In 10:5–42, the only possible allusions to the disciples' proclamation of Jesus occur in references to persecution "for my name's sake" (10:18, 22; cf. 10:25 and 10:32–33, acknowledging or denying Jesus before people). Similarly in 28:18–20 the description of the first stage of the disciples' mission, making disciples, does not mention proclaiming Jesus; yet the fact that the new disciples are to be baptized "in the name of the Father and of the Son and of the Holy Spirit" and to be taught what Jesus taught them presupposes that a proclamation of Jesus took place. The question is, What is the role of this proclamation? Why is it not made more explicit?

to conclude that it is because having an overabundant righteousness (stage 5) is, by far, the most important part of the disciples' mission. Accordingly, the way to make disciples out of people would be to perform good works, i.e., having an overabundant righteousness.[172] In order to understand that this is the case, we need to revisit stages of the plot of the story previewed in 5:3–7:12.

First, note that among the "immediate consequences" of the disciples' overabundant righteousness (stage 7) is the fact that others will "see your good works and give glory to your Father who is in heaven" (5:16). In other words, as a result of the disciples' good works, people give thanks to God and thus recognize God's goodness; or, metaphorically, they are "in the light" (5:15–16a). This means that the disciples' good works establish the basic conditions that will allow these people to become disciples themselves: having faith (see stage 3). They now acknowledge God's goodness, which they recognize in the goodness of the disciples' works (rather than in what happens to the birds and the lilies, 6:26–30); they are "full of light" and thus have a "sound eye" (6:23; stage 2).

In sum, it is not preaching but performing such good works that is the way of making disciples; these good works overcome the obstacle to discipleship for others, namely, their failure to recognize the goodness of God ("evil eye," cf. 6:23) and their failure to have faith/confidence in God's goodness (6:30).

But how will people recognize the goodness of God in the disciples' good works? We can understand it in part by noting that the very radical nature of their good works — seeking reconciliation even when one is not at the origin of the dispute (5:23–24), making no effort to protect oneself or one's belongings (5:38–42), loving one's enemies (4:43–44) — has the same effect as Jesus' exhortation to "look at the birds" (6:26); one cannot but take notice of such radical good works!

Yet why would people give thanks to God for these good works, instead of praising the disciples themselves (the most natural reaction)? The Sermon on the Mount does not provide any direct answer to this question. It is only at the very end of the actual story of the disciples, during the Passion (which ends for the disciples in 28:17), that it will be clarified that crucifixionlike persecutions are what makes it possible to recognize in the disciples' good works manifestations of God's goodness. Yet the Sermon on the Mount itself allows us to make several remarks.

For people seeing these good works, their radical character might by itself raise a question concerning the motivation of the disciples, suggesting that their will is established by God and that they act as children of God

---

172. Luz makes a similar point (although he introduces "proclamation" from other parts of the Gospel), when he writes, "The praxis of the Sermon on the Mount is conducive to the people praising the Father in heaven (5:16). Thus it is that the word of proclamation aims at deeds (Mt 18:20!), and deeds, in turn, become proclamation" (Luz, *Matthew*, 216).

(5:45) and thus in the name of God, or that they are insane. Yet the second aspect of their righteousness (6:1–21) plays an essential role; by giving alms, praying, and fasting "in secret," the disciples adopt an attitude that prevents receiving praise from people. Matthew 5:21–48 should not be isolated from 6:1–21; they are two aspects of the same overall behavior. According to 5:21–47, taken by itself, each of the disciples' good works already entails renouncing something — renouncing the condemnation of others (5:23–24); renouncing a member of one's body (5:29–30); renouncing the possibility of divorce (5:31); renouncing appeals to God or to anything else to avoid doing something or giving a straight answer (5:33–37); renouncing protection (5:38–42); renouncing hatred of one's enemies and thus accepting persecution (5:43–44; cf. 5:11–12). In addition, in light of 6:1–21, all these good works should be performed in such a way as to avoid receiving praise from other people, as the duties toward God also should be. In this way it becomes clear that the disciples' motivation is not a human motivation (receiving praise from others), and thus that its origin is in God. It becomes clear that it is God's will that they fulfill, and thus that their good works are manifestations of God's goodness.

Yet as suggested above, persecution, a form of purification of the disciples' good works and thus a form of forgiveness (cf. 6:12, 14–15) is what ultimately makes clear that these are not the disciples' good works, but indeed God's good works.[173] Consequently, seeing the disciples' good works, people give glory to God (5:16) and through this acknowledgment of God's goodness (cf. 6:22–7:12) are in the process of being made disciples, which they will become fully by being taught all that Jesus commanded the disciples (28:20; 5:17–6:21) and by doing it, as they are eager to do at this point.

◆

In sum, the ideal effect on the fishers and the crowds of the preview of the story of the disciples presented in 5:3–7:12 is that they would be willing to be made full-fledged disciples, and thus be willing to carry out their mission and to be salt and light of the world through their good works of overabundant righteousness. They should be willing to do the will of God as taught by Jesus because now they are aware that God's will is good for them and because they have a glimpse that it is also good for others.

---

173. Then 6:12, 14–15 makes sense. First, note that these verses are puzzling in that they include the affirmation that only the one who has forgiven others will be forgiven by God. This affirmation is all the more puzzling when one recognizes that forgiving others epitomizes all the good deeds described in 5:21–48 because it means that our good deeds would need to be forgiven. Indeed, they need to be forgiven! As long as we consider and implicitly or explicitly convey to others that the good things we do are *our* good deeds, (1) we are hypocritical, and (2) we prevent other people from giving thanks *to* God. Thus "our good deeds" do indeed need to be forgiven!

Reading B, CAW 7: Matthew 7:13–27 and the Urgency of the Disciples' Mission

In reading the rest of the plot dimension of the Sermon on the Mount (7:13 –
27), we proceed as we did earlier. First, we identify the stages of the story
of the disciples to which it refers, and then we discuss the ideal effect of the
passage on the hearers. We need to bear in mind that by 7:12 the hearers
have ideally been transformed into full-fledged disciples ready to carry out
their mission.

As we examine the plot dimension, we note a shift of addressees after
7:12. They are no longer people in the process of being made disciples (i.e.,
novice disciples), but full-fledged disciples, religious leaders who are supposed
to make disciples by carrying out their mission. Consequently, in the plot dimension these verses have to be read as further instructions for carrying out
their mission.[174] The section can be subdivided into three passages: 7:13–14;
7:15–20; 7:21–27.

Reading B, CAW 7.1: Matthew 7:13–14 — The Narrow Gate and the Hard Road

In light of the previewed story expressed in 5:3–7:12, the exhortation to "enter by the narrow gate" (7:13) and thus to follow "the hard way" that "leads to
life" (7:14) amounts to an exhortation to disciples to carry out their mission
(performing good works of overabundant righteousness as a way of making
disciples; stages 5 and 6), since "entering" the kingdom (here, "life") is one of
the rewards (stage 8) for doing so. Yet 7:13 is primarily a description of the
irremediable condemnation and destruction of the many who take the "wide
gate" and the "easy way," while 7:14 ends with a lament that "those who
find [the way to life] are few."

The ideal effect of Matthew 7:13–14 is to urge the full-fledged disciples
to carry out their mission. The description of the many who are going to
destruction and the few who find the way to life should have the ideal effect of underscoring the urgency of this mission. If they do not do so, many
will perish! It should be emphasized that (in an interpretation focused on the
plot dimension) these warnings about the judgment (as well as those found
in 7:15–27) are not to be interpreted as aimed at convincing the hearers to
become disciples; ideally, the hearers have already been convinced, in part
by promises of rewards (stage 1). According to the story, one becomes a disciple because one wants to receive blessings from God and trusts in God's

---

174. Thus they can be viewed at that point as "religious leaders," and thus as leaders of
the community. This change of addressees (the end of the Sermon on the Mount as directed
to leaders of the community) has been recognized by Minear, even though he places the shift
after 7:14 (rather than after 7:12). See P. Minear, "False Prophecy and Hypocrisy in the Gospel
of Matthew," in *Neues Testament und Kirche: Festschrift R. Schnackenburg*, ed. J. Gnilka
(Freiburg: Herder, 1974), 76–93 (see especially 85).

goodness, not because one fears condemnation and punishments (contrast with reading A, CAW 6.1).

Reading B, CAW 7.2: Matthew 7:15–20 as Instruction to Disciples Carrying Out Their Urgently Needed Mission

Similarly, 7:15–18, 20 contain instructions that refer to disciples in the process of carrying out their mission (stage 5); they should "beware of false prophets" and learn how to recognize them "by their fruits." In addition, 7:19 describes the irremediable destruction/condemnation of those who do not bear "good fruit."

The ideal effect of Matthew 7:15–20 is to urge the disciples to prevent the actions of false prophets that mislead people to perdition. In addition, 7:19 once again shows the urgency of their mission, since it is not only the false prophets who will be destroyed, but also their followers who, like them, will fail to bear fruit. By contrast, if the disciples carry out their vocation, the people whom they make into disciples will bear good fruit (overabundant righteousness), and thus will not be destroyed.

Reading B, CAW 7.3: Matthew 7:21–27: The Urgency for the Disciples to Carry Out Their Mission in a Proper Way

Once again we find a description of the irremediable condemnation and destruction (7:21, 23, 26–27) of people who fail to be true disciples, namely, those who fail to do the will of God (7:21) that Jesus taught (7:26), even though they acknowledge the authority of Jesus as Lord (7:21) and perform miracles in his name (7:22). Only those who do God's will shall enter the kingdom (7:21; stage 8); those who do Jesus' words and have therefore an overabundant righteousness are like a house built on the rock.

The ideal effect of Matthew 7:21–27 on disciples is similar to that of the preceding passages. In an interpretation focused on the plot dimension, these descriptions of eschatological condemnation and destruction are not warnings aimed at convincing the ideal hearers to become disciples by doing the will of God according to Jesus' teaching, since they are already convinced to have an overabundant righteousness. Rather, they are aimed at showing disciples the urgency of carrying out their mission in a proper way. It is not enough to convince people to recognize Jesus' authority (stage 1). If people merely acknowledge Jesus as "Lord" but do not do God's will, they will be condemned, even if they perform miracles in Jesus' name. Thus it is essential that the disciples through their mission convince people to do God's will as taught by Jesus. For this purpose, they do need to teach people what Jesus taught them (cf. 28:20). But the essence of their mission is to convince people to do this teaching. For this purpose, the disciples need to perform good works so that people might glorify God and acknowledge God's goodness (stages 2 and 3). Then such people will be in a position to want to do God's

will (stage 4) and to do it by having an overabundant righteousness themselves; as a consequence, these people will be in a position to carry out their
own mission as disciples (stage 5).

Reading B, CAW 8: The Sermon on the Mount Transforms Its Hearers into Full-Fledged Disciples Ready to Carry Out Their Mission

These comments on 7:13–27 are an appropriate conclusion to our study
of the plot dimension of the Sermon on the Mount, which included elucidating the story of the disciples as previewed by the Sermon. In sum, the
Sermon aims at transforming the fishers and the crowds into full-fledged disciples ready to carry out their mission. But because their mission is nothing
less than making disciples out of people, the way in which the plot dimension of the Sermon ideally affects its hearers also provides a model of the
way disciples should carry out their mission. They should call people to discipleship by proclaiming the promises of blessings that Jesus first announced,
especially the good news of the kingdom (cf. 5:3–10); they should also teach
people the nature of the mission to which they are called (cf. 5:11–16) and
how to carry out this vocation, the overabundant righteousness that is God's
will (5:17–6:21). But primarily they should convince these people of God's
goodness through their good works (cf. 6:22–7:12). Once these new disciples are ready to assume their mission, the original disciples should instruct
them concerning the urgency of carrying out this mission in order to save
people from condemnation (7:13–27). Clearly, these concluding remarks are
becoming conclusions about the teaching of the Sermon on the Mount that
readers in different settings could make their own — the issue that we will
discuss in chapter 5.

CHAPTER 4

Figurative and Thematic Interpretations of Discipleship according to the Sermon on the Mount

In this chapter I present, in the form of a twofold commentary, the different interpretations of discipleship according to the Sermon on the Mount advanced by Luz[1] and Davies and Allison,[2] on the one hand, and by myself,[3] on the other. The twofold commentary moves back and forth between the two kinds of interpretations as it presents their respective *conclusions about what the Sermon on the Mount is and says* concerning discipleship in its different sections.

This twofold commentary is androcritical. The scholarly arguments proposed by these male European-American scholars in their respective commentaries must be reexamined from this perspective. Luz and Davies and Allison fail to be fully critical because they do not conceive of their interpretation as resulting from a choice of *one among several* possible coherent interpretations. Thus they fail to bring to light for themselves and for others a part of their interpretive processes because they do not envision the possibility that a text might have several meaning-producing dimensions, each the potential basis for a coherent interpretation. They view their critical interpretation as an effort to express "the" only true teaching of the Sermon on the Mount about discipleship, even though it simply actualizes the potential of the one specific meaning-producing dimension on which it is focused.

The case of my commentary is a bit different, but it also fails to be fully critical. I recognize the existence of different meaning-producing

---

1. Ulrich Luz, *Matthew 1–7: A Commentary* (Minneapolis: Augsburg, 1989), 203–460.

2. W. D. Davies and D. C. Allison Jr., *A Critical and Exegetical Commentary on the Gospel according to Saint Matthew*, vol. 1, ICC (Edinburgh: T. & T. Clark, 1988), 410–731.

3. Daniel Patte, *The Gospel according to Matthew: A Structural Commentary on Matthew's Faith* (Minneapolis: Fortress, 1987; 3d printing, Valley Forge, Pa.: Trinity Press International, 1996), 60–108.

dimensions, each of which has the potential of being the basis of a set of interpretations, and I emphasize that this commentary is limited to the study of one of its dimensions — its convictional dimension, which expresses "Matthew's faith."[4] But my exegetical work remained one-dimensional at this stage in my research because I still presupposed that one of these dimensions represented "the" only true teaching of the text — the teaching that the author sought to convey. My goal was to elucidate "the" only true meaning-producing dimension that conveyed the faith of the author. This goal is appropriate. But in pursuing it, I pretended that the other dimensions could not be as legitimate an expression of the author's faith, although they can be as I have shown since then.[5] Thus, through this inappropriate claim, I hid the epistemology and value judgments that governed my choice of a dimension and of an interpretation.

Because of the one-dimensional character of our works, Luz, Davies and Allison, and I ended up incorporating in our (single) interpretation everything that we found significant about the Sermon on the Mount. There is confusion in each of our interpretations when we treat as central certain textual features that are actually peripheral to the focus of our reading. Through the proposed androcritical multidimensional examination, I propose to clarify the nature of the critical arguments presented by Luz, Davies and Allison, and myself in our respective commentaries so as to elucidate the differences between our *conclusions about what the Sermon on the Mount is and says* concerning discipleship. Once again, my goal is to show the legitimacy of each of these scholarly interpretations. Although each is conceived of as a quest for "the" total and only true meaning of the Sermon on the Mount, it remains basically legitimate in that it presents *one among several* possible *coherent* interpretations that can be based on the various meaning-producing dimensions of this text. Thus in this chapter, even more than in the preceding one, I strive to elucidate the coherence of each kind of interpretation by emphasizing those features of the interpretation that directly reflect the chosen dimension of the text and by bracketing out its features which, for one reason or another, focus on another dimension — most often, the historical/realistic dimension.

I now wonder why, despite my theoretical awareness, I ended up in a one-dimensional predicament similar to that of Luz and Davies and Allison. I have to conclude that we all tended to revert to an interpretation focused on the historical/realistic dimension for the same basic reason. It was a matter of plausibility and thus of epistemology, not of legitimacy. In other words, each of us could readily perceive the coherence of the respec-

---

4. Patte, *Matthew,* 13; see 1–15.
5. See Daniel Patte, *The Religious Dimensions of Biblical Texts: Greimas's Structural Semiotics and Biblical Exegesis,* SBL Semeia Studies (Atlanta: Scholars Press, 1990), 103–215. In this monograph, I show how three different dimensions express faith, each in its own way. Any one of these three can be the expression of the faith that the author seeks to convey.

tive dimensions (the figurative and thematic dimensions), which became the focus of our interpretations. But we felt uneasy about our conclusions because they did not add up to a view of discipleship as ethical practice and to an ethical teaching that readily fit the traditional preunderstanding of the moral life, as providing a knowledge of "what disciples should do." Because we were totally fascinated by this deontological preunderstanding of the moral life and of discipleship as doing God's will, an understanding associated with the historical/realistic dimension of the Sermon on the Mount (as discussed in chap. 5), we tended to combine our figurative or thematic conclusions with historical/realistic conclusions. To avoid this pitfall and to free ourselves to develop the coherence of the figurative and thematic dimensions, we need to be confident that the conclusions about what the text is and says resulting from a focus on these dimensions point toward a plausible view of discipleship. For this reason, in the presentation of the coherence and legitimacy of both the figurative and thematic interpretations, I include allusions to the other plausible view of discipleship: discipleship as "imitation" (to be further discussed in chap. 6).

After our multidimensional study of Matthew 4:18–22, a few introductory remarks regarding the meaning-producing dimensions on which these two kinds of interpretations are focused are sufficient to clarify the critical methods that help to make the legitimacy and coherence of both kinds of interpretations explicit.

Reading C: History of Traditions and Figurative Critical Interpretations Focused on the Figurative Dimension of the Sermon on the Mount

We have already noted regarding Matthew 4:18–22 that Luz as well as Davies and Allison focus their scholarly interpretations on the *figurative* meaning-producing dimension of the text (even though these critics rarely use terms like "figure" or "figurative").

A first indication that they read the text figuratively is their emphasis that the teachings of the Sermon on the Mount "are general," so much so that injunctions ostensibly addressed to the disciples during Jesus' ministry ("you") are actually addressed to the total community[6] and even to the world.[7] In other words, "a teaching addressed to the disciples of Jesus' time" is a figure for "similar teachings addressed to disciple-like people in other times and spaces," such as the community in Matthew's time. Furthermore, Luz and Davies and Allison interpret each figure in terms of other texts and traditions to which it alludes and seek to understand the place of each figure in the overall figurative organization of the text.

---

6. As Luz (*Matthew*, 249) says, for instance, about 5:13–16.
7. Luz, *Matthew*, 216.

Thus for their respective critical studies of the figurative dimension of the Sermon on the Mount, they use in part a "history of traditions" approach, which is essential for identifying the evocations of other texts and traditions by means of which figures are constructed. Davies and Allison make a particularly systematic effort to identify all possible allusions to traditions and texts, including those that at first might not seem to be relevant.[8] Since this approach also includes taking note of the way in which the redactor transformed traditions and sources in order to construct the figures of the text, a redaction critical approach is also appropriate. This is a part of the method used by Luz, although it obviously does not have the same focus as it has for Strecker (see chap. 3, reading A, CAW 1.1); a significant part of Luz's approach involves elucidating how the redactor reshapes the traditional figures into new figures.[9]

Furthermore, Luz and Davies and Allison use what can be called a *comparative critical approach* which, from our androcritical multidimensional perspective, contributes to their elucidation of the figurative dimension. As they critically review previous scholarly studies, their polemical comments against other critical studies are somewhat misguided, since they criticize what are in most instances historical/realistic interpretations for not taking into account figurative features. Yet in the process, they further elucidate the figurative dimension on which their own critical studies are focused. In their commentaries, this comparative approach also takes the form of a consideration of what Luz calls the "history of influence" (*Wirkungsgeschichte*), i.e., of the different ways in which a given passage has been interpreted through the history of the church. This *Wirkungsgeschichte* is often the occasion for Luz to take note of the possibility of a figurative interpretation.

Finally, both Luz and Davies and Allison pay close attention to the *figurative organization* of the text. This involves interpreting the Sermon on the Mount as a figurative textual unit of the Gospel according to Matthew and identifying its subunits and their interrelation with the help of certain *literary conventions*. Thus these interpreters identify inclusions, chiasms, ring compositions, use of triads, and other stylistic features of the text,[10] so as to identify the subunits of the Sermon on the Mount. This is an important step for their scholarly interpretations because in this *figurative* dimension

---

8. See Davies and Allison, *Matthew,* 34–58 — a long table of quotations of and allusions to the LXX.

9. Because of the different emphases of their respective critical studies, Davies and Allison and Luz devote more time to the elucidation of one or another aspect of the figurative dimension. Thus Davies and Allison, with their history of traditions approach, tend to emphasize the diversity of traditions to which the text alludes and thus the construction of figures. Luz, on the other hand, pays greater attention to the semantic coherence of the Sermon on the Mount, which contributes to the construction of a figurative system or symbolic world.

10. Davies and Allison, *Matthew,* 58–96. Luz, *Matthew,* 33–46, 49–73.

the *center* of each chiastic structure is one of the keys for interpreting the figures of a passage.

We will begin our discussion with interpretations of the figurative structure of the Sermon on the Mount advocated by Luz and Davies and Allison. This structure plays a most important role in this critical study and also facilitates the comparison with the study of the thematic dimension that I propose.

Finally, in order to show the coherence of the history of traditions/ figurative critical interpretations of Luz and Davies and Allison, I will seek to elucidate how their *conclusions about what specific passages are and say* are related to the figurative organization of the Sermon on the Mount, which they themselves emphasize.

Reading D: A Structural Critical Interpretation Focused on the Thematic Dimension of the Sermon on the Mount

A scholarly interpretation focused on the thematic dimension of the Gospel according to Matthew, such as the one proposed in my commentary, reaches quite different conclusions about what the sermon is and says about discipleship because, as noted in chapter 2, it focuses on another meaning-producing dimension of the text. As with the interpretations by Luz and Davies and Allison, I underscore the legitimacy of my conclusions about what the text is and says study by elucidating in this multidimensional androcritical the main characteristics of the thematic dimension that is the focus of my interpretation. I also criticize, refine, and complement these conclusions by seeking to be more self-conscious in my systematic elucidation of relevant features of the thematic dimension.

The structural critical study is deliberately focused on the thematic dimension, giving priority to the internal semantic organization of the text and to the system of convictions that this structure conveys.[11] I quite self-consciously focus my critical study on this meaning-producing dimension of the Gospel. Yet as mentioned above, my approach remained one-dimensional; consequently, I felt obliged to underscore in my interpretation aspects of other interpretations focused on other dimensions because I could not but recognize their significance. Thus my study must be submitted to the same androcritical ex-

---

11. Patte, *Matthew*, 1–15, passim. This dimension receives different names, according to the perspective from which one looks at it. When the emphasis is on its relationship with the figurative dimension, it is best called the thematic dimension. When the focus is on the way it affects readers, it can be called "semantic universe" or "system of convictions," characterized by a specific "pattern of perception" (Greimas would say "proprioceptive axiology." See these terms in A. J. Greimas and J. Courtés, *Semiotics and Language: An Analytical Dictionary*, trans. L. Crist, D. Patte, et al. [Bloomington: Indiana University Press, 1982]).

amination as the others. *This androcritical multidimensional study is needed to clarify the relationship of my study to other critical studies focused on other dimensions of the text.*

The structural exegetical method that I have used in my interpretation has been briefly presented in chapter 2.[12] *It is enough to reiterate here that "themes" can be identified formally by keeping in mind that each "thematic unit" (and the text as a whole) has a theme that is most directly expressed by its opening and its closing, and by their relations. The opening by itself presents the theme, yet in a way that is often veiled by its figurativization. This theme is restated* in another form *in the closing. The actual characteristics of the theme are most directly expressed by those features of the opening and the closing of the unit (or text) that are in* inverted parallelisms *with each other. Identifying the inverted parallelisms of the Sermon on the Mount allows us to recognize its overall theme as well as its thematic subunits and, in a first approximation, the convictions expressed by the themes of these units.*[13]

As is the case with the figurative dimension (but not with the historical/ realistic dimension and with the plot dimension), the overall structure of the thematic dimension plays an essential role in the way in which this dimension affects readers. Indeed, a close study of the thematic structure of the *Sermon on the Mount (its organization in thematic units and subunits, each with its inverted parallelisms) is essential for the identification of the themes and subthemes that establish a potentially coherent teaching of the Sermon — its thematic vision.*

The study of the theme and subthemes in themselves merely provides an approximate *identification of the thematic vision of the text and thus needs to be complemented by a study of the convictions expressed by the semantic oppositions associated with the oppositions of actions.*[14] *Thus beyond the study of the thematic organization my commentary analyzes each of these oppositions. As with other interpretations, my specific goal in this multidimensional study is to take note of the main conclusions about what the Sermon is and says about discipleship, which I reached through my systematic study of the thematic dimension of this text.*

---

12. For a systematic presentation of the method used, see Daniel Patte, *Structural Exegesis for New Testament Critics,* Guides for Biblical Scholarship (Minneapolis: Fortress, 1990; 2d printing, Valley Forge, Pa.: Trinity Press International, 1996).

13. These are, respectively, step 1 and step 5 of the method described in Patte, *Structural Exegesis,* 9–22 and 47–61. Note that by contrast with the study of the figurative organization (which focuses on the center of chiastic structures), here priority is given to the material found at the beginning and at the end of the passages (the outside of the chiasms; the inclusions themselves). Yet as we shall see, thematic and figurative units do not always correspond to each other; slight variations are possible.

14. These are steps 2, 3, and 4 of the above mentioned method. See Patte, *Structural Exegesis,* 23–45.

Reading C, CAW 1: Critical Interpretations of the Figurative Dimension — The Figurative Structure of the Sermon on the Mount

Reading C, CAW 1.1: The Center of the Sermon on the Mount, the Lord's Prayer, as Key for the Interpretation

Both Luz and Davies and Allison (although the latter are more cautious)[15] find that the entire Sermon on the Mount is an admirable literary construction centered on the Lord's Prayer, which must therefore be recognized as the primary key for understanding the figurative meaning-producing dimension of the Sermon.

The elucidation of the rest of the figurative structure of the text is also important[16] because it provides significant clues concerning the makeup of figures (which often correspond to complete subunits) and their interrelations. We will thus begin by taking note of how Luz as well as Davies and Allison have identified "inclusions" (exclusively established by parallelisms, not *inverted* parallelisms; see reading D, CAW 1.1) and other surface patterns (triadic groupings; ringlike compositions) through which the text is organized as a figurative system.

Reading C, CAW 1.2: The Ringlike Structure of the Sermon on the Mount Centered on the Lord's Prayer

As noted regarding Matthew 4:18–22, in a figurative interpretation the unit that includes the Sermon on the Mount begins in 4:23, owing to the inclusion between 4:23 and 9:35 (an almost word-for-word repetition of the summary description of Jesus' ministry in 4:23).[17] This shows that the Sermon on the Mount is encased in ringlike inclusions.[18] Between 4:23 and 9:35, verses that underscore that Jesus' ministry includes

---

15. Luz, *Matthew*, 211–13. Davies and Allison (*Matthew*, 590–617) are more cautious. Because they want to assert that the Lord's Prayer originates with Jesus, they do not want to underscore that Matthew constructed it as the figurative center of the Sermon on the Mount. But this historical/realistic concern is irrelevant for this figurative interpretation; in other words, claiming that the author-redactor of the Sermon on the Mount made the Lord's Prayer the center of the figurative organization of the Sermon is not saying anything about its historical origin! This is shown by the fact that Davies and Allison end up with the same overall structure of the Sermon as does Luz.

16. This is by contrast with critical studies of the historical/realistic dimension (for which the Sermon, as any parenetic text, is made up of a series of teachings whose order is not especially significant) and of the "plot dimension" (which is not so much concerned with the actual organization of the Sermon, but with the organization of the ideal story of the disciples that it posits).

17. Although both Luz and Davies and Allison take note of this inclusion and recognize the balanced organization of 4:23–9:38 (introduction, 4:23–5:2; Sermon and its conclusion, 5:3–7:29; series of nine healings, 8:1–9:34; conclusion; 9:35–38), they understand this figurative unit as a part of a larger section of the gospel; 4:23–11:30, for Luz (*Matthew*, 42–43, 203–4); 4:23–12:50, for Davies and Allison (*Matthew*, 68–69).

18. As emphasized by Luz, *Matthew*, 203–4, 211.

both teaching-preaching and healing, one finds a symmetric presentation of teaching-preaching (the Sermon on the Mount, chaps. 5–7) and of healings (a series of miracle stories; chaps. 8–9). Furthermore, 9:35 is followed by the instruction to the disciples (10:1–42) that describes their mission as involving both teaching-preaching and healing.

This delimitation of broad figurative units means that the introduction of the Sermon on the Mount is 4:23–5:2[19] (and not merely 5:1–2). This introduction forms an inclusion with 7:28–8:1 through the mention of "teaching" by Jesus (uses of words of the family of διδάσκω, 4:23; 5:2; and 7:28–29); of the great crowds following Jesus (ἠκολούθησαν αὐτῷ ὄχλοι πολλοί, 4:25; 5:1; and 7:28, ἠκολούθησαν αὐτῷ ὄχλοι πολλοί, 8:1); of climbing and descending the mountain (ἀνέβη εἰς τὸ ὄρος, 5:1; Καταβάντος δὲ αὐτοῦ ἀπὸ τοῦ ὄρους, 8:1).[20]

In view of the ringlike inclusions that encase the Sermon on the Mount (5:3–7:27) and delimit it as a complete unit, one is not surprised to find a similar organization in the Sermon itself.[21] The primary evidence concerning its figurative organization is the inclusion formed by the repetition of "the law and the prophets" in 5:17 ("Do not think that I have come to abolish the law or the prophets") and 7:12 ("In everything do to others as you would have them do to you; for this is the law and the prophets").

This inclusion delimits the three main parts: introduction, 5:3–16; main body, 5:17–7:12; conclusion, 7:13–27.[22] Such a triadic grouping is also found in each of the main parts (although not everything should be forced into such groupings). The introduction, 5:3–16, includes the nine (three times three) beatitudes (5:3–12),[23] followed by a threefold figurative description (salt, light, city) of the task of the disciples (5:13–16). The conclusion, 7:13–27, includes a series of three warnings (7:13–14; 7:15–20; 7:21–23) followed by the parable of the two house builders (7:24–27). Similarly, the main body, 5:17–7:12, is best subdivided into three parts

---

19. As these verses are designated by Davies and Allison, *Matthew*, 410–28.

20. See Luz, *Matthew*, 203–4; Davies and Allison, *Matthew*, 724–25.

21. I combine the proposals by Luz and Davies and Allison in this presentation.

22. With Luz (*Matthew*, 212–13). For Davies and Allison (*Matthew*, 64, 470–71), 5:13–16 does not belong to the introduction; "these verses serve as the heading for 5:17–7:12" (471). Thus they both acknowledge that the main body is 5:17–7:12, and do not include 5:13–16 in it. Actually, Davies and Allison's overall presentation of the structure of the Sermon on the Mount (64) shows that they do not know what to do with 5:13–16, which does not fit neatly in their organization of the Sermon exclusively in triadic groupings. (Note that the main body is first designated as 5:13–7:12, and then subdivided as if it were 5:17–7:12).

23. For Davies and Allison (*Matthew*, 63), the beatitudes include 5:11–12 because of the triadic organization of the rest of the Sermon on the Mount (and of the gospel); three times three. Luz (*Matthew*, 226–27) does not really justify this delimitation of the beatitudes. He notes that there is an inclusion between 5:3 and 5:10, but discounts it for the delimitation of the figurative unit. This is simply because the figure of the "blessed ones" (μακάριοι) is taken as defining the unit.

(Torah, 5:21–48; cult, 6:1–18; social issues, 6:19–7:11),[24] surrounded by an introit (5:17–20) and a conclusion (7:12).[25] Each of the three parts of the main body includes one or several triadic groupings: in 5:21–48, two sets of three antitheses; in 6:1–18, almsgiving, prayer, and fasting; in 6:19–7:11, two triads, each made up of a general principle and two parables (6:19–24 and 7:1–6), and each followed by encouragements (6:25–34 and 7:7–11).[26]

The Lord's Prayer (6:9–13) is at the very center of this ringlike composition of the Sermon on the Mount.[27] It is found at the center of a subunit about prayer (6:7–15), where it is surrounded by a teaching about the Gentile way of praying (6:7–8) and about forgiveness (6:14–15). This subunit about prayer is itself at the center of the unit on the cult (6:1–18), which is at the center of the main body (5:17–7:12). This ringlike composition is illustrated in figure 1.

Figure 1
Figurative Structure of the Sermon on the Mount (Reading C)

4:23–5:2		7:28–8:1
Followed by crowds		Jesus climbs down
Jesus climbs up		the Mountain
the Mountain		followed by crowds
	5:3–7:27	
	The Sermon on the Mount	
5:3–16		7:13–27
Introduction		Conclusion
	5:17–7:12	
	Main Body	
5:17–20		7:12
Introit of body		Conclusion of body
5:21–48		6:19–7:11
Antitheses-Torah		Social Issues
	6:1–18	
	Cult	
6:2–4		6:16–18
Almsgiving		Fasting
	6:5–15	
	Prayer	
6:7–8		6:14–15
Not as Gentiles		Forgiveness
	6:9–13	
	LORD'S	
	PRAYER	

---

24. With Davies and Allison in their presentation of the triadic groupings in the main body (cf. *Matthew,* 64).

25. With Luz (*Matthew,* 212).

26. Davies and Allison, *Matthew,* 64.

27. As is also emphasized by Luz (*Matthew,* 212–13).

*Reading C, CAW 1.3: A Figurative Interpretation Begins with
an Examination of the Center of the Figurative Dimension,
the Lord's Prayer, in Light of the Outer-Rings*

The structure of the Sermon on the Mount that Luz and Davies and Allison recognize in their commentaries demonstrates that the interpretation of these scholars is focused on the figurative dimension of the text (by contrast with the historical/realistic dimension and the plot dimension, for which the textual organization is not significant, and by contrast with the thematic dimension with its different structure, summarized in fig. 2, p. 207). Therefore, our androcritical multidimensional interpretation needs to make explicit how the conclusions of Luz and Davies and Allison owe their coherence to the figurative dimension on which the interpretation of these scholars is actually focused — although this focus is somewhat hidden by the one-dimensional and totalizing character of their works.

For this purpose, we first need to bring to light the fact that these interpretations actually use the Lord's Prayer as a key for their interpretation of the Sermon on the Mount, and more specifically for their interpretation of discipleship according to the Sermon. Using the "center" of a ring composition as a key for understanding the rest of a text is appropriate in an interpretation focused on the figurative dimension of the text, since a ring composition is a literary convention which, as a figure of speech, calls the readers' attention on its center as the most significant part of the text.

Does this mean that we must begin our investigation by considering how Luz and Davies and Allison have interpreted the Lord's Prayer by itself? Not exactly. As a figurative unit, the Lord's Prayer cannot be interpreted by itself. Saying that it is the center of the figurative dimension does not mean that the other figurative units of the text are not significant. According to their place in the figurative system, the other units reflect (as mirrors do) the central point and throw light on it. Any figure or figurative unit must be constantly interpreted in terms of the other figures and figurative units because they reflect and illuminate one another. Conversely, this means that the study of any given figure or figurative unit by itself, while a necessary step, is often inconclusive and tentative. The proper interpretation of the figurative dimension of a given text appears when the coherence of its overall figurative structure is taken into account.

Concretely, this means that my presentation of this figurative interpretation[28] will underscore how the Lord's Prayer is *reflected and illuminated*

---

28. I use the shorthand "figurative interpretation" in the narrow sense of "interpretation focused on the figurative meaning-producing dimension" *as defined above* by the interpretive practices of Luz and Davies and Allison. Actually any given text involves several figurative meaning-producing dimensions, each of which can be the focus of a legitimate interpretation that could also be designated as "figurative." Practically, I prefer to give these other dimensions more specific designations. A case in point is the "thematic" dimension and interpretation, which, broadly speaking, could also be called "figurative."

by other figurative units, and especially by those units that form the "outer rings" — the figurative setting of the Sermon on the Mount in the Gospel and its framework — which might more directly reflect and illuminate the center, the Lord's Prayer.

Reading D, CAW 1: Critical Interpretations of the Thematic Dimension — The Thematic Structure of the Sermon on the Mount

Reading D, CAW 1.1: The Inverted Parallelisms between the Introduction and the Conclusions as Key for the Interpretation

The elucidation of the thematic structure of the text is the first step of the study of the thematic dimension of the Sermon on the Mount presented in my commentary (as it also is for the study of the figurative dimension, see reading C, CAW 1.1). By recognizing the thematic units and subunits and by studying the "inverted parallelisms" (as distinct from the inclusions and ringlike compositions, see reading C, CAW 1.2) that delimit them one is able to discern the main themes and subthemes of the Sermon on the Mount as well as the basic convictions expressed by the thematic dimension. The key to understanding the thematic meaning-producing dimension of the Sermon on the Mount is found in the inverted parallelisms between the introduction and the conclusion of the Sermon as a whole, and secondarily in the inverted parallelisms of each thematic unit and subunit.

We shall consider how the thematic units and subunits have been studied in my commentary by elucidating how they interrelate specific themes (such as the theme of "vision," "seeing," the "eye") and how semantic oppositions help refine the themes and convictions identified. These considerations will help us to elucidate the themes and convictions of the Sermon on the Mount and to underscore the coherence of the thematic meaning-producing dimension. In this way, we will have identified the conclusions about what the Sermon is and says (CAWs) about discipleship of the structural interpretation presented in my commentary, which can serve as the basis for drawing conclusions about the teaching (CATs) regarding discipleship (see chap. 6, reading D, CATs).

Reading D, CAW 1.2: The Inverted Parallelisms of the Thematic Structure of the Sermon on the Mount between the Beatitudes and the Final Judgment

The thematic unit of the Gospel according to Matthew, which includes the Sermon on the Mount, begins in 5:1, since, as we discussed in chapter 2 (reading D, CAW 2), according to the structural interpretation of my commentary,[29] the previous thematic unit is 3:1–4:25.

---

29. See Patte, *Matthew*, 60–65. I briefly summarize these pages in the following paragraphs.

Since 5:1-2 describes Jesus as beginning to teach (ἀνοίξας τὸ στόμα αὐτοῦ, "opening his mouth" [author's translation], 5:2), this thematic unit ends with 7:28-29, which states that Jesus concluded his teaching (ὅτε ἐτέλεσεν ὁ Ἰησοῦς τοὺς λόγους τούτους, "when Jesus had finished saying these things," 7:28). This is taking note of a first inverted parallelism within the framework of the Sermon on the Mount. Other inverted parallelisms will appear as we look at it more closely and seek to identify the theme underscored by 5:1-2 and 7:28-29. Yet we need to take note of one of them: in 5:1-2, the Sermon on the Mount is addressed to the disciples, with the crowds as, at best, second-rank addressees; in 7:28-29, the crowds are the only ones responding to Jesus' teaching. The inversion of the place of the crowds is certainly significant. We will have to take into account that there are two distinct audiences. (Beyond this, we do not need to take into account the inverted parallelisms of the framework of the Sermon because the theme it underscores concerns Jesus' authority, not discipleship.)[30]

Since the framework underscores that there are two kinds of audience for the Sermon on the Mount, we have to take into account the shift from impersonal style (5:3-10, the Sermon as addressed to the impersonal crowds) to personal style (5:11-7:20, addressed to "you," the intimate group of disciples), and back to impersonal style (7:21-27). Thus we have to identify the introduction as 5:3-10 and the conclusion as 7:21-27.

Matthew 5:3-10 and 7:21-27 are parallel, in part through their impersonal style, and are set in inverted parallelisms through their respective form: words of blessing (beatitudes, 5:3-10) and words of judgment, which include both condemnation and blessing (the final judgment, 7:21-27).

Let us explore the inverted parallelisms between these two passages a little more by clarifying the characteristics (in 7:21-27) of the features that set them in inverted parallelisms, "condemnation" and "blessing." For what is one condemned or blessed in 7:21-27? Condemnation is for not doing Jesus' teaching ("everyone who hears these words of mine and does not act on them," μὴ ποιῶν αὐτοὺς, 7:26), as well as for being "evildoers" (7:23, οἱ ἐργαζόμενοι τὴν ἀνομίαν). Blessing is entering the kingdom; it is for those who are doing the will of Jesus' Father (7:21, ὁ ποιῶν τὸ θέλημα τοῦ πατρός μου). Consequently, the features of the beatitudes (5:3-10) that set up the parallelism is the description of the blessing as having the kingdom (αὐτῶν ἐστιν ἡ βασιλεία τῶν οὐρανῶν, "theirs is the kingdom of heaven") both in 5:3 and 5:10 (thus also part of the inverted parallelism of the subunit; a confirmation), and the description of the proper acts (being poor in spirit, mourning, etc.) would be a description of Jesus' words that is God's will that one needs to do in order to enter the kingdom.

These first general observations identify, at least approximately, the main theme of the Sermon on the Mount as concerning doing or not doing the

---

30. See Patte, *Matthew*, 60-62.

right acts, i.e., righteousness (see 5:6) as what opens or closes the kingdom. This preliminary identification of the theme of the Sermon on the Mount gives us a clue for identifying the thematic subunits: the passages that emphasize some aspects of this general theme are certainly delimiting thematic subunits.

Matthew 5:20 with its emphasis on "overabundant" or "better righteousness" (we will need to decide how to designate it here) as a condition for entrance into the kingdom appears to be the beginning of a thematic unit on this issue. Since 5:20 is presented in a negative form (ἐὰν μὴ...οὐ μὴ, "unless your righteousness exceeds that of the scribes and Pharisees, you will never enter the kingdom of heaven"), the conclusion of this thematic subunit would need to involve a more positive outlook on similar issues, so as to form an inverted parallelism. Beginning in 5:20, we find a series of teachings about behavior toward other persons (5:21–48), followed by teachings about behavior toward God (giving alms, prayer, fasting, 6:1–18). The verses about gathering treasures in heaven, 6:19–21, since they conclude on the positive side, seem to be an appropriate conclusion for this subunit. A close study of it will confirm this first tentative identification of a subunit in 5:20–6:21, which includes sub-subunits: 5:21–47 and 6:2–18 (with 5:47–6:1 as framing material).

Proceeding outward from this central unit shows that 5:17–19 and 6:22–7:12 constitute inverted parallelisms that expresses different kinds of conditions that must be met in order to have a life characterized by overabundant or better righteousness. The introductory verse, 5:17, expresses in a negative form the relationship of all the teaching in 5:20–6:21 to Scripture: "Do not think that I have come to abolish the law and the prophets." The concluding verse, 7:12, expresses the same point in a positive form: "In everything do to others as you would have them do to yᶜu; for this is the law and the prophets."

We can expect that the two remaining passages, 5:11–16 and 7:13–20, are themselves in inverted parallelism, as it soon becomes clear. In 5:11–12 the disciples are presented as "like the prophets"; 7:15 refers to false disciples as false prophets. The largely positive definition of the vocation of the disciples as being prophetlike, as being salt of the earth, and as light of the world in 5:11–16 occurs in an inverted parallelism with the largely negative definition of the vocation of the disciples in 7:13–20, emphasizing the vocation of discipleship as leading people through the "narrow gate" and the "hard road," unlike false prophets who lead people to destruction. This preliminary identification of the thematic organization of the Sermon on the Mount is summarized in figure 2, on the following page.

Reading D, CAW 1.3: A Thematic Interpretation Begins with an Examination of the Units in Inverted Parallelisms —
The Judgment Scene (7:21–27) and the Beatitudes (5:3–10)

Figure 2 shows the thematic structure of the Sermon on the Mount that I identified in my commentary focused on the thematic meaning-producing

Figure 2

Thematic Structure of the Sermon on the Mount (Reading D)

A1 — 5:3 - 10. Beatitudes. Characteristics of the Disciples

    B1 — 5:11-16. The Disciples' Vocation

        C1 — 5:17-19. Conditions for Implementing the Vocation

            D1 — 5:20. Introduction of Antitheses

                E1 — 5:21- 47. Antitheses: Overabundant Righteousness

            D2 — 5:47- 48. Conclusion of Antitheses

            D3 — 6:1. Introduction to Next Unit

                E2 — 6:2-18. Overabundant Righteousness

            D4 — 6:19 -21. Conclusion of Preceding Unit

        C2 — 6:22-7:12. Conditions for Implementing the Vocation

    B2 — 7:13 -20. The Disciples' Vocation

A2 — 7:21-27. Judgment Scene. Characteristics of the Disciples

dimension and its system of convictions of the text. Our androcritical multi-dimensional interpretation needs to examine how my former conclusions owe their coherence to the thematic dimension — although I hid my actual procedures as I presented my conclusions in a commentary format, in a linear fashion following the textual order.[31]

For this purpose, we first need to make more explicit than my commentary does that I used the inverted parallelisms as an essential key for my interpretation of the Sermon on the Mount, in addition to the formal semantic oppositions. Using the inverted thematic unit as a key for understanding a text is appropriate in an interpretation focused on the thematic dimension of the text. While the introduction expresses the theme in a figurative, ambivalent way for the sake of the intended readers (as noted above), the conclusion expresses the theme more directly, with the expectation that the body of the discourse has transformed the intended readers' view of this theme.

This means that we must begin our investigation by exploring how the inverted parallelisms between the beatitudes (5:3 -10) and the judgment scene (7:21-27) express the main theme of the Sermon on the Mount. We have to resist the fascination that the beatitudes will have for readers who play the role that the discourse assigns to its implied readers.[32] *This is an essential part of the discursive strategy of the Sermon on the Mount: inviting readers to*

---

31. The actual procedures I followed in order to reach my conclusions have been presented in detail in Patte, *Structural Exegesis.*

32. In this case the "implied reader" is defined as the enunciatee's role inscribed in the text, or better, inscribed in the discursive structure of the text. Thematization is an aspect of the discursive structure. See Greimas and Courtés, *Semiotics and Language,* 85–86, 103–5, 344. Patte, *Religious Dimensions,* 129–72, 258–64.

share in the euphoric vision of the beatitudes, which they are ready to affirm, in order to lead them to accept the radical transformation of their view of an essential issue embedded in the beatitudes. The conclusion, the judgment scene (7:21–27), clearly identifies this essential issue – the main theme of the Sermon – and makes explicit the proper view of this issue according to the Sermon on the Mount.

In an androcritical interpretation of the thematic dimension, we must take note of its effect on us who performed an interpretation focused on this particular dimension. For this, we must self-consciously retrace the interpretive path that we followed and through which our vision was transformed regarding a certain theme. Concretely this means that we must begin retracing our interpretive path by considering the concluding thematic unit, 7:21–27. It is in terms of this judgment scene that we need to understand the beatitudes, as well as the rest of the Sermon, and thus progressively elucidate the thematic view of "discipleship according to the Sermon on the Mount."

As such, an interpretation of the Sermon on the Mount focused on its thematic dimension proceeds in a different way from an interpretation focused on its figurative dimension.

Reading C, CAW 2: Primary Figures of the Sermon on the Mount, Lord's Prayer, and Discipleship as Imitation of Christ

Reading C, CAW 2.1: Matthew 4:23–9:35 — Ambivalence in the Imitation of Christ

It is significant that the Sermon on the Mount is a part of a larger figurative unit delimited by the inclusion between 4:23 and 9:35. As we noted, 4:23 is followed by the Sermon (5–7) and a series of miracles (8–9), while 9:35 is followed by the instruction to the disciples (10:1–42). This broad organization underscores that the disciples' ministry is *like Jesus' twofold ministry* to the crowds (teaching-preaching and healing).[33] As Jesus did (4:17; 4:23), they are to teach-preach that "the kingdom of heaven is at

---

33. In a figurative interpretation, despite the emphasis on triads, Jesus' ministry is not threefold (teaching, preaching, and healing), but twofold as suggested by the clearly defined two-part division (5–7; 8–9) of the material bracketed by the inclusion between 4:23 and 9:35. Thus Luz concludes that "'preaching' and 'teaching' do not mean two different things"; they "cannot be separated"; at best, "the evidence is ambivalent" about any difference between the two terms. The only difference is that the addressees of "preaching" are "the people of Israel and the Gentiles (24:14; 26:13), never the disciples" to whom teaching is addressed. But for Luz and his figurative interpretation, this is not sufficient to separate the two. Luz, *Matthew*, 205, 206–8. By contrast, a clear distinction is made both for the interpretation of the plot dimension and of the thematic dimension.

hand" (10:6); as Jesus healed every disease and infirmity (4:24), so also the disciples (10:1).

Such observations support Davies and Allison's critical conclusion that the disciples' "missionary activity is part of the *imitatio Christi.*"[34] In other words, Jesus is a figure or model of discipleship; his activities are figures of the disciples' activities; "Jesus teaching-preaching the Sermon" is a figure of the disciples' teaching-preaching. More concretely, as Luz indicates, this means that the Sermon on the Mount is not a teaching merely addressed to the disciples-apostles; it is addressed to all those (the whole world, 28:20) to whom the disciples will teach-preach it, as Jesus did.[35]

Luz's comment points out the way in which we need to understand the conclusions (CAWs) of an interpretation focused on the figurative dimension of the Sermon on the Mount. A figure affirming that X *is like* Y (regarding specific features) also expresses that X *is unlike* Y (regarding other features).[36] The disciples, who are *like Jesus*, also are *unlike Jesus;* they are not the Son of God as he is (Luz),[37] and thus they cannot literally imitate him. Yet as they envision their own ministry, disciples should constantly hold up Jesus as an ideal model; their ministry should be *like* Jesus' ministry. This does not mean that their ministry should duplicate and prolong that of Jesus; Jesus' ministry is unique because of its very special revelatory and soteriological character.

Yet discipleship remains an *imitation of Christ;* Jesus and his performance of his ministry are a figure of discipleship. For Matthew, figures of discipleship are not (realistic) "examples" that disciples/church members can readily and completely emulate (as the examples and teachings identified and underscored in a historical/realistic interpretation). Figures of discipleship are ideals toward which people can and should orient their lives in order to envision their discipleship in terms of them. Disciples are people who have been formed or conformed to these figures.[38]

---

34. Davies and Allison, *Matthew,* 411–12.

35. Luz, *Matthew,* 216–17.

36. This comment expands what Ricoeur says about the metaphor (a specific figure) to figures in general. For a concise treatment of this issue, see Paul Ricoeur, *Interpretation Theory: Discourse and the Surplus of Meaning* (Fort Worth, Tex.: Texas Christian University Press, 1976), 45–69 ("Metaphor and Symbol"). For a more complete discussion, see Ricoeur, *The Rule of Metaphor* (Toronto: University of Toronto Press, 1977), especially chapters 5, 6, and 7. See also Patte, *Religious Dimensions,* 129–72.

37. This distance between Jesus and the disciples and the high Christology it involves are underscored, according to the figurative interpretation (and also a historical/realistic interpretation), in chapters 1–4 of the Gospel. See, for instance, Luz, *Matthew,* 215: "Jesus the Son of God speaks" (in the Sermon on the Mount).

38. Note the passive forms, "formed or conformed." People "are made" fishers of people or disciples. They do not make themselves disciples.

Reading C, CAW 2.2: Matthew 4:23–5:2 and 7:28–8:1: Jesus as Moses-like Messiah and the Crowds as Disciple-like, Two Figures of Discipleship and Their Ambivalence

The introduction of the Sermon on the Mount, 4:23–5:2 (not merely 5:1–2), and its conclusion, 7:28–8:1 (not merely 7:28–29), posit two very different figures of discipleship: Jesus and the crowds. Since, as discussed above, discipleship involves imitating Jesus, the figure of Jesus constructed by these verses is also a figure of discipleship, which we first examine. Then we shall consider the crowds as a figure of discipleship.

In the framework of the Sermon, 4:23–5:2 and 7:28–8:1, Jesus is presented as a Moses-like figure, a first manifestation of the ambivalence of the symbolic world conveyed by the Sermon on the Mount. Jesus climbing up the mountain (ἀνέβη εἰς τὸ ὄρος, 5:1) in order to deliver a discourse concerning the law and God's will and Jesus climbing down the mountain (καταβάντος δὲ αὐτοῦ ἀπὸ τοῦ ὄρους, 8:1) have to be understood as allusions to Moses climbing up and down the mountain (Sinai; see Ex 19:3, 12; 24:15, 18; 34:1–2, 4). Thus one can say with Davies and Allison and with Luz that Jesus is presented as "the mosaic Messiah" "delivering messianic Torah," on the Sinai-like mountain of revelation.[39]

This figure (like any figure) involves ambivalence: Jesus is both "like Moses" and "unlike Moses"; his teaching is both "like" and "unlike" the law and the covenant revealed by Moses on Mount Sinai. The tension inherent to this figure of Jesus as the new Moses is open to two kinds of interpretations: either as the expression of discontinuity between Jesus and Moses — the teaching of the new Moses invalidates the Mosaic covenant and its law — or as the expression of continuity — the teaching of the new Moses elucidates the teaching of Scripture.

The former interpretation (discontinuity between Jesus and Moses) is further suggested by the clear opposition between the authority of Jesus and the authority of "their (the crowds') scribes" (7:29); the law of the old covenant (taught by the scribes) is set in tension with the law of the new covenant taught by the mosaic Messiah. But in support of the latter interpretation (continuity between Moses and Jesus), 7:29 can also be interpreted in light of 5:17, which is read to say that Jesus' teaching does not invalidate Moses and the old law. One might be tempted to "reduce" these tensions to one or the other of its poles, so as to have an unambiguous interpretation. But doing so is destroying the figure (which brings together the old and the new) and dissolving the symbolic world it helps to convey.

Since Jesus is also a figure of discipleship, this ambivalence is compounded. Disciples are people who believe in Jesus as the new Moses (both in continuity and discontinuity with Moses); as imitators of Christ, they

---

39. Davies and Allison, *Matthew*, 423–27; Luz, *Matthew*, 224, 455–56.

have to conceive of their own vocation as a religious leadership that is both Moses-like and Moses-unlike.

Note that this figure of Jesus as the new Moses is also an eschatological figure: it is a messianic figure (as both Luz and Davies and Allison note). As this Moses-like figure becomes a figure of discipleship, it posits what we can call an "eschatological horizon" against which disciples are expected to envision themselves as disciples.[40]

The direct figurative context of the Sermon also proposes the crowds as a figure of discipleship. Since in this perspective 4:23–25 is a part of the framing material of the Sermon (as is especially emphasized by Davies and Allison),[41] the role of the crowds is more apparent: from the outset it is clear that the Sermon is addressed to both the disciples and the crowds, an interpretation confirmed by 7:28–8:1. There are indeed two concentric circles of hearers of the Sermon, but they are not to be contrasted (as is done in a historical/realistic interpretation). The Sermon is equally addressed to both groups because they belong together, as is emphasized by both Luz and Davies and Allison.[42] Since the mention that "the crowds followed [Jesus]" (4:25) is here understood metaphorically (as discussed in chap. 2), the crowds "by following, belong together with the disciples."[43] The crowds are a figure of discipleship.

Once again, this means that the crowds are both like and unlike the disciples: the crowds are a figure of discipleship in that they follow Jesus after he healed their sick (4:24–25) and in that they recognize his superior authority (7:28–8:1). Thus Davies and Allison conclude, "So grace comes before task, succor before demand, healing before imperative."[44] Expressing this point in the vocabulary I introduced above, Davies and Allison's statement about the crowds as a figure of discipleship posits another *horizon* — which can be provisionally called the horizon of present powerful manifestations of divine[45] grace — against which disciples are expected to envision themselves as disciples.

In sum, disciples are to be both Jesus-like and crowd-like, both Moses-like religious leaders and people who acknowledge and submit to the

---

40. By speaking of such an eschatological horizon, I begin to show that, on the basis of our discussion of Matthew 4:18–22, I conceive of the teaching of the Sermon on the Mount about discipleship as a vision of discipleship or (better) as a symbolic world in which disciples have to be socialized. See chapter 6.

41. Davies and Allison, *Matthew,* 410–28, a section that they entitle "Introduction to the Sermon on the Mount (4:23–5:2)." Luz treats 4:23–25 by itself, as the introduction of the new section that includes the Sermon. Luz, *Matthew,* 203–8.

42. Luz, *Matthew,* 224; Davies and Allison, *Matthew,* 422, 427.

43. Luz, *Matthew,* 201.

44. Davies and Allison, *Matthew,* 427.

45. It might be closer to the text of 4:23–25 to use the term "supernatural" instead of "divine." Even if this might not be absolutely clear in these verses, it is made clear by the figurative context, in terms of which these verses must be interpreted here, that this second horizon concerns present *divine* manifestations.

authority of a Moses-like figure. This means that the distinction between disciples and most other people is blurred because disciples need to see themselves both as part of the crowds and as leaders of the crowds. Consequently, one can already note here that, according to this figurative dimension of the Gospel, the church is perceived as a mixed body: it is never clear who belongs or does not belong to the church. (On this point, which Luz repeatedly underscores, see our discussion of 7:13–27.)

Conversely, this also means that the Sermon on the Mount is a message addressed to the broader audiences: to the crowds, indeed to all people who are called to follow Jesus; as Luz underscores, discipleship expands into the church[46] and beyond it into the whole world.[47] Consequently, the Sermon "cannot be an ethics for the disciples in the *more narrow sense*, not an ethics only of the perfect. A two-level ethic is excluded."[48] Rather as a message addressed by a Moses-like figure, the Sermon on the Mount is a covenantal ethic, offered to all and open to all.

Reading C, CAW 2.3: The Lord's Prayer (6:5–13) as Prayer of the New Covenant: The Eschatological and Theological Horizons of Its Symbolic World (Compare with Reading D, CAW 3.7)

The Lord's Prayer as the central figurative unit of the Sermon on the Mount is read in light of the outer ring of the figurative structure, as taught by the new Moses, and thus as "the prayer of the new covenant." Here I am *not* saying that it *is* the prayer of the new covenant — this would go against Luz's interpretation, for whom this is one of several potential interpretations of the prayer.[49] I am speaking of the Lord's Prayer as the prayer of the new covenant in the same way in which we discussed Jesus as Moses-like; in its figurative sense, this phrase expresses both that "it *is*" and that "it *is not.*"

Another way to express the same point is to say that this prayer is both *in discontinuity* and *in continuity* with Jewish prayers, as is emphasized by both Luz and Davies and Allison. The ambivalence becomes visible as soon as one asks (Luz's explicit question), In which sense and to what extent is this prayer "new" as compared with Jewish prayers? Luz and Davies and Allison answer that, actually, the Lord's Prayer fits the style and content of private Jewish prayers well;[50] all its features can be found in Jewish

---

46. Luz, *Matthew,* 206.

47. Ibid., 216.

48. Ibid., 224.

49. Ibid., 374–75. Davies and Allison (*Matthew,* 590–615) provide, as usual, a mass of information, which supports Luz's point, but it is difficult to have any clear perception of how they interpret the Lord's Prayer in the context of the Sermon on the Mount (many of their comments are concerned with the prayer of the historical Jesus).

50. As both Luz (*Matthew,* 386; see 369–89) and Davies and Allison (*Matthew,* 595–97) note. The plural forms (e.g., "our") that associate the praying believer with the community is also a characteristic of private Jewish prayers.

prayers.[51] Thus the prayer of the new covenant is *in continuity* with prayers of the old covenant.

The distinctiveness of the Lord's Prayer is due to the way in which it brings together Jewish elements.[52] It is "stamped by Jesus," as Luz says, in that it is centered on "the petition of the poor for bread for the morrow" (6:11; cf. 5:3) and receives its perspective from the coming kingdom of God, rather than "the history of Israel's salvation."[53]

Luz's interpretation clarifies that the distinctiveness of the Lord's Prayer — what is "new" in it — is in the kind of symbolic world it sets up (and therefore neither an ethical nor a dogmatic teaching, as one concludes when one reads it by focusing on other dimensions). To begin with, Luz repeatedly reminds us that 6:9–13 is a prayer. "Thus the Lord's Prayer is an *aid in praying* and is intended to help the person who recites it to discover the loving closeness of the Father. It wants to make prayer possible ... [it is] a basic text which, beyond the borders of the church, can help people in praying and discovering the love of God."[54]

In saying so, Luz also indicates that the Lord's Prayer is to be understood in terms of its figurative dimension. By praying, one envisions the world in a new way: one perceives "the love of God" as a fundamental characteristic of this world. Or, better, since we are speaking of the heavenly Father's care for human beings and their needs, one of the horizons against which we see the rest of our world is the *horizon of the present manifestations of God's love*. In terms of our earlier, provisional formulation we found this as one of the two horizons of the symbolic world posited by the outer ring of the Sermon on the Mount (see above, reading C, CAW 2.1).

Luz also insists that in praying in this way, anyone "beyond the borders of the church" enters the world of discipleship which, as Luz's following paragraph suggests, can be called the "symbolic world of the disciples."

> The Lord's Prayer is not intended to make theology possible, but prayer. Matthew was very much aware of this. Deliberately, he led the disciples in his Sermon on the Mount, after confronting them with the demand of higher righteousness and perfection, into the inner space of prayer. Here is the center of the Sermon on the Mount. Thus Matthew leads the human being through action of grace. The person who is on the way to perfection (5:20–48) learns in the heart of the Sermon to

---

51. See I. Abrahams, "The Lord's Prayer," in *Studies in Pharisaism and the Gospels* (1917–24; reprint, New York: KTAV, 1967), 2, 94–108 (cf. 98–99, where the author proposes a composite prayer made out of lines from Jewish prayers that parallel the lines of the Lord's Prayer).

52. Thus Davies has proposed that the Lord's Prayer could have been viewed by Matthew and his community as the Christian counterpart of the Eighteen Benedictions (*Shemoneh 'Esreh*). W. D. Davies, *The Setting of the Sermon on the Mount* (Cambridge: Cambridge University Press, 1964), 309–13.

53. Luz, *Matthew*, 386–87.

54. Ibid., 387.

understand the will of God that makes demands on him or her, as the will of *the Father* . . . as the will of God who brings salvation.[55]

In light of the twofold horizon that we found in the outer ring of the Sermon on the Mount, and as Luz's last phrase suggests, the symbolic world of the disciples is framed not only by the *horizon of the present manifestations of God's love,* but also by an *eschatological horizon:* the coming of salvation, i.e., the coming kingdom of God.

The twofold horizon of this symbolic world necessarily generates tensions. Which of the two parts of the horizon is perceived as predominant? The eschatological horizon? Or the horizon of God's love? These tensions generated by the twofold horizon that distinguishes the Lord's Prayer compound the usual tensions between the old and the new found in any symbolic world (here between Jewish teaching and Jesus' teaching). Ambivalence and tension are necessarily intrinsic to the symbolic world of the Sermon on the Mount, if it is indeed characterized by *a twofold horizon* — the heavenly Father's present care and the coming kingdom. It is even clearer here than in the case of the figure of the new Moses that "reducing" these tensions to one or the other of its poles, so as to have an unambiguous interpretation, means dissolving the very core of the teaching of the Sermon on the Mount — its symbolic world.

Far from reducing these tensions, both Luz and Davies and Allison systematically underscore the ambivalence of each passage of the Sermon. If one reads their commentaries with hope of discovering in them the unambiguous teaching of the Sermon on the Mount about discipleship (or any other theme), one is in for a frustrating experience. We have to enter with them into the ambivalence of the figurative dimension of the Sermon on the Mount, first by reading with them the Lord's Prayer.

Reading C, CAW 2.4: Ethical and Eschatological Interpretations of the Lord's Prayer in Tension

Luz's overall *conclusions*[56] *about what the Lord's Prayer is and says* are, therefore, that by praying it, one is invited to enter the disciples' symbolic world with its twofold horizon — the horizon of God's present loving care and the eschatological horizon of the coming kingdom. In other words, one is invited to envision the world and one's entire human experience as a disciple does (or should do), i.e., in terms of this symbolic world. In order to understand more specifically what this symbolic world of the disciples is, I propose to reread the Lord's Prayer (following the interpretations of Luz

---

55. Luz, *Matthew,* 388.

56. These conclusions, since they involve an invitation to the practice of prayer, might seem to be *conclusions about the teaching* of the Lord's Prayer, rather than conclusions about what the text is and says. Indeed, they are very close to CATs, but as we shall see (chap. 6, reading C), in addition the CATs themselves include a way of practicing discipleship with such a vision.

and, secondarily, Davies and Allison) from the perspective of Luz's overall conclusions about the Lord's Prayer.

By praying "Our Father" (Πάτερ ἡμῶν), the believers address a God who, even though "in heaven," is not distant and indifferent (as the Gentiles think, 6:7), but close and caring, as 6:8 emphasizes, "Your Father knows what you need before you ask him."[57] They express their complete trust that God, their Father, will answer their prayer, and indeed *already does so before they ask him* (5:45; 6:25–34).[58] Thus even as they utter the prayer, *believers are enticed to look for such fulfillments*. This requires discernment. Where can we find manifestations of God as a caring Father? Which of the many happenings around us are such manifestations of God's care?

The form of the prayer gives a focus to this discernment: the individual who prays associates herself or himself with the community;[59] *it is in this community that fulfillments of the prayer can already be found*. This community is not clearly delimited,[60] as the open form of the prayer shows; it includes all those who address God as "our Father." Thus one always needs to discern those who truly belong to it — among whom are people from the crowds (4:23–5:2; 7:28–8:1) and children (18:1–4), as well as disciples — from those who do not belong to it. Among the latter are Gentiles and hypocrites (mentioned in 6:5–7), and more generally all those who because of their self-sufficiency and hypocrisy are not hungry and thirsty for God's loving care (God's rewards, 6:1, 2, 5, 16) and for God's righteousness (6:33; cf. 5:6). It is among those who belong to this community and who believe in a loving and caring God that this prayer invites disciples to find models of discipleship to imitate.

The tension and ambivalence of the moral discernment involved in the Lord's Prayer begin to appear. On the one hand, believers are expected to believe in a loving and caring God, asking for God's interventions in the

---

57. Luz (*Matthew*, 375) follows Jeremias and his claim that "Father" is a translation of the familiar "abba," J. Jeremias, "Abba," in *The Prayers of Jesus* (Minneapolis: Fortress, 1967), 11–65. Davies and Allison (*Matthew*, 601–2) express reservations on this point — and appropriately so, in my view. The evidence for this conclusion is quite weak. But this does not change Luz's main point: even without Jeremias's interpretation, the closeness of the Father in heaven remains, although it means that one does not need to perceive this closeness as "intimacy"; rather, it needs to be perceived as a manifestation of God's love, or care, *in the present*.

58. As in Isaiah 65:24: "Before they call I will answer." But neither Luz (*Matthew*, 365–66) nor Davies and Allison (*Matthew*, 589–90) see how 6:8 leads to the figurative interpretation of the prayer that they themselves partly envision.

59. As was also the case in Jewish prayers; Luz, *Matthew*, 377. Davies and Allison, *Matthew*, 600–602.

60. Against Davies and Allison (*Matthew*, 601), who emphasize that this community is clearly limited to Jesus' followers ("because sonship depends on Jesus, the Son of God," a point that they fail to support convincingly), and thus exclude "the populace at large." Here they have adopted the perspective of reading A (Strecker), for which the Sermon on the Mount clearly delimits the boundaries of the community.

near future as well as in the eschatological future — *an eschatological interpretation.* On the other hand, they are expected to identify models they should imitate, duplicating their moral behavior — *an ethical interpretation.* These two interpretations should be held together, as Luz underscores and Davies and Allison concede because it is impossible to reach a definite conclusion in favor of one or the other. The prayer should be kept *open;* the tensions that it represents should be preserved, not artificially dissolved.

The first three petitions, "Hallowed be thy name, Thy kingdom come, Thy will be done, on earth as it is in heaven" (6:9c–10),[61] are enough to illustrate this point. These petitions, taken together, have traditionally been interpreted *either* ethically (in terms of the present theological horizon of the caring Father) *or* eschatologically (in terms of the eschatological horizon). According to the ethical interpretation, human beings (with the help of their caring Father) are expected to bring about the hallowing of God's name, the kingdom, and the time when God's will shall be fully done, by imitating (in the sense of emulating the example of) models of discipleship. According to the eschatological interpretation, God is expected to fulfill these petitions at the end of times; people are formed as disciples by being conformed to those who do God's will in heaven — eschatological models of discipleship. But for an interpretation focused on the figurative meaning-producing dimension, this is a false alternative; the prayer involves *both* envisioning God's fulfillment of these petitions at the end of time (eschatological interpretation) *and* recognizing, in light of this vision, God's proleptic fulfillments of them in the time of Jesus and in the present through members of the community who are then models whom the praying disciples are to imitate with God's help (ethical interpretation).[62]

The tensions between the ethical and eschatological interpretations, between the horizon of the present manifestations of God's care and the eschatological horizon, and between continuity with the old Jewish traditions and discontinuity that emphasizes the newness of Christ and his teaching are all brought together in the first petition (6:9c).

"Hallowing the name" [of God] is in Jewish tradition "giving glory" to God in prayers, but also obeying God's commands (up to martyrdom).

---

61. On this and what follows see Luz, *Matthew,* 374–80; Davies and Allison, *Matthew,* 593–607.

62. Thus this figurative interpretation acknowledges a realized eschatology, as a historical/realistic interpretation also does. But the relationship between future and realized eschatology are reversed. In a historical/realistic interpretation, realized eschatology is predominant, the future eschatology being merely the horizon in which realized eschatology is perceived; so to speak, one understands the future eschatology on the basis of the realized eschatology (the realistic component). By contrast, in this figurative interpretation the future eschatology is predominant; it provides the vision necessary for recognizing the instances of realized eschatology; one understands the realized eschatology on the basis of the envisioned future eschatology.

This is an ethical interpretation, according to which believers are to bring about the "hallowing of the name" by doing good deeds before people so that "they may see your good works and give glory to your Father who is in heaven" (5:16). But the passive form, ἁγιασθήτω (hallowed be), can be interpreted as a divine passive, the petition asking that God fully manifest himself so that everyone will truly glorify his name, something that is to take place only at the eschaton — this is an eschatological interpretation.

Which interpretation should we adopt? Both. The complete glorification of the Name is a vision of what God will bring about that is perceived over against the eschatological horizon. Here and now, it is the vocation of the disciples — a very demanding vocation that needs to be formed in them, as 5:21–48 shows (see reading C, CAW 4). A person who brings glory to God through his or her righteous deeds is a model of discipleship. Or one can revert to the eschatological interpretation: by bringing glory to God, this person has met one of "the conditions of entry into the kingdom of God";[63] this person has demonstrated that she or he "has been trained for the kingdom of heaven" (13:52) and thus belongs to the future kingdom.

Conversely, when taking as a starting point the eschatological interpretation — the glorification of God's name will be completely brought about by God's own intervention — one can revert to the ethical interpretation by emphasizing that God plays an essential role in the person's righteous deed. This is why a person's righteous deed can become a model of discipleship despite its radical nature; other people can truly view it as feasible because the eschatological perspective reveals that God plays a role in it.[64]

The preceding comments apply to the next two petitions when they are taken together because they balance each other; one is primarily eschatological, the other primarily ethical. The second, "Your kingdom come" (6:10a), calls for an eschatological interpretation: the kingdom is an eschatological reality that God alone can bring about.[65] Yet the lack of specific definition of the kingdom and the unusual (for Jewish tradition) description of the kingdom as "coming" leave the interpretation of this petition

---

63. Luz, *Matthew,* 217. The "glance at the [future] kingdom of heaven" that brackets the Sermon on the Mount (4:17, 23; 5:3, 10; 7:21) refers to what the Christian community progresses toward. It is what frames the vision of Christian practice offered by the Sermon on the Mount. Thus from this figurative perspective, in the Sermon Matthew (by contrast with Jesus) defines "the conditions of entry in the kingdom of God," understood as a vision of a reality that is still future and around which the community is gathered.

64. This formulation seeks to account for Luz's conclusion that Matthew and his community underscore "the priority of grace," without understanding the practice of the disciples as signs of the kingdom already dawning (as Strecker and Kingsbury do in their historical/realistic interpretation, according to which the church is then the sphere of God's eschatological rule, i.e., the kingdom). See Luz, *Matthew,* 217–18.

65. While an ethical interpretation is not impossible (see Georg Strecker, *The Sermon on the Mount: An Exegetical Commentary,* trans. O. C. Dean Jr. [Nashville: Abingdon, 1988], 114, who proposes an ethical interpretation as is consistent which his historical/realistic interpretation), the eschatological interpretation is primary, as Strecker himself concedes.

open; this is not simply a traditional eschatological petition. The third petition, "Your will be done" (6:10b), is similarly open, in the sense that it is a very general reference to the will of God, although it is clear that the petition aims at active human behavior: an ethical interpretation. Yet the will that is to be done is the will of an active God. Thus Luz concludes, "An alternative between divine action and human action would be a false alternative."[66]

In sum, for Luz (and for Davies and Allison, although less explicitly), when believers pray the Lord's Prayer, they *envision* Jesus' ministry and their own experience in a way that takes into account (1) that God is a caring, close, and active Father and (2) that the kingdom and the judgment are coming. As they pray with the community, they are formed in the image of this vision and its twofold horizon and thus discover themselves disciples with a twofold vocation: to manifest the care of God, the loving Father, and to warn about the judgment of those who fail to serve God. This *conclusion about what the Lord's Prayer is and says* according to an interpretation focused on this figurative dimension is consistent with the conclusions of the figurative interpretation of Matthew 4:18–22 discussed in chapter 2 (reading C, CAWs).

Reading D, CAW 2: The Main Theme of the Sermon on the Mount—Judgment (7:21–27), Beatitudes (5:3–10), and Moral Discernment

Reading D, CAW 2.1: Moral Discernment as the Essential Characteristic of Disciples according to the Judgment Scene, 7:21–27 (Compare with Reading C, CAW 3.9)

We identified (see reading D, CAW 1) the concluding thematic unit of the Sermon on the Mount (7:21–27) by taking note of the formal inverted parallelisms with 5:3–10. Their respective designations as the judgment scene and the beatitudes were chosen because they represent an aspect of their inverted parallelisms. But such representations (which have a figurative character) should not be confused with the main theme around which the Sermon on the Mount is organized in its thematic dimension. In order to identify this main theme, we first need to examine 7:21–27 more closely, noting that my commentary elucidates the passage's formal semantic oppositions. "Through the oppositions of this passage Matthew contrasts those who say 'Lord, Lord' and do not do the will of Jesus' Father (7:21a) or who hear Jesus' words and do not do them (7:26) with those who say 'Lord, Lord' and do the will of his Father (7:21b) or who hear his words and do them (7:24)."[67] The ques-

---

66. Luz, *Matthew,* 380. For the similar "open" interpretation of the other petitions, see Luz, *Matthew,* 380–89. See also Davies and Allison, *Matthew,* 607–17.

67. Patte, *Matthew,* 100; see also 408, where the formal oppositions are listed.

tion becomes, What is the difference between false disciples (who merely say "Lord, Lord" and do not do his teaching) and true disciples (who do what he taught them)? What makes them behave in such radically different ways?

The concluding parable of the houses built on rock and on sand, 7:24–27, sets a contrast between a "wise man" (ἀνήρ φρόνιμος, i.e., a man with practical wisdom), who has moral discernment, and a "foolish man" (ἀνήρ μωρός, 7:26) who lacks such wisdom and discernment. The wise man is the one who identified a good foundation for the house — solid rock rather than unstable sand. This is what distinguishes people who are blessed and will withstand the flood of the last judgment from those who will be destroyed by it: they identify a good foundation and build on it.

Note also that according to this interpretation, what happens at the time of the flood/judgment is not what is emphasized by the opposition. The focus is on the decision to build on the rock or on the sand, much before the time of the judgment. The flood/judgment reveals the kind of discernment on which the behavior of people (building a house) is based. The good or bad foundation of the house is hidden until the judgment, but a wise person (φρόνιμος) identifies this good foundation already in the present.

The emphasis of the thematic dimension is, therefore, on the importance of having here and now the appropriate moral discernment. In effect, the importance of knowing about the eschatological judgment is minimized; it is too late at the time of the judgment/flood to do anything to correct the situation. It is at the building time that one needs to use moral discernment in order to make the right decision. The eschatological framework of the text is a part of an existing symbolic world, which the thematic dimension of the Sermon does affirm. But the primary goal of the Sermon according to this thematic interpretation is to teach its main theme to readers, not this symbolic world (by contrast with the figurative interpretation, see reading C, CAW 2). The symbolic world is a means for expressing the main theme, namely, the importance of moral discernment (practical wisdom, φρόνησις), and more specifically, the importance of identifying the good on which one's life/house must be based.

Faithful disciples (who do Jesus' teaching, 7:24, and God's will, 7:21) are people who know how to discern the "good" that is hidden (the foundation of a person's life) before it is revealed at the judgment. They know how to recognize those words that one should do — Jesus' words and the expressions of God's will. They already, here and now, use the same discernment that the Judge will use at the end of time. Thus they do not stop with appearances when they evaluate someone.

In this way, they know not only how to discern a good foundation (rock) from a bad one (sand), but also a good builder from a bad one. Similarly, they know how to identify people who are models of discipleship and whom they should follow and imitate. Indeed, one who says "Lord, Lord," prophesies, casts out demons, and performs other miracles in the name of Jesus (7:21–23) might be a disciple that one should take as a model; but not necessarily *so. It all depends on whether or not this person does God's will, i.e., if that person truly uses moral discernment and finds a solid foundation for his or her life. In sum, this (brief) examination of the thematic dimension of 7:21–27 shows that the main theme of the Sermon on the Mount concerns (true) moral discernment as the foundational characteristic of discipleship.*

Reading D, CAW 2.2: Moral Discernment as a Condition for Saying the Beatitudes, 5:3–10 (Compare with Reading C, CAW 3.1)

As one ponders the beatitudes from the perspective of the judgment scene (7:21–27), it soon appears that despite their exclusively euphoric character the beatitudes (5:3–10) are directly related to moral discernment. To begin with, in order to proclaim these beatitudes, and in order to appropriate them and repeat them, one must have the true discernment emphasized in 7:21–27. Conversely, the beatitudes exemplify this discernment and thus provide the readers of the Sermon with the lenses they need to achieve the true discernment of faithful disciples.

In each beatitude, the description of the behavior or attitude (e.g., "poor in spirit," "peacemaker") is a description of doing Jesus' words and God's will, i.e., building on a good foundation. The choice of such behaviors does not appear, at first glance, to be necessarily wise (to say the least), in the same way that the foundation of a house remains hidden until the flood. The description of the eschatological blessing (e.g., "theirs is the kingdom"; "they will be called children of God") reveals that the choice of this kind of behavior was wise indeed, in the same way that the flood reveals which house is actually built on the sound foundation, the rock. In the present, when there is no flood, they choose a certain kind of behavior because they already discern that it is the will of God and thus that it is the kind of behavior that will withstand the judgment.

Thus someone with true discernment recognizes that persons who are "poor in spirit" (5:3)[68] do not assert their own will (they are "poor in spirit") because inwardly they have made God's will their own will (cf. 7:21). Because they belong to the kingdom of heaven, they submit to the yoke of heaven: "theirs is the kingdom of heaven." The same can be said about people who are "persecuted for righteousness' sake" (5:10); this behavior shows that inwardly they are indeed people who have made God's will (righteousness) their own will, no matter what might be the consequences for them; they submit to the kingdom of heaven. "Theirs is the kingdom." Similarly, for all the beatitudes, someone with true discernment should recognize people who have inwardly made God's will their own.

1. People who "mourn" (5:4), because they have deprived themselves of the loved ones who demand their allegiance, are people who inwardly are

---

68. Here and in what follows I paraphrase my conclusions regarding the significance of the beatitudes (Patte, *Matthew*, 101) in the clearer perspective provided by an interpretation that already presupposes the interpretation of 7:21–27 and its emphasis on moral discernment.

committed to serving God and God alone with the confidence that true comfort (from God) will be given to them. "They will be comforted."

2. People who are "meek" (5:5) do not assert their rights (when others want to take advantage of them) because inwardly they are confident that their rights will nevertheless be asserted. "They will inherit the earth."

3. People who "hunger and thirst for righteousness" (5:6) eagerly look at everything around them for signs of God's righteousness; they are people who seek to discern manifestations of God's righteousness because inwardly they are confident that they will find such manifestations. "They will be filled."

4. People who are "merciful" (5:7) possess inward confidence that "they will receive mercy" (from God).

5. People who are "pure in heart" (5:8) and have undivided devotion to God (cf. 6:2–6) feel inwardly confident that "they will see God."

6. People who are "peacemakers" (5:9) by seeking reconciliation at all cost and loving their enemies know inwardly that they are children of God (cf. 5:44–48) and thus are confident that "they will be called children of God" (by God and by others).

In sum, the beatitudes help the disciples to develop their moral discernment by providing them with a series of exemplary cases of people who perform outward actions which, despite the appearances, are a solid foundation (rock) chosen with true moral discernment. Through the beatitudes used as lenses, the readers/disciples are invited to look around themselves and to identify those who are "blessed," that is, those whom they should imitate as models of discipleship. The impersonal form ("they") of the beatitudes suggests that one can expect to find such models of discipleship anywhere in society, not merely in the church.

Reading D, CAW 2.3: Representation of the Theme of Moral Discernment in the Figures of "Vision," "Seeing," and "Eye" — Discernment as Clear Perception of Manifestations of God's Goodness (Compare with Reading C, CAW 3.6)

If we have properly identified "moral discernment as the foundational characteristic of discipleship" as the main theme of the Sermon on the Mount through our study of 7:21–27 and 5:3–10, we should also find this theme holding a prominent place in the body of the Sermon. Yet we should also expect that this main theme will be presented figuratively. We have to understand how these figures express the main theme.

Three interrelated and recurring figures found throughout the Sermon on the Mount clearly exhibit features that express the theme of moral discernment: the figurative uses of "vision," "seeing," and "eye." Let us examine how these figurative usages express the theme of moral discernment before reading systematically the rest of the Sermon on the Mount.

There are many references in the Sermon on the Mount to seeing, some about appropriate ways of seeing, some about wrong ways of seeing, *some about the way God sees, some about the way disciples should see. Appropriate ways of seeing include:*

- *"Seeing the crowds," Ἰδὼν δὲ τοὺς ὄχλους, 5:1, a phrase that is here interpreted as referring to Jesus who perceives the positive attitude of the crowds toward him, since they followed him, 4:25.*

- *Seeing God, τὸν θεὸν ὄψονται, as one of the blessings of the king-dom, 5:8.*

- *Seeing the good works of disciples, ἴδωσιν ὑμῶν τὰ καλὰ ἔργα, 5:16, an appropriate kind of seeing that leads people to give glory to God.*

Wrong ways of seeing include:

- *Looking at a woman with lust, βλέπων γυναῖκα πρὸς τὸ ἐπιθυμῆσαι αὐτὴν, 5:28; this amounts to having an evil eye that "causes you to sin" (ὁ ὀφθαλμός…σκανδαλίζει σε, 5:29).*

How God sees:

- *God sees in secret (βλέπων ἐν τῷ κρυπτῷ) acts of righteousness, such as the giving of alms, prayer, fasting (6:4, 6, 18). God's way of seeing is contrasted with seeing what people want you to see (πρὸς τὸ θεαθῆναι, 6:1; cf. 6:16), namely, outward acts (6:5).*

How the disciples should see:

- *Being a faithful disciple involves having a "healthy" or "sound" (ἁπλοῦς) eye, rather than an "unhealthy" or "evil" (πονηρὸς) eye (6:22–23).*

- *Those with a sound eye can "look (ἐμβλέπω) at the bird of the air" (6:26) and look at "the lilies of the field" and be instructed by them (καταμνθάνω, 6:28) regarding how God cares for them. By contrast, those with an evil eye see "the speck in [their] neighbor's eye but do not notice the log in [their] own eye" (7:3; see 7:4–5).*

From these repeated mentions of "visual" thematic features in various fig-urative usages, we can conclude in this thematic interpretation that a basic condition for discipleship is having a "sound eye" (6:22). What is a "sound" (ἁπλοῦς) eye and what does it mean to have one?[69] Having a sound eye includes:

- *Having a vision of reality that includes God's manifestations in the present and thus the manifestations of the coming kingdom in the present.*

---

69. See the detailed discussion of the texts on this important theme in Patte, *Matthew*, 90–98.

- Having faith (rather than "little faith," 6:30), i.e., seeing that God takes care of the birds (6:26) and the lilies of the field (6:28–30), and also that God makes the rain fall and the sun rise on the righteous and on the unrighteous (5:45).

- "Seeing God" (5:8) in the good works of disciples and giving thanks to God for these deeds (rather than thanking the disciples).

- Seeing things as God sees them and thus "seeing" what is "in secret" (6:2–18), i.e., what is hidden, what comes from the heart.

- Having the ability to discern what is pure (rather than impure), what is precious (rather than worthless, 7:6), what are good things for one's children (7:9–10) as well as for oneself and others (7:12).

From the contrast with having an evil eye (πονηρὸς, 6:23), we can also conclude that having a sound eye is having an "undivided" eye (a possible meaning of ἁπλοῦς), i.e., an eye that is exclusively focused on what God is doing and on the good things people are doing. Having faith, i.e., having true moral discernment, is seeing how God takes care of the creation (6:26, 28) and of human beings (5:45), and not worrying about the rest (6:25–34), i.e., not seeing the rest (evil, lack of food, clothing, etc.) as something that should determine one's action.

To practice such moral discernment is not to deny the existence of evil or the power of evil. The point of 6:25–34 (according to this thematic interpretation) is that one sees good manifestations of God's loving care in the midst of a worrisome situation in which being anxious is the common "reaction." Faith is the trust and confidence that God takes care of us in the midst of these and worse situations. Then one does not need to allow evil to determine one's behavior. Doing good is not defined as striving to overcome evil; it is not a reactionary attitude.

Such a reactionary attitude occurs when one has an "evil eye," i.e., an eye focused on evil. One becomes anxious and ends up trying to serve two masters (6:24) instead of serving God and giving glory to God. A divided eye produces a divided allegiance. Similarly, if one has an evil, "divided" eye, one continually judges and condemns others (7:1–5), even if it only is for minute deficiencies; one can see other people (including disciples and the community of disciples) as a "mixed bag" of good and of evil that one must criticize rather than as models that we are called to imitate. The one who has an evil eye is content to see the outward acts. Totally confused, such a one follows false prophets who look good from the outside (because they are "in sheep's clothing"), without noticing that "inwardly [they] are ravenous wolves" (7:15), and condemns people with minute (outward) deficiencies ("speck in the eye," 7:1–5), even though they might have hidden (ἐν τῷ κρυπτῷ) good deeds and be good inwardly (7:17; cf. 6:4, 6, 18). Thus "beware of (προσέχετε ἀπὸ) false prophets" (7:15), religious leaders who mislead one into joining the many who are going to destruction through the wide gate and the easy road (7:13). Conversely, those who bear good fruit (7:17) out of their inward goodness are true prophets; following them leads to life (7:14).

In sum, viewed from the perspective of an interpretation that is focused on the thematic dimension, the Sermon on the Mount emphasizes that true moral discernment, which distinguishes faithful discipleship, is characterized by clarity and straightforwardness. Being a faithful disciple involves being totally focused on the manifestations of God's goodness, the good works of people, and the hidden good in righteous people. The person who has such vision knows what direction to go in — imitating God and anyone else who performs good works.

These conclusions are far from the conclusions of a figurative interpretation, that emphasize the ambivalence of the symbolic world. At this point, it is essential to go back to the figurative interpretation, lest we think that the thematic interpretation is the only legitimate interpretation (an obvious temptation for me!).

Reading C, CAW 3: A Figurative Interpretation — Discipleship in between the Two Horizons of the Symbolic World of the Sermon on the Mount

In effect, for Luz and Davies and Allison, the rest of the Sermon on the Mount is interpreted from the perspective of the Lord's Prayer. *In effect*, for them, it specifies what discipleship involves when it is conceived of in the tensions between the now and the not-yet between the present of the caring Father and the eschatological future, i.e., in the tensions between the two horizons of the symbolic world. Disciples need to live in this symbolic world in order to be formed in the image of the models of discipleship, especially Jesus, the primary model they are to imitate — the *imitatio Christi* mentioned by Davies and Allison.[70] In this symbolic world, disciples also learn to identify those they should not view as models because they are false religious leaders — false prophets. The symbolic world and its twofold horizon posited by the Sermon on the Mount are the necessary context for faithful discipleship.

The phrase "in effect," as I used it above for Luz and Davies and Allison, is a reminder that these scholars do not conceive of their interpretation as "figurative" — that is, as focused on one of the several meaning-producing dimensions of the Sermon on the Mount — because of their one-dimensional interpretations. These scholars find themselves in a dilemma in this case. On the one hand, they clearly pursue a figurative interpretation. As we already noted regarding other passages, and as I will underscore below regarding the rest of

---

70. Davies and Allison, *Matthew*, 411–12.

the Sermon, they pay close attention to the figures of the text and to the figurative organization, often drawing "figurative conclusions" — among them the remarkable conclusions of Luz regarding 5:21–48 (see reading C, CAW 3.4). On the other hand, their one-dimensional approach compels them to include in their interpretation the results of historical/realistic interpretations, which are often at odds with their figurative interpretation. In the process, the coherence of their figurative interpretation is obscured.

In the following pages, I strive to show as clearly as possible the coherence of the important interpretation of the symbolic world of the Sermon on the Mount by Luz and Davies and Allison. I justify my interpretation of their work by showing in an introductory section the extent to which their interpretation is "figurative" (in some instances, totally, in others, very little). I leave off doing this when I have clarified the markers with which they repeatedly signal their figurative comments. So that the coherence of this important figurative interpretation might be perceived more readily, I present without interruption its conclusions about what all the sections of the Sermon express about the symbolic world of discipleship — rather than provide immediately after the comments on each section the counterpoint found in the alternate interpretation. In order to make the comparison easier, I cross-reference the comments on each section of the Sermon on the Mount with the corresponding comments of the alternate interpretation.

Reading C, CAW 3.1: Matthew 5:3–12 — The Beatitudes as Expressions of God's Present Loving Care and of Eschatological Promises (Compare with Reading D, CAW 2.2)

Davies and Allison's and Luz's Figurative Interpretations and Their Conclusions about What Matthew 5:3–12 Is. There are three main indications that Davies and Allison interpret the beatitudes as a part of the figurative dimension of the Sermon on the Mount.[71]

1. They argue that the beatitudes include 5:3–12 (and not merely 5:3–10), giving priority to the repetition of μακάριοι as a formula of blessing (and thus possessing significant emotional appeal) and to the triadic organization (nine beatitudes; three times three).

2. They identify all the possible allusions to biblical texts and Jewish traditions in each of the beatitudes.

3. They insist that the beatitudes are to understood as "blessings," not as ethical instructions (against Strecker's interpretation of the historical/realistic dimension).

The indications that Luz interprets the beatitudes as a part of the figurative dimension of the Sermon on the Mount are not as striking, but

---

71. Davies and Allison, *Matthew*, 429–69.

ultimately no less clear.[72] While he makes the first two of the above points, he does so with less emphasis than Davies and Allison because by means of his redaction critical and comparative approaches, he finds that he can bypass *neither* the ethicization of the beatitudes by Matthew (who, as Strecker emphasizes, transformed them into ethical admonition and order for the life of the community), *nor* the beatitudes as an "impartation of grace." Luz concludes (with Luther) that the beatitudes are both ethical admonitions and an impartation of grace. In this way, he anchors his interpretation of the beatitudes even more clearly on the figurative dimension than Davies and Allison do: yes, the beatitudes are ethical admonitions; yes, they call for an internalization of God's will; but these ethical admonitions are a figure of grace. It is not that the ethical admonitions are a gift (grace), as Strecker says,[73] but rather that "the gospel also contains commandments" as something toward which one should "strive" (Luz citing Luther).[74] Because of the beatitude form, these ethical admonitions are set in a framework of grace; they point to present blessings (the utterance of beatitudes, as well as the rest of Jesus' ministry and what is like it in the present) and to future blessings. The ethical is thus framed in the twofold horizon of God's present blessings and of God's eschatological blessings (which remain future and are not realized, as Luz insists). Beyond Luz's comments (but in the perspective of his comments on 5:21–48), we can say that the eschatological horizon and the internalizing of God's will clarifies that these beatitudes are not commandments but figures of life in the kingdom, and that the present horizon means that there are people who already do these things in the present and are thus models of discipleship whom disciples are called to imitate.

Conclusions about What Matthew 5:3–12 Says according to This Figurative Interpretation. When read with a focus on the figurative meaning-producing dimension of the Sermon, each beatitude directly expresses the twofold symbolic horizon. Obviously, the eschatological promises (e.g., "for theirs is the kingdom of heaven," 5:3, 10) express the eschatological horizon, the coming kingdom. The declarations of blessing ("Blessed") express "the present theological horizon" (a shorthand for "the horizon of the present manifestations of God's care as our heavenly Father"). The descriptions of the blessed ones (e.g., "the poor in spirit") are then read in this twofold horizon.

Taking into account continuity and discontinuity between old and new,

---

72. Luz, *Matthew*, 224–46.

73. Georg Strecker, "Die Makarismen der Bergpredigt," *New Testament Studies* 17 (1970/71): 255–75 (esp. 274).

74. Luz, *Matthew*, 246. I stress the distinction between Strecker's and Luther's interpretation beyond what Luz says here, in view of what Luz himself says about the antitheses (see below).

Luz and Davies and Allison read the declarations of blessing ("blessed," μακάριοι) as present manifestations of God's loving care comparable to the "blessings" and "beatitudes" in cultic, wisdom, and apocalyptic texts of the Hebrew Bible and the LXX.[75] As a religious word of blessing uttered by one who has religious authority, Jesus, such a blessing is a word that has the power of positing a new reality, as a curse also does.[76] Such persons *are* "blessed" by God, and they are in a special relation with God (as in Ex 19:4–5); they *are* "chosen" of God; God's "own."[77] The readers/hearers are then invited to identify certain characters in the Gospel or people in their present as blessed ones,[78] i.e., people who have benefited from the care and love of the Father. The present theological horizon of the symbolic world begins to be posited.

The descriptions of those who are blessed can then be understood (so Luz) as reflecting an ethicization of the tradition by Matthew, without conceiving of them as commands that should be obeyed. These descriptions provide a means for identifying the blessed ones as people to be imitated. For instance, in 5:3, "poor in spirit" (οἱ πτωχοὶ τῷ πνεύματι) is to be understood metaphorically without completely excluding a reference to actual poverty;[79] it points toward "the religious state of poverty"[80] and thus "the ethical attitude of humility"[81] exemplified by the actual poor who will be comforted, as prophesied by Isaiah (61:1–2; cf. Mt 11:5). Thus people

---

75. Davies and Allison, *Matthew*, 431–34. These blessings include those uttered by the Levites on those who "obey the voice of the Lord" (Dt 28:1–14, particularly relevant because of the "ethical" descriptions of the blessed ones). These blessings are preceded (Dt 27:15–26) and followed (Dt 28:15ff.) by curses on those who do "not obey the voice of the Lord." This remark is important, even though Matthew, unlike Luke (6:20–26), does not directly associate blessings with curses (woes); the negative counterpart of the beatitudes is found in the conclusion of the Sermon, Matthew 7:24–27.

76. William F. Beardslee, *Literary Criticism of the New Testament* (Minneapolis: Fortress, 1971), 27–39.

77. One can thus say with Davies and Allison (*Matthew*, 439–40) that the beatitudes as proclamations of blessedness are an expression and manifestation of God's grace. This emerges for Davies and Allison in the process of rejecting an ethical interpretation of the beatitudes, which Luz (*Matthew*, 229–30) wants to maintain without denying Davies and Allison's interpretation. This debate arises because they consider each beatitude as a whole, rather than focusing on its three components. Yet they end up in agreement. Davies and Allison agree that "it would be foolish to deny the imperatives implicit in 5:3–12" (440). Luz underscores, as we noted, that the demands ("imperatives") are themselves an expression of grace: "grace happens in the proclamation of the demands of Jesus" (215).

78. As the macarism of the *Homeric Hymn to Demeter,* "Happy is he among men on the earth who has seen these mysteries," discussed by Betz, allowed the initiated (during the initiation liturgy of the Eleusian mysteries) to recognize himself and others who had "seen these mysteries" as the happy ones. See Hans Dieter Betz, *Essays on the Sermon on the Mount,* trans. L. L. Welborn (Minneapolis: Fortress, 1985), 26–28.

79. Let us keep in mind that a metaphor brings together two semantic fields, here that of "actual poverty" and that of a "humility," a spiritual attitude.

80. In agreement with the Jewish *'anawim* "piety." Davies and Allison, *Matthew,* 442–43. Betz, *Essays,* 33–34.

81. Luz, *Matthew,* 232–34. Betz, *Essays,* 34.

who can be identified as "in the religious state of poverty" are blessed ones whom one should imitate, even though it might not yet be apparent that they belong to the eschatological kingdom.

Reading C, CAW 3.2: Matthew 5:13–16 — Positive and Negative Figures of the Disciples' Vocation of Religious Leadership (Compare with Reading D, CAW 3.1)

Davies and Allison's and Luz's Figurative Interpretations and Their Conclusions about What Matthew 5:13–16 Is. The rest of the introduction of the Sermon, 5:13–16, is readily interpreted for its figures. Thus Davies and Allison underscore the triad of figures, "salt of the earth," "light of the world," and "city on a hill," and the allusions to biblical texts and Jewish traditions that construct these figures. By conceiving of these figures as simply referring to "the task of the people of God in the world" and to "the Gentile mission," they basically revert to an interpretation of the historical/ realistic dimension. They nevertheless come back to the figurative dimension when they note that "in being lights, the disciples are imitating Jesus, who was a light to those sitting in darkness (4:15–16)," and consequently that "the evangelist [has an] exalted estimation of the ecclesia's role in the religious life of humanity." They note in a typical figurative interpretation that these three figures of discipleship indicate that the disciples' religious leadership has the same goal as and thus "is like" that of Jesus (bringing glory to God, who is both Jesus' and the disciples' "Father in heaven," as Luz underscores). Similarly, these figures show that the church (the community of disciples) "must be the primary locus of God's activity in and for all people."[82]

Furthermore, in response to his review of the *Wirkungsgeschichte,* Luz stresses that these figures express that "the light of the world takes shape in the *works* of the Christians," once again noting the relationship between commandments and grace for Matthew. The most distinctive signal that Luz does interpret the figurative dimension of these verses is his comment regarding the openness of the vision of the church proposed by these verses; becoming disciples involves encountering people who are "light" for us. The teaching of the rest of the Sermon, presenting what these good works/ lights are (cf. 5:17–7:12), gives the readers the vision they need to recognize models of discipleship.[83]

Conclusions about What Matthew 5:13–16 Says according to This Figurative Interpretation. In 5:13–16, the three figures "salt," "light," and "city on a hill," which as open metaphors can have many possible connota-

---

82. Davies and Allison, *Matthew,* 470–80. Quotations are from 471, 478, 479.
83. Luz, *Matthew,* 246–55. Quotation from 255.

tions,[84] express the disciples' vocation as religious leaders. About "salt," it is enough to note that as "salt" does not exist for itself, so disciples do not exist for themselves, but for "the earth." Discipleship is a vocation of religious leadership. About "light," 5:16 shows that letting one's light shine in the world is performing "good deeds"; since the same metaphor describes Jesus' ministry in 4:16, the disciples' mission is to be *like* Jesus' mission. Finally, we note that both metaphors point out the universal character of the disciples' mission as religious leaders: they are to be salt *of the earth* and light *of the world* (τοῦ κόσμου).

It is quite significant for this figurative interpretation that 5:13–16 includes negative figures of discipleship: the salt that has lost its taste (μωρανθῇ; literally, "caused to become foolish") and should be thrown out (5:13); the light under a bushel (5:15). These negative figures complement the symbolic world and function as the positive ones do. They are an invitation to identify (both among the characters of the Gospel and among the members of the Christian community) people who are not disciple-like. People who lose their character as disciples (salt that has lost its taste, hidden light), i.e., members of the community who, even though they are still in the community, are not truly disciples because they have become foolish (without moral discernment) and thus are unable to carry out their vocation of religious leadership.

Since this is clear about the negative figures, it follows that the positive figures in 5:13–16 are themselves an invitation to identify people who are positive models of discipleship, truly salt of the earth and light of the world, who are worthy of imitation.

Reading C, CAW 3.3: Matthew 5:17–20 — Jesus as a Model of Discipleship (Compare with Reading D, CAW 3.3; 3.5)

Luz's Figurative Interpretation and Its Conclusions about What Matthew 5:17–20 Is.   The first signal that Luz's interpretation is focused on the figurative dimension is his opening acknowledgment that these "verses belong to the most difficult ones of the Gospel." Luz chooses the most difficult reading and underscores the ambivalence of the text.[85] The discussion of two central issues will suffice here.

First, Luz outlines the diverse possibilities for interpreting the statement that Jesus has come not to "abolish" (καταλύω) but to "fulfill" (πληρόω) the law and the prophets (5:17). The basic question is, Does Jesus fulfill the law and the prophets by his teaching or by his actions?

An interpretation focused on the historical/realistic dimension answers, By his teaching (so Strecker; see chap. 3, reading A, CAW 4.1), an interpretation that seems natural in the context of the Sermon. Davies and Allison

---

84. For the various possibilities, see Luz, *Matthew*, 247–55; Davies and Allison, *Matthew*, 470–79.

85. Luz, *Matthew*, 255–73.

adopt this interpretation, oscillating as they often do between a historical/ realistic interpretation and a figurative one.[86]

Luz answers, By his actions, and more specifically, By his obedience, the way in which he keeps the law. In this way, *Jesus' praxis* during his ministry, his fulfillment of the law and the prophets, *is a model that disciples are to imitate.* Thus Luz opens the way for interpreting the central part of the Sermon (5:21–7:12) as *the description of the "righteousness" that Jesus practices* in his ministry — a praxis that disciples are called to imitate.

Second, in which sense is this "righteousness" (δικαιοσύη) "more" (πλεῖον) than that of the scribes and Pharisees (5:20)? Is it "more" in a quantitative sense or in a qualitative sense? Instead of choosing one of these traditional options, Luz (joined by Davies and Allison)[87] notes that the text is *ambivalent,* keeping both options in tension. It is a matter of doing everything prescribed by the law (the quantitative interpretation in terms of 5:18–19) and also of doing the law as the will of God that needs to be envisioned in terms of the love commandment (the qualitative interpretation in terms of 5:21–48). We will see below that the phrase "higher righteousness" designates this ambivalent understanding.

This tension, which is typical of figurative textual features, can be illustrated by noting that doing the entire law is an expression of the continuity of Jesus' ministry with Judaism that involves (1) doing the ritual commandments (in this interpretation of Matthew, Jesus does and teaches; see 23:23, 26; 24:20) and simultaneously (2) giving priority to mercy and love above ritual (as is expressed by Jesus both in his teaching, e.g., 5:23–24, and in his ministry, e.g., 9:10–13, quoting Hos 6:6, "I desire mercy, not sacrifice"). In this way, Luz shows that the figurative dimension of the Sermon seeks to convey *either* that discontinuity with Judaism (resulting from giving priority to mercy over sacrifice) must be accepted without abandoning and denying the continuity that exists *or* that continuity must be maintained despite the discontinuity that necessarily characterizes discipleship lived in imitation of Jesus' radical ministry.

Conclusions about What Matthew 5:17–20 Says according to This Figurative Interpretation.   In Matthew 5:18–20, the eschatological horizon reappears so as to clarify the difference between the *present* (of Jesus' ministry and of the church), when the law and the prophets are to be fulfilled, and the *eschatological future,* when the law and the prophets will pass away, as well as their interrelation — what one does in the present affects one's eschatological future.

In this figurative interpretation, one can note that Jesus' statement about

---

86. Davies and Allison, *Matthew,* 484–89.

87. Ibid., 498–502 (with, once again, a focus on the figurative dimension and its ambivalence).

not abolishing the law and the prophets but fulfilling them (5:17) is a description of Jesus' mission ("I have come," 5:17) as comparable to, i.e., a model of, what disciples should do (as expressed in 5:19–20 and 5:16). More specifically, following Luz, one notes that the verb πληρόω refers to the fulfillment of the law and the prophets (1) *in an ethical sense:* Jesus obediently fulfills all their demands (5:19) by fulfilling "all righteousness" (3:15);[88] (2) *in a theological and eschatological sense:* in Jesus' life the prophecies are fulfilled (by God), as in the formula quotations with πληρόω (1:22; 2:15, 17, 23; 4:14);[89] (3) *in Jesus' teaching* (especially 5:21–48), which "fulfills" the law in the sense of "completing" it, "making it perfect."

Through Jesus' teaching (3), he makes explicit that disciples should imitate him by obediently fulfilling the law and the prophets as he did (1) and by fulfilling all righteousness (3:15; 5:20) as they carry on Jesus' teaching.[90] Yet the *imitatio Christi* should not be viewed as merely following the example of Jesus and implementing his teaching (ethical interpretation) because being like Jesus involves being the fulfillment of the prophecies (2), which is accomplished by God. The ethical interpretation is qualified and modified by the theological and eschatological features of the *imitatio Christi*.

It remains that the most marked characteristic of Jesus as a model of discipleship is that he obediently fulfills the demands of the law and the prophets. By fulfilling "all righteousness" (3:15) through his obedience to all the commands of the law and the prophets (5:17), Jesus invites disciples to envision for themselves a life characterized by a righteousness greater than that of the scribes and Pharisees (5:20) — and thus to take Jesus as a model of righteousness rather than the scribes and Pharisees, who are false models because of their limited righteousness. Just as fulfilling the Scripture is for Jesus the very core of his mission (what he has come to do, 5:17), so it is for the disciples.

The eschatological horizon is set by the phrases "until heaven and earth pass away" (ἕως ἂν παρέλθῃ ὁ οὐρανὸς καὶ ἡ γῆ) and "until all is accomplished" (ἕως ἂν πάντα γένηται) in 5:18, which are understood in this

---

88. For Matthew, the prophets also contain demands, such as the prophetic command of mercy, Hosea 6:6 quoted in Matthew 9:13 and 12:7; furthermore, in both 7:12 and 22:40, the phrase "the law and the prophets" refers to commands (the Golden Rule and the two great commandments). This interpretation is emphasized by Luz. Cf. Luz, *Matthew,* 261–64; Luz, "Die Erfüllung des Gesetzes bei Matthäus (5:17–20)," *Zeitschrift für Theologie und Kirche 75* (1978): 414–15.

89. Both *the law* and the prophets contain these prophecies (cf. 11:13, where the law, along with the prophets, is said to have "prophesied until John"); Jesus also fulfills such predictions by being "like Moses." This is the interpretation emphasized by Davies and Allison, *Matthew,* 486–87; it is also retained by Luz (*Matthew,* 265). Jesus fulfills the type of Moses (cf. 5:1–3; 7:28–29). In addition, the implicit reference to Deuteronomy 18:15–20 in Matthew 17:1–5 suggests that Matthew viewed Jesus as the eschatological prophet like Moses.

90. As noted above, Luz emphasizes that Jesus' teaching about fulfilling the law is subordinated to his praxis. Thus through his teaching Jesus invites the disciples to imitate him. Luz, *Matthew,* 265.

interpretation as references to the last judgment.[91] In the "mixed" situation in that the readers are — where many people relax some of the laws instead of doing them (5:19),[92] where God's will is not yet done as it is in heaven (6:10) — it becomes possible to envision the higher righteousness that will be at the coming of the kingdom of God (6:10; cf. 6:10a), when God's will is to "be done on earth as it is in heaven" (6:10b). This vision of eschatological higher righteousness is already embodied by Jesus, as well as by other people, who "shall be called great in the kingdom" (5:19), and thus should be viewed as models of discipleship.

Reading C, CAW 3.4: Matthew 5:21–48 — "A Ray of Hope for a New, Better Human Being" (Compare with Reading D, CAW 3.6)

When Matthew 5:21–48 is read against the eschatological and theological horizons that the Sermon on the Mount progressively sets up for the readers (who focus on the figurative dimension), it presents the higher righteousness that will be "the order of law" of the coming kingdom and its present manifestations.[93]

The first two antitheses emphasize the eschatological horizon (the judgment, in 5:22, 25–26, 29–30), which disappears in the third, fourth, and fifth (5:31–42) to make room for the present theological horizon of the caring heavenly Father in the sixth antithesis (5:45, 48). The antithesis form expresses the tensions between the old and the new that we have found elsewhere; here it is the tension between Jesus' teaching and the law (see especially the fifth antithesis, 5:38–42, but also the third, 5:31–32, and the sixth, 5:43–48). The significance of this tension appears more clearly through the repetition of this antithetical form, as Luz indicates in the conclusions of his detailed study.[94]

First Luz notes that one of the effects of the antithesis form is to make a Christological point. The antitheses "demonstrate how the Son of God fulfills in complete sovereignty God's word of law and prophets in putting his word over against Moses." They prolong and specify the figure of "Jesus preaching on the mount" as the new Moses[95] by emphasizing in what ways he is *unlike* Moses. Since Jesus is presented as a model of discipleship, this

---

91. Luz, *Matthew,* 265–67, and Davies and Allison, *Matthew,* 494–95 (but see 490! and Davies, "Matthew 5,17–20," in *Mélanges bibliques pour A. Robert* [Paris: Bloud et Gray, 1957], 440–56, in which Davies ends up espousing a historical/realistic interpretation).

92. Matthew 5:19 can be interpreted to mean either that "whoever relaxes one of the least of these commandments" is excluded from the kingdom, as the scribes and Pharisees are, 5:20 (Davies and Allison, *Matthew,* 495–98) or that such a person will nevertheless enter the kingdom and be "least" in it (Luz, *Matthew,* 267–68). Luz's interpretation is the most consistent in this figurative perspective, which presupposes that the present situation is "mixed."

93. Here and below, Luz's interpretation is obviously focused on the figurative dimension. It is enough for me to present his conclusions. Davies and Allison continue to move back and forth between different types of interpretations.

94. See Luz, *Matthew,* 273–351. It is enough here and below to present Luz's conclusions.

95. Ibid., 279.

Christological point is also a point about discipleship. Disciples are people (characters of the Gospel or people around the readers) who, either as a community (the plural "you") or as individuals (the singular "you," found alternatively with the plural),[96] embody the contrast set up by the antitheses. As Jesus is unlike Moses, so disciples are unlike the "people of old" who received the law. As Jesus is like Moses by proclaiming God's word as order of law, so disciples as religious leaders are like the people of old who were called to envision a new community implementing a new "order of law." The question is, What is kept of the old? What is really new?

Regarding the first and second antitheses, Matthew 5:21–26 and 5:27–30, Luz underscores that the teaching of Jesus ("But I say to you that if you are angry with a brother or sister, you will be liable to judgment," 5:22; "that everyone who looks at a woman with lust has already committed adultery with her in his heart," 5:28) is *"nothing new* within contemporary Jewish parenesis."[97] These antitheses contrast two aspects of the commandments of Torah already distinguished in Judaism: (1) Torah as a legal system that provides "civil order" in society (or in the community) and is implemented by courts of law; and (2) Torah as the will of God that claims the whole person through its moral requirements (the more demanding parenesis to the individual). Civic order of law demands the punishment of murder and adultery. In Jewish ethics, being wrathful and being lustful (having lustful intention) is being sinful. Thus the content of Jesus' teaching in 5:21–30 in and of itself is not new.

It is the antithesis form that creates newness. By opposing the two aspects of the commandments as two "sentences of law," the antithesis *gives to the moral demands of God's will the very status that "the order of law" has.*[98] Of course, this teaching is unrealistic in present society; the commands prohibiting wrath and lust cannot be enforced by courts so as to provide the basis for an actual civic order. The only court that can enforce it is the eschatological judgment, as the descriptions of the punishment in Gehenna (5:22, 29–30) make clear. What the antitheses envision is thus *the fulfillment of the law in the kingdom.*

In sum, the first and second antitheses set up a contrast between the fulfillment of Torah in the present evil society (where the law alone can be implemented as a civic order) and its fulfillment in the kingdom (where the moral teaching becomes law of civic order).[99] Disciples are to abide by the "law of the kingdom," that is, by Jesus' "demands [that] surpass those of

---

96. The second person *singular* (σου) is used in 5:23–26, 29–30, 36, 39b–42, 43.

97. Luz, *Matthew,* 284 (italics mine), 295, and notes. See also Davies and Allison, *Matthew,* 511–21, 522.

98. Against Luz, *Matthew,* 285 (who here is inconsistent with the rest of his figurative interpretation), this is not devaluating the law of the civic order, but rather increasing the value of the moral demands; with Davies and Allison, *Matthew,* 507, 521–22.

99. Luz, *Matthew,* 285–86, following L. Goppelt, *Theology of the New Testament* (Grand Rapids: Eerdmans, 1982), 40.

the Torah, without contradicting the Torah."[100] In the words of Luz, these antitheses are "a ray of hope for a new, better human being in the coming of the kingdom of God," that contrasts with the present situation where hatred and lust (and related sexist attitudes) are omnipresent.[101] Furthermore, when in the midst of present (evil) society one recognizes people who behave according to this teaching of Jesus, these people are signs of the coming kingdom, models of discipleship that one should imitate.

The third antithesis, Matthew 5:31–32, must be interpreted in the same way as the preceding ones, despite the fact that it clearly alludes to a practical regulation used in Matthew's community (cf. the exception to the prohibition of divorce; παρεκτὸς λόγου πορνείας, "except on the ground of unchastity," 5:32).[102] Here a regulation of the community is presented in the form of an antithesis that can be interpreted as the preceding ones by reading it in terms of 19:3–9 and the statement that Moses' teaching about divorce (5:31; 19:7; Dt 24:1–4) was a mere concession granted because of "your hardness of heart" (19:8). Once again, the antithesis contrasts the *"order of law" in present evil society* (in which because of the hardness of heart of its members, divorce and remarriage of divorced people may legally take place) with the *"order of law" in the kingdom* (the prohibition of divorce and of remarriage — marrying a divorced woman is committing adultery). Those who abide by Jesus' teaching are, once again, "a ray of hope for a new, better human being in the coming of the kingdom of God." This is an "order of 'law of the kingdom,'" and not of the world."[103]

The fourth antithesis, Matthew 5:33–37, seems to present a different case, since the antithetical teaching, "Do not swear at all" (ὅλως), is in contradiction with the implication of the teaching of Scripture (the law and the prophets) as summarized in 5:33.[104] Since "swearing falsely" was prohibited, swearing truthfully was permitted and even advocated. Furthermore, the categorical prohibition of oaths of any kind[105] is not found in the Jewish moral teaching. Nevertheless Luz finds in Jewish moral teaching related to the prophetic teaching (e.g., Hos 4:2) exhortations to avoid the unnecessary use of oaths (especially to avoid misusing the divine name). Actually, this critical attitude toward oaths was widespread in both Hellenism and

---

100. Davies and Allison, *Matthew*, 508.

101. Luz, *Matthew*, 431 (cf. 328–29, 341–42). Luz says this about other antitheses, but it also applies here.

102. As Luz (*Matthew*, 298–310) and Davies and Allison (*Matthew*, 527–32) note.

103. As Luz (*Matthew*, 322) says about the next antithesis.

104. Matthew 5:33, is not a quotation of a specific passage of the law. See Luz, *Matthew*, 313, and Davies and Allison, *Matthew*, 533–34.

105. Against the historical/realistic interpretation of Strecker, Luz underscores that the "yes, yes" and "no, no," 5:37, should not be viewed as an alternate oath formula. The two examples of the use of the double yes as a substitute oath formula (2 Enoch 49:1 and *b. Seb.* 36a) are counterbalanced by the many instances of the use of the double yes to mean "a true yes." See Luz, *Matthew*, 317–18 and notes.

Judaism.[106] But the categorical prohibition of oaths was unthinkable (as well as impractical) because the use of oaths was necessary in court proceedings (e.g., to authenticate witnesses). Thus once again, the teaching of this antithesis is " 'a law of the kingdom,' and not of the world."[107]

In the fifth antithesis, Matthew 5:38–42, the teaching "do not resist an evildoer" (or, "do not resist evil," μὴ ἀντιστῆναι τῷ πονηρῷ, 5:39a) is in contradiction with Torah, "an eye for an eye and a tooth for a tooth" (5:38; Ex 21:24; Lv 24:20; Dt 19:21). Once again, "the general admonition to suffer injustice is widespread in all antiquity,"[108] and thus is not new in and of itself. The newness is created by the antithetical form and by the lack of any mention of motivation (e.g., resignation to one's powerlessness or hope of making friends out of one's enemies) for the renunciation of revenge.[109] The "parodic" illustrations (not practical injunctions, 5:39b–42) of the general command, "do not resist an evildoer," bring to the fore its "shocking" character; they include overlooking vehement insults (5:39b), giving up one's legal rights (5:40; according to Ex 22:26–27 and Dt 24:12–13 — the law prohibited taking the cloak of a poor man),[110] and not resisting the demands of foreign powers (5:41). The last illustration, which reflects the situation of Matthew's community, does not weaken the shocking character of the antithesis; giving up one's possessions,[111] rather than lending them, is impractical in the world. This antithesis once again *contrasts the order of law of the kingdom with the order of law of the present world*, which is ruled by revenge, the use of force, and the exploitation and oppression of the powerless. Thus those who do not resist evil among the readers and in the Gospel (Jesus during his Passion) are models of discipleship as they represent the better human being of the coming kingdom, whom disciples should imitate in various situations.

In the sixth antithesis, Matthew 5:43–48, and its extreme demand to "love your enemies" with an *unconditional* love, the figurative interpretation of the preceding antitheses finds its ultimate justification. There is no suggestion that one should love one's enemies with the hope of making friends of them — love-with-the-hope-of is not love![112] In no other antithesis does Jesus' teaching fulfill (surpass without invalidating) the Torah as

---

106. Luz, *Matthew*, 314 and notes.

107. Ibid., 322.

108. Ibid., 326 and notes. See Davies and Allison, *Matthew*, 543–48.

109. See examples in Hellenistic and Jewish literature in L. Schottroff, "Gewaltverzicht und Feindesliebe in der urchristlichen Jesustradition (Mt 5,38–48; Lk 6,27–36)," in *Jesus Christus in Historie und Theologie: Festschrift H. Conzelmann*, ed. G. Strecker (Tübingen: Mohr, 1975), 207–11.

110. This is clearly parodic, since, if one would follow it literally, one would have to go away naked! See J. D. Crossan, "Jesus and Pacifism," in *No Famine in the Land*, ed. J. W. Flanagan and A. W. Robinson (Atlanta: Scholars Press, 1975), 195–208.

111. Matthew 5:42 echoes the injunction in 5:23–26 to reconcile oneself with others at all costs, including economic costs — cf. "until you have paid the last penny."

112. Luz, *Matthew*, 350.

clearly as here. The love of enemies is the "more" (περισσὸν) that the higher righteousness involves (5:46–47; cf. 5:20). It is not by chance that Matthew bracketed the antitheses by teachings involving love of enemies: the first antithesis also emphasized it by calling for reconciliation with anyone who has a grievance (5:23–24).

The figurative character of this teaching is clarified by a strong emphasis on the theological horizon — behaving as one's Father in heaven does (5:45) and thus being "perfect as your Father in heaven is perfect" (5:48; this, of course, does not mean that one should literally do what God does). But surprisingly, the eschatological horizon that was emphasized in the first set of antitheses is nowhere explicit.

The significance of this shift of horizon can easily be overlooked. With Luz, one can interpret the sixth antithesis like the preceding ones. This injunction to love one's enemies is impractical and unrealistic (even when it is actualized by Matthew who identifies the enemies as "persecutors" of the community; 5:44). Thus one *could* say that here also it is "the order of law of the kingdom," which is contrasted with the order of law of the world, and that those who behave in this way are "children of God" in an eschatological sense (as in 5:9). One *could* say that they manifest the better human being in the coming kingdom, who is perfect, τέλειός, i.e., completely fulfills all demands of God's will and has thus the higher righteousness (περισσὸν, 5:47; cf. 5:20), which results from an undivided commitment.[113]

Yet when the shift to the theological horizon (the Father's *present* care for all human beings, including evil ones) is taken into account, it becomes clear that this new "order of law" is not merely future (the order of law of the eschatological kingdom); it also is a *present* reality. This presence of the "new order of law" is manifested in natural phenomena (sunshine, rain) governed by the heavenly Father. This presence of the "new order of law" is also manifested by people (around oneself or among characters of the Gospel) who are perfect as their Father in heaven is perfect. The better human being of this new order of law is a present reality in such people, who are therefore models that disciples are called to imitate. As such, they become figures of the love of God for evil people as well as for good people.

The "new order of law" is not a purely future eschatological reality (a utopian vision), but also a present reality as the Father's care is a present reality. True discipleship as religious leadership includes helping other people to recognize this present reality and thus to envision and strive to bring about the community that would live according to this (eschatological) "order of law."

---

113. Ibid., 346.

Reading C, CAW 3.5: Matthew 6:1–18: Fusion of the Eschatological and Theological Horizons into a Single Symbolic World (Compare with Reading D, CAW 3.7)

Once again, in and of itself the teaching of this passage is not strikingly new.[114] The injunction to give alms without boasting and secretly (6:3–4) is found in Jewish (and Hellenistic) literature,[115] as is the injunction to avoid exaggerated display while fasting;[116] and prayer in seclusion was not unknown in Judaism.[117] The newness of this teaching is once again created by the twofold figurative horizon in which it is set.

The introductory verse, 6:1, refers only to the eschatological horizon: the judgment at which one would not receive rewards. The heavenly Father is mentioned as the one who will give or not give rewards. In all the rest of the unit, the eschatological horizon (the repeated mentions of eschatological reward) is thoroughly integrated with the present theological horizon of the close and caring heavenly Father "who sees in secret" (ὁ βλέπων ἐν τῷ κρυπτῷ, 6:4, 6, 18). Thus the two horizons that remained juxtaposed in 5:21–48 and 6:19–7:11 are now *fused into a single, twofold horizon.*

The negative injunctions, not to give alms, pray, and fast in such a way as to be honored by others, have weight only because of the eschatological horizon; seeking present rewards (being honored by others) becomes something that one readily forgoes when it becomes clear that this means being deprived of eschatological rewards. Conversely, the positive injunctions, to give alms, pray, and fast "in secret," have weight only because of the present theological horizon; this kind of attitude makes sense only insofar as God is the heavenly Father who cares for human beings and is close to them.

The effect of this central passage on the intended readers is, therefore, to make it impossible for them to conceive of their experience as disciples in terms of a single one of the two figurative horizons; they must imagine it against a fused twofold horizon, i.e., in terms of the entire symbolic world. The effect on the readers varies according to the convictions they held before reading the Sermon on the Mount.

- If they held strong eschatological convictions and thus envisioned their experience as disciples primarily in terms of the eschatological horizon — the coming of the kingdom, the last judgment, eschatological rewards and punishments — they are enticed to acknowledge that they should also envision their experience in terms of the other horizon, the loving care and closeness of their heavenly Father.

---

114. Betz (*Essays*, 62) goes as far as saying that "from the point of view of the history of religions, the cultic *didache* in Matthew 6:1–18 is completely in keeping with the religious thought and practice of Judaism. At no point does it betray 'Christian' influence."

115. For references, see Luz, *Matthew,* 358; Davies and Allison, *Matthew,* 582–84.

116. Luz, *Matthew,* 361; Davies and Allison, *Matthew,* 617.

117. Davies and Allison, *Matthew,* 586–87.

• Conversely, if the readers held strong convictions about the loving care and closeness of the heavenly Father and thus envisioned their experience without true recourse to eschatology (e.g., because they believed in a realized eschatology), then they are enticed to acknowledge that their own convictions do not make sense so long they are not complemented by eschatological ones.

Yet the ultimate effect on the two kinds of readers is the same. It is only in terms of the *twofold* figurative horizon that readers can be formed into disciples who will be in a position to live in the present imperfect world their discipleship as an eschatological identity of followers of the new Moses who proclaims the coming kingdom because they can count on the loving care of their heavenly Father. When disciples conceive of their identity in terms of this twofold horizon, they readily distinguish themselves from hypocrites (6:2, 5, 16), who typify false discipleship. Those who envision their discipleship according to this twofold horizon are thus ready to pray the Lord's Prayer (6:9–13) which is, as we saw, simultaneously an eschatological prayer (asking that God bring about the promises of the eschatological time) and a prayer asking for the help of the caring and close Father in fulfilling one's vocation as disciple in the present (the ethical interpretation).

Reading C, CAW 3.6: Matthew 6:19–34: Earthly Possessions,
the Present Care of the Heavenly Father, and the Kingdom
(Compare with Reading D, CAW 3.7; 3.4)

The text shows the implications for disciples of adopting the symbolic world and its twofold horizon, here regarding the relationship of discipleship and possessions. This is a central issue for those who "strive first for the kingdom of God and his righteousness" (6:33). In this verse, "the juxtaposition of βασιλεία and δικαιοσύνη...corresponds to the juxtaposition of the second and third petition of the Lord's Prayer, except that here the task of the person...stands in the foreground."[118] Righteousness as action is envisioned against the background of the theological horizon — the Father who, *in the present*, feeds the birds, clothes the lilies, and provides the necessities of life for human beings (6:26–30).

In 6:19–34, as in 5:21–48, we find teachings that affirm traditional views: in 6:19–20, a sapiential teaching about gathering heavenly treasures also found in Jewish literature;[119] in 6:22–23, the common Jewish metaphor of the "eye" as reflecting the moral character of a person;[120] in

---

118. Luz, *Matthew*, 407. Furthermore, Matthew 6:31–32, by contrasting what Gentiles ask with the attitude of disciples toward their "heavenly Father [who] knows that you need," refers back to the framing of the Lord's Prayer, 6:7–8. See above our discussion of Luz's interpretation of the Lord's Prayer in reading C, CAW 2.3.

119. For references, see Luz, *Matthew*, 395–96; Davies and Allison, *Matthew*, 628–32.

120. For references, see Luz, *Matthew*, 397–98; Davies and Allison, *Matthew*, 635–41.

6:24, an image regarding the impossibility of serving two masters based on common experience and found in both Hellenistic and Jewish literature;[121] in 6:25–34, a teaching about anxiety and divine providence with many parallels in Hellenistic and Jewish texts that express a general theological wisdom.[122] Yet these traditional views are not merely repeated; they are "sharpened" by being set in the twofold figurative horizon of the kingdom and of the Father's care.

Gathering heavenly treasures rather than gathering earthly treasures (6:19–20), which refers to performing good deeds and the rewards that they bring, as in Jewish literature (see also 6:1ff.), is sharpened by the emphasis put in 6:21 on the heart: ἡ καρδία σου. The issue is not primarily earthly possessions in and of themselves, but the attitude of the whole person (as represented by the "heart," a person's "center") toward earthly possessions. From this perspective, the metaphor of the "eye" (see above, reading D, CAW 2.3, for contrast!) refers to attitudes toward money (ἁπλοῦς, the "sound" eye, refers to "generosity" with one's possessions) and emphasizes that "the total existence of the person is at stake; it is here a question of light and darkness, of wholeness and perfection" (cf. 5:48).[123] Ultimately, it is a matter of serving (and worshiping) either God or "mammon," that is, money and earthly possessions. In sum, in 6:19–24, "on the question of possessions, there stands in the intention of Matthew the principle that perfection is the goal and that on the way to it the righteousness of the disciples must be higher than that of the Pharisees and scribes. This means that 6:19–24 in Matthew's view is an example [a model] of discipleship ethics … "[124] as 6:25–34 (and especially 6:30–33) makes clear: "Strive first for the kingdom of God and his righteousness." The passage on anxiety, 6:25–34, emphasizes that the Sermon on the Mount seeks to overcome skepticism about God's providence[125] by establishing the horizon of the close and caring Father for readers who, because of their exclusive reliance on the eschatological horizon, are skeptical about the present. Matthew 6:30–34 has the effect of continuing to fuse the two horizons: confidence in the continual care of the Father is necessary so that one can "strive first for the [eschatological] kingdom."

---

121. Davies and Allison, *Matthew,* 642.

122. For references, see Betz, *Essays,* 89–123; Luz, *Matthew,* 407–8; Davies and Allison, *Matthew,* 645–63.

123. Luz, *Matthew,* 397–98; see also Davies and Allison, *Matthew,* 637–39.

124. Luz, *Matthew,* 399 (the last sentence is in a note), in agreement with K. Bornhäuser, *Die Bergpredigt: Versuch einer zeitgössischen Auslegung* (Gütersloh: Bertelsmann, 1923), 145.

125. This skepticism is linked with apocalypticism, since it needs to be fought by apocalyptic and Jewish apologetic. Betz, *Essays,* 120–21.

*Reading C, CAW 3.7: Matthew 7:1–11: Relationship to Neighbor
and to the Heavenly Father (Compare with Reading D, CAW 3.4)*

The text continues to show the implications for disciples of adopting the
symbolic world and its twofold horizon, first regarding the issue of "judging others," which directly concerns discipleship as religious leadership.

The teaching about "not judging" taken as a whole (7:1–5) is, for Matthew, "to be understood in view of the kingdom"; it stands "under the
demand of perfection (5:48)."[126] The eschatological horizon is made explicit by the mentions of the future judgment in 7:1a–2; one should envision
one's judging of others in light of the eschatological judgment to which one
will be submitted ("you will [or will not] be judged").

Against the background of the eschatological horizon, one should not
judge: "Judge not" (Μὴ κρίνετε, 7:1a). The "parable" of the log in one's
eye (7:3–5) illustrates this principle. It is parodic and grotesque (a splinter
in an eye is realistic, but a log?) as the illustrations of the principle "not to
resist evil" (5:39–41) were. As such, this teaching takes a general scope.[127]
In light of the last judgment, one's fault appears like a log in an eye, and
thus it is obvious that one should not judge and condemn others.

Nevertheless, from this perspective, when one has removed the log from
one's eye, one is in a position to remove the splinter from the eye of a
brother or sister; his or her sin is not simply a private matter. This removal
of the splinter in others, "judging" them, is not prohibited when it is done
appropriately (after removing the log from one's eye); indeed, it is a part of
the responsibility of the disciples as religious leaders. As becomes clear in
18:12–35, this removal of the splinter (leading other members of the community to abandon their fault) is to be done on the basis of forgiveness
(cf. the Lord's Prayer, 6:12, 14–15).[128] Distinguishing between what is holy
and what is impure, what is precious and what is worthless (7:6), is something that disciples should do; they have to "judge" not only themselves
but also (and afterward) others, although this is done with a forgiving
attitude.[129]

As in 5:21–48 and in 6:19–34, the eschatological horizon (the last judgment) set by the first part (7:1–6) of this subunit makes room in the second

126. Luz, *Matthew*, 418.

127. This teaching is not restricted to one's relationship to members of the community.
The repeated mention that it is the fault of a brother or sister in the Christian community
(τοῦ ἀδελφοῦ σου) underscores the littleness of the fault (splinter), but it does not limit the
application of the principle. Luz, *Matthew*, 417.

128. Davies and Allison, *Matthew*, 673–74. Luz (*Matthew*, 418) says that, for Matthew,
this is *not* "judging." This interpretation is possible, yet it is more consistent with the thematic
interpretation. See below. In the figurative interpretation, as Luz himself will emphasize about
7:15–20, disciples have also a "judging" role.

129. Davies and Allison, *Matthew*, 674–77. Luz (*Matthew*, 419) gives up on making sense
of this verse.

part (7:7–11) for the figure of the heavenly Father and his *present*[130] care for human beings: God gives "good things to those who ask him" (7:11; cf. 7:7). As in 6:25–34, the "encouragement" (Davies and Allison) provided by 7:7–11 for the disciples faced with the difficult task of judging properly is actually the result of envisioning one's experience and one's relationship with others in the appropriate symbolic world in the context of prayer to "our Father who is heaven" (the relationship between 7:7–11 and the Lord's Prayer is clear). Thus once again, the eschatological horizon (the coming kingdom and judgment) is displaced to make room for the present theological horizon of the heavenly Father's care for human beings (all of them, without distinction; including those "who are evil," 7:11).

Reading C, CAW 3.8: Matthew 7:12: The Golden Rule—Recognizing That the "Better Human Being" of the Kingdom Already Exists (Compare with Reading D, CAW 3.4)

Familiar observations of this figurative interpretation are found once again. In one form or another, "the Golden Rule is found universally,"[131] that is, not only in the Hellenistic and Jewish world, but also in China (Confucianism) and in India. While most of the non-Christian formulations are negative ("that which you do not wish that people do to you, do not do to them"), non-Christian positive formulations ("whatever you wish that people do to you, do so to them") are also found. In and of itself, the Golden Rule is *quite ambiguous:* it can be (and has been) interpreted as a call for naive or not so naive egoism, and even as a justification for retaliation![132] Thus it "cannot be directly a normative ethical basic principle.... *The Golden Rule must already presuppose a standard of behavior.*"[133]

By placing it at the end of the main body of the Sermon on the Mount and by adding to it "for this is the law and the prophets," Matthew made it a summary of Jesus' entire teaching (which provides, therefore, the "standard of behavior" that the Golden Rule presupposes here). In brief, here as in reading A, CAW 5.21, the Golden Rule becomes another version of the commandment of love, which is radically emphasized in the love for one's enemies (5:43–48) and other parts of the Sermon on the Mount (e.g., 5:21–26; 5:38–42).[134] Thus the Golden Rule is interpreted by the Sermon on the Mount.

---

130. The present tense of the verbs "receive" and "find" in 7:8 makes it clear that prayers will be answered in the present, not merely at the coming of the kingdom. See Luz, *Matthew*, 421.

131. Luz, *Matthew*, 426, see 425–32. For the many parallels to 7:12 in Hellenistic and Jewish literature, see also Davies and Allison, *Matthew*, 686–88 and bibliography.

132. For examples, see Luz, *Matthew*, 428.

133. Luz, *Matthew*, 429.

134. As is emphasized by Davies and Allison, *Matthew*, 685–90.

Yet the Golden Rule, as a very general principle that summarizes the main body of the Sermon on the Mount and echoes the broad statement about Jesus as fulfilling the law and the prophets in 5:17, also "interprets the Sermon on the Mount."[135] It points out that the teaching of the Sermon on the Mount needs to be carried out much beyond the specific instances mentioned in the injunctions of 5:21–7:11.[136] "It excludes the thought that *only* the commandments mentioned there are meant."[137] It invites readers to *envision* for themselves the significance of these commandments in all kinds of concrete situations and thus "to invent for themselves in the light of love what is meant in the Sermon on the Mount."[138]

As we have seen, when one focuses on the figurative dimension of the text, the radical demands of the main body of the Sermon on the Mount primarily provide a vision that is "a ray of hope for a new, better human being in the coming of the kingdom of God," that contrasts with the present situation that is so dominated by "lies, power, and hatred."[139] This vision of the symbolic world is not utopian! It allows people to envision themselves as disciples, as such "better human beings" who act according to these radical demands or more generally, who act along similar kinds of ways in different situations (the Golden Rule).

Reading C, CAW 3.9: Matthew 7:13–27 — People on the "Easy Way" and "Fruitless" as Models of False Discipleship (Compare with Reading D, CAW 2.1; 3.2)

In this figurative interpretation, the concluding section of the Sermon on the Mount completes the establishment of the symbolic world into which one needs to be resocialized in order to be a faithful disciple; these verses continue to construct the eschatological horizon, focusing on the last judgment and false discipleship. In the perspective of this interpretation, Matthew 7:13–27 shows that (1) judgment is not ours but the Lord's and that it will take place at the end of time (as is also expressed by the parable of the weeds, 13:24–30, 36–43);[140] (2) the disciples themselves need to take the

---

135. As Luz (*Matthew*, 431) emphasizes.

136. "The Golden Rule is not a principle from which all of the law's commands can be deduced, nor is it the hermeneutical key to interpreting the law or for determining the validity of different commandments" (Davies and Allison, *Matthew*, 689–90, against the "historical/ realistic" interpretation). Yet we should add that it is not either "the most basic or important demand of the law, a demand which...states its true end" (690; a sentence that is another form of the historical/realistic interpretation: it would express the essence of the eternal will of God!).

137. Luz, *Matthew*, 431.

138. Ibid.

139. Ibid.; cf. 328–29, 341–42.

140. This text is *not* to be read as providing criteria for judging members of the community in order to exclude those who are false disciples, as Betz expresses (*Essays*, 156) by saying that this concluding section "serves the paraenetic attempt to label the competition as 'heretical.' " This is the historical/realistic interpretation, over against which Luz argues step by step. See

necessary steps in order to avoid being condemned at the last judgment;[141] and (3) the disciples need a clearer vision of their present situation and of their community, a vision that they gain by considering them in the light of the eschatological judgment.[142]

For a figurative interpretation focused on the symbolic world into which disciples must be socialized, having a clear vision of what is "not true" and even "false" discipleship is as essential as having a vision of true discipleship. Being a faithful disciple means avoiding being misled by wrong models of discipleship as much as it means following true models. Knowing how to recognize false disciples, false prophets, false leaders is a necessary part of knowing how to recognize true models of discipleship, i.e., of knowing how to perform a part of one's role as disciples/religious leaders.

Matthew 7:13–14 and its images of the gate (ἡ πύλη) and of the way (ἡ ὁδός) through their own ambivalence set an ambivalent picture of the present situation of the community of disciples. First, through the description of the wrong gate/way as "wide" and "easy," the text underscores the lure of nondiscipleship or false discipleship. A life of discipleship is a difficult ("hard," τεθλιμμένη) way (7:14) because the moral conduct it demands is hard.[143]

The text also contrasts the two ways in terms of their respective horizons: while the easy way is limited to a present world horizon, the hard way has also an eschatological horizon. The "easy way" and the "wide gate" (7:13) refer to those who have no concern for the eschatological time and thus will perish.[144] By contrast, the "hard way" and the "narrow gate,"[145] which lead to (eternal) life, refer to disciples who envision their lives in

---

Luz, *Matthew,* 438–54, and especially, 446–50, on the many different and problematic ways in which "the 'easy' criterion of the 'fruit' " was used throughout church history to condemn whoever was viewed as heretic at the time.

141. Matthew 7:13–27 is *not* to be read as showing to disciples the urgency of carrying out their vocation in order to avoid "many" perishing. This is the interpretation focused on the unfolding of the plot.

142. Matthew 7:13–27 is *not* read as establishing the basic characteristics of the true moral discernment that is the basic condition for faithful discipleship (the thematic interpretation focused on moral discernment; see above, reading D, CAW 2).

143. This moral connotation comes from Jewish traditions about "the two ways" based on Deuteronomy 30:19 and Jeremiah 21:8. For the many references to these images in the Jewish tradition, see Davies and Allison, *Matthew,* 696–700.

144. This is emphasized by the twofold warning that those who go to perdition are "many" (7:13) and those who go to life are "few" (7:14).

145. When this metaphor is understood as synonymous with the "hard way": Davies and Allison, *Matthew,* 696–98. "Entering by the narrow gate" might also represent entering life, since the "gate" is at the end of the "road": so Luz, *Matthew,* 436–37. In a historical/realistic interpretation (reading A), "entering by the narrow gate" is interpreted as that through which one passes to take the "hard road," i.e., as obedient submission to Jesus' call to repentance that permits entry to the life of righteousness, which is already a participation in life. See Strecker, *Sermon,* 156–58; P. Bonnard, *L'évangile selon Saint Matthieu,* CNT 1 (Neuchâtel: Delachaux & Niestlé, 1963), 102.

terms of an eschatological horizon.[146] Luz concludes that the situation in which disciples have to carry out their vocation is ambivalent, "mixed," constantly requiring new decisions from the disciples: "The community is on the way to the gate of life. It constantly faces the choice of the two ways. Being a Christian, being baptized, does not mean a tranquil certainty of salvation but the constant challenge of the decision between the broad way and the difficult way of the Sermon on the Mount."[147]

Matthew 7:15–23[148] clarifies a necessary condition for making the right decision in the ambivalent situations in which disciples find themselves: identifying false disciples. As Luz repeatedly emphasizes,[149] this identification is not in order to judge them and exclude them from the community. It is rather in order to avoid being misled by them. False prophets are not manifestations of God's grace and thus are not "opening up the way on which we can go."[150]

The rule for recognizing false prophets, "you will know them by their fruits" (7:16, 20), makes it clear that, against the eschatological horizon, disciples "can and should be concerned about the discerning of the spirits."[151] The eschatological horizon and its vision of the last judgment shows that the Christian community is a mixed body in which false prophets stand alongside true prophets. The eschatological light also shows what is behind the appearances, or more precisely, that the problem with false prophets is the discrepancy between outward appearances and inward realities, between words and deeds (understood as deeds of higher righteousness, 7:21–23, 24, 26).

Furthermore, the last judgment reveals that "false prophets" (ψευδο-προφῆται, 7:15) include charismatic leaders: actual Christian prophets who "prophesy" and perform miracles in Jesus' name (7:22). As such, they have at least the potential of misleading the community because of their special claim to authority, due to their special gifts.[152]

But "false prophets" is a much broader category that encompasses any false "disciples," since in 5:11–12 (already evoked by the preceding verses) the disciples are presented as prophetlike: they will be persecuted as the prophets were. False prophets include false disciples (tasteless salt; light

---

146. This eschatological character of discipleship is further expressed in the text in the description of the "hard" way by a term that evokes eschatological afflictions (interpreting τεθλιμμένη in terms of θλῖψις), such as the persecutions mentioned in 5:10–12, which Matthew associates with the time before the eschaton (cf. 24:9, 21, 29). Luz, *Matthew*, 435–36. Davies and Allison, *Matthew*, 700.

147. Luz, *Matthew*, 437.

148. In this figurative interpretation, these verses are read together because they are about "false prophets." See Luz, *Matthew*, 439–41; Davies and Allison, *Matthew*, 702–3.

149. Luz, *Matthew*, 438–50.

150. Ibid., 450.

151. Ibid., 443.

152. The interpretation of Davies and Allison, who overlook the ambiguity.

under a bushel) who fail to carry out their vocation. They do not do the will of the Father (7:21) and thus do evil deeds. This is what the image of the bad tree bearing evil fruits (7:16–20) indicates.

In sum, over against the eschatological horizon, the danger represented by "false prophets" appears as much more pervasive than one might have thought; one has to beware not to be misled, not merely by a few wandering charismatics (who come from the outside, 7:15), but potentially by any Christian.[153] Such false prophets are destructive ("wolves") for the community, even though they appear to be inoffensive members ("sheep," 7:15);[154] those who follow them go to destruction (as in 7:13–14).

In Matthew 7:24–27, the two parts of the judgment parable[155] of the two housebuilders are figures of "everyone who hears these words of mine" (Mt 7:24, 26), i.e., figures of all the hearers of the Sermon on the Mount: the disciples and the crowds, including all the members of the community. As in 7:13–23, the parable presents this community as a "mixed body."[156] In this interpretation focused on the figurative dimension of the text, one who shares in the symbolic world of the Sermon on the Mount and its eschatological horizon plainly sees the difference between the two houses (two groups of people in the church). Consequently, the parable functions as an affirmation that those who do Jesus' words are already blessed — their blessedness is a present reality that will endure at the judgment. Similarly, those who do not do Jesus' words are already cursed — their destruction is already a present reality, the lack of solid foundation, that will be actualized at the judgment. Once again, the figures of the parable make it clear who, among the members of the "mixed body" of the community, the readers should take as models to follow.

The relations of the conclusion of the Sermon (7:24–27) with its introduction, the beatitudes (5:3–12), appear. We have noted that the beatitudes are reminiscent of the Levites' blessings in Deuteronomy 28:1–14. The parable, 7:24–26, is also quite reminiscent of Deuteronomy 28.[157] Such

---

153. An interpretation in line with Luz (*Matthew*, 442–50), who once again emphasizes that, for Matthew, the community is a "mixed body."

154. "Sheep" has the connotation "members of the chosen people." Cf. Num 27:17; Ps 78:52. Davies and Allison, *Matthew*, 704.

155. See Daniel Marguerat, *Le Jugement dans l'Evangile de Matthieu* (Geneva: Labor et Fides, 1981), 209. Davies and Allison, *Matthew*, 721.

156. The hearers of these words fall into two groups: those who do them (7:24), and those who do not do them (7:26). As the figures of the narrow and hard gate/road and of the wide and easy gate/road did (7:13–14), the figure of the house built on rock (doing Jesus' words) shows that those who do these words will not be destroyed at the judgment, by contrast with those who do not do them and will be destroyed, figurativized by the house built on the sand.

157. The first part of the parable, 7:24, is quite reminiscent of Deuteronomy 28:1, which describes those who are blessed as those who "obey the voice of the Lord your God, being careful to do all the commandments which I command you this day." In Deuteronomy 28:15ff., the Levites' blessings are followed by curses, introduced by a parallel formula — those who are cursed are those who do "not obey the voice of the Lord..." — as 7:26 introduces the second part of the parable with a formula parallel to 7:24, this time about those

an allusion to Deuteronomy 28 shows, once again, that in this figurative dimension the Sermon on the Mount is presented by Matthew as a new Mosaic teaching, which raises once again the question of the relationship between the new covenant and the old covenant.[158] In 7:24–27, Jesus' words ("these words of mine") replace Torah, a point that could be understood either as an affirmation that Jesus' teaching is the new Torah that abolishes the old Torah, or, in light of 5:17, as an affirmation that Jesus' teaching fulfills the old Torah.

In sum, disciples as religious leaders are called to make a clear distinction between those on the way to life and those on the way to destruction, between true and false disciples, between those with a solid foundation and those with an unstable foundation. The eschatological horizon allows disciples to make such distinctions and to identify whom they should recognize as models and thus imitate and call others to imitate.

Making these distinctions by envisioning everything against the background of the eschatological horizon is necessary for faithful discipleship because of the basic ambivalence of the present situation. Because the church is a mixed body, it is essential to make a clear distinction between true and false disciples. Because the relationship between the church and Judaism is also mixed — they are both in continuity and in discontinuity with each other — it is essential to make a clear distinction between what is to be retained and what is to be rejected in Judaism. Disciples as religious leaders need to make these distinctions for themselves and also for others.

From the perspective of the thematic interpretation (see reading D, CAW 2), I read 7:21–27 in terms of the beatitudes rather than in terms of the Lord's Prayer and the twofold horizon of its symbolic world (as Luz and Davies and Allison do). As a result, my interpretation emphasizes moral discernment and its role for discipleship as the main theme of the Sermon: as a sound and undivided eye, which is focused on the manifestations of divine and human goodness.

Since in this thematic perspective, 7:21–27 is read as an exhortation to use moral discernment (to be wise, φρόνιμος, rather than foolish, μωρός), the rest of the Sermon is then read as a series of cases, which show how disciples can use an undivided moral discernment in various situations in order to identify models of discipleship whom they can imitate and follow.

We have already seen that the beatitudes (5:3–10) train the "sound eye" of

---

who do not obey Jesus' words. See Davies and Allison, *Matthew,* 719. Luz (*Matthew,* 452) emphasizes the parallelism with Deuteronomy 30:15–20, and Leviticus 26, with the same effect.

158. In fact, Matthew might presuppose that his readers would recognize the similarity of this parable with rabbinic parables, including the parable attributed to Elisha ben Abuyah in *'Abot Rabbi Nathan* 24, where the doers and nondoers of Torah are compared to houses that are not destroyed or are destroyed by water. See Davies and Allison, *Matthew,* 719.

the disciples — help them to develop their moral discernment — by providing a series of exemplary cases of people who acted out of true moral discernment. A few general comments about the main passages of the Sermon on the Mount further clarify the special kind of moral discernment that the Sermon advocates, according to the conclusions of the thematic interpretation of my commentary.

Reading D, CAW 3: A Thematic Interpretation — Perceiving Discipleship with the Moral Discernment of a Sound, Undivided Eye

This interpretation of the thematic dimension is best presented by interpreting together the thematic units of the Sermon on the Mount that are set in inverted parallelisms by the text. See again figure 2: "Thematic Structure of the Sermon on the Mount" (p. 207). Thus we proceed from the outside to the inside, first interpreting together 5:11–16 and 7:13–20, then 5:17–19 and 6:22–7:12, etc.

Reading D, CAW 3.1: Matthew 5:11–16 — Discerning True Discipleship: When Actions Fit Vocation (Compare with Reading C, CAW 3.1; 3.2)

The shift to a personal style ("you") invites readers seeking models of discipleship to turn their eyes toward the church and its members, more specifically, toward people persecuted "on my account" (ἕνεκεν ἐμοῦ), i.e., Christians associated with Jesus (instead of the more general, "persecuted for righteousness' sake," ἕνεκεν δικαιοσύνης, 5:10).

The thematic dimension of these two verses (identifiable through the explicit semantic opposition posited between 5:12a and 5:11)[159] presents two different ways of perceiving the same situation. Those who "revile you and persecute you and utter all kinds of evil against you" (5:11) perceive "you" and their situation in one way; by contrast, "you" as believers/disciples are expected to perceive the same situation in a positive way and thus "rejoice and be glad" (5:12). Thus disciples are distinguished from those who persecute them through the way in which they "see" their own situation, i.e., through their special kind of moral discernment — a sound, undivided eye. "The situation of the disciples is perceived as good, or euphoric, by the disciples themselves, while other people [those who persecute them] see it as evil, or dysphoric."[160] Disciples are those who "rejoice" and are "glad" because they perceive something good in their situation, despite what others might see in it.

The text actually specifies how they perceive this goodness in their situation despite persecutions. They look at their present both in terms of the

159. Patte, *Matthew,* 68–69, 407.
160. Ibid., 68.

eschatological future ("for your reward [will be] great in heaven," 5:12) and in terms of past *sacred history* and *Scripture* ("for in the same way they persecuted the prophets who were before you," 5:12). *True disciples* are people who discern goodness (the manifestation of God's goodness) in their present, not only by envisioning the future rewards they are confident of receiving (as was emphasized in the beatitudes) but also by recognizing that their experience is comparable to (fulfills the type of) certain events or prophecies in Scripture. Thus they can recognize themselves as prophetlike and consequently as sent by God for a special mission.[161] In sum, the disciples' *true discernment*, in light of Scripture and the eschatological future, reveals to them what is hidden from others and yet what is a sound foundation (7:24–27) of their being as disciples: their *prophetic vocation*.

The thematic dimension of the following verses, 5:13–16, is focused (by the explicit opposition in 5:15)[162] once again on the disciples' vocation. It specifies a key characteristic of true discipleship that is also found in 7:13–20: outward behavior corresponds to inner motivation (good fruit is found on a good tree; see reading D, CAW 3.2). Whatever their specific vocation, true disciples always demonstrate a particular characteristic: their actions fit their vocation.[163] Since their vocation is to be "salt of the earth," their actions are salty — or they are not disciples (i.e., worthless). Since they are to be "light of the world," they are on a lampstand and "give light to all in the house" — or they are not disciples. Thus one can recognize true disciples (models of discipleship) in those whose outward behavior fits their vocation.

The specific nature of this vocation is left open. It is only clear that it involves doing "good works" (τὰ καλὰ ἔργα) that will bring people to give glory to God (5:16). These "good works" are perceived (ἴδωσιν) by other people as manifestations of the goodness of God (since people give thanks to God because of these good works). Thus those whom one identifies as models of discipleship are people whose actions one also perceives as manifestations of God's goodness.

Reading D, CAW 3.2: Matthew 7:13–20: Recognizing True Prophets by Discerning How Actions and Inner Persons Fit (Compare with Reading C, CAW 3.9)

Matthew 7:13–20 (the passage in inverted parallelism with 5:11–16) emphasizes the eschatological judgment through a series of powerful figures. This passage is easily interpreted as an exhortation to use one's moral discernment in order to keep blessing and condemnation, good and evil in tension and thus in order to recognize the good to be followed through an identification

---

161. Ibid, 69.
162. The elliptic opposition in 5:15 is (καίουσιν λύχνον καὶ) τιθέασιν αὐτὸν ὑπὸ τὸν μόδιον ἀλλ' (=VS) ἐπὶ τὴν λυχνίαν. A similar opposition is found in 5:13, but is not as clearly marked. Patte, *Matthew*, 69, 407.
163. Patte, *Matthew*, 69–70.

of the evil to be rejected, avoided, or overcome. This is what the figurative interpretation concludes with its ambivalent symbolic world (see reading C, CAW 2.3). Yet for the thematic interpretation, such a conclusion is in contradiction with the positive moral discernment as a foundational characteristic of discipleship, which gives coherence to the thematic dimension (see reading D, CAW 2.1).[164] Such a conclusion amounts to saying that the Sermon advocates having a "divided" eye. As we saw concerning 7:21–27, faithful disciples (who do Jesus' teaching, 7:24, and God's will, 7:21) are people who know how to discern the "good" that is hidden (the foundation of a person's life) before it is revealed at the judgment. They already, here and now, use the same discernment as the Judge will use at the end of time, and thus they do not stop at appearances when they evaluate someone. In this way, they know how to identify people who are models of discipleship and whom they should follow and imitate. Is 7:13–20 in tension with this understanding of discipleship? No, if one considers the thematic dimension of the text, including the explicit oppositions it sets up.

In 7:13–14, the explicit oppositions between those who take the narrow gate/hard road and those who take the wide gate/easy road are well marked. But their metaphorical character, without descriptions of the motivation for the different kinds of actions, leaves them open to all kinds of interpretations (and not merely a figurative one). This metaphorical passage needs to be interpreted in terms of other passages with which it is associated in the thematic dimension, namely, 7:15–20 and also 5:11–12.

The explicit opposition in 7:15–20, "every good tree bears good fruit but the bad tree bears bad fruit," indicates (together with the implicit oppositions it supports) that as people can readily recognize the inner quality or nature of a tree by its fruit, so disciples with true discernment should readily recognize the inner quality, the "inward" motivation, and the actual vocation (as true or false prophet) of people around them, as they identify whom they should follow and imitate.

Of course, these verses warn disciples about the dangers of being misled by false religious leaders, i.e., by people wrongly identified as models of discipleship. False prophets (7:15) are "ravenous wolves," dangerous for disciples. Are these verses teaching that disciples should be apprehensive and anxious about the risk of being misled by false prophets? Should they allow this anxiety to define the goals of their behavior and vocation (which would then be aimed, for instance, at "identifying, neutralizing, and rejecting false prophets")? This attitude contradicts the view of moral discernment underscored in 7:21–27 through the theme of seeing, vision, and sound eye. More importantly, it would contradict what the thematic dimension of 7:15–20 underscores through its explicit and implicit oppositions.

---

164. It is also in contradiction (from the thematic perspective) with the call not to judge ("Do not judge, so that you may not be judged," 7:1).

As soon as the text has warned the readers about false prophets, it alleviates any potential anxiety by offering twice repeated reassurances: "you will know them by their fruits" (7:16, 20). In the thematic dimension, this is not a criterion for judging others. This is a word of comfort: "Beware of false prophets. But do not worry about them. You will readily recognize them when you need to. Despite their efforts, they cannot hide from you; they cannot but reveal who they truly are by their fruits!" Just as the fruit necessarily corresponds to the kind of tree that bears it (7:16–18), so false prophets, even though they might try to disguise themselves (in sheep's clothing), cannot but disclose by their fruit what they are inwardly ("ravenous wolves"): "you will know them by their fruits" (7:16, 20).

In sum, 7:15–20 posits a condition for true moral discernment: do not worry about false prophets/disciples. Simply be a good tree. The description of the false prophets helps us understand what is a good tree/disciple, by contrast with a bad tree. Bad trees/false prophets are persons for whom there is no true fit between outward deeds and inward motivations. The point is that one must discern what are the actions of a person that truly corresponds to the inner person — the motivation of this person, the "foundation" on the basis of which this person acts.[165] But the disciples do not have to worry about this; with a sound eye, they will right away recognize any discrepancies between outward actions and inner motivation and thus "they will know them."

These brief comments on 7:15–20 clarify the nature and the role of the true moral discernment (sound, undivided eye) that disciples need to have. From this perspective, the readers can make a back reading of 7:13–14. A first reading of 7:13–14 seemed to suggest that being faithful disciples and doing good works involve a special effort on the part of the disciples. Indeed, for most people (the many, πολλοί, who take the easy road and the wide gate, 7:13) discipleship appears to be too hard a road and too narrow a gate (7:14).[166] But from the perspective of 7:15–20 this interpretation is unwarranted. Thinking that doing good works involves a special effort on the part of the disciples misconstrues these verses, indeed Jesus' entire teaching (according to the thematic dimension of the Sermon). Good works are good

---

165. Thus acts of righteousness (e.g., acts of caring; feeding the hungry) might not be "good fruits" (acts of overabundant righteousness). If they do not come from a "good" inner motivation (if this righteousness is not internalized), these acts of righteousness are "bad fruits." See the very perceptive interpretation of this point in Dan O. Via, *Self-Deception and Wholeness in Paul and Matthew* (Minneapolis: Fortress, 1990), 89–92.

166. And many interpreters concur, as they read these verses in terms of various passages of the Sermon on the Mount, according to the dimension that is the focus of the interpretation. Thus for a *historical/realistic interpretation,* doing good works involves striving to carry out commandments; for an interpretation focused on the *plot dimension,* doing good work demands overcoming one's unwillingness to do it by finding a reason for doing it; for the *figurative interpretation* and its emphasis on the ambivalent symbolic world, doing good works demands the identification of false prophets and other forms of evil, which clarifies the evil that the good works are to overcome.

fruits that good trees spontaneously produce. *If disciples are good trees, i.e., if they have true moral discernment, a sound eye, they correctly perceive what is good, what is holy, what are God's blessings, who are the blessed ones. Their sound, undivided eye will give them inward motivations that produce matching outward actions; they will (spontaneously) bear good fruit.*[167]

Reading D, CAW 3.3: Matthew 5:17–19: Discerning True Discipleship — A Vocation Defined in Terms of Scripture (Compare with Reading C, CAW 3.3)

The juxtaposition of similar oppositions regarding Jesus (5:17) and disciples (5:19) about fulfilling or doing, instead of abolishing, the law (and the prophets) shows that in the thematic dimension of these verses Jesus presents himself as a model of discipleship by specifying how he relates his vocation to Scripture (5:17–18). He requires a similar attitude from disciples (5:19).[168]

We again find in 5:17–19 the two characteristics of discipleship that are underscored in 5:11–16 (and 7:13–20): (1) interpreting one's present situation in terms of both the past (Scripture) and the eschatological future; (2) the "fit" (or match) between a disciple's vocation (inward motivation) and actions. What is fitting for Jesus' vocation ("I have come to," ἦλθον) is to fulfill the law and the prophets. For Jesus (5:17–18), but also for disciples (5:19), fulfilling Scripture is equivalent to being salty (5:13) or to being a lamp on a lampstand (5:14–15) or to doing good works so that people might give glory to God (5:16). Not fulfilling the law and the prophets, i.e., either "abolishing" (καταλύω) them (5:17) or "breaking" (or "annulling," λύω) the commandments, including the least of these (5:19), is equivalent to being salt without taste or to being a light under a bushel — a contradiction of Jesus' and the disciples' vocation. In sum, models of discipleship are people who, as Jesus did, understand their vocation as involving the fulfillment of Scripture.

What does "fulfilling Scripture" mean in the thematic dimension? This will be clarified in the following verses (5:20–48). We can already say that it involves conceiving of one's vocation in terms of the present role of Scripture, by contrast with its role in the eschatological future (5:18) and with its role in the past (as is emphasized in 5:21–48). The role of Scripture changes from one period to another; at the end of time, it will be abolished (5:18); in the present, it must be taught, and thus interpreted and done (5:19). In the past, Scripture certainly had a still different role (as is made explicit in 5:21–48).

Jesus as model of discipleship fulfills Scripture by nourishing himself with every word of it (as the temptation story, 4:1–11, expresses) and therefore by fulfilling all righteousness (3:15). The prophecies are fulfilled in his ministry (e.g., 4:14–16). Thus we can conclude that "fulfilling the law and the prophets" involves allowing Scripture to establish the vocation one will carry

---

167. Patte, *Matthew*, 100–101.
168. Ibid., 70–75, 407.

out. And since one lives in a specific time, the present, which should not be confused either with the eschatological future or with the past, fulfilling Scripture necessarily involves interpreting the present in term of Scripture as well as interpreting Scripture in terms of the present.[169]

In sum, according to 5:17–19, true models of discipleship are people who allow Scripture to establish their vocation by interpreting their present situation and Scripture in terms of each other. But this understanding of the way in which the disciples' vocation is defined is not complete in itself. As the thematic structure underscores, these verses, 5:17–19, are in inverted parallelisms with 6:22–7:12, which complements and focuses the teaching of 5:17–19. While the role that Scripture played in the lives of Jesus and the disciples provides an excellent model for the way in which the vocation of disciples is established, one should not think that it is more than one model (one instance) among several. In other words, Scripture is not the only means through which the vocation of the disciples is established.

Reading D, CAW 3.4: Matthew 6:22–7:12: Discerning True Discipleship — A Vocation Defined in Terms of What a Sound Eye Recognizes as Scripture-like (Compare with Reading C, CAW 3.6; 3.7; 3.8)

This relatively long thematic unit is essential to the thematic interpretation of the Sermon on the Mount because it explicitly develops its main theme, moral discernment, represented by the figures of seeing, of vision, and especially of a sound eye. We discussed these figures above (reading D, CAW 2.3). It is enough to say that:[170]

- *6:22–23 opens this unit by positing a sound, undivided eye as a basic condition for discipleship;*

- *6:24 indicates that a divided eye makes it impossible to serve God because it leads us to seek to serve both God and mammon;*

- *6:25–34 shows that anxiety makes it impossible to seek the kingdom and righteousness, and that true (great) faith, i.e., seeing with a sound eye the manifestations of God's care and goodness, overcomes this anxiety;*

- *7:1–5 underscores that the disciples need to preserve the soundness of their eye in order to be of help to others;*

- *7:6 adds that not discerning what is holy and valuable (as alone a sound eye allows one to do) leads to disaster.*

---

169. Ibid., 73; see 70–75.
170. For a detailed study of the thematic dimension of these passages, see Patte, *Matthew,* 90–98.

Beyond the affirmation in 6:21–7:6 of the essential role of moral discernment or a sound eye as a basic condition for discipleship, 7:7–12 makes two startling points that complement and sharpen the teaching of 5:17–19. First, both 7:7–11 and 7:12 affirm that all human beings have a sound eye: they know how to discern what is good for their children and what is good for themselves. Thus anybody is a potential disciple; each has what it takes to be a true disciple, namely, true discernment.

Second, 7:12 expresses that what people (whoever they might be) perceive as "good for themselves" is equivalent to "the law and the prophets"; it is Scripture-like. As disciples should do the good things that the law and the prophets prescribe (this is fulfilling them, 5:17–19) so disciples should do the good things that they perceive when they consider what they would like other people to do for them. Thus the disciples' vocation is now defined in terms of what their sound eye perceives as good for them (or their children). This "discerned good" is the same as the teaching of Scripture, and therefore it has the same role as Scripture, according to 5:17–19.

Conversely, the way in which this discerned good defines the disciples' vocation clarifies the way in which Scripture defines it. According to 7:12, discipleship does not simply mean implementing the good one has discerned, i.e., demanding that other people do for us what we want. Rather, discipleship demands that disciples implement the discerned good beyond the realm where it was discerned. It is a matter of doing for others what we want other people to do for us. This is implementing the discerned good in an overflowing way, as the lamp on a lampstand gives light to all in the house (5:15). Then it already appears that fulfilling Scripture (5:17–19) means doing more than the good things that Scripture points out to do; the disciples' righteousness should be an overabundant righteousness.

Reading D, CAW 3.5: Matthew 5:20 and 5:45–48: Discerning True Discipleship — Overabundantly Doing the Good Things That Disciples See Scribes, Pharisees, Tax Collectors, and Gentiles Doing (Compare with Reading C, CAW 3.3; 3.4)

Matthew 5:20 and 5:45–48 (the inverted parallelisms of this thematic unit) make similar points. Disciples need to have a "righteousness that exceeds (περισσεύσῃ) that of the scribes and Pharisees" (5:20); they need to do more than the tax collectors and Gentiles (τί περισσὸν ποιεῖτε, "what more are you doing?" 7:47). The righteousness, the outward acts, of true disciples need to be overabundant (5:20). They need to overflow, so as to reach everyone (righteous and sinners) as God's sun and rain do (5:45); or, so as to reach everyone in the house, as the light of a lamp on a stand (5:14–16).

Thus we can conclude that "righteousness is the implementation of one's vocation, doing what fits one's vocation. One can have a limited implementation of one's vocation, a narrow righteousness. Such is, according to Matthew, the case of scribes and Pharisees. Such is also the case of tax collectors and

Gentiles who correctly recognize that loving is part of what they should do (their vocation) but limits its implementation to loving those who love them. The overabundant righteousness is the implementation of this vocation by loving not only one's friends but also one's enemies (5:46–47). This righteousness overflows the narrow confines of the disciples' circle of friends and applies also to those outside this circle, their enemies. The disciples' proper implementation of their vocation is the fulfillment of 'all righteousness,' by doing all that fits their vocation (cf. 5:15), as Jesus did in 3:15."[171]

A disciple can have such an overabundant righteousness by imitating models of discipleship. To begin with, disciples imitate the supreme model of discipleship, God, for the overabundance of his righteousness. As God's good deeds overflow so as to reach everybody (5:45), so disciples should allow their good deeds to overflow and reach everybody, including their enemies. This is what perfection is: "Be perfect, therefore, as your Father in heaven is perfect" (5:48).

What is this righteousness that should be overabundant? Interpreting 5:20 by itself, one might think that this is a righteousness (a kind of behavior) that is different from that of the scribes and Pharisees (the "better" righteousness of the historical/realistic interpretation, reading A, CAW 4.4, or the "higher" righteousness of the figurative interpretation, reading C, CAW 3.3). But in this thematic interpretation 5:20 must be interpreted as teaching that the disciples should have the same righteousness — the same kind of behavior — as that of the scribes and Pharisees. This interpretation of 5:20 results from the relationship of this verse with 5:45–48, with which it is in inverted parallelism. Let me explain.

In 5:45–48 the righteousness of the disciples is contrasted with that of the tax collectors and Gentiles. The difference does not concern the kind of righteousness — the kind of behavior. Disciples should have the very behavior (loving and welcoming others) that the tax collectors and the Gentiles already have. In this way the disciples' behavior (loving) affirms as valuable an aspect of the behavior of the tax collectors and of the Gentiles. The difference is simply that the disciples perform this action in an overabundant manner — loving and welcoming not only those who love them, such as their brothers and sisters, but also other people, including their enemies, i.e., those who persecute them.

Similarly, in the thematic dimension that underscores the significance of inverted parallelisms, 5:20 must be read as expressing the same view of overabundant righteousness (parallel features) as 5:45–48; but this time, the disciples' behavior is contrasted with the scribes' and Pharisees' behavior instead of the tax collectors' and Gentiles' (inverted features). This means that 5:20 must be reread in terms of 5:45–48. Of course, by itself, 5:20 might have been read as a rejection of Jewish righteousness and of Judaism. But

---

171. Patte, *Matthew*, 76.

now this first interpretation must be complemented, sharpened, and even corrected. From the perspective of 5:45–48, 5:20 requires from disciples a righteousness that affirms (and does not contradict) essential aspects of the righteousness of the scribes and Pharisees, even as they perform these same actions in an overabundant way. As in the case of the tax collectors and the Gentiles, an overabundant righteousness involves doing what is discerned as the good things that the scribes and the Pharisees do, and doing more, by implementing them in other realms also.

We can then draw an unexpected conclusion: a behavior characterized by overabundant righteousness requires moral discernment. Since overabundant righteousness involves doing overabundantly the good things that other people do, disciples first need to discern those good things, whether the people doing them are brothers and sisters in the community of disciples (as is suggested in 5:3–19 and 7:13–27) or scribes, Pharisees, tax collectors, and Gentiles. This also means that models of discipleship might be found in the behavior of people who are far from perfect. Even though tax collectors and Gentiles are not perfect (their love is limited to those who love them), a sound eye perceives in them a model to be imitated, in an overabundant way.

Reading D, CAW 3.6: Matthew 5:21–48: Discerning True Discipleship — Overabundant Righteousness as Carrying Out One's Vocation toward Others by Fulfilling Scripture (Compare With Reading C, CAW 3.4)

Since the vocation of true disciples (i.e., their inner motivation, the foundation of their behavior; cf. 7:13–27) may be established or defined in terms of Scripture (among other possibilities), one way to clarify the meaning of overabundant righteousness (5:20) is to exemplify how one makes the models of good behavior overflow, i.e., in the language of 5:17–19, clarifying what fulfilling the law (as offering models of righteousness) entails.

The first antithesis, Matthew 5:21–26 (read with a focus on its obvious opposition, a feature of the thematic dimension), proposes a first example of this overabundant righteousness. To begin with, true disciples do not limit themselves to what is written in the law; they internalize it. "You shall not murder" (5:21) also means you shall not be angry (5:22). This internalization is the way through which disciples allow the law to establish (or define) their vocation as inner motivation.

Overabundant righteousness overflows from this inner motivation. The disciples not only do not murder (5:21) but they also do not get angry with a brother or a sister and consequently do not insult him or her (5:22). But the overflowing continues! Disciples also take the responsibility to work toward reconciliation if someone has something against them (5:23–26), i.e., even in the case when anger originates with the other. This means that the teaching about the evil of anger is not to be used by disciples to condemn others; disciples should only use it in order to evaluate their own personal behavior and take the responsibility for reestablishing a good relationship with brothers and sisters, whenever necessary. For true disciples, this overabundant fulfillment of the commandment "you shall not kill" takes precedence over everything else, including worship.[172]

The second and third antitheses, Matthew 5:27–32, provide similar examples of overabundant righteousness. True disciples do not limit themselves to what the law says; they internalize it. "You shall not commit adultery" (5:27) also means "you shall not look at a woman with lust" (5:28). "As previously, evil is defined as a wrong relationship between people, although it is now the wrong union of two people instead of the estrangement of two people."[173] True disciples are people who avoid this wrong relationship by using the law to judge and condemn themselves (not others). The third antithesis, about divorce, prolongs the second: true disciples assume responsibility for other people's adultery (divorcing one's wife "causes her to commit adultery," 5:32), as they assume responsibility for someone else's anger (5:23–26). Overabundant righteousness, not divorcing even though the law would permit it, is refusing to use the law to separate oneself from someone else; it is acting in such a way as to preserve the good union that marriage is.

> In the first three antitheses (5:21–32) overabundant righteousness aims at maintaining or (re)establishing good relationships with others with the recognition that inner dispositions are essential in these relationships and that disciples have to evaluate carefully their responsibility for these relationships so as to ensure that they are in no way the cause of evil relationships.[174]

Once this pattern is understood, it is easy to recognize it in the last three antitheses as well.

The fourth antithesis, Matthew 5:33–37, emphasizes through a fourth example of overabundant righteousness that not swearing at all, despite the law that would permit it, is a way to maintain a direct, open, frank relationship with others. By introducing someone or something between the disciples and those to whom they speak, swearing would prevent a good relationship with others. Since swearing is attributing to someone else the validity or trustworthiness of one's motivation, swearing amounts to denying one's responsibility for one's own statement or intention. By not swearing, true disciples take full responsibility for their own intentions and readily reveal their inner disposition, which directly corresponds to their outward actions.[175]

The fifth and sixth antitheses, Matthew 5:38–48, underscore that the overflow of the practice of the law is not limited to members of the community ("brothers and sisters," 5:22), or the family (5:27–32), or to those with whom one is already in direct dialogue (5:33–37), as the preceding examples of

---

172. Patte, *Matthew*, 77–79.
173. Ibid., 79.
174. Ibid., 80.
175. Ibid., 80–81.

overabundant righteousness might have suggested. True disciples establish good relationships not only with those who love them (5:46) but also with evildoers (5:39) who abuse (5:40–42) and persecute them (5:44). They do not use the law to protect themselves from other people (as suggested by the allusion in 5:40 to the law that prohibits taking a cloak from a poor man)[176] and even less as an authorization to take revenge against those who mistreat them (5:38–39) or even simply to hate them.

The injunction to "love your enemies and pray" for them brings together the three thematic features of discipleship emphasized throughout the antitheses.

1. Love is an inner disposition (a vocation; an inner motivation).

2. It is an inner disposition toward others; the fundamental value of the disciples' relationships to other people whoever they may be (including those who persecute them) is reasserted.

3. The relationship with God who gave Scripture (as is repeatedly expressed by the phrase "it was said") finds expression in the prayer for one's enemies.

Disciples call on God in favor of their enemies *instead* of seeking God's protection from them—a protection that is offered in Scripture (see 4:6). But that would involve calling on God and Scripture *against* their enemies.[177] The overflowing fulfillment of the law, which once internalized defines the disciples' vocation, is thus characterized by the total commitment to establishing, reestablishing, and maintaining good relationships with other people in all dimensions of human experience.

Reading D, CAW 3.7: Matthew 6:1–21: Discerning True Discipleship— Overabundant Righteousness as Carrying Out One's Vocation toward God (Compare with Reading C, CAW 3.5; 3.6)

When 6:1 is translated literally, "Beware of practicing your righteousness (τὴν δικαιοσύνην ὑμῶν) before others" (author's translation), it is clear that 6:1–21 continues the description of the righteousness that should characterize the behavior of the disciples. We can therefore expect other models of overabundant righteousness. The focus is now on the disciples' relationship with God. It is enough here to summarize the conclusions of the interpretation focused on the thematic dimension of this passage.[178]

Those who will be shown to be truly blessed at the last judgment (with rewards from heaven, 6:1, 4, 6, 18, and treasures in heaven, 6:19–21), i.e., models of true discipleship, are people who practice their religious duties (another aspect of "righteousness") such as giving alms, praying, and fasting in an overabundant way, although this overabundant righteousness has a different

---

176. See Deuteronomy 24:10, 12–13; Exodus 22:25–26.
177. Patte, *Matthew,* 82.
178. Ibid., 84–90 and 408.

character because it now concerns the disciples' relationship to God. True disciples should give alms, pray, and fast "in secret" (ἐν τῷ κρυπτῷ, 6:4, 6, 18) because this is what is "fitting" for actions performed for God's sake. They must be performed exclusively for God in secret, where God alone can see them. For instance, true prayer is being in direct relationship with God, which is best expressed by praying in one's room after having closed the door (6:5–6).[179] This overabundant righteousness reflects a special inner disposition that characterizes true discipleship — trusting in God as one's loving, caring Father in heaven "who knows what you need before you ask him" (6:8).

Thus true disciples are called to pray the Lord's Prayer (6:9–13) with confidence in God's goodness. In this thematic dimension (where this point is emphasized by an explicit opposition between 6:8 and 6:7), praying with such a confidence also means that the disciples who have discernment (a sound eye) look for the evidence that God answers their prayer. They do this with the expectation of finding that God has indeed answered it. After all, disciples recognize themselves as children of this caring Father (6:8, 9).

In this prayer, once again, disciples neither express concern for themselves nor ask to be protected from others. They simply ask God to give them what they need in order to fulfill their vocation. This is signaled by the very first petition, "hallowed be your name" (6:9): God's name will be hallowed when people will "give glory" to him. This is what happens when disciples do good works as they carry out their vocation (5:16). The second petition asks that the ultimate fulfillment of their vocation be brought about: the coming of the kingdom (6:10a). The third one most directly asks that God help them fulfill his will in an overabundant way: "as it is in heaven" (6:10b). Then the disciples ask for the bread necessary for their subsistence (in agreement with the NRSV translation of τὸν ἄρτον ἡμῶν τὸν ἐπιούσιον by "our daily bread," 6:11), so that they might be confirmed in their faith that God cares for them.

Potential and actual anxiety is overcome, as the praying disciples see, by means of their sound eye/discernment, fulfillments of this petition and of the preceding ones. Conversely, their sound eye/discernment is reinforced — their eye does not risk being divided by anxiety (see reading D, CAW 2), and thus they can more readily perceive good manifestations of their caring Father in heaven.

In the next petition, 6:12, the disciples predicate their petition for forgiveness from God on their own performance of overabundant righteousness toward others, as becomes apparent when one notes that most of the righteousness described in 5:21–48 involves forgiving. Thus strange as it may sound, God's forgiveness is necessary precisely when disciples have performed good works (such as forgiving): this prayer asks for what disciples need in order to fulfill their vocation, the ultimate goal of which is the glorification of God (5:16), as the first petition reasserts. For this purpose, the disciples'

---

179. Ibid., 84–88.

good works need to be "purified" (forgiven) so that it might be clear that they are manifestations of God's goodness; otherwise, people would give glory to them for their good works (an interpretation comparable to the narrative interpretation focused on the plot dimension; reading B, CAW 5.2).

The last petition, 6:13, is then interpreted as the disciples' petition that God set up the essential condition for faithful discipleship: God taking care of "evil" or of the "evil one" (ἀπὸ τοῦ πονηροῦ, 6:13). If the disciples cannot trust that God takes care of evil, they will worry about evil and thus become anxious (6:25–34), having therefore a divided eye (6:22–23). They will seek other kinds of security and thus seek to serve both God and mammon (6:24), storing up treasures on earth (6:19–21). In other words, they will be "tempted" to abandon their vocation to a life characterized by overabundant righteousness. Their inner motivation, the vocation that they internalize, would no longer be defined by an undivided, clear, straightforward moral discernment focused exclusively on the manifestations of God's goodness. Their preoccupation with evil and with overcoming evil leads such persons to have a "reactionary" vocation, one defined "in reaction to" the presence of evil that one feels the need to overcome (since one does not trust God to take care of evil).

Reading D, CAW 3.8: True Discipleship — Overabundant Righteousness as a Life Totally Shaped by What One Discerns with a Sound Eye

These comments on the Lord's Prayer neatly summarize the conclusions of my thematic interpretation of the Sermon on the Mount, precisely because they bring us back to Matthew 6:22–7:12, which was discussed earlier in relationship to 5:17–19 (see reading D, CAW 3.4) and in the presentation of the importance of moral discernment, which this passage repeatedly expresses by means of the figures of vision, seeing, and the eye (see reading D, CAW 2.3).

This discernment is what allows one to identify true models of discipleship to imitate in becoming a disciple. This discernment allows a person to identify people who are already true disciples, i.e., people who live their lives in response to the manifestations of God's goodness. They take these manifestations of goodness as models of righteousness that they implement in an overabundant way in other realms of existence. The person who becomes a disciple can implement in an overabundant way, in other realms, the models that these disciples are for him or her. This ongoing process is perpetuated by praying, through which the soundness of one's eye/discernment is constantly honed. Then it appears that models of the good-things-to-do, righteousness, which disciples are to implement in an overabundant way, are not found among disciples only, but also in the law and the prophets and thus among the scribes and the Pharisees who teach Scripture (23:2). They are righteous (as Joseph was, 1:19)[180] in that they allow Scripture to govern their lives. The disciples are to implement these models of righteousness in an overabundant

---

180. See the thematic interpretation of this verse in Patte, *Matthew*, 24–28.

way, allowing them to overflow in other realms of their human experience. Furthermore, models of the good-things-to-do, righteousness, which disciples are to implement in an overabundant way, are not to be found merely among disciples, among scribes and Pharisees, and in the law and the prophets, but also among tax collectors and Gentiles, i.e., among all other people, including those who do not know anything about Scripture and Jesus (see Mt 7:21–23; 25:31–46). They know how to love and welcome people who love them and welcome them (4:46–47); they know how to give to their children what is good for them (7:7–11); they recognize the good things they would like other people to do for them (7:12). With their sound eye/discernment, disciples recognize all this as "the law and the prophets," as models of the good-things-to-do, of righteousness, which they should internalize (as Scripture) and thus implement in an overabundant way in all kinds of aspects of their lives.

Thus the interpretation of the entire Sermon on the Mount confirms what the concluding passage, 7:24–27, expresses (see reading D, CAW 2.1): true disciples are people with a special kind of moral discernment; they are "like a wise man (ἀνδρὶ φρονίμῳ) who built his house on rock" (7:24). They are people with a "practical wisdom" (φρόνησις) that allows them to build their lives (righteousness) as disciples on a solid foundation. Jesus' words are such a solid foundation because they provide examples of "overabundant righteousness," that is, of the fulfillment of a vocation envisioned as a response to the manifestations of God's goodness and to all the manifestations of righteousness. This is what being turned toward the kingdom and its blessings is all about.

PART II

A Fourfold Commentary
on the Sermon on the Mount

Four Plausible Views of Discipleship

F OUR PLAUSIBLE VIEWS of discipleship according to the Sermon on the Mount. Four ways of conceptualizing what a life of discipleship entails. Distinct potential teachings about discipleship offered to readers by the Sermon and correlated to the textual dimensions on which four kinds of interpretations are focused. This is what Part II (chaps. 5–6) of our study seeks to elucidate.

Part I (chaps. 3–4) demonstrated that each of these four interpretations — and by extension, any interpretation — chose to focus itself on a certain meaning-producing dimension in which it found a coherence for the text. Part II will show that this choice is made partially[1] on the basis of an *epistemology judgment* that implicitly or explicitly establishes that for the interpreter a given teaching of the text is more plausible than others and therefore that the meaning-producing dimension that is correlated to this teaching is the most significant one. Thus we choose to focus our interpretation of the Sermon on the Mount on a particular textual dimension because the view of discipleship it proposes makes sense for us, in the particular cultural setting in which we are. Let me explain these points.

Part I showed that four kinds of scholarly interpretations of the Sermon on the Mount are equally *legitimate*. In its *conclusions about what the text is*, each interpretation reflects a *legitimacy judgment* manifested by the use of a critical method, as is appropriate in scholarly interpretations. In each case, the interpretation made sure that its *conclusions about what the text says* were properly grounded in textual evidence, i.e., in *what the text is*. In one way or another, each scholarly interpretation expressed this role of the legitimacy judgment, be it by appealing to other studies, and/or by correlating the Sermon on the Mount to other texts and traditions and to external evidence, and/or by emphasizing methodological issues. My multi-dimensional presentation tried to make as explicit as possible the important

---

1. Legitimacy judgments and epistemology judgments are *correlated*. Therefore, according to the circumstances, the order of these two judgments varies in the interpretive process. Scholarly studies usually claim that true critical scholarship requires starting with the legitimacy judgment, and thus to raise the epistemology issues (what do the results of a scholarly study mean) in a second step. Yet the reverse order is as plausible and, I suspect, at least as frequent. In this latter case, the use of critical methods and of legitimacy judgments (i.e., scholarly studies) *brings to critical understanding* existing *conclusions about the teaching of the text and their epistemology judgment*. Nevertheless, throughout this study, I presuppose the former sequence, simply because the starting point of this androcritical study is existing scholarly studies.

role played by legitimacy judgments in these four interpretations and, by extension, in any interpretation.

By being multidimensional, my presentation deliberately brought to light another significant role of legitimacy judgments, namely, verifying that any given interpretation is *comprehensive* by accounting for all the sections of the text (rather than interpreting passages without taking into account their context in the Sermon), *consistent* by using the same kinds of criteria all along, and *coherent* by making sure that all the *conclusions about what discrete sections of the Sermon say* can be held together to form a meaningful overall interpretation of what the Sermon says regarding discipleship. Our systematic multidimensional examination of the four interpretations by male European-American scholars sought to make as explicit as possible that each of the four interpretations is indeed comprehensive, consistent, and coherent. As a result, it began to appear that despite their scholarly character these interpretations did not fully reveal the interpretive processes that led them to their conclusions.

The discussion of the second set of interpretations (comparing those of Luz and Davies and Allison with that of my commentary) showed most clearly that an excessive effort to be comprehensive — an effort to be exhaustive — led to a lack of consistency and/or of coherence in each of these interpretations, including mine. This tension between being comprehensive and exhaustive versus being consistent and coherent can of course be viewed as reflecting the polysemy of the text, as a problem to be resolved.[2] From this perspective, one can hold on to a one-dimensional practice of critical interpretation. Yet this tension can also be viewed as evidence that an interpretation involves choosing one of the potentialities offered by a text. Then the polysemy of the text appears in a positive light as a set of potentialities offered by the text. Written from this latter perspective, the preceding chapters have shown the plausibility of viewing each of the four kinds of interpretations as legitimate in the sense that its consistency and its coherence are due to its focus on a specific textual dimension, and that it is comprehensive by following this dimension throughout the text (but not by being exhaustive).

Thus the multidimensional presentation has brought to critical understanding that in each interpretation a legitimacy judgment made sure that the conclusions are properly grounded in textual evidence and that the interpretation is comprehensive (accounting for all the sections of a text,

---

2. For instance, Strecker, Davies and Allison, and Luz explain the polysemy of the beatitudes by underscoring the tension between the beatitudes of the historical Jesus (and of early traditions) and of Matthew. See Georg Strecker, *The Sermon on the Mount: An Exegetical Commentary*, trans. O. C. Dean Jr. (Nashville: Abingdon, 1988), 27–47; W. D. Davies and D. C. Allison Jr., *A Critical and Exegetical Commentary on the Gospel according to Saint Matthew*, vol. 1., ICC (Edinburgh: T. & T. Clark, 1988), 429–69; Ulrich Luz, *Matthew 1–7: A Commentary* (Minneapolis: Augsburg, 1989), 224–46.

but not all of its features), consistent, and coherent, by focusing the interpretation on a specific meaning-producing dimension of the text — such as those that I called the historical/realistic, story/plot, figurative, and thematic dimensions. In effect, the legitimacy judgment of each interpretation has ascertained that its *conclusions about what the text is and says* are based on appropriate textual evidence by pointing to a meaning-producing dimension that is itself comprehensive, consistent, and coherent. Our multidimensional study also implies that other such textual dimensions would be appropriate bases for other interpretations.

By means of a legitimacy judgment, an interpreter chose an interpretation that can be shown to be grounded in textual evidence rather than one that is not.[3] The fact that each interpretation and its *conclusions about what the text is and says* are focused on one of several equally legitimate meaning-producing dimensions of a text shows that the interpretive process also included making a choice among these legitimate dimensions and the interpretations based on them. In order to bring to critical understanding this second kind of choice, we must repeatedly ask the question, Why? Why was any particular meaning-producing dimension chosen as the focus for the interpretation rather than any other one? Since the first kind of choice was concerned with textual evidence, i.e., with *conclusions about what the text is*, we can expect that this second kind of choice concerns the *conclusions about what the text says*, which are closely linked with the former ones, and indeed, cannot be separated from them.

The question becomes, Why were certain *conclusions about what the text says* chosen rather than another set of such conclusions? As I have suggested in the introductory part of this book,[4] and as I will illustrate in chapters 5, 6, and 7, this choice is implicitly or explicitly made on the basis of both epistemology and value judgments. In Part II (chaps. 5–6) of our multidimensional androcritical study of selected interpretations of discipleship according to the Sermon on the Mount, I seek to bring to critical understanding the *epistemology judgments* that governed the choices involved in each interpretation. In Part III (chap. 7), I will raise the issue of the *value judgments* that these choices also involved.

Why were certain *conclusions about what the Sermon says* regarding discipleship chosen rather than another set of such conclusions? First, because these conclusions made sense for the interpreter. By acknowledging the presence of the interpreter, I move from one aspect of the interpretive process to another. The *conclusions about what the Sermon says* regard-

---

3. It is important to note that far fewer interpretations lack such grounding in textual evidence than practitioners of one-dimensional interpretation commonly think. This is so because in a one-dimensional interpretation, all the interpretive choices are ascribed to legitimacy judgments, even though from a multidimensional perspective it appears that choices were also made on the basis of epistemology and value judgments.

4. See introduction, chapter 1, and chapter 2.

ing discipleship are simply descriptive[5] of the semantic content of a given meaning-producing dimension. But these conclusions and their semantic descriptions do not express the "meaning" of the text, which is always a meaning "for" certain individuals or groups. Meaning begins[6] to occur when readers envision how specific *conclusions about what the text says* (CAWs) have the potential to affect them and thus to be a *teaching* for them because they make sense for them. Thus as we consider *conclusions about the teaching* (CATs) of the Sermon regarding discipleship, we examine how readers (be they readers in the present rhetorical contexts or in the original one) conceptualize what the text says about a theme, so as to relate it to the rest of their experience.[7] This includes considering how the interpreters relate (positively or negatively) what the Sermon says about discipleship[8] to their existing understanding of discipleship.

To summarize, while the *conclusions about what the Sermon says* (CAWs) of each scholarly interpretation reflect and express the coherence of one meaning-producing dimension of the text, *conclusions about the teaching* (CATs) of the Sermon regarding discipleship reflect and express how these CAWs *make sense* for an interpreter and other people in the interpreter's culture, both because what the text says regarding discipleship is *recognizable and conceivable* in the semantic world of that culture and because people can readily perceive that *different conceptualizations of this theme affect them differently.*

The close relationship between *conclusions about what the text says* and *conclusions about the teaching* of the text needs to be underscored. The *conclusions about the teaching* are framed by the conceptualization of a theme *on the basis of epistemological categories of an interpreter's culture,* and are thus culturally marked. Yet they remain *conclusions about the teaching* of the text, because the culturally marked conceptualization of the theme merely provides the questions to be addressed to the text, not the answers.[9] *Conclusions about the teaching* of the text and *conclusions about what the text is and says* are correlated.[10]

Our study of Matthew 4:18–22 in chapter 2 has already illustrated this point in a general way. It has shown that choosing to focus the in-

---

5. A descriptive "hermeneutical practice" would say Elisabeth Schüssler Fiorenza, *Revelation: Vision of a Just World* (Minneapolis: Fortress, 1991), 1–20.

6. The full occurrence of meaning also involves value judgments, to be discussed in Part III (chap. 7).

7. As I noted in the introduction, epistemology judgments and CATs concern "rhetorical" interpretive practices, as Schüssler Fiorenza calls them (*Revelation: Vision of a Just World,* 1–20).

8. According to an interpretation focused on a certain meaning-producing dimension.

9. The conclusions themselves might be that the text has nothing to say about such a theme.

10. I deliberately emphasize that these choices are "correlated" in order to avoid any suggestion that one of the two is superior or anterior to the other. As noted in chapter 2, according to circumstances, one might be first and the other second, or vice versa.

terpretation either on the historical/realistic dimension (with Strecker and Kingsbury) or on the story/plot dimension (with Edwards) is correlated with conceptualizing discipleship as what one should do as disciples or in short *discipleship as doing God's will.* By contrast, choosing to focus the interpretation of Matthew 4:18–22 either on the figurative dimension (Luz, Davies and Allison) or on the thematic dimension (Patte) is correlated with conceptualizing *discipleship as imitation* and with the *conclusion that the teaching* of Matthew 4:18–22 offers a vision of discipleship as a distinctive type of religious leadership.

Having reviewed four kinds of scholarly interpretations of a much richer text, the Sermon on the Mount, we can now envision much more developed conceptualizations of discipleship according to these interpretations. Since these conceptualizations result from choices among semantic categories available in the culture of the interpreters — all of whom are male European-Americans — the androcritical task involves identifying and making explicit in each case the European-American categories implicitly used to conceptualize discipleship. Since discipleship is readily conceived of as an ethical practice (as discussed in chap. 1), the categories that we need to identify belong to *preunderstandings of the moral life* available in the European-American cultures of the interpreters (often in the form of ethical theories).

In chapter 5 I propose to show that Strecker's overall *conclusion about the teaching* of the Sermon on the Mount regarding discipleship as doing God's will (reading A) is that *the Sermon provides ideal norms for discipleship*, not only in Matthew's time, but also today. I will also argue that such a view of the teaching of the Sermon makes sense when discipleship is conceptualized in terms of a *deontological* preunderstanding of the moral life. Similarly, I will show that in reading B the alternative overall *conclusion about the teaching* of the Sermon on the Mount regarding discipleship as doing God's will is that *the Sermon provides a blueprint for becoming disciple and carrying out one's mission as disciple* (rather than ideal norms). This latter interpretation makes sense when discipleship is conceptualized in terms of a *consequentialist* preunderstanding of the moral life.

In chapter 6 I propose to show that, in reading C, the *conclusion* of Luz (and Davies and Allison) *about the teaching* of the Sermon on the Mount regarding discipleship as imitation is that the Sermon provides for its readers *a vision of discipleship as part of a symbolic world in which disciples need to be resocialized.* By contrast, in reading D, my conclusion on the same point is that the Sermon teaches its readers *moral discernment.* I will also argue that these two distinct views of the teaching of the Sermon make sense when discipleship is conceptualized in terms of two kinds of *perfectionist* preunderstandings of the moral life.

I do not imply in any way that the use of European-American categories for conceptualizing these two sets of conclusions about discipleship according to the Sermon on the Mount makes these interpretations illegitimate in any way, shape, or form. We have established in the preceding chapters that each of them is legitimate. These different conceptualizations represent appropriate choices of specific themes or subthemes in terms of plausible epistemology judgments in European-American cultural contexts. The use of these culture-specific preunderstandings of the moral life is quite appropriate in a critical interpretation. In fact, one fails to be critical when one does not acknowledge that one's interpretation (whatever it might be) involves epistemology judgments in terms of culture-specific categories.

Finally, chapter 7 raises the question of the relative value of these different interpretations. This question needs to be addressed by all critical interpretations. Elucidating the interpretive processes involved in one's interpretation — what a critical study pledged to do — involves making explicit the role played by value judgments in our interpretations, in addition to legitimacy and epistemology judgments.

CHAPTER 5

Doing God's Will

Deontological and Consequentialist Views of Discipleship according to the Sermon on the Mount

The ethical practice associated with discipleship according to the Sermon on the Mount is envisioned as two different kinds of ethical practice by reading A and reading B, even though both readings view it as the implementation of God's will. The difference is due, as we saw in chapter 3, to the fact that in reading A Strecker and Kingsbury focus their interpretations on the historical/realistic dimension of the text, while reading B is focused on the story/plot dimension. Each focus is shown to be legitimate through a legitimacy judgment that has intuitively (in *pro me/nobis* interpretations) or self-consciously (in scholarly interpretations) established that the chosen focus is a comprehensive, consistent, and coherent textual dimension. But the choice of a focus also reflects the epistemology judgment that the given set of *conclusions about what the Sermon says* about discipleship makes sense and is a teaching with the potential to affect readers. Since this teaching concerns discipleship as an ethical practice, we can even say that it has the potential to affect readers in their concrete lives — whether it is practiced by the readers themselves or by people around them.

In this chapter I want to argue that reading A conceptualizes the teaching of the Sermon on the Mount regarding discipleship in terms of a *deontological* preunderstanding of the moral life, while reading B conceptualizes it in terms of a *consequentialist* preunderstanding of the moral life. Keeping the corresponding ethical theories in mind will help us not only to sharpen our understanding of the plausibility of each view of discipleship but also to gain a clear sense of the kind of practice it entails. The point is that the respective *conclusions about the teaching* of the Sermon of reading A and reading B invite the readers to two different kinds of life of discipleship.

Before examining how a life of discipleship as ethical practice is conceptualized in each of these interpretations, I briefly explain the differences between deontological and consequentialist preunderstandings of the moral life and suggest in general terms why I believe reading A and reading B are related to them. For this purpose, I follow Ogletree (*The Use of the Bible in Christian Ethics*), who provides clear analytical distinctions among different preunderstandings of the moral life, including the deontological, the consequentialist, and the perfectionist.[1]

Reading A and a Deontological Preunderstanding of the Moral Life

According to Ogletree,[2] a deontological preunderstanding of the moral life underscores *intersubjective relations in a community* (or even in the world at large). These relations should structure the moral life, which is defined in terms of obligations toward others.[3] "We characteristically express our obligations . . . in terms of laws, codes, and regulations, in terms of general principles and rules."[4] The moral life is thus conceptualized as the implementation of laws, regulations, principles, and rules. As their designations indicate, these rules are largely regulative in significance, as they posit the possibility of community life in terms of the basic requisites of human life. As such, "they set inviolable limits to action. In this function they are predominantly negative. Their theme is, 'harm not.' They also assert minimal duties, one's necessary share of responsibility in the human enterprise: in labor and work, in truthfulness and fidelity."[5] Since laws, general principles and rules are based on "the basic requisites of human life," they are viewed by Immanuel Kant, the major proponent of deontological ethical theory, as universal principles that express the moral imperative.

Once one conceives of ethical practice in terms of such a deontological preunderstanding of the moral life, the question becomes, How do human beings *know* these universal principles that express their duty toward others? In order to do good, one needs to know what is the good one should do. For Kant, popular knowledge of what is good remains problematic and uncertain as long as one does not advance to the stage of rationality; one does not truly know the good as long as one does not transcend concrete cases to reach through reason the abstract, metaphysical level of universal principles. Thus Kant argues that these universal principles that define our duty can be determined by reason, a universal characteristic of human beings.[6] This rationalistic point of view is plau-

---

1. Thomas W. Ogletree, *The Use of the Bible in Christian Ethics: A Constructive Essay* (Philadelphia: Fortress, 1983), 15–45.

2. Ibid., 24–25.

3. Ibid., 23–24.

4. Ibid., 25.

5. Ibid., 26.

6. Ibid., 24 and 43. Ogletree quotes Immanuel Kant, *Fundamental Principles of the Metaphysics of Morals* (New York: Bobbs-Merrill, 1949), 24–30. Kant's ethical theory is also presented in his *Critique of Practical Reason and Other Writings in Moral Philosophy* (Chicago: University of Chicago, 1949).

sible, even though it is rejected by proponents of other ethical theories.[7] Religious people with a deontological preunderstanding would conceive of these universal moral principles and rules as the eternal will of God, which people do not know until it is revealed to them.

In order to test whether or not Strecker (and secondarily Kingsbury) read the Sermon on the Mount with a deontological preunderstanding of the moral life, we need to consider the *conclusions about what the Sermon says* about discipleship we identified above (reading A, CAWs), and ask ourselves questions, such as:

- Does this interpretation (reading A) understand the Sermon on the Mount as the revelation of universal principles of the moral life that people would not know apart from their being revealed?

- Does the teaching of the Sermon primarily set up limits on the disciples' behavior?

- Is the community posited as the ultimate good?

- Does the Sermon emphasize that the community's boundaries and cohesion are maintained by strengthening the intersubjective relations among its members? Does it emphasize positive duties toward other members? Does it include negative admonition that set the limits of the community of disciples?

- Are the disciples' duties minimally defined as their participation in the collective enterprise of the community?

Strecker himself indicates that he conceptualizes the teaching of the Sermon on the Mount in deontological categories in his comments on the Golden Rule. He says that "the standard of value that is established by the Golden Rule" and the rest of the Sermon on the Mount is comparable to "the categorical imperative of Immanuel Kant, according to which a person should act 'so that the maxim of your will could at any time also be valid as a principle of general legislation.'"[8] For Strecker, the Sermon offers what a deontological preunderstanding of the moral life posits as "the basic requisites of human life," i.e., the standards of behavior that must be implemented in the human community, beginning with the community of disciples (the church).

---

7. Such as Ogletree (see *Use of the Bible*, 24–28) and Habermas. See the critique of Kant in Jürgen Habermas, *Theory and Practice* (Boston: Beacon, 1973), and *Communication and the Evolution of Society* (Boston: Beacon, 1979).

8. Strecker, *Sermon*, 153, quoting Kant's *Critique of Practical Reason*.

Reading B and a Consequentialist Preunderstanding of the Moral Life

According to Ogletree, consequentialist (also called teleological and utili-
tarian) preunderstandings of the moral life "call attention to the fact that
our actions are in our power and that we are answerable for their conse-
quences."[9] Following John Stuart Mill,[10] Ogletree emphasizes that from this
perspective one pays close attention to the value issues inherent to any
decision and is thus more self-conscious about value commitments.[11] The
ways in which individuals act are of interest, as well as the ways in which
they move from being interested in an action to formulating a project to
act, and to actually deciding to act. In sum, "consequentialist theories of
the moral life presuppose and articulate the intentional structure of human
action."[12]

The conclusions about what the Sermon says regarding discipleship ac-
cording to reading B focus on the unfolding of the plot. This leads reading B
to notice and emphasize what the text says about the ways in which would-
be and novice disciples make or fail to make decisions to act as full-fledged
disciples. Ogletree adds:

> *Consequentialist theories more readily bring to consciousness the pos-*
> *itive values that provide the justifying grounds of action, the "for-the-*
> *sake-of-which" that renders action humanly important. When linked to*
> *a general theory of values, they articulate the total good to which a*
> *human being aspires. They state not simply what we are obliged to do,*
> *but what it might be desirable or worthwhile to do.[13]*

Is this not precisely the way in which the Sermon on the Mount functions
according to reading B and its conclusions about what the text says regard-
ing discipleship? Does it not articulate "the total good to which a human
being aspires" by emphasizing the rewards and other consequences of good
deeds? Does it not articulate what is "desirable or worthwhile to do" by pro-
viding a clear blueprint of the steps that readers-would-be-disciples must take
again and again in order to discover in each new situation what are the deeds
that are really "desirable or worthwhile"? According to reading B, the Sermon
envisions discipleship as a constant quest for what is truly desirable for the
disciples and for other people. Furthermore, the conclusions about what the
Sermon says presuppose that the teaching of this text is primarily understood

---

9. Ogletree, *Use of the Bible*, 20.

10. Marshall Cohen, ed. *The Philosophy of John Stuart Mill* (New York: Modern Library, 1961), and David Lyons, *The Form and Limits of Utilitarianism* (New York and London: Oxford University Press, 1965). Ogletree, *Use of the Bible*, 42, n. 9.

11. Ogletree, *Use of the Bible*, 21.

12. Ibid., 18.

13. Ibid., 26.

as setting up goals for the disciples' life; among these goals is a vocation to manifest God's goodness so that other people might give glory to God and might become disciples themselves.

At any rate, here we have moved away from the deontological interpretation that sees the Sermon as laying out moral principles and rules that disciples/readers are expected to readily implement. What is foregrounded here is the preliminary question, Why would one want to do all these things? In sum, in view of its focus on the story/plot and in view of its conclusions that the Sermon seeks to convince its readers to become disciples and to carry out their vocation, we can anticipate that reading B conceives of the teaching of the Sermon about discipleship from the perspective of a consequentialist preunderstanding of the moral life.

◆

One might think that consequentialist and deontological preunderstandings amount to simply highlighting certain features of the moral life and that it would be appropriate to bring them together into a single, comprehensive ethical theory, as Ogletree tends to do.[14] Yet these are quite distinct conceptualizations of the moral life. They cannot be reduced to each other without losing their most characteristic features. So it is with the conceptualization of discipleship as ethical practice presupposed by reading A and reading B. They are quite dissimilar understandings of discipleship whose distinctiveness must be respected. Yet both are plausible in the European-American cultures because they are related to preunderstandings of the moral life that make sense in these cultures — the deontological and the consequentialist ones.

In order to show the plausibility of the suggestion that Strecker's interpretation (focused on the historical/realistic dimension of the Sermon) conceptualizes discipleship in terms of a deontological preunderstanding of the moral life, the first task at hand is to identify his broad conclusions about the teaching of the Sermon regarding discipleship. This amounts to identifying Strecker's conclusions about the ways in which readers are affected by what the Sermon says on this issue and the conceptualization of discipleship that it involves.

---

14. Ogletree, *Use of the Bible,* 34–41. After showing the distinctiveness of the several theories, Ogletree proposes a way of bringing them together in what is, from my point of view, nothing else than another distinct theory (focused on the temporal horizon of existence).

Reading A, CATs: Preliminary Identification of Strecker's Conceptualization of "Discipleship according to the Sermon on the Mount"

In a part of the first chapter of his book, *The Sermon on the Mount: An Exegetical Commentary*,[15] Strecker reviews what he calls the "types of exegesis" of the Sermon on the Mount proposed through the centuries.[16] These types of exegesis refer to the significance (and thus to *conclusions about the teaching)* of the Sermon for the church in various historical contexts. Strecker returns to them in his concluding chapter, primarily in order to emphasize the views of the significance of the Sermon that (from the perspective of his critical study) are inappropriate — "wrong paths" for relating the teaching of the Sermon on the Mount to the present.[17] In this negative fashion, he defines what are his *conclusions about the teaching* of the Sermon regarding discipleship for readers in different contexts. Since Strecker is somewhat explicit in these two sections of his book about the teaching of the Sermon for its readers, we need to consider closely these suggestions. They provide for us six categories, which we shall use to regroup Strecker's diverse *conclusions about what the Sermon says* about discipleship (CAWs from chap. 3), as a first step toward clarifying his *conclusions about the teaching* of the Sermon (CATs) and the conceptualization of discipleship they involve.

Discipleship according to the Sermon on the Mount means "doing God's will." In Strecker's (and Kingsbury's) interpretation, everything in the Sermon concerns doing God's will. This is true even in the case of the beatitudes, which are at the same time "indicative" and "imperative," admonition and command (reading A, CAW 2.2). It is true of Matthew 5:17–19, which is a rule "obligatory for all followers of Jesus" (reading A, CAW 4.3) and of Matthew 7:24–27, which underscores that obeying or not the teaching of the Kyrios (which is God's will) is pronouncing a judgment on oneself (reading A, CAW 6.4).

The Sermon on the Mount provides the knowledge of God's will, which all people need in order to be faithful disciples. For Strecker, the Sermon is an absolute expression of God's eternal will because it is presented as an

---

15. I shall further clarify this view of discipleship and its significance in European-American cultural contexts by showing that other scholars — among whom Gerhard Barth, "Matthew's Understanding of the Law," in *Tradition and Interpretation in Matthew,* by G. Bornkamm, G. Barth, and H. J. Held, trans. P. Scott (Philadelphia: Westminster, 1963), 58–164; Jan Lambrecht, *"Eh bien! Moi je vous dis": Le discours-programme de Jésus (Mt 5–7; Lc 6,20–49),* Lectio Divina 125 (Paris: Cerf, 1986); Jean Zumstein, *La condition du croyant dans l'Evangile selon Matthieu* (Göttingen: Vandenhoeck & Ruprecht, 1977) — reach similar conclusions: the Sermon on the Mount presents discipleship as doing God's will.

16. Strecker, *Sermon,* 15–23.

17. Ibid., 182.

eschatological teaching, since the Sermon is proclaimed by Jesus speaking as the eschatological Lord (reading A, CAW 1.1, 1.2, 1.3). Matthew 5:21–7:12 is the authoritative proclamation of God's eternal will by the exalted Kyrios and eschatological Judge. This teaching of God's will in the Sermon is addressed by Jesus to the disciples for the sake of the crowds (to whom the disciples should teach it, Mt 28:20). Thus all people need it in order to be faithful disciples (reading A, CAW 5.1). What is this "knowledge of God's will" that people need? Matthew 5:21–7:12 offers hermeneutical principles for "fulfilling the law" and having a better righteousness in view of the impending eschatological judgment: the hermeneutical principles of love, perfection, and judgment (reading A, CAW 5.2)

These first two points clarify Strecker's insistence in the introduction to his commentary that one should not introduce into the Sermon any differentiation between gospel and law, including the corresponding differentiation between indicative and imperative, "such as we find in the theology of the Apostle Paul" — a tendency that he also finds in Lutheran types of exegesis.[18] One has no choice but to see the Sermon as demanding "concrete ethical behavior,"[19] that is, as an expression of God's will that must be obeyed.

Discipleship, conceptualized as doing God's will, does not require a special, gracious, intervention of God — the "gospel as indicative" in Lutheran interpretations — which would subsequently enable people to obey God's will — the "law as imperative" in Lutheran interpretations. Indicative and imperative are not differentiated. In terms of Strecker's conceptualization of discipleship, those to whom the teaching of the Sermon is addressed already are in a position of doing it, without additional divine help. As we saw regarding Matthew 4:18–22, for Strecker, the authoritative call of Jesus is all that was needed for transforming the four fishers into disciples; by obediently responding to this call, they have shown themselves to be disciples. *The only thing they need is a knowledge of God's will,* and this is what the Sermon on the Mount provides, in the same way that in reading A, Matthew 4:18–22 offers an ideal norm of discipleship for its readers. This expression of God's will, which disciples must do, is both gospel and law (in Paul's sense) and thus both indicative (gracious gift of God) and imperative. The knowledge of God's will — what they must do, the imperative — is the only gracious gift from God that people need.

The Sermon on the Mount as expression of God's will is practicable by those to whom it is addressed, namely, disciples, people who have already repented, who are Jesus' followers, and who form the church. For Strecker, the disciples to whom the Sermon is addressed have already aban-

---

18. Strecker, *Sermon*, 15–16.
19. Ibid., 179.

doned everything to follow Jesus in obedience to his authoritative call. The beatitudes indicate that the disciples *are* "blessed." As soon as they are taught God's will, they have everything they need to carry it out (reading A, CAW 2.1). Thus "salt" and "light of the world" are descriptions of the state of discipleship, i.e., both who they are and what they do (reading A, CAW 3.1). More generally, God's eschatological rule is proleptically realized in the community of disciples because they carry out God's will (reading A, CAW 2.3).

This important aspect of the conceptualization of discipleship is expressed by Strecker in his introduction. He emphasizes that it is not impossible to carry out the teaching of the Sermon on the Mount. Again Strecker rejects the traditional Lutheran interpretations affirming that the Sermon as a full expression of God's will (i.e., as the "law of Christ") simply demonstrates our sinfulness. "The law of Christ... leads people to the knowledge of sin."[20] By contrast, Strecker concludes that the Sermon is *not* a call to repent from our sins, which it would reveal to us by confronting us with God's will (the content of the Sermon on the Mount). Rather, the Sermon is admonition, a call to action, an ethical command for people who have already repented, i.e., for followers of Jesus. For such people, the teaching of the Sermon is *practicable*. This teaching is indeed for "all the nations" (Mt 28:19–20), but only after they repent and accept being made disciples.[21] These comments suggest what is at stake in the epistemology choices presupposed by Strecker's conceptualization of discipleship and of the teaching of the Sermon as providing the knowledge of God's will.

Discipleship according to the Sermon on the Mount involves a better righteousness in the form of concrete deeds, with a social dimension; it is not a private ethic.   For Strecker, what is demanded from the disciples is a "better" righteousness, i.e., a righteousness that encompasses both the private and the public dimensions of concrete life in the community of disciples (the sphere of God's eschatological rule) and beyond (reading A, CAW 4.4).[22]

Discipleship is not legalistic; it is not the literal application of the ethical demands of the Sermon on the Mount without regard for the concrete circumstances.   For Strecker, the Sermon teaches basic ethical principles rather than a series of parenetic instructions demanding literal and thus legalistic implementation. The redactor illustrates this point through the Sermon itself, which applies the basic principles of Jesus' teaching to the

---

20. Strecker, *Sermon*, 16, 183.

21. Ibid., 179.

22. "...the Preacher on the mount, with all his own radicalism, demands concrete ethical behavior. For Matthew, the Sermon on the Mount is first of all admonition, which is directed toward the followers of Jesus...." Strecker, *Sermon*, 179.

church situation, as exemplified by each of the antitheses (Mt 5:21–48). It is also shown by the beatitudes, which reflect the self-consciousness of the community (reading A, CAW 2.0), and by Matthew 7:13–14, a call to practice Jesus' teaching that reflects the situation of Matthew's church (reading A, CAW 6.1).

These conclusions are related to Strecker's rejection of another type of conceptualization of the teaching of the Sermon on the Mount, namely, that of liberal scholars from the turn of the century (such as Herrmann and Harnack). For Strecker, these scholars overemphasize individualism and see the Sermon as teaching an "ethic of attitude." Accordingly, "it was no longer the concrete deed that counted as fulfillment of the better righteousness, but the attitude in the depth of one's heart. . . . "[23] For Strecker, the Sermon demands a better righteousness in the form of concrete deeds that have a social dimension; this is not a private ethic. Yet Strecker warns that emphasizing the concrete character of the ethical demands of the Sermon should not lead to legalism, which involves applying the literal application of its teaching in the same way in all circumstances.[24]

Finally, discipleship according to the Sermon on the Mount is the concrete ethical behavior that the entire Christian community is called to and is expected to implement, so as to be "the light of the world." For Strecker, being "salt" and "light of the world" involves, for the disciples, carrying out a universal mission, which is demanded from all the members of the church (reading A, CAW 3.2). This concrete ethical behavior is to be carried out beyond the borders of the community, since it includes the disciples' relationship with other people and thus also deals with economic issues (see reading A, CAW 5.35 on Mt 6:19–24). Yet the descriptions of "salt without taste" and light "under a bushel" must be understood as rules of community discipline; not carrying out the universal mission is tantamount to excluding oneself from the church (reading A, CAW 3.3). Thus the Sermon sets up rules for the life of the community of disciples (reading A, CAW 4.1), as Strecker emphasizes in his detailed comments on Matthew 5:21–7:12 and in the conclusions he draws from the study of this central passage (reading A, CAW 5.3, see 5.31 to 5.39). These rules are for the *entire* community, not for an elite. Strecker emphasizes that the Sermon does not teach a two-stage ethic. Thus he rejects the late medieval interpretation according to which the Sermon is directed to a special group of Christians who want to be perfect.

---

23. Strecker, *Sermon*, 183. Important features of this "liberal" conceptualization can be found in the conceptualization of discipleship according to reading D — which emphasizes that the Sermon teaches "moral discernment," a kind of ethical attitude.

24. Ibid., 184.

[The Sermon] is an unconditional, general call to discipleship!...
no special ethic for a Christian elite.... The Christian community is
called to place itself under the word of its Lord, to shape the realm of
the church in accordance to the Sermon on the Mount, and to realize an exemplary existence that will shine into the world like the light
into the darkness (5:16).[25]

  This summary of Strecker's *conclusions about what the Sermon says*
regarding discipleship, as well as the negative points he makes in his introduction, clearly emphasizes a view of discipleship characterized by a
"concrete ethical behavior." This is consistent with his interpretation of
Matthew 4:18–22 (discussed in chap. 2). Discipleship is doing God's will,
as revealed by Jesus in the Sermon on the Mount, by those who have responded to Jesus' call by abandoning everything to follow him and thus
implementing the ideal norm posited by 4:18–22.
  Strecker's interpretation of the Sermon is indeed related to a *deontological preunderstanding of the moral life.* These general observations are
enough for us to suspect that Strecker conceptualizes "discipleship according to the Sermon on the Mount" as a deontological ethical practice. By
saying so I am not putting into question the legitimacy of his interpretation. This legitimacy has been shown in chapter 3. I am simply identifying
the broad epistemology categories that Strecker used and that are correlated
to his choice of the historical/realistic dimensions as a focus for his interpretation. These deontological categories provide us with an additional critical
perspective for understanding the details of Strecker's interpretations of the
various passages of the Sermon. In this way, we will be in a better position
to perceive the plausibility, significance, and appeal for people in European-
American cultures of this interpretation of discipleship according to the
Sermon on the Mount.

Reading B, CATs: Preliminary Identification of an Alternate Conceptualization of "Discipleship according to the Sermon on the Mount"

*Clearly, Strecker's conclusions regarding discipleship are framed in terms a
particular preunderstanding of the moral life — a deontological one. This
suggests that the alternate interpretation, which is focused on the plot
meaning-producing dimension of the text and generates very different conclusions about what the Sermon says about discipleship, is quite probably framed
by another preunderstanding of the moral life. I have already suggested that
reading B conceptualizes its conclusions about the teaching of the Sermon*

---

25. Strecker, *Sermon,* 182, 184.

regarding discipleship in terms of a consequentialist preunderstanding of the moral life, and that this conceptualization of discipleship is correlated with the choice of the plot dimension of the text as the focus of this interpretation. This suggestion is confirmed in a preliminary way by a brief review of some of the conclusions of reading B about what the Sermon says regarding discipleship that have been identified in chapter 3.

Discipleship according to the Sermon on the Mount means "doing God's will." *This conclusion initially seems to be identical with the corresponding one in Strecker's interpretation, yet it is not. Here doing God's will is conceived of as an overabundant righteousness (see reading B, CAW 5.12 and 6.32). This is so because the rest of the teaching of the Sermon regarding discipleship is understood quite differently.*

The Sermon on the Mount is a "sermon" and thus a call to discipleship. *The nature of the Sermon's teaching is construed quite differently than in reading A. Here, the Sermon aims at establishing the will of the hearers to do God's will. See reading B, CAW 1.3 and 3.3 (see also 1.1, 1.2, 2.2, 6.2). Many of the CAWs underscore how the hearers' will is established.*

The Sermon on the Mount teaches how to recognize the goodness of God so as to entice the hearers to want to do God's will (see reading B, CAW 5.14). *This is so because according to this interpretation, the Sermon emphasizes that as long as one is anxious and has a divided eye that does not recognize God's manifestations and their goodness, one cannot want to be a disciple (reading B, CAW 6.11, 6.12, 6.14). So the Sermon teaches novice disciples and would-be disciples how to see God's goodness.*

In order to do God's will and their mission, disciples need to be aware of the good consequences of their deeds for themselves (rewards), for others, and for God. (See reading B, CAW 2.0, 2.1, 3.1, 3.2, 4.2, 4.3, 5.11, 7.11, 7.12, 7.3, 7.4). *These summaries call to mind the characteristic orientation of the conclusions about what the Sermon is and says regarding discipleship of reading B, which is focused on the plot dimension. For the time being, this should suffice to explain why it is appropriate to suggest that reading B and its conclusions about the teaching of the Sermon might be shaped by a conceptualization of discipleship as a consequentialist ethical practice.*

Since the conceptualizations of discipleship as deontological and consequentialist practices both assume that discipleship is primarily characterized by "doing God's will," they can be presented in a point-counterpoint manner (as we did in chap. 3).

Reading A, CAT 1: The Plausibility of Conceptualizing Discipleship with a Deontological Preunderstanding of the Moral Life

Strecker's scholarly interpretation includes the conclusion that the Sermon on the Mount gives its intended readers, Matthew's church, the knowledge of God's will, without which it is impossible to be faithful disciples because discipleship is "doing God's will."[26] Accordingly, the most significant teaching of the Sermon is a unique knowledge of God's will. Since discipleship is "doing God's will," this knowledge is the only thing we are truly lacking in the same way that in Matthew 4:18–22, Matthew provides us with an ideal norm for discipleship as an expression of God's will for us.

We can begin to explore the conceptualization of discipleship implied by these conclusions by noting that emphasizing (with Strecker) that discipleship is "doing God's will," raises the possible question, What is God's will? The essential condition to being a disciple is having an appropriate knowledge of God's will.

This presupposes that the basic human predicament that would prevent one from doing God's will and from being a faithful disciple is *a lack of knowledge of God's will*. From this perspective, anyone who has an appropriate knowledge of God's will is in a position to do it. Conversely, anyone who does not do God's will probably does not have an appropriate knowledge of God's will.

This perspective is consistent with a deontological preunderstanding of the moral life. Unlike consequentialist views, which see the basic problem with human beings as a lack of will to do good, a deontological preunderstanding of the moral life affirms that human beings do *have the will to do good*. It is rooted in a deep sense of duty toward others — toward neighbors and toward God. This deep sense of duty is a part of the fabric of human existence because of its intersubjective character; there are necessarily "other persons in our field of action," who have "a dignity like our own, a dignity requiring our respect and beneficence."[27] This sense of duty engenders in us a will to do good, the will to do God's will.

The problem is that human beings *do not know* what God's will is, i.e., what the good that they should do is, what their duty toward others is. One possibility is that the particularities of each situation and of each relationship prevent one from apprehending the abiding duty that would define the good that one should seek to do in all circumstances — God's eternal will. Another possibility is that one does not know how to perform one's duty in the particularities of concrete situations because one does not fully understand God's eternal will. According to deontological ethics, human

---

26. See again chapter 3, reading A, CAWs 1.2, 1.3, 4.3, 5.1, 5.3, 6.1, 6.4.
27. Ogletree, *Use of the Bible*, 23.

beings need and constantly strive for a formulation of our universal duties toward others, for a law based on universal moral principles. In theological vocabulary, they need to receive a revelation of God's eternal will.[28]

For people who share this deontological preunderstanding of the moral life, including many European-Americans, Strecker's conclusion that Matthew presents the Sermon on the Mount as a revelation of God's eternal will by Jesus the exalted Lord and Judge (reading A, CAW 5.1) is readily recognized as a *plausible expression* of the significance of the Sermon for its readers — a *conclusion about the teaching* of the Sermon. From a deontological perspective, human beings need to receive a revelation of God's eternal will; nothing is more significant for them. Readers also need a more concrete presentation of God's will for them, in the form of ideal norms, such as the one presented in 4:18–22. But this ideal norm becomes authoritative only when it clearly conforms to God's eternal will as revealed by Jesus.

Reading B: CAT 1: The Plausibility of Conceptualizing Discipleship with a Consequentialist Preunderstanding of the Moral Life

The alternate scholarly interpretation (focused on the story/plot dimension by its narrative critical method) includes the conclusions that the Sermon on the Mount functions in the story as a "sermon" aimed at convincing both the novice disciples (the four fishers) and the crowds to become full-fledged disciples who "do God's will."[29] This is to say that the Sermon on the Mount seeks to overcome what would prevent novice disciples and crowds from doing God's will, namely, not wanting to do it. The fundamental reason for this unwillingness to do God's will is apparent in the conclusions of reading B about what the text says regarding the unfolding of the story of the disciples.[30] In brief, people do not want to do the actions that they should do according to God's will, not because of a lack of knowledge (they already know God's will as expressed in the "law and the prophets"), but because doing God's will appears to be too costly. They do not recognize that acting according to God's will has good consequences. As Matthew 4:18–22 shows, discipleship needs to be viewed as the ongoing process of being made fishers of people because in order to decide to do God's will, people need to be able to anticipate the implications of doing so.

---

28. These very brief remarks regarding deontological preunderstandings of the moral life represent my interpretation of ethical theories (including Kant's) with the help of Ogletree (*Use of the Bible,* 23–28) and of Greimas's structural semiotics (Greimas and Courtés, *Semiotics and Language,* 93–94, 193–95, passim).

29. See chapter 3, reading B, CAWs 1.1, 1.2, 1.3, 1.4, 2.0, 2.2.

30. See the summary presentation in reading B, CAW 6.3, "Overall Plot of the Story of the Disciples."

From these conclusions about what the Sermon is and says, *it is easy to en-vision what is, generally speaking, the teaching of the Sermon on the Mount for its readers/hearers. What is most significant for the readers is that the Ser-mon shows them why they should want to do God's will, and thus calls them to discipleship.*

As we begin pondering how reading B conceptualizes discipleship, we can note that when one conceives of discipleship as "doing God's will," one of the possible questions is, Why would one want to do it? In this case, the essential condition for being a disciple is having the will to do God's will. The basic human predicament, which would prevent one from doing God's will, is lacking the will to do it.[31]

These conclusions are consistent with a consequentialist preunderstand-ing of the moral life. Unlike deontological preunderstandings (see reading A, CAT 1), a consequentialist preunderstanding[32] *emphasizes the "intentional-ity" (or intentional structure) of moral actions, i.e., the process through which people decide to act, which is far from being always self-conscious! For our purpose, the most important characteristic of consequentialist ethical theo-ries is that they underscore, in Ogletree's words, that "actions involve values. We adopt projects because of the values we expect to promote or protect by means of them. Values supply the essential content of our reasons for committing ourselves to our chosen projects."*[33]

What makes us decide to do or not to do something is our conscious or subconscious evaluation of the anticipated consequences of our action. Will this action be beneficial or not? For whom? We "calculate the likely results of our actions" and "assess their relative goodness (or badness)" before com-mitting ourselves to do them. If we are not convinced that the goodness of the outcome of a proposed action clearly outweighs its "cost" (its negative consequences), we refuse to do it; we do not want to do it.

This point needs to be emphasized because many of us in European-American cultures are deeply influenced by a deontological perspective (see reading A). It might seem obvious (as it is from a deontological perspective) that God's will is good for us. Is it not clear that God is good? That God wants good things for us? And that God's will is good for us? For people who do not share the deontological perspective, just the opposite is obvious. Clearly,

---

31. This lack of will might be caused by a recognition that one does not have the means to do it. When this is emphasized, one might want to formulate the question in a broader way: How can one do God's will? What makes it possible to do God's will? In this case, the essential condition for being a disciple would be *having the means to do* God's will; if one has the means to do it, one will want to do it. I did not formulate the question in this way because there is no indication in the Sermon on the Mount that human beings lack the power or the ability to do God's will.

32. These very brief remarks regarding consequentialist ethical theories represent my in-terpretation of these theories with the help of Ogletree's phenomenological approach (*Use of the Bible*, 18–22) and of Greimas's structural semiotics (Greimas and Courtés, *Semiotics and Language*, 93–94, 157, 193–95, passim).

33. Ogletree, *Use of the Bible*, 19.

many of our contemporaries are not persuaded that God's will is good for us. Even many believers do not practice the teaching of the Sermon on the Mount. Why? Because we are not convinced that it is "good" (beneficial) for us and others. We are not convinced that it is good for us to forgive those who strike us or steal from us (5:38–42). By forgiving, we might lose our property, our well-being, our honor. Would such forgiveness not encourage criminals to continue in their evil ways? In fact, most of us are convinced that resisting evil people is the right thing to do! Even though we know that love — radical love for neighbors, including one's enemies — is God's will, the fact is that we do not practice such a love, fundamentally because we are not truly convinced that it is the good thing to do.

Thus a conceptualization of discipleship according to the Sermon on the Mount as a consequentialist ethical practice is also plausible in European-American cultures. People in these cultures use this perspective, which includes John Stuart Mill's utilitarianism,[34] in many aspects of their daily lives — including most business transactions. Even if a consequentialist perspective is not dominant in these cultures, it still makes sense for people who, for one reason or another, seek an alternative to the deontological perspective. People in European-American cultures should recognize such a plausibility, since they use this perspective in many aspects of their daily lives.

Adopting this consequentialist perspective means that the teaching of the Sermon on the Mount for readers is to be found in its discursive (or rhetorical) force, its ability to convince its hearers, including us, of the goodness of God's will and thus of discipleship as doing God's will, and not so much in the "knowledge-content" of the Sermon. The plausibility of this teaching is found in the Sermon on the Mount as a sermon seeking to entice people to accept God's will, not in the Sermon as a lecturelike presentation of "God's will." In this way Matthew 5–7, as legitimately read with a focus on the story/ plot dimension, offers readers a message that is plausible, insofar as they recognize the plausibility of some kind of consequentialist preunderstanding of the moral life — as European-American people should be able to do.

Reading A, CAT 2: The Plausibility of Claiming that the Sermon on the Mount Reveals God's Eternal Will to Disciples

From a deontological perspective, the suggestion that Strecker's interpretation does not really read the Sermon on the Mount as a sermon seems nonsensical. Once again, what is obvious and plausible from one perspective is nonsensical and implausible from the other. Indeed, Strecker's and Kingsbury's interpretations account for the rhetorical force of the Sermon

---

34. As Ogletree (*Use of the Bible*, 42) emphasizes. See Mill's essay, "Utilitarianism," in *The Philosophy of John Stuart Mill*, ed. Marshall Cohen (New York: Modern Library, 1961).

on the Mount. But its role looks quite different from their deontological perspective.

It is clear that for Strecker (and Kingsbury) the Sermon on the Mount is not to be read as a sermon that seeks to convince hearers and readers to change their mind/will (by contrast with the consequentialist interpretation; reading B). Such a sermon is unnecessary, since according to this interpretation those to whom the Sermon on the Mount is directed are already committed to being disciples and to doing God's will. This view is plausible from a deontological perspective, for which a deep sense of duty is part of the fabric of human existence (see reading A, CAT 1). Nevertheless the Sermon on the Mount must have a rhetorical force because it still needs to convince hearers and readers that its teaching is indeed a revelation of God's eternal will (rather than another human moral teaching).

Strecker's and Kingsbury's interpretations, focused as they are on the historical/realistic dimension of the text, conclude that the Sermon on the Mount (together with earlier sections of the Gospel of Matthew, including 4:18–22) presents Jesus as having an exceptional authority — indeed, as already having "all authority in heaven and earth" as the exalted Kyrios (see reading A, CAW 1.2). Because the Sermon on the Mount makes explicit this eschatological authority of the Preacher on the mount, his teaching (the content of the Sermon on the Mount) can be recognized as an absolute expression of God's eternal will (see reading A, CAW 1.3).

This rhetorical effect must be a part of the teaching of the Sermon on the Mount for its readers because there is so much at stake for discipleship in the authority of Jesus (see reading A, CAT 4, for further discussion of this issue). It is enough here to note that those who recognize the authority of Jesus as that of the exalted Kyrios, Son of God, and eschatological Judge (see reading A, CAW 5.1) will base their entire lives on the Sermon on the Mount because *the Sermon will have become a moral imperative that shapes their relationships with others and with God in all aspects of their lives.* This is what it means to recognize the Sermon on the Mount as an (the) expression of God's eternal will![35]

Deontological preunderstandings of the moral life include the conviction

---

35. Strecker does not suggest in any direct way in his introductory and concluding comments that we should give a central place to the extraordinary authority of Jesus in our conclusions about discipleship, except in the penultimate sentence of his book: "This path of signal existence [shaping the realm of the church in accordance with the Sermon on the Mount and realizing an exemplary existence] will best do justice to the missionary claim of the exalted One, as emphasized by Matthew at the end of his Gospel." Strecker, *Sermon,* 184–85. Yet it is enough to show how Strecker's relentless references to the "exalted *Kyrios*" and his authority might be integrated to plausible *conclusions about the teaching* of the Sermon on the Mount in a deontological perspective. A similar but more tentative comment is found on p. 177. All the other references to Jesus' authority, including in the introduction and the conclusion (11–23, 174–85), are conclusions about what Matthew says regarding his view or his community's view (in the past).

that the fundamental principles of morality are universalizable.[36] Besides the use of practical reason advocated by Kant, one of the ways of universalizing foundational moral teaching is assigning to it a mythical origin. This is what Strecker does by underscoring that the Sermon on the Mount is taught by the resurrected and exalted Kyrios, who is also the eschatological Judge; he also does it by arguing that Matthew has "historicized" Jesus' ministry and teaching, i.e., has set them in an "unrepeatable past" that is a sacred and ideal time.[37] In effect, Strecker suggests to his readers that they should acknowledge the authority of the teaching of the Sermon on the Mount as God's eternal will because of its mythical character. Thus it becomes plausible, from this particular deontological perspective, to recognize the teaching of the Sermon as actually providing a knowledge (a revelation) of God's eternal will, which should be received as a moral imperative.

I can now summarize this important point. In various ways, the Sermon calls its hearers/readers to carry out its teaching; i.e., to do "the will of my Father in heaven," as the Preacher on the mount says (7:21). For Strecker and other deontological interpretations, what would prevent people from acting according to these instructions include (1) the failure to recognize them as expressions of God's eternal will (a problem overcome by believing that the Preacher on the mount is the exalted Kyrios — a point to which we shall come back, see below reading A, CAT 4) or (2) the failure to understand properly what this eternal will of God requires from them (see below reading A, CAT 3).

Reading B, CAT 2: The Plausibility of the Sermon on the Mount as "Sermon" Proclaiming a Good News to Convince People to Do God's Will

As we have seen, the interpretation focused on the Sermon on the Mount as part of the plot of the story of the disciples and as preview of this story understands that the Sermon functions as a sermon aimed at convincing the novice disciples and the crowds to do God's will and to become disciples.[38] Establishing their will to adopt such a way of life is a necessary step in the process through which they will eventually be made full-fledged disciples and fishers of people. The Sermon has the same role for readers who identify themselves with these characters, i.e., for people who show at least some interest in becoming disciples (be it in the time of Matthew or today). The question is, Are the "arguments" used by the Sermon plausible for European-American readers who envision discipleship as a consequentialist ethical practice?

---

36. As Ogletree (*Use of the Bible*, 24) notes, referring to Kant (*Metaphysics of Morals*, 24–30).

37. Strecker, "The Concept of History in Matthew," 67–84.

38. See reading B, CAT 1 and chapter 3, reading B, CAWs 1.1, 1.2, 1.3, passim.

In addressing this question, it is useful to raise two interrelated theoretical questions: How does one establish or change someone's will? How does someone agree to perform a new kind of action?

Consequentialist ethical theories and semiotics[39] recognize two basic reasons for adopting a new kind of behavior (through which a new kind of will is established): being convinced that a failure to "do these things" would bring bad consequences (including punishments) or being convinced that "doing these things" would bring about good consequences (including rewards).

According to the first model, the hearers of the Sermon on the Mount would be convinced to do God's will (and be disciples) because they would fear the judgment, the hell of fire (e.g., 5:22, 28-29; 7:19), which would be the consequence for not doing God's will. In this case, one wants to do God's will because one has to do it. It is an obligation. One does not do more than what is absolutely necessary to avoid this threatened punishment; God's will is conceived in a negative way. "You shall not" (do this or that) because it is against God's will.

This first consequentialist model can be related to and associated with a deontological reading that would emphasize the parenetic character of the Sermon (rather than its historical/realistic dimension) and thus would be more legalistic than Strecker's and Kingsbury's interpretations. The Sermon would still be read as a (the) revelation of God's eternal will (see above, reading A, CAT 2), but with a heavier emphasis on this point. Thus the Sermon would be read as a series of duties commanded by the Kyrios as eschatological Judge who threatens the nondoers with eschatological punishments. This plausible conclusion about the teaching of the Sermon cannot be based on conclusions about what·the Sermon is and says reached by an interpretation focused on the story/plot dimension; it cannot be based on reading B and its CAWs. It could be shown to be legitimate by a scholarly interpretation focused on another dimension of the text, namely, on the Sermon as an eschatological (apocalyptic) parenetic text, comparable to the Rule of the Community of Qumran (1QS). This interpretation would emphasize the punishment pronouncements throughout the Sermon and especially in 7:12-27, such as 7:19, "Every tree that does not bear good fruit is cut down and thrown into the fire," and on the presentation of Jesus as eschatological Judge in the Sermon and in the rest of the Gospel according to Matthew in passages such as 3:10-12; 11:21-24.[40]

---

39. Ogletree, *Use of the Bible*, 18–22; Greimas and Courtés, *Semiotics and Language* (all the articles concerning the "modalities" [will, knowledge, and ability] and related issues); see also Paul Ricoeur, *Freedom and Nature: The Voluntary and the Involuntary* (Evanston, Ill.: Northwestern University Press, 1966).

40. Thus this interpretation of the passages about the judgment as a threat emphasizing that one "must" do these things is both legitimate and plausible. Despite its close relationship to the deontological interpretation — for which one of the basic hermeneutical principles is the principle of judgment — it is consequentialist because it emphasizes the establishment of the will of the readers/hearers, though as "having to do" established by means of threats.

By contrast, according to the second model (adopting a new kind of behavior because one is convinced that "doing these things" would bring about good consequences), the hearers/readers would be convinced to do God's will because they would recognize that God's will presented in the Sermon is good for them and for others. In this case, one is willing to do God's will because one "wants to do it." One does not put limits on doing God's will, since the more one does God's will, the more good consequences (for others and for oneself) there will be; God's will is conceived in a positive way. While retaining the negative commandments as guardrails, God's will is primarily conceived as a vocation, as a task one is called to do because of the goodness of its consequences.

The interpretation focused on the plot dimension and its conclusions about what the Sermon is and says (see chap. 3, reading B, CAWs) are readily related to and associated with this second plausible consequentialist perspective, and not at all with the former model. From the point of view of reading B, if the Sermon on the Mount would aim at convincing people to do God's will by threatening them with eternal punishments for not doing it or for doing things contradictory to it, the result would be the very hypocrisy that is denounced in 6:1–21 and the minimal compliance to the letter of the law that is systematically rejected by the antitheses in 5:21–48. By contrast, if the Sermon convinces us to do God's will by showing us the good consequences of doing it, we would not want to limit righteousness — the performance of God's will — in agreement with the conclusion that the Sermon conceives of the disciples' faithful behavior as an overabundant righteousness (see chap. 3, reading B, CAW 5.12, 5.14, etc.).

Similarly, according to reading B, repeated references to the judgment should not be read as threats of punishment ("you will do it or you will burn in hell"). In the body of the Sermon (5:17–7:12), they function as warnings, i.e., as negative forms of promises. A warning, "not doing God's will is depriving yourself of God's blessings," is quite different from a threat, "if you do not do God's will, you will burn in the hell of fire" (see reading B, CAW 5.11). The references to the judgment in the concluding part of the Sermon, 7:13–27, are a different case but do not constitute a threat aimed at convincing people to do God's will. As reading B underscores in its conclusions about what this passage, 7:13–22, is and says (see reading B, CAW 7.1–7.3), these verses do not describe what will happen to "you," the hearers/readers, if you do not become disciples. Rather, they describe what will happen to other people — those who take the wide gate and the easy road (7:13–14), bad trees (7:15–20), or other people who are not among the true disciples (as the impersonal style of 7:21–27 shows). Thus we conclude that these verses should not be read as a threat aimed at forcing people to accept becoming disciples and doing God's will, but rather as an admonition seeking to convince disciples of the urgency of carrying their mission for the sake of others.

In sum, when the Sermon on the Mount (in 5:33–7:12) seeks to convince

its hearers/readers to do God's will and to become disciples, it is a proclamation of good news, emphasizing the good consequences of discipleship. This
means that this consequentialist interpretation understands God's will, which
disciples are expected to do, differently from a deontological interpretation.

Reading A, CAT 3: The Plausibility of the View of God's Eternal Will That Disciples Should Do

According to the Sermon on the Mount, what is God's eternal will that
disciples should implement? The interpretation focused on the historical/
realistic dimension and its *conclusions about what the Sermon is and says*
are clear.

Negatively, one should not conceive of God's eternal will in the Sermon
as a series of specific commandments demanding a *literal* implementation
(a point made in terms of the genre of the Sermon, not a parenetic text but
an "epitome"; see reading A, CAW 1.4). Rather, *God's will is expressed
in the principles used in the Sermon on the Mount for reinterpreting the
law and the prophets.* Through his radical reinterpretations of the law in
the antitheses (5:21–48)[41] as well as through his teaching in 6:1–7:12, "the
Preacher on the mount does not want to teach a new law but rather to
bring to expression the sovereign Will of God in and in contrast to the
Old Testament Torah."[42] This is what he does as he "fulfills the Law" by
reinterpreting it and as he provides hermeneutical principles — the principles of love, perfection, and judgment — for the interpretation of Torah. As
Strecker's redaction critical study shows, the church tradition and Matthew
reinterpret Jesus' own teaching, as well as Torah, using the same hermeneutical principles so as to illustrate what it means to be disciples doing
God's will in new situations. As we have noted (reading A, CAW 5.39),
the entire set of community rules presented in Matthew 5:21–7:12 "fulfills" Jesus' teaching as Jesus' teaching "fulfills" the law (see reading A,
CAW 5.1–5.39).

Thus Strecker vehemently rejects viewing the Sermon on the Mount as
a series of specific commandments demanding a *literal* implementation because it transforms the Sermon into a *legalistic* teaching. He insists that this
legalistic interpretation is to be rejected because seeking to practice "the
original literal meaning" of the Sermon is not only an impossibility (despite
the claim of the Anabaptists),[43] but also in contradiction with the "very
teaching" of the Sermon about the law.[44] Such vehement reactions reflect

---

41. Cf. Strecker, *Sermon*, 94.
42. Ibid., 95.
43. Ibid., 17.
44. This kind of statement is typical of one-dimensional interpretations, which want
to present themselves as the only legitimate interpretations, and do not take into account
that their central affirmations (e.g., a parenetic interpretation would be legalistic) are value

a value judgment (see chap. 7). They also reflect an epistemology judgment. A legalistic interpretation is not plausible because it is not supported by Strecker's scholarly investigation focused on the historical/realistic dimension of the Sermon and by its *conclusions about what this text is and says.*

Strecker seeks to show the plausibility of his conclusions that God's eternal will is expressed in the basic hermeneutical principles used for the interpretation of Torah by linking these conclusions with what he views as true obedience, "obedience in spirit," in contrast to obedience to "the original literal meaning" of the Sermon. Obedience in spirit might involve deviating from what is literally commanded, as Dietrich Bonhoeffer exemplified by plotting against the Third Reich.[45] Proposing to perform the literal commands of the Sermon is being "fanatical" (as the Anabaptists were)[46] and "legalistic" (as in the case of the two-stage ethic). Rather, one should recognize that in his formulation of the Sermon on the Mount Matthew provided us with examples of "what the church in all ages has the task of doing: it must comprehend and interpret anew in a changed situation the Will of God as expressed in the message of Jesus."[47] "Obedience in spirit," true obedience to the teaching of the Sermon, begins with interpreting and reinterpreting God's will in terms of the church's present circumstances and *according to the principles of interpretation exemplified in the Sermon itself.* Then one will truly do God's will in the present situation.[48]

This view of God's eternal will as the hermeneutical principles of love, perfection, and judgment that disciples implement always anew is quite plausible for a deontological perspective, according to which basic moral principles are universalizable in that they are "ground rules which order [human] interactions" and thus should be implemented at all times and in all places, even though the course of events constantly requires different concrete implementations.[49]

---

judgments (legalism is sin for most liberal Protestants!). Strecker's conclusion is justified by reference to a critical interpretation (his own, of course). Yet one should not forget that this interpretation is focused on *one* specific dimension of the text, and ignores other dimensions, which could justify the rejected interpretation.

45. Strecker, *Sermon*, 22, 181–82.

46. Ibid., 16–18. Yet note that Strecker underscores that "fanatical" is not used with a negative connotation.

47. Ibid., 180.

48. For Strecker, writing during the cold war, a time when humankind was faced with a daily feeling of threat to existence "through a self-initiated atomic blast of annihilation," the teaching of the Sermon and especially its "key word 'love of enemy' acquires importance in the rational calculation of survival" (Strecker, *Sermon*, 181). Yet this word and the rest of the teaching of the Sermon will truly be significant and effective in that situation only insofar as it is interpreted as a call to concrete actions following the basic principles enunciated in it (rather than seeking to obey its literal teaching in a legalistic and individualistic way).

49. As is emphasized by Ogletree, *Use of the Bible*, 24.

Furthermore, and by contrast with the consequentialist interpretation with its emphasis on blessings, good consequences, and rewards (see reading B, CAT 2 and 3), the emphasis on the principle of judgment as the primary hermeneutical principle (see reading A, CAW 5.21) is plausible from a deontological perspective. As Ogletree says:

> Deontological perspectives are strongest in calling attention to those obligations that are entailed by the basic requisites of human life. In regard to these requisites they are largely regulative in significance. They set inviolable limits to actions. In this function they are predominantly negative. Their theme is, "harm not." They also assert minimal duties, one's necessary share of responsibility in the human enterprise: in labor and work, in truthfulness and fidelity.[50]

From this perspective it is quite plausible to read the Sermon as teaching that the basic hermeneutical principles of love, perfection, and judgment—as expressions of God's eternal will—are the means through which authoritative rules for community life should be formulated. The "authoritative" character of these community rules (as Strecker emphasizes; see reading A, CAW 5.3–5.39), which are to be used for community discipline, including excluding people from the church, show that the principles that engendered them imply a certain conception of the church and of its structure, to be discussed below (see reading A, CAT 5).

Reading B, CAT 3: The Plausibility of Good Consequences of Doing God's Will as Reasons for Wanting to Do It

For a consequentialist interpretation, it is plausible to emphasize that people already know God's will but do not want to do it. In its conclusions about what the Sermon says this interpretation emphasizes that people had the law and the prophets prior to Jesus. The problem is that they failed to internalize them and thus failed to make of God's will their own will (see reading B, CAW 5.13). They even have an innate knowledge of God's will, since it simply asks from them to "do to others as you would have them do to you" (7:12, see reading B, CAW 6.2). Thus from a consequentialist perspective, it is plausible to conclude that the primary goal of the Sermon on the Mount is to convince disciples to do God's will by emphasizing the good consequences of doing it (reading B, CAT 2).

This interpretation and its conclusions about what the Sermon is and says have also shown that this text underscores the good consequences of doing God's will, be it a reward (ὁ μισθὸς, 5:12; 6:1–6, 16–18), a blessing (μακάριοι οἱ..., 5:3–11), or a benefit of one kind or another (ταῦτα πάντα προστεθήσεται ὑμῖν, 6:33; cf. 6:8; 7:7–11), for the disciples themselves (the

---

50. Ibid., 26.

most numerous mentions), or for other people and for God. (See especially reading B, CAW 3.1, 3.2, 3.3.)

The plausibility of drawing from a consequentialist perspective conclusions about the teaching of the Sermon for the readers needs to be carefully examined because at first it seems that such conclusions go against all the preunderstandings of what Christian discipleship is all about for many people in European-American cultures.

What is puzzling is that we are led to conclude that the teaching of the Sermon on the Mount for readers is that they should want to do God's will by self-interest. This conclusion is based on textual evidence that is readily recognizable; there is no doubt that the Sermon stresses the disciples' self-interest in doing God's will, as the numerous promises of rewards (beginning with the beatitudes) show. Yet we question the plausibility of such conclusions. Is this to say that the Sermon teaches that we shall be rewarded for our good works (τὰ καλὰ ἔργα, 5:16)? That we should do good deeds in order to be personally blessed?

From a deontological perspective, these ironic questions have an obvious negative answer. The Sermon teaches, on the contrary, that we should not consider our own self-interest because according to the Sermon (i.e., its historical/realistic dimension) the interests of the community, and thus of other people, are primary (see below reading A, CAT 5).

From a consequentialist perspective, our answer is a resounding yes. It is in our self-interest to do God's will; we will be blessed, we will be rewarded, if we do so. The Sermon does not see any problem with people doing God's will because they want to be blessed. It has a very pragmatic perspective: people will not want to adopt such a radical way of life as long as they are not convinced that doing so is more beneficial for them than doing something else. In sum, doing God's will involves being convinced that God's will is "good for oneself."

Yet the very formulation of the preceding sentence shows that according to this consequentialist interpretation the teaching of the Sermon about rewards for good deeds is not necessarily antithetical to a recognition of the graciousness of God. If God's will is indeed "good for us," this means that to know God's will is to have received a gracious gift from God. It also means that God himself is "good for us" as "our Father in heaven" who is always ready to give us the good things we need (6:8-9; cf. 5:45-47; 6:33; 7:7-11). It follows that in order to be convinced to do God's will, we ultimately need to be convinced of God's goodness.

In this perspective, the question becomes, How, according to the Sermon on the Mount, are people convinced of the goodness of God and thus of the goodness of God's will? The conclusions of reading B about what the text presents as various stages of the story of the disciples (see the summary presentation in reading B, CAW 6.3) provide an answer — authoritative words are important for convincing people that God's will is good for them. Prom-

ises of rewards need to be trustworthy; thus the trustworthiness of Jesus as proclaimer of these promises plays an essential role (see below, reading B, CAT 4). For a deontological interpretation, this is enough to establish the reliability of the knowledge of God's will, but from a consequentialist perspective it soon appears that words, even if they are authoritative, are not sufficient to convince people of the goodness of God's will or of God's goodness toward them. No promise is fully trustworthy as long as it is not confirmed by concrete manifestations of God's goodness in human experience. Only if they can recognize the good things that God is doing for them now will people be in a position to give thanks to God (5:16). Good deeds by other people are such manifestations of God's goodness toward us.

Then there is the importance of the several mentions of the good consequences for God and for others of doing God's will. Our own good deeds on behalf of others most directly benefit these people. Yet they are also of benefit to God: these people give thanks to God because of our good deeds (5:16). God receives praises. God's name is hallowed (6:9). It also means that the people who benefit from our good deeds now recognize God's goodness. In sum, beyond the direct benefit others receive from our good deeds (e.g., a concrete manifestation of love), others benefit from these deeds by being convinced that God is good toward them. This recognition of God's goodness opens the way for these people to become themselves disciples willing to do God's will. Once they are convinced of God's goodness, they can recognize the goodness of God's will for them. Then they can recognize that it is good for them to do God's will; thus they will want to do it. They have become disciples and act as such.

Envisioned from a consequentialist perspective, this alternative interpretation (reading B) and its conclusions about what the Sermon says clearly teach that the self-interested recognition that God's will is "good for us" remains at the very center of the process of becoming disciple. This summary also makes clear that while self-interested deeds are ultimately good deeds for others and for God, altruistic deeds are also and primarily self-interested. This consequentialist conclusion about the teaching of the Sermon on the Mount regarding a fundamental aspect of discipleship as ethical practice needs to be clarified.

The Sermon on the Mount does not hesitate to promise rewards (e.g., 5:12, 46; 6:1–6, 16–18) for doing God's will or to present doing God's will as "good works" for which one should expect remuneration (μισθός). The Sermon (according to this interpretation) does not pretend to be disinterested. When one does something, e.g., pray in a certain way, one does it hoping to receive certain rewards. Thus as 6:1–18 expresses with three examples, the question is, What kind of rewards do you want? Rewards from human beings or from God? Should you not choose to do God's will in order to receive rewards from God (6:1)? These are the better rewards, the true blessings, the true treasures: "store up for yourselves treasures in heaven" (6:20).

What are these better rewards according to the Sermon on the Mount? Are they exclusively rewards in heaven – the future eschatological kingdom? The answer is an emphatic no. There are present as well as future positive consequences for doing God's will. In fact, the Sermon insists on the present manifestations of God's goodness by using the present tense in 5:3, 10, "theirs is the kingdom of heaven," as well as by making statements such as "he makes his sun rise on the evil and on the good, and sends rain on the righteous and on the unrighteous" (5:45, see also 6:25–34; 7:7–11).

What, according to the Sermon, are the present "good consequences" of doing God's will? What does "theirs is the kingdom of heaven" (5:3, 10) mean? Three examples are sufficient to explain: the good consequences for us of praying, of forgiving others, and of preserving marriage.

Regarding the good consequences for us of praying, Matthew 7:7–11 is significant. God's will requires disciples to pray (7:7; 6:9); if we do so, we will receive the things we need (7:8–11; 6:7–8; see also 6:25–34). Yet there is another blessing: by trusting (believing) in the goodness of God who gives us the good things we need, we recognize ourselves as children of "our Father in heaven." This trusting faith (contrasted with "little faith," 6:30), which is a necessary motivation for praying, is itself a blessing because having this trusting faith is being freed from anxiety (6:25–34) and from the stress of having to strive to serve two masters (6:24). It is also having a sound eye, which recognizes both the authority/power and the goodness of God who, as King of this present "kingdom," is in complete control of what happens in the world (6:25–34; 5:45) and who, as our caring Father in heaven, gives us to be in control of our lives in the world (freed from anxiety and from serving other masters). (See reading B, CAW 6.1ff.)

From these present blessings that result from praying according to God's will, one can infer that doing the rest of God's will, as presented in 5:21–48, has similarly good consequences for disciples. We can clarify this by considering these verses in terms of other passages in Matthew that express it more directly.[51]

The first (5:21–26), fifth (5:38–42), and sixth (5:43–47) antitheses demand that disciples maintain, restore, or establish a positive relationship with others (be they brothers and sisters within the church or outsiders) by being reconciled with them whatever might be the cost, including not resisting evil and loving one's enemies. All the aspects of this radical behavior involve or are comparable to forgiving people who have sinned against us. It is clear that such behavior is good for others. But is it good for us who behave in this way?

At first glance, it may seem to be costly self-denial. But from the consequentialist perspective, such a view would contradict the Sermon's teaching in regard to "overabundant righteousness" (doing God's will; doing good works).

---

51. Remember, we are interpreting the Sermon on the Mount as a part of the Gospel according to Matthew!

Conceiving of forgiving and loving others as a costly self-denial, performed exclusively for the sake of others and God, is necessarily leading us to put limits on our righteousness (even if we feel magnanimous and generous) instead of practicing an "overabundant righteousness" (5:20) that overflows the limits of the commandments by implementing their implications as well as their literal meaning.

Peter's attitude illustrates this misinterpretation when he asks, "How often should I forgive? As many as seven times?" (18:21). Is he not generous? In the previous verses, Jesus has presented a church regulation according to which forgiveness must be offered three different times to a sinful member (18:15-20). Now Peter proposes to forgive seven times! But he has totally misunderstood Jesus' teaching. It is not for the sake of the other (the sinner) that we seek to bring him or her back into the church and that we forgive, but because it is "gain" for us: "if he or she (who has sinned against you) listens to you, you have gained your brother or sister" (18:15, author's translation). I hear someone objecting, "Indeed, forgiving, being reconciled, not resisting evil, loving enemies might, sometimes, make us gain a brother or a sister. But is it worthwhile in view of the high cost?" Oh yes, it is worth it! When one has gained a brother or a sister, one can pray with her or him. Then the blessing becomes clear: "Truly I tell you, if two of you agree on earth about anything you ask, it will be done for you by my Father in heaven. For where two or three are gathered in my name, I am there among them" (18:19-20). If one does not forgive, it will not be long before one does not have any brother or sister! Then two essential blessings will be missing: God's response to one's prayers; Jesus' presence. Yes, forgiving, gaining brothers and sisters, is good for us! So why would we want to put any limitation to forgiving? "Not seven times, But I tell you, seventy-seven times" (18:22).

Similarly, the second and third antitheses (5:27-30), which require that disciples avoid lust (as well as adultery) and preserve marriage, are demands that disciples should meet, not only for the sake of others but also for their own sake. This is made explicit in 19:3-9, where Jesus emphasizes that avoiding divorce is "good for us," insofar as marriage is a good gift from God (19:4-6; divorce being permissible when this is not the case, 5:32; 19:9). If one understands that marriage is a good gift from God (as the disciples do not in 19:10-12), who would want to divorce? This would be depriving oneself of a good gift from God! Once again, God's will, despite its radical character, is good for us.

In sum, when we truly recognize that God's will is good for us, we are ready, indeed eager, to make God's will our own will. According to this interpretation of the Sermon, nothing else (beyond a lack of will) prevents us from doing God's will, so our righteousness shall become overabundant (5:20), overflowing the limitations of usual human behavior (5:46-47), as the light on a lampstand lights all in the house (5:15). Consequently, the central issue — indeed, the only issue — for the Sermon on the Mount (according to this interpretation) is, How shall we truly believe that God's will is good for us?

Why should we believe all the promises and affirmations we read in the Sermon on the Mount? These promises are very easy to brush aside as "too good to be true," "too idealistic," or again as "leading to a fanatical behavior."[52] Actually, the Sermon itself addresses this question. Having the slightest doubts about the goodness of God and of his will is to have "little faith" (6:30), anxiety (6:25-34), a divided eye (6:22-23). Then as we strive to serve two masters (6:24), we are in fact unwilling to make God's will our own will. The question becomes, Is the Sermon on the Mount in itself — as a sermon, as a discourse — enough to convince us to trust completely in the goodness of God and God's will?

The Sermon and its teaching give a negative answer to this question. We give thanks to God and thus acknowledge God's goodness only when we recognize this goodness as manifested for us in concrete ways: in the form of good works performed by people acting in the name of God (5:16). In sum, we can expect the Sermon to convince hearers and readers to do God's will and to be disciples, only insofar as its promises and commands are uttered by someone (Jesus or one of the disciples after him, 5:19; 28:20) who manifests the goodness of God among us. This is already speaking of the conclusions about the Christological teaching of the Sermon reached by this consequentialist interpretation (see below, reading B, CAW 4). Yet this goodness of God should also be recognizable in the disciples' good works (5:16).

The disciples' good deeds are perceived as manifestations of God's goodness, when it is clear that the disciples are themselves totally dependent on God, their heavenly Father. This point is repeatedly emphasized in the second part of the Sermon. Ideal disciples are aware that their Father knows what they need before they ask (6:9) and is ready to give them the good things they need (7:7-11). Therefore, they are aware that they do not need treasures on earth (6:19-21); that they do not need to serve mammon (6:24); that they do not need to be anxious about their lives, food, drink, and clothing (6:25-34). "Your heavenly Father knows that you need all these things. But strive first for the kingdom of God and his righteousness, and all these things will be given to you as well" (6:32b-33).

Consequently, disciples can afford to make themselves totally vulnerable, giving to others both their coat and their cloak (5:40), as well as anything that belongs to them (5:41). By being meek (5:5), by accepting vulnerability in all kinds of ways — loving their enemies (5:44), being peacemakers (5:9), being persecuted, taunted, reviled (5:10-12), as well as by taking no money, no bag, or other supplies (according to the missionary discourse, 10:9-10) — the disciples demonstrate their own weaknesses, their lack of personal resources. Whatever they do is done with God's resources. Anyone who sees the disci-

---

52. Strecker, *Sermon,* 17, and reading A, CAT 3.

ples' good works recognizes the appropriateness of giving thanks to God for them — these good deeds could not have been performed without the help of God and are manifestations of God's goodness.

The disciples' lowliness is what makes them true disciples. Conversely, any expression of self- confidence in doing good works is actually a sin that tarnishes them and prevents them from manifesting God's goodness. This interpretation might explain why one needs to be forgiven precisely when one has done good works — such as forgiving others (the attitude that summarizes most of the teaching in 5:21–48). Although it may sound strange, from the perspective of this consequentialist reading the petition about forgiveness in the Lord's Prayer might be interpreted as follows. According to this prayer, we are supposed to ask for forgiveness ("forgive us our debts," 6:12) precisely when we have done good works (when "we have also forgiven our debtors," 6:12; see also 6:14–15, which underscores this point). Is it because receiving forgiveness is a reward for our having forgiven others? In a sense it is. But in the context of the Lord's Prayer, consisting as it does of petitions for the things we need in order to fulfill our vocation as disciples (see reading B, CAW 5.14, 5.2, 6.3), it appears that we need forgiveness precisely when we have done good works. So that seeing our good works people might give glory to God (5:16), "our" good work (forgiving others) must be shown to be a manifestation of God's goodness, and thus must be purified. The implicit or explicit claim that such good works are ours (e.g., done out of some qualities that are ours) must be forgiven so as to make clear that this is God doing good things through us; true forgiveness on our part is possible only insofar as God works it in us.[53]

Whether or not these suggestions about the petition regarding forgiveness are plausible, from the consequentialist perspective it appears that a similar point can be made regarding Jesus' own good works. As long as they are perceived as Jesus' good works, one celebrates Jesus' fame and follows him for inappropriate reasons, as the crowds did (4:24–25). It is only when it becomes clear that Jesus' deeds are manifestations of God's goodness, God's deeds for us because Jesus is Emmanuel, God among us, that one can become a disciple. This clarification (purification) of the meaning of Jesus' ministry will ultimately occur on the cross. In this consequentialist interpretation, the Sermon on the Mount, and more generally the Gospel according to Matthew, underscores the lowliness of Jesus during his ministry — in direct contrast with a deontological interpretation.

---

53. From such a perspective, one can understand why Jesus himself needs to be baptized (3:15) — his good deeds must also be cleansed to make it clear that he does manifest God's goodness among us (as is indeed manifested after his baptism, 3:16–17).

Reading A, CAT 4: The Plausibility of Discipleship as Submitting to the Authoritative Teaching of the Exalted Lord and Judge — A High Christology

Several conclusions of Strecker's interpretation, focused on the historical/realistic dimension of the Sermon on the Mount, need to be taken into account, even though they are more about Christology than about discipleship. As we have already noted, the logic of understanding discipleship as deontological ethical practice recognizes the Sermon as authoritative in order to be received as the true expression of God's will, i.e., as a series of hermeneutical principles that are to guide the implementation (fulfillment) of the law and the prophets and of Jesus' teaching in the concreteness of the life of the community.

In this interpretation, the Sermon on the Mount owes its authority to Jesus, the Preacher of the mount, whose extraordinary authority puts him in a position *of revealing God's eternal will* (note Jesus' very different function according to a consequentialist interpretation; see below, reading B, CAT 4). Jesus has this authority when he preaches the Sermon because, according to this interpretation of Matthew, he is not only the Son of God but also the exalted Kyrios who has "all authority in heaven and on earth" and will be the eschatological Judge. This high Christology, believing in a Christ who has an extraordinary authority, is an intrinsic part of discipleship as a deontological ethical practice.

The Authority of the Son of God. The scholars who propose a deontological interpretation[54] reach this *conclusion about the teaching* of the Sermon on the Mount because for them Matthew 1–4 as the prologue to Jesus' ministry establishes the identity and authority of Jesus as *the Son of God.*[55] As soon as he begins his ministry, the Son of God exercises his extraordinary authority by calling four disciples with an unconditional command, "Follow me." As we saw in chap. 2, they submit to it by abandoning everything and obeying. It is to such disciples that the Sermon is addressed (5:1–2); it is another authoritative word to which they must submit. Such demonstrations of extraordinary authority over both supernatural powers (Satan, angels, 4:1–11; diseases and demon possession, 4:23–24) and

---

54. This brief paragraph summarizes salient points of the interpretations of Matthew 1–4 by Georg Strecker, *Der Weg der Gerechtigkeit: Untersuchung zur Theologie des Matthäus* (Göttingen: Vandenhoeck & Ruprecht, 1962; 3d ed., 1971), and Jack D. Kingsbury, *Matthew: Structure, Christology, Kingdom* (Philadelphia: Fortress, 1975), and *Matthew as Story* (Minneapolis: Fortress, 1986).

55. This is first expressed by the story of the miraculous birth of Jesus (1:18–25), and repeatedly confirmed by the magi's acknowledgment of his authority as king of the Jews (2:1–12), by his fulfillment of the prophets (1:22–23; 2:5–6, 13–15; 4:14–16), by the voice from heaven at his baptism (3:13–17), and by the story of the temptation (4:1–11) that ends with a demonstration of the authority of the Son of God: commanding the devil ("Away with you, Satan!") and being obeyed by him and served by angels.

human beings (disciples, 4:18–22) demonstrates Jesus' authority as the Son of God, even as he preaches the Sermon. Thus the scholarly interpretation focused on the historical/realistic dimension of the Gospel of Matthew (as illustrated by our discussion of 4:18–22 in chapter 2) supports the conclusion that the teaching of the Sermon is an authoritative revelation of God's will, and thus supports the broader conclusion that discipleship according to the Sermon on the Mount is a deontological ethical practice.

The Authority of the Exalted Kyrios.   As Strecker says, the Sermon is preached by the "exalted Lord" (or the "resurrected and exalted *Kyrios*").[56] According to reading A, the authority of Jesus as the exalted Kyrios is manifested throughout the Sermon, but especially in the antitheses (5:21–48; note the formula, "You have heard that it was said...but I say to you"; see reading A, CAW 5.1). In sum, "the Kyrios stands over the Torah; his authority makes it possible to be critical of the Torah, which leads even to dissolving individual commandments and setting up new instructions."[57] Thus as Strecker says about Jesus' fulfillment of the law (5:17), "By power of his authority, Jesus, as God's ambassador, reveals the intended meaning of the Old Testament Torah and thus leads to its actualization (cf. 19:8)."[58] In sum, while the law and the prophets do teach God's eternal will, one can truly have access to their teaching only when they are authoritatively interpreted by the exalted Kyrios.

The Authority of the Eschatological Judge.   This radical reinterpretation of Scripture (as well as the other expressions of God's will found in the Sermon) is also shown to be authoritative by the fact that the Preacher on the mount is the eschatological Judge. Jesus is identified as the eschatological Judge in 7:22–23: "On that day many will say to me, 'Lord, Lord, did we not prophecy in your name....' Then I will declare to them, 'I never knew you, go away from me, you evildoers.'"[59] This means that Jesus' teaching ("these words of mine," 7:24) is God's will as he utters it ("the will of my Father in heaven," 7:21) and as such is binding. It has a juridical status. It decides "who belongs" and "who does not belong" in the eschatological kingdom (7:21–23), and therefore (cf. 5:19–20) who belongs and does not belong to the church, i.e., to the group of disciples of Jesus, the Son of God, the exalted Kyrios, the eschatological Judge.

---

56. As Strecker repeatedly expresses throughout his study of the Sermon on the Mount, beginning with his discussion of 5:1–2: Strecker, *Sermon,* 26.

57. Strecker, *Sermon,* 62; see also 56.

58. Ibid., 55; see also 56, 62–95, 178–79.

59. Ibid., 164–68; see also 168–72 on 7:24–27.

The various scholarly interpretations supporting the conclusion that discipleship according to the Sermon on the Mount is a deontological ethical practice note the high Christology of this text. Yet some scholars are more tentative than Strecker and Kingsbury. For instance, Lambrecht[60] and Barth[61] express such a hesitation (see also Zumstein[62] and Marxsen[63]). They recognize that while a high Christology is consistent with Matthew's overall presentation of Jesus, one cannot simply ignore the passages that emphasize Jesus' lowliness. The ambivalence in Matthew's presentation is interpreted as coming from Matthew's effort to express both Jesus' extraordinary authority, which makes him unique, and the continuity of his teaching with past revelations, which makes him recognizable as one of us (a low Christology).[64] But in these deontological interpretations, it is clear that the Sermon underscores Jesus' extraordinary authority.[65]

Reading B, CAT 4: The Plausibility of Discipleship as a Continuation of Jesus' Ministry — A Low Christology

An understanding of discipleship as a consequentialist ethical practice involves a relationship with Jesus that presupposes a low Christology, in contrast to the high Christology associated with the understanding of discipleship as a deontological ethical practice. According to the alternative interpretation (reading B),[66] while readers need to acknowledge Jesus' authority, it is also important not to overvalue his authority (see reading B, CAW 4.3). According to this interpretation, people are convinced to do God's will (1) if they can

---

60. Lambrecht, *Eh bien*, 195–200. He notes that the Sermon on the Mount is not focused on Jesus, and thus that its Christology should not be overemphasized, since it is only implicit. Yet he acknowledges that the Christology implied by the Sermon on the Mount is clearly a high Christology, as is shown by the kind of teaching found in the Sermon on the Mount: God's command.

61. Barth, "Matthew's Understanding," 125–37.

62. Zumstein, *La condition du croyant.*

63. Willi Marxsen, *New Testament Foundations for Christian Ethics*, trans. O. C. Dean Jr. (Minneapolis: Fortress, 1993), 231–48.

64. Barth, "Matthew's Understanding," 137–59. For Barth, this concern for continuity is mainly meant to express that Jesus' teaching is not a "new" law in any sense of the term, but rather an expression of God's eternal will and an authoritative admonition that needs to be heard against the background of the forthcoming eschatological judgment.

65. In these deontological interpretations, the very textual features that express continuity between Jesus' teaching and the law and the prophets (e.g., 5:17) and which, in other interpretations, are viewed as expressions of Jesus' lowliness, are viewed as expressions of the extraordinary authority of Jesus and of his teaching. Note again the reverse interpretations of Matthew 5:17 in Strecker's and Kingsbury's interpretation (reading A, CAW 4.2) and in the alternative interpretation (reading B, CAW 4.2 and especially 4.3, "Matthew 5:17 Is a Warning against Overvaluing Jesus' Authority").

66. I refer to the alternative interpretation focused on the story/plot dimension of the Sermon, its *conclusions about what the Sermon is and says* (reading B, CAW 1ff.) and the preceding consequentialist *conclusions about the teaching* of the Sermon (reading B, CAT 1, 2, 3).

trust in Jesus' promises; (2) if they can recognize his teaching as a true expression of God's will; and (3) if it is clear that God's will is "good for us." The first condition demands acknowledgment of Jesus' authority; but the second and third conditions cannot be truly met if one overvalues his authority.

The Preacher on the mount meets all these conditions, being presented by Matthew as a manifestation of God's authority and power as well as God's goodness, i.e., as Emmanuel, "God with us." Jesus manifests God's authority, power, and goodness among us and for us by showing that the good deeds he performs and the good words he proclaims are not his deeds and words, but God's. Like anybody else, he receives all the good things (including power and authority) that he needs for his ministry from the God whom he invites us to call "our Father in heaven" because we also can depend on him as the provider of all the good things we need.

Jesus as a Child of God.   *These suggestions, which originate in the logic of a consequentialist interpretation, can be supported by an interpretation of the Gospel of Matthew focused on its story/plot dimension.*[67] *According to such a narrative interpretation, Matthew 1–4 establishes that Jesus is a child of God almost in the same sense as disciples are children of God (5:9, 45; cf. 6:9), thus my use of the phrase "child of God," instead of the title "Son of God." This is not to deny his special status; yet Jesus' relationship to us is emphasized. Matthew 1 emphasizes the extraordinary character of Jesus' conception and birth, and thus sets him apart as an extraordinary child of God who, in a unique way, will manifest God among us — Emmanuel (1:18–25). As son of David and son of Abraham (1:1), he is also inscribed in a long genealogy, if in a somewhat strange way (1:2–17).*[68] *In this perspective, it becomes clear that God's interventions in Jesus' birth (1:18–25), infancy (2:1–23), and baptism (4:1–11) are in continuity with God's interventions in the history of*

---

67. I suggest here an interpretation of the entire Gospel along the lines suggested in chapters 2 and 3 for reading B, by contrast with an interpretation of the Gospel in terms of its ending (where Jesus has all authority) as a historical/realistic interpretation (reading A) does.

68. In a patrilinear perspective, this genealogy unfolds through the agency of fathers who beget sons. But Matthew notes the role of five women: Tamar (1:3), Rahab (1:5), Ruth (1:5), the wife of Uriah (1:6), and Mary (1:16). If it had not been for them, the unfolding of this genealogy would have been interrupted repeatedly. The case of Mary clarifies the significance of the mentions of the four other women: as God through Mary provides a son of David, son of Abraham "conceived in her ... from the Holy Spirit" (1:18–25), so God intervened through the four named women to maintain the continuity of the genealogy. According to this interpretation focused on the unfolding of the plot, these women are manifestations of God's powerful interventions in human affairs; they are manifestations of God's goodness among us, as Jesus is in another way. The lesson of this genealogy is that being children of Abraham and of David (a blessing) is not merely due to human begetting, but also to divine intervention, without which this genealogical continuity would have been repeatedly interrupted. To those who do not recognize the benevolent hand of God in human affairs and claim a special status due to their human ancestry, John the Baptist says, "God is able from these stones to raise up children to Abraham" (3:9). For these and many other connotations of Matthew 1, see the insightful and detailed study by Robin D. Mattison, *To Beget or Not to Beget: Presupposition and Persuasion in Matthew Chapter One* (Ph.D. Diss., Vanderbilt University, 1995).

Israel (who, as God's child, was also called out of Egypt, 2:15, and was also tempted in the wilderness for "forty" years, 4:1-2). Thus God's interventions in Jesus' life could have been foreseen by the prophets, whose words are fulfilled in what happens to Jesus (1:22-23; 2:5-6, 15, 17-18; 4:14-16). Jesus is an extraordinary child of God, not because he would have in himself (as a part of his nature) a special power/authority, as John wrongly thinks (3:11-15)[69] and as the devil intimates ("if you are the Son of God...," 4:3, 6), but because he faithfully fulfills God's will.[70]

In sum, it is by fully assuming his humanity — that is, his dependence on God's interventions, his need for God's word as nourishment, his submission to God's will — that Jesus is an extraordinary child of God, the Son of God, who shares in God's authority and power. As such he can be seen by his hearers as having an exceptional authority for proclaiming an authoritative teaching (7:28-29). Yet this recognition of Jesus' authority is quite ambiguous. Why are the crowds alone in acknowledging his authority? Do the novice disciples share the crowds' view? Is this recognition truly appropriate?

Jesus as Emmanuel. *Jesus is truly Emmanuel, the manifestation of God's power and authority and of God's goodness among us because it is with God's power and authority that he proclaims "good" news and performs good deeds such as healings (4:23).[71] This is not to deny that the Preacher on the mount displays an exceptional authority. He blesses people. The beatitudes (5:3-10) are "words of power" that bring about the transformation of a reality.[72] Thus he has an extraordinary "priestly" authority. Similarly, through the antitheses ("you have heard... but I tell you," 5:21-48), as well as through his teaching on alms, prayer, and fasting (6:1-18) and elsewhere in the Sermon on the Mount (e.g., 7:12), Jesus presents himself as the authoritative interpreter of Torah, indeed, as having an authority comparable to that of Torah (the word of God), since his teaching is an expression of God's will*

---

69. This interpretation of 3:11–15 is the same as the one in Patte, *Matthew*, 50–51.

70. Jesus is an extraordinary child of God because he makes God's will his will and thus "fulfill[s] all righteousness" (3:15), or, as is expressed in 4:1–11, he acknowledges that God's word is the good food that he needs as other human beings also do (4:4; quoting Dt 8:3), and thus readily submits to God's good authority as any human being should (4:7, 10). It is as a consequence of his submission to God's will that he is the Son, "the Beloved, with whom I am well pleased" (3:17), who has power/authority to command ("Go") and be obeyed by Satan (4:10–11).

71. Jesus does not have power/authority on his own, as the eschatological Judge would have, and thus contrarily to the expectation of John the Baptist (3:11–12). This interpretation focused on the unfolding of the plot dimension underscores that Jesus rebuked John for his "high" view of him that John expressed when he initially refused to baptize Jesus as he baptized everybody else (3:13–14). Jesus does not proclaim the coming of the judgment, but the good news of the kingdom (4:23). Edwards makes similar remarks, but without drawing as clear a conclusion, because he does not focus as much on the unfolding of the plot. Edwards, *Matthew's Story of Jesus*, 15–18.

72. See William A. Beardslee, *Literary Criticism of the New Testament*, Guides to Biblical Scholarship (Philadelphia: Fortress, 1970), 36–39.

(7:21, 24). Finally, in 7:21-23, the Preacher presents himself as the eschatological Judge, and identifies his own words (7:24) with God's will (7:21). In a sense, the Preacher on the mount suggests that the origin of his manifold authority is in his special relationship with God, about whom he speaks as "my Father in heaven" (7:21).

Nevertheless, the Preacher on the mount emphasizes that the authority he uses is not his, but God's. The beatitudes are indeed words of power that affect those who receive them, but their actual power resides in what they proclaim — the kingdom of heaven as a present and future blessing from God. The good news (τὸ εὐαγγέλιον) is that God is in the process of bringing about his kingdom (4:17) and its blessings (5:3, 10).

Similarly, Jesus displays an authority comparable to that of Torah, yet this is not because he has authority over Torah. He is not superior to the law and the prophets, as he would be if he had come to abolish them (5:17a). Rather, he totally submits himself to their authority: "I have come not to abolish but to fulfill" (οὐκ ἦλθον καταλῦσαι ἀλλὰ πληρῶσαι, 5:17b). It is because the Preacher on the mount fulfills Torah — nourishes himself with God's words in Scripture (4:4), internalizes it, making God's will his own will — that he has the authority to exhort the disciples to do the same. It is precisely because he submits to the authority of the Torah that Jesus has the authority to radically interpret it for the new situation of the disciples in the time when the kingdom is coming, as he does in the antitheses (5:21-48) and the rest of the Sermon. The authority of the Preacher on the mount is an authority that he receives from the law and the prophets (words "from the mouth of God," 4:4) to which he submits — as he is declared God's Son (3:17) after "fulfilling all righteousness" (3:15), and as he h s the authority to send away Satan (4:10-11) after nourishing himself with Scripture and submitting to it (4:3-10).

This means that disciples who submit to God's will and authority, as Jesus does, can expect to have the same authoritative position that he has. This is what the Preacher on the mount means when he emphasizes that the disciples are themselves children of the Father in heaven. Consequently, they should behave as their Father does (following Jesus' example, 5:45), and they should pray, together with Jesus, "Our Father in heaven" (6:9). As he is a child of God, so they are children of God, even if many people do not yet recognize it (a recognition promised for the future, 5:9, but lacking in the present, 5:10, 11-12).

Jesus' and the Disciples' Comparable Authority.   *The authority of Jesus and that of the disciples (as fishers of people faithfully doing God's will) are comparable. This suggestion is confirmed by passages throughout the gospel.*

1. The description of the disciples' ministry in 10:5-8 is strikingly parallel to the description of Jesus' ministry in 4:17-9:38; the disciples are to preach the same message and perform the same miracles that Jesus performed; they have the same power/authority that he has.

2. Several passages about the disciples' "little faith" suggest that if they had true faith they would have at their disposal as much power/authority that Jesus has because in each case it is God's power/authority; e.g., Peter could have walked on the water (14:28–33), the disciples could have cured the epileptic boy, or could have moved a mountain (17:14–20; see 21:18–22).

3. The statements in which Jesus promises the disciples that they will be eschatological judges together with him (19:28) make the same point; indeed, they already have the power of the keys of the kingdom, which includes having the authority to judge who will and will not enter the kingdom (18:18; see 16:19).

Since according to this interpretation Jesus' authority and ministry are comparable to the disciples', what we have just learned about discipleship can lead to a greater understanding of Jesus' status and function.

As we have seen ("Overall Plot of the Story of the Disciples," chap. 3, reading B, CAW 6.3), according to this alternative interpretation the goal of the disciples' ministry is to perform good deeds (stage 5), so that others may "see your good works and give glory to your Father in heaven" (5:16; stages 7 and 2), and consequently recognize the goodness of God, trust in God and have faith (stage 3), want to do God's will (stage 4), and thus become disciples (stage 5). It is not difficult to recognize that Jesus' ministry is similar. One of its goals, if not its main goal, is also to "make disciples" (cf. stage 7), — i.e., to make fishers of people (4:19), out of the four fishers and the crowds. For this purpose, as in the case of the disciples' ministry, Jesus performs good works (e.g., his healings; stage 5), so that people might perceive God's goodness (stage 2), glorify God (stage 3), make God's will their own will (stage 4), recognizing it as "good for them" and thus being willing to have an overabundant righteousness (cf. 5:20; stage 5).[73]

As in the case of the disciples, the positive result of Jesus' ministry (people being willing to do God's will and to become disciples) can only be expected if these people actually give glory to God when they see Jesus' good works. How is it that people recognize manifestations of God's goodness in Jesus' good works? As in the case of the disciples (see reading B, CAT 3), when the lowliness — the humanity — of Jesus is clear, and thus when it is apparent that without God he could not do the good things he does.

---

73. This clarifies (for this interpretation of Mt) the relationship between Jesus' preaching and teaching (including the Sermon on the Mount, Mt 5–7) and his healings and other acts manifesting God's "mercy" (Mt 8–9; cf. the quotation of Hos 6:6 in Mt 9:13, "I desire mercy and not sacrifice"). Without good deeds manifesting the goodness of God and of his will, the teaching of his will would be pointless; the people taught would not want to do it! Conversely, without the teaching of God's will, good deeds would not engender new good deeds performed with the help of God's authority and power by new disciples; the beneficiary of the good deeds would not perceive them as an invitation to serve God and neighbor.

We have noted how Jesus' lowliness is indicated in the Sermon on the Mount, despite the fact that this Sermon must also be an authoritative speech as an expression of God's will.[74] Jesus' humanity and his total dependence on God's power and authority are most directly visible in the crucifixion. When he is abandoned by God (27:46), Jesus loses the power that allowed him to save (heal) others (27:38–42), as well as the knowledge of God's purpose and will that he taught with so much authority – he does not even know why he is crucified (27:46). In sum, the death of Jesus on the cross most clearly demonstrates that all his good deeds were manifestations of God's power, authority, and goodness. All his teaching (including the Sermon) is an expression of God's will – a will that we should want to do because it is good for us.[75] The more he submits in obedience to God's will (26:39, 42), even death on the cross, the more his entire ministry – words and deeds – gains in authority, as God's, indeed, the more authority he receives: "all authority in heaven and on earth" as the exalted Lord and the eschatological Judge (28:16–20), an authority that he did not have during his ministry.

In sum, according to this consequentialist interpretation, the Sermon on the Mount itself requires that Jesus be recognized as our brother who became our Lord, the exalted Kyrios, through his humble obedience to God's will. The more the limitations of his humanity during his ministry are recognized, the more authoritative is his teaching because it becomes clear that it is truly an expression of God's will, which is good for us and thus good to do.

---

74. We can also note that it is when he submits like anybody else to John's baptism (3:11), that it is made manifest for the crowds that he is truly God's son (3:16–17). The voice from heaven is addressed to other people, since it speaks of Jesus in the third person: "This is my Son" (and not, "you are my Son," as in Mk 1:11 and Lk 3:22).

75. This final and radical demonstration of Jesus' humanity and his dependence on God is necessary because, for all the people who witness his deeds and who hear his teaching, the temptation is to believe that the extraordinary power and authority that Jesus displays are his, rather than given to him by God. For instance, in 7:28–29 the crowds' response to the Sermon on the Mount is ambivalent: they affirm Jesus' authority without acknowledging that this is God's authority that Jesus manifests. Even though it is called "great faith," the centurion's recognition of Jesus' great power/authority might itself be ambiguous, unless one keeps in mind that for him authority is necessarily something granted by superiors — not a permanent attribute of the person (8:5–13). The disciples' response to the calming of the storm is most inappropriate; although Jesus emphasized his lowliness in 8:20, the disciples express their amazement by saying, "What kind of person is this, that even the wind and the sea obey him?" (8:27, author's translation). They attribute the authority to calm the sea to Jesus, without even suspecting it might be God's authority! Yet an appropriate response to Jesus' ministry is possible. For instance, following the forgiving and healing of the paralytic in 9:2–7, the crowds have the appropriate response: "When the crowds saw it, they were filled with awe, and they glorified God (ἐδόξασαν τὸν θεὸν, not Jesus!) who had given such authority to human beings (τὸν δόντα ἐξουσίαν τοιαύτην τοῖς ἀνθρώποις, and not merely to Jesus!)" (9:8). Such a response elucidates the significance of Jesus' healings: in the same way that forgiveness of sins is given by Jesus in the name of God, so Jesus' miracles are performed with the power/authority of God; they are manifestations of God's goodness or "mercy" (as is emphasized in Jesus' explanation of his eating with sinners, 9:12–13); God is the one who should be glorified (9:8).

Reading A, CAT 5: The Plausibility of Discipleship as Implementing the Sermon's Regulations for Life in the Church as the Sphere of God's Eschatological Rule

In sum, according to the *conclusions about the teaching* regarding discipleship of the Sermon on the Mount read with a deontological pre-understanding of the moral life (reading A, CAT 1, above), the Sermon is a proclamation of God's eternal will (reading A, CAT 2) addressed to the disciples (reading A, CAT 3) by the Son of God — the exalted Kyrios and eschatological Judge (reading A, CAT 4). As such the Sermon expresses the requirements for belonging to the βασιλεία τῶν οὐρανῶν. This Greek phrase refers not only to the future "kingdom of heaven" but also to God's eschatological rule (or "reign") as realized in the church, i.e., the community of disciples who take on themselves "the yoke of the reign of God" by agreeing to fulfill God's eternal will according to the teaching of the eschatological Lord. Thus the Sermon on the Mount is the promulgation by the eschatological Lord of the regulations that govern life in the community that is the "sphere of God's eschatological Rule."[76] Conversely, these regulations serve as a basis for judging whether or not someone belongs to the church (see reading A, CAW 5.3–6.3, which I summarized in a few sentences).

In this perspective, the beatitudes (5:3–12) are read "as the entrance requirement(s) for the kingdom of God,"[77] which spell out what one must have achieved before being counted as belonging to the kingdom. This includes being "poor in spirit," i.e., totally submitting to the demands expressed in the words of the exalted Kyrios who preaches the Sermon on the Mount. For this, one must adopt a radical way of life already spelled out in the beatitudes: "active deeds that fulfill the new law of Christ: active dedication to the high goal of meekness, friendliness, and gentleness — deeds that are determined not by anger, brutality, or enmity, but entirely by goodness," as Strecker says about 5:5.[78] Because of the radical character of the way of life demanded from disciples — a righteousness qualitatively better than other kinds of righteousness because it implements the law in terms of the principles of love, perfection, and judgment revealed by the exalted Lord — the demarcation between insiders and outsiders is clear. Those who do not exhibit this better righteousness do not belong to the kingdom and to the church (5:20).

Matthew 5:17–20 and the entire Sermon on the Mount function as "sentences of holy law," as Käsemann says regarding 5:19,[79] i.e., they are

---

76. Kingsbury's most appropriate phrase, in *Matthew as Story*, 104–8.

77. Strecker, *Sermon*, 33, passim.

78. Ibid., 36.

79. Ernst Käsemann, "Sentences of Holy Law in the New Testament," in *New Testament Questions of Today* (Philadelphia: Fortress, 1969), 66–81 (especially 78). Käsemann says this regarding 5:19 (because of its specific form); in effect a deontological interpretation expends this qualification to the entire Sermon on the Mount.

regulations on the basis of which the behavior of the members of the community can be judged, to the extent of being eventually excluded from the
church. People who do not practice the better righteousness demanded by
Jesus' teaching in the Sermon on the Mount — and thus do not fulfill their
vocation as salt and light of the world (5:13) — are to be excluded from the
church as the sphere of God's eschatological rule.[80]

Strecker and Kingsbury do not emphasize this point (although they clearly
express it) because they are preoccupied with insisting that the Sermon not
be construed as a rigid, legalistic set of regulations. Since the better righteousness required from disciples (church members) is characterized by a practice
of the law constantly being reinterpreted for new, concrete situations in
terms of love, perfection, and judgment, the use of the Sermon as a set of
church regulations must always be contextualized. To begin with, one should
remember that "with the judgment you make you will be judged" (7:2).
More specifically, one should judge others as one judges oneself (7:5; 5:29–
30), or better, one should judge others as one would like to be judged by
others (according to the Golden Rule, 7:12). The flexibility of the regulations
on which this judgment of others is based is due in part to the fact that the
regulations take into account the specific situations in which the teaching is
to be implemented, as is exemplified by the several stages of reinterpretation
still recognizable in several passages (e.g., 5:21–26, 38–42; 6:19–34).[81]

It remains that judging others in terms of the Sermon on the Mount as
a set of church regulations is part of what is expected from disciples because without such an enforcement of ecclesiastical rules the community
of disciples would become unable to perform its vocation of salt and light
of the world (5:13–16). For the sake of its vocation, the church must be
characterized by a way of life clearly different from that of the world; as
the sphere of God's eschatological rule, the church must be clearly distinct
from its environment. The boundary between inside and outside must be
clearly marked. Thus the good behavior (better righteousness) of a disciple must clearly identify him or her as belonging the church, not the
world.[82]

---

80. The tasteless salt is to be "thrown out" (5:13), as the false prophets who fail to bear
good fruit are to be "thrown into the fire" (7:15–19), and as those who do not do Jesus'
teaching are told to "go away" by the eschatological Judge (7:21–23). In other cases, the sentence is not exclusion: members of the community can be judged to be "least" or "great in
the kingdom of heaven" (5:19), and consequently least or great in the church as the sphere of
God's eschatological rule, according to whether or not they practice and teach others to practice the least of these commandments. Here, I underscore points that Strecker makes without
emphasis or that he simply implies. This is the case with his comments on 5:19; he mentions
Käsemann's interpretation, and actually defends it against opposite views, but does not make
explicit the ecclesiology implied by it. See Strecker, *Sermon*, 56–57. Yet, this ecclesiological
teaching is in the logic of the CATs that he underscores.

81. Strecker, *Sermon*, 64–70, 81–85, 130–41.

82. Ibid., 184–85.

In this perspective, the teaching of the Sermon on the Mount is primarily understood as setting up limits to the disciples' behavior. It defines their behavior negatively to ensure that the distinctiveness of the community is apparent; the disciples' duties are minimally defined as their participation in the collective enterprise of the community (its vocation as salt and light of the world). Thus the Sermon includes, on the one hand, negative admonitions, such as "do not resist an evildoer" (5:39), which set the community of disciples apart from the rest of society because of the distinctive behavior of its members, and on the other hand, positive expressions of duties vis-à-vis other members of the community — maintaining or reestablishing good relationships with them, as expressed in the first four antitheses (5:21–37) and the Golden Rule.[83] The community is posited as the ultimate good; it is the present manifestation of the kingdom. Belonging to it is a proleptic participation in the kingdom. Thus the disciples' vocation as salt and light of the world is to draw people into this community. For this purpose, disciples need to make this community clearly visible (as "a city built on a hill," 5:14). Emphasizing the community's boundaries, maintaining its cohesion, and strengthening the intersubjective relations within it are primary duties for its members. Thus whatever a member of the community (a disciple) does should be something readily acceptable by the rest of the community — something that would reinforce the cohesion of the community rather than be divisive. For this reason, the disciples' behavior should be consistent with the general principles that govern the life of the community. In sum, "the standard of value that is established by the Golden Rule" and the rest of the Sermon on the Mount is, according to Strecker, comparable "to the categorical imperative of Immanuel Kant, according to which a person should act 'so that the maxim of your will could at any time also be valid as a principle of general legislation.' "[84]

The fact that Strecker interprets the Golden Rule in terms of Kant once again shows that his interpretation of the Sermon is deontological.[85] Actually, his conclusions (as summarized above) directly reflect a deontological preunderstanding of the moral life for which, as we have seen, intersubjective relations in a community are primary. For Strecker, the Sermon offers what a deontological preunderstanding of the moral life posits as "the basic requisites of human life," i.e., the standards of behavior that must be implemented in the human community, beginning with the community of disciples (the church). Without such an implementation there is

---

83. For Strecker, the Golden Rule in the Sermon on the Mount is the equivalent of the commandment of agape, as expressed in 5:21–48 (*Sermon*, 155). Consequently, as one implements the Golden Rule one envisions "others" as disciples, i.e., members of the church whose behavior would be characterized by love.

84. Strecker, *Sermon*, 153, quoting Kant's *Critique of Practical Reason*.

85. Contemporary deontological ethical theories are based on Kant's work. See Ogletree, *Use of the Bible*, 24–25.

no hope that humankind can break out of its race toward annihilation —
"through a self-initiated atomic blast of annihilation," as Strecker says in
the midst of the cold war,[86] or through an ecological disaster resulting from
ongoing neglect of our duties toward each other, as we could say after the
cold war. The only hope for humankind is that the teaching of the Sermon
on the Mount be used to shape the church community, so that it might
become a proleptic manifestation of the kingdom in which the rest of the
world would be invited to participate. Strecker concludes his study of the
Sermon on the Mount with these words:

> Thus as Jesus himself, in his life and death, set a universally valid
> example, the Christian community is called to place itself under the
> word of its Lord, to shape the realm of the church in accordance with
> the Sermon on the Mount, and to realize an exemplary existence that
> will shine into the world like the light into the darkness (5:16). This
> path of signal existence will best do justice to the missionary claim
> of the exalted One, as emphasized by Matthew at the end of his gos-
> pel. With these words let us remember the Christians' commission:
> "Go therefore and make disciples of all nations . . . teaching them to
> observe all that I have commanded you."[87]

Reading B, CAT 5: The Plausibility of Discipleship as Implementing the Sermon's Blueprint for the Processes of Becoming Disciples and of Making Disciples

The conclusions about the teaching *regarding discipleship of the Sermon on
the Mount read with a consequentialist preunderstanding of the moral life
(reading B, CAT 1) can be summarized in a few sentences. The Sermon is predominantly a call to discipleship seeking to convince people to want to do
God's will (reading B, CAT 2), which is primarily addressed to people (the
crowds) who are not yet disciples (reading B, CAT 3) by Jesus, the beloved
child with whom God is well pleased (3:17) because of his obedience (reading B, CAT 4). The Sermon is also addressed to (novice) disciples (reading B,
CAT 3) and is useful in the practice of discipleship because it provides a
blueprint for the process of becoming a disciple (a process that every disciple must undergo constantly in order to remain faithful), as well as for the
process of making disciples (the vocation of all disciples, including those who
have just become disciples).*

*This twofold process can be summarized by the first five stages of the
overall story/plot of the disciples posited by the Sermon on the Mount. It
is enough here to list the stages (see the complete discussion in chap. 3,
reading B, CAW 6.3).*

---

86. Strecker, *Sermon*, 181.
87. Ibid., 184–85.

Stage 0: Prior to Becoming Novice Disciples: Knowing God's Will

Stage 1: Becoming Novice Disciples: Acknowledging the Authority/ Trustworthiness of Jesus

Stage 2: Recognizing God's Goodness

Stage 3: Trusting in God's Goodness, Having Faith

Stage 4: Making God's Will Their Own Will; Appropriating Jesus' Teaching, Internalizing the Law, Praying

Stage 5: Doing God's Will: a. Having an Overabundant Righteousness; b. Carrying Out One's Mission

For novice disciples and full-fledged disciples, the Sermon on the Mount is a reminder that they must themselves constantly undergo this process in order to (continue to) do God's will faithfully and thus to receive their rewards: the kingdom (5:3, 10, 12, 20); divine rewards (6:4, 6, 18); being comforted, inheriting the earth, being satisfied, obtaining mercy, seeing God, being called children of God (5:4–9; 6:14), and sharing in Jesus' authority, including as eschatological Judge (cf. 19:28). The necessarily ongoing character of the process of becoming disciples becomes clear as we review it in reverse.

In order to have an overabundant righteousness and to fulfill their vocation (stage 5), disciples must internalize God's will (stage 4). For this, they must have faith, i.e., trust that God's will is good for them and trust that God does provide for them all the good things they need to do his will (stage 3). To attain this true faith, they must identify around them the manifestations of God's goodness (stage 2). It is only if they see the good works of other servants of God — Jesus, other disciples (stage 1) — and give glory to their Father in heaven that they themselves can be faithful disciples, i.e., continue to become disciples because discipleship is something one always becomes. If they stop this process, i.e., if they believe that they are disciples (as a rock is a rock) or that they have all that it takes to carry out their mission on their own, they have renounced discipleship. If they step out of the process of becoming disciples, their behavior, even if it includes spectacular deeds (7:21–23), is nothing more than a parody of discipleship that is powerless to manifest God's goodness (because they themselves end up conceiving of them as expressions of their own goodness!) and that soon brings about denials and betrayals, as the story of the Twelve illustrates (e.g., 17:14–21; 26:20–75).

By contrast, when their discipleship is a process that they undergo again and again in response to the call that the Sermon on the Mount again and again addresses to them and to their recognition of manifestations of God's goodness, their good works (their righteousness) can be perceived by others as "overabundant," extraordinary, and thus as manifestations of God's goodness. As other people give glory to God because of the disciples' good works, these people are themselves in the process of becoming disciples: the disci-

ples are in the process of making disciples (28:19-20), of being "fishers of people" (4:19); they are in the process of fulfilling their vocation as disciples.

In this perspective, the teaching of the Sermon on the Mount is primarily understood as setting up goals for the disciples' lives. It defines their behavior positively as a vocation to manifest God's goodness, so that other people — any other people! — might give glory to God and might become disciples themselves. In this consequentialist interpretation, the Sermon on the Mount does not demand that disciples maintain a clear distinction between their community and the world, but rather that they overcome the boundaries that separate community and world. Not resisting evil (5:39), giving of themselves beyond what abusive people demand from them (5:40-42), or more generally, love, forgiveness, and reconciliation (5:22-26, 43-47) are attitudes that one must have not only toward one's brothers and sisters in the community of disciples but also toward anybody else, even one's enemies. What characterizes disciples and makes their behavior so radically different is precisely the fact that they ignore the boundaries that separate friends from foes (5:46), righteous from unrighteous (5:45), insiders from outsiders (5:47). The fulfillment of their vocation as disciples requires that they cease understanding God's will as a series of prohibitions — which in the form of negative admonitions hide rather than reveal that God's will is good for us. Rather, they must conceive of it as revealing that God's will is nothing else than the good for which disciples grope, together with any other human being. This is why all the teaching of the Sermon on the Mount culminates in a positive version of the Golden Rule.[88] What disciples perceive to be good for them (what they want others to do to them) is precisely God's will (the law and the prophets), i.e., the good deeds that they should perform for others (whoever they might be), who in turn should perceive them as manifestations of God's goodness toward them.

This interpretation of the Sermon on the Mount as providing readers with the means to discover the good that they will want to do is typically consequentialist, as we noted following Ogletree. "Consequentialist theories more readily bring to consciousness the positive values that provide the justifying grounds of action, the "for-the-sake-of-which" that renders action humanly important."[89] For a consequentialist interpretation, the Sermon on the Mount precisely functions in this way. It emphasizes the rewards and other positive consequences of good deeds. It provides for readers a clear blueprint of the steps that they must again and again take in order to discover in each new situation what are the deeds that are really good (manifestations of God's goodness) because they are grounded in faith, i.e., in the trust that God, "our Father in heaven," provides with the good things they need. The Sermon on

---

88. For other versions of the Golden Rule, see Strecker, *Sermon*, 150–55. From his deontological perspective, Strecker does not perceive any special significance to the "positive" form of the Golden Rule in the Sermon on the Mount — although he takes note of it.

89. Ogletree, *Use of the Bible*, 26.

the Mount is thus a blueprint for a discipleship that is a constant quest for what is truly desirable for the disciples and for other human beings.

At the end of this review one cannot but be struck by the glaring differences between the two views of discipleship found among the *conclusions about the teaching* of the Sermon on the Mount of Strecker's and Kingsbury's deontological interpretation and of an alternate consequentialist interpretation developed out of Edwards's suggestions. My hope is that the use of ethical categories and the references to the text have shown the *plausibility* of each of the two views of "discipleship according to the Sermon on the Mount," for people who because of their cultural background can envision these two kinds of preunderstandings of the moral life — at any rate, European-American people, since these preunderstandings have found expression in their ethical theories.

Saying that these two types of interpretations and their respective conclusions about "discipleship according to the Sermon on the Mount" are *governed by preunderstandings* of the moral life does not mean that they are not legitimate. This is clear in the examples we used, namely, scholarly interpretations, which began by elucidating the coherence of specific meaning-producing dimensions and thus showed that, out of these *conclusions about what the Sermon is and says* (CAWs), it is legitimate to draw *conclusions about the teaching* (CATs) of this text regarding discipleship and to ponder their significance for us. Interpretations governed by preunderstandings are legitimate, even if they are *"pro me/nobis* interpretations." These interpretations emphasize their *conclusions about the teaching* of the text for me or for us. Even these interpretations do not project preunderstandings on the text or read them into the text. Rather, they lead the interpreters to address certain questions to the text — questions regarding *"what* disciples should do" if they go to the text with a deontological preunderstanding, or questions regarding *"how* to become disciples" if they approach the text with a consequentialist preunderstanding. When readers address such "practical" questions to the text, their attention is focused on certain features of the text, which interestingly scholarly interpretations can show to provide a legitimate coherence for an interpretation of the text — respectively, features that form the historical/realistic meaning-producing dimension of the text that can be systematically elucidated by means of either a specific redaction critical method (as used by Strecker) or a specific literary method (as used by Kingsbury); or features that form the story/plot meaning-producing dimension that can be elucidated by means of a specific narrative method.

As we shall see presently, the same can be said about interpretations approaching the Sermon on the Mount with other preunderstandings, namely, perfectionist preunderstandings of the moral life.

CHAPTER 6

Imitation

Two Perfectionist Views of Discipleship
according to the Sermon on the Mount

This chapter is devoted to a comparison of the *conclusions about the teaching* (CATs) of the Sermon on the Mount regarding discipleship that can be drawn on the one hand from the figurative interpretation of Luz[1] (and also Davies and Allison)[2] and on the other hand from the thematic interpretation of my commentary.[3] The goal in chapter 6 is similar to that in chapter 5, i.e., to show the *plausibility* of each understanding of discipleship as ethical practice. Yet there is a significant difference: contemporary European-Americans (and possibly others) may have some difficulty envisioning the plausibility of discipleship as (two kinds of) perfectionist ethical practice.

The conceptualizations of discipleship as *deontological* and as *consequentialist* ethical practices can be readily recognized as plausible by most people in European-American cultures, since most people commonly use the corresponding preunderstandings of the moral life as they make decisions.[4] But the conclusions of the figurative and thematic interpretations point toward conceptualizations of discipleship as perfectionist ethical practices, which are not self-evident in contemporary European-American cultures.

This is not to say that perfectionist preunderstandings are completely nonsensical. They are not foreign to European-American cultures, with

---

1. Ulrich Luz, *Matthew 1–7: A Commentary* (Minneapolis: Augsburg, 1989), 203–460.

2. W. D. Davies and D. C. Allison Jr., *A Critical and Exegetical Commentary on the Gospel according to Saint Matthew*, vol. 1, ICC (Edinburgh: T. & T. Clark, 1988), 410–731.

3. Daniel Patte, *The Gospel according to Matthew: A Structural Commentary on Matthew's Faith* (Minneapolis: Fortress, 1987; 3d printing, Valley Forge, Pa.: Trinity Press International, 1996), 60–108.

4. I suspect that while deontological preunderstandings govern decision making in the personal life, consequentialist preunderstandings primarily govern decision making in the business world and the rest of public life.

which they share roots in the Aristotelian tradition. Indeed, these pre-understandings and the corresponding conceptualizations of discipleship remain etched somewhere in our subconscious, even though at present they seem to be minority views. Their plausibility is only acknowledged when our imagination is piqued by someone who evokes them for us. Then we recognize them and welcome them as old friends we had almost forgotten. But at first, these evocations merely produce fleeting images that we have a hard time pinning down.

In many ways, this is the situation experienced by Luz, Davies and Allison, and myself as authors of our respective commentaries. As we read the Sermon on the Mount, flashes of unexpected but fascinating and plausible images of discipleship attracted our attention to figurative or thematic features of the text. These glimpses were enough to lead us to focus our interpretations on these meaning-producing dimensions. But (as noted in chap. 4), as we sought to elucidate the coherence and legitimacy of such interpretations, we could not stay consistently focused on these dimensions because the plausibility of our conclusions regarding discipleship kept fading away in our minds, clouded as they were by one-dimensional and androcentric perspectives. Deontological (and consequentialist) conceptualizations of discipleship superimposed themselves on perfectionist views and obscured them.

Reading C and Reading D: The Plausibility of Discipleship as Perfectionist Ethical Practices — Imitation

Luz, Davies and Allison, and I could not let go of the preunderstanding of discipleship as "doing God's will" with its presuppositions that all we need in order to have a good moral life is either the knowledge of God's will or the will to do it. Thus even as we had fleeting glances that the Sermon on the Mount offered an eschatological vision of life in the kingdom (so Luz) or a complex figurative world constructed out of allusions to many Jewish and Hellenistic traditions and biblical texts (so Davies and Allison), or again a view of discipleship characterized by moral discernment (so Patte), none of us could conceive of discipleship as fundamentally defined in terms of a perfectionist preunderstanding of the moral life that foregrounds either *(re)socialization in a symbolic world* or *moral discernment*. Similarly, while each of us referred or alluded to *discipleship as "imitation,"* it was always about one point or another, rather than about the entire teaching of the Sermon on the Mount; we did not recognize that discipleship as imitation is quite different from a deontological conceptualization of discipleship. Consequently, our commentaries are constantly in the process of losing sight of discipleship as "imitation" — and thus, ironically, they repeatedly lose sight of the symbolic world of the Sermon on the Mount and of what one discerns with a "sound eye."

As a result, in quite a number of instances, Davies and Allison, and also Luz, reverted to interpretations focused on the historical/realistic dimension of the text (as noted in chap. 4) because these interpretations provide conclusions that they readily apprehend as plausible, since they are consistent with a deontological preunderstanding. Similarly, in my commentary, I quite often concluded that what disciples perceive with true moral discernment provides them with the knowledge needed to do God's will; in effect, I found plausibility for the conclusions of my thematic interpretation in a deontological preunderstanding, and in discipleship as "doing God's will." This amounted to denying the plausibility of conceiving of discipleship as "imitation" (of Christ), in spite of centuries of church life during which this was the predominant conceptualization of discipleship. In sum, the one-dimensional androcentric commentaries by us as male European-American exegetes end up not only hiding but also betraying the *conclusions about the teaching* (CATs) of the Sermon on the Mount regarding discipleship toward which our own *conclusions about what the Sermon is and says* point.[5]

In view of this state of affairs, the multidimensional androcritical study must read these commentaries "against the grain," at least to some extent. In chapter 4 I deliberately bracketed out all our *conclusions about what the sermon is and says* that were not pertinent to the interpretation of the figurative and thematic dimensions of the sermon, respectively. In so doing, the multidimensional analysis elucidated something to which we constantly referred, even though we did not really consider it: the coherence and the distinctiveness of one or the other of these meaning-producing dimensions. Similarly, the present chapter seeks to envision the plausible conceptualizations of discipleship that our commentaries have not formulated, but that are in the logic of our scholarly interpretations and their *conclusions about what the sermon is and says.*

The study of these scholarly interpretations "against the grain" of their own practices is facilitated by the earlier multidimensional study of these interpretations of the Sermon on the Mount in chapter 4 and of Matthew 4:18–22 in chapter 2.[6] These two chapters suggest that, in order to

---

5. In their respective interpretations, there is inconsistency between their performance of the legitimacy judgment and their performance of the epistemology judgment, quite possibly because they were not self-conscious regarding the epistemological choices involved in their interpretation (at least, I know this was the case for my own interpretation).

6. These two chapters have shown that both kinds of interpretations reached comparable CATs: Matthew 4:18–22 offers a "vision of discipleship," i.e., a model or "type" of discipleship (as Luz suggested in "The Disciples in the Gospel according to Matthew,"in *The Interpretation of Matthew*, ed. Graham Stanton [Philadelphia: Fortress; London: SPCK, 1983], 98–128) that can be used in order to identify those who fulfill this type and who therefore are people whom one should *imitate* in order to be a faithful disciple. The differences between these two kinds of interpretations concern the understanding of this vision: for Luz and Davies and Allison, it is a *vision of authentic religious leadership* (which includes a certain vision of the Christian community and its relationship with the rest of society); for me, it is a *vision of*

understand the plausibility of these two kinds of teachings of the Sermon regarding "discipleship as imitation," we need to consider perfectionist pre-understandings of the moral life. As suggested, discipleship as imitation is best understood in terms of perfectionist ethical practices.

Reading C, CATs and Reading D, CATs: Perfectionist Preunderstandings of the Moral Life and Discipleship as Imitation

As Meeks emphasizes in the opening paragraphs of his study *The Moral World of the First Christians,*[7] "We tend to think of ethics as moral argument or rules." In other words, those of us in modern European-American culture conceive of ethics either in consequentialist terms ("as moral argument" helping us to decide what is the best course of action, a decision in which clear examples of courses of action play an essential role) or in deontological terms ("as moral rules" that provide us with a well-defined ground for discerning what actions are appropriate or not in a given community or society). Is it not the primary concern of ethics to elucidate the relative value of different courses of action, as the consequentialist theories emphasize? Or to determine what are the "obligations" that one ought to observe in a community, as the deontological theories insist? It might be for many people. Yet perfectionist preunderstandings are also plausible.[8] Ethicists regularly and strongly advocate perfectionist theories of the moral life.[9] In addition, as Meeks points out, perfectionist theories cannot be overlooked as a possibility when one studies texts written in the Greco-Roman world, where Aristotle and his followers developed them.[10]

It might be surprising that from a perfectionist perspective, the Sermon on the Mount is read neither as a series of rules or principles that one must implement ("do") as a member of the community under God's eschatological rule, nor as a blueprint for becoming and being disciples, which one

---

people associated with Jesus' ministry (a much more focused vision). Each of these has been shown to be legitimate through a different critical interpretation focused on a given dimension of the text (either the figurative or the thematic dimension) — as discussed in chapter 4.

7. Wayne A. Meeks, *The Moral World of the First Christians* (Philadelphia: Westminster, 1986), 11.

8. See Thomas W. Ogletree, *The Use of the Bible in Christian Ethics: A Constructive Essay* (Philadelphia: Fortress, 1983), 28–34.

9. See for instance Stanley Hauerwas, *A Community of Character: Toward a Constructive Social Ethic* (Notre Dame and London: University of Notre Dame, 1981), and also his "A Sermon on the Sermon on the Mount" in *Unleashing the Scripture: Freeing the Bible from Captivity to America* (Nashville: Abingdon, 1993) — an insightful and delightful application of his perfectionist ethical theory to the interpretation of the Sermon on the Mount. A perfectionist ethical perspective is also adopted by Peter Paris in his analysis of *The Social Teaching of the Black Churches* (Philadelphia: Fortress, 1985).

10. In addition to Meeks, *The Moral World of the First Christians,* see Wayne A. Meeks, *The Origins of Christian Morality: The First Two Centuries* (New Haven and London: Yale University Press, 1993).

must implement in one's life. From this perspective, the Sermon is neither revealing God's will that one needs to receive before doing the right things, nor seeking to establish the reader's will to do God's will. Thus for instance, Hauerwas writes regarding the beatitudes:

> The temptation is to read the Beatitudes as a list of virtues that good people ought to have or as deeds they ought to do. We thus think that we ought to try to be meek, or poor, or hungry, or merciful, or peacemakers, or persecuted. Yet we know that it is hard to try to be meek — either you are meek or you are not. Even more difficult is it to have all the characteristics of the Beatitudes at once! Yet that is not what it means to be blessed.[11]

From the perspective of perfectionist preunderstandings of the moral life, directly or indirectly the Sermon on the Mount offers an ideal vision of discipleship that is beyond what any disciple can expect to do, as one recognizes when, with Hauerwas, one evaluates one's life without false pretense. Thus the Sermon does not prescribe for us what we should do.

It is true that the teaching of the Sermon, which in one way or another provides for its readers an ideal vision of discipleship, is an ethical teaching that should lead us to act in specific ways. From this perspective, an essential (although negative) condition for practicing — for "doing" — the Sermon is not conceiving of it either as a list of virtues or as a blueprint for deeds that one ought to do.

Ogletree's explanation of basic characteristics of perfectionist theories clarifies what is at stake:

> Perfectionist theories stress the remoteness of value concepts and moral principles from concrete experience. If we are to apprehend what is going on in concrete situations and respond appropriately to them, we need more than our abstract moral notions, no matter how clear and precise they may be. We need a developed capacity for moral discernment; we need prudence, "practical wisdom" (Aristotle).... For perfectionist theories, it is the fullest realization of virtue by concrete human persons which is the primary substance of the ethical.[12]

Let us review each of Ogletree's points, comparing them with Meeks's presentation. In this way we shall clarify the main characteristics of perfectionist preunderstandings of the moral life and put ourselves in a position to understand that there are at least two possible kinds of perfectionist interpretations of the Sermon on the Mount.

---

11. Hauerwas, *Unleashing the Scripture,* 71.
12. Ogletree, *Use of the Bible,* 31–33.

Perfectionist theories emphasize that values (on which any action is based; they are posited by deontological and consequentialist understandings of the moral life) are constructs, or more specifically, parts of the *symbolic world* or semantic universe in which we live and which defines them.[13] This world in which we live might seem natural and/or factual to us. Yet as cross-cultural studies show, it is a construct that interrelates the various features of concrete human experience in specific ways and attaches values to each of them. This is what Ogletree means when he speaks about "the remoteness of value concepts and moral principles from concrete experience" in our daily life. Most often we are not aware of their role in our behavior.

Perfectionist theories also point out that to be a moral agent is to have "character" (*êthos*), including "moral discernment," "prudence, 'practical wisdom' (Aristotle)." It is not simply a matter of mastering this wisdom intellectually — this would be learning *about* virtues as abstract moral notions instead of *learning virtues,* i.e., learning "how to do one's functions well" (a rough definition of virtue) in the process of character formation.[14] Learning virtues is a matter of moral discernment; it is discerning good ways of doing things in concrete situations. Practical wisdom is a matter of *practice;* moral discernment is something that one cultivates, as one acquires "culture." To put it more concretely, one acquires practical wisdom by learning to perform well one's function, as apprentices hone their woodcarving skills. A virtue (good woodcarving skill) and *a fortiori* practical wisdom as a series of virtues cannot be gained by oneself (although acquiring virtues demands effort from the individual). Apprentices need to learn in an actual workshop (with tools and benches) from a master cabinetmaker, and learning involves observing (discerning the useful gestures) and imitating the expert. Similarly, Christian virtues, as virtues of practical wisdom, are learned in the concreteness of human experience by imitating the way in which "experts" perform them. The issues regarding the specific realm(s) of human experience — among which the "community of disciples" — in which models "of discipleship" or models of "behavior for disciples" can be found are, therefore, essential in perfectionist ethical practice.

Two kinds of perfectionist preunderstandings of the moral life can be distinguished. One that I call "resocialization/perfectionist" preunderstanding gives priority to the *resocialization in a symbolic world* (the focus

---

13. See Meeks, *Moral World,* 13–14.

14. As Hauerwas (*A Community of Character,* 111) puts it: "For the Greeks the term virtue, *arete,* meant that which causes a thing to perform its function well. *Arete* was an excellence of any kind that denotes the power of anything to fulfill its function." See also C. B. Kerferd, "Arete," in *Encyclopedia of Philosophy,* ed. Paul Edwards (New York: Free Press, 1967), 1:147–48; and O. Bauernfeind, ἀρετή, in *Theological Dictionary of the New Testament,* ed. G. Kittel, trans. G. W. Bromiley (Grand Rapids: Eerdmans, 1964), 1:457–61.

being on the community and its symbolic world as the necessary context of moral discernment and of the rest of the moral life); another, which I call "discernment/perfectionist" preunderstanding, gives priority to the *establishment of moral discernment or character formation* (here, the focus is on the acquisition of virtue as a condition for the community and its symbolic world or for participation in them). Clearly, it is a matter of emphasis. But the shift in emphasis regarding these key features of perfectionist views of the moral life is quite significant.

Reading C, CAT 1: The Plausibility of a Resocialization/ Perfectionist Preunderstanding of the Moral Life

Meeks underscores socialization in a symbolic world in his work on New Testament ethics.[15] For him, one becomes a moral agent primarily by maturing in a culture, i.e., by being "socialized" in the symbolic world of that culture; or by being "resocialized" in the symbolic world of a Christian community. Then one develops "moral discernment" through which one distinguishes in the ambiguities of concrete life how one should act as a member of that community, i.e., how one should conform in one's behavior to the community's symbolic world and to the models this community and its symbolic world offer. "Imitating" is being conformed and conforming one's behavior to the community and its symbolic world.

The commentaries of Luz and Davies and Allison, through their focus on the figurative dimension of the Sermon on the Mount, seem to imply a resocialization/perfectionist preunderstanding of the moral life, according to which the Sermon on the Mount contributes to the formation of disciples by establishing for its readers an appropriate symbolic world.

Reading D, CAT 1: The Plausibility of a Discernment/ Perfectionist Preunderstanding of the Moral Life

Ogletree and Hauerwas in their works on ethics understand perfectionist preunderstanding of the moral life as character formation by means of moral discernment. Becoming a moral agent is primarily a matter of moral discernment and character formation; one becomes a moral agent by identifying models of behavior (people who manifest virtues in their lives) by means of moral discernment and by "imitating" these models (as an apprentice imitates experts). As persons who exercise moral discernment (and who are "cen-

---

15. See Meeks, *Moral World*, 11–17. Note how he pushes aside the question of character formation (*êthos*) so as to foreground the role of the symbolic world, following the classical essay by Clifford Geertz, "Ethos, World View, and the Analysis of Sacred Symbols" in *The Interpretation of Cultures* (New York: Basic Books, 1973), 126–41.

ters of meaning and values"),[16] we form a "community of characters" with a particular symbolic world.[17]

My commentary, through its focus on the thematic dimension of the Sermon on the Mount, seems to imply a discernment/perfectionist preunderstanding of the moral life, according to which the Sermon on the Mount teaches such moral discernment to its hearers/readers. This is directly expressed by its conclusions about what the primary theme of the Sermon on the Mount is — a specific kind of moral discernment that characterizes discipleship (see reading D, CAW 2.1).

As a first step toward a clarification of the differences between these two conceptualizations of the teaching of the Sermon regarding discipleship as perfectionist ethical practice, I propose to explore the features of these interpretations that most directly suggest that they presuppose a perfectionist understanding of the moral life.

Reading C, CAT 1.1: Signs of Luz's and Davies and Allison's Perfectionist Interpretation of the Sermon on the Mount

In his introductory comments on the Sermon on the Mount and in his review of the "history of influence" (*Wirkungsgeschichte*),[18] Luz underscores what are not his *conclusions about the teaching* of the Sermon on the Mount regarding discipleship. He strongly rejects the Reformers' interpretation according to which the Sermon is unfulfillable. In his view, the Anabaptist and the traditional Catholic interpretations are closer to the teaching of the Sermon (as he interprets it). He notes that the Anabaptists are faithful to "the basic elements of Matthean theology: the priority of practice before teaching, the will to obedience, the fact that the individual command is taken seriously, that it does not simply dissolve in the commandment of love, the will to the formation of brotherly and sisterly community."[19] The Reformers and their followers betray these basic features of the teaching of the Sermon because they understand it as a series of commands or of radical ethical principles (such as the commandment of love), which they subsequently judge to be not practicable. Whatever might be the theological and ecclesiological reasons for this interpretation by the Reformers,[20] Luz's rejection of it amounts to a rejection of a deontologi-

---

16. Ogletree, *Use of the Bible*, 28.
17. See Hauerwas, *A Community of Character*.
18. Luz, *Matthew*, 214–23.
19. Ibid., 220.
20. See Luz, *Matthew*, 221–22, where the author raises three questions concerning "the reasons why a real praxis of Christianity based on the Sermon on the Mount did not spread widely in the realm of the churches of the Reformation." These questions concern: the view of sin and of the Sermon on the Mount as unfulfillable; the application of the Sermon on the Mount as it affects individual Christians and as it also affects other people; the relationship between individual and community.

cal interpretation: the Sermon on the Mount is not "Christian halakah."[21] Then what kind of understanding of discipleship as ethical practice does he affirm?

He articulates it. When speaking about the interpretations of the Sermon on the Mount in the classical Catholic tradition since Augustine and in marginal groups (including the Anabaptists) throughout church history, Luz underscores that "Matthean theology is basically perfectionist." Thus he quotes Augustine about the Sermon on the Mount, "The perfect . . . sermon shapes through its commandments the 'Christian life,' " and Thomas Aquinas, "In the Sermon on the Mount 'the whole perfection of our life is contained.' "[22]

Luz did not use this perfectionist technical vocabulary lightly.[23] When he emphasizes the practicability of the teaching of the Sermon on the Mount, Luz once again underscores that a deontological interpretation is inappropriate. Indeed, the Sermon is practicable; but this is not the practicability of a series of commands by Jesus that the community would be obliged to keep and that Matthew or the tradition would have made practicable by adapting them for the new situation of the church (with the exceptions of 5:32 and 42).[24] Luz expresses his perfectionist understanding of the teachings of the Sermon as follows:

> They are not laws that prescribe accurately how a Christian must act in every situation. They are not sentences of law but exemplary demands that portray in examples the manner and radicalism in which God demands obedience. The freedom to invent new examples is always a part of exemplarity. Therefore, it is for Matthew neither an unambiguous definition of Christian action nor a complete freedom in the sense of "dilige et fac quod vis" (love and do what you wish)! He thinks of the Christian life most easily as a way that has the goal of perfection (5:20, 48) and whose direction and radicalism are clearly marked by the individual commands, like tracers that are lighted by their goal.[25]

In sum, Luz uses perfectionist categories to express his conclusions regarding the significance of the Sermon on the Mount for us, yet without referring directly to perfectionist theories and their technical vocabulary. He clearly does not have in mind in his commentary the range of ethical theories (deontological, consequentialist, perfectionist) with which I seek to

21. Luz, *Matthew*, 215.
22. Ibid., 219.
23. It is important to note that all interpretations that speak about perfection are not "perfectionist." How could one not speak about perfection when dealing with 5:48? By the phrase "perfectionist interpretation" I exclusively designate those interpretations that, consciously or not, involve a perfectionist preunderstanding of the moral life.
24. Ibid., 215.
25. Ibid., 216.

understand a sample of male European-American exegetical interpretations (thus his use of deontological vocabulary, such as "commands"). Nevertheless Luz stresses the importance of the symbolic world that the Sermon on the Mount conveys. For him, this symbolic world provides the perspective from which one should view each of the teachings of the Sermon: "the individual commands, like tracers that are lighted by their goal," i.e., by the kingdom as an ideal, symbolic world (see my comments about Luz's interpretation of 5:21–48 in chap. 4, reading C, CAW 3.4).

The perfectionist character of the interpretation proposed by Davies and Allison in their commentary is readily apparent in their repeated emphasis that the sermon or its various sections conveys "a new vision." Quoting one of their concluding comments on 5:21–48 is sufficient for our present purpose:

> What is being added [to Torah] over and above the tradition is...a new attitude, a new spirit, a new vision. This is why 5:21–48 is so poetical, dramatic, and pictorial, and why a literal (mis)interpretation creates absurdities. The text functions more like a story than a legal code. Its primary character is to instil principles and qualities through a vivid inspiration of the moral imagination.[26]

In other words, for them, 5:21–48 and the rest of the Sermon on the Mount "instil" virtues ("principles and *qualities*") by communicating to its readers a symbolic world "through a vivid inspiration of the moral imagination."

Reading D, CAT 1.1: Signs of a Perfectionist Reading of the Sermon on the Mount in My Commentary

I can say without any hesitation that when I wrote my commentary, including its section on the Sermon on the Mount, I did not approach the text with ethical categories (including perfectionist categories) in mind. Yet as becomes clear when one considers my commentary, a perfectionist classification of its conclusions and their clarification and amplification along this line are quite appropriate.

In my introduction, as well as throughout the commentary, I emphasize that my goal is to elucidate the "system of convictions" conveyed by the Gospel according to Matthew. Through my definition of "system of convictions" I make clear that I want to study the system of values conveyed by this gospel (a basis for moral discernment) and expressed through its symbolic (or figurative) world. Note that from this perspective a system of convictions (deep values and the pattern that interrelates them) provides a basis for moral discernment and has priority over the symbolic world, which expresses it. A system of convictions gives believers a "vision" of everything in their experience, "vision" being understood as a process (and not in the static sense it has when used

---

26. Davies and Allison, *Matthew,* 566.

to designate the symbolic world). *This vision is appropriately called* discernment, *since it involves discerning the relationship among all things, including
new and unexpected things, in one's experience according to the pattern of
the system of conviction.*[27] *In other words, a system of convictions gives believers the ability of envisioning everything in terms of a system of values; it
provides* moral discernment.

A system of convictions, through the discernment it supplies, establishes
the identity (and thus the êthos or character) of the author as believer as well
as of the readers as believers. "[Convictions] establish for believers what they
spontaneously perceive as their true identity as well as the true character of
the world (the human community, the natural world, and their eventual relationship to a supernatural world) in which believers are to implement their
identity."[28] Since convictions establish the identity of believers, they have
power over them. Convictions "drive" believers to act in certain ways rather
than others; they provide moral discernment and thus establish believers as
moral agents. "Following one's convictions, being driven by them, is nothing
else than 'being oneself,' implementing one's true identity."[29] Since Matthew writes his Gospel because he is driven by his convictions, his discourse
necessarily reflects and conveys his system of convictions.

The question then becomes, What system of convictions is conveyed by
the Sermon on the Mount? How does this vision, this moral discernment,
allow one to envision discipleship? More specifically, how does the Sermon
teach moral discernment by communicating to its readers a specific system
of convictions?[30] My commentary has reached conclusions regarding each of
these issues, although they still remain to be presented systematically in terms
of a perfectionist preunderstanding of the moral life.

As a first step in this direction, it is helpful to note generally how convictions are conveyed: always indirectly. Only self-evident truths are actual
convictions with the power to form the character of people. They cannot be
communicated directly, e.g., through a rational argument that would demonstrate their truth. Someone who tried to do so would end up conveying

---

27. Patte, *Matthew,* 7; see also D. Patte, *The Religious Dimensions of Biblical Texts:
Greimas's Structural Semiotics and Biblical Exegesis* (Atlanta: Scholars Press, 1990), 115–19.

28. Patte, *Matthew,* 5.

29. Ibid.

30. I suggested that seeking to elucidate the system of convictions conveyed by a text
amounts to studying the *moral discernment* it communicates. I can be more specific. A system
of convictions posits as self-evident not only what characterizes the real and the illusory —
providing means for discerning between "true" and "false" — but also what characterizes the
euphoric (what is felt to be good for us) and the dysphoric (what is felt to be bad for us). In
this way it provides means for discerning between good and bad, and especially between good
behavior and bad behavior, since a system of convictions drives believers to act by setting up
goals for their lives. The question is then: What is the specific way in which the Sermon on the
Mount does this? For a discussion of the "proprioceptive" semantic categories ("felt" rather
than "thought" values), see A. J. Greimas and J. Courtés, *Semiotics and Language: An Analytical Dictionary,* trans. L. Crist, D. Patte, et al. (Bloomington: Indiana University Press, 1982),
248, 346; and Patte, *Religious Dimensions,* 119–22.

ideas (demonstrated truths) without any power to inspire people, rather than convictions (self-evident truths) that do.[31] *Thus convictions must be communicated through poetic means, such as themes, thematic systems (and their structures), figures, and symbolic worlds (and their structures). This indirect communication of convictions takes many different forms, according to the nature of the system of convictions.*

My interpretation of the Sermon on the Mount includes conclusions which emphasize that readers can only hope to practice the discernment that is characteristic of discipleship by identifying people who already practice this discernment, such practices being models of discernment *that disciples are to imitate. Yet having moral discernment and "practical wisdom" allows disciples to identify people who perform the kinds of behavior that disciples should practice. In other words, moral discernment allows disciples to identify* models of behavior for disciples.

In sum, as I seek to clarify the conclusions about the teaching *of the Sermon regarding discipleship toward which my interpretation points, I have to concede that, even though I did not have these theories in mind when preparing and writing my commentary, perfectionist theories of the moral life provide categories that allow me to begin bringing these conclusions to understanding by formulating them more clearly.*

We can then provisionally conclude that the interpretations of commentaries by Luz and Davies and Allison on the one hand, and of my commentary on the other, are perfectionist, although in different ways. This preliminary discussion suggests that Luz and Davies and Allison would agree with me in affirming that faithful discipleship requires the three main conditions for moral agency posited in perfectionist theories: (1) being resocialized in a symbolic world; (2) having moral discernment in terms of a vision of life that allows one to identify the virtues that one must strive to bring to their "fullest realization";[32] (3) imitating the exemplary behavior (by someone in a concrete situation) that one identifies as fulfilling this vision of life.

The differences between the two kinds of perfectionist interpretations are expressed in two questions.

1. What is viewed as playing the primary role in forming the character of disciples? Resocialization in a symbolic world? Moral discernment? What difference does it make in the conceptualization of discipleship as perfectionist ethical practice? Such are the questions we shall explore in reading C, CAT 2 regarding the interpretation of commentaries by Luz and

---

31. For the distinction between ideas and convictions, see Patte, *Matthew,* 4–5, and *Religious Dimensions,* 106–215.

32. Ogletree, *Use of the Bible,* 32.

Davies and Allison and in reading D, CAT 2 regarding the interpretation of my commentary.

2. How do we identify "models of discipleship" (for the resocialization/ perfectionist interpretation) or "models of discernment" and "models of behavior for disciples" (for the discernment/perfectionist interpretation)? Who does one identify as offering such models? Among the characters (personages) of the Gospel? Beyond it? Exclusively among people from the church community — as a social entity comprised of people who have been resocialized in it by sharing the specific symbolic world of the Sermon on the Mount? Or people from all walks of life, who are discovered to be true disciples belonging to the kingdom (the church as a spiritual reality), even though they may lack any connections with the church as a social entity? Such are the questions we shall explore in reading C, CAT 3 and in reading D, CAT 3.

Reading C, CAT 2: The Plausibility of Discipleship as Resocialization/Perfectionist Ethical Practice

Reading C, CAT 2.1: Resocializing Would-be Disciples in the Symbolic World of the Sermon on the Mount — Faith before Discipleship

From Luz's and Davies and Allison's figurative interpretations and their *conclusions about what the sermon is and says* regarding discipleship (reading C, CAWs), we can conclude that (the figurative dimension of) the Sermon aims at communicating to its readers an appropriate symbolic world. Moral discernment plays a secondary role; it helps in the practice of discipleship in this symbolic world; it is the means through which one can distinguish true models of discipleship from false models — true religious leaders from false prophets. Thus discernment takes place within a previously established symbolic world.

More concretely, in this conceptualization of the teaching of the Sermon, discipleship involves (re)socialization in a particular symbolic world. The specific practice of discipleship called for by the Sermon cannot make sense as long as one does not share this symbolic world, i.e., this "faith" as belief in the truth of this symbolic world. The plausibility of this conceptualization of discipleship begins to appear. It makes sense to affirm that the practice of discipleship requires faith as a prerequisite!

That "discipleship presupposes faith" is not unique to this interpretation. It is also presupposed by the other interpretations. Yet what constitutes faith varies quite radically from one to the other of these conceptualizations of discipleship.

For the deontological interpretation, it is a belief in the extraordinary authority of Jesus as the exalted Lord — a necessary condition for receiving the Sermon on the Mount as the expression of God's eternal will (see reading A, CAT 4). For the consequentialist interpretation, faith includes a belief in Jesus' promises, and thus in his authority, but it is primarily a belief/trust in the goodness of God and of God's will (see reading B, CAT 6.12). For the discernment/perfectionist interpretation, as one might expect, faith is closely associated with moral discernment (see reading D, CAT 2).

By contrast with all of these, for the resocialization/perfectionist interpretation, faith is living in the symbolic world of the Sermon on the Mount. It is holding this symbolic world as the context in terms of which everything in human experience must be understood so as to make sense. It is seeing oneself in this world and recognizing oneself as a disciple with an identity that is also a vocation: discipleship.

From this perspective, having faith is necessarily a community experience. One cannot have this kind of faith by oneself, although one can receive a revelation of (i.e., a knowledge about) the will of God by oneself, as is the case according to the deontological interpretation.[33] Similarly, one cannot have this kind of faith by encountering a few people who manifest the goodness of God through their good works, as is the case according to the consequentialist interpretation.[34] For the resocialization/perfectionist interpretation, one can have faith only when a community shares its symbolic world with that person. Therefore, a person must be invited to participate in the community *before he or she has faith.* This is so because having faith is the same thing as being socialized or resocialized[35] into a community, which is held together by its belief in a symbolic world. In sum, becoming a disciple, i.e., becoming a moral agent acting according to the Sermon on the Mount, entails being "socialized" in the "community of characters" (Hauerwas) — in the church as community of disciples — which embodies the symbolic world posited by the Sermon on the Mount.

From such a resocialization/perfectionist perspective, it becomes understandable why the church community is a "mixed body" in which there are true and false prophets (7:15), true disciples and people who are not really disciples (7:21-23), as an interpretation focused on the figurative dimension of the Sermon (and of the Gospel according to Matthew), such as Luz's, underscores.[36] If the church community did not include people who lack faith and thus are not disciples, how would it share its faith with them? This mixed character of the community reflects the ambivalence of

---

33. From the perspective of the deontological interpretation, faith ends up being an individual submission to Jesus' authority, for which one needs to have faith in order to enter the community or to remain in it.

34. From the perspective of the consequentialist interpretation, joining the community would eventually occur after having faith.

35. "Resocialize" rather than "socialize" in the case of any adult conversion.

36. See Luz, *Matthew,* 438-50, and especially 450, where Luz refers to the history of interpretations of this passage, including the traditional ecclesiological interpretation of the church as *corpus permixtum* (mixed body).

the symbolic world of the Sermon and requires the use of discernment by the members of the community.

Reading C, CAT 2.2: The Plausibility of Discipleship as Shaped by the Ambivalent Symbolic World of the Sermon on the Mount

The figurative interpretation of the Sermon on the Mount and its *conclusions about what the sermon says* (reading C, CAW 2.2ff.) provide a clear picture of this symbolic world. I do not need to repeat these conclusions here. It is enough to evoke a few of the characteristics of this ambivalent symbolic world, which is reflected by the mixed church body. Our goal is simply to clarify how this particular symbolic world gives shape to a conceptualization of discipleship that is plausible from a perfectionist perspective.

On the basis of the interpretation of Luz, we have noted that the Lord's Prayer sets up a symbolic world with a twofold horizon: the heavenly Father's present care for human beings and their needs, and the coming kingdom of God (reading C, CAW 2.2, 2.3). This symbolic world keeps the present theological horizon in tension with the eschatological horizon. Discipleship as ethical practice in this symbolic world embodies this tension and its different manifestations.

The tension generated by the twofold horizon compounds the usual tensions between the old and the new (in the Sermon, primarily between the law and the prophets and Judaism on the one hand and Jesus' teaching on the other) found in any symbolic world. Any figurative system involves such a tension because the communication process can hope to be successful only insofar as the "new" to be communicated is expressed in terms of the "old" knowledge of the addressees — a process exemplified by the figure of Jesus as the new Moses, which presents the newness of Jesus' ministry and teaching in terms of the biblical tradition. But in the figurative dimension of the Sermon on the Mount, this ambivalence and the tensions it generates are intrinsic to the symbolic world. "Reducing" these tensions to one or the other of its poles, so as to have an unambiguous conceptualization of discipleship as ethical practice, would be dissolving the very core of the symbolic world of the Sermon. In other words, discipleship embodies the tensions between the old and the new as well as between the theological horizon of God's present care and the eschatological horizon of the kingdom.

We noted in chapter 2 (reading C), regarding the figurative interpretation of 4:18–22, that this scene of the call of the disciples is a figure of repentance (4:17). Those who become disciples are "people who sat in darkness [who] have seen a great light" and on whom "light has dawned" (4:16). They repent, turning away from darkness, from "the region and shadow of death" (4:16), from their jobs and families (4:18–22), in order to turn toward this great light — which is, in the usual ambivalence of this symbolic world, either the kingdom that Jesus announces or Jesus himself.

Thus as the other figures of 4:18–22 express, discipleship is *in discontinuity* with Judaism, with one's *past*, but also with one's *present* (jobs, families), as can be expected if discipleship is conceptualized in terms of the eschatological future of the kingdom. Or as Luz points out regarding 5:21–48 (see reading C, CAW 3.4), discipleship as ethical practice is to be envisioned in terms of the "order of 'Law of the Kingdom,' and not of the world" that the antitheses present and that is "a ray of hope for a new, better human being in the coming of the Kingdom of God."[37] As such, the practice of discipleship has to be envisioned as involving a radical way of life in discontinuity with any kind of worldly ethical practice.

This *discontinuity* is also inscribed in the very practice of discipleship as it reflects another aspect of the eschatological horizon, namely, the final judgment. As the figurative interpretation of 7:13–27 indicates, disciples are expected to anticipate the eschatological judgment in their own ministry by making a clear distinction between true and false prophets (7:15), between true and false disciples (7:21–23) within the mixed body of the church, and also by clearly identifying outsiders, i.e., those who are not disciples, such as the scribes and Pharisees (5:20), the tax collectors and the Gentiles (5:46–47). In other words, as we saw in chapter 2 (reading C, CAW 3), the figure of "fishers of people" (4:19) indicates that the disciples' vocation includes a judgmental component.

We should not forget that this figure expresses the judgmental and soteriological ambivalence of the disciples' vocation. Discipleship involves expressions of a radical love (5:21–48; 7:12) that strives to overcome any obstacle or rift separating us from others, including enemies. The exclusivism of the judgmental aspect of the disciples' vocation, which reflects the eschatological horizon of the symbolic world of the Sermon on the Mount, is balanced by and is in tension with the *inclusivism* of the soteriological aspect of their vocation, which reflects the theological horizon of the present loving care of their heavenly Father. Indeed, disciples are to envision their vocation and their practice in terms of the horizon of the *present* manifestations of God: "Love your enemies...so that you may be children of your Father in heaven; for he makes his sun rise on the evil and on the good, and sends rain on the righteous and on the unrighteous" (5:44–45).

This inclusivism of discipleship as ethical practice opens the community of disciples to all those who want to join it, even if at first they have antagonistic attitudes. As we noted (see reading C, CAW 2.1) regarding Luz's figurative interpretation, the crowds are described in the framework of the Sermon (4:23–5:2; 7:28–8:1) as disciples who before and after the Sermon follow Jesus (4:25 and 8:1), despite the ambivalence introduced

---

37. Luz, *Matthew*, 431 (cf. 328–29, 341–42).

by the distinction between disciples and crowds in 5:1–2. But 5:21–48 also suggests that enemies (5:44) and evildoers, including Gentiles (the Romans as oppressors, to whom 5:41 alludes), are to be viewed as potential members of the community (thus one should pray for them, 5:44). This suggestion is supported not only by the mixed body of the community (as discussed above) but also by the rest of the Gospel, which presents as faithful, i.e., *as people who share the symbolic world of the community of disciples*, Gentiles such as the Roman centurion (8:5–13) and the Canaanite woman (15:22–28), as well as other people who at first glance are viewed as outsiders — such as the woman suffering from hemorrhages (9:20–22), the "little ones" (10:42; 18:10), and the children (18:2–5; 19:13–15), to mention only three examples.

Discipleship as a practice envisioned in terms of the theological horizon of God's present loving care conceives of itself *in continuity* with the past — with the law and the prophets, with Judaism, with the world. It does not mean that *the discontinuity* that is inscribed, for instance, in the judgmental aspect of the disciples' vocation and in repentance as the necessary turning away from — renunciation of — the evil of the world is to be dismissed as irrelevant. On the contrary, discipleship must hold together all the features of its practice envisioned in terms of the two horizons of the symbolic world of the Sermon on the Mount, which itself holds together these horizons in a single twofold horizon in which they are kept in tension. This fusion of the two horizons-in-tension, which respects their tension (by contrast with what would happen in the logic of other symbolic worlds where one or the other would be suppressed), takes place in the cult (as is expressed in 6:1–18; see reading C, CAW 3.5). This is best expressed in terms of the last antithesis (5:43–47). As mentioned above, this passage demands that disciples *pray* for their enemies. In prayer the disciples, who envision their practice in terms of the theological horizon of God's present loving care, can see these enemies as potential brothers and sisters with whom they hope to share the symbolic world of their open community. Yet this is not blind naivete. They still recognize their enemies as persecutors of the community (5:44b) or more generally as evildoers (5:39). With the judgmental perspective of a practice of discipleship envisioned in terms of the eschatological horizon, evildoers and enemies must also be recognized for what they are, as false prophets are also recognized (7:15–20).

The inclusive and exclusive horizons of the symbolic world, as well as the soteriological and judgmental aspects of the disciples' vocation, are held together without canceling each other in the context of the cult of the community i.e., in the context of the community engaged in the ritual reenvisioning of its practice of discipleship. This ritual involves the reaffirmation of its vocation as a community, a universal vocation as salt of the earth and light of the world (5:13–14). Thus disciples have to see their vocation as encompassing all evildoers, including their enemies and their persecutors. They have to be ready to welcome them into the community. The ritual affirms the soteriological aspect of the disciples' vocation.

The community ritual also shows that the judgmental aspect of the disciples' vocation is necessary for the performance of its soteriological function. This judgmental perspective is a part of the very worship service, which separates them from those who do not participate in the community; from those who cannot pray with them because for them God is not a loving Father (e.g., people like Gentiles, 7:8), and from those who are hypocrites (6:2, 5, 16) because they make a show of their piety instead of truly doing God's will.[38]

That the judgmental aspect is necessary to the performance of the disciples' vocation is demonstrated in teachings that the disciples need to avoid becoming like salt that has lost its taste (5:13), or people who are misled by a lustful eye (5:29), or people led back into darkness by an unhealthy eye (6:23). In sum, they need to grow in discipleship so that they do not lose it.

Growing in discipleship involves being conformed and conforming oneself to the symbolic world, a process that involves imitating members of the community who can be recognized as models of discipleship. In the context of the community, these are true religious leaders (true prophets) who again and again confirm and reinforce the faith of community members by representing for them the symbolic world, for instance, by leading them in worship. From these models of discipleship the disciples also need to learn, always anew, how to practice discipleship in ever new situations. In sum, any disciple is always in need of models of discipleship to follow.

Then the problem is to make sure that one follows an authentic model of discipleship, not false disciples and false prophets. While all disciples are potentially models of discipleship — all of them are to be fishers of people, salt, light, and thus religious leaders — one cannot be sure that all the members of the community as a mixed body are true disciples. Indeed, many in the community might be false prophets. In order to identify these models of discipleship whom they need to follow, they need to use *discernment*, discerning between good and evil fruit (7:16–20) in order to sort out true prophets/disciples from false prophets/disciples as one sorts out good and bad fish (13:47–48). This is the necessary judgmental aspect of the disciples' vocation. They must be able to recognize, for their own sake as well as for the sake of others, true models of discipleship. For this they must be able to identify and denounce false religious leaders.

Thus in the context of the cult of the community, yes, they can pray for enemies, persecutors, and evildoers of all kinds, with the hope of welcoming them one day in the community. But this does not prevent the

---

38. With Luz, it is important to note that this text should not be viewed as a call to reject a specific group of people (Jews), but a certain type of behavior, no matter who demonstrates it. Luz, *Matthew,* 357, 360, see 352–66; Davies and Allison, *Matthew,* 572–90.

disciples from using their judgmental discernment to identify these enemies and evildoers for what they are rather than taking them as models
to be imitated. In such cases, discerning that these people are evildoers who
should not be imitated does not seem to present any difficulty (but note
the ambivalence of 7:15–20). At any rate, it remains to be understood how,
according to this resocialization/perfectionist interpretation, one identifies
models of discipleship. Before doing so, let us consider how the alternative discernment/perfectionist interpretation of the Sermon on the Mount
envisions discipleship.

Reading D, CAT 2: The Plausibility of Discipleship as a Discernment/Perfectionist Ethical Practice

Reading D, CAT 2.1: Moral Discernment at the Heart of Discipleship as Practical Wisdom; Faith as Discerning Whom to Imitate

*The thematic interpretation of my commentary and its conclusions about
what the Sermon is and says underscore that the communication of moral
discernment (vision as process, characterized by a certain convictional pattern) is the primary goal of the Sermon on the Mount (see reading D, CAW 2).
One of these conclusions is that the Sermon on the Mount presupposes that
its readers already share the author's symbolic world. But they lack the moral
discernment that would allow them to be disciples who act according to the
teaching of the Sermon. They are like the foolish man (ὁμοιωθήσεται ἀνδπὶ
μωρῷ) who does not know how to discern a solid foundation for his house
(7:26–27) or like the salt that lost its flavor (τὸ ἅλας μωρανθῇ, 5:13), or
like people with bad eyes (6:22–23); in sum, they are people of little faith
(ὀλιγόπιστοι, 6:30). In order to become faithful disciples, such foolish readers need practical wisdom that comes from having moral discernment, like
the wise man (ἀνδρὶ φρονίμῳ) who knows how to discern a solid foundation
for his house (7:24–25), like salt, like people with a sound eye (6:22–23). In
sum, they need great faith, like the Canaanite woman whose persistent behavior demonstrates a discernment and practical wisdom that Jesus calls her
"great faith" (15:28, μεγάλη σου ἡ πίστις), and also like, for instance, the
centurion in 8:5–13 and the woman in 9:20–22, whose respective behavior
demonstrates exemplary faith because it involves discernment and practical
wisdom.*

*Thus moral discernment and the practical wisdom it provides are so cen-
tral to discipleship that they are identified with true faith. Having faith is not
primarily "believing in" a symbolic world (by contrast with reading C, CAT 2).
People might "believe in" Jesus and in his power/authority and thus recognize him as the eschatological Judge and call him "Lord" (7:21–22) and yet
not have actual faith, as is shown by the fact that such people are rejected.
People might "believe in" Scripture as an expression of God's will but show*

lack of actual faith by failing to discern other expressions of God's will — failing to recognize expressions of God's will in the attitude of tax collectors and Gentiles, in the spontaneous recognition of what one needs to give to one's children and of what one wishes others to do to oneself (7:7–12), and also in the manifestations of divine providence (5:45; 6:25–34).

Having faith is having the moral discernment that allows one to have an overabundant righteousness. *This specific kind of practical wisdom overflows all the limitations that symbolic worlds posit for those who believe in them, including the symbolic worlds centered on Scripture as an expression of God's will and centered on Jesus as the authoritative eschatological Judge.* This faith/moral discernment recognizes manifestations of divine providence as models of overabundant practice:

- In 5:45, the Father in heaven who "makes his sun rise on the evil and on the good," not merely on the good, "and sends rain on the righteous and on the unrighteous," not merely on the righteous, is a model for a practice that overflows the boundaries between evil and good or between righteous and unrighteous, however one or another symbolic world might define these distinctions;

- In 6:25–37, the Father in heaven of human disciples, who overabundantly takes care of birds of the air and of lilies of the field of so little value, and who will do even more for human disciples (6:26; 6:30, οὐ πολλῷ μᾶλλον ὑμᾶς, ὀλιγόπιστοι);

- In 6:8 and 7:11, the Father in heaven whose care for the disciples is much more than what Gentiles expect from their gods and is also much more than the care of human parents for their children.

It is this kind of divine overabundant practice, overabundant righteousness, that disciples are called to emulate: "Be perfect, therefore, as your heavenly Father is perfect" (5:48). In order to be such faithful disciples, people need faith/moral discernment, something that the Sermon on the Mount seeks to communicate to its readers. The question is, How does the Sermon communicate it? By providing us with models of discernment as practiced by Jesus.

Faith/discernment is the means for identifying the kind of behavior that needs to be practiced in an overabundant manner. It allows disciples to identify people whose concrete practices should be viewed as models of behavior for disciples, i.e., as the kinds of behavior (righteousness) that disciples need to perform in an overabundant way. We shall discuss these below (reading D, CAT 3.2). We need to note that the people whose behavior must be imitated might or might not belong to the Christian community. Although the Sermon on the Mount teaches moral discernment by expressing it in terms of a specific symbolic world, this moral discernment is not tied to it and thus is not tied to the community, in contrast to the resocialization/perfectionist interpretation *(see reading C, CAT 2). In both cases, the community is a "mixed body." Certain members of the community might indeed be identified as models, but others might be identified as false prophets (7:15-20) and as people who are far from being models of discipleship, since the Son of man will not recognize them (7:21-23). The difference is that in this discernment/perfectionist interpretation, models for disciples — be they models of discernment or models of behavior — are to be found as much (if not more) outside the community as inside it — as the examples of the Canaanite woman and the centurion suggest. Similarly, in the parable of the great judgment (25:37-40), Matthew gives as models for disciples people with compassionate behavior, who are clearly outsiders to the Christian community since they do not know that they have performed these acts to the Son of man and for his sake.*

In sum, the perspective of a discernment/perfectionist interpretation gives priority to the identification of virtues, good kinds of behavior, and ways of performing one's function well as a disciple in concrete situations. This perspective resists giving priority to the identification of persons who can serve as models of discipleship through all that they do as persons because as members of the community they embody in their lives the symbolic world proclaimed by the Sermon on the Mount (as is the case according to the resocialization/perfectionist interpretation; see reading C, CAT 2). Since virtues as expressions of practical wisdom[39] are to be identified one at a time in each concrete situation, they might be manifested by people who are far from being models for disciples in other aspects of their lives. Similarly, being faithful disciples is not embodying the symbolic world of the community but practicing in an overabundant way the good behavior that one discerns to be appropriate for a disciple in each given situation.

Reading D, CAT 2.2: Discipleship Shaped by the Moral Discernment of an Undivided Eye

After these preliminary observations and the thematic interpretation of the Sermon on the Mount and of Matthew 4:18-22 (see reading D, CAWs in both chap. 4 and chap. 2), we can now understand the plausibility of the conceptualization of discipleship from the perspective of this discernment/perfectionist interpretation. An overview of this conceptualization is the best way of showing its plausibility.

Let us remember that discipleship is being "like a wise man (ἀνδρὶ φρονίμῳ) who built his house on rock" because one "hears these words of [Jesus] and acts on them" (7:24). "These words of Jesus" include the call/command to

---

39. Speaking of "convictions" as values that are "felt" as euphoric or dysphoric in concrete situations — as I do in my commentary (see Patte, *Matthew*, 4–8) — or "proprioceptive values" as Greimas and Courtés do (see *Semiotics and Language*, 248) are two other ways of speaking about virtues. On practical wisdom, see above the section entitled "Reading C, CATs and Reading D, CATs: Perfectionist Preunderstandings of the Moral Life and Discipleship as Imitation."

*follow him (4:19), which is understood here as an invitation to join in Jesus'
ministry (as we saw in chap. 2, reading D, CAT 2). This ministry involves presenting to all (crowds of Israel at first, then crowds of Gentiles) the good news
of the nearness of the kingdom, both in words (preaching, teaching) and in
acts (healings, good deeds toward others), as is attributed to Jesus (4:23–25)
and his disciples (10:7–10; 28:18–20). This is a prophetic ministry in continuity with the prophets of Scripture, as we noted regarding 4:18–22 and as is
also indicated in 5:12 regarding disciples. It involves not only proclaiming the
dawning of the light (of the kingdom) as Isaiah had done (4:15–16) but also
being a manifestation of that light as Jesus was when he went to Capernaum
(4:13–14): "You are the light of the world" (5:14). Being a true disciple (like a
wise housebuilder) includes discerning that one is associated with this eschatological ministry of Jesus and thus that one's actions must be manifestations
of the light (of the kingdom) for others.*

*Being a true disciple also includes discerning how one's actions can be
such manifestations of the light for the world, and thus discerning how one
can "do" Jesus' word about this: "Let your light shine before others, so that
they may see your good works and give glory to your Father in heaven"
(5:16). The thematic dimension of the Sermon demonstrates that for this
purpose, one's practice of good works (righteousness) needs to be overabundant (5:20), as the light on the lampstand overflows and "gives light to
all in the house" (5:15). In order to understand how to practice this overabundant righteousness so that it may manifest the light of the kingdom for
others, i.e., in order to understand how to "strive first for the kingdom of God
and his righteousness" (6:33), one needs to discern and observe (see 6:26:
ἐμβλέψατε) God's righteousness, namely, the manifestations of divine providence. As discussed above (reading D, CAT 1), these are overabundant; they
are manifestations of God's goodness and care not only toward those who
deserve it but also toward those who do not deserve it. Conversely, in order
to be a faithful disciple manifesting God's kingdom and righteousness, one
must choose one's course of action exclusively on the basis of these manifestations of goodness that one has perceived, rather than choosing it on the
basis of the manifestations of evil that one also perceives. The person oriented
toward the perception of evil would end up striving for food, clothing (6:25–
34), and whatever else might seem to provide security and ward off anxiety,
such as wealth (mammon, 6:24), instead of striving for God's kingdom and
righteousness.*

*These verses are not merely describing how disciples should overcome
anxiety by recognizing manifestations of divine providence. They express thematically fundamental patterns that must characterize a life of discipleship.
More precisely, they posit two basic conditions for faithful discipleship, i.e., for
performing one's function as a disciple well (the definition of virtue): having
a sound eye and overabundant righteousness.*

The first basic condition is to have a sound eye, an undivided (ἁπλοῦς) eye

(6:22) that is totally focused on manifestations of goodness because it is from this perspective, and from this perspective alone, that one can discern the course of action that disciples must follow in any given concrete situation. In order to be light of the world — manifestations of the good news of the kingdom and of its nearness — disciples should not and need not develop courses of actions that are designed to ward off evil in any of its manifestations. These reactionary attitudes deny the nearness of the kingdom and therefore contradict the very vocation of discipleship. As is expressed by the parable, reacting to the presence of weeds in a wheat field and deciding to pull out the weeds is a disastrous course of action because the wheat would be pulled out along with the weeds (see Mt 13:24–30). But one can choose not to worry about weeds/evil, preferring a course of action that is focused on wheat/goodness because this very presence points to the nearness of the kingdom, which is also the harvest when the proper Judge, the Son of man, will destroy all evil (see 13:37–43). This is why a first basic condition for faithful discipleship is having a sound eye: true moral discernment that allows one to identify true manifestations of goodness.

The second basic condition for faithful discipleship is that the disciples' actions be characterized by overabundance, as are God's providential manifestations. As we have already seen, a good deed needs to be practiced so that it positively affects not only good people but also evildoers (such as our enemies). As presented in 5:20–48, overabundant righteousness involves perceiving (with a sound eye) in something that might appear to be negative (such as the law, You shall not murder) a good, positive injunction (such as, Preserve, uphold, and restore good relationship with others) and practicing this positive injunction not only in the realm ח which it was intended (a people, a community, cf. 5:21–26) but also beyond that realm (with outsiders, enemies; cf. 5:38–48).[40]

Does this mean that it is in "the law and the prophets" that disciples are expected to find what they should do in an overabundant way? Not directly, otherwise they would not need to have a sound eye — moral discernment. It is in the law and the prophets as practiced by people, and in the equivalent of the law and the prophets as practiced by people (7:9–12) that disciples are expected to find with their sound eye manifestations of goodness, which they are supposed to emulate in an overabundant way.

Consequently, discipleship involves joining in the performance of good by someone else and pursuing this righteous practice beyond the realm in which this person performed it. It is in this sense that discipleship involves being associated with Jesus' ministry, in order to carry out this ministry beyond its original geographical and temporal borders. But it also appears that discipleship involves following models other than Jesus (reading D, CAT 3.1; 3.2; 3.3).

---

40. See again Patte, *Matthew*, 77–84.

For an interpretation in terms of a resocialization/perfectionist perspective, the preceding conclusions do not make sense. This is to be expected since instead of looking for models *of behavior* that one should practice in an overabundant way, in a resocialization/perfectionist interpretation disciples are to look for models *of discipleship*, i.e., for people who are embodying the symbolic world of the Sermon in an exemplary way.

Reading C, CAT 3: The Plausibility of Conforming to the Twofold Symbolic World of the Sermon by Imitating Models of Discipleship

From the perspective of the resocialization/perfectionist interpretation centered on the symbolic world with a twofold horizon of the Sermon on the Mount, readers can readily identify in the Gospel characters (and possibly in people of their experience) models of discipleship whose exemplary behavior they should imitate, as well as antimodels of discipleship whom they should distrust. This conception of imitation embodies the ambivalence of this symbolic world, which keeps in tension an ideal eschatological future and a flawed, mixed present. The correlation between the ambivalent symbolic world and imitation can be put in one formulaic sentence: the relationship of "models of discipleship" to "imitators" is similar to the relationship between the eschatological future and the present. Since models of discipleship are religious leaders who should be followed, for the imitators (the other disciples) they represent "the new, better human being in the coming of the kingdom of God";[41] they are models of "higher righteousness."[42] And yet these models are found in the present, where one also finds other manifestations of the loving care of God.

The ambivalence of the symbolic world is also reflected by the fact that imitating these models means being both in continuity and in discontinuity with them; being both like them and unlike them. In this symbolic world, discontinuity is an intrinsic part of the conception of discipleship as religious leadership. A model of discipleship is a religious leader whom other disciples should *follow* (thus continuity), but at some distance because following implies being behind (and thus some discontinuity). Models are ideals that one strives to imitate by duplicating their behavior without ever fully succeeding, in the same way that the higher righteousness presented

---

41. Luz, *Matthew*, 431.

42. A righteousness that belongs to another order of law ("the order of law of the kingdom") as compared with the usual kind of righteousness of this world. See Luz, *Matthew*, 269–70, 273, passim. Davies and Allison (*Matthew*, 498–501, 504, passim) call it in the same sense, "better righteousness." Note that this is a category that is different as compared with the "qualitative" interpretation (the "better righteousness" of the deontological interpretation) and with the "quantitative" interpretation (the "overabundant righteousness" of the consequentialist and of the discernment/perfectionist interpretations); reading A, CAW 4; reading A, CAT 3; reading B, CAW 5; reading B, CAT 2, 3; reading D, CAW 3; reading D, CAT 3.

in the Sermon on the Mount is an ideal vision of life in the eschatological kingdom.

No wonder, therefore, that Christ is almost the only one worthy of being viewed as a model for disciples and that discipleship might readily be conceived of as an "imitation of Christ" (*imitatio Christi*), even if Christ is not the only model. It is not surprising either that besides presenting Christ as an ideal model that disciples should imitate, the Gospel according to Matthew (in its figurative dimension) presents many antimodels of discipleship, among which the models of failed discipleship represented by most of the story of the Twelve!

Reading D: CAT 3: The Plausibility of Discerning What Discipleship Entails by Identifying Appropriate Models

The discernment/perfectionist interpretation involves a very different understanding of discipleship as imitation because (1) "what" must be imitated according to true moral discernment is not a person, but a specific attitude (a moral discernment) and/or a specific behavior performed by that person; and because (2) "imitating" does not mean following at a distance, but participating in the action of that person by performing it beyond its original realm in an "overabundant" practice.

Regarding the first point, we have already noted that according to the discernment/perfectionist interpretation, disciples need to learn true moral discernment by following models of discernment. Furthermore, as they use this moral discernment (a sound eye), disciples need to identify positive behaviors that are models of behavior. This does not mean that these kinds of behavior are in themselves extraordinary. They might be nothing more than the most ordinary behavior of ordinary people who love their families and welcome their friends (5:46 – 47), or the kind of behavior that common people like others to show toward them (7:12). This means that models of behavior for disciples might potentially be found in all contexts of human experience. It might be an attitude or an act performed by someone who otherwise is far from being perfect – his or her other attitudes and/or actions should not be imitated. Thus models of behavior might be found among people who are not at all related to the community of disciples. Conversely, the fact that a behavior is performed by disciples, even if it is in the community, does not guarantee that it is a model of behavior. The identification of actual models of behavior demands the true moral discernment (a sound eye) that the Sermon on the Mount (and the rest of the Gospel according to Matthew) teaches by providing models of discernment.

This understanding of "what" needs to be imitated also transforms the way in which "imitation" itself is practiced. As has already been suggested, imitating Jesus, in this discernment/perfectionist interpretation, involves following him by being associated with his ministry (see chap. 2, reading D,

CAT) and thus prolonging his ministry in new locations and historical periods. As we consider specific examples, we shall see that the same applies for any "models for discipleship"; by practicing in an overabundant way behavior demonstrated by certain people, one participates in what they are doing in an overabundant way — beyond the realm in which they circumscribe their actions.

While Jesus is viewed in both perfectionist interpretations of the Sermon on the Mount as the primary model for disciples, the function of this model is quite different in the discernment/perfectionist interpretation — according to which Jesus is a model of discernment, but not necessarily of behavior — and in the resocialization/perfectionist interpretation — according to which Jesus is a model of behavior.

Reading C, CAT 3.1: *Jesus as the Primary Model of Discipleship* — Imitatio Christi *as Resocialization*

Discipleship has been defined traditionally as imitation of Christ (*imitatio Christi*)[43] because Jesus is presented as *"the" primary model of discipleship* in the Gospel according to Matthew (or, more specifically, in its figurative dimension). In terms of the symbolic world on which this resocialization/ perfectionist interpretation is centered, it is plausible to recognize Jesus as "the" model of discipleship because he is presented as fulfilling in an ideal way the higher righteousness that the Sermon on the Mount allows its readers to envision.

Jesus "does" the will of God, which he discloses in the Sermon on the Mount. As the eschatological Lord, the new Moses, the fulfillment of the prophets, Jesus fulfills throughout his ministry the eschatological vision of life that he unveils in the Sermon on the Mount: he fulfills the type of the better human being; he manifests the higher righteousness throughout his ministry. Thus disciples must strive to do as he did, i.e., to duplicate his actions, even though it is clear that here and now they cannot reach the ideal that Jesus represents.

Since in this interpretation the Lord's Prayer plays such a central role (see reading C, CAW 2.2, 2.3), it is enough to take note of how Jesus (during his ministry as presented by Matthew) fulfills its petitions — understood here both as setting ethical demands for the one who prays and as petitions for eschatological fulfillments (the moral and eschatological dimensions of the Lord's Prayer).

1. Jesus "hallowed" God's name (6:9), not only by giving thanks to God (11:25) but also by fulfilling all righteousness (3:15) and by manifesting God's mercy (9:13); in this way he brings people to glorify God's name (e.g., 9:8; 15:31; 21:9, 15–16).

---

43. Davies and Allison, *Matthew*, 411–12.

2. Regarding the coming of the kingdom (6:10), he preached it (4:23) when he said, "Repent for the kingdom of heaven has come near" (4:17) and when he uttered parables of the kingdom (e.g., 13:24–33).

3. Regarding doing God's will ("your will be done," γενηθήτω τὸ θέλημά σου, 6:10), he totally submitted to God's will for mercy (9:13; 12:7), including during the Passion: "not as I will, but as you will" (26:39); "your will be done" (γενηθήτω τὸ θέλημά σου, 26:42, with the same wording as in the Lord's Prayer).

4. Regarding the petition about bread (6:11), he gave bread to the hungry (14:15–21; 15:32–38) and met people's needs, whatever they might be, with compassion.

5. Regarding forgiveness (6:12), he ate with sinners (9:10–13), a prefiguration of the Messianic banquet and a sign that he forgave their sins (as well as healing their diseases). Elsewhere, he explicitly forgave people their sins (cf. 9:1–8), including the disciples' denials of him (he commissioned such disciples, 28:16–20).

6. Regarding temptation (6:13), he was tempted (4:1–11) and afflicted (the Passion and the cross, which Matthew presents as a temptation, "If you are the Son of God," 4:3, 6; 27:40; cf. 27:43), but he was delivered from the evil one (Satan, 4:10–11) and from evil (the Passion; cf. the resurrection).

Similarly, Jesus can be identified as one of the blessed ones described in the beatitudes (5:3–12), as Davies and Allison point out: "Jesus was himself meek (11:29; 21:5). Jesus mourned (26:36–46). Jesus was righteous and 'fulfilled all righteousness' (3:15; 27:4, 19). Jesus showed mercy (9:27; 15:22; 17:15; 20:30–1). And Jesus was persecuted and reproached (26–27)."[44]

He also acted according to the teaching of the antitheses. For instance, Luz notes that Jesus' strikingly relaxed relationship to women (as in 8:14–15; 9:20–22; 15:21–28; 20:20–28; 26:6–13) should be seen as an implementation of the teaching of the second antithesis (6:27–30).[45] Furthermore, regarding the fourth antithesis (5:33–37), during the Passion Jesus avoids using an oath by answering "you have said so" to the high priest who "adjures" him to utter an oath (26:63–64). Similarly, Jesus is presented as implementing the teaching about treasures in heaven (6:19–34), for instance, in 8:20, "the Son of man has nowhere to lay his head."

In sum, Jesus is presented as a model of discipleship to be imitated, since he fulfills all these teachings of the Sermon on the Mount.[46] Yet he is not presented as systematically fulfilling all the teachings of the Sermon on the

---

44. Davies and Allison, *Matthew*, 467.

45. Luz, *Matthew*, 296.

46. Thus Luz (*Matthew*, 408) underscores that Jesus as presented in the Gospel according to Matthew served as a model for representants of "early Christian itinerant radicalism."

Mount. For instance, Jesus (as a character in the Gospel according to Matthew) who calls his followers to seek reconciliation at all costs (6:21–26) and to love their enemies (5:43–48) is far from doing so, when he curses the cities in 11:20–24 and the scribes and Pharisees in Matthew 23. In the symbolic world of the Gospel, this is another tension arising from Jesus' dual role as model of discipleship and eschatological Judge.

Just as disciples should not pretend to duplicate the role of Jesus as the eschatological Judge (see reading C, CAW 3.9),[47] in the same way they cannot pretend to duplicate Jesus' fulfillment of the higher righteousness proclaimed by the Sermon on the Mount. Jesus typifies the better human being of the vision of eschatological life presented by the Sermon.

Reading C, CAT 3.2: Other Characters of the Gospel as Models of Discipleship

According to the resocialization/perfectionist interpretation, although other characters of the Gospel are far from being ideal models as Jesus is, they are nevertheless presented as models of discipleship. These other characters, e.g., the Twelve, are models only through a few aspects of their behavior because the rest of their behavior is not worthy of imitation. Of course, the failures of the Twelve (e.g., their lack of faith, 14:28–33; their misunderstandings, 16:21–23; 20:20–23; their denials, 26:69–75) are not to be imitated. Yet they remain models of discipleship to be imitated because of their other deeds (e.g., abandoning everything to follow Jesus, 4:18–22; 19:27, 29) and because of the description of what they are supposed to do (e.g., their itinerant missionary activity, 10:7–10). In sum, they are models of discipleship only insofar as their attitude and behavior reflects Jesus' and his teaching

This ambivalence of the Twelve — who are and are not models of discipleship — is an appropriate reminder that the teaching of the Sermon on the Mount is a vision of the ideal eschatological community, which is only partially fulfilled in the present time by "the community . . . on the way to the gate of life,"[48] which the present church is.

From this perspective, it becomes clear that other characters of the Gospel are also models of discipleship because they fulfill one or another of the teachings of the Sermon on the Mount. For instance, using once again the petitions of the Lord's Prayer as lenses, we have to wonder, Were not those who were healed or those whose sick were healed (e.g., 4:23–24) delivered from evil (6:13)? Is it not the case that those who followed Jesus repented (and thus accepted God's will, 6:10) in response to his proclamation of the kingdom (see chap. 2, reading C, CAW, the figurative interpretation of

---

47. Identifying the false prophets in order to avoid following them and to warn others about them is not "judging" them.

48. Luz, *Matthew*, 437.

4:18–22)? Were not the children who cried "Hosanna to the Son of David" (21:15) hallowing God's name (6:9, uttering "perfect praise," 21:16)? Was not the unnamed woman hallowing God's name when she poured ointment on Jesus' head (26:6–13)?

Similarly, the crowds (who follow Jesus, 4:25; 8:1), the children (cf. 18:1–4; 19:13–15), the "little ones" (10:42; 18:6), the women (throughout the Gospel, see below), and other characters — such as Gentiles (e.g., 8:5–13; 15:21–28), the "blind and the lame" (21:14) — who are, in one way or another, reviled or rejected by other people can all be said to be "blessed ones" (5:3–12), and thus models of discipleship.[49] Insofar as these characters have one or several of the characteristics of the "blessed ones," they should themselves be considered as models of discipleship.

These diverse characters are in most instances presented as *positive* models of discipleship, by contrast with the Twelve who often end up being presented as *negative* models of discipleship. In all the scenes involving them as characters, women are presented as positive models of discipleship through one or another aspect of their behavior. I include here the five women of the genealogy — Tamar, Rahab, Ruth, the wife of Uriah, and Mary, 1:1–25; Peter's mother-in-law, 8:14–15; the ruler's daughter and the woman in the crowd, 9:18–26; the Canaanite woman, 15:21–28; the woman who anoints Jesus, 26:6–13; the women at the scene of Peter's denial, 26:69–75; the wife of Pilate, 27:19; the "many women" at the cross, among whom "Mary Magdalene, Mary the mother of James and Joseph, and the mother of the sons of Zebedee," 27:55–61; the women as Easter witnesses, 28:1–10. The only two exceptions to this positive portrayal of women include Herodias and her daughter, 14:1–12, and the mother of the sons of Zebedee in 20:20–28.[50] By contrast, the male disciples are presented as negative models in many scenes. Even though they are presented in a less negative light than in the Gospel according to Mark, they still are presented negatively (even at the time of their commissioning, "some doubted," 28:17)!

These positive models of discipleship reflect for the readers of the Gos-

---

49. Thus in agreement with Luz (*Matthew*, 242, passim), the second-person teaching (in 5:11–12 and in the rest of the Sermon on the Mount) is addressed to the total community, indeed, to the world. This is so, not merely because the vocabulary about defamation and persecution is quite general, and thus is an adequate description of the situation of the community (so Luz) but also and mainly because the "you" (disciples) is a figure of discipleship.

50. As Amy-Jill Levine points out: "Women who appear apart from husband, father, or son assume positive, active roles in the Gospel (8:14–17; 9:20–22; 12:42; 13:33; 15:21–28; 21:31–32; 25:1–13; 26:6–13; 27:55–61; 28:1–10)" ("Matthew," in *The Women's Bible Commentary*, ed. Carol A. Newsom and Sharon H. Ringe [Louisville: Westminster/John Knox, 1992], 253; see also 252–62). Our respective lists are slightly different because Levine takes into account other passages that include women as characters in parables or other discourses, and because she highlights in this quotation women "apart from husband, father, or son." But her comment does not exclude that, in Matthew, women in relationship to husband, father, or son might also (but not always) have "positive, active roles."

pel according to Matthew the twofold symbolic world of the Sermon on the Mount and its ambivalence. As such, they typify the concrete ways in which actual disciples, members of the church as religious leaders, might be expected to carry out their discipleship in the flawed, mixed present situations. These models help readers/disciples identify religious leaders whom they can follow on the road to the kingdom, in the steps of Christ who alone fulfills the eschatological vision of the better human being.

Reading C, CAT 3.3: The Identification of False Models of Discipleship Not to Be Imitated

Because the identification of religious leaders plays such a significant role in the resocialization of the readers/disciples in the symbolic world of the Sermon, the identification of false religious leaders, false prophets, and other negative models of discipleship becomes essential. Without such an identification of false models, faithful discipleship is not possible; in the "mixed" situation that exists at present (before the end of time), we must strive to overcome the evil that these false disciples (false prophets, etc.) promote.

By contrast, according to the discernment/perfectionist interpretation, identification of these false models does not need to be a concern of true disciples because (1) it is clear who they are, because (2) one can be confident of God's protection from the evil they might devise, and because (3) deciding on a course of action can only be wrongheaded when this decision is made in a reactionary way.

Such negative models of discipleship are not difficult to identify in the Gospel itself. For instance, the Twelve (as characters) are often presented as negative models of discipleship. They are described as having "little faith" (6:30; cf. 8:26; 14:31; 15:33; 17:20); being unable to envision suffering, hardship, or to resist evil (5:10, 12, 39; 7:14; cf. 16:21–23; 17:23; 26:51); wanting to be "great" and being self-confident rather than poor in spirit and meek (5:3, 4; cf. 18:1; 20:20–23; 26:33–35); wanting to limit forgiveness (5:21–26; 6:12, 14–15; cf. 18:22); judging and rejecting the good deeds of others (7:1–4; cf. 26:6–13).

Identifying negative models of discipleship has been necessary for the church from the time of Jesus' ministry to the present. But today identifying positive and negative models of discipleship is much more complex because the church is "mixed" and ambivalent. It is easy to be seduced into following and imitating people who are models of false discipleship. Thus according to this interpretation, 7:13–27 urges readers to identify false prophets in the Christian community, who should not be imitated.

In this interpretation, as Luz notes, in and of itself, the criterion of the "fruit" is not sufficient for identifying these false prophets. Identifying models of false prophets (false disciples) in the Gospel is thus necessary in order to identify them in our present and to avoid being misled by them. The Pharisees, scribes, and Sadducees as characters of the Gospel are presented by the text as models of false discipleship. This is indicated by the relationship that the text establishes between 7:15–23 and 3:7–10: the image of the bad tree bearing evil fruit, which is used in both texts, is directed against the Pharisees and Sadducees in 3:7–10. "Every tree that does not bear good fruit is cut down and thrown into the fire" (3:10b, repeated in 7:19). As is clear from 7:15–23, the problem with such false prophets is not so much their teaching (they say the right thing, calling Jesus "Lord") as their deeds;[51] similarly, the teaching of the scribes and Pharisees remains valid ("do whatever they teach you and follow it," 23:3a); the problem is that "they do not practice what they teach" (23:3b). This is the attitude that Matthew calls ἀνομία, lawlessness (7:23). It does not involve completely discarding the law, but rather failing to have the higher righteousness that characterizes true disciples (5:20; cf. also 23:13ff.). The scribes and Pharisees do many things demanded by the law, but they neglect "the weightier matters of the law: justice and mercy and faith" (23:23) or fail to have deeds that befit repentance (3:8).[52]

Another model of false discipleship to which the teaching of 7:15–23 points is the figure of the false prophets who "will arise and lead many astray" (24:11) in the end time. They will bring about ἀνομία, lawlessness (24:12; 7:23), with the result that "love" will cool down. In sum, in the present time, when the church approaches the end time as described in 24:11–12,[53] the identification of the false disciples, with the help of the model of false discipleship that the Pharisees and Sadducees provide in the gospel, is all the more important. But the false disciples should not be ejected from the church. The wheat will be separated from weeds at the judgment. While the Pharisees and Sadducees are identified as unfaithful members of the community (the chosen people), and thus as persons whom one should not take as models of discipleship, they remain part of the "mixed body" of the community in the same way that the old and the

---

51. As Luz (*Matthew,* 442–43) emphasizes, taking into account the redaction of the Q material about the bad tree bearing evil fruit (cf. Lk 6:43–45 and Mt 12:33–35).

52. Thus "false prophets" and their models, the scribes and Pharisees, are not necessarily people who proclaim false words of revelation. Yet the ambiguity remains because the same image of the bad tree bearing evil fruits is once again used in 12:33–35 about the Pharisees, this time with an interpretation of the evil fruit as evil words, namely, saying that Jesus' authority to cast out demons comes from "Beelzebul, the prince of demons" (12:24) — instead of saying that he is Lord (7:21–23). This seems to be inconsistent with the figure of false prophets in 7:15–23, until one takes note that in 7:23 the false prophets are rejected at the judgment as people who are unknown to the Lord. In other words, these false prophets do not acknowledge the true authority of Jesus as Lord; their words, including "Lord, Lord" are false words; even though they appear (in their "sheep's clothing") to acknowledge the authority of Jesus, they do not. Truly acknowledging Jesus' authority as Lord is acknowledging the authority of his teaching by obeying it.

53. As Luz (*Matthew,* 442) and Davies and Allison (*Matthew,* 705, 718–19) suggest; against Schweizer, *Matthew,* 198–99.

new Mosaic covenants should not be separated, torn apart from each other, at least "until heaven and earth pass away" (5:18).

Reading C, CAT 3.4: A Resocialization/Perfectionist Interpretation of Discipleship according to the Sermon on the Mount

The teaching of the Sermon on the Mount regarding discipleship according to this resocialization/perfectionist interpretation can now be summarized. The figurative interpretation has shown the legitimacy of concluding that the Sermon offers its symbolic world to readers. As readers make this symbolic world theirs and are resocialized, the Sermon on the Mount enables them to identify models of discipleship that they should imitate as well as false prophets and false disciples whom they should not imitate. By identifying such models and antimodels in the rest of the Gospel, and most importantly by identifying them in the church of their time, such readers assume the role of disciples as religious leaders. They show that they conceive of themselves, in light of the twofold horizon of the Sermon's symbolic world, as people with an ambivalent mission in the flawed, mixed situation of the church — indeed, of the entirety of human experience. Having identified models of discipleship and false prophets, they find themselves obligated to imitate the former, to reject the latter, and to call others to do the same. In so doing, they assume religious leadership, becoming models of discipleship. They carry out both the positive (soteriological) and judgmental aspects of their vocation by giving as examples those they identified as models of discipleship and by denouncing false prophets. Furthermore, despite their limitations, they strive to be faithful disciples by living in the flawed, mixed present situation in light of the vision provided by the eschatological and theological horizons of the symbolic world presented in the Sermon on the Mount. Ideally, these readers are resocialized in the symbolic world of the Sermon on the Mount, which they share and now embody with the other faithful members of the church.

The discernment/perfectionist interpretation of the teaching of the Sermon on the Mount regarding discipleship differs significantly, although these two perfectionist perspectives are closely related in their conceptualizations of discipleship.

Reading D, CAT 3.1: Jesus as Model of Discernment and as Model of Overabundant Righteousness

For the discernment/perfectionist interpretation, discipleship is also defined as imitation of Christ (imitatio Christi). Because Jesus fully shares our human condition, he is a model for disciples. Jesus is "like a wise man" (ἀνδρὶ φρονίμῳ, 7:24) who demonstrates his moral discernment by fulfilling "all righteousness" (3:15; see 5:17). He is thus a model of discernment as well as a model of overabundant righteousness. By imitating him (by giving the same

*"overabundant" character to their lives), disciples are associated with Jesus'
ministry, which they prolong; they "follow him," as they were called to do
(4:19).*

*From this perspective, disciples are not confronted by the dilemma of
being called to imitate Jesus and of being totally unable to fulfill the
higher righteousness that he exemplifies (according to the resocialization/
perfectionist interpretation; see reading C, CAT 3.1). Jesus' behavior needs
to be imitated by disciples; it is a model of righteousness for them. But imitating Jesus is a matter of having the same pattern of behavior (and not the
same behavior): a pattern of overabundance.*

*Overabundant righteousness (5:20, 47–48) is not an extraordinary right-
eousness that could only be practiced by an extraordinary person (Jesus as
Christ) or in an extraordinary time (the future eschatological time). It is not
a "higher" righteousness (as it is in reading C), but a common kind of good
behavior (righteousness) that is applied beyond the realm in which it is usually applied. Since discipleship involves practicing common kinds of behavior
in an overabundant way, one also needs a model for discerning the types of
behavior that should be practiced in this extravagant way. The Sermon on the
Mount as proclaimed by Jesus (and the rest of Jesus' ministry in the Gospel
according to Matthew) offers such a model of discernment.*

Reading D, CAT 3.2: Jesus as Model of Discernment — Recognizing Righteousness in the Behavior of Ordinary People and Offering It as Model

*As the "I" who pronounces the Sermon on the Mount, Jesus is presented
as a model of discernment who identifies people with righteous behaviors.
With the moral discernment of his particular practical wisdom, Jesus points to
and affirms certain kinds of behavior that, in view of the kingdom, should be
extended beyond what is customary and thus be imitated in an overabundant
way. Disciples should have the same kind of moral discernment.*

*In this interpretation, Jesus' utterance of the beatitudes (5:3–10) is a
demonstration of his practice of moral discernment. This can be seen when
the beatitudes are interpreted in terms of the entire thematic organization of
the Sermon and especially in terms of 7:13–27 (see reading D, CAW 2.2). As
a first model of discernment, the beatitudes provide lenses the readers need
in order to have the true discernment that will allow them to identify models
of behavior, as Jesus did. Actually, the beatitudes straightforwardly provide
criteria for identifying people who demonstrate the kinds of behavior that
distinguish them as models. These are ordinary behaviors of ordinary people
who find themselves (or put themselves) in certain types of situations: ordinary people who are poor in spirit, who mourn, who are meek, who hunger
and thirst for justice[54] (because they suffer from injustice), who are merci-*

---

54. "Righteousness" is understood here as the practice of justice.

ful, pure in heart, peacemakers, and/or persecuted for righteousness' sake (5:3–10).

Disciples are called to discern, as Jesus did, models of righteousness in the behavior of people in the concrete situations around them. There is no suggestion that any of these people show extraordinary or heroic behavior. This is the behavior of ordinary people who may not feel they have any choice in life (and thus are poor in spirit); the behavior of ordinary people who are grieving for one reason or another; who might be co-opted and alienated (and thus are meek); who suffer from injustice (and thus thirst for justice) and are persecuted; who show compassion, are pure in heart, and are peacemakers, as many people are in various situations of their daily lives. Following Jesus, disciples who practice this moral discernment should recognize models in the behavior of ordinary people leading ordinary lives. By proclaiming the Sermon, Jesus teaches his disciples appropriate moral discernment.

Reading D, CAT 3.3: Disciples Affirming and Practicing in an Overabundant Way the Models of Righteousness They Have Discerned in the Behavior of Ordinary People

Disciples who practice this moral discernment and recognize models in the behavior of ordinary people in their daily lives should also affirm this behavior as a manifestation of righteousness worthy of the kingdom; they should do so by imitating these people's behavior. For the disciples this involves associating themselves with those who are poor in spirit, who mourn, who are hungry and thirsty for justice, who are peacemakers, etc., and thus learning from these people. But this does not mean doing as they do. For instance, disciples who follow these models of behavior are not to share the mourning, the meekness, or the thirst for justice of oppressed people in whom they discern such models. The disciples can "sympathize" with the oppressed, but they cannot truly share their situation or share their feelings as victims of oppression and of injustice, and they are not asked to pretend to do so. Disciples are to fulfill these models of behavior in an overabundant way by practicing them in a different realm — the realm of their own concrete lives. Through this overabundant righteousness they become the light of the world; they manifest the kingdom in their lives, and they proclaim the ways in which the victims of oppression manifest the kingdom.

Following this model and using the beatitudes as general criteria, disciples "following Jesus" (here as a model of discernment) are thus invited to identify models of righteousness in the behavior of ordinary people around them (thus the importance of the impersonal form of the beatitudes, 5:3–10). This means that faithful disciples follow/imitate Jesus by following/imitating the models of righteousness that they discern in ordinary people around them. For this, disciples need to recognize in the actual behaviors of these ordi-

nary people true models of righteousness, i.e., ways of behaving that are right before God.[55]

Reading D, CAT 3.4: From True Moral Discernment to Overabundant Righteousness

The discernment/perfectionist interpretation shows the plausibility of this view of discipleship as ethical practice by referring to the body of the Sermon on the Mount (5:17–7:12). This interpretation points out how the presentation of Jesus' fulfillment of the law provides a model of the way in which true moral discernment leads to the practice of overabundant righteousness. As the disciples/readers implement the teaching of the beatitudes about discernment, they are expected to recognize that Jesus points to models of behavior in the tax collectors and the Gentiles, who love those who love them and salute those who salute them (5:46–47). These are good behaviors that disciples should affirm by practicing in an overabundant way; for instance, if they are persecuted (5:11–12; 5:44), by loving and saluting those who persecute them (5:45). Reading 5:17–45 from this perspective, disciples should recognize that the law as taught and practiced by scribes and Pharisees (5:20; see 23:3) presents good behaviors that should be affirmed and viewed as models of behavior for the disciples (see reading D, CAW 3.5).

As in the previous cases, the models of behavior represented by each of the commandments (5:19) should be "fulfilled" (5:17) by being practiced in an overabundant way, as Jesus exemplifies in the following verses. This involves (as we noted in reading D, CAW 3.5 and 3.6) discerning how each commandment and how its ordinary, literal practice (e.g., not murdering, 5:21) includes a model of behavior—for instance, avoiding anything that would destroy good relationships with others and doing whatever it takes to preserve and reestablish such relationships (5:22–26). But such models of behavior are to be carried out in an overabundant way only in situations where they are appropriate, as the next examples about commandments concerning adultery and divorce show (5:27–32). Disciples must discern whether or not a good relationship (such as marriage) still exists before doing whatever it takes to preserve and reestablish it[56] or whether or not a wrong relationship (such as adultery) already exists, before doing whatever it takes to avoid it.[57] Thus discerning models of behavior (models of righteousness) also involves discerning how to practice this righteousness in an overabundant way by internalizing it

---

55. From the perspective of this discernment/perfectionist interpretation, one can even say that the behavior that is taken as a model of righteousness should itself actualize a motivation based on true discernment/faith — since what one is inwardly (one's deepest motivations) is necessarily revealed by one's outward actions ("you will know them by their fruits...every good tree bears good fruit," 7:16–17). This is what the disciples should have recognized as they identified this behavior as a model of righteousness.

56. The point emphasized in 19:3–9.

57. Thus the exception "except on the ground of unchastity" (5:32) is included in the prohibition of divorce.

and considering how it applies in concrete situations in all aspects of one's life (such as those given as examples in 5:21–48).

Faithful disciples (true prophets) are those who internalize such models of righteousness, who allow these models to define their vocation, intention, and thus their will, and who consistently act in conformity with these inner intentions by practicing this kind of righteousness in an unfailing, unwavering, steady way in all aspects of their lives – thus practicing it as an overabundant righteousness.

The thematic interpretation and its conclusions about what the Sermon is and says have identified these points (see reading D, CAW 3.1–3.8), which I do not need to repeat here. It is enough to emphasize how the teaching of 5:17–7:12 further expresses this process.

Jesus finds models of righteousness, i.e., specific instances of behavior that fit the criteria posited by the beatitudes, by observing with a sound, undivided eye the behavior of people around him: the behavior of the scribes and Pharisees as they follow their Scriptures; of the tax collectors and the Gentiles as they follow their own traditions; and even of the disciples as they follow their natural inclinations (7:9–12). Observing these people with a sound eye does not mean being blind to the evil in their behavior. The disciples are described as evil ("you then, who are evil," 7:11). The very mention of "tax collectors" and "Gentiles" evokes the dubious morality of their lives (see 6:7, where Gentiles are described as pagans; see also, e.g., 18:17). The mention of "scribes and Pharisees" has the same effect (see 23:2–35). Nevertheless, observing these people with a sound eye involves bracketing out all this evil so as to discern in their concrete ways of behaving models of righteousness that disciples should affirm, internalize, and then practice in all aspects of their own lives, and thus in an overabundant way.

This discernment involves recognizing and affirming that these "evil people" (such as the disciples, in 7:9–12, but also by implication, the tax collectors, the Gentiles, and the scribes and Pharisees) have good motivations, at least for the specific actions viewed as models of behavior. Such people have an instinctive knowledge of what is good to do (for their children, 7:11); what they deeply wish[58] is the right thing to do ("the law and the prophets," 7:12). Thus these specific righteous behaviors of "evil people" reflect true discernment/faith; these "evil people" also are models of discernment/faith for disciples, however surprising this may seem.

We can perceive the plausibility of this overabundant righteousness as a practice through which disciples fulfill their vocation as light of the world. When disciples practice these good works (5:16) of overabundant righteousness before scribes and Pharisees, or tax collectors and Gentiles, or people like them, these people readily recognize these actions as good works because they are nothing other than the implementation of their own positive

---

58. "Do to others as you [would wish, θέλητε] them do to you," 7:12.

*values (virtues) written large. Then the disciples are "light" for them, manifesta-
tions of the kingdom for them. Then these people cannot remain indifferent;
either they give glory to God for what they perceive as glorious fulfillments
of their own values (5:16) or they laugh at and persecute the disciples for
what they perceive as grotesque and vicious caricatures of their views and
their lives (5:11–12). Those who give glory to God might want to become
disciples by recognizing the legitimacy of their own discernment that the
disciples have affirmed and by allowing this discernment to guide them not
only into discrete acts of righteousness but also into a life of overabundant
righteousness.*

Reading D, CAT 3.5: Jesus as Model of Overabundant Righteousness Who Points to Other Models of Righteousness and of Faith/Discernment

*The rest of Jesus' ministry as presented in the Gospel of Matthew can be read
as descriptions of overabundant righteous practice. The list of passages would
include all those mentioned in the resocialization/perfectionist interpretation
(see reading C, CAT 3.1) where Jesus actualizes the vision of (eschatological) higher righteousness. I do not need to list them again. Since here Jesus
is understood to exemplify overabundant (not "higher") righteousness, I need
to demonstrate with a few examples how these models of overabundant righteousness in Jesus' ministry are to be understood from the perspective of the
Sermon on the Mount (read in this discernment/perfectionist way).*

*Models for disciples are found in people who can be recognized as
"blessed." Jesus is clearly presented by Matthew as one of those who are
"blessed." His "blessedness" — his status as "true prophet" (cf. 7:15), i.e., a
true manifestation of God's goodness — is authoritatively declared throughout
the Gospel: he is called Emmanuel (1:23); he fulfills the prophecies (e.g., 1:22;
4:14; 8:17); the voice from heaven declares, "This is my Son, the Beloved,
with whom I am well pleased," at both his baptism (3:17) and transfiguration
(17:5).*

*Jesus' blessedness is confirmed by his resurrection through which he re-
ceives "all authority in heaven and on earth" (28:18), while for other models
of discipleship it will only be confirmed at the last judgment (cf. 7:24–27).
Yet people with moral discernment recognize Jesus' blessedness by taking
note, in Matthew's description of his ministry, of the different ways in which
his good works reflect his faith, i.e., his discernment of righteousness and/or
true discernment/faith in people around him. Let us recall that according to
this interpretation overabundant righteousness involves (1) discerning righteous behaviors in other people (necessarily based on true discernment/faith),
(2) affirming these behaviors and discernment/faith as righteous and true, and
(3) internalizing them and acting them out in an overabundant way.*

*These features are made explicit in models of overabundant righteousness
that Jesus offers the disciples. First, Jesus publicly affirms the faith that he identifies in people and then acts according to their faith. Thus he affirms the*

faith — indeed, the "great" or extraordinary faith — of the Canaanite woman (15:28), of the centurion (8:5–13), and of the woman with a hemorrhage (9:20–22). He goes on to perform the miracles they were hoping for. Exploring these passages and many others in greater detail, examining how the respective faith/discernment and behavior of these people are appropriated and practiced in an overabundant way by Jesus, might result in a reorientation of Jesus' proposed actions in his ministry. Such is clearly the case with the centurion (Jesus does not go to his house, as he planned) and even more so with the case of the Canaanite woman (who transforms the scope of Jesus' ministry).

Once we begin to recognize this pattern, we need to reread the entire Gospel of Matthew with new eyes — or better, with a sound, undivided eye — and thus with true discernment. After affirming the woman with a hemorrhage has a model of faith and of righteousness (9:20–22), did Jesus internalize the pattern of her behavior and make it his own, practicing it in other realms of experience? We could ask the same question regarding the woman who poured ointment on his head and whom he praises for her discerning action (26:6–13): Did Jesus' actions and attitudes during the Passion rehearse in an overabundant way her own gesture?

As soon as one begins asking such questions (and many similar ones need to be raised),[59] we begin to perceive the entire Gospel in a different light. Instead of a Jesus who brings from the outside a remedy to correct an evil situation — a physician-surgeon who cuts off the malignant tumor and transplants in its place a sound organ (as in reading C)[60] — in the discernment/perfectionist interpretation focused on the thematic dimension of the Gospel, Jesus is perceived as a homeopathic physician who recognizes the good that is present in an apparently desperate situation and enhances it. In 9:10–13, many tax collectors and sinners join Jesus for dinner. The Pharisees see the evil: you should not eat with such people. Jesus affirms the Pharisees' view: yes, these are evil/sick people. But he practices their view in an overabundant way: they need a physician (according to God's will for mercy) and he becomes such a physician for them. What kind of physician? Before curing the paralytic, "when Jesus saw their faith, he said to the paralytic, 'Take heart, son; your sins are forgiven'" (9:2). Jesus affirms the faith of the paralytic's friends. They brought the paralytic to him; he not only cured him but also forgave his sins — an overabundant prolongation of their actions. Then he calls a tax collector to join him in his ministry, "Follow me" — an affirmation of Matthew's

---

59. This is what I do in my commentary (Patte, *Matthew*), even though it is now clear that it needs to be read with a multidimensional, androcritical eye, so as to verify that it is indeed consistent, coherent, and comprehensive as it interprets the thematic dimension of the entire Gospel according to Matthew.

60. This is a very powerful reading because of its focus on the most preeminent dimension of the Gospel text, namely, its figurative dimension, which includes the figure of Jesus as the eschatological Judge already *during his ministry* (as is also emphasized by reading A).

worth (9:9). In this perspective, how should one read the following verses (9:15–17)? Since the bridegroom is Jesus, the wedding guests are the disciples (see 9:14) – including Matthew the tax collector! But should the "piece of unshrunk cloth" and the "new wine" (9:16–17) be identified with Jesus (as is usually done) or with the sinners and tax collectors? In this interpretation it amounts to the same thing. Since Jesus emulates the sinners and tax collectors (by practicing in an overabundant way the model of righteousness he perceived in them), sinners and tax collectors end up being, together with Jesus, the new piece of cloth that would tear the old one and the new wine that would break the old wineskins – manifestations of the kingdom.

Obviously, this is not the place to proceed to a systematic interpretation of the Gospel according to Matthew from the perspective of this discernment/perfectionist interpretation of the Sermon on the Mount. The above comments are made to suggest that such an interpretation is not implausible. Its plausibility would demand a review of the entire thematic interpretation of the Gospel according to Matthew (provided in my commentary). Yet whether or not the rest of the Gospel presents Jesus as a model of overabundant righteousness, the above comments should suffice to show the plausibility of the conclusions about the teaching of the Sermon on the Mount regarding discipleship understood from the perspective of a discernment/perfectionist interpretation.

The discernment/perfectionist conceptualization of discipleship according to the Sermon on the Mount can be summarized in three points. Discipleship involves (1) discerning true models of righteousness and of faith/discernment in the concrete behavior of any persons around oneself;[61] *(2) affirming these models as preliminary manifestations of the kingdom and of God's righteousness; and (3) practicing righteousness by fulfilling these models in an overabundant way.*[62]

---

61. Including people like the tax collectors and Gentiles who love those who love them (5:46–47), or people who wish that people do good things for them (7:12).

62. Loving those beyond the realm of those who love us, including our enemies (5:44); reorienting our wishes, and doing to others as we would have others do to us (7:12).

PART III

A Fourfold Commentary
on the Sermon on the Mount

Assessing the Relative Values of Four Legitimate and Plausible
Interpretations of Discipleship according to the Sermon on the Mount

P ART 3 of our multidimensional study of discipleship according to the Sermon on the Mount is the shortest of the three, consisting of a single chapter. But for you, my reader, it has the potential of being the longest and the most important one, since it offers you the opportunity to become an active participant in this study. It is an overture.[1]

As the preceding multidimensional study makes clear, this concluding part cannot bring to closure our investigation of discipleship according to the Sermon and its interpretations. Many other interpretations should be brought into the discussion.[2] There is much unfinished business.[3] Similarly, closure is unthinkable as we consider the overall implications of this multidimensional study for interpreters of the Bible. Assessing the overall effect

---

1. It is both a "proposal," inviting your participation, and a "prelude" to many multidimensional studies.

2. See the massive bibliographies of studies on the Sermon on the Mount in Hans Dieter Betz, *The Sermon on the Mount, Including the Sermon on the Plain (Matthew 5:3–7:27 and Luke 6:20–49): A Commentary on Two Early Christian Manuals of Discipleship*, Hermeneia, ed. Adela Yarbro Collins (Minneapolis: Fortress, 1995), and Marcel Dumais, *Le Sermon sur la montagne. État de la recherche, Interprétation, Bibliographie* (Paris: Letouzey & Ané, 1995).

3. One would need to bring into the discussion the recent studies of New Testament ethics so as to identify the kind of preunderstandings of the moral life they posit as they relate the teaching of the Sermon on the Mount to the ethical teaching of other New Testament texts. I have presented such a study at the Studiorum Novi Testamenti Societas (SNTS) meeting in Prague, August 1995, in a paper discussed in the "Ethics of the New Testament" seminar. This paper emphasized that a series of studies conceive of their task as the elucidation of "what" believers should do; together with Strecker and Kingsbury, they posit one or another kind of deontological preunderstanding. In this category I included Eduard Lohse, *Theological Ethics of the New Testament* (Minneapolis: Fortress, 1991); L. William Countryman, *Dirt, Greed, and Sex: Sexual Ethics in the New Testament and Their Implications for Today* (Philadelphia: Fortress, 1988); J. L. Houlden, *Ethics and the New Testament* (New York: Oxford University Press, 1977); Jack T. Sanders, *Ethics in the New Testament: Change and Development* (Philadelphia: Fortress, 1975); as well as most "conservative" introductions to Christian ethics, such as Roger H. Crook, *An Introduction to Christian Ethics*, 2d ed. (Englewood Cliffs, N.J.: Prentice-Hall, 1995). I contrasted these with interpretations that posit one or another kind of perfectionist interpretation, among which are the magisterial studies of Wolfgang Schrage, *The Ethics of the New Testament*, trans. D. Green (Philadelphia: Fortress, 1988), and of Wayne A. Meeks, *The Origins of Christian Morality: The First Two Centuries* (New Haven and London: Yale University Press, 1993), and *The Moral World of the First Christians* (Philadelphia: Westminster, 1986). In this paper I related to the latter set of studies those that underscore the theological context of ethics, among which are Willi Marxsen, *New Testament Foundations for Christian Ethics* (Minneapolis: Fortress, 1993), and Jean-François Collange, *De Jésus à Paul: L'éthique du Nouveau Testament* (Genève: Labor et Fides, 1980), as well as D. H. Dodd, *Gospel and Law* (New York: Columbia University Press, 1951), and T. W. Manson, *Ethics and the Gospel* (New York: Charles Scribner's Sons, 1960) — who respectively raise the ethical question in the context of either the creative tension between kerygma and didache or the community life marked by the kingdom.

of the multidimensional character of this study on interpreters involves taking into account a diversity of responses, since it is legitimate and plausible for different readers to learn different things from the same text. Thus in this concluding part I cannot present what "we" have learned from the preceding chapters, but simply what "I" have learned. There is room for you and your assessment, which might be quite distinct from mine because of the different interpretation, convictions, interests, and concerns that you started with.

What did I learn from the preceding study? One of its goals was to bring to critical understanding my own interpretation,[4] and many of its features were indeed elucidated and refined. But before considering these results, in order to avoid any misunderstanding, it is important to clarify what I did *not* learn about my interpretation.

First, this study did not demonstrate to me that my interpretation is legitimate and plausible. I already knew this, having verified it by rigorously applying to the text a well-defined critical method;[5] the warranting conclusions that I proposed as a basis for understanding the teaching of the Sermon on the Mount were solidly grounded in textual evidence. Thus I was convinced of the legitimacy of my interpretation. Similarly, I already knew that my interpretation was basically plausible. Even though my *conclusions about the teaching* of the Sermon regarding discipleship needed to be made more explicit and needed to be developed further, I was fully convinced they made sense — they had epistemological coherence. A similar point could be made about the three other kinds of interpretations discussed above — their authors did not need a demonstration of the legitimacy and plausibility of their interpretations. They already knew this was the case. Furthermore, I anticipate that all interpreters could say the same regarding interpretations in which they have invested themselves. Before getting involved in a detailed critical examination of our interpretations, all of us can determine on our own which of our interpretations are or are not legitimate and plausible. We have a pretty good sense of this, even when we are not ready to demonstrate it, as we show in a pragmatic way by committing ourselves "to live by" certain of our interpretations but not others.

Second, even though this study helped me refine my critical arguments and my conclusions, it did not make my interpretation legitimate and plausible. The process of bringing to critical understanding an interpretation

---

4. The interpretation I presented in Daniel Patte, *The Gospel according to Matthew: A Structural Commentary on Matthew's Faith* (Minneapolis: Fortress, 1987; 3d printing, Valley Forge, Pa.: Trinity Press International, 1996).

5. This method is presented in a short methodological book, Daniel Patte, *Structural Exegesis for New Testament Critics* (Minneapolis: Fortress, 1990; 2d printing, Valley Forge, Pa.: Trinity Press International, 1996), which was developed on the basis of detailed theoretical research. See Daniel Patte, *The Religious Dimensions of Biblical Texts: Greimas's Structural Semiotics and Biblical Exegesis* (Atlanta: Scholars Press, 1990).

does not produce a new interpretation; it simply makes explicit the interpretive processes involved in an existing interpretation. Thus the preceding study contributes to bringing my own interpretation to critical understanding by highlighting the textual evidence on which it is based (so that its legitimacy is more readily recognizable) and by clarifying the coherence of its *conclusions about the teaching* of the Sermon (so that their plausibility is apparent). Similarly, since the three other kinds of interpretations discussed above were already legitimate and plausible, the multidimensional critical study did not make them so, but simply elucidated what they were. The same could be said about many other interpretations, especially *pro me* and *pro nobis* interpretations; interpreters commit themselves to live by them because they are convinced of their legitimacy and plausibility. For these interpreters, as for me, bringing these *pro me/nobis* interpretations to critical understanding involves making explicit what the interpreters already know to be the case. Simple respect for these interpreters demands that we presuppose that their *pro me/nobis* interpretations be considered as basically legitimate and plausible until proven otherwise — as we must do with scholarly interpretations as well.

So what did I learn from the preceding multidimensional study? The first part (chaps. 3–4), surprisingly, taught me that my interpretation is not the only legitimate one; it is *one among several legitimate interpretations*. I anticipate similar surprise among the proponents of the three other kinds of interpretations. Yet this plurality of legitimate interpretations could be expected because of the plurality of accepted critical methods. Similarly, the second part of this study (chaps. 5–6) surprised me by showing that all of the interpretations are *plausible*, despite their very different conclusions. I had not anticipated that several distinct kinds of *conclusions about the teaching* (CATs) of the Sermon regarding discipleship could be plausible. In sum, this multidimensional investigation taught me that, as an interpreter with a particular interpretation, I actually had a choice among equally legitimate and plausible options.

Thus the question that this study raises for me is, Why did I choose one rather than another of these interpretations? The question itself demonstrates that this critical study is not finished. It has not yet made explicit all the interpretive processes that my interpretation involves. Beyond demonstrating the legitimacy and plausibility of my interpretation, I need to clarify why I chose it. My choice is neither a matter of legitimacy (I had several legitimate interpretations among which to choose) nor a matter of plausibility (several interpretations are plausible, even from my particular cultural perspective); rather, it is a matter of value judgments. From my perspective, the interpretation I chose has a greater relative value than the three other kinds of interpretation. My choice reflects my convictions, my interests, my concerns. Of course, these are not mine alone; I share them with a certain interpretive community. Yet they remain quite personal.

How can I make explicit the value judgments involved in my interpretation? Even though these are quite personal, I do not propose an introspective analysis. By myself, I cannot truly know what characterizes my value judgments. It is only by encountering others who have different convictions, interests, and concerns that I discover the particularities of mine. Once again I need to proceed comparatively, contrasting my choice with those represented by the three other interpretations discussed above. Yet the range of differences in convictions, interests, and concerns is limited by the fact that all of us are male European-American academics. For this reason (and others to be discussed), the bringing to critical understanding of my interpretation needs to be pursued beyond the pages of this book through comparisons and contrasts with other interpretations, including yours, my reader.

This is one of the reasons why this concluding part calls for your participation. At the very least, it is an invitation to you, my reader, to become partisan either by choosing one interpretation as the teaching by which you want to live or, negatively, by rejecting those interpretations by which you do not want to live. It is an invitation to participate in the assessment of the relative value of the different *conclusions about the teaching* of the Sermon on the Mount regarding discipleship.

This invitation is addressed to you regardless of your concerns and/or interests in discipleship according to the Sermon on the Mount and regardless of the type of relationship you may have to the four kinds of interpretations discussed in the preceding chapters. If you are committed to practicing Christian discipleship, it is fairly clear why you need to choose one teaching "by which to live": the conclusions of the several legitimate and plausible interpretations are so different that nobody can simultaneously practice such diverse teachings about discipleship. Making such a choice involves assessing which teaching is the closest to your commitments and thus has a greater relative value for you. Conversely, if your primary interest in discipleship according to the Sermon on the Mount lies in your observation of negative effects that certain ways of practicing Christian discipleship have for other people, the question is, By which of the teachings of the Sermon on the Mount do these believers live? For you it is a matter of assessing which interpretations propose teachings with negative relative values, i.e., teachings by which one should *not* live. In both instances, the chosen teaching(s) about discipleship by which to live (or not to live) might be one of those proposed by the four kinds of interpretations discussed above, or it might be the conclusion proposed by a different interpretation of the Sermon — possibly your own. In the latter case, your participation as a reader of this study involves introducing your own interpretation into the discussion. One of the goals of Part III is to facilitate this process by suggesting how the relationship between the four readings discussed above and different readings, including yours, can be envisioned.

This invitation to participate in assessing the relative values of different interpretations of discipleship according to the Sermon on the Mount has been indirectly extended to you from the very beginning of this multidimensional study. At this point I make the invitation explicit through the personal style I have to adopt as I perform this assessment from my own perspective. In so doing, I simply pursue the task I laid down for myself from the outset: bringing to critical understanding my own interpretation by acknowledging its specificity — here, the specificity of the value judgments it involves.

Such a conceptualization of the critical task is *androcritical;*[6] it is governed by the preunderstanding that all interpretations reflect their interpreters' contextual perspectives and thus that no interpretation can claim to be universal.[7] As a male European-American interpreter, I must deny any implicit or explicit androcentric claim that a scholarly interpretation is a quest for "the" single universally true interpretation of the text. Positively, I must acknowledge the specificity of my interpretation and affirm it by making explicit the legitimacy and plausibility of its characteristics and their relative value. This androcritical perspective requires one to remain open to acknowledging and affirming the legitimacy and plausibility of new interpretations and their relative value. This openness to other interpretations involves acknowledging the specificity of one's own interpretation. This is what I seek to do regarding my own interpretation. This is why I invite you to elucidate and affirm the specificity of your own interpretation.

Bringing to critical understanding our own interpretations in this multidimensional way greatly benefits each of us. Unlike one-dimensional critical practices, this critical practice does not require us to abandon our own interpretations for the sake of an ever elusive universal interpretation, but to assume responsibility for them. By acknowledging their specificity and our reasons for our interpretive choices, we affirm ownership of our interpretation. Furthermore, since this acknowledgment concerns interpretations regarding discipleship, it amounts to assuming responsibility also for our specific practice (or lack of practice) of discipleship, and thus of claiming ownership of our own identity. As we gain control over the original interpretations that we might have adopted without realizing that we had a choice and without being aware of the negative implications of those choices, we now have the freedom to choose another interpretation or to keep the same one. Such valuable benefits justify the effort that is required to bring to critical understanding our own interpretations.

---

6. As was emphasized above in the introduction.

7. Paraphrasing Paul, I would say that no interpretation is universal because none is complete until the time "when the complete comes" (1 Cor 13:10) and we gain a complete, transcendent understanding.

CHAPTER 7

Choosing a Teaching by Which to Live

The Relative Values of Interpretations of Discipleship according to the Sermon on the Mount

What are the results of the preceding multidimensional study of "discipleship according to the Sermon on the Mount"? First, there are results in regard to the four kinds of interpretations we have discussed. So far we have shown that four kinds of *conclusions about the teaching* of the Sermon regarding discipleship are equally legitimate and plausible. The question is, What is the relative value of each interpretation? There are also more general results concerning the nature and task of critical biblical studies. What are the implications for biblical studies of recognizing that quite different interpretations can be consistent, coherent, and thus have appropriate textual grounding by being focused on different meaning-producing dimensions of a text? Of understanding that the teaching of the Sermon about discipleship as ethical practice can be conceptualized in quite different yet plausible ways? Although less tangible and less easily described, these general results of the preceding study have the potential to be the most significant for readers of the Bible. Ultimately, this study affects our views of ourselves as interpreters of the Bible, our views of scriptural authority (regardless of our belief in it), and our views of discipleship (regardless of our practice of it).

In this chapter I first seek to assess the relative value of a multi-dimensional critical practice of biblical studies by considering its effects on interpreters. These effects vary from person to person since they are closely associated with the interests, concerns, and convictions of each interpreter. Thus it is best that I reflect on the ways in which I am affected by this multidimensional critical study.

Assessing the Relative Value of a Multidimensional Critical Practice of Biblical Studies

How am I affected by the preceding multidimensional study? What are its less tangible effects on me? Generally speaking, it has left me with ambivalent feelings, primarily a diffuse sense of dissatisfaction, incompleteness, disorientation, betraying; then, progressively, a sense of responsibility, freedom, openness, motivation.

Positively, this multidimensional study calls me to assume responsibility for my own interpretation vis-à-vis other biblical scholars and other people who are affected by it, without renouncing my responsibility vis-à-vis the text, whose role in the interpretive process I continue to acknowledge. In sum, it gives me freedom, openness, and motivation to complete the process of bringing my interpretation to critical understanding. Negatively, as I affirm the results of this multidimensional study, I have a feeling of having betrayed both my vocation as a biblical scholar and my convictions about the authority of Scripture. No wonder it took me so long to adopt a multidimensional practice! Even though I began envisioning the legitimacy and plausibility of multidimensional studies more than ten years ago,[1] I would not practice it because I could not perceive any value in it. Now I can. Yet the diffuse sense that this multidimensional practice is inappropriate lingers with me and needs to be accounted for.

Assuming Responsibility for Our Role as Interpreters and for Decentering Biblical Interpretation

Recognizing that my interpretation of the Sermon on the Mount and its teaching about discipleship is one of several equally legitimate and plausible interpretations forces me to acknowledge that I am responsible for my interpretation: I chose it among several legitimate and plausible ones because of certain value judgments that were governed by specific interests and concerns. The preceding two parts of the multidimensional study have put me in a position to assume responsibility for my interpretation by elucidating the value judgments it involves and by assessing its own relative

---

1. The legitimacy and plausibility of a multidimensional critical interpretation of text is posited by semiotic theories, at least since the 1978 French publication of A. J. Greimas and J. Courtés, *Semiotics and Language: An Analytical Dictionary*, trans. L. Crist, D. Patte, et al. (Bloomington: Indiana University Press, 1982). Among my works, it is made explicit in Daniel Patte, *The Religious Dimensions of Biblical Texts: Greimas's Structural Semiotics and Biblical Exegesis*, SBL Semeia Studies (Atlanta: Scholars Press, 1990), and in *Structural Exegesis for New Testament Critics*, Guides to Biblical Scholarship (Minneapolis: Fortress Press, 1990; 2d printing, Valley Forge, Pa.: Trinity Press International, 1996), but it is already mentioned as a possibility in the introductions of *The Gospel according to Matthew: A Structural Commentary on Matthew's Faith* (Minneapolis: Fortress, 1987; 3d printing, Valley Forge, Pa.: Trinity Press International, 1996), and even of *Paul's Faith and the Power of the Gospel: A Structural Introduction to the Pauline Letters* (Philadelphia: Fortress, 1983).

value. This multidimensional exegetical practice is, therefore, a moral duty that I should not skirt in any way if I want to be accountable to those who are affected by my interpretations of the Bible as well as to the scholarly guild.[2]

Together with this sense of moral responsibility, the preceding multidimensional study leaves me with a diffuse sense of having betrayed both the expectations that others have of me and my own basic convictions. Do I not betray the scholarly guild inasmuch as my practice of "multidimensional" critical biblical studies directly challenges the practices of the guild? But as I have already explained (introduction and chap. 1), I am convinced that far from forsaking critical standards, a multidimensional study seeks to bring more rigor to critical biblical studies. In subsequent chapters, I have carefully documented my case for the legitimacy and plausibility of the various interpretations. Thus I am satisfied that my multidimensional study serves the scholarly guild and its academic goals. Yet this sense of betraying the guild persists because the multidimensional component of the study contradicts the *alleged goal* of critical biblical study, namely, establishing "the" (single) legitimate and plausible interpretation of the teaching of the text. This goal is not necessarily what biblical scholars themselves claim about their own work (although some do), but it is what both students and laypersons expect from our work. They are disappointed when we tell them that we cannot teach them the true meaning of a text. Their disappointment prompts a nagging question, Am I not forsaking the role I am expected to play as a biblical scholar?

So I am. I deliberately challenge these expectations. But my betrayal of this aspect of the traditional conception of scholarly practice is not a betrayal of critical biblical study. On the contrary, by assuming responsibility for our interpretations and recognizing that each of us has chosen to focus our reading of a text on one of its several meaning-producing dimensions and to conceptualize its teaching in terms of a specific preunderstanding of a given theme, we practice biblical scholarship in a truly critical way. We strive to make explicit the various interpretive processes involved in each of our interpretations.

Similarly, by betraying the expectations held by laypeople and our students, we biblical scholars open the possibility of becoming accountable to them. By acknowledging that each of our interpretations is one among several legitimate and plausible ones, we free these people from feeling obliged to adopt the interpretation we propose and thus from feeling compelled to abandon their own interpretations. Since we fail to provide for them the absolutely true interpretation that they could appropriate without having to assume responsibility for it, we disappoint them. We are not meeting the

---

2. See Daniel Patte, *Ethics of Biblical Interpretation: A Reevaluation* (Louisville: Westminster/John Knox, 1995).

high expectations that our students or our parishioners have of us. Thus we lose authority. But in so doing we give back to them their dignity as responsible readers of the Bible from which they were alienated by our one-dimensional practices.

Actually, when we comply with our students' and parishioners' wishes by providing them with what they expect from us — an authoritative interpretation — we belittle them. We must acknowledge and confess (as a sin) that each time we consciously or not pretend to teach "the" single true interpretation to "ordinary readers," we reduce them to the status of "ordinary readers." These are second-class readers, childishly inept, who are unable to produce legitimate and plausible readings of biblical texts on their own, who cannot handle the complexity of an ambivalent text, and who, therefore, need to rely on the interpretations of "expert readers" such as ourselves. A multidimensional practice of biblical studies avoids belittling the many readers of the Bible around us. For upper middle-class male European-American scholars, such a practice is one way to decenter our androcentric and Eurocentric interpretations, as we were called to do by Elisabeth Schüssler Fiorenza in her presidential address to the Society of Biblical Literature,[3] by African-American biblical scholars,[4] as well by other "voices from the margin."[5] This decentering of androcentric and Eurocentric interpretations is all the more urgent[6] because such interpretations serve, promote, and reinforce patriarchalism, colonialism, apartheid, and liberalism (as a form of classist alienation of less privileged classes)[7] through their a priori dismissal of all other interpretations as inept and childish.

In sum, I refuse to be swayed by suggestions that conducting a multidimensional biblical study betrays my vocation as a critical biblical scholar and teacher. On the contrary, for us, male European-American scholars, it is one of the very few ways (in addition to other postmodern critical

---

3. Elisabeth Schüssler Fiorenza, "The Ethics of Interpretation: De-Centering Biblical Scholarship," *Journal of Biblical Literature* 107 (1988): 3–17.

4. For instance, Randall C. Bailey, Charles B. Copher, Thomas Hoyt Jr., Lloyd A. Lewis, Clarice J. Martin, William H. Myers, David T. Shannon, John W. Waters, Renita Weems, and Vincent L. Wimbush, who contributed to *Stony the Road We Trod: African American Biblical Interpretation*, ed. Cain Hope Felder (Minneapolis: Fortress, 1991).

5. R. S. Sugirtharajah, ed., *Voices from the Margin: Interpreting the Bible in the Third World* (Maryknoll, N.Y.: Orbis, 1991). Musa Dube and Gerald West, eds., *"Reading With": An Exploration of an Interface between Critical and Ordinary Readings of the Bible, African Overtures*, Semeia 73 (Atlanta: Scholars Press, 1996).

6. Patte, *Ethics of Biblical Interpretation*, 17–36.

7. I abruptly summarize here what I learned from both African-American and Latin American theologians, in particular James Cone, *Martin & Malcom & America: A Dream or a Nightmare* (Maryknoll, N.Y. Orbis, 1991), especially 244–71 (where Cone emphasizes the necessary complementarity of Martin and Malcom); Enrique Dussel, *Philosophy of Liberation*, trans. A. Martinez and C. Morkovsky (Maryknoll, N.Y.: Orbis, 1985), in which he relentlessly unmasks all kinds of forms of alienation hidden under the cover of liberal cultural manifestations.

approaches such as intertextual and ideological criticism)[8] to decenter our interpretations of the Bible in order to be accountable to those who are directly or indirectly affected by our work and teaching as we carry out our task as critical biblical scholars, which is to empower people to be responsible readers of the Bible.

Acknowledging the Role of the Text and Affirming Scriptural Authority

By alluding to different ways of decentering our interpretations, I signal that I deliberately chose a multidimensional approach, although at first I was not aware of my reasons for preferring this option. While all postmodern critical approaches recognize the plurality of plausible interpretations (an emphasis that is sufficient for decentering interpretations), only a multidimensional approach emphasizes that each plausible interpretation is also legitimate in the sense that it is grounded in one of the several meaning-producing *dimensions of the text*.

Why this emphasis? Does it not convey that meaning is located in the text? Is it not a subtle way of preserving for scholars a status of being "better interpreters" than "ordinary readers"? There is no easy answer to these questions.[9] Here, it is enough to say that my choice of a multidimensional approach is a deliberate effort to acknowledge the important role of the text in any interpretive process,[10] and in the case of a biblical text, to acknowledge its scriptural authority (and/or power) for its readers, especially if they are believers, but even if they are not (when they directly

---

8. See The Bible and Culture Collective, *The Postmodern Bible* (New Haven and London: Yale University Press, 1995); George Aichele and Gary Phillips, eds., *Intertextuality and Reading the Bible*, Semeia 69/70 (Atlanta: Scholars Press, 1995); David Jobling and Tina Pippin, eds., *Ideological Criticism of Biblical Texts*, Semeia 59 (Atlanta: Scholars Press, 1992); Giles Gunn, *The Culture of Criticism and the Criticism of Culture* (New York: Oxford University Press, 1987).

9. These questions merely allude to a few of the issues concerning the respective roles of readers and texts in the interpretive process. See Robert C. Culley and Robert B. Robinson, eds., *Textual Determinacy: Part I*, Semeia 62 (Atlanta: Scholars Press, 1993), and *Textual Determinacy: Part II*, Semeia 71 (Atlanta: Scholars Press, 1995). For further developments on my position, see Daniel Patte, "Textual Constraints, Ordinary Readings, and Critical Exegesis: An Androcritical Perspective," in *Textual Determinacy: Part I*, 59–79.

10. Postmodern colleagues disagree with my affirmation that a critical study must account for the role of the text in the plural interpretive process, seeing in my emphasis on the role of the text a conservative streak, which the following comments on scriptural authority admittedly seem to confirm. See The Bible and Culture Collective, *The Postmodern Bible*, 113–17. While I do not want to deny the plausibility of their radical postmodern semantic universe, to show that mine is equally plausible it is enough to point out that, as far as I am concerned, they deny their own objection as long as they are producing texts that they expect to somehow affect their readers. I can add that since in itself the multidimensional approach prevents any attempt to conceive of the teaching of the text as a content of the text container, I am not seeking to maintain the text as an object in a subject-object dichotomy or to return to a logocentrism.

or indirectly interact with believers). What believers mean by "scriptural authority" is clarified when one considers the relationship between the respective roles of the reader and of the text from the perspective of our multidimensional study.

Assuming responsibility for my own interpretation — as the preceding multidimensional study entices me to do — involves acknowledging that my role as a reader is limited, framed, and channeled by the text. Of course, this power of the text to affect its readers is exercised in diverse ways according to the circumstances. In each specific case the text affects readers primarily through one of its several meaning-producing dimensions to which the readers might be more sensitive because of the peculiar context from which they make sense of the impact of the text on them.[11] Yet, in each given case, the distinctive effect of a text on its readers is related to the given dimension through which it touches them.[12] In most cases readers overlook this impact of the text on them,[13] neglect it, or dismiss it.[14] By contrast, when readers affirm the canonical status of a text — whether this status is perceived as intrinsic to the text or as originating with institutions, traditions, and/or cultural ethos — the impact of this text on the readers is amplified. The text has now authority and/or power for its readers. It has authority in the sense that its teaching (as perceived by the readers) has import for them, for their vision of life, for their conceptualization of human

---

11. For this theoretical view of the relation between text and reader, see again the introduction and chapter 1.

12. In most instances, as modern (and postmodern) readers in a busy technological world, we do not pay much attention to the effects of texts on us. We might simply think that a given text (be it a newspaper article, a textbook, a travel brochure, an e-mail message, or a biblical text) either contains or does not contain the information we are looking for, without taking note that it does not contain it but conveys it (through one of its dimensions) along with many other messages that affect us in various ways (through the other dimensions of the text). But, in a hurry, we run away with the piece of information we were looking for, brushing aside the rest of the text and its effects, even forgetting the text from which we obtained the information.

13. When one keeps in mind texts in all kinds of media, it is easy to recognize that in most instances we overlook the effect on us of all the popular fictions we read or look at — in the case of shows (including operas) and films — by considering them as pure entertainment. Yet this does not prevent them from having an effect on us. Actually, speaking of entertainment and of "the pleasures of readings" is referring to the effect of the text on the readers. See Robert Alter, *The Pleasures of Readings in an Ideological Age* (New York: Simon and Schuster, 1989), who emphasizes the distinctive effects of literary texts on readers, against the emphasis on the role of the readers and their ideologies as underscored by Mieke Bal in *Lethal Love: Feminist Literary Readings of Biblical Love Stories* (Bloomington: Indiana University Press, 1987). In my view, both perspectives must be included in an understanding of the complementary role of readers and text in the interpretive process. On movies see Robert Jewett, *Saint Paul at the Movies: The Apostle's Dialogue with American Culture* (Louisville: Westminster/John Knox, 1993), and Margaret R. Miles, *Seeing and Believing: Religion and Values in the Movies* (Boston: Beacon, 1996). Both emphasize that even though movies are most often regarded as primarily "entertaining," they communicate values, social expectations, social roles, "constructions of desire and the desirable."

14. As when we push aside a book or an article because we have concluded that it does not apply to us or does not deal with the topic we are investigating.

experience and reality, for setting up their individual and collective voca-
tions, and for their daily life (providing rules of behavior). The text has
power over its readers in the sense that it affects them, transforming them,
converting them, drastically changing their behavior, sending them out in
mission. For me as a reader, the teaching of this authoritative and powerful
canonical text is *pro me* and indeed *pro nobis* (when I perceive myself as
related to an interpretive community). It offers "the" teaching by which I
must live.

Word of God for Us: The Scriptural Authority of One of the Several Teachings of the Text

When this canonical text is a biblical text, such as the Sermon on the
Mount, this *pro me/nobis* teaching is what believers receive as the word
of God for them. Believers must allow this word of God to mold their lives,
especially in reference to discipleship.

By showing and affirming that four distinct sets of *conclusions about the
teaching* of the Sermon on the Mount regarding discipleship are plausible
(see Part II, chaps. 5–6) and by insisting that these plausible conclusions
concern discipleship as ethical practice, the preceding multidimensional
study ends up saying that I have a choice among *pro me/nobis* interpretations — and thus for me and other believers, a "choice among potential
words of God." But is this not an oxymoron? If we choose it, is it still the
word of God with power and authority for us? Can we speak of "words
of God" (in the plural)?

A multidimensional approach shows that the reader who formulates an
interpretation chooses this interpretation neither because it is the only legitimate one nor because it is the only plausible one, but because of certain
value judgments and thus because of certain interests and concerns related
to the pragmatic aspects of experience. Thus a believer/reader chooses a
given interpretation because it is "the" (single) interpretation *by which to
live*, i.e., because it allows him or her to conceive of discipleship as a way
of life that is most consistent with his or her values and circumstances.
Yet this is not to say that this choice is made on a whim, independently
of the text. We might choose a legitimate textual dimension and a plausible interpretation precisely because they have power and/or authority for
us in that they stir up deep emotions, perhaps reawakening some of our
long established interests and concerns, while other textual dimensions do
not affect us as directly. Bringing to critical understanding our own interpretation involves reexamining why we spontaneously responded to a text
as we did, thus reevaluating our emotionally charged convictional interests
and concerns, so as to assume responsibility for our choice of a word of
God for us. In the process, we pass from the emotional, instinctive, esthetic
religious experience of the text (the power of the text on us), to the self-

conscious affirmation that we are deliberately assuming responsibility for this choice by saying, This is indeed what "I" believe (*credo*); this is what the word of God is for me (*pro me*).[15] In so doing, I assume responsibility for the power/authority of the text on me — meaning that I might choose to reject what I took to be the word of God in an original interpretation and select another one.

From this perspective, am I not betraying the very view of the Bible as Scripture(s) and as word of God? I am, if the Bible is conceived as Scripture (in the singular), instead of Scriptures (in the plural). I am, if the word of God revealed through the Bible is conceived as a monolithic revelation that does not change whatever might be the circumstances and that is imposed on believers who cannot but accept it, as puppets cannot but follow the script and cannot but obey the commands of the puppeteer. I am, if word of God is conceived as a total and complete revelation that we can fully possess because it is the fixed content of the biblical text-container.

But I do not believe in such a word of God, a deadly letter carved in stone ministering death. I believe in the living word of God offered to us through the ministry of the life-giving Spirit (cf. 2 Cor 3:6–8). Of course, we need a solid foundation (the rock, Mt 7:24–25) and a clearly defined orientation (toward the kingdom, Mt 6:33) for our lives. We need a clearly defined word of God by which to live. But I do not believe this word to be an immutable teaching/content which, like a law, is forced on us as soon as we enter the sphere of the authority of Scripture. Otherwise the very process of so strongly affirming biblical authority/power would end up denying it. After all, this teaching/content of Scripture — be it the fundamentals of Christian life or the orthodoxy that defines the true church — can be passed down independently of the biblical text from generation to generation by an institution and its hierarchy, which becomes the filter that screens out and silences all the other voices of the text. I do not and cannot believe that this is the true word of God. I cannot disavow my Huguenot ancestors who, rather than confessing a gospel handed down to them by the church hierarchy, died or were imprisoned for daring to read the Bible on their own with the conviction that through the Spirit it had for them a living, powerful, ever new and renewing word that kindled fires in their lives that the flames of their martyrs' pyres only intensified. With Luther, I cannot be content with the "letter" of Scripture, but have to be open to the Spirit that inspired the Scriptures in their diversity and that inspires ever renewed readings among which God's word for us (to be preached)

---

15. The relationship between the powerful emotional effect of the text and assuming responsibility for our interpretation is comparable to that between convictions and theological reflections, and in semiotics between the proprioceptive deep and narrative semantics and the logical deep and narrative syntax. See Daniel Patte, *The Religious Dimensions of Biblical Texts: Greimas's Structural Semiotics and Biblical Exegesis*, SBL Semeia Studies (Atlanta: Scholars Press, 1990), 111–28 and 173–207 (especially the conclusions in 202–7).

and God's word for me (*pro me*) are chosen.[16] With Augustine, I am reminded that claiming that a biblical text reveals "the" single truth — the
one revealed in my interpretation, of course — manifests a lack of charity toward other interpreters, even though Christ has shown that the law
and the prophets depend on the twofold commandment of love. Thus as I
envision God's words as expressed in the various interpretations of each
given biblical text, I keep in mind Augustine's prayerful queries, which
warn us against hiding our lack of charity behind a quest for what the
author meant:

> What harm comes to me, O my God, "light of my eyes" in secret, . . . if
> various meanings may be found in these words, all of which are true?
> What harm comes to me, I say, if I think differently than another
> thinks as to what he who wrote these words thought? All of us who
> read strive to trace out and understand what he whom we read actu-
> ally meant, and since we believe him to speak the truth, we dare not
> assert that he spoke anything we know or think to be false. There-
> fore, while every [one] tries to understand in Holy Scripture what the
> author understood therein, what wrong is there if anyone understand
> what you, O light of all truthful minds, reveal to him [or her] as true,
> even if the author he [or she] reads did not understand this, since he
> also understood a truth, though not this truth?[17]

With Paul, I cannot but conceive of any revealed knowledge, including
of God's word, as partial, biased, or incomplete because "for now we see
in a mirror, dimly, but then we will see face ⟨⟩ face. Now I know only in
part (ἐκ μέρους); then I will know fully, even as I have been fully known"
(1 Cor 13:12). Thus the revelation of the complete (τὸ τέλειον, 1 Cor
13:10) and final word of God is future (not past); I cannot expect to find it
contained in the past Scriptures; Scriptures are not "archetypes" but "prototypes."[18] The Scriptures and their various interpretations *point toward*
the perfect (τὸ τέλειον); this is all they can do. Expecting to find the perfect
in the present, conceiving of our interpretation as a quest for the perfect
or (worse) as the successful outcome of this quest, is idolatry — claiming

---

16. For an excellent study of Luther's contrast between "letter" and "Spirit" and his theology of preaching, see Regin Prenter, *Spiritus Creator*, trans. J. M. Jensen (Philadelphia:
Muhlenberg, 1953), 115–16.

17. Augustine, *Confessions*, trans. John K. Ryan (Garden City, N.Y.: Doubleday, 1960),
12:18, 320.

18. At this point I follow Elisabeth Schüssler Fiorenza, *In Memory of Her: A Feminist
Theological Reconstruction of Christian Origins* (New York: Crossroad, 1983), 33–36, and
Bread Not Stone: The Challenge of Feminist Biblical Interpretation (New York: Beacon,
1984), ix–xxv, 93–115, passim, who underscores that the Scriptures should not be read as
"archetypes" but as "prototypes."

that the relative (τὸ ἐκ μέρους) is absolute (τὸ τέλειον). This understanding of the word of God in an eschatological mode[19] is at least as plausible as another view of Scripture as word of God, especially when considering New Testament Scriptures that reflect both Jesus' proclamation of the kingdom and the church's proclamation of Jesus as the Lord who will be the eschatological judge (Mt 7:21–23).

From this theological perspective, I cannot claim anything other than a *relative value* for the biblical teaching that I hold to be word of God for me. In saying so, I also express a critical understanding of the interpretive process that leads me to this conclusion. I acknowledge that I apprehend this teaching through an interpretation that I focused on one of the several meaning-producing dimensions of the text (legitimacy judgment) and that I find this teaching to be plausible because of my contextually marked pre-understandings (epistemology judgment). I only see "in a mirror, dimly." Yet, by affirming that this teaching is word of God for me and/or for us, I acknowledge its authority and power for me, and I submit to it by appropriating it as a teaching by which to live as I confess: I believe (*credo*), that this is the word of God *for me in this specific context*. This confession reflects a value judgment regarding the relationship of this teaching both to my basic convictions and to my contextually marked interests and concerns.

In sum, I acknowledge that the teaching I identify in my interpretation of a text, be it in a theological eschatological mode or in a critical mode, does not have an absolute but a relative value, even if I commit to live by it because I hold it to be word of God for me. The multidimensional andro*critical* practice that I advocate here is rigorously critical — it demands that each of us strive to elucidate the various aspects of the interpretive process involved in our interpretations — even as it makes explicit how this critical practice is related to my theological interests and my ethical concerns.[20]

The Critical Task of Elucidating the Role of Value Judgments and the Theological/Ethical Task of Choosing a Teaching by Which to Live or Not to Live

The preceding discussion suggests what the procedures should be both *for the critical task* of elucidating the role of value judgments in the four kinds of interpretation of discipleship according to the Sermon on the Mount and *for the theological/ethical task* of choosing (and/or confirming our choice

---

19. See David Schnasa Jacobsen, *As Seeing the Invisible: The Cosmic Scope of Apocalyptic Preaching* (Ph.D. diss., Vanderbilt University, 1996), especially chapter 1 in which the author develops "a theology of the Word in an apocalyptic mode."

20. As discussed in Patte, *Ethics of Biblical Interpretation*.

of) a teaching about discipleship by which to live or not to live. These two tasks are closely interrelated because they deal with two aspects of the same phenomenon; value judgments are the means by which each interpreter chooses a specific interpretation by which to live. Yet the two tasks remain distinct.

The critical task aims at elucidating the specific value judgments that govern the original choice of an interpretation, as well as the convictions, interests, and concerns on which these judgments are based. This elucidation involves comparing the different interpretations in terms of their respective value judgments. Yet because of the contextual and often very personal character of these value judgments, this comparison has to be made self-consciously from the critical interpreter's own perspective, i.e., from a perspective that ascribes a higher relative value[21] to the interpretation chosen by the interpreter and lower values to other interpretations. This is what I do below as I seek to elucidate why I chose reading D by first trying to understand why I did not choose the three other kinds of interpretation.

The theological/ethical task involves assessing the relative value of the original choice of an interpretation by which to live or not to live. The question is, What is the relative value of this interpretation as word of God, i.e., as a teaching by which to live (or as a dangerous teaching by which no one should live)? Raising this question is an essential component of the multidimensional critical study; it is also a critical question. I call it a theological/ethical question because, as we saw above, identifying the *relative* value of an interpretation does not deny its scriptural authority, when one conceives of the word of God in an eschatological mode.[22] Since this theological/ethical assessment of the relative value of an interpretation involves elucidating its *specific* value as a teaching by which to live, we need to compare interpretations that make explicit their respective theological/ethical values. Thus before assessing the relative value of my interpretation, I first need to elucidate the value judgments that it implicitly involves.

---

21. The same procedure would be followed by reversing the values when the interpreter's primary concern is to identify the interpretation by which *not* to live, i.e., the one with the lowest relative value, for example, because it involves a teaching that is most dangerous — as compared with the other interpretations that have a relatively higher value.

22. I paraphrase Jacobsen's subtitle, "Word in an Apocalyptic Mode" (see David Schnasa Jacobsen, *As Seeing the Invisible*, chap. 1). My reformulation still refers to the same important dimension of New Testament texts and still focuses attention on the perception of the present in terms of the end time, but without pointing to a specific figurativization of it.

Bringing to Critical Understanding My Interpretation: Elucidating Its Value Judgments and Assessing the Relative Value of Its Teaching about Discipleship

Why I Did Not Choose Reading A: The Dangers of a Deontological Interpretation of Discipleship according to the Sermon on the Mount

Both Strecker's (and Kingsbury's) interpretation and my interpretation (readings A and D, respectively) have been shown to be equally legitimate (see chaps. 3 and 4) and equally plausible (see chaps. 5–6). Therefore the question is, What convictions, interests, and/or concerns led me, in my commentary, to accept one set of *conclusions about the teaching* (CATs) of the Sermon about discipleship and to reject the other? I progressively discover the answer to this question through this multidimensional study, since it helps me bring to critical understanding my interpretation and the choice it involves. Yet this choice is not as clear-cut as it may seem. Again and again I find myself living by and making decisions on the basis of a deontological interpretation that I have self-consciously rejected after recognizing its dangers.[23] The deontological interpretation remains very attractive for me — it has a relative value that I cannot ignore — even though I am convinced that ultimately it is a very destructive and dangerous interpretation that must be resisted and avoided.

As I explain in chapter 1, I ultimately opted against a conceptualization of discipleship as "implementation" of God's will (however it might be construed) and in favor of a view of discipleship as "imitation" of Christ, i.e., as an intuitive ethical practice. This choice is not simply for the sake of pedagogical effectiveness, as chapter 1 might suggest. It also reflects fundamental convictions about the basic human predicament that the teaching of the Sermon as word of God contributes to overcoming by helping people to be faithful disciples. Because of the detailed discussion in chapter 5 of the *conclusions about the teaching* (CATs) of the Sermon regarding discipleship, we can directly go to the heart of the matter.

According to reading A (Strecker and Kingsbury), discipleship according to the Sermon on the Mount is the implementation of a norm (see chap. 2, reading A on Mt 4:18–22) which, as the Sermon specifies, is a set of universal principles of the moral life — the eternal will of God — that sets limits on the disciples' behavior for the good of the community. Thus according to reading A (see chap. 3, reading A, CAWs 2–3; chap. 5, reading A, CAT 3)

---

23. Autobiographically I can note that through this multidimensional study I discover to my surprise that even though this process was subconscious, it was an actual interpretive choice with which I was constantly confronted during the years following World War II as a young adult in the Reformed Church of France and (regarding moral preunderstandings) in French culture and society of that time.

the Sermon is a moral imperative that shapes the disciples' relationships with others inside and outside the community and with God in all aspects of their lives. It offers a set of community rules that must be continuously reinterpreted so as to be appropriately implemented by the community of disciples in changing situations (see reading A, CAWs 4–5).[24]

Such conclusions, as well as their conceptualization of discipleship, are very attractive to me because they provide a well-defined framework for life, which nevertheless retains the flexibility of adapting itself to new contexts and situations. This appears to be a good compromise between artificial legalistic certainties and the ambivalence and laissez-faire mentality of secular culture. These conclusions also offer me the possibility of belonging to a community — an extended family with clear boundaries — which can give me a sense of belonging that I crave in a fragmented and individualistic European-American culture.

Yet these *conclusions about the teaching* of the Sermon make me uneasy because they require individual disciples to sacrifice themselves for the sake of the community. Am I reluctant to commit myself? This is indeed part of the issue. But for me the important question is, Disciples sacrificing themselves for the sake of what (or of whom)? Having their relationships with others reshaped by what (or by whom)? I become even more nervous when answers to these questions posit the community as the ultimate good — here, by identifying it with the kingdom, God's eschatological rule, which is proleptically realized in the community of disciples who carry out God's eternal will (see reading A, CAW 2.3). Despite its cautious denials that the community is absolutized — the community of disciples is merely a preliminary realization of the kingdom (reading A, CAW 2.3), which can then fulfill its mission of being the light of the world (reading A, CAW 3.2) — this interpretation posits the community as the ultimate good, which the disciples' entire behavior is aimed at bringing about and which the disciples must serve.

When it becomes clear that reading A posits such a pattern of relationships between community and individual disciples, this interpretation and its conclusions about discipleship become highly problematic for me because they call for the control of individuals by the community. Personally I do not care to be controlled by a community and its hierarchy — after all, I am a Huguenot who was raised on a farm with a farmer's spirit of independence.[25] But what is even more problematic for me is that these *conclusions about the teaching* of the Sermon open the door to all kinds of deplorable abuses. Thus I refuse to adopt reading A and its conclusions as a teach-

---

24. Unless otherwise noted, the cross references, such as reading A, CAWs 4–5, refer to the readings of *the Sermon on the Mount,* and thus to the relevant chapters in Part I (chaps. 3 and 4) or in Part II (chaps. 5 and 6) — here to chap. 3.

25. As I was reminded by Bill McKibben, "Some Versions of Pastoral," *The New York Review of Books,* 11 July 1996, 42–45.

ing by which I would want to live. A teaching that demands me to view a human community as the ultimate good cannot be word of God for me.

If I agreed to view such a community as the ultimate good, I would self-lessly pledge to sacrifice myself for its "construction" and "maintenance,"[26] and as a faithful member of this community I would have to demand similar sacrifices from others. The danger of such a teaching is clearly man-ifested when this view of discipleship is *implemented* in sects that require their members to lay down their lives for the sake of the sect (tragedies such as those of Jonestown and Waco are in the logic of this teaching). But this danger is no less clear when this teaching is implemented in high churches for which there is no salvation outside of the church. In such cases the Christian mission involves bringing lost people into the church where they will be saved by submitting to its teaching. The threat of exclusion from the church becomes the ultimate form of coercion. Such *implementations* of discipleship (whether high church or sectarian) condone and even promote the same pattern of relationship in the political realm (where it easily takes the form of fascism), in the economic and cultural realm (where it takes the form of colonialism, oppression, and all kinds of racism, since all those who, unlike us, are not members of the church are lost, less than human), and in the family realm (where abusive relationships should be accepted as parts of the self-sacrifice for the good of the community unit that the family is). Thus one is not surprised to find that both Strecker and Kings-bury present the Sermon on the Mount as a sex-exclusive and patriarchal teaching (see chap. 3, reading A, CAW 7).[27]

A teaching with such implications cannot be word of God — good news, gospel — for me. If reading A with its conclusions were the only possible reading, I would have to say that the Sermon on the Mount cannot be word of God for me and that the Gospel of Matthew is a straw gospel that has no place in my canon.

Have I condemned reading A too harshly? One could wonder, since Strecker and Kingsbury strongly reject legalistic interpretations of the Sermon and carefully avoid any suggestion that it would call for the im-

---

26. I purposefully use the vocabulary of the sociology of knowledge in order to emphasize that my comments apply to all kinds of community maintenance endeavors that involve the di-rect or indirect absolutization of the community. See Peter Berger, *The Sacred Canopy* (Garden City, N.Y.: Doubleday, 1967), and Peter Berger and Thomas Luckman, *The Social Construc-tion of Reality: A Treatise in the Sociology of Knowledge* (Garden City, N.Y.: Doubleday, 1967).

27. Remember Kingsbury's conclusion: "The nature of this new community derives from the call Jesus extends: through Jesus, who is God's unique Son in whom God's Kingdom is a present reality, those who make up this community live in the sphere of God's eschatological rule where God is their Father (6:9) and they are sons of God [cf. 5:9, 45; 13:38], disciples of Jesus (10:1; 26:18), and brothers of Jesus (28:10) and of one another (23:8). In a word, the new community Jesus forms is a brotherhood of the sons of God and of his disciples." Jack D. Kingsbury, *Matthew as Story* (Minneapolis: Fortress, 1986), 104. (The references in brackets are from a footnote in Kingsbury's book.)

plementation of its teachings as a literal and rigid legal code. Does not Strecker circumvent the oppressive burden of legalism when he emphasizes that the eternal will of God revealed by the Kyrios is a set of hermeneutical principles for constantly reinterpreting the law and the prophets in new situations, as well as Jesus' teaching (see reading A, CAW 5.2, and CATs 2–3)?

It is true that legalism exemplifies the oppressive and alienating character of the teaching about discipleship, which disturbs me. But rejecting legalism is not enough. The problem remains as long as one conceives of discipleship as "implementing God's will," whether one conceives of it as a legalistic code or as a set of hermeneutical principles. This becomes clear when one notes that Strecker explains that the implementation of the hermeneutical principles of love, perfection, and judgment insures that Jesus' teachings function as practicable rules for the community life (see reading A, CAW 5.2–5.3). As clearly as in legalism, we find here the problematic pattern according to which the ultimate goal of the implementation of God's will is the establishment of a community under God that is a preliminary manifestation of the kingdom. Individual disciples must sacrifice themselves for the good of the community; other people must either submit to the community and conform to it, or they are rejected from it as "sinners,"[28] as "lost," and thus as less-than-human beings who can be demonized.

As it seeks to implement the teaching of the Sermon, the community of disciples cannot but condone and promote the very things it condemns, namely, oppressive and abusive relationships of all kinds. Matthew 5:20 and other passages are read as a confirmation that Jews are lost, damned, and excluded, as long as they stubbornly refuse to turn away from Judaism and to join the church in response to "the mission to the Jews." No Jew, regardless of positive personal qualities, can do anything truly good; as long as he or she remains a Jew, by definition, he or she is a sinner — lost, damned, and excluded. This is not a simple proclamation of the differences between two religious traditions; it is anti-Judaism (indeed anti-Semitism), which opens the door to all the monstrous atrocities of the Nazi Holocaust. Even though speaking of the Jews as belonging to a race (the Semitic race) and of anti-Semitism is scientifically and historically wrong, anti-Semitism is nevertheless the appropriate term here:[29] in the logic of this interpretation and of its twisted "gospel," members of the community are the only true human beings — those who are saved — while all other human beings are less-than-human beings. It is a small step to add that these people belong to lost races, and this is especially true in the case of Jews.

---

28. Accordingly, members of the community are unlike these sinners.

29. As was underscored by Samuel Sandmel, *Anti-Semitism in the New Testament?* (Philadelphia: Fortress, 1978), xi–xxi, passim.

These disparaging comments seem out of place. After all, this deontological interpretation underscores the disciples' duties that make possible intersubjective relations. It calls for a community of disciples where love is preached and implemented toward other members of the community as well as toward outsiders. Yet I see a first little worrisome step. This love for outsiders, for sinners, for the lost, for enemies is expressed in the church's mission through which these people are called to join the church by "repenting." Am I not carried away by my suspicion? Love for outsiders is expressed in concrete deeds. This mission is not merely in words (a call) but also in good works (5:16) aimed at alleviating in many different ways the pain, anguish, and suffering of those who are stricken by illness, poverty, natural disasters, as well as by crimes and other forms of injustice. Oppressive, exploitive, and abusive relationships are thus condemned in deeds as well as in words, as the disciples seek to construct and maintain a community characterized by selfless love, which is open to everyone who would join it by abandoning their former lives in the world and by selflessly forsaking anything that would differentiate them and thus separate them from other members of the community. From the perspective of the community, then, those who refuse to become members condemn themselves to oppressive, exploitive, and abusive relationships in which they are both victims and perpetrators. They demonstrate it by refusing to participate in the selfless life of the community and by affirming their difference, be it a difference in religion, culture, race, or sexual orientation. Thus when they are excluded, they are not really victims of discrimination; they have excluded themselves. All the other kinds of discrimination that they suffer fade out and become quasi-invisible for the disciples in the community. This is what these sinners should expect after choosing the sad and self-destructive way of life in the self-centered world outside of the sphere of God's rule.[30] The more the disciples selflessly devote themselves to the construction and maintenance of their community, the more they exclude those who fail to implement this teaching and the more they discriminate against all those who are different from the members of the community in terms of race, religion, or culture. As far as they are concerned, the responsibility for oppression, injustice, discrimination, racism, and all other kinds of social evil is out there in the unrepentant world — as if disciples were no longer sinners and as if their community were not a human community necessarily tainted by its participation in the life of a human society. The love feast of the kingdom in the community means a hell of fire, oppression, exploitation, dehumanization for outsiders.

---

30. On the invisibility of the monstrous oppression of black women (raped and used as breeders) as well as of other sins, see the powerful comments by Delores S. Williams, "Sin, Nature, and Black Women's Bodies," in *Ecofeminism and the Sacred*, ed. Carol J. Adams (New York: Continuum, 1993), 24–29.

I do not deny the importance of self-sacrifice in discipleship; but, as I already said, I contest self-sacrifice for the sake of a human community as ultimate good. Similarly, I do not deny that doing God's will is a central characteristic of discipleship and that the community of disciples is important. But I contest the specific way in which reading A and its deontological interpretation of the Sermon on the Mount conceptualize these two aspects of discipleship. I do not deny the value of a deontological preunderstanding of the moral life; but I contest its use to make universal claims about a particular community and the teaching by which it lives.

As we noted in chapter 5 (reading A, CAT 1), a deontological preunderstanding of the moral life emphasizes duties that make possible *intersubjective* relations in *any human society* and that are understood in terms of basic requisites of *human life*, expressed in *universal* principles. This is a plausible preunderstanding positing that all human communities are imperfect and need to strive to implement the ideal intersubjective relations expressed in universal principles accessible to all human beings through reason. But when this rationalistic preunderstanding is used for interpreting and making sense of the teaching of the Sermon on the Mount, it is distorted by exclusively applying what was said regarding humanity as a whole to the community of disciples — which is universalized in the sense that it represents ideal humanity in the kingdom. Since the teaching of the Sermon is the revelation of God's eternal will (universal principles), the church is an ideal community — the only community where God's will is implemented; the sphere of God's eschatological rule; a preliminary manifestation of the kingdom. This is not to say, as Strecker and Kingsbury acknowledge, that the church is perfect; it is not the kingdom, but a proleptic manifestation of it. Its members are sinners, but they are repentant and forgiven sinners. Thus the church is the sphere of God's eschatological rule, the community of those who implement God's will (even if they have temporary lapses), the locus of salvation, from which all unrepentant sinners are excluded even as they are invited to join the community by turning away from their sins, i.e., by abandoning everything in their lives that does not conform to the church community.

This plausible but most problematic view of the community of disciples is based on the conviction that the basic human predicament is a lack of knowledge of God's will — rather than a lack of will or a lack of ability (see below). Human beings do not do God's will and are thus lost because they do not know what they should do; they do not know the duties they should implement in their lives. The Sermon overcomes this lack of knowledge by revealing to the disciples God's eternal will proclaimed by Jesus as the exalted Kyrios (reading A, CAT 2). If they do not do God's will after receiving this revelation, they show who they truly are — people in rebellion against God, wolves disguised in sheep's clothing, hypocrites like the scribes and Pharisees and indeed like all the Jews, since they refuse to repent. The community of disciples has a unique status because it alone has access to God's will; it alone has the key to truly good intersubjective relations; it alone is the door giving access to the kingdom. Damned are those who do not enter by this narrow door.

In sum, the view of discipleship and of the community that I find so problematic is based on the convictions that

- the basic human predicament is a lack of knowledge of God's will, as a body of knowledge about what to implement and about how to do it (hermeneutical principles);

- the Sermon on the Mount is the revelation of the eternal (and thus universal) will of God by the exalted Kyrios who has all authority in heaven and on earth;

- the community of disciples has a unique status as the sphere of God's eschatological rule, a preliminary manifestation of the kingdom under the Kyrios;

- the community is the ultimate good (and the locus of salvation) to be constructed and maintained at all cost by self-sacrifice and by the exclusion of all those who are not worthy to be in it.

Why Reading B Is Not a Satisfactory Alternative for Me: Limitations of a Consequentialist Interpretation of Discipleship according to the Sermon on the Mount

As is clear, I did not choose as my interpretation either the consequentialist (reading B) or the first perfectionist interpretation (reading C). Why did I not choose them? My first reaction is one of surprise. In its own way, each of these seems to address the concerns I have with the deontological interpretation. But as I ponder the ways in which each differs from the interpretation I chose (reading D), their respective limitations appear. Albeit in different guises, each includes a problem similar to one of those I perceived in the deontological interpretation.

The consequentialist interpretation (reading B) seems to be in an ideal position to address the concerns I expressed about the deontological conclusions, since it bases its own conclusions about discipleship according to the Sermon on a totally different set of convictions. As was emphasized in chapter 3, it is clearly legitimate to read the Sermon on the Mount as a sermon that seeks to convince the hearers/readers to do God's will. Seemingly, the basic human predicament that Jesus overcomes is a lack of *will* to do God's will (rather than a lack of knowledge of God's will). Instead of being the exalted Kyrios who lays down God's demands, Jesus is our brother, the lowly Son of man, who manifests God's goodness among us through his good deeds, proclaims the good news of the kingdom, and teaches the goodness of God's will. Because disciples recognize the goodness of God expressed and manifested by Jesus' ministry and the benefits of doing God's will for themselves (present and future rewards), they want to do God's will in overabundant ways by performing good deeds for the benefit of others and of God (Mt 5:16). In the process, the disciples' vocation is established; it involves being prophet and manifesting the goodness of God as salt and light of the world, so that others might in turn glorify God and become disciples. From this perspective, discipleship and the mission it involves are the direct prolongation of Jesus' ministry. Thus discipleship involves implementing the model of discipleship that Jesus' ministry is. For disciples, this is an awesome responsibility, since the salvation of other people depends on the good performance of their mission.

This is a very attractive teaching about discipleship. It has other features (described in chaps. 3–5), such as the view of discipleship as an ongoing process that different people enter in their own ways, that make it even more appealing. Yet the question remains, Why do I prefer reading D? What am I lacking in this view of discipleship? Or, alternatively, what bothers me about it?

Let me first specify the points that I am ambivalent about. First, I am not at all confident that "I" know the will of God that I should carry out. In many situations, I do not clearly recognize the best course of action. Although this might simply be a professional handicap — academics raise too many questions — I believe this is true at least in large segments of the European-American cultures, which, whether they like it or not, are postmodern.[31] Yet I have to acknowledge that there are many people in these cultures who are confident that they actually know what God's will is. These include members of extremist groups (including neo-Nazi militia), sects, fundamentalist churches, and other churches that have adopted the deontological interpretation of discipleship. After Jesus' proclamation of God's eternal will in the Sermon on the Mount, they know what God's will is; what remains is to want to do it. Now I understand my instinctive suspicion of the conclusions of reading B. Most of the problems I discussed regarding the preceding interpretation could be once again listed here. I should have anticipated it. The basic pattern remains the same; discipleship is still understood as implementing God's will — here the model offered by Jesus' ministry.

The emphasis in reading B that our will as disciples also needs to be established and that for this we need a clear sense of vocation remains an important point. Nevertheless, I have some doubts about the conclusions regarding the nature of the disciples' vocation and mission. The claim that disciples prolong Jesus' ministry and that they are to make disciples by manifesting God's goodness through their good works is problematic for

---

31. See chapter 1.

me. I am not concerned by the low Christology and its emphasis on the humanity of Christ, which allows disciples to share Jesus' ministry; it challenges patriarchal and other hierarchical interpretations. What concerns me is that as long as other people do not respond positively to the disciples' missionary activity they are on the wide road to perdition (see chap. 3, CAW 7, and chap. 5, CAT 5). Once again, this conception of the mission opens the door to all kinds of discrimination; the disciples are the only true human beings — the saved ones — who bring salvation to the lost, the damned, the less-than-human beings. This is the humiliating and dehumanizing gesture of the rich handing out their leftovers to the worthless poor. No reciprocity, and thus no true love, is envisioned.

This interpretation could include such a reciprocity. But it remains an unrealized possibility. For reading B, those who are not yet disciples, whoever they might be, should already have a knowledge of God's will (their problem is that they do not want to do it). If we envision the possibility that they have a knowledge of what God wants to be done in a specific situation — rather than a general knowledge of God's will — they might have something that the disciples would need to receive from them. There would be reciprocity. But in reading B the interpretation is totally focused on what allows someone to enter the process through which a disciple goes before being ready to carry out his or her mission. Thus his or her "sound eye" is directed toward the manifestations of God's goodness in the lives of a previous generation of disciples and in Jesus' ministry (see chap. 3, CAW 6). Whatever other people might have to contribute is out of sight, as for the most part the community also is. The primary concern is with the way in which individuals are made fishers of people.

Why Reading C Is Not Quite Satisfactory for Me: Limitations of the First Perfectionist Interpretation of Discipleship according to the Sermon on the Mount

Why did I not choose as my interpretation the first perfectionist interpretation (reading C)? I wondered. When I first encountered the perfectionist interpretation of the Sermon on the Mount in W. D. Davies's work,[32] I readily recognized and appreciated the effort to underscore the ambivalence of the relationship between Jewish teachings and the Sermon on the Mount. This interpretation recognized that the community of disciples is rooted in Judaism, with which it was engaged in a heated debate — a family dispute. In this way, Davies seemed to address one of the central concerns I have with the deontological interpretation — its anti-Judaism. Yet I was not quite satisfied by this interpretation, even as the commentaries

---

32. W. D. Davies, *The Setting of the Sermon on the Mount* (Cambridge: Cambridge University Press, 1964).

and other studies of Luz and Davies and Allison clarified its *conclusions about the teaching* of the Sermon regarding discipleship and how different they are as compared with those of Strecker's deontological interpretation. But as I compare its conclusions with those of the interpretation I chose (reading D), the limitations I instinctively perceived in this interpretation appear.

According to both readings C and D, discipleship according to the Sermon on the Mount is a faith venture (as intuitive ethical practice) rather than the implementation of a code of behavior (legalistic interpretations), of hermeneutical principles (reading A), or of a process exemplified by Jesus' ministry (reading B). Discipleship still involves doing God's will and acting on the basis of Jesus' teaching (Mt 7: 21–27). But in the perfectionist interpretations, doing God's will means acting according to the faith[33] that the Sermon conveys to the disciples and that allows them to identify what they should do. When discipleship is conceptualized from this general perspective, it has a drastically different texture and quality, amounting to a much better relative value from the standpoint of my convictions, interests, and concerns.

According to the deontological and consequentialist interpretations of the Sermon, in one way or another Jesus reveals "what" disciples should do and/or "how" they should do it — in such cases "faith" is limited to trusting that Jesus has indeed provided such a revelation. As a result the community as exclusive possessor of this revelation engenders and promotes problematic patterns of behavior. By contrast, according to the perfectionist interpretations, through the Sermon on the Mount (as well as through the rest of the Gospel according to Matthew), Jesus offers faith. Whether it is understood as the vision one has when one is socialized in a specific symbolic world or as the moral discernment (sound eye) that allows one to recognize what is God's, it is *with the help of this faith* that subsequently disciples discover what they should do. In sum, discipleship as faith venture involves the acknowledgment that disciples do *not* possess a knowledge of either "what" God's will is or "how" to do it in order to enter life (Mt 7:13–14), and thus *cannot* claim that their community is in any way a manifestation of the kingdom and that its pattern of behavior somehow embodies the way to implement God's will. Disciples in this faith venture *"seek* the kingdom of God and his righteousness" (6:33, author's translation).[34] And when these seekers have found either kingdom or God's righteousness, they should indeed rejoice and act on it. But they should also

---

33. Here as in chapter 5 I use the term "faith" in an attempt to express the differences between the conclusions of these perfectionist interpretations and those of deontological and consequentialist interpretations.

34. ζητεῖτε is read here as "try to find," "seek information about," "desire," "try to obtain," that is, with all its connotations emphasizing that one does not know either kingdom or righteousness.

acknowledge that they merely got a glimpse and that they must keep seeking; disciples have constantly to *discover* by means of faith what specifically they must do, since this is neither once and for all established nor deduced by adapting old teachings for new settings by means of the same eternally appropriate hermeneutical principles.

Because of the perception they have of themselves in this faith venture, disciples/seekers cannot approach others as possessors of life or of the way to it (with all the oppressive patterns of relationships this involves). All they can do is to invite others to participate with them in the search for the kingdom and for God's righteousness. The oppressive pattern that ends up marring all relationships because of its weight is still massively present. But maybe a few cracks begin to appear.

Another characteristic shared by the two perfectionist interpretations is that one cannot be involved in this faith venture by oneself. This is an intrinsic part of a perfectionist preunderstanding of the moral life; one cannot gain virtue without others whom one observes and imitates. From this perspective, I can venture to say that one of the reasons for the emphasis on reconciliation, forgiveness, and love for others in the Sermon is that these are conditions for seeking the kingdom and God's righteousness. It is only with the help of others that disciples can progress in their search. A few other cracks seem to appear on the oppressive pattern of relationships. Is this an illusion?

At this point the two perfectionist interpretations go their separate ways. By focusing on the Lord's Prayer as the center of the Sermon, Luz (and Davies and Allison) indicate that the faith conveyed by the Sermon is a communal faith — the faith of a community praying together, "Our Father in heaven, hallowed be your name, Your kingdom come...." (Mt 6:9–10). In praying together in this way, the community enters and is being socialized in the symbolic world with its twofold horizon of the present loving Father and of the coming kingdom. The members of the community learn to share this twofold vision of what they are to search for: the righteousness of their Father in heaven and the kingdom. Who is included in this worshiping community? Of course, disciples already involved in the faith venture, as well as all kinds of other people who have been invited to join the search, who might be novice disciples, would-be-disciples, or simply curious onlookers. Consequently, the church community is always, as Luz emphasizes, a *corpus permixtum;* because it is a mixed body, everyone can enter it, whatever clothing they might wear (cf. Mt 7:15). Is this the sound of crumbling? Is this the good news that the structure of oppression in relationships is finally crumbling and falling?

The ambivalence that inheres all aspects of the symbolic world is underscored, again and again. The fact that the various teachings of the Sermon are not new, but are borrowed from the Jewish or Hellenistic traditions, is emphasized; the newness is in the twofold horizon that these teachings project by the new way in which they are held together (a point repeatedly emphasized by Luz and Davies and Allison). Yes, the contributions of all these very different people who form the mixed body of worshipers is necessary, so that all may share in this vision of the kingdom and God's righteousness.

But just as the oppressive pattern seems to crumble in Luz's interpretation, it is quickly shored up by the interpretation of Matthew 7:13–27 — the community is called to identify and reject the false prophets in its midst, even if it must proceed with caution.[35] And so the oppressive pattern is rebuilt in Luz's general conclusions. There it becomes clear that for Luz the vision of the kingdom is nothing other than "the vision and standard for a future shape of the *church*" (Luz's emphasis), which must be implemented in the present church so as to avoid "a pretense for a 'laissez faire' attitude and for the neglect of a common church form out of a falsely understood respect for the individual."[36]

I understand Luz's concerns as originating in Switzerland, where an intense debate regarding the "form of the church" is taking place in reference to the future of "state churches." But with these concluding comments, disappointingly, he brings back all the problematic features of Strecker's deontological interpretation. Yet, as I pointed out in chapter 6, I should not be surprised. A figurative perfectionist interpretation cannot but take into account the ambivalence of the disciples' vocation. Yes, it is inclusive — it recognizes models of discipleship among women, Gentiles, children — and yes, it is salvific; as fishers of people, the disciples throw out their nets to pull everybody inside the church. But it is also judgmental; it involves identifying the false prophets and casting them out along with other evil religious leaders, such as the Pharisees and the scribes (see chap. 2, reading C). This is necessary because the church is not only the place of worship where disciples can gain a vision of the kingdom and of the Father's present care but also the place where the kingdom is proleptically manifested. Thus it is in the church itself that one should look for models of discipleship who manifest the kingdom and God's righteousness. It is true that one might find such models of discipleship outside the usual leadership of the church — children, women — and even outside the church — Gentiles, little ones; but as the parable of the sheep and the goats expresses (Mt 25:31–46), even though they themselves do not know it, they are already members of the church. Through this co-optation, everything is back in order: the manifestations of God's righteousness belong to the church, and it is the vocation of the disciples to establish the church as a preliminary manifestation of the kingdom. This is the goal of the resocialization of church members by means of worship; the goal of constructing and maintaining the com-

---

35. Ulrich Luz, *Matthew 1–7: A Commentary* (Minneapolis: Augsburg, 1989), 433–54.
36. Luz, *Matthew*, 457–58.

munity of disciples; the goal of clearly marking its boundaries so as to exclude all those who do not conform. The faith venture is largely confined within these boundaries because the goal of this venture is the church itself. Although the process of constructing and maintaining the community is understood quite differently, in this figurative perfectionist interpretation (as in the deontological interpretation), the reasons for constructing and maintaining this community are the same: a church is to be the preliminary manifestation of the future kingdom. Thus the oppressive pattern of relationships is back, almost as heavy as before.

Why I Chose Reading D: Discipleship as Faith Venture; Imitating God's Righteousness Wherever It May Be Found

My reasons for choosing the second perfectionist interpretation (reading D), with its focus on the moral discernment emphasized by the thematic dimension of the Sermon, are at last clarified for me. Since I have already explained why I did not choose the three other kinds of interpretations, I can be brief.

I envision *discipleship as a faith venture* that involves following Jesus and whoever else one identifies as manifesting the kingdom and God's righteousness. Unlike Luz, I do not see the Sermon teaching that this faith venture and its search for God's righteousness and the kingdom is to be confined within the boundaries of the church. This choice of interpretation is a matter of personal conviction — together with my Huguenot ancestors and many contemporary European-Americans, I cannot envision God being confined within the church. In the same way that the boundaries of the Chosen People have been opened to include many other people because "God is able from these stones to raise up children to Abraham" (Mt 3:9), so God is able to cause people to perform righteousness even if they are outside the church. Therefore, one of the features of reading D that is very attractive for me is its conclusion that we should expect to find people manifesting God's righteousness outside the community of disciples (as the beatitudes express from the outset in this interpretation). Similarly, the negative corollary that the community of disciples is *not* the privileged locus of the manifestations of God's righteousness fits well with these convictions. The church is not and never has been a community of righteous people, but a community of sinners — as Luther and the other Reformers appropriately emphasized and as is confirmed in my own experience (there is at least one sinner involved in every church activity). My conviction — and my hope — is that the church is neither the kingdom nor a preliminary manifestation of the kingdom. If it were, I am not sure I would want to pray, "Thy kingdom come"!

Yet I find it difficult to avoid being trapped into a deontological interpretation. For instance, the confession of our sins at almost each worship service raises for me a nagging question: What does it mean to repent from our sins, since we have to repent from the same sins the following week? Is this anything other than hypocrisy? By raising these questions, I show that I am still thinking of discipleship as the *implementation* of a teaching that defines "what" a righteous behavior is or "how" to achieve it. I am still thinking that "repenting" means "turning *away*" from one's sinful life in order to adopt a different, righteous way of life. In sum, I am still thinking in deontological categories. But from the perspective of the thematic perfectionist interpretation, it is not the repeated repentance which is hypocritical, but the fact of raising such questions about it because they involve pretending that we, disciples, could and should be righteous and that the community of disciples could and should be a preliminary manifestation of the kingdom.

The significance of the observation that according to this thematic perfectionist interpretation "repenting" primarily means "turning *toward*" the kingdom[37] finally appears. For those engaged in the faith venture of discipleship, repentance is an essential first step in their search for God's righteousness and the kingdom. The question is, Where shall I find manifestations of God's righteousness? In which direction should I turn to see these manifestations of righteousness? By confessing my sins, I eliminate one sector. Even if there are some manifestations of righteousness among my own deeds, it is not there that I should look for them. I have to turn my sights in another direction. Similarly, when we, as a community of disciples, repent and ask for forgiveness ("forgive *us* our debts," Mt 6:12), we express that we should not first turn toward our community to find the kingdom and God's righteousness. So where should we turn? Where can we expect to find renewing and transforming manifestations of God's righteousness and of the kingdom? The answer must be, outside the community of disciples — outside the church.

This is the surprising news of the gospel, the surprising news to the Chosen People. Where is God's renewing righteousness manifested in the person of the Messiah? Not in Judea, but in the "land of Zebulun, land of Naphtali, on the road by the sea, across the Jordan, Galilee of the Gentiles" (Mt 4:15). The surprising news to the disciples is that it is not among the disciples, but among the crowds of "little ones" who are poor in spirit, mourning, meek, that one finds manifestations of God's transforming righteousness in people who really are thirsty and hungry for it, merciful, pure in spirit, peacemakers, and persecuted for it (5:3–10). Does this mean that the disciples and the Jewish people are condemned? Of course not. This would be the case if their respective mission was to be the holy people or a community that is the *primary* locus of the manifestations of God's righteousness and of the kingdom — and thus the locus of salvation (as is

---

37. See chapter 2, reading D, CAW 4, and CATs 1 and 2.

the case in different ways according to readings A and C). But this is not the case in this interpretation. The call to repentance and the call to look outside the community (among the Gentiles and the little ones) for manifestations of the kingdom and of God's righteousness are essential lessons in moral discernment; a sound eye is useless if it looks in the wrong direction.

What, then, is the mission of the disciples? It is not to preach righteousness by telling others what they should or should not do (reading A). It is not to perform better acts of righteousness that could serve as examples that others should emulate (reading A) or that others could discern as expressions of God's goodness as they progress toward discipleship (reading B). In one phrase, the mission of the disciples is to perform acts of *overabundant* righteousness. Without repeating what I demonstrated in chapter 6 (CAT 3), I can now express it in a more direct way. The mission of the disciples involves:

- Identifying *outside* the community expressions of God's righteousness — among the little ones (Mt 5:3–10); in the teaching (the law and the prophets) and the practice of the scribes and the Pharisees (5:20–45); in the behavior of tax collectors and of Gentiles (5:46–47); in parents taking care of their children (7:9–11); and, most generally, in the acts of righteousness that everyone would like others to perform for them (7:12);

- Amplifying each expression of God's righteousness (5:20, 46–47); affirming it; putting it in the spotlight; acknowledging it as an expression of the righteousness of God that the disciples are seeking (6:33), and thus as a righteousness that should be practiced in all kinds of circumstances and thus beyond its original context;

- Practicing "overabundant righteousness," that is, practicing other people's righteousness — a righteousness that is not ours because we have learned it from someone else; as we practice it in a new, broader setting, we emulate someone else; acknowledging that any righteousness by which we choose to live ends up being an overabundant righteousness both because we practice it overabundantly and because we have received it from other people.

Thus the community of disciples is not the *primary* but always a *secondary* locus of the manifestations of God's righteousness and of the kingdom. Disciples do "strive...for the kingdom of God and his righteousness" (as the NRSV translates Mt 6:33) with the hope of bringing about preliminary manifestations of the kingdom. But these manifestations of the kingdom are not centered on the community of disciples (as they are according to readings A, B, and C). Actually, they are not centered anywhere — *they are decentered* — because the good news is that God's righteousness and God's kingdom encompass east and west (8:11), all the nations (here including

Israel, 28:19), even when people do not know that their righteousness is God's righteousness (25:36–40). The task of the disciples is indeed to make disciples by teaching others what Jesus has commanded them, which from this perspective means teaching others to practice overabundant righteousness — not their own righteousness, but the righteousness of God that they should discover in still other people.

Discipleship is indeed a faith venture. But such a venture involves risks — possibly too many risks for some. Where are the criteria to control the identification of the manifestations of God's righteousness among outsiders? Are we in a situation where everything goes? Do we end up with the laissez-faire atmosphere that Luz and many with him fear? I do not think so because of the role of the community of disciples. The interpretation of the Sermon in reading D has merely hinted at it. A multidimensional study of the ecclesiology of the Gospel according to Matthew would be necessary at this point. Here this point is best clarified in an indirect fashion through a few additional reflections on the implications of this multidimensional study.

My Choice of a Teaching about Discipleship to Live By: The Theological and Communal Dimension of the Multidimensional Critical Study

From the beginning, this multidimensional study has been my effort to practice the teaching of the Sermon on the Mount that I chose as a teaching to live by. References to the "decentered" character of the disciples' mission as overabundant righteousness intentionally evokes the decentering of androcritical interpretations discussed above. Through this multidimensional approach I decentered my interpretation by affirming and amplifying the legitimacy and plausibility of three other interpretations. I did so by actually practicing each of these interpretations; indeed, I was astonished to find myself convinced that each is a coherent and consistent interpretation of the Sermon on the Mount and that it fully makes sense for me. Thus in Part I and Part II my interpretation has been decentered in the sense that it was shown to be one among several equally legitimate and plausible interpretations. This is roughly equivalent to what I said above about overabundant righteousness.

In Part III I recentered my interpretation by raising the question of the relative values of the four interpretations. Since I did so from the only value perspective I could really adopt, namely, "mine," from the outset it was clear which interpretation would be rated as the best and thus as worth living by: "mine," of course. It is clear from its passionate tone that I am quite convinced of the dangers of other interpretations and of the positive value of "mine." I end up "centered" on an interpretation. Interpretation matters. The interpretation of discipleship according to the Sermon on the Mount by which I live matters. There is nothing wrong with centering oneself on an interpretation.

Yet my interpretation remains somewhat decentered because it is now clear that "I" chose it. Furthermore, the quotation marks signal that this choice and this interpretation are "mine" in a special sense. Is reading D "mine"? Yes, it is the one "I" chose to live by. But "I" did not make this choice by myself. Is this not the interpretation "I" personally chose as I wrote my commentary? Yes and no. As I noted in both chapter 4 and chapter 6, in the process of this multidimensional study many characteristics of my interpretation that were barely mentioned in my commentary became apparent for the first time; for instance, I was not aware that my *conclusions about the teaching* of the Sermon regarding overabundant righteousness and discernment (a sound eye) made sense for me through a perfectionist preunderstanding of the moral life. In sum, I significantly refined my interpretation as I brought it to critical understanding through constant comparison with the three other kinds of interpretation: Strecker, Kingsbury, Edwards, Luz, Davies and Allison played an essential role in shaping "my" interpretation. Since they primarily play a contrasting role, it might still be appropriate to call this interpretation "mine." But I can no longer see it as fully "mine" as soon as I acknowledge (as I do) the full hermeneutical circle in which it is involved. This interpretation is thus a product of a multidimensional study that practices the teaching of the interpretation "I" chose to live by. The point is that, as I underscored in *Ethics of Biblical Interpretation*,[38] most of the features of this androcritical multidimensional practice of critical biblical study are *not mine* at all; they are my effort to affirm, amplify, and practice in a different context (a male European-American context) — and thus in an overabundant way — certain important practices of biblical studies by feminist, African-American, and Two-Thirds World scholars.[39]

I want nevertheless to claim this reading for myself; it is the one I want to live by. But as is clear, this is no longer an androcentric or Eurocentric claim: the interpretation is no longer viewed as a universal teaching everyone must choose. It is word of God for me, and thus the word I am ready to preach to others. This is a high claim, but it does not deny that another

---

38. Daniel Patte, *Ethics of Biblical Interpretation: A Reevaluation* (Louisville: Westminster/ John Knox, 1995).

39. While the conception of the biblical text as multidimensional originates for me in semiotic theories, its heuristic qualities were confirmed for me as I found it used by two African scholars who use a distinction either between different historical dimensions or literary (natural and symbolic) levels to explain the distinctive textual grounding of their contextual interpretations. See Itumeleng J. Mosala, *Biblical Hermeneutics and Black Theology in South Africa* (Grand Rapids: Eerdmans, 1989), and Teresa Okure, SHCJ, "The Mother of Jesus in the New Testament: Implications for Women Mission," *Journal of Inculturation Theology* 2, no. 2 (1995): 196–210, and *The Johannine Approach to Mission: A Contextual Study of John 4:1–24* (Tübingen: J. C. B. Mohr, Paul Siebeck, 1988).

interpretation might truly be word of God for you, and indeed for us in another situation, or even in the same one, if you convince me by advocating another interpretation and its greater value. Let us not forget that I took a risk as part of a faith venture when I chose this interpretation. Thus this choice can never be final and permanent.

The question becomes, How do believers identify the teaching that is for them the word of God by which they live? I long struggled with this question, as I studied various biblical texts seeking to identify criteria that individual interpreters could use and the foundation on which these criteria could be grounded. Finally, it dawned on me during a short visit in the Philippines. While conversing with students and colleagues at Union Theological Seminary (Dasmariñas, Philippines), who cannot think of themselves apart from the community to which they belong, it became clear to me that I was looking in the wrong direction. The word of God is never "for me" by myself; it is always "for us." Indeed, it is as an individual that "I" must confess, "I" believe (*credo*). But there is a secret of faith: this most personal human experience requires other people's faith.[40] I cannot believe by myself. Before I believed, someone already believed. My confession of faith expresses that I share the faith that other people already have and that they shared in passing down to me. In order to assume authentically my faith, I must acknowledge my indebtedness (*utang na loob*, as one would say in Tagalog) to the community that confirmed and thus established the value of my personal religious experience.

The same applies to faith interpretations. Before affirming that an interpretation is *pro me* (the interpretation by which I should live), I had to recognize it as *pro nobis*. I should not try to discern what is the word of God by myself, as an isolated individual. Actually, as I interpret I never truly succeed in isolating myself. Behind its closed door, my quiet study is soon invaded by a crowd of other interpreters whom I brought with me or who were already there, on the bookshelves. As Fish points out, there is no interpretation outside of an interpretive community.[41] Or as Habermas indicates,[42] truth claims are constantly negotiated in such interpretive communities because they are always partial. The *pro me/nobis* interpretation, which is recognized as good for us — indeed as the best for us and thus as the teaching by which we should live, word of God for us — is a result of negotiations with others in the context of an interpretive community. Thus

---

40. I follow de Certeau who calls a secret of believing the fact that "so that belief might exist, believing must *already* exist somewhere." See Michel de Certeau, S.J., *Croire: une pratique de la différence* (Urbino: Centro Internazionale di Semiotica e di Linguistica, 1981), 12; cf. 8–13.

41. Stanley E. Fish, *Is There a Text in This Class? The Authority of Interpretive Communities* (Cambridge: Harvard University Press, 1980).

42. Jürgen Habermas, *Knowledge and Human Interest,* trans. J. J. Shapiro (Boston: Beacon, 1971), and *Moral Consciousness and Communicative Action*, trans. C. Lenhardt and S. W. Nicholsen (Cambridge: MIT Press, 1990).

the value of our choice of an interpretation as word of God for us cannot but reflect the value of the community itself.

By underscoring the necessary role of an interpretive community in our choice of a teaching by which to live, I once again suggest why I as an individual cannot conclude this study. The assessment of the relative values of the different interpretations of discipleship according to the Sermon on the Mount needs to be prolonged in the context of one or another specific community. It is only in such concrete contexts that the effects of the various teachings about discipleship on other people can be assessed. It is only if this assessment is shared by other members of the community and thus confirmed by them that I am empowered to abide by my choice of a *pro me* interpretation and thus to strive to live by it. In sum, as became clear for me in the Philippines, while individual interpreters can distinguish "good" and "helpful" interpretations from "bad" and "harmful" ones — as I tried to do above — only a community is in a position of discerning what is word of God for us in a specific context.

Is this to say that I posit "community" as an absolute good or as an ultimate foundation? Of course not. From the eschatological perspective (also a postmodern perspective), which I adopt here, I cannot do so. Furthermore, I do not prescribe a course of action. I simply attempt to describe how we practically discern the word of God — different words of God in various communities. Interpretive communities, even if they are religious and are called churches or the church, are neither infallible nor perfect. While the churches might appropriately seek to secure themselves on a solid foundation, such as the rock of Jesus' words (Mt 7:24), or might envision themselves in terms of the kingdom that Jesus proclaimed and that they seek (Mt 6:33), it is only through interpretations and reinterpretations that they have access to Jesus' teaching. In sum, any interpretive community, including the holiest of churches, remains a human community, with a relative value that we must assess by comparing it with other communities.

It is indeed good, helpful, self-affirming, empowering, freeing, constructive, beneficial for diverse people to form a community held together by a sense of indebtedness (*utang na loob*, so strong in Philippine cultures) or a sense of solidarity (as European-American might call it, although it is quite weak in our cultures). Thus when interpretive communities are characterized by a *reciprocal* sense of indebtedness and of solidarity, they are "dialogical communities" whose members discern together what is word of God for them through a dialogue in which the interpretation of each is respected, even as its relative value is assessed. It is this respect for other people's interpretations that this multidimensional study seeks to promote. It asks each of us to consider any interpretation as legitimate and plausible until proven otherwise (rather than the opposite), even as its relative value needs to be debated through comparison with the relative values of other legitimate and plausible interpretations. This dialogical interpretive process is not very efficient; it often takes much time and patience to understand how the interpretation of someone else might indeed be legitimate and plausible. Before this dialogue, we might never have perceived the dimension of the text on which an interpretation is focused; yet now that we have allowed this interpreter to help us see this textual dimension, we can readily recognize the legitimacy of this interpretation. Similarly, we might never have conceptualized a given teaching (such as discipleship) in terms of the culturally marked preunderstanding that a given interpretation presupposes. But as we recognize that this preunderstanding has the same status as our own, even though it might be expressed differently,[43] we find that we have to acknowledge the plausibility of this interpretation in its own cultural setting. As we patiently and respectfully listen to each other in the context of an interpretive community, an actual dialogue can take place regarding the relative values of diverse legitimate and plausible interpretations. Then the dialogical community can determine what is the *pro nobis* interpretation — the best interpretation for us — that I might want to adopt as a *pro me* interpretation if I choose to remain a member of this community.

Unfortunately, such dialogical communities are the exception rather than the rule, as the daily experience of women exemplifies according to Elisabeth Schüssler Fiorenza quoting Richard J. Berstein:

> There is no guarantee... no "logic of history" that must inevitably lead to dialogical communities that embrace all of humanity in which reciprocal judgment, practical discourse, and rational persuasion flourish. If anything we should have learned how much the contemporary world conspires against it and undermines it.[44]

Conversely, it is true that in many instances membership in a community is suffocating, burdensome, onerous, oppressive, enslaving, tyrannical. This happens when the threads that bind together the members of the community are transformed into chains; when the sense of indebtedness is turned upside down and is viewed by those in power as a right to demand compensations for the favors they have "graciously" granted or might provide in the future for the powerless; when the sense of solidarity degenerates into exploitive relationships by becoming either a means of co-opting the contributions of others or an expression of condescending superiority through which the one-way sharing of material, intellectual, or religious resources becomes a source of humiliation, alienation, and colonialism.

Interpretive communities easily become such oppressive communities. They still establish what is the "best" interpretation — the "word of God

---

43. This is the essential contribution of the collection of African biblical interpretations presented in Dube and West, eds., *"Reading With."*

44. Richard J. Berstein, *Beyond Objectivism and Relativism: Science, Hermeneutics, and Praxis* (Philadelphia: University of Pennsylvania Press, 1983), 231, quoted in Elisabeth Schüssler Fiorenza, *Bread Not Stone*, xxiii.

for us." But instead of doing it through a dialogical negotiation that shows respect for the diverse interpretations represented in the community and their relative values, these communities decree what the word of God is and, without any true consideration, dismiss as valueless, illegitimate, and implausible — indeed, as heretical, irresponsible, and foolish — all other interpretations advanced by members of the community. These members are condemned to alienation, oppression, co-optation, acculturation if they accept the choice of the community's hierarchy of an interpretation as word of God for them; or, if they refuse it, to exclusion from the community, excommunication, and indeed persecution as heretics.

Those who are thus excluded form communities "in the wilderness" (as my Huguenot ancestors did) or "on the margin" of the dominant interpretive community, be it a church, an academic institution, or a culturally marked scholarly guild.[45] There are many reasons why human beings need to belong to a community in order to survive. Participation in an interpretive community is no less necessary. For Christian believers for whom the Sermon on the Mount is part of the Scriptures, participation in such an interpretive community is necessary because without it we are unable to discern among the available interpretations which one is word of God for us, and thus which one we should personally confess by saying, *Credo*, I believe.

Thus ultimately, choosing a teaching about discipleship by which to live involves choosing to participate in a specific interpretive community, rather than in one of the others. As suggested above, a multidimensional critical practice involves opting for specific kinds of dialogical communities that are open to a broad diversity of interpretations, including feminist, African-American, and Two-Thirds World interpretations. In such interpretive communities, the bringing to critical understanding of our interpretations is never finished, and their choice as word of God for us is always called into question. But this is as it should be; the word of God is a living word, not a dead letter.

"Reading with" Other Interpreters: An Ongoing Venture

One of the points that was clarified for me by the preceding multidimensional study is that I had (and still have) a choice among several interpretations, since there are several legitimate and plausible interpretations, and that I made this choice on the basis of passionate value judgments.[46] I had no idea that I had so much at stake in the interpretation

---

45. See R. S. Sugirtharajah, ed. *Voices from the Margin: Interpreting the Bible in the Third World* (Maryknoll, N.Y.: Orbis, 1991), 1–6. See also Fernando F. Segovia and Mary Ann Tolbert, eds., *Reading from This Place*, vol. 2 (Minneapolis: Fortress, 1995).

46. This is old news for preachers, who are quite aware that their choice of an interpretation directly reflects their interests and their concerns. Each week, as they study the text

that I presented in my commentary. The androcritical edge of these remarks is that in each of their works other biblical scholars also choose one interpretation rather than others *on the basis of value judgments* passed on the conclusions about the teaching (CATs) of these interpretations. I am aware that this statement is counterintuitive for most male European-American scholars. We are ready to concede that over the years of our careers as biblical scholars our interpretations of specific texts have changed; indeed, progress in our research may have led us to deliberately choose a "better" interpretation. The new interpretation is "better" in the sense that it is either more legitimate (it better represents the textual evidence) or more plausible (its presentation of the teaching of the text about a certain topic makes more sense). This disinterested view of our scholarly choices is indeed plausible in the one-dimensional androcentric and Eurocentric world (a semantic universe) for which a text has a single legitimate and plausible teaching. But as I emphasized elsewhere[47] and repeatedly suggested since the beginning of this book, the cost of remaining in this world is too high for me or for any biblical scholar. It involves depriving myself of the great benefit of talking *with* others (something I cannot do as long as I talk *for* them or *about* them)[48] and reading the Bible *with* others, including at least two-thirds of the persons in the world — the entire Two-Thirds World — and ultimately many more because in this perspective scholars end up alienating *all* other readers of the Bible because they speak and read *for* them. In this world, a scholar cannot but alienate even his or her colleagues because the quest for "the" single true interpretation demands that we speak *about* other scholars and their interpretations, but *never with* them.[49]

Thus one of my deepest aspirations is to escape this desolate universe

---

on which they will preach, they deliberately choose one of the several and quite different teachings presented in the variety of commentaries they consult. They might simply conceive this choice as the selection of the most insightful commentary. Yet, for many, this is the self-conscious choice of the interpretation that is *the most valuable* for them and their congregation because it underscores the teaching that they feel their congregation needs to hear at this point in time; the teaching that is word of God for us today. Furthermore, these preachers, if they are conscientious, do not repeat the same sermon twice: the next time they preach on this text they emphasize another of its teachings — and at times a very different one — because circumstances have changed. In sum, preachers are commonly aware that they choose one interpretation rather than others *on the basis of value judgments* regarding the conclusions about the teaching (CATs) of these interpretations.

47. See Patte, *Ethics of Biblical Interpretation*, 17–36.

48. I use categories derived from the important essay by Gayatri C. Spivak, "Can the Subaltern Speak?" in *Marxism and the Interpretation of Culture,* ed. G. Nelson and L. Grossberg (London: Macmillan, 1988), 277–313. See also Patte, *Ethics of Biblical Interpretation,* 23–25, 33, and Dube and West, eds., *"Reading With."*

49. This depersonalization of other scholars is one of the consequences of the mode of discourse of one-dimensional (traditional) scholarship, as is emphasized in Stephen Moore, "True Confessions and Weird Obsessions: Autobiographical Interventions in Literary and Biblical Studies," in *Taking it Personally: Autobiographical Biblical Criticism,* by Janice Capel Anderson and Jeffrey L. Staley, Semeia 72 (Atlanta: Scholars Press, 1996).

where other people are hellish[50] because they reduce me to the status of subaltern-things[51] when they speak *about* me as a static thing and *about* my immutable interpretation of an immutable text, and where I do the same to them in a hellish circle out of which there is No Exit. I know. It is not very realistic to seek *"un petit coin de Paradis,"* — a piece of the kingdom and the righteousness/justice (δικαιοσύη, Mt 6:33) through which the "blessed ones" interact *with* each other. But it is also not very realistic to ignore the fact that there are many people who are speaking and reading *with* each other, recognizing each other as persons to be respected in their distinctiveness — as children of God. These people give me hope, even as they give me a craving to speak *with* and read *with* them because when I affirm them as persons by reading *with* them, I am in turn affirmed as a person.

Only when I read *with* others do I become aware of my *personal* investment in *my* interpretation, am I free to affirm it, and do I find myself affirmed as a person. Noting that I emphasize the subjective aspect of interpretation, someone might be tempted to object that I reduce reading to a subjective endeavor. But I do not. I seek to keep a balance by emphasizing just as strongly both the role of the text and the intersubjective character of the interpretive process. Although at any given moment one necessarily foregrounds one of them. Text, reader, and those *with* whom the reader reads are closely intertwined.

The role of the text cannot be separated from the interested role of the reader: I would not invest myself in an interpretation if I did not have at least a strong sense that it is legitimate and plausible and thus solidly grounded in textual evidence. Otherwise how could it be valuable for me? Conversely, this legitimate and plausible interpretation is not simply imposed on me by the text and its constraints. I chose it.

It is only as I read *with* others that I own up to this role and assume my interpretation as "mine." Reading *with* other persons involves respecting them and their interpretations even (and especially) when they are different from mine. Consequently, "reading with" cannot but expose the role of my personal convictions, interests, and concerns in my choice of an interpretation. I have to acknowledge the reasons for my interpretive choice. Furthermore, reading *with* others reveals to me treasures of the text that were hidden from me, as well as dangerous traps of the text, into which I could have fallen, that need to be marked with a red flag, and/or quagmires and quicksand from which I need to be rescued. Reading — and especially, reading the Scriptures — *with* others is an ongoing process of empowerment that constantly calls me to reassess my interpretive choices because I

---

50. A paraphrase of the famous phrase "l'enfer c'est les autres" in Sartre's play, *No Exit*. See Jean Paul Sartre, *No Exit, a Play in One Act & The Flies, a Play in Three Acts*, trans. S. Gilbert (New York: Knopf, 1948).

51. I allude to Spivak, "Can the Subaltern Speak?"

now have more interpretations to choose from. Simultaneously, by my participation in this reading process *with* others, I contribute to keeping the reading process alive and empowering for them.

From this perspective, the drastic limitation of legitimate and plausible interpretations and readers found in any one-dimensional interpretive practices — including androcentric and Eurocentric practices — tragically and irresponsibly impoverishes the intersubjective relations with other readers, the reading process, and the text itself. Furthermore, this limitation denies much of our common reading experience. This is, in brief, why I believe we must stay open to envisioning the possibility that other interpretations may be legitimate and plausible, even if they differ from ours, as happens when we take the risk of reading *with* others.

Reading *with* others involves doing to others as we would have them do to us (Mt 7:12). It involves respecting them as readers and respecting their interpretations. It involves acknowledging that these other interpreters are themselves personally invested in their own interpretations — a personal investment that in most instances is different from mine, even if we end up with the same choice of interpretation. Thus when we read *with* each other, we always have much to discuss and even to debate regarding our respective personal investments. This exchange helps me clarify my (often subconscious) reasons for choosing this interpretation and puts me in a position to proceed to a self-conscious reevaluation of my choice. Reading *with* others also involves acknowledging their basic competence as interpreters, as I would like them to acknowledge mine. This means that I cannot any longer play the role of an expert who reads *for* (or *instead of*) incompetent readers — by providing them with the true interpretation or by assessing the deviations of their interpretations from this "norm." Rather, reading *with* others involves presupposing that they have at least a basic interpretive competence to discern and adopt interpretations that are legitimate and plausible, that, until proven otherwise, are basically legitimate and plausible.[52]

---

52. This presumption that all interpretations are basically legitimate and plausible until proven otherwise is not idealistic naivete. The presumption that one is innocent of interpretive crimes until proven guilty applies to interpretations by ordinary readers, such as beginning students. Believe me, I am well aware that my students' interpretations need improvement. They have much to learn in order to bring their interpretations to critical understanding, and thus to be in a position to present their interpretations in a way that makes sense for others. Yet I can conceive of their interpretations as basically legitimate and plausible because regarding any interpretation I make a sharp distinction between "performance" and "explicit presentation" of legitimacy, epistemology, and value judgments. Thus I can recognize that a given interpretation is basically legitimate and plausible when its conclusions about what the text says (parts of its CAWs) and its conclusions about the teaching (CATs) of the text for a certain audience show that appropriate legitimacy and epistemology judgments were *performed* during the process of reading, even if the presentation of these conclusions fails to present how these judgments were performed and justifies them on other grounds (e.g., value judgments). See again in the introduction the discussion of the ways in which diverse presentations of inter-

It now is clear that throughout this multidimensional study I have attempted to read *with* a group of male European-American biblical scholars. The scholarly character of our presentations helped me recognize the legitimacy and the plausibility of our very different interpretations, which I could therefore affirm. As I elucidated the respective value judgments involved in our respective interpretations, I learned much about what was at stake for me in my choice of an interpretation. As is clear, "reading *with*" does not require forsaking our own interpretations. On the contrary, reading *with* empowers each of the reading partners to own up to her or his own interpretation. This cannot really take place as long as the reading partners do not affirm their own interpretation.

Because it is written, this book could misrepresent the process of reading *with*. Since I have to speak for myself when dealing with value judgments, it may seem that I have closed the process by forcefully presenting my interpretation as the most valuable one. Thus a proper conclusion to this study must introduce a different interpretation of the Sermon on the Mount that would reopen the process by suggesting the possibility that another interpretation might be more valuable than mine. In this way, it would be clear that the interpretation by which I chose to live has a *relative* (not absolute) value, even though it is word of God for me. This new interpretation would at least suggest that in the other situations my interpretation might not be the best, possibly even suggesting that my interpretation might not even be the best for me in my present situation.

This is not some kind of masochistic exercise through which I would take perverse pleasure in destroying what I have so painstakingly built. On the contrary, it is the gratifying pursuit of my search for the kingdom and God's righteousness, constantly punctuated by the joyful discovery of mostly significant and valuable interpretations. This newly encountered interpretation calls me to continue bringing to critical understanding my interpretation and helps me to make explicit others of its characteristics, be they related to its legitimacy, epistemology, and/or value judgments.

A most powerful and significant interpretation of the Sermon on the Mount, which had this effect for me as I attempted to read *with* its author, is the one offered by Alice Walker in *The Temple of My Familiar*,[53] which she calls "The Gospel according to Shug." By saying that I attempted to read the Sermon on the Mount *with* Alice Walker, I do not claim to be an expert who because of detailed studies is competent to lecture on Walker's remarkable literary corpus. I read her fiction and poetry for the pleasure of

---

pretations made explicit or not the roles of the value, epistemology, and legitimacy judgments and the corresponding conclusions (CARVs, CATs, and CAWs).

53. Alice Walker, *The Temple of My Familiar* (New York: Pocket Books, 1990), 287–89. Monya Stubbs, as I was reading the Sermon on the Mount with her, called my attention to this text, closely related to her own interpretation. I am deeply indebted to her generosity in introducing me to the interpretive community to which she belongs with Alice Walker.

it — and what a pleasure it is! But the three pages of "The Gospel according to Shug" stopped me. She was inviting me to read the beatitudes (and, I soon discovered, the entire Sermon) *with* her.

"Helped are those who are enemies of their own racism...." By themselves, these first words of "The Gospel according to Shug" opened for me a totally new reading of the Sermon. They include *conclusions about the teaching* of the first beatitude which are most striking. A few brief remarks on these first words are sufficient to show how reading *with* Alice Walker both insures that my reading remains decentered and furnishes the exhilarating experience of discovering a different way of reading the Sermon and of envisioning discipleship that casts my own reading in a new light.

"Helped" is a translation of μακάριοι. Why not? Its potential *legitimacy* is readily recognizable (and was recognized when the beatitudes are interpreted in terms of the poor of Israel). The teaching of the beatitudes (what the text says) shifts in a remarkable way. This word does not point toward a simple euphoric situation — bliss — given as a reward in the present or the future (readings A and B), or toward the mark of those who should be imitated because they manifest the kingdom and/or God's righteousness. Here those who are blessed — the "helped" ones — are those who are *empowered*.

This interpretation is a *plausible* conclusion regarding the teaching of the beatitudes (and of the entire Sermon, although showing it would require a detailed examination of the text). Walker presupposes that the basic human predicament is a situation of powerlessness, not a lack of knowledge or a lack of will, as we middle-class, male European-American scholars presuppose. Her presupposition is at least as plausible as ours. All of our presuppositions are clearly marked by the social contexts out of which we read. It does not occur to us, middle-class male European-Americans, that the Sermon on the Mount might address the needs of oppressed people who desperately need to be empowered. But from her perspective as an African-American woman, Alice Walker saw this dimension of the text and its plausibility.

Finally, with this first word Alice Walker forces me to recognize that my interpretation, reading D, which I *value* so much, is far from having a universal value. Its limitations appear; it is clear that my interpretation is not the best (at the very least) for African-Americans.

"Those who are enemies of their own racism" as a translation of οἱ πτωχοὶ τῷ πνεύματι. Who are those who are "helped"? As above, much could be said about the legitimacy, plausibility, and value of this interpretation. Those who are "helped" are people who acknowledge their own sinfulness and repent of it, since for its victims racism is the ultimate manifestation of evil and sin. But by this comment I reduce Walker's interpretation to a traditional one (see Luther), and in the process I obscure the oppressive character of sin as evil that has power over human beings. Those who are enemies of their own racism — of this evil power within them and outside of them — are indeed helped, empowered. How? When? Walker's concluding beatitudes might provide a clue: "Helped are those who *know*" (Walker's emphasis). Is it those who *recognize* (know) racism within themselves who are empowered? The *legitimacy* of this interpretation can be substantiated by noting that several passages of the Sermon might be read as calling the disciples to direct their moral discernment toward themselves so as to identify evil in themselves (the most obvious passages are 5:29–30 and 7:5) — a very different emphasis from the one found in my interpretation. This is a sign that Walker focuses her interpretation on a meaning-producing dimension of the text that might be different from any of those on which are focused the four kinds of interpretations that we discussed. Therefore, I should not attempt to force her interpretation into the mold of one of the methodologies we used. Another critical method might be necessary. This is another sign for me that I cannot deny the legitimacy of an interpretation simply because it is not based on a dimension (and method) that I readily recognize.

Similarly, the *plausibility* of Walker's interpretation is certainly not to be understood in terms of a traditional European-American preunderstandings of the moral life and/or ethical theory. This is suggested by the direct or indirect references to the stories of the interrelationship among people, which seem to replace abstract moral values (such as righteousness). "They shall live in harmony with the citizens of this world." Similarly, while Walker's second beatitude ("Helped are those born from love: conceived in their father's tenderness and their mother's orgasm") might be surprising at first, it makes perfect sense as a part of her interpretation of the Sermon on the Mount, when one keeps in mind the long history of rape and sexual exploitation (even being used as breeders) to which black women were subject under slavery (and after it) in North America, so poignantly presented by Delores Williams as the deepest, most violent, and yet invisible sin against black women.[54] This narrative presentation of values is of course to be expected in a literary work. But it may reflect what Katie Cannon calls "the moral wisdom of Black women," which is shaped by the form of the story in which it is expressed and yet plays the same role and has the same status as the "ethical theories" proposed by European-American ethicists.[55]

The decentering of my interpretation and my empowerment as a reader continues and goes on and on, as long as I continue to read *with* others, and as long as others show their willingness to read *with* me by quietly affirming the interested character of their interpretations. From the perspective

---

54. See Williams, "Sin, Nature, and Black Women's Bodies," 24–29.

55. See Katie G. Cannon, *Black Womanist Ethics,* AAR Academy Series (Atlanta: Scholars Press, 1988), and *Womanism and the Soul of the Black Community* (New York: Continuum, 1995).

of my own reading, these are blessed ones who manifest God's righteousness, and whom I am called to imitate in an overabundant way. For Alice Walker, they might rather be the "helped ones" "who know" and who, in turn, help us as we read *with* them. So, read on and on *with* Alice Walker, beginning with her first beatitude.

> Helped are those who are enemies of their own racism: they shall live in harmony with the citizens of this world, and not with those of the world of their ancestors, which has passed away, and which they shall never see again.

Appendixes

Conclusions about What Matthew 4:18-22 Is and Says

Reading A, CAW 1:
Mt 4:18–22 as a
window on an event
of "history" or a
scene of a "realistic
narrative"

Reading B, CAW 1:
*Mt 4:18–22 as the
beginning of the
unfolding of a plot or
of a history*

Reading C, CAW 1:
Mt 4:18–22 as a
figurative text and
the appropriate
critical method

Reading D, CAW 1:
*Mt 4:18–22 as a
thematic text and
the appropriate
critical method*

Reading A, CAW 2:
The representation
of an event of
history or a scene of
a realistic narrative
in Mt 4:18–22 as a
meaning-producing
dimension of the
text

Reading B, CAW 2:
*The plot of Mt 4:
18–22 as a meaning-
producing dimension
of the text*

Reading C, CAW 2:
The figurative unit
to which Mt 4:
18–22 belongs
delimited by literary
conventions

Reading D, CAW 2:
*The thematic unit to
which Mt 4:18–22
belongs delimited
by intratextual
structures*

Reading A, CAW 3:
Time and space
notations as
particularly
significant

Reading B, CAW 3:
*The interplay
among charac-
ters as particularly
significant*

Reading C, CAW 3:
A vision of disciples
as religious leaders
with an ambivalent
mission: metaphors
and figures

Reading D, CAW 3:
*A vision of dis-
cipleship as being
associated with Jesus'
ministry: Jesus' and
John's ministries in
inverted parallelisms*

Reading A, CAW 4:
Personages or char-
acters as particularly
significant

Reading B, CAW 4:
*The characters
as actors/active
participants in the
unfolding of the plot
and their significance*

Reading C, CAW 4:
A vision of disciple-
ship as a prophetic
vocation: allusions
to other texts and
traditions

Reading D, CAW 4:
*Mt 4:18–22 as vision-
type of discipleship:
trusting response to
the coming of the
kingdom*

Reading A, CAW 5:
The features of the
scene emphasized
by the redactor
as particularly
significant

Reading B, CAW 5:
*The process of
becoming a disciple*

Reading C, CAW 5:
A vision of disci-
pleship as repenting
from one's sins:
organization of the
figurative unit

Reading D, CAW 5:
*The thematic con-
notations of Jesus'
calling of disciples
and the thematic
vision of discipleship*

Reading A, CAW 6:
The historical/
realistic situation
constructed by
the text and its
institutional features

Reading B, CAW 6:
*The relationship of
Mt 4:18–22 with the
rest of the history*

Reading C, CAW 6:
A vision of disciples
associated with
other followers of
Jesus and contrasted
with Pharisees and
Sadducees

Conclusions about the Teaching of Matthew 4:18–22 Regarding Discipleship

Reading A, CAT 1:
Mt 4:18–22 as ideal norm of discipleship

Reading B, CAT 1:
Discipleship as an on-going process of transformation

Reading C, CAT 1:
Mt 4:18–22 conveys a vision of discipleship

Reading D, CAT 1:
Mt 4:18–22 conveys a vision of discipleship

Reading A, CAT 2:
Discipleship as unconditional and costly submission to Jesus' words

Reading B, CAT 2:
Mt 4:18–22 as one of the diverse ways of entering the process of discipleship

Reading C, CAT 2:
Distinguishing "authentic" from "inauthentic" religious leadership

Reading D, CAT 2:
Discipleship requires identifying those who are associated with Jesus' ministry

Reading A, CAT 3:
Discipleship as acknowledging the authority of the exalted Kyrios

Reading B, CAT 3:
Discipleship as a voluntary decision to follow Jesus

Reading A, CAT 4:
Mt 4:18–22 as apostolic "ideal" in terms of which the relative status of church members can be assessed

Reading B, CAT 4:
From "would-be disciples" and "novice disciples" to "full-fledged disciples"

Conclusions about What the Sermon on the Mount Is and Says

Reading A, CAW 1: Critical interpretations of the historical/realistic dimension: The Sermon's framework (5:1–2; 7:28–29)	**Reading B, CAW 1:** *A critical interpretation of the plot dimension of the sermon's framework (5:1–2; 7:28–8:1)*	**Reading C, CAW 1:** Critical interpretations of the figurative dimension: the figurative structure of the Sermon on the Mount	**Reading D, CAW 1:** *Critical interpretations of the thematic dimension: the thematic structure of the Sermon on the Mount*
CAW 1.1: What the Sermon is: A teaching addressed to the disciples for the sake of the crowds	**CAW 1.1:** *What Mt 5:3–7:27 is: A sermon addressed to both novice disciples and crowds*	**CAW 1.1:** The center of the Sermon on the Mount, the Lord's Prayer, as key for the interpretation	**CAW 1.1:** *Inverted parallelisms between the introduction and the conclusions as key for the interpretation*
CAW 1.2: Who is Jesus, the Preacher on the mount? The eschatological Lord?	**CAW 1.2:** *What Jesus' twofold role is: Preacher and teacher of the sermon*	**CAW 1.2:** The ringlike structure of the Sermon on the Mount centered on the Lord's Prayer	**CAW 1.2:** *The inverted parallelisms of the thematic structure of the Sermon on the Mount between the beatitudes and final judgment*
CAW 1.3: What the Sermon as an eschatological teaching is: An absolute expression of God's eternal will	**CAW 1.3:** *The Sermon on the Mount is a call to discipleship*	**CAW 1.3:** A figurative interpretation begins by an examination of the center of the figurative dimension, the Lord's Prayer, in light of the outer-rings	**CAW 1.3:** *A thematic interpretation begins by an examination of the units in inverted parallelisms: the judgment scene, 7:21–27, and the beatitudes, 5:3–10*
CAW 1.4: The Sermon is an epitome; it teaches basic ethical principles rather than parenetic sayings demanding literal implementation	**CAW 1.4:** *The Sermon contributes to making fishers of people out of the novice disciples*		

Reading A, CAW 2:	Reading B, CAW 2:	Reading C, CAW 2:	Reading D, CAW 2:
Mt 5:3–12: The beatitudes: An ethical teaching for the eschatological community under God's rule	*Mt 5:3–10: The beatitudes — a preview of important stages of the disciples' story and a call to discipleship*	Primary figures of the Sermon on the Mount, Lord's Prayer, and discipleship as imitation of Christ	*The main theme of the Sermon on the Mount: judgment, 7:21–27, beatitudes, 5:3–10, and moral discernment*
CAW 2.0: The beatitudes reflect the self-consciousness of the community	*CAW 2.0: The beatitudes are addressed to both the disciples and the crowds*		
CAW 2.1: Disciples are "blessed"	*CAW 2.1: The beatitudes give a preview of the story of the disciples*	CAW 2.1: Mt 4:23– 9:35: ambivalence in the imitation of Christ	*CAW 2.1: Moral discernment as the essential charac-teristic of disciples according to the judgment scene, 7:21–27 (compare with CAW 3.9)*
CAW 2.2: The "indicative" of the beatitudes is also "imperative," admo-nition, command	*CAW 2.2: The ideal effect of the beatitudes upon the crowds as a verbal call to discipleship. Many are called to discipleship!*	CAW 2.2: Mt 4:23– 5:2 and 7:28–8:1: Jesus as Moses-like messiah and the crowds as disciple-like, two figures of discipleship and their ambivalence	*CAW 2.2: Moral discernment as condition for saying the beatitudes, 5:3– 10 (compare with CAW 3.1)*
CAW 2.3: God's eschatological rule is proleptically realized in the community of disciples who carry out God's eternal will	*CAW 2.3: The ideal effect of the beatitudes on the novice disciples: a call to a more permanent commitment*	CAW 2.3: The Lord's Prayer (6:5– 13) as prayer of the new covenant: the eschatological and theological horizons of its symbolic world (compare with reading D, CAW 3.7)	*CAW 2.3: Represen-tation of the theme of moral discernment in the figures of "vi-sion," "seeing," and "eye": discernment as clear perception of manifestations of God's goodness (compare with CAW 3.6)*
CAW 2.4: What the beatitudes are: a realistic description of the historical disciples	*CAW 2.4: Ideally, the beatitudes establish both the fishers' and crowds' will*	CAW 2.4: Ethical and eschatological interpretations of the Lord's Prayer in tension	

Reading A, CAW 3:	Reading B, CAW 3:	Reading C, CAW 3:	Reading D, CAW 3:
Mt 5:13–16: The nature of discipleship as setting up duties for disciples and boundaries for the church	*Mt 5:11–16: The disciples' vocation; further preview of their story; further establishment of the will to be disciples*	A figurative interpretation: discipleship in between the two horizons of the symbolic world of the Sermon on the Mount	*A thematic interpretation: perceiving discipleship with the moral discernment of a sound, undivided eye*
CAW 3.1: "Salt" and "light of the world" are descriptions of the state of discipleship — the indicative	**CAW 3.1:** *The preview of the story of the disciples in 5:11–16: the performance of their vocation as prophets, salt, and light and its consequences*	**CAW 3.1:** Mt 5: 3–12: the beatitudes as expressions of God's present loving care and of eschatological promises (compare with reading D, CAW 2.2)	**CAW 3.1:** *Mt 5: 11–16: discerning true discipleship: when actions fit vocation (compare with reading C, CAW 3.1 & 3.2)*
CAW 3.2: Being "salt" and "light of the world" involves carrying out a universal mission — the imperative	**CAW 3.2:** *The ideal effect of Mt 5: 11–16 on novice disciples: benefits for others and God as additional reasons to be disciples*	**CAW 3.2:** Mt 5: 13–16: positive and negative figures of the disciples' vocation of religious leadership (compare with reading D, CAW 3.1)	**CAW 3.2:** *Mt 7: 13–20: recognizing true prophets by discerning how actions and inner persons fit (compare with CAW 3.9)*
CAW 3.3: "Salt without taste" and light "under a bushel" are expressions of a rule of community discipline	**CAW 3.3:** *The establishment of the hearers' will to be disciples is a major purpose of the Sermon on the Mount*	**CAW 3.3:** Mt 5: 17–20: higher righteousness: Jesus as a model of discipleship (compare with reading D, CAW 3.3 & 3.5)	**CAW 3.3:** *Mt 5: 17–19: discerning true discipleship: a vocation defined in terms of Scripture (compare with CAW 3.3)*
Reading A, CAW 4: Mt 5:17–20: Sentences of "holy law" for reproving or rejecting people from the church	Reading B, CAW 4: *Mt 5:17–19: conditions for being great in the kingdom*	**CAW 3.4:** Mt 5: 21–48: "a ray of hope for a new, better human being" (compare with reading D, CAW 3.6)	**CAW 3.4:** *Mt 6: 22–7:12: discerning true discipleship: a vocation defined in terms of what a sound eye recognizes as Scripture-like (compare with CAW 3.6, 3.7 & 3.8)*
CAW 4.1: Rules for determining the status of people vis-à-vis the community in 5:17–20	**CAW 4.1:** *A passage limited to Mt 5: 17–19*	**CAW 3.5:** Mt 6: 1–18: fusion of the eschatological and theological horizons into a single symbolic world (compare with reading D, CAW 3.7)	**CAW 3.5:** *Mt 5: 20 and 5:45–48: discerning true discipleship: over-abundantly doing the good things that disciples see scribes, pharisees, tax collectors, and Gentiles doing (compare with CAW 3.3 & 3.4)*

Reading A, CAW 4.2: Jesus' sovereign authority to fulfill the law and the prophets	**Reading B, CAW 4.2:** *The preview of the story of the disciples in 5:17–19: conditions for being "great in the kingdom of heaven"*	**Reading C, CAW 3.6:** Mt 6:19–34: earthly possessions, the present care of the heavenly Father, and the kingdom (compare with reading D, CAW 3.7 & 3.4)	**Reading D, CAW 3.6:** *Mt 5:21–48: discerning true discipleship: overabundant righteousness as carrying out one's vocation toward others by fulfilling Scripture (compare with CAW 3.4)*
CAW 4.3: Mt 5:17–19 is a rule "obligatory for all followers of Jesus"	**CAW 4.3:** *Mt 5:17 is a warning against overvaluing Jesus' authority*	**CAW 3.7:** Mt 7:1–11: relationship to neighbor and to the heavenly Father (compare with reading D, CAW 3.4)	**CAW 3.7:** *Mt 6:1–21: discerning true discipleship: overabundant righteousness as carrying out one's vocation toward God (compare with CAW 3.5 & 3.6)*
CAW 4.4: The *better* righteousness of the sphere of God's eschatological rule	**CAW 4.4:** *The ideal effect of Mt 5:17–19 on novice disciples: establishing their will to become fully faithful disciple*	**CAW 3.8:** Mt 7:12: the golden rule: recognizing that the "better human being" of the kingdom already exists (compare with reading D, CAW 3.4)	**CAW 3.8:** *True discipleship: overabundant righteousness as a life totally shaped by what one discerns with a sound eye*
CAW 4.5: In sum: Mt 5:3–20 provides rules for inclusion and exclusion from the church as the sphere of God's eschatological rule		**CAW 3.9:** Mt 7:13–27: people on the "easy way" and "fruitless" as models of false discipleship (compare with reading D, CAW 2.1 & 3.2)	

Reading A, CAW 5: Mt 5:21–7:12: The revelation of God's eternal will to be implemented by the eschatological community

CAW 5.0: What is the historical/realistic dimension of Mt 5:21–7:12?

CAW 5.1: Mt 5:21–7:12 is the authoritative proclamation of God's eternal will by Jesus, the exalted Kyrios and eschatological Judge

CAW 5.2: Mt 5:21–7:12: Hermeneutical principles for "fulfilling the law" and having a *better* righteousness in view of the impending eschatological judgment

CAW 5.21: The hermeneutical principle of love

CAW 5.22: The hermeneutical principle of perfection

CAW 5.23: The hermeneutical principle of judgment

CAW 5.3: Mt 5:21–7:12 is a series of laws (rules) governing the life of the community of disciples as a redaction critical study shows

CAW 5.31: Matthew's redaction applies the first antithesis (5:21–22) to the life of his church

CAW 5.32: Matthew's redaction applies the other antitheses (5:27–48) to the life of his church

CAW 5.33: Matthew's redaction reinforces the character of community rules of the teachings in 6:1–18

CAW 5.34: The Lord's Prayer, 6:9–13, is also a set of indirect admonitions

CAW 5.35: The teachings of 6:19–24 are practical injunctions challenging the absolutization of the economic order

CAW 5.36: The teaching about anxiety, 6:25–34, is also a rule for community life

Reading B, CAW 5: *Mt 5:20 – 6:21: Conditions for entering the kingdom: adopting a radical behavior*

CAW 5.1: *The preview of the story of the disciples in 5:20 – 6:21*

CAW 5.11: *Entering or not entering the kingdom as receiving or being deprived of a reward*

CAW 5.12: *The disciples' behavior as they fulfill their vocation: overabundant righteousness*

CAW 5.13: *Three conditions for wanting an overabundant righteousness: acknowledging Jesus' authority; internalizing the basic intention of the law; recognizing that God's will is good to do*

CAW 5.14: *A condition for wanting to internalize God's will: being convinced of the goodness of God*

CAW 5.2: *The ideal effect of Mt 5:20 – 6:21 on novice disciples*

CAW 5.21: *Mt 5:20 – 6:21 as threatening the novice disciples' resolve to be made disciples*

CAW 5.22: *Mt 5:20 – 6:21 as inviting novice disciples to pray the Lord's Prayer and to acknowledge that without God's help they lack the will to carry out their mission*

Reading B, CAW 6: *Mt 6:22–7:12: Basic condition for overabundant righteousness: a sound eye*

CAW 6.1: *The preview of the story of the disciples in 6:22–7:12: how the lack of will to adopt such a radical behavior is overcome*

CAW 6.11: *Mt 6:22–24: The nature of the problem: a divided will resulting from a divided eye*

Reading A, CAW 5.37: Matthew's redaction transforms the radical prohibition of judging, 7:1–5, into a community rule

CAW 5.38: Mt 7:7–11 is a practical admonition for a distinctive way of praying by the community

CAW 5.39: In sum: this entire set of community rules "fulfills" Jesus' teaching as Jesus' teaching "fulfills" the law

Reading B, CAW 6.12: *Mt 6:25–34: Anxiety is the source of divided eye and divided will; the overcoming of anxiety by a sound eye seeing manifestations of God's goodness (=faith)*

CAW 6.13: *Mt 7:1–6: A sound eye to be used for helping others, not for condemning*

CAW 6.14: *Mt 7:7–12: Consequences of having a sound eye: faith/confidence in God and being willing to do God's will*

CAW 6.2: *The ideal effect of Mt 6:22–7:12 upon novice disciples: fully establishing their will to carry out their mission as disciples*

CAW 6.3: *Overall plot of the story of the disciples*

CAW 6.4: *The overall ideal effect of this preview of the story of the disciples*

CAW 6.41: *Mt 5:3–7:12 ideally transforms the former fishers and the crowds into disciples ready to carry out their mission*

CAW 6.42: *The mission of the disciples: performing good works toward others in order to make disciples out of them*

Reading A, CAW 6: Mt 7:13–27: Closing admonitions

CAW 6.1: Mt 7:13–14, a call to practice Jesus' teaching which reflects the situation of Matthew's church

CAW 6.2: Mt 7:15–20: Apocalyptic warnings which become criteria for exclusion and inclusion in the church as eschatological community

CAW 6.3: Mt 7:21–23 applies the preceding criteria to all church members

CAW 6.4: Mt 7:24–27: Obeying or not the Kyrios's teaching is pronouncing a judgment upon oneself

Reading A, CAW 7: The Sermon on the Mount as a law that determines the boundaries of the Christian community

Reading B, CAW 7: *Mt 7:13–27 and the urgency of the disciples' mission*

CAW 7.1: *Mt 7:13–14: The narrow gate and the hard road*

CAW 7.2: *Mt 7:15–20 as instruction to disciples carrying out their urgently needed mission*

CAW 7.3: *Mt 7:21–27: The urgency for the disciples to carry out their mission in a proper way*

Reading B, CAW 8: *The Sermon on the Mount transforms its hearers into full-fledged disciples ready to carry out their mission*

APPENDIX 2B

Conclusions about the Teaching of the Sermon on the Mount Regarding Discipleship

Reading A, CAT 1: The plausibility of conceptualizing discipleship with a deontological preunderstanding of the moral life	*Reading B, CAT 1: The plausibility of conceptualizing discipleship with a consequentialist preunderstanding of the moral life*	**Reading C, CAT 1:** The plausibility of a resocialization/perfectionist pre-understanding of the moral life	*Reading D, CAT 1: The plausibility of a discernment/perfectionist pre-understanding of the moral life*
		CAT 1.1: Signs of Luz's and Davies and Allison's perfectionist interpretation of the Sermon on the Mount	*CAT 1.1: Signs of perfectionist reading of the Sermon on the Mount in my commentary*
Reading A, CAT 2: The plausibility of claiming that the Sermon on the Mount reveals God's eternal will to disciples	*Reading B, CAT 2: The plausibility of the Sermon on the Mount as "sermon" proclaiming a good news to convince people to do God's will*	**Reading C, CAT 2:** The plausibility of discipleship as resocialization/perfectionist ethical practice	*Reading D, CAT 2: The plausibility of discipleship as a discernment/perfectionist ethical practice*
		CAT 2.1: Resocializing would-be disciples in the symbolic world of the Sermon on the Mount: faith before discipleship	*CAT 2.1: Moral discernment at the heart of discipleship as practical wisdom; faith as discerning whom to imitate*
		CAT 2.2: The plausibility of discipleship as shaped by the ambivalent symbolic world of the Sermon on the Mount	*CAT 2.2: Discipleship shaped by the moral discernment of an undivided eye*

Reading A, CAT 3: The plausibility of the view of God's eternal will that disciples should do	**Reading B, CAT 3:** *The plausibility of good consequences of doing God's will as reasons for wanting to do it*	**Reading C, CAT 3:** The plausibility of conforming to the twofold symbolic world of the sermon by imitating models of discipleship	**Reading D, CAT 3:** *The plausibility of discerning what discipleship entails by identifying appropriate models*
Reading A, CAT 4: The plausibility of discipleship as submitting to the authoritative teaching of the exalted Lord and Judge: a high Christology	**Reading B, CAT 4:** *The plausibility of discipleship as a continuation of Jesus' ministry: a low Christology*	**CAT 3.1:** Jesus as the primary model of discipleship: *imitatio Christi* as resocialization	**CAT 3.1:** *Jesus as model of discernment and as model of overabundant righteousness*
		CAT 3.2: Other characters of the gospel as models of discipleship	**CAT 3.2:** *Jesus as model of discernment: recognizing righteousness in the behavior of ordinary people and offering it as model*
		CAT 3.3: The identification of false models of discipleship not to be imitated	**CAT 3.3:** *Disciples affirming and practicing in an overabundant way the models of righteousness they have discerned in the behavior of ordinary people*
Reading A, CAT 5: The plausibility of discipleship as implementing the Sermon's regulations for life in the church as the sphere of God's eschatological rule	**Reading B, CAT 5:** *The plausibility of discipleship as implementing the Sermon's blueprint for the processes of becoming disciples and of making disciples*	**CAT 3.4:** A resocialization/ perfectionist interpretation of discipleship according to the Sermon on the Mount	**CAT 3.4:** *From true moral discernment to overabundant righteousness*
			CAT 3.5: *Jesus as model of overabundant righteousness who points to other models of righteousness and of faith/discernment*

Bibliography

Abrahams, I. *Studies in Pharisaism and the Gospels*. Reprint ed. New York: KTAV, 1967, 2:94–108.

Aichele, George, and Gary Phillips, eds. *Intertextuality and Reading the Bible*. Semeia 69/70. Atlanta: Scholars Press, 1995.

Albright, W. F., and C. S. Mann. *Matthew*. The Anchor Bible, vol. 26. Garden City, N.Y.: Doubleday, 1971.

Alter, Robert. *The Pleasures of Reading in an Ideological Age*. New York: Simon and Schuster, 1989.

Augustine. *Confessions*. Translated by John K. Ryan. Vol. 12. Garden City, N.Y.: Doubleday, 1960.

Bal, Mieke. *Narratology: Introduction to the Theory of Narrative*. Translated by C. van Boheemen. Toronto: University of Toronto Press, 1985.

———. *Lethal Love: Feminist Literary Readings of Biblical Love Stories*. Bloomington: Indiana University Press, 1987.

———. *Murder and Difference: Gender, Genre, and Scholarship on Sisera's Death*. Bloomington: Indiana University Press, 1988.

Banks, R. "Matthew's Understanding of the Law: Authenticity and Interpretation in Matthew 5:17–20." *Journal of Biblical Literature* 93 (1974): 223.

Barth, Gerhard. "Matthew's Understanding of the Law." In *Tradition and Interpretation in Matthew*, by G. Bornkamm, G. Barth, and H. J. Held, 58–164. Translated by P. Scott. Philadelphia: Westminster, 1963.

Beardslee, W. *Literary Criticism of the New Testament*. Guides to Biblical Scholarship. Philadelphia: Fortress, 1970.

Beare, Francis W. *The Gospel according to Matthew*. San Francisco: Harper & Row; Oxford: Basil Blackwell, 1981.

Berger, Peter. *The Sacred Canopy: Elements of a Sociological Theory of Religion*. Garden City, N.Y.: Doubleday, 1967.

Berger, Peter, and Thomas Luckman. *The Social Construction of Reality: A Treatise in the Sociology of Knowledge*. Garden City, N.Y.: Doubleday, 1967.

Berstein, Richard J. *Beyond Objectivism and Relativism: Science, Hermeneutics, and Praxis*. Philadelphia: University of Pennsylvania Press, 1983.

Betz, Hans Dieter. *Essays on the Sermon on the Mount*. Translated by L. L. Welborn. Minneapolis: Fortress, 1985.

———. *Synoptische Studien*. Tübingen: J. C. B. Mohr, 1992.

———. *The Sermon on the Mount, Including the Sermon on the Plain (Matthew 5:3–27 and Luke 6:20–49): A Commentary on Two Early Christian Manuals of Discipleship*. Hermeneia. Edited by Adela Yarbro Collins. Minneapolis: Fortress, 1995.

Betz, Otto. "Die Proselytentaufe der Qumransekte und die Taufe im Neuen Testament." *Revue de Qumran* 1 (1958): 223.

The Bible and Culture Collective. *The Postmodern Bible*. New Haven and London: Yale University Press, 1995.

Blount, Brian K. *Cultural Interpretation: Reorienting New Testament Criticism*. Minneapolis: Fortress, 1995.

Bonnard, P. *L'évangile selon Saint Matthieu*. Commentaire du Nouveau Testament 1. Neuchâtel: Delachaux & Niestlé, 1963.

Bornhäuser, K. *Die Bergpredigt: Versuch einer zeitgössischen Auslegung*. Gütersloh: Bertelsmann, 1923.

Bornkamm, G., G. Barth, and H. J. Held. *Tradition and Interpretation in Matthew*. Translated by P. Scott. Philadelphia: Westminster, 1963.

Bultmann, Rudolf. *Existence and Faith: Shorter Writings by Rudolf Bultmann*. Edited by S. Ogden. Cleveland and New York: World Publishing Company, 1960.

———. *History of the Synoptic Tradition*. Translated by S. Marsh. New York: Harper & Row, 1963.

———. "Πένθος, Πενθέω." In *Theological Dictionary of the New Testament*, edited by G. Kittel and G. Friedrich. Vol. 6. Translated by G. W. Bromiley. Grand Rapids: Eerdmans, 1968.

Cannon, Katie G. *Black Womanist Ethics*. Atlanta: Scholars Press, 1988.

———. *Womanism and the Soul of the Black Community*. New York: Continuum, 1995.

Cargal, Timothy. *Restoring the Diaspora: Discursive Structure and Purpose in the Epistle of James*. Atlanta: Scholars Press, 1993.

Certeau, Michel de, S.J. *Croire: une pratique de la différence*. Urbino: Centro Internazionale di Semiotica e di Linguistica, 1981.

Chatman, Seymour. *Story and Discourse: Narrative Structure in Fiction and Film*. Ithaca, N.Y.: Cornell University Press, 1978.

Coalter, Milton J., John M. Mulder, and Louis B. Weeks. *The Re-Forming Tradition: Presbyterians and Mainstream Protestantism*. Louisville: Westminster/ John Knox, 1992.

Cohen, Marshall, ed. *The Philosophy of John Stuart Mill*. New York: Modern Library, 1961.

Collange, Jean-François. *De Jésus à Paul: L'éthique du Nouveau Testament*. Genève: Labor et Fides, 1980.

Collins, Raymond F. *Introduction to the New Testament*. Garden City, N.Y.: Doubleday, 1983.

Cone, James. *Martin & Malcom & America: A Dream or a Nightmare*. Maryknoll, N.Y.: Orbis, 1991.

Cook, Roger H. *An Introduction to Christian Ethics*. 2d ed. Englewood Cliffs, N.J.: Prentice-Hall, 1995.

Countryman, L. William. *Dirt, Greed, and Sex: Sexual Ethics in the New Testament and Their Implications for Today*. Philadelphia: Fortress, 1988.

Crossan, John Dominic. *In Parables: The Challenge of the Historical Jesus*. New York: Harper & Row, 1973.

———. "Jesus and Pacifism." In *No Famine in the Land*, edited by J. W. Flanagan and A. W. Robinson, 195–208. Atlanta: Scholars Press, 1975.

———. "Parable and Example in the Teaching of Jesus." *Semeia* 1 (1974): 63–104.

Culley, Robert C., and Robert B. Robinson, eds. *Textual Determinacy: Part I.* Semeia 62. Atlanta: Scholars Press, 1993.

———. *Textual Determinacy: Part II.* Semeia 71. Atlanta: Scholars Press, 1995.

Davies, W. D. "Matthew 5:17–20." In *Mélanges bibliques pour A. Robert.* Paris: Bloud et Gray, 1957.

———. *The Setting of the Sermon on the Mount.* Cambridge: Cambridge University Press, 1964.

Davies, W. D., and D. C. Allison Jr. *A Critical and Exegetical Commentary on the Gospel according to Saint Matthew.* International Critical Commentary, vols. 1–2. Edinburgh: T. & T. Clark, 1988, 1991.

Derrida, Jacques. *Of Grammatology.* Translated by Gayatri Chakravorty Spivak. Baltimore: Johns Hopkins University Press, 1976.

Dibelius, Martin. *From Tradition to Gospel.* Translated by B. Woolf. New York: Charles Scribner's Sons, 1917.

———. *James.* Hermeneia: A Critical and Historical Commentary on the Bible. Revised by H. Greeven. Philadelphia: Fortress, 1975.

Dodd, C. H. *Gospel and Law.* New York: Columbia University Press, 1951.

Dube, Musa, and Gerald West, eds. *"Reading With": An Exploration of an Interface between Critical and Ordinary Readings of the Bible. African Overtures.* Semeia 73. Atlanta: Scholars Press, 1996.

Dumais, Marcel. *Le Sermon sur la montagne. État de la recherche, Interprétation, Bibliographie.* Paris: Letouzey & Ané, 1995.

Dupont, Jacques. *Etudes sur les Actes des Apôtres.* Paris: Cerf, 1967.

———. *Les béatitudes.* Paris: Gabalda, 1969–73.

Dussel, Enrique. *Philosophy of Liberation.* Translated by A. Martinez and C. Morkovsky. Maryknoll, N.Y.: Orbis, 1985.

Eco, Umberto. *A Theory of Semiotics.* Bloomington: Indiana University Press, 1976.

Edwards, Richard A. *Matthew's Story of Jesus.* Minneapolis: Fortress, 1985, 47–61.

———. "Uncertain Faith: Matthew's Portrait of the Disciples." In *Discipleship in the New Testament*, edited by F. F. Segovia. Minneapolis: Fortress, 1985.

Felder, Cain Hope, ed. *Stony the Road We Trod: African American Biblical Interpretation.* Minneapolis: Fortress, 1991.

Fish, Stanley E. *Is There a Text in This Class? The Authority of Interpretive Communities.* Cambridge: Harvard University Press, 1980.

Gaechter, Paul. *Das Matthäusevangelium.* Innsbruck: Tyrolia, 1963.

Geertz, Clifford. *The Interpretation of Cultures: Selected Essays.* New York: Basic Books, 1973.

Greimas, A. J., and E. Landowski, eds. *Introduction à l'analyse du discours en sciences sociales.* Paris: Hachette, 1979.

Greimas, A. J., and J. Courtés. *Semiotics and Language: An Analytical Dictionary.* Translated by L. Crist, D. Patte, et al. Bloomington: Indiana University Press, 1982.

Guelich, Robert A. *The Sermon on the Mount: A Foundation for Understanding.* Waco, Tex.: Word Books, 1992.

Gundry, Robert H. *Matthew: A Commentary on His Literary and Theological Art.* Grand Rapids: Eerdmans, 1982.

Goppelt, L. *Theology of the New Testament.* Grand Rapids: Eerdmans, 1982.

Gunn, Giles. *The Culture of Criticism and the Criticism of Culture.* New York: Oxford University Press, 1987.

Habermas, Jürgen. *Knowledge and Human Interest.* Translated by J. J. Shapiro. Boston: Beacon, 1971.

———. *Theory and Practice.* Boston: Beacon, 1973.

———. *Communication and the Evolution of Society.* Boston: Beacon, 1979.

———. *Moral Consciousness and Communicative Action.* Translated by C. Lenhardt and S. W. Nicholsen. Cambridge: MIT Press, 1990.

Halleux, R. D. A. de, ed. *Mélanges bibliques en hommage au R. P. Béda Rigaux.* Genbloux: Duculot, 1970.

Halliday, M. A. K. *Explorations in the Functions of Language.* London: Edward Arnold, 1973.

Harvey, Van. *The Historian and the Believer: A Confrontation of the Modern Historian's Principles of Judgment and the Christian's Will-to-Believe.* New York: Macmillan, 1966.

Hauerwas, Stanley. *A Community of Character: Toward a Constructive Social Ethic.* Notre Dame and London: University of Notre Dame Press, 1981.

———. "A Sermon on the Sermon on the Mount." In *Unleashing the Scripture: Freeing the Bible from Captivity to America.* Nashville: Abingdon, 1993.

Hengel, Martin. *The Charismatic Leader and His Followers.* Translated by J. Greig. New York: Crossroad; Edinburgh: T. & T. Clark, 1981.

Heschel, Abraham J. *The Sabbath: Its Meaning for Modern Man.* New York: Farrar, Straus, and Young, 1951.

Houlden, J. L. *Ethics and the New Testament.* New York: Oxford University Press, 1977.

Hummel, R. *Die Auseinandersetzung zwischen Kirche und Judentum im Matthäusevangelium.* Munich: Kaiser, 1963.

Iser, W. *The Implied Reader: Patterns of Communication in Prose Fiction from Bunyan to Beckett.* Baltimore: Johns Hopkins University Press, 1974.

———. *The Act of Reading: A Theory of Aesthetic Response.* Baltimore: Johns Hopkins University Press, 1978.

Jacobsen, David Schnasa. *As Seeing the Invisible: The Cosmic Scope of Apocalyptic Preaching.* Ph.D. diss., Vanderbilt University, 1996.

Jaggar, Allison M. "Love and Knowledge: Emotion and Feminist Epistemology." In *Gender/Body/Knowledge: Feminist Reconstructions of Being and Knowing,* edited by Allison M. Jaggar and Susan R. Bordo, 145–71. New Brunswick, N.J.: Rutgers University Press, 1989.

Jeremias, J. *The Prayers of Jesus.* Minneapolis: Fortress, 1967.

Jewett, Robert. *Saint Paul at the Movies: The Apostle's Dialogue with American Culture.* Louisville: Westminster/John Knox, 1993.

Jobling, David, and Tina Pippin, eds. *Ideological Criticism of Biblical Texts.* Semeia 59. Atlanta: Scholars Press, 1992.

Kant, Immanuel. *Critique of Practical Reason and Other Writings in Moral Philosophy*. Chicago: University of Chicago Press, 1949.

———. *Fundamental Principles of the Metaphysics of Morals*. New York: Bobbs-Merrill, 1949.

Käsemann, Ernest. *New Testament Questions of Today*. Philadelphia: Fortress, 1969.

Kennedy, George A. *New Testament Interpretation through Rhetorical Criticism*. Chapel Hill, N.C., and London: University of North Carolina Press, 1984.

Kerferd, C. B. "Arete." In *Encyclopedia of Philosophy*, edited by Paul Edwards. Vol. 1. New York: Free Press, 1967.

Kingsbury, Jack D. *Matthew: Structure, Christology, Kingdom*. Minneapolis: Fortress, 1975.

———. "The Verb *Akolouthein* ('to Follow') as an Index of Matthew's View of His Community." *Journal of Biblical Literature* 97 (1978): 56–73.

———. *Matthew as Story*. Minneapolis: Fortress, 1986.

Kittel, G., ed. *Theological Dictionary of the New Testament*. Translated by G. W. Bromiley. Grand Rapids: Eerdmans, 1964–74.

Lachs, Samuel Tobias. *A Rabbinic Commentary on the New Testament: The Gospels of Matthew, Mark and Luke*. Hoboken, N.J.: KTAV, 1987.

Lambrecht, Jan. *"Eh bien! Moi je vous dis": Le discours-programme de Jésus (Mt 5–7; Lc 6, 20–49)*. Lectio Divina 125. Paris: Cerf, 1986.

Léon-Dufour, X. "The Synoptic Gospels." In *Introduction to the New Testament*, edited by A. Robert and A. Feuillet. Translated by P. W. Skehan et al. New York: Desclée, 1965.

Levine, A.-J. *The Social and Ethnic Dimension of Matthean Salvation History*. Lewiston, N.Y.: Edwin Mellen, 1988.

———. "Matthew." In *The Women's Bible Commentary*, edited by Carol A. Newsom and Sharon Ringe. Louisville: Westminster/John Knox, 1992.

Lohmeyer, E. *Das Evangelium des Matthäus*. 4th ed. Revised by W. Schmauch. Göttingen: Vandenhoeck & Ruprecht, 1967.

Lohse, Eduard. *Theological Ethics of the New Testament*. Minneapolis: Fortress, 1991.

Luz, Ulrich. "Die Erfüllung des Gesetzes bei Matthäus (5:17–20)." *Zeitschrift für Theologie und Kirche* 75 (1978): 414–15.

———. "The Disciples in the Gospel according to Matthew." In *The Interpretation of Matthew*, edited by Graham Stanton, 98–128. Philadelphia: Fortress; London: SPCK, 1983.

———. *Matthew 1–7: A Commentary*. Minneapolis: Augsburg, 1989.

———. *The Theology of the Gospel according to Matthew*. Cambridge: Cambridge University Press, 1995.

Lyons, David. *The Form and Limits of Utilitarianism*. New York and London: Oxford University Press, 1965.

Manson, T. W. *Ethics and the Gospel*. New York: Charles Scribner's Sons, 1960.

Marguerat, Daniel. *Le Jugement dans l'Evangile de Matthieu*. Geneva: Labor et Fides, 1981.

Marxsen, Willi. *New Testament Foundations for Christian Ethics*. Minneapolis: Fortress, 1993.

Mattison, Robin D. *To Beget or Not to Beget: Presupposition and Persuasion in Matthew Chapter One.* Ph.D. Diss., Vanderbilt University, 1995.

McEleney, N. J. "The Principles of the Sermon on the Mount." *Catholic Biblical Quarterly* 41 (1979): 552–70.

McKenzie, Steven L., and Stephen R. Haynes, eds. *To Each Its Own Meaning: An Introduction to Biblical Criticisms and Their Application.* Louisville: Westminster/John Knox, 1993.

McKibben, Bill. "Some Versions of Pastoral." *The New York Review of Books,* 11 July 1996, 42–45.

Meeks, Wayne A. *The Moral World of the First Christians.* Philadelphia: Westminster, 1986.

———. *The Origins of Christian Morality: The First Two Centuries.* New Haven and London: Yale University Press, 1993.

Meier, John P. *Law and History in Matthew's Gospel: A Redactional Study of Mt. 5:17–48.* Rome: Biblical Institute Press, 1976.

———. *Matthew.* Wilmington, Del.: M. Glazier, 1980.

Miles, Margaret R. *Seeing and Believing: Religion and Values in the Movies.* Boston: Beacon, 1996.

Minear, P. "False Prophecy and Hypocrisy in the Gospel of Matthew." In *Neues Testament und Kirche: Festschrift R. Schnackenburg,* edited by J. Gnilka, 76–93. Freiburg: Herder, 1974.

Moore, Stephen. *Literary Criticism and the Gospels: The Theoretical Challenge.* New Haven: Yale University Press, 1989.

———. "True Confessions and Weird Obsessions: Autobiographical Interventions in Literary and Biblical Studies." In *Taking It Personally: Autobiographical Biblical Criticism,* by Janice Capel Anderson and Jeffrey L. Staley. Semeia 72. Atlanta: Scholars Press, 1996.

Mosala, Itumeleng J. *Biblical Hermeneutics and Black Theology in South Africa.* Grand Rapids: Eerdmans, 1989.

Newsom, Carol A., and Sharon H. Ringe, eds. *The Women's Bible Commentary.* Louisville: Westminster/John Knox, 1992.

Ogletree, Thomas W. *The Use of the Bible in Christian Ethics: A Constructive Essay.* Philadelphia: Fortress, 1983.

Okure, Teresa, S.H.C.J. *The Johannine Approach to Mission: A Contextual Study of John 4:1–24.* Tübingen: J. C. B. Mohr, Paul Siebeck, 1988.

———. "The Mother of Jesus in the New Testament: Implications for Women Mission." *Journal of Inculturation Theology* 2, no. 2 (1995): 196–210.

O'Neill, J. C. "Biblical Criticism." In *The Anchor Bible Dictionary.* Edited by David Noel Freedman. New York: Doubleday, 1992, 1:725.

Paris, Peter. *The Social Teaching of the Black Churches.* Philadelphia: Fortress, 1985.

Patte, Daniel. *Paul's Faith and the Power of the Gospel: A Structural Introduction to the Pauline Letters.* Philadelphia: Fortress, 1983.

———. *The Religious Dimensions of Biblical Texts: Greimas's Structural Semiotics and Biblical Exegesis.* SBL Semeia Studies. Atlanta: Scholars Press, 1990.

———. "Textual Constraints, Ordinary Readings, and Critical Exegesis: An Androcritical Perspective." In *Textual Determinacy: Part I,* edited by Robert C.

Culley and Robert B. Robinson, 59–79. Semeia 62. Atlanta: Scholars Press, 1993.

———. *Ethics of Biblical Interpretation: A Reevaluation.* Louisville: Westminster/ John Knox, 1995.

———. *The Gospel according to Matthew: A Structural Commentary on Matthew's Faith.* Minneapolis: Fortress, 1987; 3d printing, Valley Forge, Pa.: Trinity Press International, 1996.

———. *Structural Exegesis for New Testament Critics.* Guides to Biblical Scholarship. Minneapolis: Fortress, 1990; 2d printing, Valley Forge, Pa.: Trinity Press International, 1996.

Prenter, Regin. *Spiritus Creator.* Translated by J. M. Jensen. Philadelphia: Muhlenberg, 1953.

Ricoeur, Paul. *Freedom and Nature: The Voluntary and the Involuntary.* Evanston, Ill.: Northwestern University Press, 1966.

———. *The Symbolism of Evil.* Translated by E. Buchanan. Boston: Beacon, 1967.

———. *Interpretation Theory: Discourse and the Surplus of Meaning.* Fort Worth, Tex.: Texas Christian University Press, 1976.

———. *The Rule of Metaphor.* Toronto: University of Toronto Press, 1977.

———. "The Hermeneutics of Symbols and Philosophical Reflection." In *The Philosophy of Paul Ricoeur*, edited by C. E. Reagan and D. Stewart, 36–58. Boston: Beacon, 1980.

Robinson, James M., and John B. Cobb Jr., eds. *The New Hermeneutic.* New York: Harper & Row, 1964.

Sanders, Jack T. *Ethics in the New Testament: Change and Development.* Philadelphia: Fortress, 1975.

Sandmel, Samuel. *Anti-Semitism in the New Testament?* Philadelphia: Fortress, 1978.

Sartre, Jean-Paul. *No Exit, a Play in One Act & The Flies, a Play in Three Acts.* Translated by S. Gilbert. New York: Knopf, 1948.

Schmid, J. *Das Evangelium nach Matthäus.* RNT 1. Regensburg: F. Pustet, 1959.

Schottroff, L. "Gewaltverzicht und Feindesliebe in der urchristlichen Jesustradition (Mt 5,38–48; Lk 6,27–36)." In *Jesus Christus in Historie und Theologie: Festschrift H. Conzelmann*, edited by G. Strecker, 207–11. Tübingen: Mohr, 1975.

Schrage, Wolfgang. *The Ethics of the New Testament.* Translated by D. Green. Philadelphia: Fortress, 1988.

Schulz, Anselm. *Nachfolgen und Nachahmen: Studien über das Verhältnis der neutestamentlichen Jüngerschaft zur urchristlichen Vorbildethik.* Munich: Kösel-Verlag, 1962.

Schüssler Fiorenza, Elisabeth. *In Memory of Her: A Feminist Theological Reconstruction of Christian Origins.* New York: Crossroad, 1983.

———. *Bread Not Stone: The Challenge of Feminist Biblical Interpretation.* New York: Beacon, 1984.

———. "The Ethics of Interpretation: De-Centering Biblical Scholarship." *Journal of Biblical Literature* 107 (1988): 3–17.

———. *Revelation: Vision of a Just World.* Minneapolis: Fortress, 1991.

Schweizer, Eduard. *Lordship and Discipleship.* London: SCM, 1960.

———. "Gesetz und Enthusiasmus bei Matthäus." In *Beiträge zur Theologie des Neuen Testaments*, edited by E. Schweizer, 49–70. Zurich: Zwingli Verlag, 1970.

———. *Matthäus und seine Gemeinde*. Stuttgart: KBW Verlag, 1974.

———. *The Good News according to Matthew*. Atlanta: John Knox, 1975.

———. "Matthew's Church." In *The Interpretation of Matthew*, edited by G. Stanton, 129–55. Minneapolis: Fortress, 1983.

Scott, Bernard Brandon. *Hear Then the Parable: A Commentary on the Parables of Jesus*. Minneapolis: Fortress, 1989.

Segovia, Fernando F., and Mary Ann Tolbert, eds. *Reading from This Place*. Vol. 2. Minneapolis: Fortress, 1995.

Spivak, Gayatri C. "Can the Subaltern Speak?" In *Marxism and the Interpretation of Culture*, edited by G. Nelson and L. Grossberg, 277–313. London: Macmillan, 1988.

Stanton, Graham, ed. *The Interpretation of Matthew*. Philadelphia: Fortress, 1983.

Stendahl, K. "Biblical Theology, Contemporary." In *Interpreter's Dictionary of the Bible*. New York and Nashville: Abingdon, 1962, 1: 418–32.

Strecker, George. *Der Weg der Gerechtigkeit: Untersuchung zur Theologie des Matthäus*. Göttingen: Vandenhoeck & Ruprecht, 1962; 3d ed., 1971.

———. "Die Makarismen der Bergpredigt." *New Testament Studies* 17 (1970/71): 255–75.

———. "The Concept of History in Matthew." In *The Interpretation of Matthew*, edited by Graham Stanton, 70–74. Philadelphia: Fortress, 1983.

———. *The Sermon on the Mount: An Exegetical Commentary*. Translated by O. C. Dean Jr. Nashville: Abingdon, 1988.

Sugirtharajah, R. S., ed. *Voices from the Margin: Interpreting the Bible in the Third World*. Maryknoll, N.Y.: Orbis, 1991.

Tilborg, Sjef van. *The Jewish Leaders in Matthew*. Leiden: Brill, 1972.

Trilling, W. "Amt und Amtsverständnis bei Matthäus." In *Mélanges bibliques en hommage au R. P. Béda Rigaux*, edited by A. Descamps and R. D. A. de Halleux, 29–44. Genbloux: Duculot, 1970.

Via, Dan O. *The Parables: Their Literary and Existential Dimension*. Philadelphia: Fortress, 1967.

———. *Self-Deception and Wholeness in Paul and Matthew*. Minneapolis: Fortress, 1990.

Walker, Alice. *The Temple of My Familiar*. New York: Pocket Books, 1990.

Williams, Delores S. "Sin, Nature, and Black Women's Bodies." In *Ecofeminism and the Sacred*, edited by Carol J. Adams, 24–29. New York: Continuum, 1993.

Wuellner, Wilhelm. *The Meaning of "Fishers of Men."* Philadelphia: Westminster, 1967.

Zumstein, Jean. *La condition du croyant dans l'Evangile selon Matthieu*. Göttingen: Vandenhoeck & Ruprecht, 1977.